THE RENAISSANCE

THE RENAISSANCE

ROBERT ERGANG

D. VAN NOSTRAND COMPANY, INC.
Princeton, New Jersey Toronto London Melbourne

Van Nostrand Regional Offices: *New York, Chicago, San Francisco*

D. Van Nostrand Company, Ltd., *London*

D. Van Nostrand Company (Canada), Ltd., *Toronto*

D. Van Nostrand Australia Pty. Ltd., *Melbourne*

Published simultaneously in Canada by
D. Van Nostrand Company (Canada), Ltd.

L.C. card number
67-8363

PRINTED IN THE UNITED STATES OF AMERICA

Preface

When I stated in my *Europe from the Renaissance to Waterloo* that the secularization of life, thought, and culture is the essence of the Renaissance, friends urged me to develop the idea on a broad scale. This book, therefore, offers an interpretive account of the beginnings of our modern secular civilization, with special emphasis on culture. The narrative, as the chapter headings indicate, contains discussions of the developments in politics, science, commerce, and industry, in addition to the changes which took place in the various cultural fields, including painting, sculpture, literature, music, and the drama. Considerable attention has been devoted to the lives and contributions of notable Renaissance figures. The scope of the book embraces the major countries of Western Europe.

As in most projects of this kind, the execution progressed more slowly than anticipated. Prior commitments, workaday duties, and eye disease necessitated the shelving of the project for long periods and at other times slowed the progress to a snail's pace. Nevertheless, when I was able to work at it, the self-assigned task was both interesting and pleasant. Opening new historical paths is most often stimulating as well as rewarding. As the book goes out to the public, it is accompanied by the wish that readers will derive from it some degree of the pleasure I experienced in writing it.

This book owes much to others. Professor Marshall W. Baldwin of New York University gave freely of his time to read the manuscript and of his expert knowledge to make emendations and constructive suggestions. For this I am deeply grateful. My sincere thanks also to Professor Wilbur Hollman of Cedar Crest College for spending so many hours discussing Renaissance music with me, for his suggestions, and for his critical reading of the chapter on drama and music. Last but far from least I am indebted to my wife (née Mildred Overbeck), junior partner in the project, who not only functioned as typist and critic, but also read to me for hours on end when my eyes became too weary to use. The responsibility for all errors and shortcomings, whatever their nature, is solely my own.

ROBERT ERGANG

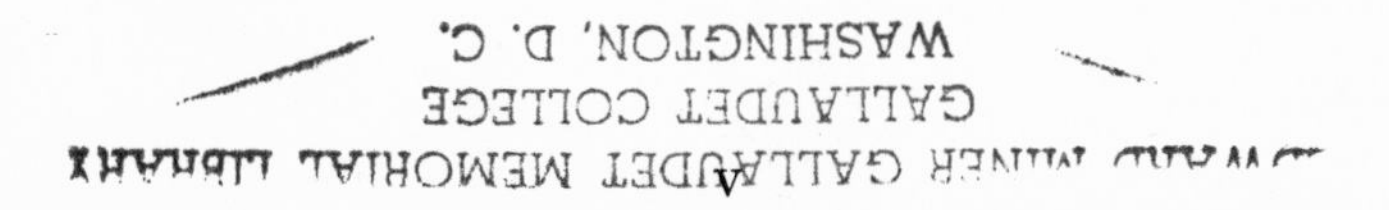

Illustration Acknowledgments

Alinari Art Reference Bureau: Fig. 4

Archives Photographiques: Figs. 7, 8, 11, 13, 18, 26, 27a, 29, 31, 33

The Bettmann Archive: Figs. 3, 9, 20, 21, 22

Brogi Art Reference Bureau: Figs. 14, 15

Galleria Degli Uffizi, Firenze: Fig. 5

Reproduced by courtesy of the Trustees, The National Gallery, London: Figs. 6, 10, 12, 28, 35

Queens Gallery, reproduced by gracious permission of Her Majesty Queen Elizabeth II: Fig. 27b

Tutta L'Opera del Cellini, a cura di Ettore Camesasca (Milano: Rizzoli Editore, 1955): Fig. 19

The quotations from Vasari which appear with Figs. 18 and 21 are taken from *The Lives of the Artists*, a selection translated by George Bull (Baltimore, Md.: Penguin Books, 1965).

Contents

Illustrations

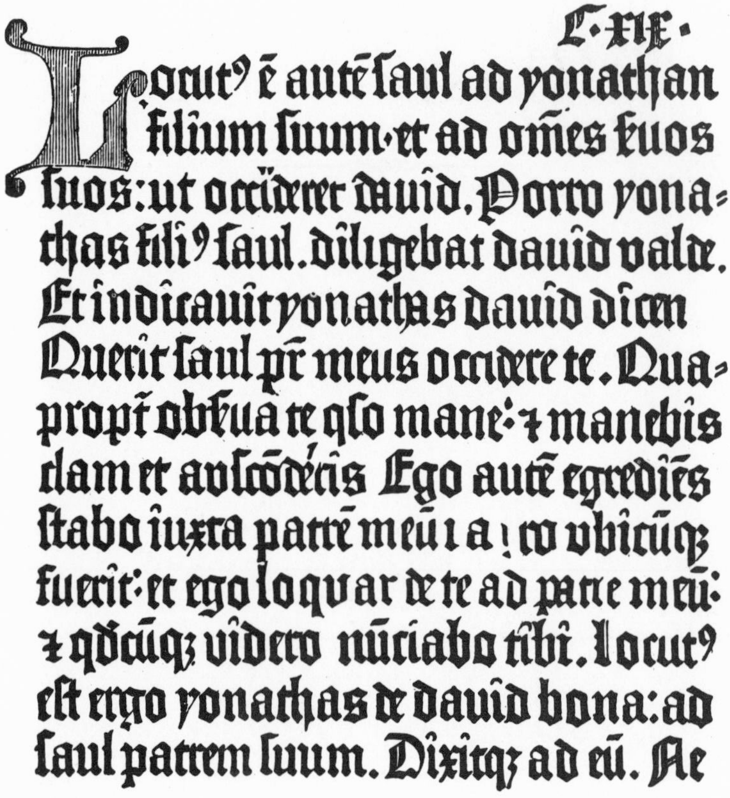

C·XIX·

Locut9 ē autē saul ad yonathan
filium suum·et ad omēs suos
suos: ut occideret david. Porro yona=
thas fili9 saul. diligebat david valde.
Et indicavit yonathas david dicens
Querit saul pr̄ meus occidere te. Qua=
propt̄ obsua te qso mane: ⁊ manebis
clam et absconderis Ego autē egrediēs
stabo iuxta patrē meū i agro ubicūq3
fuerit: et ego loquar de te ad patrē meū:
⁊ qdcūq3 videro nūciabo tibi. Locut9
est ergo yonathas de david bona: ad
saul patrem suum. Dixitq3 ad eū. Ne

Figure 1. Facsimile of a portion (I Samuel xix, 1-5) of the 42-line Latin Bible, printed by Johann Gutenberg at Mainz in 1456. The 1282 double-column pages were divided into two, three, or even four volumes. The estimated printing of 150 copies was a considerable number for the 16th century. This work is also known as the Mazarin Bible, because the first copy described was found in the great Bibliothèque Mazarine, established in 1642 by the French prime minister, Cardinal Mazarin.

Figure 2. Although originally attributed to Cimabue, later research has established that this "Madonna and Child with Angels" was painted by Duccio for the chapel of the Rucellai in Santa Maria Novella, Florence.

Figure 3. "The Presentation of Christ in the Temple" is part of a fresco cycle, "The Life of Christ." It was painted by Giotto for the Arena Chapel (so named because it was built on the site of an ancient amphitheater) in Padua.

Figure 4. In this detail of the "Expulsion of Adam and Eve from the Garden of Eden," the lifelike rendering of the two grief-stricken figures represents one of Masaccio's most important contributions to the development of painting.

Figure 5. Botticelli often used mythological subjects to portray his love of earthly beauty. In this detail from the "Garden of Venus," or "Primavera," Flora and Zephyrus, the West Wind, are gently urging Spring into the garden.

Figure 6. Leonardo da Vinci painted two versions of the "Madonna of the Rocks," one *c*. 1483 and the other *c*. 1506. The second, pictured above, is believed by some to be largely the work of Ambrogio de Predis, one of Leonardo's pupils.

Figure 7. Leonardo's "Mona Lisa" is one of the most famous paintings of all time. It beautifully illustrates the artist's genius for expressing subtle psychological values.

Figure 8. The influence of the four years Raphael spent in Florence is evident in "La Belle Jardinière." He has used, for example, the pyramidal grouping found in Leonardo's "Madonna of the Rocks."

Figure 9. Twenty-five years after the completion of the Sistine ceiling, Michelangelo returned to the chapel to paint the monumental "Last Judgment" for Pope Paul III. The fresco measures 48 by 44 feet, and took five years to complete.

Figure 10. Giovanni Bellini's "Portrait of the Doge Loredano" is a masterpiece of serenity and power. Leonardo Loredano was the Doge of Venice who, with incredible perseverence and calm courage, led his people in a successful battle for survival against the League of Cambrai in 1508.

Figure 11. The Venetians were the first among the Italians to realize the possibilities inherent in the use of landscapes in painting. "The Tempest" shows both this awareness of nature, and Giorgione's mastery in the handling of light.

Figure 12. Titian's "Bacchus and Ariadne" shows the artist's perfection of composition and his assured handling of minute details. The scene, because of the Corona Borealis in the upper left-hand corner, appears to be just prior to Ariadne's death when the jewels of her crown became stars.

Figure 13. With his "Sacrifice of Isaac," Ghiberti won the competition to design a set of bronze doors for the baptistery at Florence. The trial panel, a technical triumph because it was cast in one piece, is still in existence.

Figure 14.

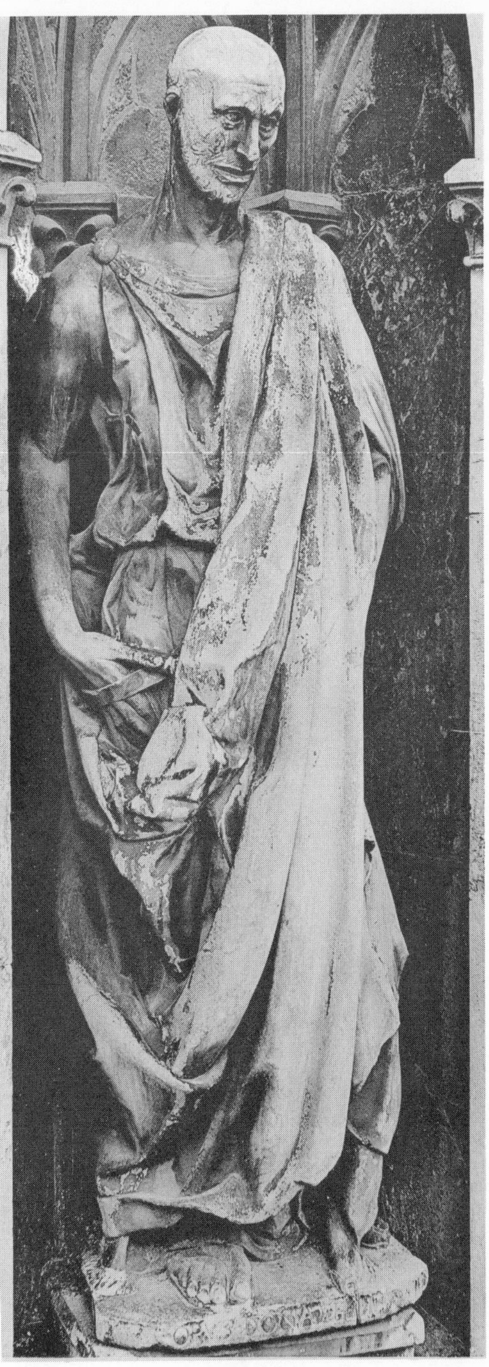

Figure 15.

Donatello's sculptures of David (Fig. 14) and Habakkuk, or "Il Zuccone," (Fig. 15) illustrate the range and diversity of the great artist. Michelangelo's "David" (Fig. 17) offers a striking contrast in artistic interpretation.

Figure 16. When Verrocchio died in 1488, he had completed only the model of his "Colleone." The statue was cast in bronze by Alessandro Leopardi, who signed his own name on the saddle girth.

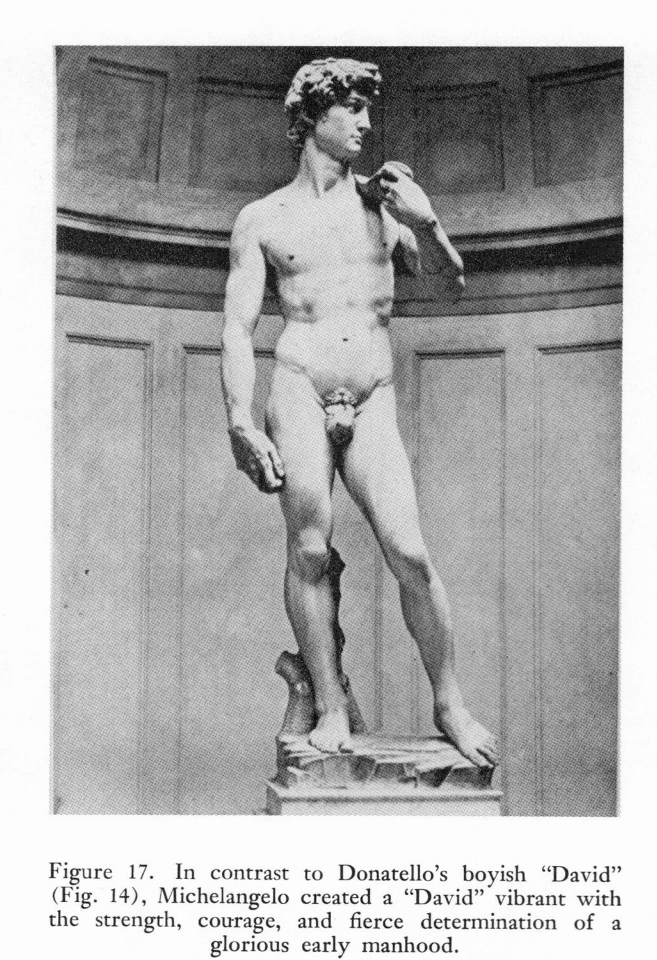

Figure 17. In contrast to Donatello's boyish "David" (Fig. 14), Michelangelo created a "David" vibrant with the strength, courage, and fierce determination of a glorious early manhood.

Figure 18. The beautiful "Pietà" was completed *c.* 1499 when Michelangelo was only about 24 years old. Said Vasari, "The lovely expression of the head, the harmony in the joints and attachments of the arms, legs, and trunk, and the fine tracery of pulses and veins are all so wonderful that it staggers belief that the hand of an artist could have executed this inspired and admirable work."

Figure 19a. The two figures in Cellini's gold salt cellar represent Neptune and Earth. On the sea side (shown) are fish and sea horses, and a ship to hold the salt. An Ionic building and land animals decorate the land side. Several figures on the pedestal are direct copies from Michelangelo's Medici tombs.

Figure 19b. Made in 1527 by Cellini for Francis I, this gold seal was affixed to a secret treaty between France and England, whereby Henry VIII agreed to refrain from further intervention in the wars between Francis and the Holy Roman Emperor, Charles V. The front of the seal (shown) bears a likeness of Francis I; on the reverse are the royal arms of France.

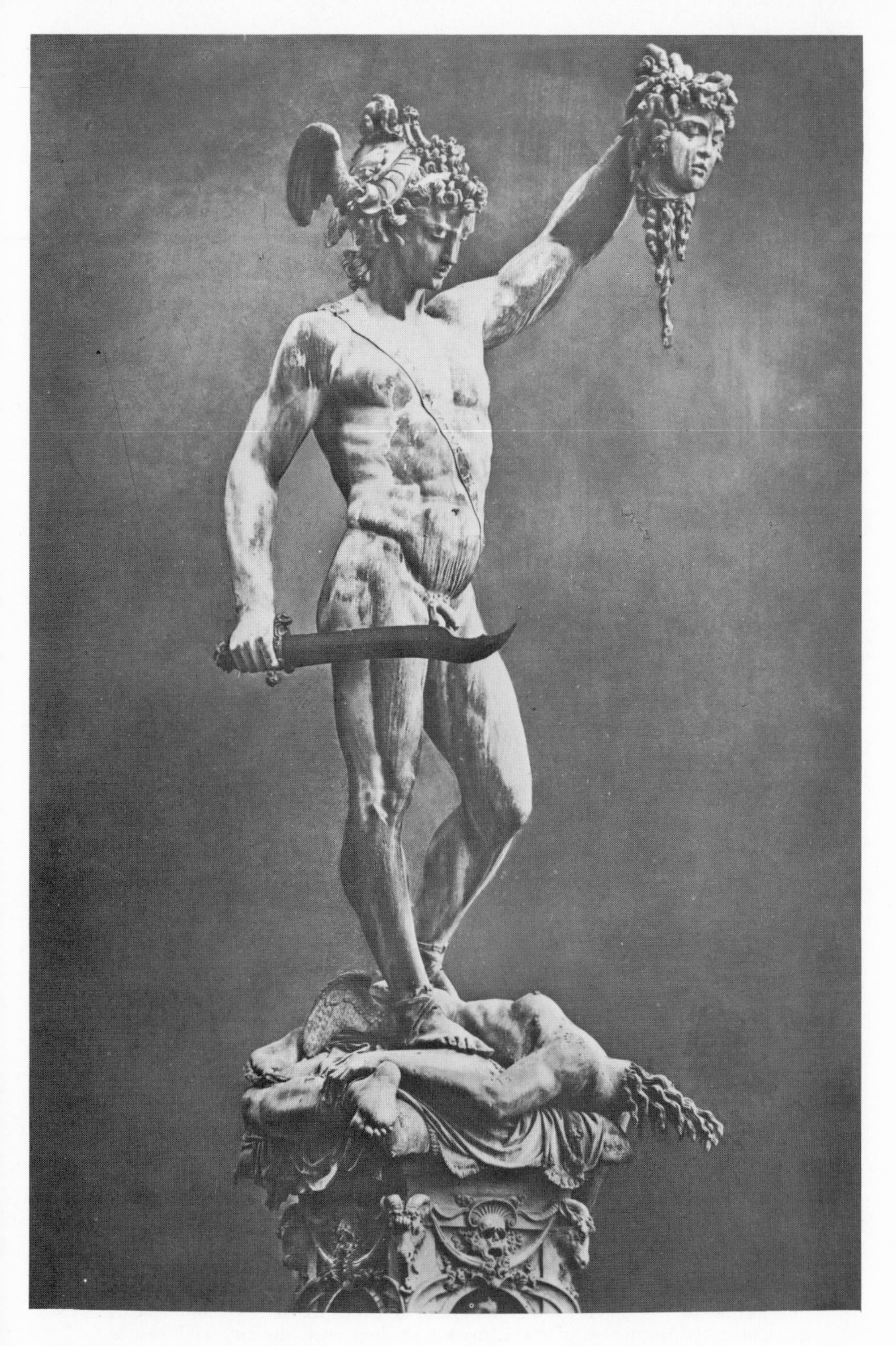

Figure 20. Cellini spent the last nine years of his life working on his "Perseus." He considered the monument to be his masterpiece, an opinion which critics, however, have not shared.

Figure 21. After years of wardens' misgivings, citizens' interference, and a feud with Ghiberti, in 1436 Brunelleschi brought to completion the main portion of the dome of the Cathedral of Santa Maria del Fiore. Vasari ended his description of the dome which dominated the city of Florence by remarking that the "heavens themselves seem to be envious of it since every day it is struck by lightning."

Figure 22. The reconstruction of St. Peter's Cathedral in Rome was commissioned by Pope Julius II in 1505. Originally designed by Bramante, who died in 1514, later directors of the gigantic project included Raphael, Michelangelo, and Bernini. The cathedral was finally completed in 1663.

Figure 23. "The Tree of Jesse" is from a miniature in a 15th-century manuscript breviary. In this celestial concert, the ancestors of Jesus Christ are playing such medieval instruments as the portable organ, bagpipe, harp, double flute, veille (hurdy gurdy), and psalterion.

The facing page shows some of the instruments which were widely used during the Renaissance.

Great organ with bellows and double keyboard (12th century)

Vielle (15th century)

Vielle (13th century)

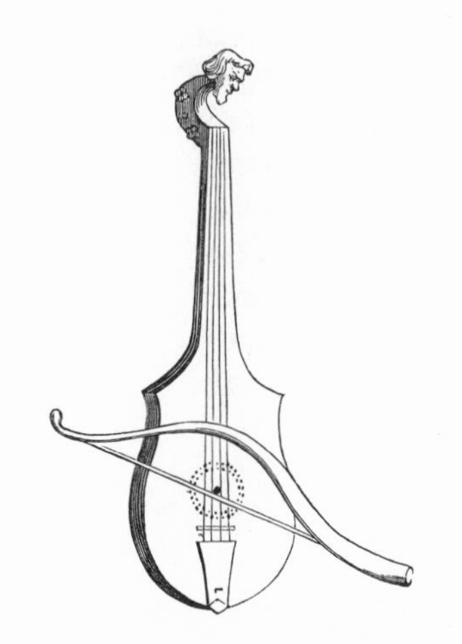

Rebec (16th century)

Monochord (15th century)

Psalterion (12th century)

Organ with single keyboard (14th century)

Figure 24. A fresco series painted by Orcagna represented the four destinies of man—death, judgment, hell, and paradise. The rich and happy "Dream of Life" shown here will be displaced in the next segment by the "Triumph of Death."

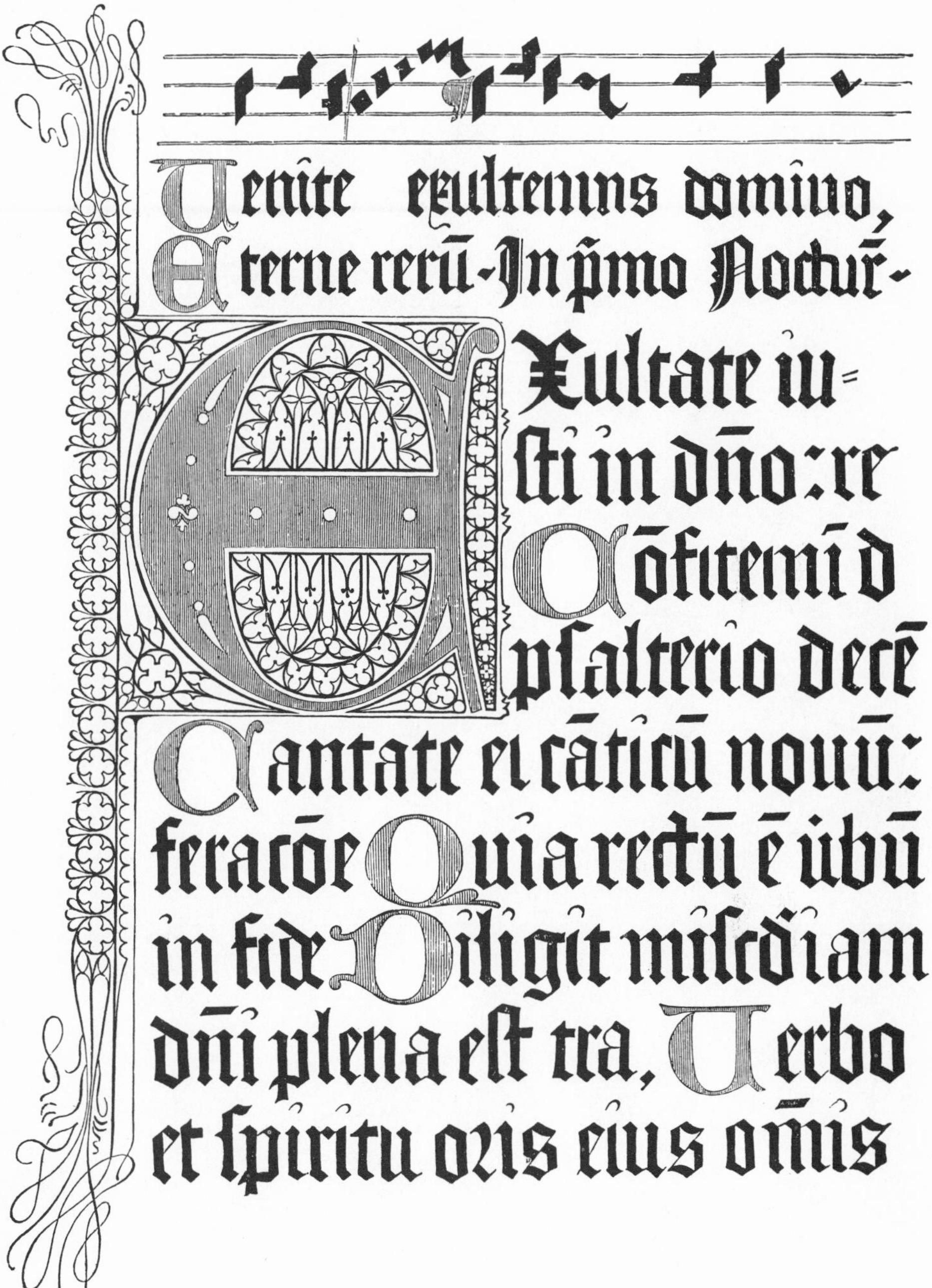

Venite exultemus domino,
Eterne rerū. In p̄mo Noctur̄.
Exultate iu-
sti in dn̄o: re
Cōfitemī d
psalterio decē
Cantate ei cāticū nouū:
feracōe Quia rectū ē ūbū
in fide Diligit misc̄diam
dn̄i plena est tra. Verbo
et spiritu oris eius omīs

Figure 25. The *Psalter*, published at Mainz in 1457 by Fust and Schoeffer, was the first printed book with a complete publication date. The large initials were printed in red and blue from type made in two pieces. The page above is from the second (1459) of the four editions.

Figure 26. This portrait of Francis I was painted by Titian about 1536. The artist, who never actually saw the French king, obtained his likeness from a medal.

Figure 27a. Holbein's portrait of Anne of Cleves reportedly made a most favorable impression on Henry VIII. He was, however, less impressed with Anne herself, and the marriage lasted only six months.

Figure 27b. Although Holbein the Younger was a native of Augsburg, much of his work was done in England. This drawing of Sir Thomas More was executed during Holbein's first visit to London.

Figure 28. Famous for his religious paintings, Jan van Eyck was also a master of portraiture. "The Marriage of Giovanni Arnolfini and Giovanna Cenami" shows van Eyck's striking ability to portray character and to integrate a wealth of detail.

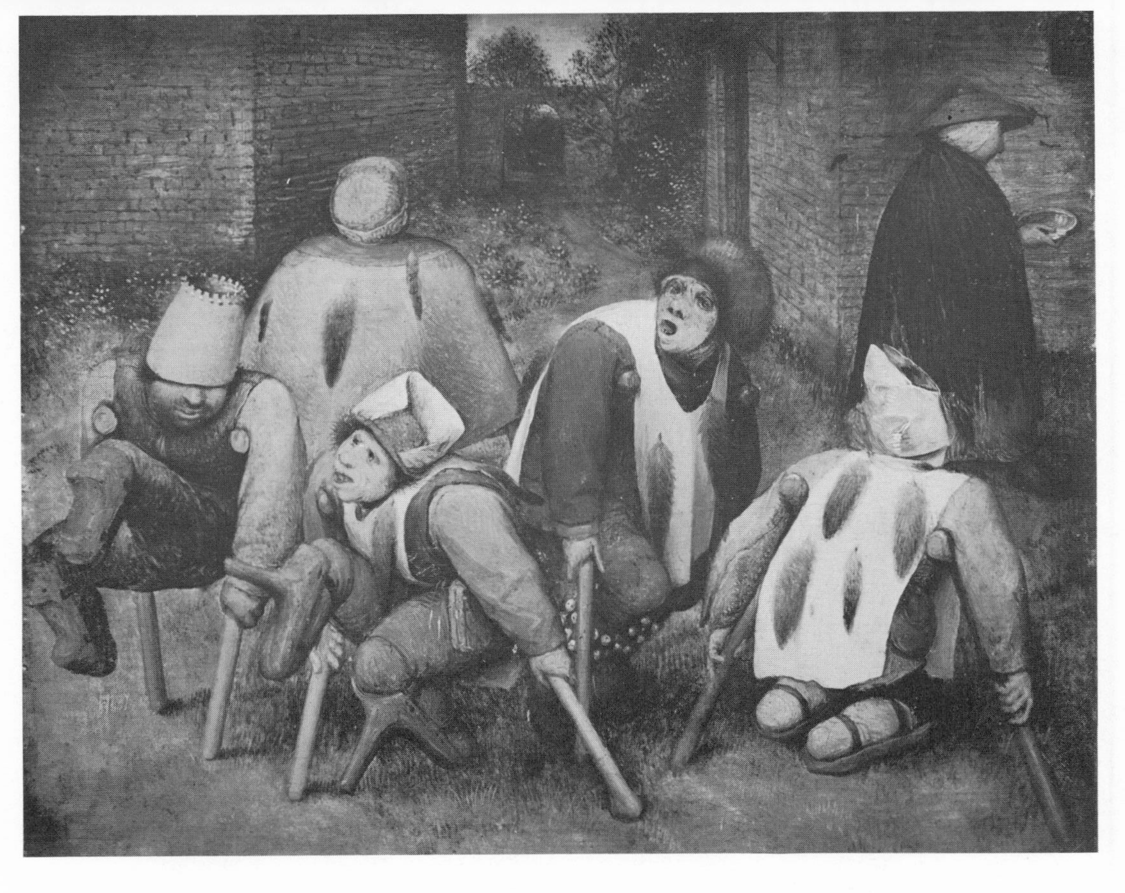

Figure 29. Bruegel the Elder earned the nickname "Peasant Bruegel" and "The Droll" by his realistic portrayal of village life. His peasant scenes were often humorous and charming, but sometimes—as in "The Beggers"—distinctly unpleasant.

Figure 30. The 14th-century Flemish sculptor Claus Sluter brought a new naturalism and refinement to stone carving. The figures of Philip the Bold, Duke of Burgundy, and his Duchess Margaret, protected by St. John the Baptist and St. Anne, were executed for the portal of the Carthusian monastery at Champmol, Dijon.

Figure 31. François Clouet introduced the full-length portrait into French Renaissance painting. The drawn curtains, such as those framing the figure of Henry II, were often the setting for royal portraits.

Figure 32. Germain Pilon, a favorite court painter of Catherine de Medici, was one of the major figures of the French Renaissance. He designed "Les Trois Grâces" to hold an urn containing the heart of Catherine's husband, King Henry II of France.

Figure 33. The best sculptures of Jean Goujon are noted for their combination of strength and delicacy. Both of these characteristics are evident in "Diana and the Stag," but there is now considerable doubt as to whether or not it is actually Goujon's work.

Figure 34. In Dürer's famous engraving "The Knight of Death," a fully-armed knight travels to battle in the company of Sin and Death, who are personified as footman and esquire. Dürer's brilliant engravings and woodcuts were his most valuable contribution to Western art.

Figure 35. In 1538 Holbein, now court painter to Henry VIII, journeyed to Brussels to paint a portrait of Christina of Denmark. Daughter of King Christian II of Denmark, niece of Emperor Charles V, and widow of the Duke of Milan, 16-year-old Christina was considered a possible fourth wife for Henry.

THE RENAISSANCE

1

The Renaissance: The Word and the Concept

The age of the Renaissance is one of the great creative periods of history. Few historical eras have displayed greater intellectual and artistic vitality or have been richer in conspicuous genius. To find its equal in previous history, one must go back to the great days of Athens during which the genius of Greece reached its highest development. The age of the Renaissance is a picturesque age which one historian has described in these words, "Never was virtue more heroic or vice more refined." Like all other ages it had its contradictions and illusions, but they did not dampen the eager curiosity about the unknown or interfere with the probings into it. The Renaissance period was, above all, a time which gave new direction to intellectual endeavor by turning the thoughts and strivings of men into paths leading to what is now called modern civilization.

In a more specific sense the Renaissance stimulated a deep interest in man as a terrestrial being and in the world as his abode. It is common knowledge that the Renaissance period was a great age for the development of painting and sculpture. Artists awakened to a love of natural beauty for its own sake, creating works of unsurpassed excellence. In the field of literature the Renaissance witnessed the rise of the great national literatures of Western Europe written in the slowly-developing vernacular languages. In the realm of science the modern scientific spirit began to make itself felt. By approaching nature through the medium of observation and experimentation, students of natural science laid the foundations for the structure of modern science. The earth was given its proper place in the universe by the revival of the heliocentric theory, support for which was gathered through the use of the new methodology. At the same time the inventive spirit was at work facilitating progress in many directions. The art of printing with movable type, for example, appeared just in time to make possible the swift and easy diffusion of knowledge. This was followed by the invention of the telescope which was an invaluable aid in the study of the heavens. An equally invaluable aid in the exploration of uncharted seas and in the discovery of theretofore unknown lands was the mariner's compass. Equipped with the compass and other improved navigational devices, explorers set out to find an all-water route to the riches of India. Their efforts resulted not only in the finding of the all-water route, but also in the discovery of America. Riches in the form of spices and other products as well as precious metals greatly increased the wealth of the European states. Furthermore, the discoveries also opened a wider world for both the intellect and the imagination.

The era of the Renaissance was also an age of great social, economic, and political changes. While the old feudal order was disintegrating, the rising middle class or bourgeoisie was injecting new life into the social body by giving it new bones, muscles, and nerves in the form of commerce, industry, and banking. New exchange and credit techniques revolutionized business methods, enabling a rigorous expansion of commerce and industry. Merchants, industrialists, and bankers challenged the medieval concept of economic behavior by giving free rein to their acquisitive instincts without any feeling of social responsibility. In the realm of statecraft it was the period of the rise of the national state, the political unit about which the affairs of modern Europe were to revolve. The national state, in turn, introduced into the political arena a new force called national patriotism. This force, an adhesive which held the citizens of a national state together, also had major importance as a fomenter of national rivalries and wars.

The era of the Renaissance produced many men of extraordinary genius. The list of men of distinction is so long that only a few can be mentioned. Among those whose names are emblazoned in large letters in the annals of great achievements are such Italian figures as Botticelli, Leonardo da Vinci, Raphael, Michelangelo, Titian, Dante, Petrarch, Benvenuto Cellini, and Machiavelli. The countries north of the Alps produced such immortals as Chaucer, Shakespeare, Marlowe, Sir Thomas More, and Sir Francis Drake in England; Jan van Eyck, Holbein, Dürer, and Erasmus in Germany and the Netherlands; Villon, Rabelais, and Montaigne in France; Prince Henry the Navigator and Vasco da Gama in Portugal; Cervantes and Lope de Vega in Spain, not to overlook an Italian named Columbus who was in the employ of the Spanish rulers. Among the eminent rulers were Lorenzo the Magnificent of Florence, Ferdinand and Isabella and their great-grandson Philip II in Spain, Henry VIII and his daughter Elizabeth in England, Francis I in France, and Charles V who ruled Spain as well as the Holy Roman Empire in Germany.

Few historical periods have evoked such widespread and unflagging interest. In addition to those who have chosen the Renaissance as their special field, many historians, scholars, philosophers, artists, students of literature, and the history of science turn repeatedly to the Renaissance period to study one or more of the early phases of Western civilization. In the Western world generally there is a wide public of cultured men and women who are interested in the literary and art treasures, the philosophy and mode of life, the achievements and failures, the strivings and adventures, the virtues and vices of the Renaissance. Many examples of the literature of the period are now available in translations as well as in the original languages. It would indeed be rare to find an educated Western man completely unacquainted with the sonnets of Dante and Petrarch, Boccaccio's *Decameron*, the autobiography of Benvenuto Cellini, the poems of François Villon, Chaucer's *Canterbury Tales,* the dramas of Marlowe and Shakespeare, and Cervantes' *Don Quixote.* Modern transportation has made it comparatively easy to see the great works of art in the country of their origin. Although many paintings and sculptures of the Italian Renaissance are now in Northern Europe and the United States, a large number can still be seen in Italy itself. In Florence, the great center of Renaissance art, one can see Ghiberti's famous baptistery doors which Michelangelo pronounced fit to be the gates of paradise, Brunelleschi's great cathedral dome, Masaccio's "Adam and Eve," Donatello's statues in the basilica of San Lorenzo, and some of Michelangelo's great sculptures in the Medici chapels. The Pitti Palace and the Uffizi Gallery in Florence contain two of the world's great collections of Renaissance art. In Vatican City there are also priceless treasures of Renaissance painting, sculpture, and architecture, including the Cathedral of St. Peter and the Sistine Chapel.

Each year many thousands of tourists and visitors converge on Italy, and other thousands visit the art collections of Northern Europe. They frequent the dim corridors of galleries and museums and eagerly read the guidebooks and other descriptive literature. Furthermore, they buy color slides of Renaissance works of art, jewelry, and trinkets patterned after Renaissance styles, cloth woven in Renaissance designs, and articles of various kinds which bear a Renaissance label. Recently a large department store in Greater New York attracted a large crowd by advertising a sale of Renaissance merchandise. In all cases the word Renaissance is used as if its meaning is clearly understood. If one were to ask those who visit collections of Renaissance art and purchase "Renaissance" articles what the word Renaissance means to them, the answers would be as different as the individuals who give them. There would be as little agreement on the meaning of the concept as on the chronological limits of the period which produced the Renaissance movement. While some would have only the vaguest idea of its meaning, others would identify it with Leonardo da Vinci and Michelangelo. For others the word Renaissance might recall Boccaccio's *Decameron,* Cellini's *Autobiography* or perhaps even Erasmus' *Praise of Folly* or Sir Thomas More's *Utopia.* One would soon discover that Renaissance means different things to different people.

It is not surprising that there is no generally accepted definition of the Renaissance, because even historians and scholars do not agree on its meaning and historical significance. The question "What was the Renaissance?" has been answered in terms of an individual scholar's various interests and prejudices. The fact that the Renaissance concept has not been defined to the satisfaction of all historians has caused some to doubt that there ever was a Renaissance. This doubt they express in such phrases as "the so-called Renaissance." A few have flatly denied that the Renaissance ever transpired, inferring that the concept is something in the nature of a hoax which historians foisted on an unwary public. This failure to arrive at a precise definition, however, does not prove that there was no Renaissance. Such a line of reasoning would also prove the non-existence of liberty, socialism, and the fifteenth century. Occasionally an historian will object to the use of the word "Renaissance" because its etymological meaning is "rebirth." Such objections have little validity in an age of science in which every sixth-grade pupil knows that nothing can literally be reborn. Many words of the English language are used figuratively, and there appears to be no valid reason why "Renaissance" should be an exception. We have a precedent for this as far back as the biblical story of Nicodemus (John 3:1). "Renaissance" is not only a colorful word, it is a useful term when not invested with meanings which distort the facts of history.

The Use of the Word "Renaissance"

The use of the word "Renaissance" as an historical label is apparently here to stay. It is so firmly established in common parlance and historical writing that it would be futile to try to dispossess it. Any attempt to do so would, in the phrase of one historian, be tantamount "to tilting at windmills." It might therefore be well to survey briefly the historical use of the word. In the past its use has ranged from the specific to the all-inclusive. During the early decades of the nineteenth century it was applied to what was then called "the revival of learning," now better known as humanism, a movement which was based on a deep interest in and admiration for the classical literature of Greece and Rome. Other historians used the word Renaissance in a broader sense to include the new trend in art. In 1855 the French historian Jules Michelet used the word Renaissance in a still broader sense in his *History of France in the Sixteenth Century*. Michelet summed up his conception of the Renaissance in the descriptive phrase, "the discovery of the world and of man," thereby falsely implying that the Middle Ages had been aware of neither. Five years later the Swiss historian Jacob Burckhardt published his *Die Kultur der Renaissance in Italien* in which he expanded Michelet's idea to include, among other things, politics and statecraft. Burckhardt failed, however, to assign to economic factors their proper place in the scheme of things.

Toward the end of the nineteenth century a number of historians used the word Renaissance in the broadest sense. They applied it to the entire process of transition from medieval to modern civilization in Western Europe. One of the first to express this broad view of the Renaissance was the English historian John Addington Symonds who wrote a number of volumes on the Renaissance which were widely read in the English-speaking world. He stated that the Renaissance "is no mere political mutation, no new fashion of art, no new restoration of classical standards of taste." It is, he asserted, "the movement by which the nations of Western Europe passed from the medieval to the modern modes of thought and life." Thus when used in this sense the word Renaissance includes all the progressive developments of the period whether they are political, economic, social, artistic, intellectual or moral. Despite the differences in their conception of the Renaissance, these nineteenth-century historians had one thing in common; they believed that the changes they described had occurred suddenly, in other words, that they had been cataclysmic. Symonds, for example, asserted that things which had been neglected for centuries "suddenly became vital."

The use of the word Renaissance in either its broader or its restricted sense leaves much to be desired. When used in the limited sense it has the merit of assigning a name to a specific development, but it is not inclusive enough. Furthermore, it is extremely subjective, since the choice of the movement to which it is applied is directed by the interests or prejudices of the individual historian or interpreter. On the other hand, the broader concept of the Renaissance has the weakness that it is not definite enough. When the word Renaissance is used to denote the entire process of transition from medieval to modern civilization it is so general that it gives no clue as to the nature of the changes that took place. A more definite formula is needed to clarify the progressive movement.

The Renaissance Concept

The idea of the Renaissance did not originate in the works of nineteenth-century historians; it dates from the Renaissance itself. Historians, humanists, and artists of the time were conscious that something of great creative importance was taking place. This feeling was fostered by such developments as the growth of vernacular literatures, recovery of manuscripts of classical works, founding of libraries, new trends in painting, sculpture, and architecture, and geographical discoveries. All this added up to the conviction that a new age had dawned. Some even believed that they were participating in the creative activities which had ushered in the new age and which held the promise of a brilliant future. This self-awareness of the Renaissance is a distinguishing feature of the movement. It is the hallmark of genuineness which sets the Renaissance apart from all other so-called "renascences." Whereas interpretations of the Renaissance have varied, and the criteria on which they were based have changed, the fact of the self-awareness of the Renaissance has stood firm and unassailable. Anyone who wishes to deny that there was a Renaissance must find ways and means of circumventing this fact.

Many of the men living in the Renaissance period were not only convinced that they were living in a new age; they also had a definite idea as to when the new age had opened and who had inaugurated it. As early as the fourteenth century Boccaccio, for example, wrote that Dante "was the first to open the way for the return of the Muses banished from Italy. . . . By him dead poetry may truly be said to have been revived." Some years later Filippo Villani (1325-1405), in his book on famous citizens of Florence, stated that Dante brought Florence "back to light from the dark abysses of the preceding period." But as the emphasis shifted from vernacular to classical literature, more and more writers pointed to Petrarch as the man who had ushered in the new age by awakening interest in the classics. Flavio Biondo, for example, stated in his *Italia Illustrata* (1453) that Petrarch was the initiator of the new literary fashions. Leonardo Bruni, who also lived in the fifteenth century, gave the credit to Petrarch and Chrysoloras, the latter being the first outstanding teacher of Greek in Italy. By the end of the fifteenth century the activity of Petrarch was generally regarded as the turning-point from the old to the new. Men of the Renaissance also regarded the new trend in art as epoch-making. Boccaccio, for example, was so moved by the life-like qualities of Giotto's figures that he hailed the painter as having "restored the art of painting to the light." In the sixteenth century the Italian art historian, Vasari, in his *Lives of Eminent Painters* (1550) credited Giotto with having revived "the noble art of painting which had fallen on evil days" through "the life-like portrayal of living persons which for many years had been out of fashion."

In describing the break-away from the old traditions the Renaissance writers employed a number of metaphors. The one used most frequently was that of awakening from a long sleep or emerging from a state of torpor. This metaphor was used by writers north of the Alps as well as by those of Italy. In 1525 the great German artist Albrecht Dürer, for example, interpreted the change as a "Wiedererwachung" (reawakening). Another favorite metaphor was that of the light of the new age dissipating the darkness of the preceding one. This metaphor was used by Boccaccio, Rabelais, and others. The metaphor of rebirth came into use very gradually, but in time displaced the others. One of its earliest uses was in a letter written by Nicolas de Clemanges (1360-1434), one of the early French humanists who was in touch with the Italian movement. The Latin word he used was "renasci." Early in the sixteenth century the German humanist Melanchthon spoke of a rebirth of classical learning. Vasari used the metaphor in discussing Giotto's influence on the development of art. One of the first to use the word "Renaissance," which is of French origin, to describe the developments in the field of literature was a sixteenth-century Frenchman, Pierre Belon. During the seventeenth and eighteenth centuries the word was used only occasionally. About the middle of the nineteenth century John Ruskin gave it a wide circulation in the English-speaking countries when he used it in his *Stones of Venice* (1851). Jacob Burckhardt's *Kultur der Renaissance in Italien* (1860) firmly established its use in the German-speaking world. When Walter Pater published his book titled *The Renaissance* in 1873 he was able to state that the word was in general use.

The Renaissance Attitude Toward the Middle Ages

The metaphors used by Renaissance writers not only emphasized their belief that the changes which had taken place had been abrupt; they also expressed the opinion of the learned men of the Renaissance that the preceding period was the antithesis of their own age. This sharp line of demarcation constitutes the beginning of the custom of dividing history into periods. The period preceding the Renaissance was regarded as being separate and different because it had supposedly interrupted the development of classical civilization. It was, in other words, the period between their own time and the classical period. This is reflected in the adjective "medieval" and the designation "Middle Ages." Later historians perpetuated this idea by the division of European history into ancient, medieval, and modern.

The portrayal by the Renaissance writers of the preceding period as the antithesis of their own age also marked the inception of an unfavorable attitude toward the Middle Ages. In the view of most Renaissance writers there were two lofty plateaus of knowledge, their own era and ancient times. The long stretch of about a thousand years between the two lofty plateaus, extending from the fall of Rome to their own time, they regarded as a period of intellectual stagnation. In accordance with the metaphor of darkness and light the period was variously referred to as a time of benighted semi-barbarism or one of unrelieved barbaric darkness. Eventually the name "Dark Ages" became practically synonymous with "Middle Ages." This derogatory view of the Middle Ages appeared in the writings of the early humanists including those of Petrarch (1304-1374), the first outstanding Italian humanist. In the fifteenth century it was proclaimed by such eminent humanistic writers as Lorenzo Valla and Poggio Bracciolini. In the sixteenth century the French humanists Budé and Rabelais, among others, restated this view.

Disparagement of the Middle Ages expressed itself in the condemnation of almost everything medieval. Many artists and humanist writers, for example, judged medieval art according to classical standards and found it wanting. Thus they saw little merit in Gothic architecture which was one of the loftiest expressions of medieval spirituality. Some even decried it as being barbarous and grotesque. In 1410 the humanist Filarete wrote, "Accursed is he who devised this wretched Gothic style of building; only a race of barbarians could bring it into Italy." Many Italians contemptuously called Gothic architecture *maniera Tedesca* or the German manner. Michelangelo, for example, taunted Antonio de San Gallo because his plans for rebuilding St. Peter's in Rome included "too many small and petty parts and wreaths of columns, after the German manner." Renaissance humanist writers regarded medieval literature with disdain because it did not measure up to classical standards in regard to elegance of diction and clarity of expression. A favorite attack was to label as "obscure" and "inane" the writings of the scholastics or schoolmen who were the principal elaborators of Christian theology during the centuries preceding the Renaissance. Some idea of the low esteem in which scholasticism was held may be gained from the fact that the word "dunce" derives from the name Duns Scotus, one of the outstanding scholastic philosophers. The adjective medieval itself became a convenient superlative to describe anything unprogressive and obsolete.

Later historians were only too ready to imitate the scorn of the Renaissance writers for the Middle Ages. The Protestants in their struggle against the Roman Catholic Church re-echoed the old refrain of the darkness of the Middle Ages, and writers of the succeeding period followed suit. Disparagement of things medieval probably reached its peak in the Enlightenment of the eighteenth century. Many of the followers of the Enlightenment did not regard the period preceding the Renaissance as worthy of serious study. The French philosopher D'Alembert (1717-1783), for example, stated that in the Middle Ages reason had been "arrested for a thousand years." Voltaire (1694-1778) wrote in his *Essay on Manners*, "Scholastic theology, the bastard offspring of Aristotelian philosophy, badly translated and poorly understood, did more injury to reason and polite studies than the Huns and Vandals." Finally, toward the end of the eighteenth century, the pendulum began to swing in the other direction when certain forerunners of the Romantic Movement, including Herder and Goethe, made pleas for a more sympathetic approach to the study of the Middle Ages.

Twentieth-century historians have completely demolished the barriers to the study and appreciation of the Middle Ages which Renaissance writers erected. They have demonstrated, first of all, that the Middle Ages were not a time of dreary stagnation, but a period which produced a distinctive civilization that made important contributions to our modern civilization. The men of the Renaissance were not confronted with the problem of creating a civilization or a culture to fill a void. What they created was a culture which superseded that of the Middle Ages. Second, recent historiography has shown that the old view of a sharp break between the Middle Ages and the period we call the Renaissance is not in accord with the facts. The Renaissance did not slough off the past as a snake sheds its skin or a human being doffs a jacket. The changes were gradual and at times almost imperceptible. The development as a whole was evolutionary, not revolutionary. Most of the changes had taken root in the soil of the Middle Ages before they blossomed and produced fruit in the Renaissance period. The two periods are joined by many ties. In the light of these facts it is clear why present-day historians no longer use the word "Renaissance" in its literal meaning.

One must, however, be careful not to overemphasize continuity. This is as unhistorical as the idea of cataclysmic change. The search for continuity at all costs tends to cover history with a grey veil of uniformity which obliterates the peculiar and individual characteristics of historical periods. In the case of the Renaissance the changes, if less sudden than formerly portrayed, are nevertheless real and significant. The gradual development produced changes which gave a distinctive character to the Renaissance period.

Arriving at a Definition

In the chapters which follow, the word Renaissance will be used in a general way to designate the process of transition from the medieval to the so-called modern order in Western Europe. Since history never stands still, every age is a period of transition; but the Renaissance is a period of transition in a special sense. It is the bridge between the Middle Ages and modern times. The Renaissance period was a time of crisis in practically every phase of thought and culture. It was a time of warfare between the old and the new, a warfare which is the way of evolution. While the forces of conservatism were battling to stem the tide of change, the forces of change were struggling to assert themselves. The battle was being waged in literature, in art, in music, in drama, in science, in the political arena, in economic affairs, in life generally. New conceptions were slowly encroaching on old traditions, new values were displacing old ones, new standards were being accepted and old ones discarded. Almost every Renaissance writer, humanist, artist, and thinker was in a sense a rebel and to some extent an iconoclast.

But the mere assertion of change is insufficient. It does not illuminate the nature and extent of the changes. Any transition of the magnitude of the one which occurred during the Renaissance period can hardly be simple. It was, in fact, complex, many-sided, and not always orderly. If the history of the period is to be more than a melange of facts, the historian must find some unifying factor which can make the facts intelligible and meaningful by arranging them in some kind of pattern. Such a unifying and elucidating factor is the secularization of life, thought, and culture during the Renaissance period. This secularization is the essence of the Renaissance. Thus the Renaissance is the transition from a civilization which had the hereafter as its central idea to one which is rooted in mundane affairs. The acceptance of this definition does not, however, confer on the historian the right to employ procrustean methods to force all facts into an artificial harmony. Its purpose is to serve as a guide through the maze of changes which constitute the Renaissance.

The figurative rebirth or revival implied by the word "Renaissance" is the revival in some degree of the secular spirit which had prevailed before the rise of Christianity. The word "secular" pertains to the present life and the visible world as distinguished from "otherworldly" which refers to or implies concern for a future existence after death. Secularism is an interest in mundane affairs apart from any meaning they may have for the hereafter. The two words, secular and otherworldly, designate two separate areas of thought and interest, but are not intrinsically opposed to each other. (*See Chapter 3.*)

The dominant spirit of the Middle Ages was otherworldly, and life in general had a religious orientation. The first and last purpose of man's life on earth was the attainment of salvation, that is, of eternal bliss. This was emphasized again and again in the thought and culture of the period. Although the secular spirit did exist, it was largely subordinate to and controlled by otherworldly motives. As certain segments of the population became prosperous, however, conditions of earthly life improved and the interest in mundane affairs intensified. This interest stimulated the rise of a more secular spirit which, in turn, deepened the interest in life on earth. During the Renaissance period the secular spirit became a force of real proportions which penetrated in varying degrees most phases of human thought and activity. It was the relentless surge of this secular spirit which gradually rent asunder the sturdy fabric of medieval civilization and set the patterns which shaped the forms of the new civilization.

The growing interest in man as a terrestrial being and in the earth as his abode does not mean, however, that during the age of the Renaissance religion ceased to be a major concern. What transpired was that the interest in mundane affairs gradually became a major concern beside the otherworldly strivings. In time the secular spirit became so intense that it pushed the otherworldly motivations into the background. Man began to live more and more for the delights earthly life could offer and for the beauty of the visible world. Although a reaction against the rising tide of secularism did set in during the Protestant and Catholic Reformations of the sixteenth century, it was the secular standards of the Renaissance rather than the religious standards of the Reformations which ultimately prevailed.

Any attempt to confine historical changes within fixed chronological limits is always more or less arbitrary. This is particularly true of such an all-embracing movement as the Renaissance. Since the forces of change affected the different fields of activity at different times any precise date marking the beginning or termination of the movement would do violence to history. The edges of the Renaissance movement are at best ragged and blurred. In a general way the Renaissance period covers the fourteenth, fifteenth, and sixteenth centuries. Although indications of Renaissance developments are by no means rare in the preceding centuries, the developments which collectively constitute the Renaissance did not form a distinguishable area of history until the fourteenth century. After 1300 the new trends gathered momentum in such a way as to present the impression of novelty. By 1600 most of the collective strength of the Renaissance as a movement had been spent. By this time the Renaissance was regarded as something that had transpired in the past. The choice of 1600 as a convenient stopping place does not imply that the forces generated by the Renaissance ceased to be active. Some are still dynamic in the shaping of modern civilization.

2

The Role of the Medieval Church

The outlook of the Greek and Roman world was secular, that is, it was restricted to the concerns of this life. Any conception that classical man had of a future existence was very vague and indefinite. The world itself was for him the center of his imagination and endeavors. No human interest was recognized as transcending the secular conception of life. Although religion filled a dominant role in the society of the time and was in evidence in every sphere of life, public or private, it was subordinated to the secular ends to which society and the state were dedicated. Religion was, in fact, a department of the state and as such the means for promoting secular purposes. Any appeal to a higher law than that of the state would have been the supreme impiety. The governing principle of life was the ascendancy of the present. "Every man's life," said Marcus Aurelius, "lies all within the present." There was nothing higher than the forces that ruled the present and life had no meaning except in terms of the present.

The Otherworldly Idea

When Christianity appeared on the scene it gave a new meaning to mundane existence. It taught that citizenship in an earthly state does not and cannot comprise the whole of man's life. He has higher spiritual needs which secular values cannot satisfy. Mankind has an immortal destiny which can be fulfilled only by a life beyond this one. Since life in the hereafter is the true life of man, eternal or otherworldly values are the supreme ones. In support of this contention Christian theologians cited various passages from the Bible. Among the favorite ones were the statements of Jesus, "My kingdom is not of this world" and "Seek ye first the kingdom of God and its righteousness." The paramount importance of otherworldly aims is stressed again and again in the writings of the Church Fathers. St. Augustine, for example, in setting forth the dual character of man's citizenship (earthly and heavenly) emphasized the insignificance of the former in comparison with the latter. The early Christians differed on many points, but they were united in their belief that eternal values are paramount. The idea that man's true life is not in this world but in the hereafter was the principal attraction of Christianity. It was this concept which eventually enabled Christianity to triumph over Greco-Roman paganism and other religions.

According to the teaching of Christianity man's main purpose on earth is to make certain his salvation, that is, to insure his entrance into heaven. The earth is the stage on which the drama of salvation is being played, and each individual member of the great cast must play his part well if he is to escape eternal punishment. The attainment of eternal felicity is of such overriding importance that all other purposes are insignificant in comparison. Since every Christian has only a short probationary stay on earth during which his eternal fate is decided, he must be on his guard lest he put his salvation in jeopardy. He must take heed not to become too deeply involved in secular affairs lest the weeds of mundane cares, worldly riches, and fleshly pleasures choke the seeds of faith so that they cannot sprout, grow, and bear fruit. The assertion of the supremacy of otherworldly values and interests carried with it the implication that secular affairs have little or no meaning by themselves. They are servants of the otherworldly purpose, and must be used to promote the salvation of souls. In this way Christianity brought the secular and the otherworldly into a vital relationship which resolved the tension which had existed between the two in the early Christian era. More than this, when Christianity enlisted the secular in the service of its teachings it created a synthesis of the secular and the otherworldly. This synthesis became the theoretical basis of medieval civilization. It was as dominant as any particular Weltanschauung can be in any age and was the factor which gave medieval civilization its distinctive character.

The sphere of Christianity was not limited to a small part of Europe. It gradually extended its influence over practically the whole continent as well as over the Near East. All Europeans who became Christians, and there were few exceptions, were motivated at least in theory by the purpose of achieving salvation and were subject to the same moral laws. Thus Europe had a unity based on the Christian faith. It was not a unity discovered by historians at a later time. Theological writers of the time made much of it. For example, St. Augustine, seeing the world about him in a state of chaos and collapse, consoled himself with the idea, "There is one commonwealth of all Christian men." Writers of the succeeding centuries continued to echo this idea, even after the division of the Christian world into the eastern and western churches. Although the homogeneity of Christendom when viewed from the vantage point of the present appears greater than it actually was, there was unity in theory and to some extent in reality. Whatever the gulf between theory and reality, the idea of a single commonwealth of all Christians lived on in medieval writings. Machiavelli who lived in the sixteenth century was probably the first writer who did not regard the Christian peoples as one community.

The Medieval Church and Its Purpose

The visible embodiment of Christian unity was the Roman Catholic Church. Through its efforts the peoples and tribes of Western Europe had been converted and brought into its membership. Its efforts were so successful that by the time of the death of Pope Gregory the Great in 604 it was established as the sole religious authority with a prestige and a power that were generally recognized in Western Europe. Some idea of the high position of the Church in medieval society can be gained from the fact that the greatest crime was heresy or infidelity to the Church. In comparison treason against the state was immeasurably less serious. Having united Western Europe the Roman Catholic Church served as the skeleton to hold the body of believers together. Through its hierarchical organization it reached into every nook and corner of Western Europe, using the Latin language in both the classical and vulgar form as the medium of communication. But the claims of the Church were even broader than its organization. When the Roman Empire broke up in the West, the idea of universality or catholicity which it claimed to represent was not lost. It was simply taken over by the Church and changed into a religious concept. The idea of universality was, in fact, incorporated into its very name, the Roman Catholic Church.

To enable it to attend to the spiritual needs of such a great multitude of believers the Church developed an elaborate system of administration. The supreme administrator of this system was the pope whose authority rested on the claim that he was the successor of St. Peter, recognized by the Church as the first bishop of Rome. According to the teachings of the Church, Peter's authority as supreme head of Christendom was conferred on him by Jesus. From Peter this authority automatically passed on to those who succeeded him as bishop of Rome. As Pope Gregory VII put it, "Only the bishop of Rome can properly be called universal." As the supreme judge, lawgiver, and administrator the pope was and still is the sole and final authority. His immediate assistants were the members of the papal curia which included the cardinals, special administrators, and household officials, all appointed by him. Next in the hierarchical scale came the archbishops, then the bishops, and finally the parish priests. Through the administration of the sacraments, which are the means of receiving the divine grace needed for salvation, the clergy exercised control over every important event in human life. This control was so broad that it conditioned all phases of medieval civilization. There was no room in medieval society for any activity that might be independent of the moral laws of the Church.

In the fulfillment of its purpose which was the cure or salvation of souls the Church enlisted all phases of human life in the service of the otherworldly idea. In other words, it endeavored to bring the whole of human life into harmony with its teachings and its goals. It sought to make religion the dominant motive of life, thought, and action. In the pursuit of this aim the Church turned the field of learning into an ecclesiastical province. Its control was so complete that learning became a virtual monopoly of the Church. In the words of the French historian Henri Pirenne, "The intellectual history of Europe was merely a chapter in the history of the Church." All intellectual disciplines became adjuncts of theology, "the queen of the sciences." Thus logic served as the means of systematic arrangement and expression of the teachings of the Church. Philosophy, too, was not regarded as a separate branch of knowledge. Its function was that of "handmaiden of theology." The thought of the medieval philosophers (known as "scholastics" or schoolmen" from their association with schools, particularly higher schools of learning) was centered in theological problems. They discussed the relationship of reason to faith and vice versa, the relation of God to the world, the relation of universals to particulars, and the nature of man and his immortality. The scholastic philosophers did, it is true, criticize one another's opinions of various subjects, but there was no questioning of the basic teachings of the Church. The avowed purpose of scholastic thought was to construct intellectual props for the dogmas of the Church.

Even natural science was part of the pyramid of knowledge which had theology as its apex. The lines separating philosophy and natural science were so indistinct that many medieval thinkers regarded the two as one. But whereas philosophy concerned itself primarily with the laws and structure of all reality, natural science limited its efforts to obtaining knowledge of nature. Most of the early medieval thinkers did not consider the study of nature an end in itself. With philosophy, natural science shared the task of gathering evidence to support "the revealed truth" of which the Church was the custodian. For example, natural scientists and thinkers generally turned to nature for symbolical illustrations of the Trinity. One illustration of the unity of the Trinity was a three-pointed leaf. Nature was also scanned for symbolical illustrations of such other teachings as the goodness of God and His solicitude for man's salvation. At times natural scientists did discuss the composition of matter and the mechanics of the universe, but were careful to stay within the doctrinal boundaries set by Roman Catholic dogma. The circulation in the twelfth century of Latin translations of Aristotle's *Physics* and other discussions of science by classical thinkers stimulated a broader interest in nature and natural phenomena. But the basic interest continued to be closely allied with theology. Most of the "scientists" of the succeeding period were still theologians.

Ecclesiastical Culture

The Church was not interested in culture for the sake of culture. Like all other phases of medieval life, culture was given the purpose of helping the Church achieve its goals. Art was so thoroughly impregnated with a religious spirit that the Christian faith became its central theme. Under the aegis of the Church, painting performed a number of religious functions. First, it embellished and adorned the interiors of the houses of worship. Second, painting provided the means for strengthening the faith of members of the Church, particularly those whose faith was weak. Third, through some of its representations medieval painting warned members of the Church of the dire consequences of following the pathway of sin. Fourth, in an age of widespread illiteracy visual representations were an important means of teaching the doctrines, legends, and traditions of the Church. In the words of Pope Gregory the Great, "What writing is to those who can read, the picture is to those who cannot, but can only look."

The scope of medieval painting was largely limited to the representation of the basic doctrines of the Church. Accordingly such phases of the nativity and the crucifixion as "The Adoration of the Shepherds," "The Bearing of the Cross," and "The Descent from the Cross" were painted over and over again. Other popular subjects were the lives of the saints and the allegories in the writings of the Church Fathers. Painters also depicted the awesome powers of Satan. Often the forms of grotesque animals and venomous serpents were used as symbols of the forces of evil, the underlying purpose being to impress on the mind of the sinner the craftiness of Satan and the hideousness of sin. Portrayals of the crucifixion, the death of martyrs, and the sufferings of the damned were often gruesome and ghastly.

Because so many of the figures in medieval ecclesiastical paintings are stiff and angular, and often posed in unnatural attitudes, some art historians of the late nineteenth century believed that medieval artists lacked the ability to paint the natural human form. In some instances this may have been true. Medieval artists did, however, demonstrate in illuminating manuscripts that they could produce naturalistic representations. The trees, flowers, insects, and animals they depicted have a high degree of versimilitude. In the thirteenth century there was also a naturalistic strain in Gothic painting and sculpture. In general, however, pre-Renaissance painters did not aim at naturalistic representation. They endeavored to create something above and beyond visible nature, something that would open to the believer a vista of eternity and divine mystery. They sought to present imagery that would suggest a state of being outside earthly life. In its purest form, medieval ecclesiastical painting is ideational, that is, the idea suggested by a painting is more important than the representation. The visual representation is merely a symbol of something higher, something beyond the perception of the senses.

The Church also adapted sculpture to its purposes, making it didactic as well as ornamental. Like painting, ecclesiastical sculpture was ideational. Statues and reliefs were sculptured to symbolize spiritual values, not to reflect natural beauty. Consequently, medieval sculptures are charged with spiritual exaltation to a degree that has seldom, if ever, been equalled. No sooner had the Emperor Constantine (272-337) assured the final triumph of Christianity by being baptized into the new faith than he encouraged the construction of a number of basilicas which were adorned with gold and silver statuary embodying in material form the spirituality of Christian teachings. Marble was regarded as too common a substance to be used in the representation of a divine or saintly personage. Later during the struggle to convert the pagans to Christianity the Christian churches discontinued the use of statuary for a time because it was a form in which paganism had found expression. Hence cathedrals which were built as late as the sixth century contained no sculptures and only a minimum of decoration. When the Church was no longer apprehensive of a pagan revival, and the barbarian invasions were largely over, the sculptor's art was again employed in the service of religion, particularly in the Gothic churches and cathedrals. For these churches and cathedrals which were built in large numbers during the twelfth and thirteenth centuries, statues were chiseled in great profusion. Some cathedrals contained more than a thousand and the Milan cathedral six thousand. Many of the sculptors seem to have been monks, and where lay craftsmen were employed they worked under clerical supervision.

Since religion was the major factor in medieval life, it is not surprising to find that the greatest architectural works of the Middle Ages are the churches. The early Christian churches were modeled on the Roman basilicas or courts of justice. The varied forms of architecture which developed out of these circumstances are called Romanesque. In the twelfth century Romanesque was replaced by the final and most splendid form of medieval architecture, the so-called Gothic style. Gothic was primarily an ecclesiastical style. All the sculpture, the symbolism, and the stained glass of the Gothic churches was designed to lure the soul away from earthly thoughts and concerns to the contemplation of God and the hereafter. The Abbot Suger of St. Denis (1081-1151) expressed the emotion aroused in him upon entering a Gothic abbey church in these words: "I seemed to find myself in some strange part of the universe which was neither wholly of the baseness of the earth nor wholly of the glories of heaven, but by the grace of God I seemed lifted in a mystical manner from this lower to that higher sphere." As architectural gems the Gothic churches challenge comparison with the best the world has ever produced.

Literature was also inspired by and suffused with religion and religious motives. Until the fourteenth century most of the serious literature was ecclesiastical. Since Christianity originated in the Roman Empire it was but natural that Latin should become the official language of the Christian Church. This was not changed by the Germanic invasions. The invading tribes were assimilated by the Church and by what remained of Roman civilization. Up to the time of Charlemagne (768-814) there were still many laymen who had a good knowledge of Latin, but after Charlemagne this knowledge was largely a monopoly of the clergy, particularly of the monks. Hence practically all the Latin literature of the succeeding centuries flowed from the pens of clerics. Monks not only kept routine ecclesiastical and governmental records; they also served as chroniclers who recorded what they considered was important in each calendar year. In addition to historical literature the monks wrote accounts of the lives of saints with special emphasis on the miraculous and extraordinary. They also wrote many religious poems and hymns.

In the vernacular literatures of France, England, Germany, Italy and Spain, written for those who could not read or understand Latin, there was also a strong religious strain. Until the end of the twelfth century vernacular literature whether written for purposes of edification or entertainment was almost entirely in verse form. The use of prose was largely limited to legal documents and translations of the Bible. In the poetry of the early Middle Ages the idea of entertainment was still pushed into the background by religious motives. The earliest preserved poem in the German vernacular is a prayer, the *Wessobrunner Gebet.* Even in the poetry celebrating the prowess of Germanic heroes the religious tone became more marked at the end of the ninth century. Thus we find a strong religious flavor in the *Ludwigslied*, a song of war. In England, too, the earliest vernacular poetry was largely religious. The opening lines of a long Old English poem read:

> Jesus Christ, my Lord to Thee
> A guilty wretch I yield me:
> Broken I have thy commandments
> Against mine own conscience
> But though I have offended ever
> Lord I have forsook Thee never.

In France the *chansons de geste* (songs of deeds), the epic poems which mark the beginning of French literature, relate historical or legendary events enhanced by imaginative treatment. Even here the religious motive is not absent; in fact, almost all the imaginative courtly literature in both prose and verse is based on religious sentiment. The ideal of knightly virtue is upheld, and emphasis is put on the idea that the knight is the vassal of God as well as of an earthly overlord.

Medieval Education

Medieval education was also a domain of the Church. As the Roman Empire declined, and with it the Roman municipal schools, the Christian Church took charge of education and adapted it to its aims. The new Christian schools gradually displaced and superseded the old Roman schools. Only in Italy did some of the Roman secular schools survive. Otherwise, opportunities to acquire a knowledge of reading and writing were largely restricted to the Church schools. These schools were modeled after the Roman schools in that their curriculum retained the so-called seven liberal arts consisting of the trivium (grammar, rhetoric, and logic) and the quadrivium (arithmetic, music, geometry, and astronomy). Whereas the purpose of Roman education had been to prepare the individual for purely secular activities, the basic purpose of the Christian school was to teach the individual the things necessary to achieve eternal bliss; the primary purpose of the early medieval schools was not intellectual or aesthetic, but otherworldly. Whatever culture was not immediately necessary to the purpose of the Church was left aside. The idea of a school devoted to secular education as such was foreign to the early medieval conception of life. The big "R" in medieval education did not stand for reading, writing, or 'rithmetic, but for religion. Religious instruction was the heart and soul of the curriculum. The two principal types of schools were the cathedral and the monastic schools, and their major task was to instruct those who were preparing to enter the priesthood or to become monks. During the centuries preceding the Renaissance period a limited number of pupils were admitted who were preparing for a lay career. This was done to meet the need for literate laymen who could serve as government officials, administrators of large estates, and in other capacities. In their instruction, too, the emphasis was on religion.

The great achievement of the Middle Ages in the field of education was the founding of the universities. Although the origins of some universities are shrouded in obscurity, it is clear that most of the universities either originated in the Church or came under the supervision and protection of the Church soon after they were founded. In the universities which originated in the Church the basic and central subject of study was theology, to which all other studies were subservient. The whole accumulated store of learning of past ages was impregnated with the ecclesiastical or otherworldly spirit. The great center of theological knowledge was the University of Paris. This university was, in the words of the historian Hastings Rashdall who wrote a three-volume work on medieval universities, "the recognized fountainhead of the streams of knowledge which watered the whole of Christendom." Students came from the far corners of Europe to hear the lectures of famous teachers. In the twelfth and thirteenth centuries there was hardly a thinker of distinction in Western Europe who did not study or teach at the University of Paris. Because it served as a model for many German and English universities, the University of Paris has been called "the common mother of the northern universities." It was also the home of scholasticism which dominated European thought until the Renaissance. Through the application of the dialectical method to theological questions, the scholastics developed many subtle arguments in support of the teachings of the Church.

University students were the special wards of the Church and were included in the category of clerics. Many of them wore clerical garb and even the clerical tonsure. Kings and emperors as well as popes granted the students special privileges which put them directly under the authority of the Church. In the year 1200 King Philip Augustus of France freed the students of the University of Paris completely from the jurisdiction of the civil courts, decreeing that "our judges shall not lay hands on a student for any offense whatever." In case a student committed a violent crime he was to be arrested at once and handed over to an ecclesiastical judge. Before long "clerks" were everywhere exempt from the jurisdiction of civil tribunals.

The Church and Medieval Society

As the supreme authority the Church exercised a broad supervision over the social order. Members of society in all its departments from the lowest to the highest were expected to be obedient to the laws of the Church. Conduct in all walks of life was approved or condemned as it conformed to or conflicted with the standards and the aims of the Church. The laws promulgated by the ecclesiastical officials set standards of conduct for all the activities of medieval society. Moreover, the Church also assumed the task of enforcing these laws. So that justice might be established it took under its protection oaths, ordeals, and other phases of legal procedure, surrounding them with solemn ritual. Even those areas of life which were concerned with purely secular affairs and ambitions were subject to ecclesiastical "ordinance and governance." Thus the Church tried to protect non-combatants against the violence and the ravages of feudal warfare waged by barons intent on self-aggrandizement. It issued a series of decrees to establish what became known as the Peace of God. These decrees forbade the infliction of violence on non-combatants under threat of dire punishment. Although the first decrees were issued by local councils the movement became so popular that the pope proclaimed a Peace of God for all Christians. In its broadest scope the Peace of God sought to protect women, children, clerics, pilgrims, merchants, and peasants. Those waging war were warned not to damage or destroy ecclesiastical buildings and unfortified houses, crops and orchards, cattle and agricultural implements. Whoever violated the prohibition drew down on himself the anathema of the Church as well as the condemnation of public opinion.

The Church also endeavored to curb feudal warfare with the movement known as the Truce of God, the basic purpose of which was to restrict the number of days on which warfare could be waged. At first the period that was not to be profaned by fighting extended from Saturday noon to Monday morning, but the period was gradually extended to include the days from Thursday to Monday. Fighting was also forbidden during the seasons of Advent and Lent, and on festival and saints' days. This left those who wished to be obedient sons of the Church only about eighty days on which they could do their fighting. Although many barons ignored the prohibitions, the ecclesiastical decrees were not without effect. It appears that the prohibitions against violence to non-combatants was more widely respected than that which forbade fighting on certain days. In an effort to achieve greater obedience to the decrees the Church in some parts of Europe required young knights and young burghers of the town militia to take a solemn oath to observe and to enforce the Peace of God and the Truce of God.

The supervision of the Church was also extended to economic life. In its laws, called canon laws, the Church laid down principles for the guidance of industry and trade. While recognizing that both industry and trade are necessary to the existence of society, it sought to eliminate factors which might put the welfare of the soul in jeopardy. One of these was the temptation to amass wealth by making large profits. The lust for personal profit was regarded as nothing less than avarice, one of the seven deadly sins. In the medieval descriptions of punishment in purgatory and hell, those guilty of avarice always receive some of the most severe punishments. As a means of holding the acquistive appetite in check the Church issued laws against falsification of weights, measures, and coins, and gave special attention to the question of prices. The basic principle which it laid down was that of the "just price," whereby each article was priced by adding the cost of the raw materials to the value of the labor the craftsman had put into the production of it. This, the Church stated, should insure the craftsman a sufficient income to support himself and his family in the manner of the stratum of society in which his functions had placed him. If it did not, the price was too low. If he remunerated himself too highly and as a result amassed wealth, his prices were unjust and he was guilty of an unchristian attempt to rise above his fellows. This idea was expressed in two popular adages, "Wealth is robbery of the poor" and "Every rich man is either unjust or the heir of an unjust man." Thomas Aquinas put it this way, "If either the price exceeds the value of the object, or vice versa, the equality of justice is destroyed." The same principle was applied to wages, a just wage being the natural complement of the just price.

Town councils and gilds were expected to adopt the principle of the just price and many of them, perhaps most of them, did. Town councils often tried to fix the prices of foodstuffs on this basis. Forestallers who tried to "corner the market" by buying the available supply of food or raw materials while it was on the way to the market and then to sell it at high retail prices were severely punished. As for the gilds, many of them passed regulations governing the quality and the price of the goods their members produced. Measures were also taken to prevent one gildmaster from raising himself above the others financially.

Equally significant was the Church's prohibition of usury. In the Middle Ages the word "usury" did not mean, as it does now, the charging of excessive interest on a loan; it meant any payment at all by the borrower over and above the return of the capital. Anyone who charged interest on a loan was a usurer, and usury was one of the worst forms of avarice. A usurer who died unrepentant could not hope to escape eternal suffering in hell. The sin was considered grave because in the days before thte expansion of trade and the rise of capitalism, money was not borrowed for the purpose of making more money with it, but because the borrower was in dire need. Taking interest, therefore, was regarded as deriving profit from another's misfortune. Moreover, since work and inheritance were regarded as the only honest means of getting money, the charging of interest was considered an outrage because the lender enriched himself without work. As Charlemagne asserted in a capitulary of 808, "Usury is the demand for something that was not given." Another view of usury was that it was a charge for God's time. The Second Lateran Council, convened by Innocent II in 1139, issued a decree against usury which read in part, "We denounce that detestable and disgraceful rapacity condemned alike by human and divine law, by the Old and New Testaments, that insatiable rapacity of usurers whom we hereby cut off from all ecclesiastical consolation . . . usurers are to be regarded as infamous and shall, if they do not repent, be deprived of Christian burial." As late as the fourteenth century Dante still regarded usury as an infraction of the divine law.

Church and State

The supremacy of the Church also extended into the realm of politics and statecraft. Although political organizations from small baronies to large kingdoms were practically independent in the exercise of their functions so long as they stayed within the moral boundaries set by the Church, they were in theory not regarded as separate entities with aims of their own. No secular state was an independent institution. During the centuries before the thirteenth the self-assertive national state was still in the womb of history. All political organizations were in theory merely segments of a greater unity called Christendom. The citizens were, generally speaking, members of local political units and of the intermediate units of which the smaller organizations were a part. Before the rise of the national state most individuals undoubtedly felt some degree of loyalty to the feudal baronies or towns which controlled their economic and social status and also to such intermediate organizations as dukedoms and kingdoms. Their primary allegiance as Christians, however, was to Christendom and to the Church. All other allegiances were classed as being minor.

The Christendom over which the Roman Catholic Church presided and of which it was the visible form had in theory no territorial limits. It extended to wherever there were Christians. Actually, however, it was limited to Western Europe. The pope, as the head of the Church, was the ruler of Christendom. According to ecclesiastical teachings he was the sole legitimate earthly source of law, the guardian of right, and the supreme international judge. His authority was theoretically as broad as the moral laws of the Church. On this basis Pope Innocent III (1198-1216) formulated the papal prerogative, claiming that the supreme pontiff had the right to adjudicate all issues in which morality is involved. Accordingly a number of popes exercised a decisive influence in all phases of contemporary society, including politics and statecraft. Even the Holy Roman Empire with its claims to universal rule could not stand as an institution that was independent of the papacy. Its authority was not valid without the sanction of the Church. The emperor received the crown which symbolized his imperial authority directly from the hands of the pope.

Medieval ecclesiastical writings are replete with assertions, often in the form of metaphors, which aim to establish the supremacy of the papal authority. The classic statement is that of Innocent III who asserted that as God the Creator had "set two great lights in the firmament of heaven, the greater light to rule the day and the lesser light to rule the night," so He "has appointed two great dignitaries, the greater to rule over men's souls . . . and the lesser to rule over men's bodies." The two dignitaries, he stated, are the pope and the emperor. Furthermore, "as the moon derives its light from the sun, and is indeed inferior both in size and importance, so the royal power derives the splendor of its dignity from the authority of the pope." In short, all authority was ultimately a papal prerogative. The German historian, Ernst Troeltsch stated the issue succinctly in these words, "The only sovereignty that existed was that of the Church; there was no sovereignty of the State; nor of economic production, nor of science or art."[1]

This does not mean that there was no place in medieval society for the state. Actually it had an essential role to play. Its role was to function as "the secular arm of the Church." The secular rulers, as the Defenders of the Faith, had the sacred duty of wielding the sword for the furtherance of ecclesiastical purposes. This was also true of the Holy Roman emperor. Administratively he exercised the temporal power, but his empire was merely a functional part of a society in which the absolute sovereignty was exercised by the Church. The Emperor Charlemagne, for example, regarded it as a self-evident truth that the efforts of the state should be directed toward the realization of the spiritual welfare of society. Boniface VIII summed up his view in the famous bull *Unam Sanctam* (1302) when he wrote: "Both the spiritual and the secular swords are in the power of the Church, the latter to be used for the Church, the former by the Church. . . . It is fitting that one sword should be under another, and the temporal authority be subject to the spiritual power." The English historian J. N. Figgis described the situation in these words: "In the Middle Ages the Church was not a State, it was the State. The state or rather the civil authority (for a separate society was not recognized) was merely the police department of the Church."[2]

It is misleading to regard the Investiture Conflict, the long struggle be-

[1] *The Social Teaching of the Christian Churches*, Vol. I, translated by O. Wyon (1931), p. 252.

[2] *Studies of Political Thought from Gerson to Grotius*, 2nd edition (1916), p. 5.

tween the papacy and the emperors which broke out between Pope Gregory VII and Emperor Henry IV in 1075, as a contest between two separate societies. There was as yet no question of two states, one secular and the other spiritual. Actually it was a struggle between officials of the same state or Christian community. Both parties agreed that this society was Christendom; membership in it was gained through baptism and maintained through orthodoxy. The basic issue was the relative authority of the pope and the emperor in this single society. One side put the pope at the head of the great community of Christians, and the other argued for the headship of the emperor. The great question was "Who as the supreme authority should direct the great state or Christian community toward the achievement of the spiritual goals?" Whereas the emperor claimed that he had received his authority directly from God, the pope insisted that as the successor of St. Peter he was the divinely appointed head of Christendom and should therefore be the final arbiter. The *Dictatus*, found among the papers of Gregory VII, states that a papal decree "may be annulled by no one" and that the pope "alone may annul the decrees of all." A compromise was finally reached in the Concordat of Worms (1122) nearly fifty years after the opening of the conflict. Actually the settlement was a triumph for the papacy in so far as it recognized the ultimate authority of the pope. But the Concordat of Worms was only a temporary solution. The conflict between the pope and the emperor over the question of authority flared up again at a later time.

The Otherworldly Attitude: The Last Judgment and Hell

Since the salvation of mankind was the overriding aim of the Church, its representatives sought to keep the idea in the forefront of the consciousness of all members. This they did by stressing the importance of achieving salvation in their direct ministrations, sermons, hymns, and didactic literature. Eminent preachers ransacked the Bible for appropriate quotations and turned to nature for illustrations in their efforts to impress upon the hearers the necessity of making sure of salvation. Much was made of the briefness of life. the imminence of death, and the Last Judgment. All members of the Church were perpetually reminded of the coming of the Day of Judgment when they must appear before Christ, the Supreme Judge, to give account of their lives and actions. They were urged to secure a favorable balance of accounts for the final reckoning so that the verdict would be a favorable one and they would not, in the words of Anselm of Canterbury, be "hurried by the devil to everlasting damnation." Furthermore, the Church members were told that Judgment Day might come without prior warning at any moment "like a thief in the night"; therefore they must be in readiness for it at all times. As Pope Gregory the Great put it, "The soul's ceaseless business is to keep itself so that it may at last escape the sentence of the awful Judge."

The Last Judgment was the subject of many hymns. The first two verses of one of the early hymns read:

That great Day of wrath and terror,
That last Day of woe and doom
Like a thief that comes at midnight,
On the sons of man shall come;
When the pride and pomp of ages
All shall utterly have pass'd,
And they stand in anguish, owning
That the end is here at last.

And the sun shall turn to sackcloth,
And the moon be red as blood,
And the stars shall fall from heaven,
Whelm'd beneath destruction's flood.
Flame and fire, and desolation
At the Judge's feet shall go:
Earth and sea, and all abysses
Shall His mighty sentence know.

(*Translated by John Mason Neale, 1863*)

The most widely circulated Judgment hymn of the Middle Ages was undoubtedly *Dies Irae* (The Day of Wrath) written about 1250 by Thomas of Celano, a town near Naples. His *Dies Irae*, which has been called the highest poetic expression of the teachings of the Church on the subject, was written in Latin, but soon translated into the various vernacular languages of Europe. The fact that no less than eighty-seven versions of this hymn are known indicates how widely it was circulated. The *Dies Irae* reads in part:

Day of Wrath! Oh, day of mourning!
See fulfilled the prophet's warning,
Heaven and earth in ashes burning.

Oh, what fear man's bosom rendeth
When from heaven the Judge descendeth,
On Whose sentence all dependeth.

Lo! the Book exactly worded,
Wherein all hath been recorded:
Whence shall judgment be awarded.

When the Judge His seat attaineth,
And each hidden deed arraigneth,
Nothing unavenged remaineth.

Righteous Judge! for sin's pollution
Grant Thy gift of absolution,
Ere that day of retribution.

While the wicked are confounded,
Doomed to flames of woes unbounded,
Call me with Thy saints surrounded.

(*Translated by William J. Irons.*)

Christians were also perpetually reminded of the unending torments of hell. There appears to have been little doubt regarding the existence of hell. Such differences of opinion as existed were concerned with its location and description. Although some theologians placed it on a distant island and others suggested that it was "somewhere in the west," the favorite location was in the center of the earth. Many believed that the hot lava ejected by volcanoes came from hell and that the mouths of volcanoes were entrances to hell. As for the physical appearance of hell, some pictured it as a deep dark abyss filled with fire, brimstone, and a horrible stench, and others described it as a huge lake of fire or a pool of molten metal. In France there were some who conceived of hell as a huge grill on which devils prepared gruesome viands. The French poet Raoul de Houdenc, in his poem *La Songe d'Enfer* (*c.*1179), described an infernal banquet for which tablecloths had been made from the skin of usurers and napkins from the skin of old harlots. On the menu there were such delicacies as basted usurers, hashed robbers and murderers, broiled heretics, ragout of hypocrites, and fried tongues of lawyers. As indicated, the principal means of punishment was heat. Caesarius of Heisterbach (1180-1240), a Cistercian monk who recorded many medieval tales, relates a story in which a certain Walter who, becoming curious as to the whereabouts of his dead master, went directly to Satan for information. Instead of answering Walter's question directly, the Devil became coy and said that the master could be found in a place where the heat was so intense that if two huge mountains of iron were thrown into it they would be molten metal in less time than it takes to wink. Even though heat was the primary means of punishment cold was also involved as, for example, in Dante's *Inferno*.

But plain burning or freezing was not enough punishment for those who were guilty of committing the more heinous sins. The most horrible torments imaginable were prescribed for them by medieval theologians and mystics. Many of these punishments were borrowed from the "hells" of other religions, and others were based on visions purportedly experienced by members of both the laity and the clergy or on information gained during alleged visits to the abode of the damned by individuals who were in a state of coma. Visions of hell were so numerous as to give rise to an extensive literature on the subject which included Dante's "Inferno." Dante was so specific that he set down the exact day and hour of his visit. But there were many others who had visions of the next world. In the *Dialogues* of Pope Gregory the Great, for example, mention is made of a monk who claimed he had seen "the torments and innumerable places of hell." Matthew Paris (1200-1259) in his *Chronicles* tells of a number of persons who had seen hell or purgatory. He relates, for example, how a monk of Eversham had on Good Friday in the year 1196 lapsed into a coma which lasted for several days and during this time had in a vision seen the sufferings of the damned. The Venerable Bede tells in his *Ecclesiastical History* how St.

Fursa or Fursey lapsed into a comatose state and his soul was taken by an angel on a visit to the land of the dead. Even those who made no claim to having seen hell were eloquent in describing its punishments. Peter Damiani said after preaching on the horribleness of hell, "I shudder all over at the mention of the place and all my bones tremble." St. Stephanus is reported to have said that the miseries and torments of the damned are so horrible that if a living person were to witness them for any length of time he would be paralyzed by fear and die forthwith.

One of the most elaborate descriptions of the torments of the damned is that of Richard Rolle of Hampole, an English monk. It is in the nature of a summary of the conceptions of hell of the centuries preceding the fourteenth. He asserts, for example, that the pains of hell are without number and of a severity that is beyond the conception of the human mind. In addition to fire there is in hell a cold so intense that it would freeze a burning mountain. There is also a stench so obnoxious that it beggars description. The damned suffer from such severe hunger that they tear at their own flesh and from an unquenchable thirst that causes them perpetual torment. "Fire, smoke, and stench are their drink, and the venom of snakes their wine." In the darkness of hell, which is so thick that no man can grasp it, horrible venomous vermin endlessly gnaws the flesh and bone, and sucks the blood of the damned who are chained hand and foot with red-hot chains. Moreover, innumerable devils beat the damned unceasingly with glowing hammers. The least of the pains inflicted on them are more severe than all earthly pains added together. And there is no possibility of escape. The damned long for death, but there is no death in hell, only suffering, despair, tears, and sorrow. More tears of sorrow are shed than there are drops of water in the sea. These tears scald and burn, for they are hotter than molten lead or boiling brass. While the devils keep up an unceasing din of roaring and bellowing, the damned in their despair scratch and tear at each other's face.

As regards torments and pain the line of demarcation between purgatory and hell was not distinct, the principal difference being that the torments of purgatory were temporary. One of the fullest and best-known accounts of the punishments of purgatory is that of Tundale, an Irishman. When Tundale fell into a coma his soul left his body and soon found itself in a dark valley filled with burning coals which threw off an obnoxious stench. Over the coals was a huge grill onto which demons were throwing the souls of patricides and other murderers. The intense heat melted the souls as if they were lard and in liquid form they would seep through a metal strainer as molten wax filters through cloth. Then the souls would be reconstituted and the process of cleansing by fire would be repeated. Continuing the journey Tundale's soul came to a monster, larger than a great mountain and horrible to behold, into whose great maw a host of demons were throwing the souls of usurers and other covetous persons. The monster would crush the souls with his immense teeth, crunch them into bits, swallow them, and after digesting them evacuate the residue into a nearby lake. There the souls would be revived and after a time both men and women would give birth to serpents and vermin which would torture them exceedingly. After visiting other places of punishment including one that was bitter cold, Tundale's soul came to a great furnace into which demons were tossing souls with their tongs. When the souls began to melt the demons would place them on a large anvil and hammer them into a solid mass. Tundale's soul was also subjected to this cleansing process, but was finally rescued by his guardian angel and returned to his body. All this terrified Tundale to the extent that he questioned God's mercy, whereupon the angel informed him that God was not only merciful but also just. If they did not fear God's anger, the angel said, sinners would have no reason to repent. This story, first written in Latin, was soon translated into the vernacular and was widely circulated in a number of countries.

The Otherworldly Attitude: The World and the Devil

One way to escape the punishments of hell, the medieval Christians were told, was to guard against becoming preoccupied with worldly pleasures and ambitions. Christian thought did not totally reject all secular values as evil. Secular pleasures and ambitions were permitted as long as they did not turn a Christian's attention away from the attainment of salvation. But the danger of becoming absorbed in earthly pleasures and pursuits and thereby jeopardizing the soul was regarded as being very real. "Is not the life of man on earth," St. Augustine asked, "a constant temptation?" Every Christian was therefore admonished to be constantly on his guard against temptation. Mundane pleasures, he was told, are but dross in comparison with the joys and pleasures of the Heavenly Jerusalem. Anselm (1033-1109), archbishop of Canterbury, said, "You love the world and it swallows you; its wont is to devour, not to elevate."

A long succession of medieval poets and writers accounted false and frivolous the most coveted prizes of this life. The entire body of religious verse was, in a sense, a long refrain on the theme, "De Contemptu Mundi" (On the Contempt of the World). For example, in "Poema Morale" the author says: "Oh turn aside from the broad paths of this world, for they lead to a horrible hell." Pietro Damiani wrote:

Fleshly pleasure's feigned sweetness
Then to bitterness is turned
When the endless torment follows
By its short-lived transports earned
What he once thought great, already
To be nothing is discerned.

One of the most severe condemnations of worldly pleasures and pursuits is the "De Contemptu Mundi" of Bernard of Marlais. "Weep for your harmful joys," he wrote; "drive them away with your tears. Let every man tremble for himself! Banish your evil and seek the stars, ye children of Eve! They that burn with the flame of Venus now shall be roasted by the fiercest fires of Gehenna."

The grim censure of earthly pleasures was also stated in two medieval student songs. One of these, titled "On the Contempt of the World" reads in part:

> De contemptu mundi: this the theme I've taken
> Time it is from sleep to rise, from death's torpor waken.
> Brief is life, and brevity briefly shall be ended
> Death comes quick, fears no man, none hath his dart suspended:
> Death kills all, to no man's prayer hath he condescended.
> Rise up, rise, be vigilant; trim your lamp, be ready.

Part of another student song, "Vanity of Vanities," reads as follows:

> This vile world
> In madness hurled
> Offers but false shadows
> Joys that wane
> And waste like vain
> Lilies of the meadows.
>
> Worldly wealth,
> Youth, strength and health
> Cramp the soul's endeavor
> Drive it down
> In hell to drown
> Hell that burns forever.
>
> Carnal life
> Man's law of strife
> Hath but brief existence
> Passes, fades
> Like wavering shades
> Without real subsistence.

(*Translated by J. A. Symonds*)

Dante also regarded all secular things as transitory phantoms. He believed that he had sinned in taking seriously "the things of the present." In the *Divine Comedy* he referred to the vanity of all earthly things when he wrote:

> And into ways untrue he turned his steps
> Pursuing the false images of good
> That never any promise fulfill.

The Church also warned its members to be ever on their guard against the wiles of Satan lest they be lured from the path of salvation. No one was safe from the temptations instigated by this archenemy of mankind. Caesarius of Heisterbach stated that since Satan even presumed to tempt Christ there is no one in the world whom he will leave untempted. This archtempter of mankind was depicted in various guises. In medieval art he often appeared as a large serpent with a human head, probably in reference to the role he played in the drama of the Garden of Eden. In some of the crude illustrations which have come down to us he is represented as being a large goat walking on its hind legs. In Dante's *Inferno* he is pictured as an atrocious monster, the incarnation of ugliness, foulness, and corruption. In the later Middle Ages the most common picture of him was that of a tall man who is red, green, or sooty in color with horns on his forehead, bat's wings on his shoulders, at least one cloven hoof, and a tail of exceeding length studded with sharp barbs. But Satan was not restricted to the above forms. It was believed that he could assume any disguise that might aid him in carrying out his nefarious schemes. He was particularly fond of appearing as a beautiful woman or a black tomcat. A monk in one of the tales of Caesarius of Heisterbach saw him in such varied forms as men, beasts, and serpents. According to this author, even such high dignitaries of the Church as a bishop or an abbot might in actuality be manifestations of the Devil. Whatever the form may have been in which he appeared, Satan's purpose was ever the same. He was endeavoring to increase the population of hell by entrapping as many unwary Christians as possible.

The medieval period was Satan's heyday. Never was he so powerful, so important, and so much feared. Priests dreaded the inroads he might make into the membership of their churches. Monks, as their writings show, were preoccupied with his presence, for he and his demons were always tempting them, interfering with their prayers, and causing them discomforts to keep them from concentrating on otherworldly matters. Leading churchmen wrote long dissertations on the origin, nature and influence of Satan. He was woven so inextricably into the fabric of medieval theology that the belief in him became an essential part of the creed. Any doubt regarding his existence would have undermined the whole structure of Christian theology. In the life of the common man, Satan and his demons were everywhere, setting their snares with diabolical cunning and generally putting every soul in mortal peril. In the popular belief sin seems to have been regarded more as something instigated by the devil than the expression of a corrupt heart. Satan was also the central subject in many of the best medieval folk tales and in the mystery plays he was by all odds the most popular actor. On occasion he would cavort on the stage to the accompaniment of shouts of laughter. But the laughter was not an expression of doubt regarding Satan's existence; it was the expression of a temporary relief from the mortal fears of him and his guile. But the believer had a way out of his dilemma. In his struggles against the temptations of Satan he could enlist the aid of the saints and particularly of the Virgin Mary who was reported to have helped many to frustrate Satan's efforts to lure them from the path of salvation.

The fact that the representatives of the Church were constantly admonishing all members to be in readiness for the Day of Judgment and to be vigilant lest they be ensnared by the wiles of Satan might well lead to the conclusion that all or at least most of the people who lived in the Middle Ages concentrated their thought and attention on the hereafter. Backsliding must, however, have been a common problem, because the sermons and didactic literature of the period show that the clergy found it necessary to exhort the people again and again to turn from the secular to the otherworldly. Bishops and priests were also unable on occasion to resist the blandishments of mundane pleasures and pursuits.

What the Church set up was an ideal, one that was too lofty to be translated into practice in its entirety. As in every other age man's attachment to the things of this world made it impossible for most believers to keep their eyes on the hereafter. On the other hand, those who permitted secular pleasures and pursuits to distract their attention realized that they were guilty of wrongdoing. They knew that they were neglecting the one thing that mattered. This they had learned from the Church which was their authority for the truth. What reason could medieval men and women in general have for not accepting the teachings of a Church which was the source of practically all knowledge? Moreover, the people of the Middle Ages had the saints and ascetics as visible examples of the world to come. If many turned temporarily away from the otherworldly values sponsored by the Church to pursue secular pleasures, riches, and power, this does not contradict the fact that the world to come was the over-mastering reality of medieval life.

3

The Intensification of the Secular Spirit

The power and influence of the Roman Catholic Church reached its high-water mark in the thirteenth century. By the opening of this century the task of converting the various heathen tribes was completed and all of Western Europe except southern Spain was under the rule of the Church. The hierarchical machinery to rule this large ecclesiastical empire had also reached its full development and was in full operation. The power of the papacy which had been growing over the centuries reached its pinnacle during the pontificate of Innocent III who, as stated earlier, claimed that the final authority in secular as well as spiritual matters rested with the pope. Innocent had the support of some of the most eminent jurists of the time, and he proceeded at once to enforce his decree. His efforts miscarried in some instances, but in others he was eminently successful. For example, he instructed the papal legate to order the ruler of Castile and the ruler of Aragon to stop warring against each other and the order was obeyed. Upon receiving complaints from the Aragonese regarding the debasement of their coinage, Innocent III enjoined the king of Aragon to restore the coinage to its full value. In this case, too, his order was carried out. Furthermore, he compelled King Philip Augustus of France to take back as queen Ingeborg of Denmark whom he had divorced after falsely claiming that the blood relationship was too close. Finally, Innocent also succeeded in forcing King John of England to accept Stephen Langton as archbishop of Canterbury. This setting-aside of the royal prerogative was unprecedented in the history of the English Church. Thus Innocent III was the dominant figure of his time. He was the visible embodiment of the idea of universal rule which had originally been promulgated by the Old Roman Empire. Thomas Hobbes described the situation in these words, "If a man consider the original of the great ecclesiastical dominion, he will easily perceive that the papacy is no other than the ghost of the deceased Roman Empire, sitting crowned upon the grave thereof." The successors of Innocent III made less use of the great papal power; nevertheless, the period to the death of Innocent IV in 1254 is generally regarded as a great epoch in the history of the medieval papacy.

The thirteenth century was also the great century of the consolidation of Roman Catholic philosophy. A group of scholars which included Thomas Aquinas, Albertus Magnus, and Duns Scotus carried scholastic philosophy to its greatest heights. Thomas Aquinas harmonized the knowledge of his time with the teachings of the Church in his *Summa Theologica* (Summary of Theology), a work which many contemporaries believed would never be superseded. It was a century of considerable religious fervor, stimulated in part by the Crusades and by the mendicant orders (Dominicans and Franciscans) founded early in the century. These new orders preached the renunciation of earthly pleasure, admonishing sinners to concentrate their attention on preparing for the great Day of Judgment. In the thirteenth century, too, medieval art produced the most perfect embodiment of Christian ideals in the great cathedrals of Paris, Chartres, Amiens, Cologne, Westminster, and Canterbury.[1]

The Growth of the Secular Temper

The power and splendor of the Church did not, however, conceal the fact that the forces of secularism were struggling to assert themselves over the ascetic and otherworldly teachings. While the Church was powerful it was able to curb these forces, even though it did not succeed in suppressing them. It was aided by the fact that life in the Middle Ages was, by and large, harsh and dreary with few comforts and little leisure. An English historian wrote about the Middle Ages, "The Middle Ages . . . if they were not dark, or fruitless, or unprogressive . . . were centuries of extreme hardship, of chronic war, of devastating pestilence, of recurrent famine, of prevailing ignorance, of degrading superstition, of paralyzing terror, of furious passion and consuming lust." [2] Despite the glamor with which romantic writers have surrounded chivalry and other phases of medieval life, the earlier centuries of the Middle Ages were a dreary time on the material side. Even among the upper classes the standard of comfort was surprisingly low. The great castles were cold and cheerless fortresses and those who lived in them did not enjoy a fraction of the comforts which the ordinary citizen now considers necessities. For the masses life was a struggle to eke out a mere subsistence amid hardship, disease, and famine. Such conditions excited a nostalgia for a better existence. It was, therefore, not difficult for men and women to turn their minds to the contemplation of a happier future in the next world. Members of all classes found happiness in looking away from their stern existence to a future life without suffering, want, and fear. Thus the idea of a heavenly utopia was distinctly a means of escape from an unpleasant existence.

Gradually, however, a more distinctly secular spirit began to prevail. The development of this spirit was fostered by a number of factors, of which the general rise in the standard of living was probably the most im-

[1] There is a study by the Roman Catholic historian James J. Walsh titled *The Thirteenth, the Greatest of Centuries*, 3rd edition (1924), which contains some interesting materials, but the author fails to substantiate his thesis.

[2] F. J. C. Hearnshaw, *Medieval Conributions to Modern Civilisation* (1921), p. 16.

portant. This was not true in the same degree of the peasantry as it was of the middle class. While there was some improvement in the living conditions of the peasants, the principal beneficiary was the new middle class which included merchants, industrialists, bankers, skilled artisans, and other townspeople. As the conditions of earthly life improved, the interest in things secular grew commensurately. Many of those who enjoyed the improved conditions and the increasing comforts became so interested in mundane affairs, earthly riches, and worldly pleasures that the otherworldly became vague.

Another factor in the intensification of the secular spirit was the decline in the power and prestige of the Church which had previously held secularism in check. This is illustrated by the fact that although the popes of the late thirteenth and succeeding centuries continued to reassert the claims of papal supremacy in secular as well as in spiritual matters, they no longer had the power to enforce them. For example, the efforts of Pope Boniface VIII (1294-1303) to do so ended in failure. Then, too, the hold of scholasticism on the mind of Western Europe was gradually loosening. It seemed as if the springs which were the source of the vitality that had raised scholastic philosophy to its heights were running dry. The Church also lost prestige because the secular spirit was making inroads into the ranks of the clergy where it caused irregularities of conduct. All this gave the secular spirit the opportunity to assert itself in life and thought generally. More emphasis was put on the "here" and less on the hereafter. Cosimo de Medici, one of the great patrons of Renaissance humanists and artists, is reported to have said, "You follow infinite objects; I follow finite ones. You place your ladders in the heavens; I on earth, that I may not seek so high or fall so low." As the secular spirit grew stronger it became more self-assertive and independent. Mundane life began to take on a meaning for itself as well as for the hereafter. Secular and otherworldly interests, which had previously complemented each other, began to separate into two distinct spheres.

More and more individuals gave expression to the growing secularist spirit by trying to extract more pleasure and greater enjoyment from this life. Although they realized that mundane life is transitory and that certain earthly pleasures were sinful in the eyes of the Church, they nevertheless believed that life was something to be enjoyed. For them the ascetic ideal of sacrificing the present to the future had little meaning. This does not mean that they denied the ecclesiastical doctrine of the hereafter. They simply adopted an attitude of indifference toward it. Others were intent on deriving the greatest possible enjoyment from this life while remaining in good standing as members of the Church. One historian has described the situation in these words, "Despite the many centuries that the generations of men had professed the faith, despite the length of time their 'religion' in the narrower sense had been Christian and Catholic; their thinking and their everyday actions were beginning to become emancipated." [3] The idea that no opportunity to enjoy this all-too-short life should be overlooked was expressed by Lorenzo the Magnificent in the song which has become known as "The Song of Lorenzo the Magnificent":

> Fair is youth and void of sorrow
> And it hourly flies away—
> Youths and maids enjoy today;
> Naught ye know about tomorrow.
> Every sorry thought foreswear!
> Keep perpetual holiday.
> Youths and maids enjoy today;
> Naught ye know about tomorrow.
> Ladies and gay lovers young
> Long live Bacchus, live desire;
> Dance and play; let songs be sung;
> Let sweet love your bosoms fire,
> In the future come what may!
> Youths and maids enjoy today;
> Naught ye know about tomorrow.

There was also a higher type of secular pleasures, the so-called "intellectual pleasures." They were mainly concerned with the enjoyment of the creations of the new Renaissance culture. Such pleasures included the appreciation of the elegant style of the classics, of the beautiful representations of the Renaissance artists, and of the poetry of Dante, Petrarch, Villon, and other Renaissance poets. Another source of pleasure was conversation or correspondence with the learned men of the time. These and other interests greatly enriched mundane life. Petrarch, Erasmus, Rabelais, and others expressed the sheer exuberance of such a many-sided existence. It was undoubtedly this kind of life that Montaigne had in mind when he inscribed on the ceiling of his workroom the following motto: "Rejoice in the present life; all else is beyond thee."

The Scope of the Intensified Secularism

The secular spirit gradually asserted itself in all phases of human activity. It continued to grow stronger and more insistent in the intellectual, cultural, economic, political, and social life of the time. Many who were active in the various fields chafed under the restrictions imposed on them by the traditional sanctions of religion. Consequently there was a widespread demand either stated or implied for independence from ecclesiastical control. Those who were secular-minded wanted the right to make their own decisions in secular affairs, to exercise their creative capacities without restrictions, and to set their own goals. They desired a broader scope for self-expression than they could find within the traditional framework of an

[3] W. Dirks, *The Monk and the World*, translated by D. Coogan (1954), p. 169.

ecclesiastically controlled order. They further wanted the freedom to explore the new realms of nature which were being opened. In short, secularists sought the right to order secular affairs on principles of their own choosing and to exercise the right of self-expression for purposes that were not religious. It was in many instances a question of self-interest opposing principles laid down for the common good.

In the realm of the intellect the assertion of the secular spirit wrought marked changes. Besides gradually opening new avenues of interest, it turned the studies and disciplines which had been the "handmaidens" of theology into new channels. Science slowly adopted a secular tone as scientists began to study nature for its own sake. Experimentation gradually displaced revelation and speculation as a means of ascertaining truth. But the secularization of science progressed very slowly, mainly because most of the early scientists were clerics. Philosophy, too, gradually relinquished its role as the servant of theology, and opened the way for its secularization with the doctrine of the twofold truth based on the theory that there is a secular truth which can be learned by rational processes and a divine truth which is acquired only by revelation. While refraining from attacking revealed truth which formed the foundation of ecclesiastical theology, secular-minded philosophers proceeded to investigate secular truth based on the exercise of human reason. In this way philosophy and theology slowly drifted apart, the unity of medieval thought breaking up into the multiple interests which are characteristic of modern thought. M. Jacques Maritain has summed up the shift from the theological to the secular in these words, "The radiating dissolution of the Middle Ages and its consecrated forms represents at the same time the birth of a secular civilization, one that is indeed not wholly secular, but which, as it advances, severs itself more and more from the Incarnation." [4]

The desire to be free from ecclesiastical prescription also became manifest in economic life. The rising merchant, industrial, and banking class believed that the sphere of economic affairs should be divorced from religion and governed by its own principles. Their objections were aimed particularly at the efforts of the Church to establish a "just price" for commodities and manufactured articles and at the prohibition against charging interest on loans. So long as commerce and industry played a minor role in society both the "just price" and the ecclesiastical laws against usury were relatively unimportant, but the expansion of commerce, industry, and banking on an international scale changed the whole economic structure. The need for capital forced the merchant and industrial class to borrow from the bankers at a high rate of interest. Furthermore, since international commerce entailed great risks the merchants believed they were entitled to all the profit they could make. The unlimited accumulation of wealth at the expense of the buyer was, of course, a far cry from the ideal of brotherly love set up

[4] *True Humanism* (1939), p. 8.

by the Church. This did not, however, deter the members of the new middle class. They either ignored the ecclesiastical laws or circumvented them. Ironically the papacy itself could not obtain funds for its widespread religious activities without paying interest. When the Church finally did relax its stand against usury, economic life was well on its way to becoming thoroughly secular.

One of the phases of life in which the secular spirit asserted itself very early in the Renaissance period was statecraft. In Italy the city-states had been free to shift for themselves for some time, but in northern Europe a new type of state, the national state, was rising. Most of the monarchs of the new national states were no longer satisfied to be subordinate to the papacy in what they regarded as secular or national matters; neither did they want their states to function merely as the secular arm of the Church. They were determined to put a stop to papal intervention in matters they believed to be their own private affairs. The rise of national patriotism tipped the scales in their favor and gradually became the pivotal factor in the national state. This patriotic feeling impelled the subjects to rally around the monarch, giving him a support which enabled him to limit the authority of the papacy over his state and also to nationalize the Church in the territory under his rule. In this way the unity of Western Christendom under the rule of a universal Church was disrupted. Representatives of the new national states took over some of the functions the Church had previously exercised. Thus even in religious matters secular guidance was beginning to replace guidance by the Church. Religion was no longer the primary consideration of the state, even in theory. Secular and national matters were taking precedence over it, a change which was altering the basic tone of society.

One of the factors which promoted secularization in the realm of politics and statecraft was the revival of Roman law, a development which began toward the end of the eleventh century. The Romans, possessing special gifts for jurisprudence, had while building their empire created laws to govern it, laws that were as complex as the civilization of which Rome was the center. Over a period of centuries these laws multiplied into a great accumulation. The Roman Empire was already in an advanced stage of decline when Justinian I (482-565), emperor of the Eastern Roman Empire, decided to codify the laws, that is, to put them into an accessible and manageable form. He appointed a commission of jurists who prepared the *Corpus Juris Civilis*, known as the Justinian code. In Western Europe the interest in the code was short-lived. The Germanic tribes who invaded the crumbling empire, including the Visigoths, Burgundians, Saxons, and Angles, brought their own laws under which they continued to live. This is not to say that all traces of Roman law disappeared. In Italy and in southern France some remnants were preserved in local customary laws. In other regions the laws were based on Germanic traditions. Where vestiges of Roman law did survive they regulated the simplest human relationships. The agrarian life of the time was so simple that there was no need for the complex Roman laws.

But when life became more complicated as a result of the expansion of trade and the rise of towns, jurists and officials of various kinds turned to Roman law for legal principles useful in regulating the more intricate relationships of commercial and urban life. As the interest increased, centers for the study and teaching of Roman law were established in Italy where commerce and town life were more highly developed than in the other countries of Western Europe. The most famous center for the study of both civil and canon law was the University of Bologna. There a succession of professors of law, beginning with Irnerius (1060-1125), carefully studied the Justinian code, made marginal notes, eliminated contradictions, deduced legal maxims, and explained the meaning of the laws in long commentaries. The Bolognese revival attracted students from many countries. In this way the principles of Roman law were disseminated over Western Europe. Gradually universities north of the Alps added courses in Roman law to the curriculum. No courts were established to administer Roman law in its purest form, but in time the legal principles the students learned penetrated to the law courts and modified court practices. In Italy the humanists of the fifteenth century went beyond Justinian's code to the jurists of the golden age of Roman law. Although the effects differed in the various countries, Roman law left its indelible imprint on all the legal systems of Western Europe. In some instances it modified the existing jurisprudence and in others became an integral part of growing systems. Its general effect was to disentangle the practice of law from the chaotic uncertainty caused by the mingling of Germanic, Roman, and ecclesiastical or canon law (*Corpus Juris Canonici*).

Since Roman law was thoroughly secular it gave impetus to the intensification of secularism. In the realm of statecraft it served as an instrument for centralization as well as secularization. Secular rulers used it to supplant feudal law by a uniform code which concentrated the administration in their hands. Above all, Roman law gave the dominant role in society to the secular state. The rulers of the rising kingdoms of England, France, and Spain were not slow to realize this and to act accordingly. Thus Roman law was an effective force in exciting self-consciousness in the rising national states and in impelling them to assert their independence from papal supervision. One historian wrote in reference to France that if the enhanced power of the national monarch can "be traced to any theoretical basis it rested on the authority of Roman law." In England a number of historians have developed this idea as it applies to English history. In Spain, too, historians have pointed out that Roman law exerted a profound influence as one of the factors which produced the Spanish nation and gave political unity to the kingdoms of the Iberian peninsula.

The Rise of Secular Literatures

The growing secular emphasis of the new age is also reflected in Renaissance culture which developed a character of its own apart from the ecclesiastical culture of the preceding period. Literature was one of the first phases of culture in which the process of secularization became evident. In literature secularization was also more rapid and more complete than in painting, sculpture, and architecture. Secular-minded writers no longer felt obliged to concentrate their efforts on the supernatural and otherworldly. They preferred to expound secular themes in which they were interested. The change is illustrated by the change in the type of persons featured in the new literature. Whereas the central characters in ecclesiastical literature were God, the Madonna, disciples, apostles, and saints, in the new secular literature their places were taken by knights, merchants, townspeople of various kinds, peasants, and wayfarers. For example, in Chaucer's *Canterbury Tales* butchers and fishmongers, great merchants and abbots, learned ladies and midwives, scholars and beggars, pass in review. Literature was no longer written to save souls, but to broaden the interest in and to promote the enjoyment of the things of this life. Lorenzo the Magnificent stated that he hoped someone would derive a little pleasure from reading his verses and "even if someone should laugh at them, it will be pleasing to me that he may derive enjoyment from them, even though it may be very small."

The new literature, most of which was written in the vernacular, appeared in the form of poetry, short stories, novels, and fables. Then, too, the secular drama slowly evolved out of the religious drama. Poetry gained new elegance as poets sang of the delights of earthly love and of the pleasures of mundane existence. The Italian poet Folgore de San Gemignano (1309-1379) described in his "Garland of the Months" the pleasures which each month of the year offers. He wrote of the beauty of the "flowering countryside," of "beds with deft embroideries, silk sheets and coverlets of vair," of "sweetmeats and sharp mixed wine," of "huge jellies, roasted partridges, young pheasants, and boiled capons," of "lovely damsels" who make every day "glad with joyful love." He wrote of a "utopian port" equipped with everything to make people happy, then added, "But let it have no church or convent; leave the silly priests to their gabble, for in them are too many lies and too little truth." [5]

The change in spirit from the ecclesiastical to the secular literature is exemplified in the treatment of love. In the ecclesiastical literature the central theme was divine love, more specifically God's love for man, a love which motivated Him to make provisions for man's salvation. In the new secular literature divine love was replaced by human love, more specifically by the love between the sexes. The treatment was at first highly idealistic,

[5] R. Aldington, *A Wreath of San Gemignano* (1945), p. 20.

but gradually sank to the level of a merely physiological relationship. In Italian literature, for example, Dante's love for Beatrice is an idealistic love almost wholly devoid of sensuality. Next came Petrarch's love for Laura which is still somewhat idealistic, but more sensual. The next step is the love presented by Boccaccio in his *Decameron*, a love which is almost wholly physiological or sensual without idealistic overtones. Thereafter Poggio Bracciolini, Aretino, Lorenzo Valla, and others became earthy in their treatment, descending into the pit of obscenities. The same trend is evident in French literature from the *Roman de la Rose* to Rabelais.

Secular literature was, of course, not something new created during the period of the Renaissance. There were various works of secular literature throughout the Middle Ages, even in the centuries in which the power of the Church was supreme. Much of the secular literature that was written in the vernacular languages was either inspired by the early folklore of the Germanic tribes or was a harbinger of the secular literature of the Renaissance period. When the Germanic tribes entered the Christian fold they brought with them a delight in heroic prowess which found expression in sagas and poems to which literary historians have given the name "epics" or "heroic poems." Examples of such epics are the poems of Hildebrand, of Beowulf, of Sigrid, and of Brynhild. Gradually however, Christian ideas were superimposed on the heathen legends as is exemplified by the *Niebelungenlied.* France, too, had its epics in the *chansons de geste* which celebrate the heroic deeds of Charlemagne and his knights. Most of these epic poems have some historical basis, but they are largely pseudo-history. While the songs contain strains of paganism, they are, as previously stated, also religious in that they extol the virtues of the Christian knight. The Spanish epic, *Poema del Cid*, is also suffused with a religious spirit.

During the period preceding the fourteenth century harbingers of the secular literature of the Renaissance appeared in the lyric poetry of the troubadours of Provence and of the trouvères of northern France. Of the two the songs of the troubadours were the more influential. Their theme was love between the sexes and their songs were addressed to the ladies of the feudal aristocracy. From Provence the troubadour songs were carried into the neighboring countries of Italy and Germany. In Italy they helped to stimulate the rise of vernacular Italian poetry. Dante was one of those who found troubadour songs an inspiration. In Germany love was the main theme of the Minnesinger (singers of love), the two most outstanding Minnesinger being Walther von der Vogelweide (*c.*1170-1228) and Wolfram von Eschenbach (*c.*1170-1220) who also wrote the long epic *Parzival.* Although the wandering scholars (*Goliardi*) wrote many poems which express deep religious emotions, they also sang songs that were gay, satirical, and sometimes rowdy. Their favorite subjects were wine, women, and gambling. They wrote such songs as "The Invitation to Love," "A Sequence in Praise of Wine," and "A Carol of Wine." For example, one stanza reads:

In the public house to die
Is my resolution;
Let wine to my lips be nigh
At life's dissolution:
That will make the angels cry
With glad elocution
'Grant this toper, God on high,
Grace and absolution.'

Probably the best-known student song is "Gaudeamus Igitur" which is still frequently sung at student gatherings. It reads in part:

Let us live then and be glad
While young life's before us!
After youthful pastime had,
After old age hard and sad,
Earth will slumber o'er us.[6]

According to one computation religious literature comprised about 95 per cent of the literary output of the Middle Ages. Whatever the true ratio, there can be no doubt that the bulk of medieval literature was ecclesiastical. Religious literature was the mainstream, and secular literature only a small rivulet. This changed during the centuries of the Renaissance. Great national literatures came into being in most of the countries of Western Europe. In Italy a great vernacular literature rose to unsurpassed heights in the writings of Dante, Petrarch, and Boccaccio. In England the Renaissance saw the creation of a great national and secular literature, three of the great figures in its creation being Chaucer, Marlowe, and Shakespeare. In France, too, a series of great literary figures founded a national literature and contributed much to the development of the French language. Among them were François Villon, François Rabelais, and Michel de Montaigne. A beginning was made toward the creation of a German literature in Sebastian Brant's *Narrenschiff* (Ship of Fools) and in the dramas and poems of Hans Sachs. In Germany, however, the development of vernacular literature was interrupted by the insistence of the humanists on the use of Latin as the language of learning and by the turmoil created by the religious upheaval of the sixteenth century. In Spain, where the ecclesiastical culture persisted longer, the flowering of Spanish secular literature did not come about until the last decade of the sixteenth and the early decades of the seventeenth century in the work of Cervantes and Lope de Vega.

The growing interest in things secular also led to a wider and more intensive study of the classical literatures, the Greek and Roman literatures of the period from Homer to the tribal invasions of the early Middle Ages. Although the secular spirit which caused the educated classes to turn to the classics had to exist first, the study of them served to intensify secular feeling by revealing the thought and aims of the ancient Greeks and Romans

[6] J. A. Symonds, *Wine, Women, and Song* (1912), p. 175.

whose interests were wholly secular. From these literatures the humanists, as those who studied the ancient writings are called, gained a wide knowledge of earthly life and its possibilities. The number of humanists was small, but their enthusiasm was contagious. It resulted, first, in a kind of worship of things ancient or classical and, second, in a progressive secularization of learning. This interest in the classics and classical times was, in a sense, a reaction against the Middle Ages and its preoccupation with personal salvation.

Secular Trends in Renaissance Art

Secular trends also appeared in Renaissance art. Painters, sculptors, and architects worked hand in hand with the humanists in expressing the secular spirit. Their work, like that of the literary men, reflected the gradual shift of interest from the otherworldly to the secular. In the development of Renaissance architecture the influence of classical architecture, which was thoroughly secular, was paramount. In painting and sculpture, however, nature was the principal source of inspiration. In endeavoring to portray the natural beauty of things, painters and sculptors inaugurated the trend toward naturalism. The result was that secular beauty was given a value and a purpose for itself. This beauty was depicted both in form and in color. It was true of the human body as well as of natural scenery. To many artists the human body became an object of veneration for its loveliness. Many painters and sculptors "came down to earth and showed men and nature as they were, conquered perspective, chiaroscuro, and anatomy in the search for realistic interpretation."

In the pictorial arts, secularization progressed much more slowly than in literature. It began in the fourteenth century and continued to develop through the fifteenth and during the early decades of the sixteenth century. The progress of secularization was not smooth. At times its advance was temporarily halted by reactions. With certain variations and fluctuations the trend was much the same in all the countries of Western Europe, although it did, however, develop later in some countries than in others. Secularization first became evident in Flemish and Italian painting and in Italian sculpture, although there were previous indications of naturalism in French Gothic sculpture. The earliest manifestations of change were in the proportions of religious and secular elements in the works of art that were being produced. While the secular elements were gradually increasing, the religious elements were decreasing in the same proportions. Italian painting is a good illustration of how secular or naturalistic elements were being added little by little to the old symbolical art. The work of the Italian painters of the fourteenth and of much of the fifteenth century was still predominantly otherworldly. In the works of Raphael (1483-1520) and Leonardo da Vinci (1452-1519) the proportions of religious and secular elements were somewhat evenly divided.

In the paintings of Titian (*c.*1477-1576), however, the delight in life, in form, and in color overshadows the religious elements. Thus, while sacred and profane literature soon went their separate ways, the religious and secular elements in painting and sculpture remained side by side over a long period.

In its purest form the secularized naturalistic art of the Renaissance is predominately sensate, that is, its primary appeal is to the senses rather than to the mind as was the case with ideational art. Furthermore, it deals with the visual, not with the supersensory world. It depicts what was interesting and picturesque from the secular viewpoint. It was presented as it appears to the senses, in this case to the eye, and not as a symbol of something invisible, incorporeal, and supersensory. The purpose is to demonstrate the beauty of nature. If there is idealism in it, it is in the form of idealized nature, of such things as the human body or a landscape. Actually, however, the art of the Renaissance was not purely sensate. Since it represented the transition from the religious to the secular, it was a blend of the ideational and the sensate. Its purpose during this period was twofold. On the one hand, it continued to be devotional and suggestive of the otherworldly and, on the other, it portrayed the beauty of nature, thereby stimulating a greater interest in and knowledge of the external material world. Thus it served both the religious and secular moods of the period. But as painting and sculpture turned away from the old symbolism and traditions, its spiritual significance gradually dwindled. Although it gained in natural beauty and picturesqueness, it lost much of its power to inspire reverence and to excite devotion. In short, the religious pictures and sculptures became less distinctive of the Christian faith. Even supernatural subjects and scenes were treated with earthly realism. Ordinary human beings served as models for supernatural beings. Thus, for example, the features of angels often resembled those of the painter's apprentices or of street urchins who happened to visit the studio. Peasant women often served as models for the Madonna, and the portraits of prominent persons were frequently lent to apostles and saints. It should be added, however, that if religious paintings and sculptures became increasingly secular in their representations, at no time did they become anti-Christian. When the painters and sculptors turned away from the traditional subjects, they turned to nature itself or to the rich sources of pagan mythology.

The Growth of Secular Music

The Renaissance period also saw a tremendous development in the field of secular music. There was, of course, secular music in the Middle Ages, but it was limited in both scope and quality. Until the thirteenth century most of the composers devoted themselves almost exclusively to composing sacred music and during the centuries that followed many composers continued to turn out ecclesiastical music; in fact, some of the great religious music of all time was composed during the Renaissance period. To get some idea of the quality of the religious music produced it is necessary only to mention Palestrina (*c.*1526-1594), one of the great names in the history of sacred music. But during the Renaissance, secular music displayed a vigorous growth. It was not extraordinary for composers to compose both sacred and secular music. The production of secular music, however, soon outstripped that of sacred music. As early as the thirteenth century the number of composers of secular music was greater than the number of composers of sacred music. It has been calculated that in the fourteenth century there were in Western Europe sixty-one leading composers of secular and thirty-nine of religious music. But the increase was not uniform, for in the fifteenth there were fifty-four composers of secular and forty-six of religious music. What is outstanding is both the growth of interest in secular music and the increase of the volume of its output. Furthermore, sacred music itself was becoming secularized to a degree. Composers of sacred music made use of the greater freedom of composition they were accorded to incorporate secular themes into their music.

The sacred music of the Middle Ages and the secular music of the Renaissance represented two different attitudes toward the world of sound and the world of reality. Like medieval painting and sculpture, medieval sacred music in its purest form was ideational, that is, the idea which the music suggests to the mind was of primary importance, not the music in itself. Put in another way, how the music sounded was not as important as what it suggested. The auditory in ideational music played a secondary part, as did the visual in ideational painting and sculpture. The sounds were not important in themselves, for they were merely symbols of something greater. It was their function to suggest to the mind the higher ideas it symbolized, ideas which can be grasped only by the mind, not by the ear. Hence the music could be pleasant or unpleasant, inharmonious, and even ugly, depending on the idea it was calculated to evoke. Such an idea might be the love of God or the wrath of God, the sufferings of Christ or the hideousness of sin, the tortures of the damned or the eternal bliss of the saved.

On the other hand, the secular music of the Renaissance in its purest form is sensate. It is not a symbol of something higher, something beyond the perception of the senses. It is something to be taken at face value. If it did incidentally suggest or describe something, the suggestion or description was of secondary importance. Even then the idea suggested is not other-worldly, but something based on an experience of mundane life. Its purpose is essentially pleasurable. Since it aims to please the ear, the basic criterion is its audible beauty. The ear is the supreme judge. In summary, the secular music of the Renaissance did not stand or fall on what it suggested, but on the appeal of its beauty to the senses.

The Beginnings of Secularism in Education

In education, too, there was a shift of emphasis to the secular. As the trend developed, it changed both the primary purpose and the content of education. The purpose of strengthening the faith in eternal things gradually gave way to the idea that education must basically be a preparation for this life. It should be noted, however, that religious and moral training retained an important place in the new education. As for the content of education, it became broader, more technical, more classical, and, above all, more secular. The expanding economy and urban life created a need for men possessing broad knowledge which would enable them to cope successfully with the increasing complexities of business, government, and life in general. To fill this need better educational facilities, higher standards of instruction, and a broader curriculum of studies were necessary. As most of the cathedral and monastic schools were not prepared to teach such a range of subjects, new schools had to be founded. This was done by laymen, lay groups, and municipalities in cooperation with the ecclesiastical authorities. But a tendency to free such schools from ecclesiastical supervision soon developed. Later both primary and secondary schools were opened under lay supervision, a development which put an end to the monopoly of education the Church had held since the early Middle Ages. The Church did, however, remain the major factor in education.

By the middle of the fourteenth century, and in some instances earlier, practically every commercial town of any size had one or more municipal schools whose purpose it was to educate pupils for active participation in the expanding economic life. Whether they were called *Bürgerschulen* (burgher schools) as in Germany or whether they were known by some other name, these new schools taught their pupils practical arithmetic, secular history, commercial geography, and elementary astronomy. The secondary schools offered advanced courses in the same subjects and also courses in business techniques, civil administration, and elementary law. In both primary and secondary education some attention was also given to the study of the vernacular languages which many of the Church schools neglected in favor of Latin. Students who wished to enter the professions of law and medicine could continue their studies at one of the universities which offered courses in these secular subjects. During the Renaissance period a number of schools were also opened for the study of higher mathematics, particularly algebra and geometry. A school of this kind which was opened in Florence attracted many students from nearby and far-off places. This period saw a new use for higher mathematics. Learned men began to apply mathematical principles to natural science, painting, and sculpture.

Secondary schools featuring secular training appear to have flourished earliest in Italy because of the tremendous economic expansion that was taking place there. Many municipalities founded such schools to further their commercial, industrial, and banking interests. In addition, private schools staffed by lay teachers were also opened. In some of the larger Italian cities the number of lay teachers was considerable by the end of the thirteenth century. For example, in Milan there were eighty and in Florence there were so many that they formed one of the minor gilds. Theoretically these new schools were under the supervision of the bishop or more specifically, of the scholasticus, an official appointed by the bishop. In many towns, however, this control was disputed by the municipal authorities. No sooner were the new schools opened than a struggle ensued between the civil and ecclesiastical authorities over the control of them. It was not only a question of the Church being unwilling to relinquish its age-long control; the local clergy often had special reasons for opposing lay control. For the scholasticus the removal of a school from his jurisdiction meant a loss of income, but he often acquiesced after being assured that the opening of a new school under lay control would not deprive him of a possible source of income. Since there was no doctrinal divergence involved, the members of the higher clergy who realized the need for such schools did not oppose lay control too vigorously. If the local clergy was adamant in its refusal to permit the opening and operation of municipal and private schools under lay supervision, the civil authorities could appeal to the pope who in some cases sided with them and in others effected a compromise between the clashing opinions.

The expansion of commerce and industry in northern Europe created a similar demand for men with a considerable secular knowledge. In some cities the Italian schools served as models for the new schools that were opened. Such secondary schools as the *Gymnasium* in Germany and the *lycée* in France came later. It was in elementary education that the commercial towns of the Netherlands, Germany, France, and England gained a large measure of control over education. A number of cities in the Netherlands, including Ghent, Bruges, and Brussels, had municipal schools before the end of the first quarter of the fourteenth century. Some of the town councils asserted that "instruction is the monopoly of the municipal government." Accordingly they provided the school buildings, hired the teachers, and regulated the tuition. In many German cities the opening of burgher schools took place in the thirteenth century, but since the Church was more firmly entrenched there, the efforts of the town councils to gain control of these schools often resulted in bitter struggles. In some cases schools functioned without the consent of the scholasticus, but with the approval of the people. Whatever the situation the schools were unable to instruct all those who desired instruction.

In England the tendency toward lay control developed in the fifteenth century. In the charter of a school opened in London in 1432 it was clearly specified that the master was to be "by no means in holy orders." In the same period a certain William Wykeham organized an independent self-governing corporation to open a school at Winchester. Before the end of the century English municipalities acquired considerable independence in educational matters. It must be noted, however, that the fourteenth and fifteenth centuries did not witness the establishment of independent state or national school systems. The progress made by the civil authorities during this period in gaining some measure of control over schools and universities only laid the groundwork for later developments.

Further impetus was given to the secularization of education by the humanists. Although religious training remained a part of the curriculum in their schools, the study of the secular classics became the central feature of their educational theories. Moreover, the fact that the humanists borrowed most of their ideas on education from Greco-Roman thought gave humanistic education much of the secular connotation of classical education. Their aim was to prepare the individual to derive the maximum happiness from life and also to achieve personal distinction. It was the idea of a well-rounded education which had been developed by the Greeks. The finished product must be an individual who is fully developed physically, intellectually, aesthetically, and morally. He must be "the complete man," one who is able to cope successfully with any situation that might confront him. In the northern countries the humanists put greater emphasis on morality than the Italian humanists did. Nevertheless, the outlook of the "Christian humanists," including that of Erasmus, the greatest of them, was in a large degree secular.

Significant for the education of the nobility or gentlefolk was *Il Cortegiano* (*The Courtier*) by Count Baldassare Castiglione (1478-1529), courtier, diplomat, soldier, and man of letters who wrote verse in both Italian and Latin. In English Castiglione's book is probably better known as *The Book of the Courtier* after the famous translation by Sir Thomas Hoby. The book is written in the form of a dialogue, and its locale is the court of Urbino to which Castiglione was attached for a number of years. Thus it is a record of the elegance and literary culture of one of the most brilliant courts of the Italian Renaissance. But in a broader sense it sets up a thoroughly secular social and educational ideal for the perfect courtier and his feminine counterpart, the court lady. Castiglione's courtier is a composite of the medieval knight and the Renaissance intellectual. He is the well-rounded and perfectly equipped man of the Renaissance humanists. On the one hand, he must develop skills which make the body agile and graceful, particularly in the use of arms, in horsemanship, running, jumping, and swimming. On the other, he must develop his intellectual and aesthetic faculties and cultivate social graces. The perfect courtier must have a good command of the vernacular and a reading knowledge of Latin and Greek. He must also have some knowledge of music (*see also page 215*), some skill at drawing, and be able to demonstrate some understanding of painting. He must be a graceful dancer and a good conversationalist who displays a sense of humor. Above all, he must be a gentleman who carefully avoids affectation and boasting. In Book III Castiglione sets up a similar ideal for the court lady.

Although Castiglione completed the major part of his work about 1516, he was unable to interest a publisher in it. Finally in 1528, the year before his death, it was published by the famous Aldine Press in Venice. Read and applauded not only in the aristocratic circles of Italy but throughout the rest of Europe, the book became one of the more influential treatises of the Renaissance. During the century after its publication, it went through more than a hundred editions. Its European vogue was made possible by the many translations, including one into Latin. When it was translated in Spain by the poet Juan Boscán, who has been described as the most perfect embodiment of Castiglione's ideas, it aroused widespread interest among the nobility and became a definite influence in shaping the concept of the Spanish *caballero*. It also left its mark on Spanish literature. The influence of *The Courtier* is discernible, for example, in certain parts of Cervantes' *Don Quixote*. Two French translations which appeared in France in 1537 and 1538 were factors in molding the concept of the French *honnête homme*. At the court of Francis I, it set the standard of good conduct and raised a new ideal of culture. But *The Book of the Courtier* probably exerted its greatest influence in England, where Sir Thomas Hoby prepared an English translation which is a masterpiece of Tudor prose. Eagerly read by the English nobles, it dominated their culture for generations. It was also widely imitated by writers of English handbooks of manners. Not to be overlooked is its influence on Elizabethan literature. Lyly incorporated some of Castiglione's ideas in his *Euphues*, and Spenser modeled the Knight of Courtesy in his *Faerie Queene* after Castiglione's perfect courtier.

Reaction in Florence

It should be stated emphatically that in the early stages of its development the secular spirit was not inimical to religion. The shift of emphasis from the otherworldly to the secular was not in itself a disavowal of the teachings of the Church. Neither did the love of this life imply a rejection of the idea of life hereafter. Luis de Leon, the Spanish humanist, held that since this life is joyful the next life will be still more joyful. Anti-clerical the secular spirit was in some of its phases, but not anti-religious, despite the fact that secular-minded humanists tried to revive the ancient conception of life. Even so ardent an admirer of classical literature as Petrarch believed the study of the pagan writings to be consistent with his Roman Catholic religion. In its early stage the growing emphasis on secular values was only a redressing of the balance between the secular and the otherworldly. For centuries the latter had been the dominant factor in medieval civilization. During the Renaissance period more emphasis was put on the secular to eliminate the imbalance between the two. The reconstitution of the secular meant that it was to have a place beside the otherworldly in the Christian order.

Actually the Church itself was instrumental in fostering the growth of the secular spirit in some phases of Renaissance life. Members of the clergy as well as of the laity were patrons of the new learning and the new art. For example, the enthusiasm generated for classical literature not only captured the imagination of men of letters, princes, and members of the wealthy bourgeoisie, it also won the support of many leading clergymen for the humanist movement. The enthusiasm even penetrated the walls of the papal palace with the result that several popes joined in collecting manuscripts of classical works. The role of the Church was even more important in the development of Renaissance art. Officials of the Church sponsored art because they realized that it was still an aid to religion. Thus the Church used painting and sculpture in the same way they had been used in the preceding period; that is, to illustrate its teachings and to depict its traditions and rituals. Many of the great paintings of the Renaissance period are in chapels, churches, and, above all, in the Vatican. Only when secularism tended to become the dominant factor in society, when the interest in mundane existence threatened to stifle the interest in the hereafter, did the Church begin to offer vigorous opposition.

A sharp reaction against the rising secularism took place in Florence near the end of the fifteenth century. The reaction was instigated by Girolamo Savonarola (1452-1498), a Dominican friar. When Savonarola was transferred to Florence by his order about 1490, he was appalled by what he saw there. The sheer pagan secularism of life in Florence, the frivolity of Florentine society, the luxurious mode of living of the wealthy, the flouting of Christian morality, and the general indifference to the welfare of the soul shocked him deeply. Burning with righteous indignation, he vowed to restore the supremacy of the Christian religion in Florentine life. Before the large audiences which gathered to hear him, he fiercely denounced the hollowness of all earthly things and urged his hearers to concentrate their attention on the imperishable eternal values. One of the things which he scored again and again was the secularization of culture, particularly of literature and art. This he would promptly undo and return literature and art to the service of religion. "Art for art's sake" was to him a deadly heresy. The real purpose of art, he asserted, should be the portrayal of the beauty of the immortal soul, not of the human body. Paintings of the nude or partly nude human form were special targets of Savonarola's attacks. Thus he said, for example: "What shall I say to you Christian painters who expose half-nude figures to the eye? That is a thing of evil which must cease. You who possess such paintings destroy them or paint over them. You will then do a deed pleasing to God and the Blessed Virgin." In general, Savonarola sought to restore the supremacy of religion in all phases of life and to rededicate all human activity to otherworldly purposes.

For a time Savonarola seems to have made little headway in his crusade against what he regarded to be pagan secularism, but the death of Lorenzo the Magnificent (1492) followed by the expulsion of the Medici from Florence two years later gave him his big opportunity. His fiery preaching launched a wave of Puritanism which culminated in the Burning of the Vanities (1497). Savonarola asked all citizens who earnestly desired to save their souls to prove it by bringing to the Piazza della Signoria all those things which might endanger the welfare of their souls. More than 1300 children provided with crates and baskets went from house to house to collect "the articles of sin." Alfred Austin, in his drama "Savonarola," has them urging the citizens of Florence to fill the crates and baskets:

Vanities! Vanities! Bring out your Vanities!
Rouge-pots and scented girdles, spices, gums,
Snares of the Evil One! Ferret them out,
Unguents and patches, tresses false and tricks
Of meretricious beauty, specious dyes,
Henna, vermillion, all of them Vanities,
Give them all up! Vanities! Vanities!
Give up your curls, your counterfeits, your lures,
Love-philtres, and your Lydian potions mixed
By alchemists of Hell! Give up your drugs,
Intoxicating perfumes, subtle scents,
That lull the soul to slumber and arouse
The sleeping senses in their swinish sty,
And make them pose for garbage. Give them all up!
Lascivious fripperies, corsets and the bait
Of perforated sandals!
Vanities! Vanities! Bring out your Vanities!
All of your Vanities bring out to burn.

Florentine citizens were also asked to bring manuscripts of pagan writings, obscene books, pictures and paintings of nude women, pictorial representations of incidents from classical mythology, musical instruments, playing cards, and gambling devices. Among those who responded to Savonarola's appeal were the two painters Fra Bartolommeo and Botticelli. It is reported that the latter brought a number of paintings of partly nude women to be consigned to the flames. In addition to paintings, others brought copies of works by Boccaccio and of sonnets by Petrarch, statuary, and even examples of the goldsmith's craft. All the articles were piled high in the shape of a huge pyramid in the center of the square, and while trumpets sounded, bells rang, and a huge crowd cheered, the great pyramid was set ablaze.

The Burning of the Vanities marked the summit of Savonarola's influence and activity. By his attacks he had made many enemies who were plotting his downfall. In denying the papal authority he had even lost the support of the pope. In 1498 he was condemned to death as a heretic. After he was hanged, his body was burned and the ashes were thrown into the Arno River. The religious feelings he had aroused were neither deep nor permanent. Even the crowds he had moved with his fiery oratory became indifferent to his fate once he attacked the papal authority. After his passing, new vanities were purchased and the secularization of life continued. Luca Landucci, a contemporary wrote in his diary of the reformatory surge, "It did not last long. The wicked were stronger than the good. God be praised that I saw this short period of holiness." [7]

[7] Luca Landucci, *A Florentine Diary from 1450 to 1516*, translated by A. De Rosen Jervis (1927), p. 101.

4

The Social and Economic Background of the Renaissance

The Cradles of the New Secular Culture

The cradles of the new secular culture were the commercial towns, some of them old towns which had been reactivated by the expanding commerce and others new towns founded as centers of commerce. Towns had been the core of the economic life of both Greece and Rome, but they had lost much of their importance as the western half of the Roman Empire gradually disintegrated. The resulting decline of trade deprived the towns of their basic reason for existence. Various causes were responsible for the slackening of trade. Two of the reasons were the lack of protection for merchants and the difficulty of transporting the merchandise. As the central power declined the provinces could no longer look to Rome for aid in the preservation of law and order. Since the provinces themselves did not have sufficient forces to repress internal disorders and to repel the invading barbarians, lawlessness became rife. Furthermore, most of the roads which had been the pride of the Roman government soon fell into such a state of disrepair that the transportation of merchandise even on horseback and muleback became difficult. The main roads, that is, those on which the great lords and pilgrims traveled, were kept in some repair, but roving bands of brigands lurked along such highways in wait for unwary victims. The insecurity of life, limb, and property put great obstacles in the way of trade, causing most of the merchants to turn to agriculture for a livelihood. The general decline of commerce caused many of the towns to disappear; those which survived became mere shadows of their former greatness. Their principal function was to serve as religious centers. It has been stated that the chief institutions of such towns were "the church, the gallows, and the cemetery." The fact must not be overlooked, however, that some trade was carried on in most of the towns and in many there were periodical markets for the inhabitants of the district.

When the Roman government finally collapsed in the fifth century, it left Western Europe divided into a large number of economic, and in a sense political, units which became known as manors. The manor was a large agricultural estate which included a village in which those who cultivated the manorial land lived. Since the times were not propitious for trade each village had to produce insofar as this was possible everything the villagers needed. A great lord who lived in a castle could have his own weaver, shoemaker, saddler, blacksmith, swordsmith, and armorer, but the villein or villager was largely thrown on his own resources. Considerable cooperation, however, developed among the villeins. Those who had the smaller plots of land to cultivate used their spare time for weaving a crude type of cloth, for tanning hides and making shoes, or for fashioning farm implements. Such articles of handicraft would then be exchanged for other necessities within the village group.

Although each village was to a certain extent self-sufficient, it could not produce everything the villagers needed. Hence some things had to be procured from the outside. Perhaps the most essential commodity the majority of the villages could not produce was salt. Salt was particularly important since lack of fodder made it necessary to slaughter most of their livestock in the fall and to salt away the meat for winter use. Another commodity which was in great demand was salted fish for the many meatless days of the church calendar. The villagers also needed metals, especially iron, for their implements. Thus there was at all times a modicum of trade between the villagers and merchants outside the manor or at periodical fairs and markets. In addition a handful of merchants sold luxury items to the upper classes, that is, to the great nobles and the higher clergy. Even during the period of the greatest economic depression, silk and fine woolen textiles, imported from the Near East were available to those who could afford them. While silks were used for feminine adornment and for special ecclesiastical vestments, purple textiles, which symbolized authority, were indispensable for ecclesiastical and political robes. There was also some traffic in oriental spices and in wines from the eastern Mediterranean, although the bulk of the wine came from certain districts of Western Europe. All in all, however, trade was greatly restricted.

At the beginning of the eleventh century there were indications that the great depression which had lasted many centuries was coming to an end. By this time feudalism had established a considerable degree of law and order, the pressure of invading tribes on the frontiers had ceased, and better methods of cultivation had been introduced. The result was that agricultural communities were able to produce a surplus which could be used for trade. The surge of economic activity that followed is considered one of the great turning-points in the history of western civilization. In the first stages of the economic expansion, trade was local and only a small number of merchants engaged in it. This stage saw the rise of specialized crafts. Villagers who had previously devoted only a part of their time to such handicrafts as the making of shoes, weaving, and the fashioning of implements now became full-time craftsmen. The early traders or merchants dealt with tillers of the soil who had a surplus and with craftsmen who had handicrafted more merchandise than they could dispose of in their own village. As the economic development gained momentum the scope of commerce broadened. It became interregional and international. New crafts arose which produced new articles for sale or exchange.

Probably the most striking phenomenon of the period was the rise of towns. These towns were the creations of commerce and, in turn, were also the creators of commerce. As trade expanded, the need arose for a place where merchants could congregate, store their merchandise, and where craftsmen could open shops for the manufacture of salable merchandise. This need was filled by the reactivation of old towns and by the founding of new ones. The sites of the new towns were determined by various factors, particularly the availability of protection and the opportunity for profitable trade. Since castles offered protection some towns grew up under the castle walls. Others grew up under the moral protection of the Church near monasteries. Other towns provided their own protection by surrounding the town site with high walls and entrance gates that were closed at night or when danger threatened. Business considerations influenced the founding of towns at the intersections of important land routes, at natural river fords (Oxford), at bridges (Cambridge), at strategic locations on navigable rivers, and around coastal harbors. Gradually Western Europe became dotted with towns. Those which were strategically situated for trade and industry developed more rapidly into key commercial and industrial centers. Hence there were small towns, large towns, and cities, the last being so named because they were seats of bishoprics.

Whether they were reactivated old towns or newly-founded ones, the commercial towns experienced a rapid growth of population. Merchants and craftsmen were attracted to towns that were favorably situated for trade. Many unskilled workers migrated to the towns from the villages where the population was growing at an unprecedented rate. The new towns offered the villagers greater freedom and opportunities for a better life and for raising themselves in the social scale. Apprentices, for example, could become journeymen and masters; traders could become great merchants; and poor villagers could become prosperous and even wealthy.

It was in the free atmosphere of the towns where the citizens had the opportunity to acquire more of the goods of this world and to enjoy more of its pleasures that the secular spirit asserted itself, particularly among the wealthy. The result was the efflorescence of a new culture with an ever-broadening secular influence. It generated a remarkable urban civilization which drew its basic strength from commerce, industry, and banking, and differed in many respects from the feudal civilization of lord and peasant. With the rise of towns and cities came the formation and growth of the middle class. Eventually the members of this class became both the sponsors and the bearers of the new secular culture.

The Advent of the Middle Class

The name "middle class" (*Mittelstand* in German) derives from the early position of this class between the higher clergy and the nobility, on the one hand, and the agricultural masses on the other. In France the members of this class were given the collective name of "bourgeoisie" (citizens of a burg or medival town), a word which eventually found its way into the English language. In the first stage of the revived town life the inhabitants of the towns were a small group composed of traders, artisans, and those who cultivated land near the town. As the town increased in size the cultivators of the soil either turned to other occupations or repaired to the countryside. The lowest stratum of the remaining urban society was the mass of workers who had flocked to the towns to seek a better life. Whereas some of the unskilled workers rose in the social scale by becoming traders, shopkeepers, and skilled artisans, the rest formed the basis of what later became known as the industrial proletariat. In the manufacturing centers of Flanders and Italy the members of this segment of the urban population soon developed a group consciousness. In Florence where the workers were called *ciompi* they even staged a revolt in 1378. Thus the workers gradually became a separate division of urban society.

It can be said that, in general, the rest of the townspeople composed the middle class or bourgeoisie. It was not a homogeneous group, but one made up of groups whose interest often conflicted. The middle class, included, first of all, shopkeepers, skilled artisans, small traders, and enterprising burghers in various lines of endeavor. It also included a group which has been called "lay practitioners," that is, those who had been trained to replace the ecclesiastics who had served as teachers, government clerks, and administrative officials. A further group which developed in the heart of the bourgeoisie were the intellectuals—lawyers, men of letters, architects, and also artists who were at first classified as craftsmen. The upper layer of the middle class was composed of merchant princes, great industrialists, and wealthy bankers. They constituted the high bourgeoisie, a new aristocracy of wealth which slowly absorbed much of the political power and social prestige the landed aristocracy had previously enjoyed. As feudalism declined, the upper bourgeoisie gained recruits from the lesser nobility. The "small fry" nobles were either those who did not inherit land because of the right of primogeniture which decreed that the first-born male inherit all the land, or they were landowners whose landed property was not extensive enough to support them in a manner befitting a feudal lord. Consequently such noblemen would enter a town or city to embrace a business career. This was particularly true in Italy and southern France, but somewhat exceptional in northern Europe. Furthermore, many daughters of lesser nobles did not disdain matrimonial alliances with scions of wealthy middle-class families who could offer them luxuries and the gaiety of town life.

The distinguishing feature of the upper bourgeoisie was wealth. While many professional men and skilled craftsmen enjoyed a high degree of prosperity, many members of the upper bourgeoisie succeeded in amassing great wealth. Their wealth, however, differed in form from that of the great landed nobility. Whereas the great fortunes of the feudal period had been in the form of land, the wealth of the high bourgeoisie was largely money or capital. The accumulation of this wealth was their primary goal. What they wanted was not just wealth, but unlimited wealth. This is an important factor in explaining why they were impatient of the restrictions the Church had, in the interest of the common good, imposed on the acquisition of unlimited wealth. They were individualistic in their outlook with little sense of social responsibility. Self-interest was for them the highest law, with the profit motive pushing the golden rule into the background. With such motivations coupled with the spirit of enterprise many of them succeeded in amassing wealth on a scale previously unknown. In his essay titled "The Bourgeois Spirit" (1933) Nicholas Berdiaeff wrote:

> The knight, the monk, the philosopher, and the poet have been superseded by a new type—the greedy bourgeois conqueror, organizer and trader. . . . The bourgeois, even when he is a good Catholic, believes only in this world, in the expedient and the useful, is incapable of living by faith in another world, refuses to base his life on the mystery of Golgatha. . . . The bourgeois is impressed with this visible world, stirred, tempted by it. He does not believe seriously in another existence.

In short, the interests of the bourgeoisie, and particularly of the upper stratum, were deeply rooted in things secular. The storing up of the material treasures of this world took precedence over the gathering of spiritual treasures for the next life. Although this way of life was not in accord with the teachings of the Church, it did have its apologists. One of those who looked with favor on the commercial spirit was the versatile humanist Leon Battista Alberti (1404-1472) who wrote in his *Della Famiglia* (Regarding the Family): "A man cannot set his mind to a greater or more liberal work than the increase of money. Business consists of buying and selling, and no one of any sense can consider this a base occupation, for when you sell it is not only a mercenary affair; you have been of service to the buyer and what he pays you for is your labor."

Having acquired wealth the members of the upper bourgeoisie decided to enjoy it. There was in their lives little of the spirit of renunciation which had characterized the thought and preaching of St. Francis. They delighted in luxurious living. Many built palatial houses which they furnished with fine furniture and oriental rugs, and decorated with the best available paintings and colorful tapestries which brought life and warmth into their homes. They enjoyed the best of domestic and imported foods and wines and wore costly silk brocades and furs. Aeneas Sylvius Piccolomini who became Pope Pius II in 1458 commented that many members of the middle class lived like great nobles and wore clothes "fit for a king." In his *Canterbury Tales* Geoffrey Chaucer painted a word picture of a wealthy merchant which in a somewhat modernized version reads:

> A merchant was there with a forked beard
> In motley dress and high on his horse he sat,
> Upon his head a Flanders beaver hat;
> His boots clasped fair and elegantly;
> His statements he made very solemnly,
> Stressing always the increase of his profits
> He did gain by the exchange when he did sell.

Although brief, Chaucer's picture is a sharply etched portrait of a pompous, self-important merchant whose principal interest is a gainful transaction.

Wealth brought not only luxury, but also refinement and an interest in culture. Although the Church served as the principal outlet for most of the early works of Renaissance art, and some members of the higher clergy promoted the revival of interest in the literature of antiquity, kings and princes were also instrumental in fostering the rise of the new secular culture. Besides buying works of art they served as patrons of literary men and artists whose presence at their courts gave both pleasure and prestige. All this does not, however, minimize the role of the middle class which was, in fact, so important that countries which had no vigorous middle class had no robust Renaissance (Poland is an illustration of this point). While a few wealthy merchants, industrialists, and bankers served as patrons, another minority comprised of artists, composers, and men of letters accepted the patronage so that they could function as creators of the new culture which, by and large, reflected bourgeois interests and tastes, and mirrored contemporary life in all its phases. Meanwhile the members of the middle class as a whole became the bearers of the new culture. As the works of art became more secular, wealthy members of the bourgeoisie bought an increasing number to decorate their homes and gardens. They also employed architects to design their palatial houses in the Renaissance style.

In the field of "popular" literature the members of the bourgeoisie at first read whatever literature was available, the romances of chivalry being particular favorites. As the bourgeois reading public increased, authors wrote works specifically for bourgeois readers. In France this literature was called *littérature bourgeoise* as distinguished from *littérature courtoise* or courtly literature. This bourgeois literature included religious tales and religious dramas, but also secular tales, secular poetry, and secular dramas. After the ecclesiastical authorities turned the presentation of the religious drama over to the civic authorities and the gilds the content of the dramas became increasingly secular. Many of the narrative tales of bourgeois literature contain satirical attacks on contemporary society. Special targets of these attacks were the nobility, the clergy, and certain members of the bourgeoisie. One of the subjects on which satire was poured freely was the insatiable greed of the wealthy "money bags." Some of the bourgeois literature displayed a robust, even coarse sense of humor. Examples of bourgeois literature were the fabliaux of France, the prose tales of Boccaccio in Italy, Chaucer's *Canterbury Tales* in England, Brant's *Ship of Fools* in Germany, and such picaresque novels as *The Life of Lazarillo de Tormes* in Spain.

The long French poem *Roman de la Rose* (Romance of the Rose) is a good illustration of the transition from the romances of chivalry to the more realistic bourgeois literature. It is a romance of more than 20,000 lines of verse composed by two different authors. The first part, written about 1225 by Guillaume Lorris, is a simple allegory in the courtly style based on the love of a young man for a beautiful girl. It is an exposition of what might be called Platonic Love, the kind of love Dante cherished for Beatrice. But death claimed the author before he could finish his work. About forty or forty-five years later Jean de Meung wrote the second part. Although he retained the story used as a framework by his predecessor, he wrote his part in an entirely different spirit, a spirit which foreshadowed a certain type of bourgeois literature. Thus he pulled women down to the level of an ordinary human from the high pedestal on which the courtly romances had put her. For him love was little more than a law of nature. He satirized the nobility, criticized the clergy, ridiculed chastity and described marriage as a form of servitude. His recipe for a successful marriage was "a fat purse." In some respects Jean de Meung is a forerunner of Rabelais. Biographers of Rabelais have stated that he drew many of his obscenities from the second part of the *Roman de la Rose*. Some idea of the popularity in France of this long poem may be gained from the fact that more than two hundred manuscripts of it have survived. In England John Gower wrote a poem based on it and Chaucer translated a part of it into English. In Italy Petrarch praised it in glowing terms. About the middle of the sixteenth century a French writer styled it "the Iliad" and "the Aeneid" of France.

The Sources of Middle-Class Wealth

The principal sources of middle-class wealth, as previously indicated, were commerce, industry, and banking. Commerce was the activity which stimulated the growth of the other two. Whereas the local trade, limited to a town and nearby villages, was carried on by traders and shopkeepers who belonged to the petite bourgeoisie, the broader interregional and international trade was in the hands of great merchants (merchant princes or merchant adventurers) who belonged to the high bourgeoisie. Such merchants had branches or representatives in a number of towns and derived their profits from various sources. It was from this large-scale trade over great distances and between countries that many of the large fortunes were amassed.

The most prolific source of profits was the trade with the Levant, the territories around the eastern end of the Mediterranean. During the early Middle Ages this trade was largely controlled by the Arabs or Moors, but in the eleventh century merchants from Western Europe began to take over as middlemen between the Arabs and the local merchants of Western Europe. Thereafter the trade gradually assumed tremendous proportions, receiving a special fillip from the Crusades during the twelfth century and the early part of the thirteenth. The Italian city-states, particularly Venice, Genoa, and Pisa, made the most of their geographical situation by absorbing the bulk of this trade. They built large fleets which transported crusaders, pilgrims, and supplies from Italy to the Near East and returned laden with oriental and Levantine goods. Although the crusading fervor slowly ebbed away, the demand for the goods and luxuries of Asia and the Near East increased. Because of the long distances over which these products had to be transported and the risks attending the transportation they commanded high prices. In a period of rising prosperity, however, the number of those who could afford to buy them gradually increased.

Although the Levant trade included commodities for general consumption and raw materials for a number of industries, costly luxuries predominated. Among the more important items were precious stones, including diamonds, rubies, sapphires, and emeralds. These stones, some of which were believed to possess miraculous powers, were in great demand by wealthy members of the bourgeoisie who spent large sums on personal adornment. Gems came from various parts of Asia and the Near East, for at that time the treasure troves of precious stones in the Ural Mountains were undiscovered. Other luxury items were pearls from the Indian Ocean and ivory from Africa. Then there were oriental perfumes which were prized by the nobles and high bourgeoisie in an age when the custom of bathing had not as yet come into vogue. Near the end of the sixteenth century, for example, it was proudly reported that Queen Elizabeth took a bath at least once a year even though she was not in need of it. Other luxuries were rare oriental woods, carpets, tapestries, fine furniture, and sugar which at first found its principal use in the sweetening of bad-tasting medicines before it gradually became a table delicacy.

The most important manufactured goods which merchants imported from the Orient and the Near East were textiles. Not that there was a scarcity of textiles in Europe, but for some time their quality was not on a par with that of Eastern textiles. Particular favorites were the silk brocades with gold and silver threads, and also velvets and satins before they were manufactured in the West. Other textile imports included fabrics made of the hair of camels and other animals, fine linens from Syria and Egypt, and fine cottons from India. For a time silk fabrics of various kinds were also imported into Western Europe, but by the end of the fifteenth century the tables had turned to the extent that silk fabrics were being exported to the East. The culture of the silkworm which had been practised in China for many centuries was introduced into some parts of the West during the centuries preceding the Renaissance. The Arabs or Moors introduced both the silkworm and the mulberry tree on which it subsists into Sicily and Spain. From these regions the cultivation of the silkworm and the production of silk spread to other parts of Western Europe. The silk fabrics manufactured in Italy and in Flanders attained such high quality that they could compete successfully with imported silks.

Items of the Levant trade which must not be overlooked are dyestuffs and drugs. Outstanding among the dyestuffs was the deep blue indigo (from the Greek word for India) which had been imported in limited quantities since ancient times. In addition there was Brazil-wood which yielded a red dye. It is the wood after which Brazil was named when explorers later found Brazil trees growing in South America. Another important product was saffron from which a yellow dye was made. Saffron was not unknown in Europe, but the dye made from the imported saffron was of a higher quality. In this connection the import of alum from Asia Minor must also be mentioned. Alum was not a dye, but a chemical used to fix the color in textiles. As for drugs, many products which served as drugs were imported in the Levant trade, among them rhubarb, aloes, balsam, camphor, borax, cubebs, and cardamoms.

By all odds the most important and most lucrative products of the Levant trade were spices. The demand for them was so great and the profits of the spice trade so large that the efforts of a number of nations to find a direct route to the source of production resulted in the exploration of unknown oceans and in the discovery of new worlds. Moreover, the desire to share in the spice trade became an incentive for the building of empires. The spices which were in such great demand are products of tropical vines and trees which grow only under special climatic conditions in certain parts of India, China, and the Spice Islands or Moluccas. From these regions they were transported by ships to the Red Sea or the Persian Gulf and then carried by camel caravans over the desert areas to Syria and Egypt where the European merchants purchased them. These spices were not new to Western Europe. Documents of the eighth century show, for example, that in 716 a monastery at Corby in France received from the port of Marseilles a shipment which included pepper, cloves, and other spices. What was new about the Levant spice trade was the quantity that was imported. Spices were in great demand because they relieved the monotomy of a diet which featured salted meats. Their use made food more palatable and established new standards of luxury. Spices were also useful in preserving foods beyond their season. In addition, medicinal qualities were attributed to some spices. It was believed, for example, that cloves and clove oil not only stimulated the appetite but were also an effective remedy for vomiting. Nutmeg was believed to be a cure for insomnia. The wealthy were so eager to have spices that they paid exorbitant prices for them. If less prosperous citizens were fortunate enough to acquire a small quantity it would be hoarded as a great treasure.

The Levant merchants imported into Western Europe a considerable variety of spices. "King of the spices" was pepper, the berry of a vine-like plant indigenous to certain regions of India and to the Spice Islands. It is one of the earliest known spices, its use going back to the beginnings of recorded history. During the period of the revival of trade it was prized so highly that it was used as legal tender in some transactions in England, just as tobacco was at a later time in colonial Virginia. Cloves were also an important member of the spice family. They are the dried flower-buds of certain evergreen trees native to the Spice Islands. The Chinese used them at least as early as the third century B.C. to purify and sweeten their breath. In Western Europe they were used to flavor both food and drink. A third spice that enjoyed great popularity was ginger, a root which is cultivated in a number of tropical areas. Since it was believed that ginger "made the inner man glow with pleasant warmth," it was frequently used to spice wine. Ginger, too, was believed to have medicinal qualities. King Henry VIII of England, for example, believed it to be effective in warding off the plague. A further spice that was held in high esteem was cinnamon, obtained from the bark of a tree native to India. The people of the Renaissance period used it for spicing many foods. It has been said that when they put cinnamon in their bread it became cake. Two other spices which must not be overlooked are nutmeg and mace, both being products of the same tree which grows only in the Spice Islands. While nutmeg is the dried seed of the tree, mace is the dried outer covering of the nutmeg.

But the Levant trade did not consist only of imports into Western Europe; there were also exports to the Near East. In return for the commodities and luxuries, Western Europe sent to the Levant foodstuffs, particularly grain, and raw materials in the form of wool, hides, and metals. Exported manufactured products included woolen fabrics and common linens from England, Flanders, and Italy. Quality textiles, hardware, and weapons also gained in importance.

The Levant trade, as indicated earlier, was by and large a monopoly of the Italian city-states after the eleventh century. Certain French and Spanish towns situated on the Mediterranean coast did manage to gain a small share of the trade with the Near East, but the great bulk of it was in the hands of the city-states of northern Italy. Their geographical location gave them an advantage over other towns and cities of Western Europe. When the demand for the products of the Near and Far East manifested itself, they were in a position to make the most of the opportunity to supply it. The leading competitors for the Levant trade were Venice, Genoa, and Pisa. Competition between them was keen, expressing itself at times in bloody warfare. Fortune favored first one, then another of these city-states, but finally the superior power of the Venetians prevailed. Thenceforth Venice dominated the

Levant trade until the source of supply dried up after the discovery of an all-water route to India in 1498 by Vasco da Gama.

Economic Recession

The era of the Renaissance was not, however, a period of uninterrupted economic expansion. As in the Western world of the present day, the graph which indicates economic expansion, stability or decline did not move steadily upward. At times it remained on the same level for shorter or longer periods and at other times it turned sharply downward, indicating recession or depression. Because of the dearth of statistical data on the rise and fall of the volume of trade and industrial production, there is a diversity of opinion among economic historians regarding the duration and severity of the depressions which occurred. Besides being few in number, the known statistics are in many instances not reliable indices of the economy as a whole. A drop in the output of a specific city or district may have been more than offset by expansion in the same industry in other parts of the country. Again, a declining output in one industry may in the overall picture have been compensated for by growth in other industries. Hence any attempt to use local statistics as a basis for broader conclusions produces questionable deductions and unfounded assumptions. What appears to be beyond question is that after a long period of expansion extending to the end of the thirteenth century economic progress slackened, then stopped, and about the middle of the fourteenth century was followed by a period of decline. This decline was accompanied by a temporary decrease in the population of Western Europe.

The severity of the impact of the depression and the duration of the depressed conditions varied in the different countries of Western Europe. The blow appears to have been most crippling and longer lasting in France, England, and Germany. Depression seems to have held the economies of these countries in its grip from about the middle of the fourteenth century until about the middle of the fifteenth. The economic stagnation of this period must be regarded as a major factor in any explanation as to why Renaissance manifestations appeared so much later in these countries than in Italy. What the effect of the general depression was on the economic life of the states which later comprised Spain is a challenging question for researchers in Spanish history.

The impact of the economic setback was not so devastating in the Italian Peninsula as in the countries north of the Alps. The Italian city-states with their highly-developed economic systems were able to withstand the blow better. Despite the economic slow-down and the recession which followed, the economies of the major Italian states still continued to function at a high level. As in northern Europe the decline seems to have set in during the early decades of the fourteenth century, but was much shorter in duration than in the northern countries. While the recession lasted there was not only a sharp decline in the volume of trade and production, but there was also widespread unemployment in the ranks of the working classes. Banking, too, suffered severely, with many banks forced into bankruptcy. An authoritative delineation of the causes of the economic recession in Italy must await intensive investigation of the problem. One cause which has been advanced is overproduction. Eager capitalists expanded production until Italian markets and the countries with which Italian merchants had trade relations could no longer absorb the output. It is for this reason that the recession in Italy has been called "a crisis of saturation." A further cause which has been cited is the constant warfare which the Italian states waged against each other. Many of the states were so intent on conquering other states or defending themselves against attack, with the stronger swallowing the weaker, that they had little opportunity to look for new and wider commercial fields. But the economic recession was not an unmitigated evil. The shrinking markets and the keen competition impelled industrialists to produce quality products, bankers to expand their services, and merchants to improve their marketing techniques in order to meet the needs of the situation.

The fourteenth century also saw the population decline in many parts of Italy. After the middle of the century few new towns were founded and some of the old ones which had once been fully populated had uninhabited areas within their walls. The decline of the population was due at least in part to the Black Death which swept into Italy in 1348. It will be remembered that Boccaccio described its ravages in the introduction to his *Decameron.* The overall loss of population was so large that some historians believe the Italian population was no larger in 1400 than it had been in 1300. Even though the population decline was only temporary, it was, nevertheless, a factor in the slackening of industrial production. On the whole, however, the wealth accumulated by the upper middle class kept the economic machinery moving until the trend again turned upward.

Commerce and Industry in Northern Europe

The most prosperous area north of the Alps was undoubtedly that embraced by a group of feudal provinces collectively known as the Netherlands or Low Countries. These provinces were not only inhabited by an industrious population; they were also in a geographical location favorable for trade and industry, including fishing. Furthermore, three rivers—the Rhine, the Meuse, and the Scheldt—served the people of the Netherlands as convenient arteries of trade. Then, too, the maritime provinces had a long coastline on the North Sea. Towns and cities had grown up around harbors, along inland waterways, and at crossroads. While some of the towns served as bases for fishing fleets, others became important industrial and trading centers. During the period after 1385 most of the feudal provinces came under the rule of the house of Burgundy either by marriage, inheritance, or conquest. At that time the dukes of Burgundy were among the more powerful rulers of Europe, the equals of kings in everything but name. Their rule gave the provinces of the Netherlands a certain degree of unity and a stability of government which enabled them to continue their advance toward greater prosperity.

The principal sources of income of the northern provinces differed from those of the southern provinces. Whereas the predominantly Dutch population of the northern provinces devoted themselves largely to agriculture and fishing, the inhabitants of the southern provinces, which later became Belgium, achieved a high degree of prosperity from industry and trade. The southern provinces had a number of thriving commercial and industrial centers, among them Bruges, Ghent, Ypres, Brussels, Liege, and Antwerp. In these towns there were such industries as the manufacture of metalware, weapons, and leather-goods. The major industry, which had been growing since the eleventh century, was the manufacture of woolen cloth. The great center of the industry was the province of Flanders with the towns of Bruges, Ghent, and Ypres. Eventually the wool produced in the Netherlands was not sufficient for its needs. Increasing quantities of raw wool were, therefore, imported from England. When the Flemish woolen-cloth industry was at its height in the thirteenth century the cloth it produced was sold in every part of Europe and even in the Near East.

But in the second half of the century the industry was beset by troubles of various kinds. The source of most of them was the deteriorating relationship between capitalist employers and wage-earning workmen. Previously all those connected with the industry had joined in the struggle to obtain for their respective towns a large measure of freedom from interference by the feudal overlords in civic affairs. Once this had been achieved the workmen began to express dissatisfaction with their material status. The growing disparity between the wealth of their capitalist employers and their own poverty strengthened the belief that the employers were growing richer and richer at their expense. What they wanted was a share of the earnings large enough to enable them to raise their living standards. As it was, they were living in miserable huts and working long hours for "starvation" wages. They also wanted a voice in the management of both municipal and industrial affairs. The employers, who were banded together in merchant gilds which collectively controlled the municipal governments, vigorously opposed the demands of the workmen. The merchant gilds not only set the wages and prescribed the quality of the work each workman turned out; they also forbade the workmen to organize gilds. Workmen could not even hold meetings without express permission from the merchant gilds. All this excited in the workmen a deep hostility toward their employers. This hostility vented itself in disputes, strikes, and even violence. Finally near the end of the thirteenth century the workmen of the cloth industry staged an uprising which was so successful that it broke the power of the merchant gilds. The workmen gained both the right to organize their own gilds and to have representation in the town councils.

The victory gained by the workmen did not, however, insure them a long period of prosperity. In the fourteenth century the Flemish woolen-cloth industry gradually declined. The dependence of the industry on imported raw materials was a major cause. Flemish manufacturers were unable to make certain of an uninterrupted supply of raw wool. Wars, political disputes, and the preemption of the English wool crop by merchants of other countries at times resulted in a shortage of raw materials which, in turn, generated crises and caused unemployment. About the middle of the fourteenth century the English further reduced the available supply of raw wool by turning to cloth-making. A further cause of the decline was the loss of markets. Not only did Italian and English cloth replace Flemish cloth in some markets; the sale of Flemish cloth at the fairs of Champagne, which had been one of the principal outlets, was also greatly curtailed. Disputes between Flemish merchants and the king of France impelled the latter to put obstacles in the way of the importation of Flemish cloth into France, one of them being a heavy import duty. For these and other reasons the prosperity of the Flemish woolen-cloth industry gradually faded.

How this effected the prosperity of the southern provinces as a whole is a moot question. Statistics are lacking to show to what extent the decline in Flanders was compensated by an increase in the production of woolen cloth in other provinces of the Netherlands. The woolen-cloth industry of Brabant, for example, expanded and became more prosperous as the Flemish industry declined. There is also the further question regarding the extent to which the increasing production of cotton and linen cloth, laces, tapestries, and draperies offset the declining output of woolen cloth in Flanders. Whatever the facts in the matter, the southern provinces retained enough prosperity to provide a material background for the flowering of Renaissance painting.

The principal commercial center in Flanders was the city of Bruges which, because of its location, was a convenient stopping place between the Baltic and the Mediterranean. There merchants from the north met merchants from the south to exchange their wares. Bruges was also the destination of the so-called Flanders galleys in which the Venetian merchants transported eastern and oriental goods to the Flemish city whence they were distributed by other merchants. In addition to being accessible by water Bruges could also be reached by land routes from France, Germany, and the Danubian countries. During the fourteenth and fifteenth centuries Bruges was also known for its fairs which attracted many merchants from all parts of Europe and from the Near East. A contemporary chronicler reported that buyers and sellers from thirty-four different countries registered at one of the fairs. He also stated that many people visited Bruges just to see the wares and salable items which ranged from wax candles to cloth of gold and included such members of the animal kingdom as parrots, monkeys, bears, and lions. It was said that Bruges was the best place in Europe to gather the latest news brought by foreign merchants from various parts of the world.

Near the end of the fifteenth century, however, the commercial glory of Bruges began to fade. The principal cause of the decline was the silting-up of the River Zwyn which afforded access to Bruges from the North Sea. The water became so shallow that larger ships could no longer enter the inlet and had to turn to other ports. The departure of the foreign merchants from Bruges soon emptied the quays and stilled the bustle of commercial activity. From Bruges they turned to Antwerp which became the great commercial and financial center of northern Europe. Soon its harbor was crowded with foreign ships and its wharves were piled high with merchandise from many parts of Europe and from the Near East. Thus the prosperity of the southern Netherlands continued until it was blighted by the repressive policies of King Philip II of Spain (1556-1598) who inherited the rule of the Netherlands from his father Charles V. Meanwhile the northern or Dutch provinces were building up their fishing industry and expanding their carrying trade. They also built dikes to stop the North Sea from washing away more of their land and to reclaim land which had previously been inundated so that they could use it to raise food or for dairy farming. All this ushered in what is known as the golden age of the Dutch Netherlands.

The trade of northern Europe differed from that of the Italian states with the Levant in that luxuries and fineries did not constitute so large a part of it. With the exception of fine fabrics, furs were about the only luxury item produced in northern Europe. Not that all furs are a luxury. The fur trade included such ordinary furs as sheepskins and goatskins which peasants and townspeople used to make wearing apparel to keep them warm in the wintertime. There were also such moderate-priced furs as conies from England and the Netherlands. On the other hand, such furs as marten, ermine, and sable, were rare and costly. As symbols of affluence and social standing they were prized possessions of the wealthy classes. A German bishop of that time is reported to have said, "We strive as hard to come into possession of a marten skin as if it were eternal salvation."

The principal items of the northern trade were staple commodities in the form of raw materials and processed foodstuffs. In general the merchandise that was bought and sold was both bulkier and less expensive than the wares and foodstuffs that were being transported to Western Europe from the Near East. Among the foodstuffs the principal raw material was grain. Merchants bought it in the grain-rich regions of northern and eastern Europe and transported it to areas which did not produce enough to supply the needs of the inhabitants. Such areas were Flanders which was highly industrialized, parts of Holland which specialized in dairy farming, the various wine-growing regions, and wherever the grin harvest was poor. Another staple of northern trade, as previously indicated, was raw wool and woolen cloth. Other raw materials were hemp, flax, wax, tallow, hops, hides, salt, and timber for shipbuilding and the construction of houses. During the thirteenth century much timber was exported from Germany, Scandinavia, and northern England, but during the centuries that followed Russia and Poland became the most prolific sources. Russia also supplied pitch, tar, resins, and potash.

Among the processed foods wine and beer were important items. The trade in wine had not ceased even during the worst period of the Middle Ages, for it was a product that was in constant demand by those who could afford it. With the improvement of economic conditions people of all classes consumed large quantities. For example, in 1415 England with its small population imported more than a million gallons of wine despite the economic depression which prevailed. Much of the sweet wine which was traded internationally came from Spain. Other types were produced in Germany where vineyards flourished along the banks of the Rhine, the Main, the Neckar, and the Moselle. But the great wine-producing country was France. The mention of such regions as Champagne and Burgundy calls attention to some of the famous French wines. As for beer, both Holland and Germany began to export considerable quantities in the fourteenth century. The traffic in beer was, in fact, a source of considerable income for the Dutch.

But the leading item among processed foodstuffs was salted herring which, as stated earlier, was in great demand because the laws of the Church prohibited the eating of meat on Friday and other days of the church year. In areas near the source of supply the trade in salted fish had continued throughout the Middle Ages on a limited scale, but with the revival of trade the herring industry took on a new importance, expanding both in scope and volume. At that time the largest shoals of herring were in the Baltic along the coasts of Scandinavia and Germany. The most prolific sources were the herring fisheries of Scania at the extreme southwestern tip of Scandinavia, a region which at that time belonged to Denmark. During the herring season fishermen from far and near went there to share in the great haul. When a boat was filled with herring the catch would be sold to merchants who had set up headquarters in several coastal towns of Scania. The merchants would then have the herring carted to their processing plants nearby where they employed women to eviscerate them, wash them in sea water, and finally pack them in salt in large barrels, each of which held about six Scania bushels. After a settling period of ten days the fish were ready for distribution. Some idea of the magnitude of the herring industry may be gained from the fact that in 1368 the Scania fisheries produced 34,000 barrels of salted herring. The peak of production was reached near the end of the fifteenth century when the annual output at Scania reached 50,000 barrels. But soon thereafter a great change took place. The great shoals of herring left the Baltic for other feeding grounds, thereby spelling the doom of the Scania fisheries.

All the northern countries participated to a greater or lesser extent in the northern trade, but most of the commerce was controlled by the Hanseatic League. This league, the name of which derives from the old Scandinavian word *hansa* meaning a confederacy, was organized by a group of German cities for the protection of their commerce against piracy. Although the number of towns comprising it varied, at the height of its power the league had a membership ranging from sixty to eighty, some of them located outside Germany. Hamburg, Lübeck, Danzig, and Bruges were among the more important members. Although much of the trade was carried on between the member towns, they also traded with Norway, Sweden, and Denmark. The league also had a trading station at Novgorod in Russia where merchandise could be stored under guard and where there were living quarters for foreign merchants. Products from various parts of Russia were brought to this station where they were exchanged for merchandise from other countries. The league also had a trading station in London called the Steelyard where trade was brisk.

Gradually the Hanseatic League managed to gain a virtual monopoly of the Baltic trade and a large share of the trade in the North Sea. The Hanseatic merchants, for example, had an undisputed monopoly of the herring trade. During the early years of the league's existence the herring industry was the chief source of the wealth of many Hanseatic towns. How important it was is indicated by the three herring on the armorial shield of Lübeck. Through the sale or exchange of herring the Hanseatic merchants gained a firm hold on the trade in other commodities. For example, in exchange for herring they obtained wool and woolen cloth from England, timber, furs, and tallow from Russia, and wine from the wine-growing districts of Germany and France. The expansion of commerce was accompanied by the building of strong naval forces to protect the commercial fleets. This constituted the Hanseatic League a great power in the northern countries. In Denmark, for example, the influence of the league was for a time so great that it was an important factor in deciding the succession to the Danish throne.

During the second half of the fifteenth century both the prosperity and the prestige of the Hanseatic League began to show symptoms of decline. Undoubtedly the depression which gripped the economic life of Germany was a vital factor in undermining the prosperity of the league. As trade declined, dissension broke out among the member towns. Non-members strove to keep the trouble alive. The English and particularly the Dutch seized the opportunity to make inroads into the commerce of the league. The most crippling blow to the prosperity of the Hanseatic League was the loss of the herring trade when the herring shoals left the Baltic. The loss of the Hanseatic towns was the gain of the Dutch. The migration of the herring to the North Sea enabled the Dutch to achieve domination of the industry and to retain it during the two centuries that followed.

The Beginnings of Banking

The third source of middle-class wealth was banking. Modern banking originated in the business of money-changing and grew as an adjunct of commerce and industry. The business of money-changing was called into existence by the perplexing variety of coins that were in circulation during the period of commercial expansion. The coinage confusion resulted from the fact that so many princes and cities, in addition to the rulers of larger territories, possessed minting privileges. In Italy, for example, each one of the city-states had its own special type of coins. In Germany the confusion was even worse. After 1356 (the year in which the Golden Bull gave the seven electoral princes the right to mint gold coins) a dozen officials and the free state of Lübeck issued gold coinage. The number of princelings and cities which could, and mostly did, mint silver coins numbered over two hundred. In one small area of Germany there were more than sixty different coinages. The fact that there was no common standard of coinage greatly increased the existing confusion. Nor was this all. When the petty princes experienced financial difficulties they did not hesitate to debase the coinage by reducing the amount of precious metals in the coins. This was done either by issuing smaller coins or by adding base metals to the gold or silver. Even kings, such as Edward I and Henry VIII of England, resorted to the debasement of coinage. There was also the practise of clipping coins, that is, of clipping pieces off. In this way some of the coins were reduced to half their original size. The laws that were promulgated against such practises had little effect even though they threatened such dire punishments as torture and hanging. In the thirteenth century it was reported from the Netherlands that the coinage there included many coins that were worn thin, clipped, bent, debased, perforated with holes, and otherwise mutilated.

The monetary confusion was such that most merchants were unable to cope with it. It was a situation which called for men with an expert knowledge of the various coinages, men who could assay the value of clipped and debased coins. The need for such men gave rise to the business of money-changing. At the fairs and in all the important commercial centers money-changers appeared who for a fee exchanged "foreign" moneys for local currency which was needed for business deals. These money-changers were the forerunners of modern bankers. In Italy as late as the fourteenth century the terms "money-changer" and "banker" were used indiscriminately. The word "bank" is a derivative of the Italian word *banco* meaning bench or counter. The first money-changers set up a bench or counter on which they displayed their supply of money and behind which they conducted their business. If a money-changer failed in business the populace would break the bench or demolish the counter, a practise which is expressed in the term "bankrupt" (from the Latin *bancus ruptus* or broken bench). Money-changers did so much to facilitate trade at fairs and markets that the municipal authorities made certain not only of their presence but also that they had an expert knowledge of the various coinages.

Money-changing did not remain the sole function of the money-changers very long. Their business soon expanded in a number of directions. One of these was the acceptance for safekeeping of money from merchants who had no immediate use for it. Such deposits with a money-changer relieved the merchant of the necessity of guarding his money and also enabled him to draw on it when he needed it. Other citizens who had money to deposit soon followed suit and the money-changer became a deposit banker. It is impossible to set a date for the inception of this service since the time varied in the different regions. In Italy at least some of the money-changers became deposit bankers in the thirteenth century. In Venice, for example, a law was promulgated in 1270 which required all money-changers who wished to accept deposits to post security with the government. This marks the beginning of the supervision of banking by the state. Another function of the early bankers was the acceptance of money for transportation from one city or fair to another. This was done to free the merchants from the risks of transportation which were very great. An important step forward was the issuance by the early bankers of bills of exchange which eliminated the necessity of transportation. Upon depositing money a merchant would receive a bill of exchange redeemable for an equivalent sum in another city or at another fair. Since fairs were of such importance, special bills of exchange were developed which were payable at fairs. Such bills of exchange could, of course, be issued only by banks which had a branch or an agent at the place designated for the redemption.

In accepting deposits the bankers gathered much capital which was lying idle and as such contributed nothing to the development of commerce and industry. But a use was soon found for the idle money. Bankers lent it at remunerative rates to merchants who were in need of it. Merchants would, for example, borrow money for trade expeditions to the Near East. In some instances it was borrowed for only one voyage, and the capital would then be returned together with the interest. By lending money to those who wished to embark on commercial and industrial ventures the bankers encouraged and promoted the expansion of both commerce and industry. The interest rates charged by the bankers were high according to present-day standards. They were seldom less than 20 to 25 per cent. For a hazardous undertaking, such as a Levantine voyage, the rate was often increased to 50 per cent, whereas for a voyage to Corsica or Sardinia the rate might be as low as 20 per cent. Bankers also entered into partnership with merchant adventurers in which the lender shared the profits equally with the borrower who undertook the trading voyage. But the loans early bankers made were not limited to commercial or industrial purposes. They also lent large sums to cities for the construction of public buildings and other purposes, to wealthy individuals for the building of palatial houses, to kings and princes for the raising of mercenary armies, for waging wars, and for projects of various kinds. Loans were even made to monasteries for the erection of buildings and to communities for the building of churches. When the borrower was a ruler, the banker or bankers frequently asked for the right to collect taxes as security for their loans.

Most of the money-lenders of the period preceding the expansion of commerce were of the Jewish faith. This exempted them from the laws of the Church against the charging of interest on loans. Jews had for centuries been money-lenders to kings and princes in many countries of Europe. They were so indispensable that certain kings of England and France opposed all efforts to convert them to Christianity. One of the most successful and colorful of the early Jewish financiers in England was Aaron Lincoln (1125-1186) whose operations were so extensive that he had agents in a number of English towns. Paradoxically the loans he made for the building of churches and monasteries were one of his principal sources of income. He financed the building of abbeys at Lincoln and at St. Albans and advanced the money for the construction of nine Cistercian monasteries. When Aaron died King Henry II claimed his estate for the crown on the convenient excuse that the accumulated wealth was ill-gotten since it was gained by money-lending. The English king used the confiscated wealth to wage war against King Philip Augustus of France.

When the expansion of commerce and industry multiplied the opportunities for money-leading, Christians began to enter the business. Soon there were Christian bankers in the various countries of Western Europe, but it was the Italians who led all other nationalities in this respect. During the period from the thirteenth century to the sixteenth they held what almost amounted to a monopoly of the banking business. The supremacy of the Italian bankers rested on the banking techniques they developed, as well as on the fact that they had a sufficient supply of capital to accommodate interested borrowers. Banks in the form of partnerships were organized in Siena, Piacenza, Florence, Venice, Genoa, Milan, and other cities. In some instances such banks were the headquarters for international operations with branch offices in Bruges, London, Paris, Barcelona, and Valencia. In the foreign countries the Italian bankers were called Lombards because many of them came from the cities of Lombardy in northern Italy. In London Lombard Street still marks the district in which the early Italian bankers congregated.

At the opening of the fourteenth century the banking houses of Florence assumed the leadership. The largest Florentine banks were founded by such families as the Frescobaldi, the Bardi, the Peruzzi, and the Medici. During the first decades the banking houses of the Bardi and the Peruzzi surpassed all others in size. The Peruzzi firm which was second largest had fifteen branch offices in strategic locations from Cyprus in the eastern Mediterranean to London in the north of Europe. Both the Bardi and the Peruzzi, however, put the future of their firms in jeopardy by an overextension of credit and excessive loans. Among those to whom they lent large sums were kings of England and a king of Naples. The two kings of England who borrowed freely from them were Edward I (1272-1307) and Edward II (1307-1327), but in 1343 Edward III (1327-1377) repudiated the debts. About the same time King Robert of Naples (1309-1347) took the same course. The loss of so large a part of their capital dealt the Bardi and Peruzzi banking firms a blow from which they never recovered. In 1345 both banks suspended operations. A number of other banks were also forced into bankruptcy by the banking depression that followed. The failure of so many banks cast a pall on banking activities which was not lifted until the fifteenth century.

Besides changing money, accepting deposits, issuing bills of exchange and certificates of credit, and making loans, Italian banks served the Vatican as collectors of papal revenues in the various countries of Western Europe. These revenues, which were enormous in the aggregate, included the papal share of tithes, income from the granting of dispensations and indulgences, annates, Peter's pence, and other payments. For collecting these revenues and delivering the proceeds to the Vatican in Rome the banking firms received a commission of 5 or 6 per cent of the total. Collecting papal revenues frequently presented the bankers with opportunities for additional business. Contemporary records show that bankers, while collecting papal revenues, made loans to those who were in need of funds to pay their indebtedness to the Vatican. When the banking houses of the Bardi and Peruzzi collapsed, the Vatican had considerable difficulty in finding a banking house which could assume the task of collecting the papal revenues. Finally the Florentine banking firm of the Alberti undertook the task. Later quarrels broke out between the partners, splitting the firm into a number of rival factions. The family also lost the favor of the ruling oligarchy of Florence and was exiled from the city (1393). It was while the family was in exile that its most famous member, Leon Battista Alberti, humanist and art critic, was born. As for the papal revenues, in the fifteenth century the Medici Bank served the Vatican in the capacity of collector.

During much of the fifteenth century the bank of the Medici family, which will be discussed in the next chapter, was a major factor in the banking activities of Europe. When the Medici Bank declined in the second half of the century, banking was gradually nationalized. In the sixteenth century the leading banking firm north of the Alps was that of the Fugger family of southern Germany. The most prominent member of the family was Jakob

Fugger (1459-1525). Jakob, called Jakob the Rich by his contemporaries, is the most prominent financial figure of the early capitalist period. His biography is not a "rags to riches" story. His father left him and his two older brothers a thriving business. During the years of his schooling young Jakob did not look forward to a business career. He was well on the way in his training for the priesthood when his father suddenly died and his mother summoned him to return to Augsburg to enter the business in which his two brothers were already active. Before doing so, nineteen-year-old Jakob decided to spend a year in Venice learning the latest and best business techniques. Upon his return to Augsburg he quickly demonstrated business ability of the highest order. Under his guidance the Fugger business expanded in various directions. He changed the business from one specializing in textiles to one that made the buying and selling of metals, specifically copper and silver, the primary interest. Then he expanded its activities to the ownership of mines and the production of raw metals. The company soon made such large profits that Jakob used the accumulated wealth to enter the banking business. The Fugger bank performed such services as accepting deposits, exchanging currencies, and buying and selling bills of exchange, but its most profitable venture was money-lending.

As a banker Jakob the Rich had dealings with many important persons of his time, including popes, emperors, and princes. Perhaps his most dramatic move was the financing in large part of the election in 1519 of Charles of Habsburg as Charles V, emperor of the Holy Roman Empire. Although the Holy Roman Empire which once embraced most of Western Europe had shrunk until it was restricted to Germany, Francis I of France as well as Charles competed for the emperorship. To make his election certain, Charles offered large bribes to the seven electors whose function it was to choose the next emperor. Jakob Fugger insured the election by lending Charles the cash he needed for the bribes. As security for this and other loans the Fugger firm received the right to collect certain taxes and to exploit silver mines in the Tyrol and copper mines in Hungary. The Fugger firm also served the Vatican by making loans to the pope and by collecting papal revenues in northern and eastern Europe. Jakob who was a member in good standing of the Roman Catholic Church was criticized by contemporaries for accumulating so much wealth. But Jakob defended himself against the accusations of selfishness and excessive hoarding of wealth by saying, "Many in the world are hostile to me. They say I am rich. I am rich by God's grace and without injury to any man."

When Jakob died in 1525 he was probably the richest man in Europe. His counting houses, factories, warehouses, mines, and landed properties were scattered over a wide area. In this respect he was a forerunner of the great captains of industry of more recent times. He exemplified the mentality of the high bourgeoisie in that the accumulation of wealth was the overriding purpose of his life. It should be stated, however, that he was a representative of the Renaissance in his patronage of the arts. He also built the Fuggerei in Augsburg, a collection of dwellings which he rented to poor people at a low rental. The Fuggerei was probably the first of the modern low-income housing projects. Since Jakob had no children, his nephew Anton (1493-1560) succeeded him as head of the Fugger firm. It was under Anton that the firm reached the apex of its wealth and power.

5

Renaissance Italy

The first question that presents itself in turning to Renaissance Italy is "Why did the Renaissance attain its fullest development in Italy?" The most obvious answer is that conditions in Italy were most favorable for its development. The basic factor was undoubtedly the prosperity of many of the Italian city-states. From the Crusades to the discovery by Vasco da Gama of an all-water route to the Orient (1498) the Italian city-states were collectively the dominant economic power of Western Europe. The Italians were not only the great merchants and industrialists of Western Europe; they were also the principal bankers. Various factors contributed toward making Italy the predominant economic power. Probably the most important one was the strategic trading location of many of the city-states. This gave them an advantage in establishing commercial relations with the countries of the eastern Mediterranean. They were not slow to exploit their advantage. To the Romans the Mediterranean had been *Mare Nostrum* (our sea). Although the Italians did not hold as much land along the Mediterranean as the Romans had, they did, however, extend their commercial sway over a large part of it. While most of the countries north of the Alps were still in the grip of the long depression which preceded the revival of commerce and the growth of towns, merchants from the Italian coastal towns were busy laying the foundations on which the structure of Italian prosperity was raised. Consequently the economic boom came sooner in Italy than in most countries of northern Europe. The wealth accumulated by members of the middle class from trade, industry, and banking opened the way to the enjoyment of the good things of life and generated a secular spirit which was the motive power in the rise of a new secular culture.

Other conditions in Italy were also propitious. In the prosperous city-states, most of which were autonomous in fact if not in theory, political conditions were favorable for the rise of the new Renaissance culture. In the freer communes artists, scholars, and writers could practice a large degree of self-expression. If the government was despotic, the despot was often the chief sponsor of the new culture. Furthermore, in Italy medieval civilization did not establish itself so firmly as in the rest of Western Europe. Such characteristic medieval forms as chivalry, feudalism, scholasticism, and Gothic architecture did not strike their roots so deeply into Italian soil as they did in France. England, Germany, and Spain. In some Italian circles they were regarded as something imported. Consequently the forces which dominated medieval life seem to have weakened earlier in Italy, permitting freer development of the new culture. Then, too, in Italy the break with the pagan or secular spirit of Rome had not been so sharp as in the countries north of the Alps. The secular spirit had persisted in larger degree in literature and in some forms of art. Secular schools which the Romans had founded survived in Italy long after they had disappeared in the countries north of the Alps.

There were also other links between Christian Italy and pagan Rome. Latin remained in general use, although it was corrupted by the admixture of barbarisms. Roman law continued to be an important factor in the administration of certain provinces and municipalities. As early as the twelfth century a revival of interest in Roman law had taken place. One of the results was that the study of it became a part of the curriculum of both secondary and higher schools. In some of the Italian universities Roman law together with medicine held the place accorded to theology in northern universities. Roman monuments, the remains of Roman sculpture, and the ruins of amphitheaters, temples, and other important Roman buildings served as constant reminders of the grandeur and glory of Rome. All of these links tended to make Rome a living reality to many Italians and helped to keep alive the traditions of secularism. In addition, there was the idea of a blood relationship with the Romans. Many members of the upper classes claimed a somewhat shadowy descent from the Roman patricians. No less a person than Dante believed the Italians to be the direct descendants of the Romans. As he put it, "The Romans were the first born of the Italian family." Dante was firmly convinced that the blood of the ancient Romans flowed in his veins.

The Italian City-States

The Italy of the Renaissance was not a nation like France or England. It was a country without political unity. Despite the fact that the Italians had such important common elements of unity as language, religion, customs, and history, they lacked a feeling of common interests which would have excited a desire for political unity. As it was, the desire for national unity existed only in the minds of a few writers and dreamers. The territory of Italy, and particularly of northern Italy, was divided into a multitude of political units. The largest unit was the kingdom of the Two Sicilies which included the island of Sicily and the southern end of the Italian peninsula. The rest of Italy was divided into small states, most of which were city-states. Although these city-states were nominally a part of the Holy Roman Empire, they actually enjoyed a large degree of autonomy. As the empire became more and more identified with Germany and grew weaker, the Italian cities assumed direction of their own affairs and took measures for their own defense. Both the emperor Frederick I (1152-1190), better known as Frederick Barbarossa, and Emperor Frederick II (1215-1250) sought to reestablish the imperial sovereignty over Italy, but their efforts ended in failure. At the end of the thirteenth century the Italian city-states were independent political units. Dino Campagni observed at that time that after the death of Frederick II "the fame and recollection of the empire was well-nigh extinguished." At first the rule of most of the city-states was limited to the city itself, but as the city governments grew stronger and more prosperous they extended their authority over the neighboring countryside.

The city-states differed from each other in many ways. While some were ruled by despots, others had governments that were democratic in spirit. Each city-state had its own laws, its own currency, its own military force, and its own economic interests. Even in cultural matters there was a tendency to emphasize local interests. But whatever the interests or the form of government, the relations of the city-states with one another were marred by selfish ambition, envy, and frequent wars. The relationship between the city-states was one of "dog eat dog" with the stronger trying to swallow or at least to subjugate the weaker. The basic cause of the perpetual strife and warfare was that each city-state wanted to increase its share of trade or to play a more important role in the industrial and banking activities which had developed as a result of the commercial expansion. Some of the city-states were growing wealthy from commerce and others from industry and banking. Such city-states as Venice, Genoa, and Pisa were giving their primary attention to commerce, and others, like Florence, Lucca, and Milan were centering their attention on industry and banking. In all of them the wealthy members of the middle class served as promoters of the secular spirit and sponsors of the new secular culture.

The Rise of the Venetian Empire

The city-state which developed into the greatest commercial power of the early Renaissance period was Venice. The story of the rise of Venice begins in the fifth century when a considerable number of refugees from the Italian mainland fled to a group of small islands in the Adriatic off the northeastern coast of Italy to escape the invading hordes of Goths and Huns. The marshy islands or oozy mudflats, formed by the silt deposits of a number of rivers flowing into the Adriatic were hardly an inviting terrain, but they did offer the refugees a haven where they would be safe from attack by land or by sea. The first refugees seem to have regarded the islands as a place offering temporary asylum and at various times some returned to their old homes on the mainland. But as the invasions continued and the decaying Roman Empire was unable to stop the barbarian inroads, more refugees sought safety on the islands. They represented all strata of Roman society from the plebeians to the patricians, from the very poor to the very rich. Only slaves and criminals were excluded. Gradually the settlements as a whole became known as Venetia or Venice, a name which was taken from a district on the mainland.

When the settlements became permanent, steps were taken to establish an organized government. Governmental powers were vested in a council composed of one tribune or representative from each one of the twelve settlements that had been founded on the islands. This council was, however, unable to allay the jealousies, antipathies, and bickerings between the groups which had come from various cities of the mainland. Finally, near the end of the seventh century, the highest political authority was vested in a single official called doge (dux or duke) elected for life by the citizens of Venice on the basis of universal suffrage. But during the period of the expansion of commerce a group of merchants who virtually controlled Venetian trade aspired to gain control of the government as a means of protecting their commercial interests. An important step was taken in 1172 when the selection of a doge was entrusted to a committee chosen by the Great Council (*Maggior Consiglio*). Gradually the membership of the council was restricted more and more and in 1297 was limited to the members of the families comprising the merchant oligarchy and to their descendants. Thus the commercial oligarchy gained control of the state and the doge was thenceforth little more than a figurehead. It was a government whose principal interest was the protection and expansion of commerce.

In 820 Venice also put itself under the protection of a new patron saint. The new protector was St. Mark the Evangelist. There was an old tradition that St. Mark had founded the first Christian churches on the mainland along the northern coast of the Adriatic and that he had also been forced by a storm to seek refuge on the islands on which Venice was rising. Several contemporary chroniclers state that a few years later three merchants found the remains of St. Mark in a church in Alexandria, Egypt. According to the chronicler De Canage, "They went hastily by night to the sepulchre where the body was, put it in a basket, and covered it with cabbages and swine's flesh." Then they laid another body in the tomb and took the basket with the relics of St. Mark to the ship. When the ship arrived at Venice the entire population formed a huge procession, headed by the clergy, the doge, and officials of the state, to escort the remains of St. Mark to the palace of the doge. After the three merchants were forgiven for purloining the relics, St. Mark was, with great rejoicing, officially declared the patron saint of Venice, replacing St. Theodore. At first a modest chapel was built to house the precious relics, but in the eleventh century it was replaced by St. Mark's Cathedral. The architecture of this famous cathedral is a blend of Byzantine and other styles. Many of the materials were, in fact, imported from the Byzantine Empire with which the Venetians had established trade relations. The present somewhat flamboyant appearance of St. Mark's is due to later exterior embellishment. In general, Byzantine civilization left its mark on many phases of Venetian life.

In the meantime the economic life of Venice had taken form. Since the barren islands and desolate mudflats on which the early settlers began to build Venice were unable to supply food for the growing population, the Venetians had to turn to the sea for their sustenance. The future greatness of Venice was, in fact, founded on the sea, for the Venetians derived their wealth either from marine products or trade. This close relationship with the sea was publicly acknowledged each year on Ascension Day in a ceremony called the Espousal of the Sea. As a part of the ceremony, attended by the Venetian dignitaries, the foreign representatives in Venice, and the bulk of the Venetian population, the bishop would bless a ring on the deck of the state barge. He would then hand it to the doge who would toss it into the waters, thereby symbolizing the union between Venice and the sea. One of the first products the Venetians took from the sea was salt, obtained through the evaporation of sea water. As salt was an imperative necessity the Venetians found a ready market for it on the mainland of Italy. Fish was another important item which the Venetians either took from the sea or purchased for trading purposes. In time the Venetians also turned to the manufacture of glass and other wares. Venetian glass became so famous and was in such demand that glassmakers were forbidden on pain of death to leave Venice lest they divulge the secrets of their trade to non-Venetians.

The greatness of Venice was not, however, founded on its manufactures, but on its carrying trade. This trade was not only the primary source of Venetian wealth, but the one consideration to which everything else was subordinated. At first the trade was mainly in such commodities as salt, salted fish, grain, lumber, and wine which were bought and sold in a limited area, but the Venetian merchants soon set their faces in the direction of the Levant where the opportunity to make large profits beckoned them. The return of the first fleet of galleys from the Levant with a cargo of spices marked the beginning of a new commercial era for Venice. Precious stones, drugs, dyes, textiles, and other products were also shipped in from the Levant in large quantities, making Venice the great distributing center for eastern and oriental goods.

At the height of its prosperity and power Venice had three main trade routes, two of them sea lanes and the third an overland route. The most important of the three was the eastern route which took the Venetian merchants to Egypt, Syria, Crete, Cyprus, Constantinople, and the Black Sea. From these places the products were taken to Venice whence they were distributed over the other two routes. The second sea route ran westward in the Mediterranean to the Straits of Gibraltar where it turned northward to the ports of Spain, Portugal, Flanders, and England. The English, for example, depended for their supply of spices on the arrival of the

Venetian ships. The third or overland route started at Venice and ran northward across the Alps to Germany and central Europe. On this route the Venetians traded with the German merchants of such cities as Regensburg, Ulm, Cologne, Augsburg and Nuremberg. As early as the first decades of the thirteenth century the German merchants had a trading station with living quarters and warehouses in Venice called the Fondaco dei Tedeschi. To this trading station they could take wares they had for sale and then recross the Alps with spices and other eastern products.

While their trade was increasing, the Venetians built a great commercial empire. The first step in this direction was the establishment of Venetian control over the Adriatic. This has also been called, "the transformation of the Adriatic into a Venetian lake." It was achieved by ridding the Adriatic of the pirates who had been preying on Venetian commerce. Thereafter the peoples living on the northern and eastern coasts of the Adriatic were included in the Venetian commercial empire. Meanwhile the Venetians were also busy establishing themselves in the eastern Mediterranean. Having previously gained a foothold in the Byzantine Empire, they enlisted the crusading spirit to strengthen their hold. When thousands of crusaders assembled in Venice in 1202 awaiting transportation to the Holy Land on what has become known as the Fourth Crusade, the Venetian officials prevailed upon them to turn their arms to the capture of Constantinople, the capital of the Christian Byzantine Empire. The fact that Pope Innocent III who had called the crusade denounced the venture as a perversion of the crusading spirit failed to deter both the Venetians and the crusaders. They proceeded to lay siege to the city and when it finally capitulated (1204) they sacked it, burning a section of it and destroying priceless works of art. In place of the former government the crusaders set up the so-called Latin Empire of Constantinople with Venice and its naval forces as the real power behind the throne. The Venetians then established trading stations in various places strategically located for trade and for more than half a century reaped a rich commercial harvest. But in 1261 while the Venetian fleet was occupied elsewhere the ruler of a rival Greek state managed with the help of the Genoese to topple the Latin Kingdom of Constantinople.

The loss of the capital of the Byzantine Empire and of the control it exercised over large areas dealt Venetian commerce a severe blow, but the Venetians still had the lucrative trade with Syria and Egypt. Furthermore, they had their great naval force and the determination to regain their foothold in the Byzantine Empire. A series of naval engagements with the Genoese covering a long period finally resulted in a Venetian victory. For a time it appeared as if the Genoese might be successful in driving the Venetians out of the eastern Mediterranean altogether, but the superior wealth and power of the Venetians finally prevailed. The decisive blow came in 1380 when the Venetians forced the surrender of the flower of the

Genoese fleet at Chioggia near Venice, a blow from which the Genoese never recovered. Having meanwhile also crushed the naval power of Pisa, the Venetians could now turn their attention to the conquest of certain provinces on the Italian mainland which had long been a principal source of food for them as well as an important outlet for their products. The Venetians feared that if an unfriendly power were to gain control of these territories their food supply might be cut off. Early in the fifteenth century, therefore, they extended their control over Vicenza and Verona, and annexed Padua.

Venice was now at the zenith of its power. Although it had a population of only about 200,000 it was the richest city in Europe with an income larger than that of kingdoms. It also had a larger fleet of warships than any other Christian power. Thus the claim of the Venetians that Venice was "the Queen of the Adriatic" was no idle boast. Its vast commercial empire stretched from the Black Sea to Bruges, Antwerp and London. Its commercial fleet of more than 3000 ships, manned by 35,000 seamen, traded in every important port of Western Europe and the Near East. Moreover, Venetian manufactures had a reputation for outstanding excellence. The exquisite Venetian laces were regarded so highly that Richard III of England proudly wore them at his coronation in 1483. Venetian silks and satins, brocades and velvets were the finest that could be made. Venice itself was one of the most magnificent cities of the world, artistically designed and constructed. The palatial residences of some of the merchant princes, adorned with paintings, tapestries, and fine furniture collected from both the East and the West, made the royal palaces of Europe appear somewhat shoddy.

It has been said that if there ever was "la nation bourgeoise" it was Venice. Venetian bourgeois society lived a life of unbridled luxury and inordinate display. Extravagance in food and dress was carried to such extremes that the merchant oligarchy which ruled Venice found it necessary to issue sumptuary edicts in their efforts to curb it. The edicts were, however, largely ignored. There are accounts of elaborate banquets at which Venetians gorged themselves for hours on "truffles, oysters, sausages, ham, pickled vegetables, cheese from Piacenza, lampreys from Binasco, tripe from Treviso, sturgeon from Ferrara, eel paste from Genoa, geese from the Romagna, etc." The love of gold was expressed at such banquets by gilding the shells of oysters, the candles on the tables, and even the crust of the bread that was served. At some banquets the soups and sauces were powdered with gold dust. If there was a spirit of abstinence and asceticism it was not evident. Even religious festivals were turned into occasions for pomp and display as gorgeous and colorful as any in history. The general trend was to derive the maximum pleasure from life. For the Venetians life was not something to reason about or something to be sacrificed to the hereafter; it was something to be enjoyed. In this enjoyment no sharp line was drawn between good and evil. The standard of morality was such as to move one historian to state that Venice was the meeting place of all the sins of the world. It has been calculated that in a population of about 200,000 there were as many as 14,000 professional prostitutes. In short, Venetian life was oriented earthward rather than heavenward.

But while Venice was at the zenith of its power and magnificence, a series of events was compromising its future. One of these was the capture of Constantinople by the Turks in 1453. So long as a weak government ruled the Byzantine Empire the Venetians had been able to retain a firm hold on the trade in the eastern Mediterranean, but the Turks were powerful enough to disposses the Venetians from their holdings in the Byzantine Empire. More than this, the Turks also hampered in every possible way the Venetian trade with other countries in the eastern Mediterranean. An even greater threat to Venetian prosperity was the explorations of other states of Europe. Eager to obtain a share of the lucrative trade in spices and other oriental goods, the Portuguese and Spanish governments sent out ships in the second half of the fifteenth century to search for an all-water route to Asia. The event which struck at the very root of Venetian prosperity was the discovery in 1498 by Vasco da Gama, a Portuguese mariner, of such an all-water route to India and the Spice Islands, a development which will be discussed later. (*See Chapter 14.*)

Florence

Many of the Italian cities or city-states made their own specific contributions to the development of Renaissance culture. Venice produced a number of great painters, Pisa made some important contributions to the progress of sculpture, and Rome was for a time an important center of cultural activity. But by far the greatest contribution was made by Florence. In the drama of the Renaissance, Florence played a leading role which has often been compared with that of Athens in classical thought. Had there been no Athens, the central influence in Greek thought and art would have been lacking. Without Florence there would have been no central motive force in the Renaissance. Florence was in a singular degree the source of intellectual and artistic vigor. No city of the Christian era has given to culture and to the world such a galaxy of men of high achievement. Included in the list are great names in literature, painting, sculpture, architecture, music, science, and learning in general. In literature Florence had Dante, Petrarch, and Boccaccio; in painting Giotto, Masaccio, Botticelli, Leonardo da Vinci, and Michelangelo; in architecture and sculpture, Brunelleschi, Ghiberti, Donatello, and Michelangelo; and in music, Landini. Not to be overlooked is Benvenuto Cellini, the great master of the goldsmith's art as well as a sculptor of note. In the field of political science and historical writing Florence produced Machiavelli and Lorenzo Valla. The city on the Arno was also the nursery of humanistic learning with such outstanding humanists and literary figures as Petrarch, Boccaccio, Pico della Mirandola, Marsilio Ficino, Leon Battista Alberti, Poggio Bracciolini, and Baldassare Castiglione. The outstanding figure in the realm of science was the Florentine Leonardo da Vinci. Then there was Toscanelli (1397-1482), astronomer and cartographer, who is said to have made the map used by Columbus on the voyage which resulted in the discovery of the New World. Another Florentine, Amerigo Vespucci, gave his name to this New World by his forceful descriptions of it. In addition to those named above, Florence also produced many men of lesser talents. In brief, during the Renaissance period Florence gave to the world more men of outstanding accomplishments than some nations have contributed during their entire existence.

The history of Florence during the period preceding the era of the Renaissance is the story of the achievement of independence and of its struggle against the barons whose castles and strongholds looked down on Florence from the hills surrounding the city. As a small town populated by artisans and traders Florence had been under the rule of the house of Tuscany. Countess Matilda of Tuscany (1076-1115) delegated much of her authority to the town council, leaving the town practically free to govern itself. After her death Florence openly and successfully asserted its independence. The new republic then turned its efforts to dislodging the hostile barons from their strongholds. These barons whose fortunes were declining regarded with envy the growing prosperity of the townspeople, particularly of the middle class. They relieved their financial distress and vented their hostility by making raids into Florentine territory and by attacking merchant caravans which were leaving or entering Florence. Strong Florentine forces laid siege to the strongholds of the robber barons and razed each one as it surrendered. The town of Fiesole which had been the special refuge of robber barons and other enemies of the Florentines was also besieged, and when it capitulated, its fortifications too were demolished. Thus the back of the baronial resistance was broken.

But peace did not descend on Florence. Before long internal dissension raised its ugly head. After demolishing the baronial castles and strongholds the Florentine government permitted the owners to retain posession of the estates, but compelled them to live in Florence at least part of the year. This unfortunate decision introduced dissension into the political life of the city. These nobles formed the nucleus of an opposition party which attracted some influential Florentine families and all malcontents who had any grievances against the government. Party feeling ran so high that in 1177 street fighting and the burning of houses took place. It was only the first of a long series of factional conflicts, the record of which fills so many pages in the history of Florence. The division of the population into opposing parties did not remain the same. New factions arose and declined. Although the political sands were constantly shifting, the factional feuds continued even after class distinctions had been pushed into the background. There were short periods when conflict was in abeyance, but the rancor of the opposing parties continued to smolder beneath the surface. Time and again the embers were fanned into flames of conflict by trifling incidents. Under such conditions there were frequent changes of government. No government could remain in power long enough to establish itself firmly. Dante, who was forced into exile when the faction he supported was supplanted as the controlling power by a rival faction, compared his native city in his *Divine Comedy* with a woman constantly in pain who turns and tosses in her bed, but cannot find peace and rest:

> Thou weavest such a thin web
> Of policy, that unto mid-November
> Lasts not that which was in October spun.
> How often within time of memory
> Laws, institutions, coinage and offices,
> Hast thou changed, and renewed thy citizens?
> And if thou thinkest well and seest the truth,
> Thyself to a sick woman wilt thou liken,
> Who cannot find repose upon her down
> But by tossing seeks to ease her pain.
> (*Purgatory, Canto VI, 142-151, translated by Henry Wadsworth Longfellow*)

The internal dissension did not, however, prevent the Florentines from achieving success in their business endeavors. Like the members of the Venetian middle class, those of Florence were animated by a spirit of enterprise which made them prosperous. But the prosperity of Florence did not come from the same sources as that of Venice. Florence was not a coastal town; it was situated inland on the plains of the Arno River. The Florentines did not have an outlet to the Adriatic until they conquered Pisa in 1406. Hence while Venice and other coastal towns were making the most of the opportunities to expand their seaborne trade, Florence turned to other fields of economic endeavor.

One of the pursuits for which the Florentines displayed special talent, as stated earlier, was banking. An important factor in the success of Florentine banking was the standard value of the Florentine coinage. In 1252 the government of Florence minted a gold coin called the florin which was dependable as to weight and purity. This golden florin, whose purity was carefully guarded, set the standard of value not only in Florence and other Italian cities, but also in the Netherlands, France, Germany, England, and Spain. Giovanni Villani stated in his *Chronicle of the History of Florence* (1348) that there were eighty banks in Florence during the early decades of the fourteenth century. After the bankruptcies of the two middle decades, which included the collapse of the Bardi and Peruzzi firms, the number was considerably smaller, but Florence still remained the banking center of Western Europe.

The other major source of Florentine prosperity was manufacturing. Among the manufactures of Florence the woolen-cloth industry was the leader. This industry included the refinishing of woolen cloth made in northern Europe as well as the manufacture of woolen cloth. The latter was carried on successfully despite the fact that the wool produced in the vicinity of Florence was of an inferior grade. The wool which the Florentine merchant-industrialists liked best was imported from far-away England. There were in Florence two great gilds of the merchant-industrialists dealing in woolen cloth, the *Arte di Calimala* (so named after the street on which many of the merchants had their headquarters) and the *Arte della Lana* (wool gild). The members of the first gild specialized in refinishing cloth made in Flanders, Brabant, and Holland. They imported cloth that was coarse, poorly finished, and badly dyed in unattractive colors which soon faded. This cloth was then turned over to expect craftsmen who sheared it, removed the knots, and dyed it in more permanent and attractive colors. After this transformation into high-quality merchandise, the cloth was sold in Italy, in the markets of the Near East, and in some instances in the very countries from which the coarse cloth had originally been purchased.

The *Arte della Lana* was composed of merchant-industrialists who imported raw wool from England and Spain to supplement the inferior wool of Italy. The raw wool was then let out to textile workmen who converted it into yarn and wove it into cloth which was dyed and finished with great skill. Florentine skill in dyeing seems to have been unrivalled in Europe. Some of the dyes were produced locally and others were imported from long distances. The Rucellai, one of the prominent families of Florence, became very wealthy after one of its members discovered in the orient a method of producing a purple red or scarlet dye. This dye, the secret of which was carefully guarded, soon became the prescribed shade for all robes of state in Florence and for all ceremonial tapestries and hangings. Florentine cloth-makers and dyers also gained the exclusive right to dye and finish the cloth used for the robes of Roman Catholic cardinals and for other ecclesiastical vestments.

The Florentine woolen-cloth industry reached its peak during the early decades of the fourteenth century. Giovanni Villani reported that in 1339 there were in Florence more than two hundred weaving and dyeing establishments employing 30,000 wage-earners. But by this time the industry was already declining. The output of woolen cloth had decreased from 100,000 pieces in 1310 to 70,000 in 1339. The decline continued with the result that only 30,000 pieces of cloth were produced in 1373 and by 1382 the quantity had diminished to 19,000. Two events which have been listed as contributing to the decline are the disruption of Florentine economic life by the bankruptcy of the banking houses of the Bardi and Peruzzi, and the long war with Pisa which ended in 1364. During the two decades before 1364 the Pisans closed some of the routes over which the Florentines imported raw materials and exported finished products. This made it necessary for the Florentines to use other avenues which, because they were circuitous, added considerably to the cost of production. But local causes alone do not explain the decline. Other causes were probably more basic. Among them were the loss of the Persian markets in which large quantities of Florentine cloth had previously been sold, the shrinking of the French market because the Hundred Years War was impoverishing many of the nobles who had previously purchased high-grade Florentine cloths, the restrictions imposed by the English on the sale of raw wool, and the growing competition of English cloth.

A further crisis was created in 1378 by the revolt of the textile workers who were called *ciompi* (wooden shoes), an allusion to the wooden shoes most of them wore. Hence the revolt is known in Italian history as "Tumulto dei Ciompi." For decades the ciompi had been seething with discontent because they believed they were being exploited by ruthless merchant-industrialists. As depression gripped the cloth industry more firmly, their situation deteriorated. Shrinking profits impelled greedy industrialists to endeavor to wring the last possible measure of work from their workmen. In 1361 and the succeeding years the decline of the industry resulted in the closing of many working establishments for shorter or longer periods, causing widespread hardship as well as unemployment. The textile workers had no way of protecting their interests since they were not permitted to organize gilds. They could not even hold meetings without the express permission of the merchant gilds. At various times there had been brief outbreaks of violence, but even such incidents did not move the industrialists to make concessions. Finally in 1378 the discontent erupted in bloody revolt.

The Revolt of the Ciompi differed from previous revolts by members of the working class. Whereas the revolts in Flanders, England, and France were still medieval, with the rural population participating and religious issues involved, the uprising of the ciompi was a proletarian movement. It was the first time in history that proletarians united in an association of a definitely syndicalist character. They demanded not only higher wages and better working conditions, but also an improvement of their social and political status. As protection against hardship and unemployment they demanded that their merchant-industrialist employers permit them to produce a minimum of 2,000 pieces of woolen cloth each month or a total of 24,000 pieces per year. Other demands included the right to organize gilds and also representation in the government. The latter was particularly important to them since it represented the means for improving their lot. It was also necessary for the achievement of their ultimate aim which was the establishment of a dictatorship of the proletariat. The revolt quickly degenerated into a reign of terror during which mobs pillaged and burned the houses of officials of the gilds and of others they regarded as oppressors. The Florentine oligarchy, unable to quell the revolt, had to accede to the demands of the ciompi. The government was reorganized in such a way that the wage-earners became the controlling factor in it. Several years later, however, dissension broke out in the ranks of the proletarians, giving the members of the former oligarchy the opportunity to reestablish themselves in power. The revolt of the ciompi ended in bloody repression and the status of the working class was much as it had been before the revolt.

The hope of the industrialists that the woolen-cloth industry would quickly regain its former prosperity was blasted when many of the ciompi fled from Florence to escape punishment for participating in the revolt. In this way Florence lost many of its best craftsmen. They went to such Italian cities as Siena, Pisa, and Bologna where they were heartily welcomed. Their presence enabled these cities to expand their textile industries and to give the Florentines greater competition. But the woolen-cloth industry of Florence did gradually regain a measure of its former prosperity. At the invitation of the government several groups of textile workers from Flanders, Brabant, and Holland migrated to Florence. Their arrival gave the industry a fillip. By 1427 the number of establishments refinishing or weaving woolen cloth increased to 180, enabling one merchant-industrialist to boast, "Florence produces more fine cloth than any other place in the world." In 1458 a chronicler wrote, "Our city grew great and mighty through its industry and was therefore able to defend itself against any and all attempts to subjugate it." In 1480 the number of textile workshops in Florence reached 270.

The wealth of the middle-class merchants, industrialists, and bankers of Florence gave rise to luxurious living and led to excesses in entertainment and dress. Early in the fourteenth century these excesses reached a point at which the Florentine government found it necessary to issue ordinances in an effort to curb them. Villani wrote regarding extravagance in feminine dress:

> The women of Florence were greatly at fault in the matter of excessive ornamentation. On their heads they wore tiaras of gold and silver studded with pearls and other precious stones or they wore nets covered with wreaths of pearls. Likewise they had dresses cut of several kinds of cloth, with silk ruffs of various kinds and also fringes of pearls and little buttons of gold and silver, often four or five rows together. They also wore numerous strings of pearls and other precious stones at the breast.

Ordinances issued by the government finally forbade the wearing of tiaras of any sort, including those made of paper. Dresses made with painted or embroidered figures, striped materials, and bias patterns were also prohibited. Women were also forbidden to wear more than two rings on a finger. But all the efforts of the civil authorities proved unavailing. The women simply refused to obey them. The economic depression of the fourteenth century abated the excesses to some extent, but when prosperity returned the former extravagance in dress and ornamentation reappeared. This time the civil authorities decided to leave the women to their own devices.

The Age of the Medici

One Florentine family stands out above all others as patrons of learning and the arts. It is the Medici family which became wealthy through commerce and banking. The history of the Medici Bank as a power in Florence dates from 1397, the year in which Giovanni de Medici moved his bank from Rome to Florence. Although conditions were not particularly favorable for international banking, the Medici achieved success by adopting better principles of organization and by employing superior banking techniques. This enabled them to expand their business until the Medici Bank became the largest in Western Europe. While it never did grow as large as the Bardi and Peruzzi banks had been, its managers did succeed in avoiding the pitfalls which forced the Bardi and Peruzzi into bankruptcy. The central management of the Medici Bank carefully supervised the branch managers to keep them from making excessive loans. The Medici bankers were, in fact, so successful that their bank became the controlling factor in the finances of England, France, and Naples. The Medici Bank also had branches in North Germany and Spain, and its agents were active in Poland, Hungary, and as far east as Constantinople. In various parts of the Western world the memory of the Medici is perpetuated by the three golden balls displayed by pawnbrokers which are an adaptation of the six red balls on a gold field as they appeared in the Medici coat of arms.

In the history of Florence the influence and prestige of the Medici was so great that the period of their activity is called "the age of the Medici." To the Medici Florence is indebted in no small degree for its preeminent position in the development of Renaissance learning and art. The Medici family was in many ways the quintessence of the Florentine bourgeoisie. Its leading members were ostentatious, greedy, and at times unscrupulous. They were adventurous, but their spirit of adventure was tempered with caution. Although grossly materialistic, they did not lack devoutness. Coarse-grained, they nevertheless had excellent taste for the exquisite and a passion for Renaissance learning and art. The architect of the fortunes of the Medici was Giovanni (*c.*1360-1429), a man of moderation and good sense. Possessing an extraordinary aptitude for banking and business in general, he secured the financial supremacy of his family in Italian and European markets. In his attitude toward culture he was somewhat reactionary. When a friend chided him for his lack of interest in Renaissance learning, he said, "I am too old an oak to have my branches bent in new directions." But he did insist that his sons be educated in the "new learning." Although he took a great interest in public affairs and was even elected a magistrate, Giovanni played no leading part in politics. On his death bed he gave the following advice to his sons:

> I leave you with a larger business than any other merchant in the Tuscan land, and in the enjoyment of the esteem of every good citizen, and of the great mass of the populace who have ever turned to our family as to their guiding star. If you are faithful to the tradition of your ancestors, the people will be generous in giving you honors. To achieve this be charitable to the poor, kindly and gracious to the miserable, lending yourselves with all your might to assist them in their adversity. Never strike against the will of the people unless they advocate a baneful project. Speak not as though giving advice, but rather discuss matters with gentle and kindly reasoning. . . . Have care to keep the people at peace, and to increase the commerce of the city.

Giovanni's son Cosimo (1389-1464) not only advanced the banking fortunes of his family but also managed by political craft to become the ruler of Florence. Giovanni had made many friends for the Medici by his generosity with the result that Cosimo enjoyed considerable popularity from the start. Cosimo himself was not slow to use the wealth he inherited to strengthen the party which supported him. To the Albizzi faction which ruled Florence at the time, Cosimo's popularity, his following, and his wealth were such a definite threat that they decided to destroy him. He was thrown into prison on a trumped-up charge and narrowly escaped execution, but in the end more moderate counsels prevailed. The ruling faction decided to send Cosimo into exile, believing that his support would collapse and his business would decline. No sooner was Cosimo banished from Florence than the members of the Albizzi faction started quarreling among themselves. This enabled a group friendly to the Medici to get the upper hand and Cosimo was recalled in triumph less than a year after he had been exiled. He achieved his leadership because the rich merchant families knew that their prosperity depended on their ability to control the state and to direct its policies in accordance with their interests. They realized that a strong hand was needed at the helm to control the warring factions. Cosimo's ability in addition to his popularity and wealth marked him as the man of the hour.

With the return of Cosimo from exile in 1434 the great age of the Medici which reached its zenith under Lorenzo the Magnificent (1449-1492) may be said to have begun. For the next thirty years until his death in 1464, Cosimo exercised the supreme direction of affairs in Florence. Knowing that the republican tradition did not permit him to show himself openly as the master of the Florentine state, he retained all the republican trappings. He himself held no office; nor did he have an official title. In other words, his position was not supported by law. Nevertheless, he strengthened his hold until everything of importance had to receive his sanction. He managed things in such a way as to convince the Florentines that he was simply carrying out their wishes. Actually he was a political boss who maintained his hold on the Florentine citizens through a thousand political ties. His basic strategy was to put his friends into as many key posts as possible, to restrict the membership of the chief magistracies of Florence to his supporters. Besides being generous in giving presents and making loans, he won supporters by paying the back taxes of many Florentines who under the constitution could not participate in the government because their taxes were in arrears. To hold his wider circle of friends together he did not hesitate to influence legal decisions. Another of his stratagems was to maintain in Florence a sort of perpetual carnival atmosphere in which the people lost all thought of liberty. "He was aware," Machiavelli wrote in his *History of Florence*, "that a constant exhibition of pomp brings more envy upon its possessor than greater realities born without ostentation." Banishment which often meant financial ruin was imposed on those who persisted as adversaries. Cosimo did not even hesitate to remove a troublesome adversary by violent means. A maxim attributed to him reads: "You cannot rule a state with paternosters."

Cosimo's greatest claim to fame is the fact that he used his wealth for the advancement of Renaissance learning and art. When he became ruler of Florence the Renaissance was well on its way. More than thirty years earlier Manuel Chrysoloras had accepted the chair of Greek at the University of Florence and in the succeeding years had contributed much to the revival of interest in Greek civilization. Although Cosimo did not learn Greek, he did acquire a good knowledge of Latin. The bookseller Vespasiano da Bisticci (1421-1498) wrote in his *Lives of Illustrious Men in the Fifteenth Century* that Cosimo "was well versed in Latin letters, both sacred and secular . . . he had a knowledge of Latin which would scarcely have been looked for in one occupying the station of a leading citizen engrossed with affairs." Cosimo participated in the great search for manuscripts of classical authors which was then at its height by sending agents to various parts of Europe and the Near East to look for rare and important manuscripts. Even the commercial correspondents of the Medici were instructed to purchase important manuscripts without regard for price. The manuscripts Cosimo collected became the nucleus of the celebrated Medicean Library which was steadily augmented by succeeding members of the Medici family. This library, generally regarded as the first public library in Europe, now contains about 10,000 manuscripts of the classics, many of them of great value.

Cosimo's favorite thinker was the philosopher Plato. Since he could not read Plato in the original he encouraged the translation of Plato's works into Latin. Cosimo also organized the so-called Platonic Academy for the study of Plato's works. It was not a formal institution with a charter and statutes, but a center for discussion and exchange of ideas among those interested in the Greek classics. Cosimo provided for special studies for Marsilio Ficino, a young man of his acquaintance, and then put him at the head of the academy. Nothing pleased Cosimo more than to be able to spend some time discussing the works of classical authors with the members of his academy. In one of his letters to Marsilio Ficino he wrote: "Come and join me as soon as you possibly can, and be sure to bring with you Plato's treatise, 'Of the Sovereign Good.' If you had followed my advice, you would have translated it into Latin long before this. There is no pursuit to which I would devote myself more zealously than the pursuit of truth. Come then and bring with you the lyre of Orpheus."

Cosimo also did much to encourage Renaissance architecture, sculpture, and painting. Among the magnificent edifices he erected are the monastery of San Marco and the Church of San Lorenzo. His private dwellings, one of them in Florence, for size and grandeur equalled royal palaces. In the construction and decoration of these buildings Cosimo employed the talents of distinguished architects, sculptors, and painters, among them the architect Brunelleschi, the sculptor Donatello, and the painter Fra Angelico. At all times he was most liberal in providing the means of comfortable living for both artists and men of learning. Thus he gave Donatello a pension large enough to support him and his four assistants. Others who enjoyed his patronage were Masaccio and Fra Filippo Lippi. He was not only generous in his relationships with the artists but also patient. "One must treat these people of extraordinary genius," he said, "as if they are celestial spirits, and not like beasts of burden." In his happier moments with his learned men and artists Cosimo exhibited a lively sense of humor. Machiavelli said of him that "he was generous to his friends, kind to the poor, comprehensive in discourse, cautious in advice, grave and witty in his speech." Some of Cosimo's witty sayings were quoted far and wide. But during the last months of his life he became serious and silent. When his wife remarked about it, Cosimo replied, "When you are going to the villa you are worried for a fortnight how to arrange for the move; now I must quit this life for the next! Have I not something to think over?" He died in 1464 and his remains were entombed in the church of San Lorenzo.

Lorenzo the Magnificent

Cosimo was succeeded by his son Piero who was so badly crippled by the gout that he could not walk or ride a horse. Neither did he have sufficient ability and strength of character to offset his physical weakness. Nevertheless he was recognized as the unofficial head of the Florentine government. Five years later he died, leaving as his principal legacy to Florence his son Lorenzo who earned for himself the title "the Magnificent." In his physical appearance Lorenzo was anything but prepossessing. His features were homely, his sight weak, and his harsh and somewhat hoarse voice was likened by a contemporary wit with the croaking of a frog suffering from a bad cold. His general appearance, according to contemporaries, was that of a manual laborer or tiller of the soil rather than that of a ruler. But his easy democratic ways and his vivacity charmed those about him. Living at a time when manhood meant versatility, Lorenzo was active in many fields. As a young man he was a skilled horseman and was generally active in sports. He also delighted in music. Marsilio Ficino relates that Lorenzo would sing to the accompaniment of the lute as if he were inspired. He also found time to add manuscripts to the library his grandfather Cosimo had started, to discuss philosophy and art, and to write verse. In his verses he frequently described human passion. An example of this is the poem he wrote at the death of Simonetta, one of his many loves:

> Bright shining star! Thy radiance in the sky
> Dost rob the neighboring stars of all their light.
> Why art thou with unwonted splendor bright?
> Why with great Phoebus dost thou desire to vie?
> Perchance those eyes which Death so cruelly—
> Too daring Death—has ravished from our sight,
> Have given to thee the glory of that light
> Which can the chariot of the sun defy.
> Oh newly created star, if star thou art,
> That heaven with new-born splendors dost adorn,
> I call on thee! Oh goddess, quickly hear!
> Of thine own glory grant me now a part
> To fire these eyes with endless weeping worn,
> With something of thy light that they can bear.

Lorenzo had not reached his twenty-first birthday when his father, Piero, passed away. By this time young Lorenzo already had considerable experience in statecraft. He had previously assumed some of the functions his crippled father had been unable to carry out. Thus, for example, he was sent on diplomatic missions which would have tried the sagacity of an experienced statesman. On at least one such occasion the father complained that the son was carrying out his own ideas rather than the parental instructions. As the father put it, the gosling was leading the goose to drink. Like his father and grandfather he never officially held a high office in Florence. He controlled the Florentines by commanding them, cajoling them, and amusing them. To keep them happy he staged many fêtes, carnivals, and spectacles. He himself often wrote songs and dialogue for such occasions and was not above participating in the festivities.

Historians have passed varying judgments on Lorenzo as a statesman. While some have hailed him as shrewd and farseeing, others have denounced him as a tyrant and destroyer of the liberties of the Florentines. Guicciardini (1492-1540), for example, condemned Lorenzo for sending many prosperous citizens into exile and ruin and for silencing others by oppression. He added, however, that it was better than resorting to the dagger "as is the common wont of others." The nineteenth-century historian Villari described Lorenzo as "full of prudence and acumen, dexterous in his negotiations with other powers and still more dexterous in ridding himself of his enemies, and equally capable of daring and cruelty whenever emergencies called for bold strokes." Without condoning the methods he employed, it can be said that he was successful in controlling the warring factions and in giving the strife-torn city a period of peace.

All historians agree, however, that Lorenzo did much to promote Renaissance learning and culture. It was during his rule that the Renaissance attained its greatest splendor in Florence. In his love of mundane life, of the new art, of classical learning, and of secular poetry, he was representative of the Renaissance spirit. Besides collecting manuscripts and maintaining the Platonic Academy, he was a generous patron of artists, humanists, and men of learning generally. He further established a school in the gardens of San Marco for the purpose of raising the standards of the arts. According to Vasari, the gardens were "full of ancient and modern sculptures, so that the loggia, the paths and the rooms were adorned with good and ancient figures of marble, with paintings and other masterpieces of the greatest artists of Italy and elsewhere." One of the school's most illustrious students was Michelangelo, who later stated that this was the happiest and most profitable period of his life. Lorenzo the Magnificent was so deeply interested in art that he took great delight in watching sculptors and painters at work. One of the studios he frequently visited was that of Verrocchio who was a sculptor, goldsmith, and musician as well as a painter. Another favorite of Lorenzo was the painter Sandro Botticelli who painted a number of Medici portraits, but there is no record that he painted one of Lorenzo.

Lorenzo died in 1492 at the age of forty-three. At the time of his death the financial position of the Medici was deteriorating. Lorenzo was too busy with other things to give the banking business the attention his grandfather had given it. Furthermore, bankers in other countries were offering greater competition. Consequently the Medici branches in England and the Netherlands were closed and a number of branch banks in other countries were sold. As for the political fortunes of the Medici, two years after Lorenzo's death the Florentines revolted against his son and successor Pietro, forcing him into exile. The death of Lorenzo also marked the end of the heyday of the Renaissance in Florence, for the city on the Arno, too, was soon to enter into a period of decline. The shifting of the center of trade from the Mediterranean to the Atlantic as a result of the discovery of the all-water route to India and the Spice Islands gradually dried up the springs of Florentine prosperity.

Rome and the Renaissance

As early as the reign of Charlemagne (768-814) the rule over the duchy of Rome was conferred on the papacy, but as the Carolingian empire disintegrated the popes were at times unable to enforce their political authority.

The actual political power was in the hands of a number of feudal families, including the Frangipani, the Colonna, and the Orsini. In 1143 the citizens of Rome revolted against the oppressive rule of the great feudal families and under the leadership of Arnold of Brescia (*c.*1100-1156), an eloquent theologian whose views were anti-papal, organized a commune often called the Roman Republic. For the time being the Vatican was unable to impose its rule on Rome, but during the pontificate of Innocent III (1198-1216) the political authority of the papacy was reestablished over the Eternal City and the surrounding territory. Later while the popes were residing at Avignon (1305-1376) the citizens of Rome again set up their own government; however, when Rome again became the seat of the papacy and the capital of Christendom, papal rule was reimposed. The succeeding period saw the popes extend the territory under their rule. Julius II added much territory to the Papal States. The popes continued to rule Rome and the Papal States until Italy was unified under a national government in the second half of the nineteenth century.

Rome was not a typical Renaissance city. It was a Renaissance center only in a secondary sense. Since Rome was the religious capital of Christendom the medieval atmosphere persisted longer there than in the other Italian cities. Theology continued to be the primary interest of intellectual life. Although there was much in Rome, including manuscripts, Roman monuments, and ruins of great Roman structures, to stimulate an interest in the secular culture of antiquity, Rome produced very few native sons who were leaders in the development of the new culture. There was in Rome no such surge of popular enthusiasm over the latest works of art as in Florence where, for example, masses rushed to see the most recent masterpiece of the sculptor Donatello. Furthermore, such a typical Renaissance movement as humanism never took a deep root in Rome. In general, Rome did not have a large number of wealthy merchants, industrialists, and bankers who used their wealth and influence to promote the development of art and learning. On the other hand, the Eternal City did attract artists and men of learning from other cities. So many came that for a brief period early in the sixteenth century Rome became the center of artistic and humanistic endeavor.

Most of the credit for the part Rome did play in the Renaissance must be given to certain popes. It was they who invited artists, architects, musicians, and humanists to Rome. This is why there are so many great works of painting, sculpture, and architecture in Rome, more specifically in the Vatican. Without the interest and munificent patronage of certain popes there would, for example, be no great paintings in the Vatican by Raphael and Michelangelo, no great dome of St. Peter's by Michelangelo, and no great statue of Moses by Michelangelo. Although the interest of the popes centered mainly in art, there were a few who encouraged the humanists in their search for the works of classical authors. Several even collected libraries of classical manuscripts. The patronage of the popes was so important that the artistic and intellectual interests in Rome varied according to the personal tastes of the reigning pope.

Among the popes who helped make Rome a center of Renaissance art and learning, Nicholas V (1447-1455) stands out prominently. While he was a young man at the University of Bologna and during a stay of some years in Florence he developed a deep love for all learning and a particular interest in the classics. It was probably on the strength of his reputation as a man of learning that he (Tommaso Parentucelli) became Pope Nicholas V. As pope he used his influence in many ways to promote the advancement of the new secular learning. For example, he invited many leading humanists from neighboring cities to come to Rome. Among those who came was the Florentine humanist and man of broad learning, Leon Battista Alberti. Under the patronage of Nicholas, Alberti wrote a number of philosophical and historical treatises. Nicholas V also encouraged the humanist Poggio Bracciolini to continue his search for manuscripts, giving him letters of recommendation as well as financial assistance. Nicholas further took into his service Lorenzo Valla, the outstanding philologist among the Renaissance humanists. In addition, Nicholas was a liberal patron to many other scholars, some of whom he employed to translate Greek manuscripts into Latin. The nineteenth-century German historian Gregorovius wrote of Nicholas, "This noble pope might have been well represented with a cornucopia in his hands, showering gold on scholars and artists." One of the pope's great interests was the collection of manuscripts. Already as a young man he searched far and wide for literary treasures, making some valuable finds in both France and Germany. His desire to possess manuscripts was so great that when he found one he would, if necessary, borrow the money to purchase it. As pope he spent money freely to enlarge his collection which at the time of his death included between three and five thousand manuscripts. This collection became the basis of the Vatican Library, which is now the home of many rare and invaluable manuscripts.

Two other popes who contributed to the development of Renaissance culture were Julius II (1503-1513) and Leo X (1513-1522). During the pontificates of these two popes Rome was the capital of the Italian Renaissance. Julius II who as cardinal had been the friend of artists and scholars was as pope interested in monumental works of architecture, sculpture, and painting which would make Rome the great center of aesthetic development. To this end he continued the work that had been interrupted by the untimely death of Nicholas V. Pope Julius rendered an inestimable service to art by summoning both Raphael and Michelangelo to Rome and giving them the opportunity to execute some of their greatest works. Michelangelo was called to Rome for the purpose of building the tomb of Julius II in old St. Peter's, but after Michelangelo spent eight years selecting the marble for it the pope changed his mind. The plans which the architect Bramante prepared for the imposing structure which was to replace old St. Peter's were so imposing that the pope was convinced to proceed with them. During the lifetime of Julius only the foundations of the new St. Peter's were laid. Succeeding popes carried out the plans with some modifications. After Pope Julius cancelled the original plans for his tomb, he assigned to Michelangelo the task of decorating the ceiling of the Sistine Chapel. Michelangelo proceeded to paint on fresco some of the greatest figures in the history of art. Like Nicholas V Pope Julius II was also an assiduous collector of manuscripts. Since the printing presses were by this time engaged in printing the contents of manuscripts, the pope also added books to his collection.

The most outstanding patron of art and literature was the second son of Lorenzo the Magnificent, Giovanni de Medici who in 1513 became Pope Leo X. The very name of Medici conjures up visions of the Florentine Renaissance and Giovanni was a true representative of the Renaissance spirit. He has frequently been quoted as saying after his elevation to the pontificate, "Let us enjoy the papacy since God has given it to us." Although it is by no means certain that he made the remark, there is no doubt regarding his interest in the secular culture of the Renaissance. He enjoyed music and the theater, derived great pleasure from art and poetry, and took a lively interest in classical learning. Kind and liberal by nature, he was the friend of everyone interested in the extension of knowledge and in the cultivation of the arts. During his short pontificate Renaissance culture reached its peak in Rome. Pope Leo gathered about himself humanists, artists, and musicians from all parts of Europe. Erasmus who visited Rome at that time was greatly impressed by the size of the group and by the freedom of discussion which prevailed. The pope also supported the interest in classical civilization by appointing Raphael custodian of Roman monuments and ruins of classical structures of whatever kind in Rome and its environs.

But the flowering of the Renaissance in Rome was of brief duration. In 1527, five years after the death of Leo X, the army of the Emperor Charles V of the Holy Roman Empire sacked the Eternal City, scattering the artists and scholars in all directions. By this time the Renaissance had lost much of its vitality in Italy. The interest of those who had been patrons of the new secular culture was being absorbed by other matters. For example, the economic decline which was setting in caused the members of the wealthy bourgeoisie to concentrate on salvaging what remained of their shrinking fortunes. Furthermore, the petty rulers who had previously done so much to encourage and to patronize artists, writers, and humanists were engulfed by the wars for which Italy was the battlefield in the sixteenth century. As for the popes, their attention was centered in the revolt against authority which the monk of Wittenberg had started in Germany and which was spreading to other countries. Only Venice of all the Italian states was still to make notable contributions in the field of painting to Renaissance culture.

6

The Rise of Italian Literature

Although Latin was in the Middle Ages the medium for the expression of man's deeper knowledge and his highest thoughts, the common folk in their daily affairs used dialects to express their thoughts, impulses, and longings. While the dialects of England, Germany, and a part of the Netherlands were Germanic in origin, those of France, Spain, and Italy were corruptions of Latin. In the eleventh, twelfth, and thirteenth centuries these dialects or vernacular languages became the vehicles of new literatures. Italian literature developed more slowly than the vernacular literatures of the countries north of the Alps. It can hardly be said to have existed until near the end of the thirteenth century. By this time German literature, for example, had passed the high point of its first important period which produced the *Niebelungenlied*, the *Minnelieder*, Wolfram von Eschenbach's *Parzival*, Gottfried von Strassburg's *Tristan*, and other important works. By this time the French had already stirred the imagination of Europe with their epics and songs, including the *chansons de geste* and the songs of the troubadours. Probably the most important reason for the backwardness of Italian literature was the fact that many Italians regarded Latin as their mother tongue. Whereas the use of Latin was in northern Europe largely limited to the Church, in Italy it was also the official language of the courts of law. The Italian dialects were so close to the parent language that it was comparatively easy for those who were literate to master Latin and to use it as the spoken as well as the written language. Another reason why the Italian dialects were not used for literary purposes was that there were so many of them, each one covering only a limited territory.

The earliest Italian poetry which has survived dates from the first half of the thirteenth century. The locale where the poetry was written was Sicily. During the years preceding the middle of the century Frederick II, emperor of the Holy Roman Empire, inaugurated a brief epoch of culture there. In addition to being Holy Roman emperor, he was also the king of Sicily. Frederick himself wrote some Italian poetry, but the outstanding poet in the group which congregated at Frederick's court was Pietro delle Vigne (*c.* 1190-1249). There was, however, little that was new or original in the poetry of this group. Most of it was written in imitation of the troubadours. Like the troubadours, the Sicilian poets wrote only of love and the love was chivalrous in the original sense of the word. In the verses the poet pours out protestations of love for the lady of the castle, extolling her beauty and virtue. The noble lady, for her part, treated her poet-lover with indifference and disdain. The expressions of love were repeated by the poets again and again in virtually the same words to the point of monotony. It was a love, as Pietro delle Vigne put it, that could be understood only by those who loved:

> Since love cannot be seen by human eye,
> And sense cannot discern its marked extremes,
> How can he its sweet folly well describe,
> Who of its bare existence never dreams.

When the Sicilian school disappeared after the death of Frederick II in 1250, the writing of love poetry was continued by a group of poets in Tuscany, located in Central Italy. The Tuscan poets also imitated the troubadours, but in their poems the noble lady of the castle gradually became an abstraction, foreshadowing such love poetry as that which Dante was to write about Beatrice.

Toward the end of the thirteenth century, however, a great epoch opened for Italian literature. During this period three literary figures—Dante, Petrarch, and Boccaccio—raised the Tuscan dialect to the status of the common literary language of Italy and gave to the Italian people a literature unmatched by any other European country.

Dante Alighieri

Dante Alighieri (1265-1321) was a literary figure of such magnitude that his poetry gave Italy immediate literary preeminence. In his works Italian poetry soared at once to a height it can hardly hope to surpass. Taking the Tuscan dialect as his medium of expression he enriched it until it was able to express the most sublime poetic concepts. Thus Dante more than any other person is the creator of Italy's literary language. His choice of the Tuscan dialect did much to dispel the idea that Latin is the only proper language for the expression of poetic and philosophic ideas. Dante poured forth his scorn on those who did not esteem the Tuscan vernacular highly, stating that "many disparage their own language and exalt that of others. If it is vile in anything it is vile only so far as it sounds in the prostituted mouths of these adulterers."

Dante was born in Florence in 1265 as a member of an ancient family, but not one of the highest rank. There are many portraits, miniatures, and busts which are supposed to present likenesses of him, but it is doubtful if any of them is wholly trustworthy. Boccaccio described him in these words, "Our poet was of medium height; he had a long face, an aquiline nose, large jaws, and his lower lip was more prominent than the upper; he was slightly stoop-shouldered, and his eyes were large rather than small; his hair and beard were curly and black, and he seemed always melancholy and thoughtful." We know little of Dante's boyhood except that he was a good student.

"He gave himself and all his time," Boccaccio wrote, "not to youthful lust and indolence, . . . but to continued study in his native city of the liberal arts, so that he became exceedingly expert therein." With the passing of the years he also dedicated himself to the acquisition of a complete knowledge of poetic creations. Leonardo Bruni stated that "by the study of philosophy, of theology, astrology, arithmetic, and geometry, by the reading of history, by the turning over of many curious books, watching and sweating in his studies, he acquired the knowledge which he was to adorn and explain in his verses." In short, Dante acquired as much of the knowledge of his age as he could, a fact which is plainly evident in his later writings. But his young life was not devoted entirely to study. There was in it also a rich variety of gaiety, a love of music, and an interest in art.

During early manhood Dante was active in the affairs of Florence. In 1289, for instance, he served with distinction as a Florentine soldier in the battle of Compaldino. Thereafter Dante became deeply involved in politics. Upon joining one of the gilds which made him eligible to become a gild representative in the government of Florence, he served for a number of years as one of the six priori to whom the government of Florence was entrusted in 1282. During this period he was also a member of a number of embassies to other governments. But in 1302 factional strife erupted in Florence between two rival groups known as the Whites and the Blacks. In the ensuing struggle the Blacks came into power, banishing Dante and other leaders of the Whites from Florence. The decree of banishment stated that if Dante returned to Florence he was to suffer death by fire. It is very difficult to determine with exactness the order of Dante's wanderings. He moved from place to place and even, it appears, journeyed as far as Paris. In 1292 he had married Gemma Donati who bore him seven children, but his family did not accompany him into exile. His exile was, therefore, a lonely one, one that was made worse by "pinching poverty." All this stirred in Dante a bitterness which tinged many of his writings.

Dante felt his banishment from Florence deeply. He wrote in the *Convito:* "For it pleased the citizens of Florence, the fairest and most renowned daughter of Rome, to cast me out of her sweet bosom, where I was born and bred and passed half of the life of man, and in which with her good leave, I still desire with all my heart to repose my weary spirit and finish the days allotted me." He deplored the fact that he had no permanent abode. "Truly," he wrote, "I have been a vessel without a sail and without rudder, driven about upon different ports and shores by the dry wind that springs out of dolorous poverty." In 1315 Dante was offered the opportunity of returning to Florence on condition that he and his fellow exiles pay a fine and walk in the dress of humiliation to the Church of San Giovanni to do penance. But he rejected the conditions. In a letter to the Florentine government he declined to enter Florence except with honor. "If some other [path] can be found," he wrote, "which does not derogate from the fame and honor of Dante, that will I tread with no lagging steps. But if by no such path Florence may be entered, then will I enter Florence never." And he never did. He spent the last two years of his life at Ravenna where he died in 1321 and where his remains were interred. The sentence of banishment was not formally rescinded until 1494 under the government of the Medici. Boccaccio vigorously condemned the action of the Florentine government in banishing Dante, calling it "a shameless deed." "If all the other iniquities of Florence," he wrote, "could be hidden from the all-seeing eyes of God, should not this one suffice to provoke His wrath upon her? Yea, in truth!"

If we do not have an exact record of Dante's wanderings, we do know what he wrote. Before his expulsion from Florence he had already written the *Vita Nuova* (New Life). During his exile he spent many years on the composition of the *Divine Comedy*, a long allegorical poem, which he probably did not finish until shortly before his death. Perhaps the least known of his works in Italian is the *Convito* (Banquet), a collection of a number of long canzoni (lyrical poems or songs) and many shorter ones. There are other canzoni and sonnets which bear Dante's name, but many of these are undoubtedly spurious. Another of Dante's works that is worthy of mention is his Latin treatise *De Monarchia* in which he propounded the idea that the old Roman Empire must be revived in order to establish peace and order in Europe.

Dante called his first collection of poems, which is also the first important literary work in the Italian language, *Vita Nuova*. The sonnets and canzoni which comprise it are the record of his love for Beatrice from the time he first saw her until a year after her death. Later he added a prose commentary to the poems before giving them to the world. The title derives from the words "incipit vita nuova" (the new life begins) which Dante used to describe his first sight of Beatrice. During Dante's youth troubadour poems were still in circulation. For example, Arnaud de Marvelh, a troubadour poet, celebrated his lady love in the following lines:

> Fairer than the far-famed Helen
> Lovelier than the flow'rets gay,
> Snow-white teeth and lips truth-telling,
> Heart as open as the day;
> Golden hair and fresh bright roses
> Heaven who formed a thing so fair
> Knows that never yet another
> Lived who can with her compare.

As for the Tuscan poets, Dante himself joined them in Florence where they were writing love poetry. Soon Dante, too, was writing poetry in which he expressed his youthful love. As he himself wrote:

> I am a man who, when
> Love whispers to the heart, takes note and then
> Retells the tidings to the rest of men.

Dante's conception of love, as stated earlier, differs from that of the troubadours in that it is a love refined of sensuality. In writing about Beatrice he says little about her features, her hair, or her stature. There is never the slightest suggestion of physical possession. He desires nothing from her, an attitude which would have seemed absurd to the troubadours and minnesinger. For Dante it was sufficient that he could see Beatrice. He glorified and idealized her until the real woman ceased to exist and an ideal woman took her place. He loved her for the divine essence in her nature. The apotheosis of woman had probably never been carried further outside of religious literature. His Beatrice was the abstraction worshipped by the Tuscan poets who preceded him and who were his contemporaries. Guido Cavalcanti, one of the Tuscan poets, explained the nature and operation of love in these words, "Love which enamours us of excellence arises out of pure virtue of the soul, and equals us to God."

Few works of literature have given rise to such a variety of opinions as *Vita Nuova*. Because the poet's passion is so completely non-physical some students of Dante have asserted that Beatrice (which literally means "beatitude" or "beaming happiness") is a figment of the imagination. Some have suggested that Beatrice is an intellectual abstraction representing wisdom, philosophy, or some other concept. Actually it matters little whether Beatrice was a product of the imagination or whether she was a woman in the flesh. In order to create such a figure Dante must have felt the desire for such a gentle woman as a poignant reality. If she was a real woman, Dante, according to his own statements, scarcely knew her. He saw her only rarely and then at a distance. It is questionable whether he even exchanged a few words with her. If we can accept Dante's statement he first saw her when he was a boy of nine. Dante has described the effect on him of seeing the little girl in the red dress in this way, "From this time forward love lorded it over my soul . . . and began to exercise over me such control . . . that it behooved me to do completely its bidding." Nine years later he saw Beatrice again. This time she was "clothed in purest white" and attended by two ladies. As she passed along the street Beatrice "turned her eyes very timidly toward the place" where Dante stood. He described the effect on him of her glance in these words, "It seemed to me that I had attained the very highest bliss." He then goes on to say that others were also moved by the sight of her. "Many said when she had passed, 'This is not a woman; rather she is one of the most beautiful angels of heaven.' "

But the beautiful Beatrice, who many literary historians believe became the wife of Simone de Bardi in the meantime, was not to walk long on this earth. She died at the early age of twenty-four. Her death threw Dante into such grief that he was for a time inconsolable, but finally vented his feelings in lines such as these:

> No icy chill or fever's heat deprived
> Us of her, as in nature's course;

But solely her transcendent excellence;
For the bright beam of her humility
Passed with such virtue the celestial spheres,
It called forth wonder in the Eternal Sire;
And then His pleasure was
To claim a soul so healthful and so pure,
And make it from our earth descend to Him;
Deeming this life of weariness and care
Unworthy of a thing so excellent.

After writing a number of sonnets and canzoni during the year after her death Dante concluded with this statement:

> A wonderful vision appeared to me, in which I saw things which made me resolve to speak no more of this blessed one, until I could more worthily treat of her. And to attain to this, I study to the utmost of my power, as she truly knoweth. So that if it shall please Him . . . my life shall be prolonged for some years I hope to say of her what was never said of any woman.

The Divine Comedy

Dante's masterwork is his *Divine Comedy*, a long poem in three parts. It is a poetic tale of a visionary journey through *Inferno* (Hell), *Purgatorio* (Purgatory) and *Paradiso* (Heaven). During the course of his journey, with Virgil as his guide during the first two stages and Beatrice during the last, Dante presents a vivid picture of the horrors of hell, the expiatory sufferings in purgatory, and the glories of heaven. Dante named his poem *Commedia* because, he said, it begins sadly and after many adventures ends happily. His compatriots, however, felt that the name was too mean for such a great poem and added the prefix "Divina." The events described in it supposedly occurred in 1300 when Dante was thirty-five, but the poem was not written until after his exile from Florence in 1302. There are no records which make it possible to trace the various stages of the poem's composition. Biographers are generally agreed that it took Dante ten years or more to write it. Dante himself spoke of the *Divine Comedy* as the work "which has kept me lean for many years." In planning it Dante had difficulty deciding whether to write it in Latin or in Italian; in fact, he had even begun to write the poem in Latin before he decided in favor of the vernacular Italian. The decision was a momentous one. Had he yielded to the scholarly prejudices of his time by writing it in Latin, the *Divine Comedy* would probably have shared the fate of Latin tomes which are now unread and almost forgotten.

The subject matter of the *Divine Comedy* is not secular, but religious, medieval, and mystical. The stern spirit of the Middle Ages lives in Dante's poem. It is a poem of revelation and redemption. The basic theme is moral reform, salvation of the soul, otherworldliness. Dante is the spokesman of eternal things. It is life eternal, in terms of life here and now, with which he is concerned. He sees no division between earthly life and life eternal;

for him the practical affairs of every day and the spiritual affairs of eternity are one. His primary purpose in writing the *Divine Comedy* was not basically poetic pleasure; he wrote to save misguided humanity from the eternal tortures of hell. The purpose of the poem is expressed in the words of Beatrice to him, "Have you seen? Carry your vision back as a warning to the misguided world." In trying to fulfill his purpose Dante remained within the medieval framework in his religious beliefs, in his philosophy, and in his political ideals. The poem as such voices the hopes and aspirations of medieval man. It points backward rather than forward. Far from being ahead of his time, Dante was a prophet of the past, the expounder of a passing age. Hence the *Divine Comedy* has been called "the swan-song of the Middle Ages," "the last of the great Gothic cathedrals" and "the everlasting monument of medievalism on the eve of its dissolution."

In his great poem Dante depicts not only the tortures which the damned suffer from fire and ice, but also the soul-shaking terrors of infernal winds, the persecutions by demons, the torments inflicted by monsters, the immersion in vile mud, the transformation of the damned into grotesquely deformed creatures, and other horrors and tortures the damned must suffer. The atmosphere of hell is made leaden by the utter hopelessness which is also indicated by the inscription on the gate, "Abandon every hope, ye who enter here." Had Dante written only the "Inferno" he would have left his readers in hopeless despair. But after the appalling terrors and utter hopelessness of hell he takes the reader to the mount of purgatory where there is renewal of hope. Although the punishments are of a similar nature, they are limited in duration because the sinner gave proof of penitence before his death. After having traversed the seven circles of purgatory under the guidance of Virgil, Dante moves toward heaven with its seven circles. As he approaches it Beatrice, the object of his earthly love, descends to meet him and while she is advancing toward him Virgil disappears. As Dante ascends from circle to circle, with Beatrice as his guide, he reaches an ever higher plane of mystical communion with the Infinite. He describes heaven in these words:

> One universal smile it seemed of all things;
> Joy beyond compare; gladness ineffable;
> Imperishable life of peace and love;
> Exhaustless riches and immeasurable bliss.
>
> (*Paradiso, XXVII, 4-9*)

But the *Divine Comedy* is more than just "the last full-blown rose of the Middle Ages"; it is an epitome of medieval life and thought, an encyclopedic summation of the knowledge of Dante's day. Dante had absorbed and assimilated the teachings of scholasticism so completely that he could introduce them into his poetry in picturesque language. His guide among the schoolmen was Thomas Aquinas who had incorporated the results of ten centuries of theological inquiry in his *Summa Theologica*. Both Aquinas and

Dante regarded theology as the sum of all knowledge, the key to all problems of the universe. So close is the spiritual relationship between the two men that the *Divine Comedy* has been called a summation in poetry of the *Summa* of Aquinas. In some instances in the "Paradiso" the phrases of Aquinas are introduced almost without modification. Like Aquinas, Dante also warned his fellow Catholics against heresy. In the "Paradiso," for example, he wrote:

> Be ye more staid,
> Oh Christians! Not like feathers, by each wind
> Removable; nor think to cleanse yourselves
> In every water. Either Testament
> The Old and the New is yours; and for your guide,
> The Shepherd of the Church! Let this suffice
> To save you.

The fact that Dante's ideas are in harmony with the teachings of the Church does not mean that the *Divine Comedy* lacks originality. It is original in many respects, particularly in portraying the political passions and local traditions which gave life and color to that age. Dante also boldly mingled classical and mythological with Biblical and ecclesiastical traditions.

Many literary historians regard the *Divine Comedy* as the greatest work of Italian literature. In world literature it is ranked as an epic poem of the highest order, one which makes its author worthy to sit beside Homer, Shakespeare, Milton, and Goethe on the summit of Parnassus. After its appearance the *Divine Comedy* became Italy's most admired work almost at once. Admiration for it was expressed through the establishment of professorships devoted to lecturing on and elucidating it. It was expounded and commented on in much the same way as the Bible itself. During the decade after Dante's death no fewer than eleven commentaries on it were written. It was even included in a list of holy books to be read in Lent. But when the humanist reaction set in against the Middle Ages the popularity of the *Divine Comedy* faded. By some critics it was even styled "barbarous." Furthermore, the professorships which dealt with it were abolished. But in the sixteenth century interest in the *Divine Comedy* began to revive. Michelangelo sketched designs to illustrate it and also composed several sonnets in praise of its author. In one of these he wrote:

> He sank from earth to the abysses blind,
> And saw both hells, and lived, and made ascent
> To God, led by his thought magnificent,
> Whose light of truth he poured on us mankind.
> That lordly star of price in our night shined
> Revealing the eternal.

In the other countries of Europe the *Divine Comedy* did not enjoy the same popularity as in Italy. This can be ascribed in part to the fact that translation into a foreign language robbed the poem of much of its poetic beauty. Another factor which goes far to explain the lack of interest in the *Divine Comedy* was the reaction against the Middle Ages which set in as a result of the preachments of the humanists. For these and other reasons the *Divine Comedy* excited but little interest in France not only during the period of the Renaissance, but also during the succeeding centuries. Some French critics even subjected it to sharp criticism. Voltaire said sarcastically that Dante's reputation should endure because no one reads the *Divine Comedy*. He further stated that the work is a "salmigondis" or hodge-podge rather than an epic poem. Nor did the *Divine Comedy* enjoy a wide popularity in England or Germany. Only in Spain did it evoke considerable interest because of the gruesome and pathetic scenes of the Inferno. After the interest in it reached its nadir in the eighteenth century the tide turned in the nineteenth. During the last half of this century a number of editions of Dante's masterpiece were published both in the original Italian and in translations both in Europe and in America. Scholars also wrote commentaries and prepared concordances. In the twentieth century the *Divine Comedy* has probably been more admired than read.

The Poetry of Petrarch

After Dante's death Francesco Petrarca (1304-1374), better known in the English-speaking countries as Petrarch, gradually became the central figure of Italian literature. Born in Arezzo, a little hamlet northeast of Florence, Petrarch early gave evidence of brilliant qualities of mind. His father who regarded the practice of law as the best road to preferment and honor chose this profession for his son. Francesco attended lectures on law at the University of Montpellier and then spent the next three years at Bologna, the most famous law school of that time. But he found jurisprudence dry and uninteresting. His real interest was literature. Later he wrote regarding his law studies, "In that pursuit I cannot be said to have spent seven years, but to have lost them." When his father's death freed him from the obligation of continuing his law studies, he turned wholeheartedly to literature and began to write both in Latin and in Italian. There remained, however, the problem of finding means of subsistence, for it was a time when a writer could expect no remuneration for his work. Petrarch solved the problem by taking minor orders in the Church which afforded him an income from certain benefices. There is no evidence to show that he ever became a priest. During the years that followed Petrarch never remained long at any one place. The place he called home was Avignon near France where the pope and the members of the papal court resided at that time. He also spent some time in solitude at Vaucluse which is near Avignon. But most of the time a restlessness drove him from place to place. As he put it in one of his canzoni, "From hill to hill I roam, from thought to thought." His biographers have no easy task following him on his travels. He not only traveled about in every part of Italy; he also traversed France and Germany, and went as far as Spain. He valued his freedom of travel so highly that he firmly refused offers by the popes to make him a papal secretary. He also declined with thanks Boccaccio's offer of a professorial chair at the newly-founded University of Florence. On his travels he met people in every circle of society. He counted among his friends many rulers of the day as well as several popes who often consulted him on important matters of state.

Petrarch and Dante differed greatly in their thinking. Whereas Dante was "the spokesman of the Middle Ages," Petrarch looked forward to a new age of learning and culture, regarding the medieval period as one of darkness and "deadly sloth." Although Petrarch was in many respects typical of his medieval environment, sharing the beliefs and ideals of his contemporaries, he also exhibited characteristics that can be called modern. In his writings, for example, he turned away from the scholasticism on which the *Divine Comedy* is based and from the allegory in which Dante took such delight. His writings reflect a consciousness of secular values. He enjoyed mundane pleasure with the taste of an intellectual epicure, but as he grew older he was assailed by scruples regarding his love of earthly things. The struggle in him between the secular and otherworldly was never resolved. During the period he was writing beautiful sonnets about the chaste Laura he entered into a liaison with a woman of low station which resulted in two illegitimate children. He was probably referring to this when he wrote in his *Letter to Posterity*, "I should be glad to be able to say that I have always been entirely free from irregular desires, but I should lie if I did so." While on the one hand he pretended to despise worldly honors as vain, he was, on the other, ever athirst for fame and greedy of distinction, and even resorted to intrigue to achieve them. Petrarch reached the highest moment of his life when in 1340 he was crowned poet laureate at the Capitol in Rome according to an old Greek and Roman custom which had been discontinued during the Middle Ages. He was the first poet since antiquity upon whom the honor was bestowed.

In the history of Italian literature Petrarch stands beside Dante as a consummate master of Italian verse. Through the perfection of his workmanship and the beauty of his language he, too, contributed much toward establishing the Tuscan dialect as the literary language of Italy. When we speak of Petrarch the poet we think of the *Canzoniere*, a collection of more than three hundred sonnets and forty-nine canzoni. The idealism of his poetry derives from the age of chivalry, but Petrarch's preoccupation with emotion and self-analysis places him at the forefront of modern poetry. He is supreme in self-portraiture. Every mood of passion is described and permanently fixed in his verse. With the hand of a master he touched every string of love's many-chorded lyre. The fluctuations of his subtle analyses swing from hope to despair and back. The German literary historian Gaspary put it this way: "Petrarch was a master in one respect at least, he understood how to picture himself; through him the inner world first receives recognition; he first notes, observes, analyzes, and then sets forth its phenomena."

As Dante wrote his *Vita Nuova* to exalt Beatrice, Petrarch wrote most of his sonnets to celebrate the physical charms and the manners of Laura. The golden day on his lover's calendar was a day in April of 1327 on which he saw Laura at mass in the Church of Santa Clara at Avignon. Love seized him as suddenly as it had Dante. After a time he also began to express his love in sonnets. For more than twenty years and in more than three hundred sonnets he described all the circumstances of his attachment. Everything about Laura moved him as a lover and inspired him as a poet. The sight of her or a glance by her would stimulate new outpourings. When he enjoyed the good fortune of picking up her glove Petrarch wrote four sonnets about the incident. His love, like that of Dante, was from a distance. There is no evidence to show that during the entire twenty years Petrarch ever spoke with her except in public. Nor have we reason to believe that Laura bestowed one favor on Petrarch beyond a pleasant glance. She was a married women who for two years had been the wife of Hugo de Sade when Petrarch first saw her. Petrarch himself realized the hopelessness of his love. To his friend Giocomo Colonna he wrote, "Look at what I suffer. To fall in love with a purely ideal object might be a folly, but to love as I do, without hope, is a scourge." All this notwithstanding, he persuaded the painter Simone Martini to paint a miniature likeness of Laura which he carried about with him. In gratitude Petrarch addressed two sonnets to the artist. At no time does he express an impure thought in his sonnets. But in his *Secretum*, an imaginary dialogue between himself and St. Augustine, Petrarch acknowledges that it was Laura's virtue, not his, which maintained a purely platonic relationship between them.

Some critics have ascribed the constancy of his devotion to the fact that Laura furnished him with literary inspiration. Giacomo Colonna wrote to Petrarch: "Your Laura is a phantom created by your imagination for the exercise of your poetry. Your verse, your love, your sighs, are all a fiction; or, if there is anything real in your passion, it is not for the Lady Laura, but for the laurel—that is, the crown of poets." Petrarch answered, "As to Laura, would to Heaven she were only an imaginary person, and my passion for her only a pastime. Alas, it is a madness . . . and what an extravagance it would be to affect such a passion!" In his *Secretum* he describes his love as a torment from which he has vainly attempted to emancipate himself by solitude, by journeys, by distractions, and by trying to become engrossed in his studies. At another time he decided that his love for Laura was an earthly thing, an error, a sin and he prayed to God to turn him to a better life:

> Father of heaven! despite my days all lost
> Despite my nights in doting folly spent
> With that fierce passion which my bosom rent
> At sight of her, too lovely for my cost;

Vouchsafe at last that by Thy grace I turn
To wiser life, and enterprise more fair,
So that my cruel foe, in vain his snare
Set for my soul, may his defeat discern.

Nevertheless, torn by opposing desires, he continues to celebrate Laura's charms.

In his sonnets Petrarch humanized the love theme and brought it down to earth. Whereas Dante's Beatrice is the allegorical incarnation of theology, Petrarch's Laura is a real flesh and blood woman. She is not an ideal figure like Beatrice, but merely a figure idealized. It is her body as a human body that excites Petrarch's imagination. His muse is a feeling for lovely form, for lovely nature, for a lovely woman. His poetry mirrors the female form depicted in Renaissance art as the incarnation of the beautiful. Although Petrarch spoke of Laura's inner nature only in vague generalities, he carefully recorded every detail of her physical perfection with the single exception of her nose. Thus he referred to her "golden tresses," "slender white arms," "glowing cheeks," "milk-white bosom," "angelic smile," "gentle face," and "beauteous eyes that reflect the light of heaven." In the following sonnet, he paints the beauty of Laura in glowing colors and also declares his love for her:

Loose to the breeze her golden tresses flowed,
  Wildly in thousand mazy ringlets blown,
  And from her eyes unconquered glances shone,
Those glances now so sparingly bestowed.
And true or false, meseemed some signs she showed
  As o'er her cheek soft pity's hue was thrown;
  I, whose whole breast with love's soft food was sown,
What wonder if at once my bosom glowed?
Graceful she moved, with more than mortal mien,
  In form an angel; and her accents won
  Upon the ear with more than human sound.
A spirit heavenly pure, a living sun,
Was what I saw; and if no more 'twere seen,
  To unbend the bow will never heal the wound.

(*Translator anonymous*, *Oxford*, *1795*)

Over and over again in his many sonnets he expounds the same theme:

Say from what part of heaven 'twas Nature drew,
  From what idea that so perfect mold
  To form such features, bidding us behold,
In charms below, what she above could do?
What fountain nymph, what dryad maid e'er threw
  Upon the wind such tresses of pure gold?
  What heart such numerous virtues can unfold?
Although the chiefest all my fond hopes slew.
He for celestial charms may look in vain
  Who has not seen my fair one's radiant eyes,
  And felt their glances pleasingly beguile.

How Love can heal his wounds, then wound again,
He only knows who knows how sweet her sighs,
How sweet her converse, and how sweet her smile.
(*Translation by the Rev. Dr. Nott*)

In 1348, at the age of forty-one, Laura fell victim to the Black Death, a pestilence of extreme virulence. She was mourned not only by her husband and her ten or eleven children, but especially by Petrarch. His sonnets now became sublime as he pictures her amid the saints looking down upon him. But she is still the earthly woman and not the mystic ideal created by Dante:

The eyes, the arms, the hands, the feet, the face
Which made my thoughts and words so warm and wild,
That I was almost from myself exiled,
And rendered strange to all the human race;
The lucid locks that curl'd in golden grace,
The lightening beam that, when my angel smiled,
Diffused o'er earth an Eden heavenly mild;
What are they now? Dust, lifeless dust, alas!
(*Translation by A. Morehead*)

In later life Petrarch regarded his Italian poetry less highly than his Latin writings. "I must confess," he wrote, "that I look with aversion on the silly boyish things I once produced in the vernacular." The fact that the interest in his Italian poetry was much greater than in his Latin humanistic writings puzzled him. He failed to understand why the vernacular poems of his youth attracted more attention than, as he put it, "the serious works which with more highly developed faculties I have written since." Petrarch was certain that his fame would endure after his death, but he based his hopes on his Latin writings. This was a miscalculation. His sonnets and canzoni earned for him a place among the great poets of the world. They quickly made him Italy's favorite poet. Not only were they widely read; they were also widely imitated. In Italy a host of poets and would-be poets became Petrarchists. For a time the writing of sonnets was a fad in which merchants, bankers, courtesans, soldiers, and men and women from the humbler walks of life participated. Even after the fad declined, Petrarch's poems retained their popularity. Some idea of how great was the interest in them may be gained from the fact that in the sixteenth century they went through 167 distinct editions. In 1768, almost four centuries after Petrarch's death, an English historian wrote, "Witness the celebrated volumes of Italian verses by Francis Petrarca whose amorous and yet most chaste Platonic sentiments for the beautiful Laura have rendered him the most favorite poet of Italy for these last centuries." All Italian poets since Petrarch's day are indebted to a greater or lesser extent to his lyrical genius.

Petrarch's influence was by no means restricted to Italy. The poets of all Europe came under the spell of his sonnets. His influence penetrated to wherever lyric poetry was written. Petrarchism as the movement was called is one long anthem of the praise of woman as God's most perfect creature.

During the first half of the sixteenth century Petrarchism was introduced into France by Clément Marot and others. In England the sonnets of Sydney and Spencer, among others, show the influence of Petrarch. In Catalonia and Castile, which were later to become a part of Spain, Petrarch's sonnets were imitated by a number of poets. Auzias March, a Catalan poet of the fifteenth century, even wove a tale of love around his Teresa which is analogous to Petrarch's love for Laura. Since that time there have been many Petrarchists, for Petrarch's sonnets have retained their freshness and grace to this day.

Boccaccio's Decameron

The third member of the triumvirate which raised the Tuscan dialect to the status of the literary language of Italy was Giovanni Boccaccio (1313-1375). Boccaccio was the first great writer of Italian prose. The spirit of his writings was wholly secular. Whereas mundane life was in Dante's *Divine Comedy* still a school for eternity, in Boccaccio's writings it was something to be lived and enjoyed for itself. The world he portrays is a world of human things, not of things divine. Very little is known about Boccaccio's life apart from the references he makes to it in his writings, and most of these are in the guise of fiction. He was a product of the very bourgeois society he depicted so well. Although he is generally regarded as being a Florentine, he was actually born in Paris. His mother was a Parisian whom the father had met on one of his business trips to France. After Giovanni's birth the father deserted his mother and married a Florentine woman, whereupon the boy was taken to Florence to live with his father and stepmother. The elder Boccaccio wanted the son to follow in his footsteps as a merchant, but the boy showed neither aptitude for nor interest in a business career. When he was fourteen his father sent him to Naples to study business methods and when the lad found this uninteresting the course was changed to canon law. But young Boccaccio disliked canon law as heartily as he did business. In Naples he did, however, meet a number of scholars and writers who impressed him so favorably that he resolved to devote himself to a literary career. In 1340, after an unfortunate love affair with Maria (the Fiametta of his later writings), the natural daughter of King Robert of Naples, he returned to Florence where he spent his time writing Italian and Latin works. At various times he also went on diplomatic missions for the Florentine government.

Boccaccio was a man of many achievements. Besides his work as a humanist which will be discussed in the next chapter, he wrote poetry in Italian which would have been outstanding in any age except that of Dante and Petrarch, half a dozen works of fiction in Italian, the earliest biography of Dante, and a commentary on part of Dante's "Inferno." Toward the end of his life he also lectured for a short time on the *Divine Comedy*. But everything he wrote and did is overshadowed by his *Decameron* (from the Greek meaning "Ten Days"). If all his other achievements were wiped out, Western culture would be poorer, but Boccaccio's reputation would be undiminished, for it rests mainly on the *Decameron.* It is as the author of the *Decameron* that he earned his high rank in the history of literature.

The *Decameron* is a collection of one hundred prose tales written with a background of the Black Death which visited Florence in 1348. As an introduction to the *Decameron* Boccaccio wrote a vivid description of the plague, painting a graphic picture of the stricken city, of the terror and confusion that reigned, of the decimation of the population, and of the disorderly burials. He states that the malignancy of the plague was such that "neither the counsel of a physician nor the virtue of any medicine whatever seemed to avail or have any effect"; consequently "only very few recovered, but almost everyone attacked died by the third day." Boccaccio goes on to state that in some houses all persons died, a fact that was "only discovered by the stench of their dead bodies." The Black Death claimed so many victims that the dead were "laid before the doors" whence they were hauled away in wagons for mass burial. As the plight of the city grew more desperate many of the citizens fled to the surrounding country, leaving families and relatives behind. This is supported by the contemporary chronicler Filippo Villani who wrote, "So completely were all obligations of blood and of affection forgotten that men left their nearest and dearest to die alone rather than to incur the dangers of infection."

The idea of fleeing from the pest-ridden city was used by Boccaccio to construct a framework for his stories. One Tuesday morning in the late spring of 1348, while the plague was raging, seven young women met at mass "not by arrangement, but by chance" in the Church of Santa Maria Novella. While they were discussing the gravity of the situation, they were joined by three young men. On the spur of the moment the group decided to leave the plague-stricken city for the country. They forthwith went to a beautiful country mansion situated on one of the hills overlooking Florence. This mansion was surrounded by "beautiful lawns and marvelous gardens" in which there were arbors of vines laden with fruit and "the sides of the paths were closed in by red and white roses and jasmine." There was also a lawn "colored by a thousand varieties of flowers" and surrounded by orange and lemon trees. In the center there was "a fountain of the whitest marble with marvelous sculptures." The entire beauty of the place "was so pleasing to the ladies and the three youths that all declared that if Paradise could be found on earth, they could not conceive what other form than that of this garden could be given to it, nor what beauty could be added to it." In the cellars of the house there were "fine wines, more suitable to wine connoisseurs than to sober and virtuous ladies." The stay of the group at the mansion was joyful from the beginning to the end. After "singing six songs and dancing six dances" the group gathered about a table in the garden which was laden with delicious foods. Later there were more songs and dances; also games and general merrymaking. In the evening the group turned to story-telling. For a period of ten days each member of the group told a story every day. The resulting one hundred stories make up the *Decameron.*

The stories of the *Decameron* cover almost every phase of human life, the comic, the tragic, the ironic, the pathetic, the base, and the noble. All this makes the book a mirror of life in fourteenth-century Italy, including its vice, its fine manners, its brutality and heartlessness, its strange mixture of Christianity and paganism. In the *Decameron* Boccaccio broke completely with the ascetic tradition of the Middle Ages. He presented the society of his time completely from the secular point of view, with a wide tolerance for human foibles and errors. He accepts his fellow human beings as they are. Since the *Decameron* is a portrait of the world which presents human life as lived on this earth, it has often been called "the Human Comedy" in contrast to the *Divine Comedy* of Dante. In describing many kinds of lives, each one in its general relation to humanity, Boccaccio exhibited a keen observation of the character, habits, and dispositions of men. While some of the tales accent feminine guile, others heap ridicule and contempt on the conduct of priests, monks and nuns. Again others are humorous anecdotes of the French fabliaux type. Some critics have roundly denounced the *Decameron* as being sensuous and indecent in parts. Boccaccio does at time transgress the limits of delicate taste. On the other hand, some of the stories are notable for their delicacy and beauty. In the entire book he never uses a coarse word. Frequently a story actually preaches morality by pointing out the dangers of folly, vanity, and passion. The first story of the first day, for instance, offers a notable example of hypocrisy, while the last story of the same day celebrates the virtue of patience. Few books contain finer traits of humanity, courtesy, and generosity.

Most of the plots on which the stories are based were not invented by Boccaccio. He picked them up wherever he found them. Some are undoubtedly based on the French fabliaux and on the tales of oriental and classical writers. Others he probably collected in a rough hearsay form as he heard them on the street or in a tavern. The most precious bequests are those founded on contemporary incidents for they throw light on Boccaccio's time. To a greater or lesser extent he wove the manners and morals, the customs and foibles of his time into all the stories. Because it is filled with observations of contemporary life and because it presents realistic people, the book is as fresh, mirthful, and zesty today as it was when Boccaccio gave it to the public.

In later life when Boccaccio became absorbed in the Greek and Roman classics he frowned on his writings in the vernacular, referring to them as his "youthful follies." But posterity did not share his opinion. Literary critics are agreed that the *Decameron* was not only the first great prose work in the Italian language; it was also a great influence in the development of Italy's literary language. One literary historian, for example, styled the *Decameron* "a well of Tuscan undefiled, whence, as from the purest source, all future writers drew the rules and examples which form the correct and elegant style of Italian composition." By some the *Decameron* is still regarded as the greatest prose work in the Italian language. But the influence and example of the *Decameron* was not limited to Italy. Writers in other European countries soon read it either in the original or in translation. Its material was used in narrative verse as well as in prose. Dramatists also drew from it plots for both comedies and tragedies. Furthermore, Boccaccio's idea of putting a succession of dissimilar tales into the mouths of people brought together by some special occasion was widely adopted. Chaucer, for example, used this device in his *Canterbury Tales*, although there is considerable doubt that he ever read the *Decameron* itself. Many other English writers used materials borrowed directly or indirectly from the *Decameron*, including Shakespeare, Ben Jonson, Dryden, Swift, Pope, Goldsmith, Byron, Keats, Tennyson, and George Eliot. In Germany the sixteenth-century poet and dramatist Hans Sachs borrowed freely from it; in France Margaret of Navarre imitated it in the *Heptameron*, and La Fontaine was deeply influenced by it. In Spain the influence of the *Decameron* continued for centuries. The *Patrañuelo* (*c.*1566), contains three stories taken from the *Decameron*. Lope de Vega (1562-1635) also borrowed from it; in fact, during the entire seventeenth century Spanish writers turned to the *Decameron* not only for material for short stories, but also for plots for romances and plays. Thus the influence of the *Decameron* in the development of European literature was considerable. As author of the *Decameron Boccaccio* is in a number of respects the ancestor of modern writers of fiction.

Italian Literature in the Fifteenth Century

During the century after the death of Boccaccio, humanism constituted the major interest in the intellectual life of Italy. Most of the gifted minds, intoxicated by visions of the Greco-Roman world, devoted themselves to the study and teaching of classical literature. The humanists insisted that Latin was the only proper language for the expression of poetic and philosophic ideas. The Italian language they regarded as a corruption of Latin and fit only for use in the common converse of everyday life. Some even went so far as to look down on Dante's *Divine Comedy* because it was written in Italian and to despise the Italian works of Petrarch and Boccaccio. This caused many poets and writers who could have expressed themselves more naturally in the vernacular to follow the fashion of writing in Latin. The result was a vast output of Latin poetry and prose, but not one outstanding work was written in Italian. Since the common people did not share the humanist opinion that the Italian language was inferior, Italian literature continued to flourish on the folk level, particularly in the popular forms of poetry and song.

The Italian language also had its defenders in humanistic circles, especially in Florence where many had not forgotten that Dante, Petrarch, and Boccaccio wrote their great works in the vernacular. Prominent in the group which defended the Italian language and advocated its use as a literary medium was Leon Battista Alberti (1404-1472), a humanist of extraordinary versatility. The contemporary humanist Cristoforo Landino called Alberti "the foremost advocate of the Italian language." Alberti believed that the prejudice against the use of the Italian language for literary purposes was absurd. He advocated the use of it to the writers of Italy despite the fact that he had a thorough command of Latin. The Italian language, he stated, is the only language understood by everyone living in Italy. If the learned men of Italy, he continued, would devote themselves to its use and improvement, it might well command a respect in Italy equal to that enjoyed by Latin. Alberti did not stop at urging his countrymen to use the vernacular as a means of literary expression; he also wrote a number of his own works in Italian. The best known of these works are his long dissertation on family life titled *Della Famiglia* (On the Family) and *Della Pittura* (On Painting), his short essay on the mathematical approach to painting.

Alberti's plea for the Italian language did not fall on deaf ears. A number of Florentine humanists gradually rallied to its use. Of this group the most talented was probably Angelo Politian or Politianus (1454-1494), protegé of Lorenzo the Magnificent. Although Politian wrote some of the best Latin poetry the age produced, he was also the most accomplished Italian poet of the time. He wrote ballate (dance songs), madrigals (part songs), rispetti (love songs), and carnival songs. The world Politian depicts in his poetry is not profound, but has great beauty. The scenes in his dance songs and love songs are often laid in gardens reminiscent of the Garden of Eden. In his poetry he also reveals a novel understanding of popular emotions. Like the artists of his day he painted poetic pictures of Renaissance feelings and joys in bright colors. The following is an example of a rispetto written in the eight-line stanza which Politian helped to make popular. Unfortunately translation robs it of much of its melodiousness.

> I ask not, Love, for any other pain
> To make thy cruel foe and mine repent,
> Only that thou shouldst yield her to the strain
> Of these my arms alone, for chastisement;
> Then would I clasp her so with might and main,
> That she should learn to pity and relent,
> And in revenge for scorn and proud despite,
> A thousand times I'd kiss her forehead white.

In general, Italian literature of the fifteenth century was a literature of the people. Many poets turned to popular or semi-popular forms as vehicles for their poetry. This was particularly true of the songs of the period. Some of these songs were of such high quality that they achieved a permanent place in literature. The one that follows is characterized by a lyrical grace and a refreshing naiveté.

O swallow, swallow, flying through the air
Turn, turn, prithee, from thy flight above.
Give me one feather from thy wing so fair,
For I will write a letter to my love.
When I have written it and made it clear;
I'll give thee back thy feather, swallow dear,
When I have written it on paper white,
I'll make, I swear, thy missing feather right;
When once 'tis written on fair leaves of gold,
I'll give thee back thy wings and flight so bold.

7

Italian Humanism

Another manifestation of the progressive secularization of life and culture was the Renaissance interest in the literature of ancient Greece and Rome. The scholars who devoted themselves to the rediscovery, study, and imitation of the classical literatures referred to their studies as "studia humanitatis" or studies of humanity, and the literatures themselves were known as "litterae humaniores" or literatures based on the human side of man's nature as opposed to divine letters or the literature of theology. As a result those who studied and taught the classical languages and literatures, and imitated the classical writers, became known as humanists. This designation, first used in the fifteenth century, passed into general use in the sixteenth. The word "humanism" did not make its appearance until the nineteenth century. Although the word has been variously interpreted, the essence of the humanist movement of the Renaissance period was the appreciative study and imitation of the classics. The humanists were attracted to the classics by the wealth of information they contain on secular life, the perfection of their style, and their free outlook on life. To the humanists the classics were both a source of inspiration and a helpful guide to a better understanding of secular life and its problems. They imitated the classical writers not only because of the elegance of their style, but also because they found in them the most satisfactory expression of a philosophy of life which appealed to them.

Classical Literature in the Middle Ages

Nineteenth-century historians believed that in the Middle Ages the classical writings were not only unread, but also virtually unknown. Hence they regarded Renaissance humanism as a sudden radical departure from the Middle Ages. More recently, however, historical scholarship has shown that the lamp of classical knowledge continued to burn even during the darkest period when invasion, pillage, and confusion was the order of the day. At all times there were in the midst of the confusion various oases where the classics were read and copied. The great guardians of manuscripts were the monks of both the East and the West. Present day knowledge of the classics is based largely on copies of manuscripts which they made. But the monks and the secular clergy did not stop at multiplying the manuscripts through the laborious work of copying them. Attracted by the perfection of style attained by some of the ancient authors, they used the Latin classics as models of literary style and as textbooks for the study of grammar. Undoubtedly there were some who read the classics for their content. For those who wished to sample classical knowledge there were brief excerpts from the classics available in the anthologies which were in circulation. Thus at least a fragmentary knowledge of the classics was an important element in the stream of medieval culture.

Since the classics contain ideas which were not in harmony with the teachings of the Church many of the early fathers and the later ecclesiastical leaders frowned on the reading of them. Some even warned those who were interested in the classics that they were putting their souls in jeopardy. Tertullian, for example, contemptuously asked what the ancient philosophers had achieved with their speculations, adding that the most simpleminded Christian knew more about God than all the philosophers put together. St. Augustine, among others, regarded the Greek and Roman gods as demons employed by Satan to tempt and perplex faithful Christians. Bishop Gregory of Tours (*c.*538-594) said regarding the classical poets, "Let us shun the lying fables of the poets and forego the wisdom of the sages at enmity with God, lest we incur the doom of endless death by sentence of our Lord." In the ninth century Ermenrich of Elwangen (d.866), fearing that he might be suspect because he had quoted Virgil an inordinate number of times in a grammatical treatise he sent to the abbot of St. Gall, attached a letter to the treatise in which he stated that when he read the classical poets he was often haunted by "a dark monster" whom he would drive away by making the sign of the cross.

If the Latin classics were copied and read during the early centuries of the Middle Ages, this was not true of the Greek classics. Because of the commercial intercourse between Byzantium and certain of the Italian cities there were many Italians who had a working knowledge of Greek, but these traders and merchants do not seem to have been interested in the classical literature of Greece. Any acquaintance with Greek literature in its original form was individual and exceptional. Furthermore, there was almost no opportunity to learn Greek since the teaching of it was not a part of the curriculum of Western schools and universities. Then, too, Greek manuscripts were rarities in Western Europe. Such knowledge of Greek literature as existed was based almost entirely on Latin translations of the original Greek works. Even these were comparatively scarce. Only a few of the many writings of Plato and Aristotle were available in Latin translations. Whatever knowledge the medieval intellectuals had of Homer's works was based on concise Latin summaries. Short Latin excerpts from some of the Greek classics could be found in such compilations as that of Isidore of Seville. But an important exception must be noted here. In the province of Calabria in southwestern Italy where many Greeks from the Near East settled, Greek remained a spoken language and Greek studies were pursued in the monasteries throughout the Middle Ages.

Twice during the centuries preceding the great Renaissance of the period from 1300 to 1600 there were important revivals of interest in the classics. The first occurred during the reign of Charlemagne (768-814) and is often called the Carolingian Renaissance. Those who participated in it spoke of it as a "renovatio," or renewal. There was no mention of rebirth. At that time education, the arts, the liturgy of the Church, and even the system of governmental administration were in need of renewal and scholars turned to pagan as well as to Christian writings for ideas. The underlying motives were religious and the renewal was carried out by representatives of the Church. Although there was no attempt to reactivate the pagan classics as literature, the Carolingian scribes did make one important contribution to the study of the classics. By transcribing many of the classics they helped to preserve them for posterity. After the death of Charlemagne the interest that had been stimulated in the classics gradually declined.

The second important surge of interest in the classical writings took place in the eleventh and twelfth centuries and has been called "the Renaissance of the Twelfth Century" by some historians. This revival was more spontaneous than the previous one. The principal centers in which it developed were the monasteries, the cathedral chapters, and the universities. During the first stage the important classical writer was Virgil. His writings appear on every list of books of that period. Many of those who read Virgil's poems were inspired to write Latin poetry of their own. During the next stage, interest in classical writings was stimulated by the introduction into Western Europe of the works of many Greek authors in Latin translations. These translations made by Arabic scholars from Arabic or Greek manuscripts came from such centers of Arabic learning as Bagdad in the Near East, Toledo and Córdoba in Spain, and Palermo in Sicily. Through these translations the intellectuals of Western Europe became acquainted for the first time with many writings by Greek authors previously known only from excerpts which were included in medieval compilations from the classics. The most important translations were undoubtedly those of the works of Aristotle, some of which became available for the first time. Most of the translations were poorly done, but they did reveal Aristotle's philosophy, his logic, and his ideas on natural science.

The use of the phrase "the Renaissance of the Twelfth Century" to describe the revival of interest in the classics during the eleventh and twelfth centuries is unfortunate because it implies greater identity with the real Renaissance than the facts warrant. Professor Charles Haskins, author of *The Renaissance of the Twelfth Century*, stated, "It was a revival rather than a new birth." There was in the twelfth century no such idea of the rebirth of classical civilization as was expressed in the Renaissance of the period from 1300 to 1600. The scholars of the twelfth century did not believe that they were introducing something from a distinct civilization which preceded their own. They regarded the classics as part of their own civilization, as a phase of their civilization which had been somewhat neglected. They had such a strong sense of continuity that they believed antiquity was still with them. The idea of antiquity as a distinctly separate period did not as yet exist. There was as yet no sharp distinction between ancient and medieval culture.

The increase of interest in the classical writings during the eleventh and twelfth centuries was a development within the framework of medieval civilization and the primary inspiration of the movement was religious. There were undoubtedly some scholars who read and studied the classical writings as a means of living a fuller life, but in most cases the ideas of the pagan writers were carefully subordinated to the teachings of the Church. The purpose of most of the scholars was to marshal classical ideas for the enrichment of ecclesiastical culture. At that time the ecclesiastical culture was still in a growth stage approaching its great flowering period. It was, in fact, so dynamic that it absorbed the antique elements which either fit or could be made to fit into the pattern set by the Church. These elements were so completely absorbed that they did not inspire progress toward a new culture. The schoolmen or scholastics, for example, appropriated much from the classical writings on logic and philosophy, employing it to build rational supports for the teachings of the Church. Some scholastics were, in fact, convinced that the works of the classical writers held the key to the understanding of the deepest mysteries of the Christian faith.

In a more general way, a Christian meaning was superimposed on pagan writings to bring them into harmony with the teachings of the Church. The ideas of Aristotle, for example, were interpreted in such a way as to reconcile them with the prevailing conceptions of the truth. Virgil was made to appear as a pre-Christian witness to the faith. In the same way the *Iliad* of Homer and the *Metamorphoses* of Ovid were transformed into profound allegories of Christian truth. The scientific writings of the Greeks were, it is true, instrumental in generating interest in the field of natural science as will be shown in the chapter on Renaissance science. The science they stimulated was, however, not modern science. It was medieval science which, like philosophy, was the handmaiden of theology. In one respect the twelfth-century revival did open the way for the coming of Renaissance humanism; in Italy the literary cultivation of the classics was abbreviated into a preparation for the study of Roman law which became an important factor in arousing interest in Roman civilization.

Despite the fact that the pagan spirit was being carefully exorcised from the classics, there were still leaders in the Church who feared that scholars might imperil their souls by drinking too deeply from the flacon of pagan knowledge. Hence they warned against the dangers inherent in the study of the classics. Their warnings might be summed up in the words which Christopher Marlowe has the good angel address to Faustus:

O Faustus, lay that damned book aside,
And gaze not on it, lest it tempt thy soul
And heap God's wrath upon thy head.
Read, read the Scriptures! That is blasphemy!

Pietro Damiani (1007-1072), adviser to several popes, inveighed ceaselessly against "the beguiling songs" of the classical poets and "the golden phrases" of the classical philosophers, although his writings show that he was well versed in classical literature. Honorius of Autun (*c.*1150) asked, "How does the soul profit from the strife of Hector and the arguments of Plato, the poems of Virgil, and the elegies of Ovid?" Finally, Bernard of Clairveaux (1091-1153), the great medieval preacher, said in one of his sermons, "What good is philosophy? The apostles are my teachers! They did not teach me to unravel the complexities of Aristotle, but they did teach me how to live! Believe me, knowing how to live is no minor item! It is the greatest of all!"

The enthusiasm for the classics which developed in the eleventh and twelfth centuries was transitory. The actual period during which it existed was from 1050 to 1150. The second half of the twelfth century saw a decline, followed by a period during which classical studies suffered considerable neglect. But the tide turned with the appearance on the scene of the Renaissance humanists.

The Early Stages of Renaissance Humanism

There was a significant difference between the attitudes of the medieval scholars and the Renaissance humanists toward the classics. The difference was relative rather than absolute, but nevertheless real. Whereas the medieval scholars quietly reshaped what they knew of classical thought so that it would fit into the pattern of ecclesiastical dogma, the humanists read and studied the classics for their intrinsic values. They no longer looked at the classics through the spectacles of scholastic philosophy and theology, but sought to make the study of the classics an end in itself. "Let us," Petrarch said, "have nothing but a simple and pure study of antiquity." This approach was in a deeper sense a step in the direction of broader mental horizons and greater knowledge of mundane life. It was a manifestation of man's rejuvenated sense of the importance of life apart from its importance for the hereafter. It was a shift of emphasis from the otherworldly to the secular. There were some humanists who endeavored to balance and coordinate classical and Christian thought without subordinating one to the other, but most of the humanists sought to discover the meaning the classics had for the men who wrote them. They regarded humanism as the return to a way of thought which had disappeared a thousand years before their time. This interest in antiquity was accompanied by a turning-away from the immediate past and a growing distaste for things medieval.

The early humanists were mostly laymen with a considerable admixture of clerics. There were those who began reading the classics for their style and then became interested in the subject matter. Others read and studied the classics because of their admiration for the aesthetic achievements of the Romans and Greeks. Then there were those who turned to the classics because they had lost faith in the ability of scholasticism to provide a solution for the problems of the day. Some were carried away by their interests in the classics to the extent that they looked to them for new standards of morals and conduct. The most enthusiastic of the early humanists were students of law and those associated with the legal profession, including lawyers, judges, glossators, and notaries. Besides being the most literate section of lay society, they were in almost daily contact with the Roman law and Roman tradition. Since Roman law was such an important phase of Roman civilization, many of those who were interested in law broadened their interests to include Roman thought and culture.

Many historians have long regarded Petrarch as the first humanist. Petrarch himself, who can hardly be accused of excessive modesty, did not recognize any precursors. In one of his last works he took credit for reviving the neglected study of the classics and for initiating a new age of literature and learning. His contemporaries, too, credited him with having ushered in "the new learning." Nevertheless, Petrarch was not the first humanist. The new interest in the classics manifested itself toward the end of the thirteenth century, some years before Petrarch was born. In Padua, for example, humanistic interests were cultivated in the last decade of the thirteenth century by Lovato Lovati and his associates. In Bologna, Giovanni del Vergilio was such an enthusiastic admirer of Virgil that he adopted the name of the Roman poet. Like the later humanists Giovanni esteemed the Latin language so highly as a means of expressing poetic thought that he denounced Dante for writing the *Divine Comedy* in Italian. There were also other scholars with humanistic interests in such cities as Verona, Florence, and Milan as well as in Padua and Bologna.

If Petrarch was not the first or the only star in the firmament of humanism, he was by all odds the brightest. Very early in life he developed a fondness for the Latin language and for the Latin classics. He took such delight in Cicero that he often read the master's prose aloud. At the University of Bologna his interest in the classics became more intense. He became so engrossed in them that he would deprive himself of necessities in order to purchase copies of the works of Cicero and Virgil. When the father discovered that young Petrarch was devoting more attention to the classics than to the study of law, he roundly berated his son. One story has it that he even burned some of his son's treasures. It was all to no avail. When his father died soon thereafter, Petrarch dedicated himself entirely to being a humanist and poet. In his *Epistle to Posterity* he stated that he devoted himself to the study of antiquity because "our age has been distasteful to me," "consequently I have delighted in history." By "history" Petrarch meant antiquity, not the period preceding his own which we call the Middle Ages, a period of which he was an uncompromising critic. He firmly believed that the study of the classics would inaugurate an age in which the light of classical knowledge would dispel the darkness of ignorance and superstition. In his *Africa* he wrote:

> To thee, perchance, if lengthened days are given
> A better age shall mark the grace of Heaven;
> Not always shall this deadly sloth endure:
> Our son shall live in days more bright and pure;
> Then with fresh shoots our Helicon shall glow;
> Then the fresh laurel spread its sacred bough;
> Then the high intellect and docile mind
> Shall renovate the studies of mankind,
> The love of beauty and the cause of truth
> From ancient sources draw eternal youth.

But Petrarch was not content with being the prophet of a new age; he also worked to hasten its arrival by pleading the cause of humanism in his writings and by endeavoring to restore the pristine beauty of the Latin language. Elegance of style, he stated, is indispensable to a work of merit. In his own writings he strove to replace the prevailing barbarous forms by using as his models the best of the Roman writers. He believed that his *Africa*, on which he labored half a lifetime, would assure for him an immortality such as Virgil had earned. He even used Virgil's works as the model for his long epic which celebrates the deeds of Scipio Africanus during the later years of the Second Punic War. Before he finished the poem its fame was such that Petrarch was crowned poet laureate in Rome, an honor which Dante had coveted in vain. But posterity has not set the same high value on it. The long poem which before its completion was compared with Virgil's *Aeneid* and even labeled "homeric" was later regarded as something artificial and consigned to the realm of forgotten things.

Petrarch's widest claim to renown as a humanist is the part he played in awakening an interest in antiquity. The classics and classical thought became such a passion with him that he devoted himself unsparingly to the search for neglected works of classical authors. The discovery of such a manuscript not only gave him great satisfaction; it also made another classical work available to his fellow humanists. He was especially interested in finding works of Cicero, his favorite author. He was overjoyed, for example, when he found the only authentic manuscript of Cicero's letters in a church at Verona. He proceeded at once to make a copy which can still be seen in the Medicean Library in Florence. To the owner of another Cicero manuscript which Petrarch had borrowed for the purpose of copying it he wrote, "As I progressed I was so enchanted with certain passages, and so powerfully excited, that the copying and the reading became one, and my only dread was that the eyes would outrun the pen, and thus deaden the ardor of my writing." At times Petrarch employed others to help him copy and decipher manuscripts. In this way he managed to accumulate a library of about two hundred manuscripts. Some of these he studied critically, jotting down annotations. In general, Petrarch made the classical authors his friends and confidants, holding converse with them and writing them letters. Among those to whom he wrote letters were Cicero, Virgil, Seneca, and Homer.

Petrarch was also one of the first to appreciate the value of ruins, inscriptions, coins, and statuary as sources of historical knowledge. Time and again he urged his countrymen to search out and preserve the precious relics of Rome's greatness. He was so moved by the idea of the greatness of Rome that he exclaimed at the sight of Roman ruins, "Where can the empire of the world be found except in Rome? Who can dispute the Roman right? What force can stand against the name of Romans?"

Italian humanism was in its early stages a Latin revival. Petrarch himself never learned Greek. His interest in classical thought and literature, however, was such that the ownership of Greek manuscripts was a source of great pleasure to him. In his library he had a number of Plato's works in the original Greek and also a manuscript of the works of Homer. To Sygéros who sent him the Homer manuscript he wrote, "Thy Homer lies mute at my side. I am deaf to him, but I nevertheless delight in the sight of him, and often embrace him."

Petrarch's influence on the development of humanism was tremendous. His name stands out prominently among the scholars who were instrumental in stimulating interest in the classics and classical thought. His prestige was such that his example made humanism fashionable. Not only did many scholars turn to the classics, but cultured people generally began reading and studying them. Among those whose interest was stimulated were many university students. Fathers chided Petrarch for enticing their sons from the study of law and other subjects to the study of the classics and the writing of Latin verse. His disciple Giovanni Boccaccio wondered whether there would have been a revival of classical learning if Petrarch had not appeared on the scene. At the time of Petrarch's death Giovanni of Ravenna wrote to the humanist Coluccio Salutati that Petrarch through his "divine labors had earned for himself a place in heaven and a glorious immortality on earth."

The most distinguished of Petrarch's disciples was the author of the *Decameron*, Giovanni Boccaccio, who was nine years younger than his humanist master. Long before the two men met, Boccaccio had expressed his admiration for Petrarch's Italian poetry. He also held Dante's *Divine Comedy* in high esteem. In this he differed from Petrarch who evinced no interest in it and even claimed that he had never read it. Some historians have ascribed Petrarch's coldness toward Dante to the fact that his inordinate pride could brook no rival, not even a dead one. Boccaccio in his efforts to convince his friend of Dante's greatness went so far as to make with his own hands a copy of the *Divine Comedy* which he presented to Petrarch. But the latter remained unmoved. The first meeting between the two had taken place in 1350 when Petrarch stopped at Florence en route to Rome to gain the indulgences of the Jubilee Year. The next year Boccaccio visited Petrarch at Padua, where he was staying at that time, to offer him a chair at the new University of Florence. Although Petrarch declined the offer with thanks, the meeting of the two strengthened the bonds of their friendship which remained unbroken for the rest of their lives. Boccaccio regarded himself as particularly fortunate to have as his friend one who was the friend of popes and princes. Whenever he wrote Petrarch's name he expressed his admiration for his friend by adding such laudatory phrases as "illustrious and sublime master," "marvel and glory of our age," "man descended from heaven to restore to poetry her throne," and "a poet who is rather of the company of the ancients."

One result of the association of the two literary figures was that Boccaccio plunged eagerly into the study of classical antiquity. His delight over the discovery of a new manuscript was as great as that of Petrarch, but as humanist he was of a lesser stature. His greatest distinction as a humanist was his industry. During the last years of his life he compiled several ponderous Latin works which humanists regarded as mines of information and erudition, but which posterity has deemed commonplace and dull. In one respect, however, Boccaccio surpassed his master. He acquired a rudimentary knowledge of Greek. He was so eager to learn Greek that he prevailed on Leontius Pilatus who possessed a practical knowledge of Greek to come to Florence and live with him. Besides teaching Boccaccio Greek, Pilatus also lectured for a time on Homer at the University of Florence. Together the two men prepared a somewhat crude translation of Homer's *Iliad* and *Odyssey*. It was probably the first translation of Homer in the Renaissance period.

A much broader revival of interest in the Greek language took place some years after Boccaccio's death. Near the end of the fourteenth century a Florentine delegation succeeded in inducing Manuel Chrysoloras, a Byzantine by birth, to leave the service of the Byzantine government and accept the chair of Greek in the University of Florence. Chrysoloras, who was an eloquent lecturer as well as a gifted scholar, attracted large audiences. His lectures were attended not only by many humanists and students interested in the humanities, but also by eminent men from other walks of life. His success as a teacher resulted in his being invited to lecture in Rome, Padua, Milan, and Venice. In all of these cities he evoked a considerable interest in Greek thought as well as in the Greek language. The humanist Leonardo Bruni reported that the knowledge of Greek grew mightily after Chrysoloras brought Greek learning to Italy. But the influence of Chrysoloras was not limited to his teaching. As an aid in the teaching of Greek he prepared an elementary Greek grammar which was the first of its kind in Western Europe and long remained the only introduction to the study of Greek. A century later Erasmus used it as the basic textbook when he taught Greek at Cambridge. In Italy the work Chrysoloras had started was carried on by his students, including Leonardo Bruni and Poggio Bracciolini. They were also joined by a number of Chrysoloras' countrymen who migrated to Italy in response to the demand for teachers of Greek.

Humanist Activities

The tremendous impulse which the early humanists gave to the interest in the Greek and Roman classics caused many scholars and others to turn to the search for hidden or neglected manuscripts. So intense was the enthusiasm that it resulted in "the great hunt." Men made long journeys and suffered incredible hardships to find and then to copy or gain possession of manuscripts theretofore unknown or only slightly known. Every nook and cranny of Europe and the Near East was carefully searched in the quest for "the hidden treasures." The searchers found manuscripts in the abbeys of Germany, Switzerland, and France, in the museums and monasteries of the Byzantine Empire, and in many other places. The search was conducted with such zeal and thoroughness that few manuscripts were overlooked. When the patient quest resulted in the discovery of a poem by Horace, a discourse of Cicero or a longer manuscript, transports of joy were unbounded and friends were promptly advised of the discovery. Thus when Poggio Bracciolini found the writings of Quintillian in the monastery of St. Gall in Switzerland, he wrote to his humanist friend Leonardo Bruni: "In a well-stocked library we discovered Quintillian safe and sound, though covered with dust and filthy with neglect and age. The books, far from being housed according to their worth, were lying in a foul and obscure dungeon at the foot of a tower." Bruni was overjoyed. In answering the letter he wrote:

> What a glory it is for you to have brought to light by your exertions the writings of the most distinguished authors! Posterity will not forget that manuscripts which were bewailed as lost beyond the possibility of restoration, have been recovered, thanks to you. As Camillus was called the second founder of Rome, so may you receive the title of the second author of the works you have restored to the world. Through you we now possess Quintillian entire. Before we boasted only of the half of him, and that defective and corrupt in text. O precious acquisition! O unexpected joy! . . . I beg you to send it to me at once, that I may at least set eyes on it before I die.

Although the search was at first concentrated on Latin classics, Greek classics were soon no less coveted, particularly the Greek authors mentioned by Cicero and other Roman writers. Most of the Greek manuscripts came from the Near East. Although many Greek scholars migrated to Western

Europe after the fall of Constantinople bringing manuscripts with them, the bulk of Greek manuscripts arrived in Italy during the first half of the fifteenth century. One of the largest collections of Greek manuscripts reached Italy in 1423 when Giovanni Aurispa, a Sicilian, landed at Venice with 238, including copies of almost all Greek works that were to be recovered. During the same period the humanist Filelfo brought back almost as many when he returned to Italy from Constantinople. Another humanist, Guarino of Verona, lost part of his collection in a shipwreck, but was still able to save more than two hundred manuscripts. So many manuscripts were brought to Italy and so many Greek scholars came that Filelfo was moved to say, "Greece has not fallen; it seems to have migrated to Italy." By 1460 almost every classical work known today was rediscovered and put into circulation.

The search for manuscripts gave a great impetus to the founding of private libraries. Humanists vied with one another in accumulating as many manuscripts as possible. But the collecting of manuscripts was not limited to humanists. Many who were not primarily humanists were also collectors. Among these were Ghiberti and Donatello, two of the great Renaissance sculptors. Among the wealthy merchants, industrialists, and bankers the ownership of manuscripts was a status symbol which gave the owner intellectual prestige. To achieve the distinction of owning a large library, merchant princes employed agents to purchase manuscripts for them. The Medici family is an outstanding example of those who adopted this method of obtaining manuscripts. In general, there was probably never a time when money was spent so freely for manuscripts.

Collecting the manuscripts was only the first step. Next came the task of establishing, insofar as possible, the accuracy of the text by comparing it with other manuscripts of the same work. This was followed by the making of new copies which incorporated the corrections and revisions. Most humanists made the corrections and performed the work of copying the text themselves, particularly if the text was not a long one, but men of wealth hired either humanists or merely scribes for this work. Some manuscripts were also translated from Greek into Latin or from Greek or Latin into Italian. Many copies of the classics which the humanists edited found their way into the libraries of secondary schools and universities where they were made available to all who could appreciate their value. Many of the humanists also found their way into schools and universities. At first they traveled about from city to city lecturing and teaching whenever the opportunity presented itself. As the study of the classics was added to the curriculum of more and more schools and universities a growing need for teachers was promptly filled by the humanists.

During their heyday the humanists, composing so-to-speak a distinct social caste based on learning, were held in high esteem and their services were in great demand. Honors were heaped on them and many received munificent salaries. In the universities, for example, they were so popular that they commanded higher salaries than the doctors of law and divinity. But they also served in other capacities. Some were employed as secretaries. It has been said that they were indispensable to republics, princes, and popes. Whatever the truth of the matter, large numbers were employed by the papal curia in Rome. Other humanists served various governments as ambassadors and were sent on important diplomatic missions. Humanists also held other important governmental positions. Coluccio Salutati, for example, was appointed chancellor of the signiory of Florence. His successor was the humanist Niccolo Niccoli. The services of the humanists were also in demand as public speakers. Practically all public events, including baptisms and funerals, became occasions for speeches by humanists. In addition to holding public positions the humanists wrote poetry, historical works, and treatises of various kinds. The bulk of the literature they produced is enormous.

Fifteenth-Century Humanism

There were many outstanding humanists in fifteenth-century Italy, some of whom have been mentioned in passing. Among these was Poggio Bracciolini (1380-1459) who was probably the most industrious and most successful searcher for manuscripts of his day. After achieving proficiency as a Hellenist under the tutorship of Chrysoloras, Poggio lectured on the classics in both Florence and Venice; then he went to Rome to carve out a career for himself. In Rome, where his reputation for learning had preceded him, he was appointed papal secretary, a position he held under eight successive popes. Whatever time he could spare from his official duties he devoted to the search for manuscripts. Territorially his search was not confined to Italy. When his duties took him across the Alps he missed no opportunity to ransack the monastery libraries of Switzerland, Germany, and France. Upon discovering a coveted manuscript he did not scruple to resort to bribery and trickery to gain possession of it if ordinary methods failed. Thus he was able to take back to Italy the manuscripts of many missing classics. In the meantime Poggio also translated a number of Greek classics into elegant Latin and achieved a wide reputation as a public speaker. He spoke at the funerals of so many eminent men that he earned the title of "panegyrist of the dead." Poggio was also one of the first antiquarians. As such he collected Roman sculptures, Roman coins, and Roman curios of various kinds.

Despite his many other activities, Poggio managed to spare enough time to achieve distinction as an author. While he was in Rome he prepared a guide-book based on a careful study of Roman monuments, ruins, and inscriptions in the Eternal City. This book, titled *Urbis Romae Decriptio* (A Description of the City of Rome), was one of the first of its kind. When he was finally permitted to leave Rome at the age of seventy-two, Poggio returned to Florence. He was appointed chancellor of the Florentine state, but found the duties too strenuous for his age. Hence he retired to a suburb to write the *History of Florence*, covering the period from 1350 to his day. Poggio's best known work is his *Facetiae*, a collection of gay anecdotes and humorous tales. It appears that for purposes of recreation Poggio and his friends were wont to meet on winter evenings in a room they called *bugiale* (lie factory) to regale each other with humorous tales. Underneath some of these tales there was a strong current of caustic satire which spared no class of society, including the clergy. Some of them, for example, hurl barbed shafts at monks who don the cowl for purposes of easy living and at those who through outward sanctity hope to attain the worldly honors they affected to despise. In some of the tales ceremonies of the Church are even burlesqued. Poggio who collected the tales seems to have had no deeper purpose in giving them to the public than jest and amusement. Contemporaries, who do not seem to have found them offensive, read them with great relish. They enjoyed great popularity in the rest of Western Europe as well as in Italy and were imitated by a number of writers. After printing with movable type was invented, the *Facetiae* were printed in numerous editions.

In his personal life Poggio was representative of the humanists who openly flouted Christian morality. While he was throwing stones at the moral indiscretions of the clergy, he himself was living in a glass house. His position as a papal secretary notwithstanding, he had a mistress who bore him fourteen children. When he was past fifty he abandoned the mother of his fourteen children to marry a woman of noble birth. A biographer has described Poggio as being "jealous, irascible, and always inclined to carp at others." In his many quarrels with other humanists, he did not hesitate to hurl the most scurrilous invectives at his opponents. This he did in the most impeccable Latin.

Another important figure among fifteenth-century humanists was Leon Battista Alberti, whose activities as the champion of the Italian language have already been discussed. A man of extraordinary versatility, Alberti expressed in his many activities the idea, current in his time, that man can do whatever he wills to do. In the breadth of his interests he was the prototype of Leonardo da Vinci. Besides being a humanist, Alberti was an architect, a sculptor, a painter, a poet, a musician, a mathematician, a scientist, an engineer, and the author of a number of books. He was also a noted gymnast and athlete, skilled in running, jumping, fencing, archery and horsemanship. His contemporaries hailed him as "a man of miraculous intelligence." As a boy he attended a humanist school in Padua where he learned both Latin and Greek and later studied Hebrew and Arabic. At the age of twenty he was so proficient in Latin that he wrote a comedy titled *Philodoxius* which was given to the public as the work of a classical author and was accepted as such by the learned men of the time. He also wrote Latin orations, elegies, and eclogues which posterity has not found interesting. He is remembered for his Italian rather than his Latin writings. His long treatise *On the Family* and his short treatise *On Painting* have been mentioned earlier. To these must be added his longer work *On Architecture.* His great interest was to make mundane life better and happier for all. The ascetic conception that happiness cannot be found in this life was entirely foreign to his thinking.

Italian humanism probably reached its highest level in Angelo Politian whose achievements as an Italian poet were discussed in the previous chapter. Early in his life Politian demonstrated an extraordinary talent for both Latin and Greek. Before he was thirteen he was writing Latin poetry and coining Greek epigrams, and a few years later he was distributing his Greek poems among the learned men of Florence. At eighteen he finished translating the first five books of Homer's *Iliad* into Latin verse. Lorenzo the Magnificent, impressed by young Politian's achievements, took him into his household, making him the tutor of his sons Pietro (who succeeded him briefly as ruler of Florence) and Giovanni (who later became Pope Leo X). At the age of twenty-six Politian was appointed professor of Greek and Latin in the University of Florence. This was extraordinary not only because of Politian's youth, but also because he was the first Italian to occupy the chair, the previous occupants having been Greeks. Politian taught with such enthusiasm that his fame penetrated to every corner of Europe. Students came from France, Germany, Portugal, Spain, and England to hear him expound Homer and Virgil. Frequently he had more than five hundred students in his audience. His learning and eloquence inspired students from countries north of the Alps to launch humanistic movements in their respective homelands. Among them were William Grocyn and Thomas Linacre of England and Johann Reuchlin of Germany.

During his short life Politian also made important contributions to the humanist cause in other ways. For example, he translated into Latin many Greek classics which had previously been neglected. He also wrote Latin verse characterized by grace and perfection of style. Furthermore, Politian's *Orfeo*, a lyric tragedy, was the first Italian drama written on the model of the classical Greek drama and based on a subject taken from Greek mythology. Politian was generally regarded as the foremost classical scholar of his time. Erasmus was so impressed with his knowledge that he labeled Politian "a miracle of nature." In his outlook on life Politian was, like Alberti, a secularist. In Petrarch and to a lesser extent in Boccaccio the secular and the otherworldly struggled for mastery. In Politian's mind, however, there was no such struggle; the secular reigned supreme. Scholasticism meant nothing to him and asceticism played no part in his thinking; in fact, theology was something apart from his culture. When the classics did not occupy his mind, Politian was either enjoying life or celebrating its joys in poetry and song. A literary historian summed up the basic philosophy of his poems and songs as "Pick rosebuds while you may! It is springtime now and youth!

Winter and old age are coming!" Politian did not live to see old age. He died suddenly at the age of forty, just when he was at the height of his mental powers.

The Weaknesses and Contributions of Italian Humanism

By the end of the fifteenth century Italian humanism had become decadent. Although individual humanists continued to be active, humanism as a movement had largely run its course. In Florence, which had been the principal center of humanist activities since Petrarch and Boccaccio, the termination of Medici rule deprived the humanists of the patronage they had enjoyed so long. In general, the conditions which had been favorable to the cultivation of humanism were changing. The march on Naples of King Charles VIII of France with his army opened a period of foreign invasions which caused disintegration and turmoil in Italy. The attention of the patrons of learning turned to more pressing problems. Humanism did, as stated in an earlier chapter, continue to flourish in Rome during the first quarter of the sixteenth century, but the group of humanists assembled there was scattered in various directions when the army of the Emperor Charles V of the Holy Roman Empire took Rome and sacked it in 1527.

By this time much of the work the humanists set out to do had been accomplished. For example, since almost all the manuscripts that were ever to be found had been discovered, the services of the humanists were no longer needed to search for more. Much had also been done toward improving the quality of the manuscripts by eliminating the errors which had crept into the text. In addition, many manuscripts had been translated from Greek into Latin or from both languages into Italian. Other functions which the humanists had performed were absorbed toward the end of the fifteenth century by the new art of printing with movable type. Thus printing helped to lessen the importance of the humanists by issuing large numbers of printed books which deprived the humanists of their work as copyists. The printing industry also assumed the responsibility for the dissemination of learning, a function which had previously been exercised by the humanists. Hence there was little left for the humanists to do. Individual humanists did find employment in the printing industry as compositors and editors. A few, Aldus Manutius for example, even opened their own printing establishments. Others continued to hold teaching positions in schools and universities. But humanism as such gradually disappeared.

Once the humanists were no longer indispensable their foibles and faults, which had previously been tolerated, were held up to censure and ridicule. The accusations against the humanists included inordinate pride, insincerity, excessive flattery, moral laxity, and irreligion. Some of the humanists were undoubtedly guilty of looking with some degree of contempt on those who did not share their interest. That they resorted to excessive flattery, particularly in their dealings with the patrons who supported or employed them, is also a matter of record. But the humanists were most vulnerable to attack in the region of their morals. It can be said that the moral standards of some humanists were not very high. While most humanists lived decent and honorable lives, a few openly flouted the moral laws of the Church. There were humanists, for example, who made no secret of the fact that they had mistresses by openly acknowledging their illegitimate offspring. Such conduct was overlooked in the fifteenth century, but the new piety of the sixteenth condemned it severely. Certain historians have exaggerated the opposition of the humanists to the teachings of the Church. Some humanists undoubtedly absorbed skepticism from the classical writers. In some cases they gave vent to it by scoring ecclesiastical abuses. Humanists were at times indifferent to ecclesiastical teachings, rather than openly hostile to them. They became so engrossed in the classics that they merely ignored Christian dogmas, the actual rejection of which would have been tantamount to courting martyrdom.

Humanism in itself also deteriorated in its later stages. When the early humanists looked "backward" to classical times their purpose was to move "forward" through the liberalizing influence of Greek and Roman thought. But some of the later humanists lost Petrarch's broad concept of learning. Giving themselves up to indiscriminate admiration for everything classical, they regarded inferior classics higher than the best works in the vernacular. This spirit fostered imitation rather than creation. At first emphasis was put on content as well as on style, but for some, style or form gradually became the all-important factor. The final stage saw the imposition of restrictions even on form. The classical models of composition were gradually reduced in number until only Cicero remained. Admiration for Cicero developed into a servile cult which prescribed that the vocabulary, metaphors, and general structure be taken from his works. As a result the writings of the Ciceronians became little more than dilettante exercises in composition. Fortunately the influence of the Ciceronians was limited. Among the humanists of northern Europe Erasmus poured scorn on Ciceronianism. In Italy the Florentine reformer Savonarola roundly denounced the humanist imitators as "servile beasts." His denunciation read in part:

> There are those who pretending to be poets follow in the footsteps of the Greeks and Romans, keep the same meter, invoke the same gods, use only the words used by the ancients. We are not made on a different pattern from the men of oldtime. We have received from God similar faculties so as to give to things which vary every day variable names. But the poets I am speaking of have made themselves such slaves that they can only say what has been said before them and they repeat it in exactly the same terms.

Despite its shortcomings Renaissance humanism made some important contributions to the development of modern culture. Some historians have emphasized the fact that humanism was the culture of an elite few. This is true, but it was also more. It was the major intellectual current of Italy in the fourteenth and fifteenth centuries, and its influence went far beyond those who actually studied the classics. The humanist Coluccio Salutati wrote, "The man who does not profess to feel, even if he really does not feel, a delight in the classics is looked upon as a *rara avis* (rare bird)." Actually humanism left its mark directly or indirectly on many phases of Italian thought. First, in making the wisdom of the ancients and their varied interests in secular life available the humanists contributed greatly to the broadening of the intellectual horizon and the enrichment of human life. Second, by setting up high standards of elegance the humanists ruled out the uncouth Latin of the scholastic and monastic writers. The humanist Lorenzo Valla described the situation in these words, "Present conditions are such that every true friend of literature can scarcely restrain his tears. The Latin language is now in no better plight than the city of Rome after its capture by the Goths." The high standards of style upon which the humanists insisted not only improved Latin writings greatly, but also affected the style of Italian writings when this language became the chief medium of literature in Italy.

Third, through its efforts to insure the authenticity of texts and to make certain that the words, spelling, and grammar, were correct, the humanists laid the foundations of modern textual criticism. In other words, such investigations gave rise to the critical approach. The outstanding example of this critical spirit operating on specific historical problems was the discovery by Lorenzo Valla that the so-called Donation of Constantine, a document on which the papacy had based its claim to temporal power, was a forgery. It had purportedly been issued in the fourth century by the Emperor Constantine (272-337) at the time he left Rome to take up residence at Constantinople. The gist of the document is that Constantine, since he was leaving the West, bestowed on the papacy the temporal rule over the West. In 1440 Valla proved on philological grounds that the document was drawn up in the eighth and not in the fourth century. The evidence presented by Valla was so conclusive that few attempts have been made to contradict it.

Fourth, as stated earlier, the humanists also made their influence felt in education. Through their efforts the study of the classics was introduced into most of the existing secondary schools and universities. They also founded new schools and universities whose primary purpose was the teaching of the classics. Probably the earliest university of this kind was the University of Florence which was founded in the fourteenth century. During the succeeding period other humanist universities were founded in various parts of Europe. In the established universities, particularly those that were strongholds of scholastic learning, the efforts of the humanists to add classical studies to the curriculum at first met with resistance. Gradually, however, most of the higher schools opened their doors to "the new learning." By the end of the fifteenth century the study of the classics had found a secure place in the curriculum of most Italian universities. Moreover, in most universities they became the central feature of higher education. Once they were firmly established, classical studies were not displaced until they had to give way before the advance of scientific studies in the nineteenth century.

The humanists also succeeded in adding the study of the classics to the secondary-school curriculum. In some instances this study was started during the early years of a pupil's attendance at school. Probably the most famous of the humanist schools was that founded at Mantua in 1425 by Vittorino of Feltre (1379-1446). Vittorino, generally regarded by his Italian contemporaries as one of the great teachers of his day, introduced a broad curriculum of liberal studies into his school, one that stressed the harmonious development of mind and body. He retained the old Seven Liberal Arts, but he vitalized them with human interest. After acquiring a sound knowledge of Latin and Greek the pupils were required to read widely in history and classical literature. There were also tutors to instruct them in good manners, dancing, drawing, painting, gymnastics, and martial exercises. In brief, the curriculum represented a fusion of scholastic, chivalric, and humanistic ideas. Poor boys of promise were admitted as well as the scions of wealthy families. The only distinction between the rich and the poor was that the former had to pay, while the poor were admitted free of charge. Vittorino's school quickly became so famous that pupils came from all parts of Italy and even from Germany. Many of the men who won distinction in Italian life during the succeeding decades, including Lorenzo Valla, were educated in the school at Mantua. Vittorino's influence on the education of the future was great. An English historian wrote in 1913: "There is hardly a teacher of repute even at the present day who does not consciously or unconsciously follow the methods of Vittorino." In general, the idea of the well-rounded individual which the humanists sponsored has continued to influence educational thought and practice to the present day.

Fifth, the humanists also contributed much toward the development of modern historiography. It may be said, in fact, that modern historiography had its origin in the writings of the Renaissance humanists. It was the humanists who secularized the writing of history. Previously the medieval chroniclers had looked at the past through religious spectacles. What they saw was a working-out of the divine plan of salvation; hence they ascribed all historical events to divine causes. The humanist historians, however, did not write in a religious vein. Since many of them were lawyers, businessmen, and government officials they brought to the writing of history a knowledge of practical affairs. Their approach was secular and realistic. Unfortunately their view of history was a narrow one, for it included only politics and statecraft, but in their writings they displayed a critical attitude and a sense of perspective. Above all, they regarded the past as the record of human achievement, not as the divine plan of salvation.

8

The Invention and Spread of Printing with Movable Type

The invention of printing with movable type is one of the great landmarks in the history of Western civilization. Victor Hugo, one of the major literary figures of nineteenth-century France, regarded the new technique of printing as the greatest invention of all time. Even those who feel that Victor Hugo's estimate of the importance of the invention is somewhat arbitrary will agree that it is undoubtedly the greatest mechanical invention of the Renaissance era. Its major importance lies in the fact that it greatly facilitated the spread of knowledge by providing the means for producing books by the hundreds and thousands instead of by single copies painfully written by hand. The new technique enabled authors to present their ideas to a vastly larger number of readers, particularly after the increase of literacy among the masses. It must be noted, however, that the invention of printing was not one of the basic causes of the Renaissance; it was rather a result. By the time the new technique came into wider use during the decades after the middle of the fifteenth century the intellectual and artistic developments denoted by the word Renaissance were well on their way to maturity. What it did do was to facilitate the spread of secular knowledge. In its earliest stages the new art was, it is true, used largely in the service of religion, but printers soon devoted more and more of their attention to the production of purely secular books, including the classics. Thus the printed book became a major factor in the spread of Renaissance ideas. The new art of printing also made a tremendous impact on education. Books could now be produced at a cost which made it possible for students to buy them, thus freeing the teacher from the necessity of spending so much time dictating the text.

The beginnings of the art of printing must not, however, be sought in Renaissance Europe. Printing originated in Asia, probably in China. There are indications that the art was practised as early as the beginning of the eighth century A.D., perhaps even earlier. Some historians believe that printing dates from the third century B.C. The earliest known printed book, now in the British Museum, contains the statement that it was printed in 868 A.D. The book was not, however, printed with movable type. The method employed was block printing, that is, characters and pictures were carved by hand on the face of wooden blocks and, after ink was applied, an impression was made on parchment or papyrus. This method was also used to make playing cards and paper money, and to stamp designs on cotton cloth. Between the tenth century and the fourteenth attempts were made to produce movable type. About 1040 A.D., a Chinese named Pi Sheng experimented with movable type made of baked clay or porcelain. Movable type was also made of metal, but the experiments did not produce practical results. The fact that there are several thousand different characters in the Chinese language made it necessary for the printers to have too many different pieces of type. It was much easier and less expensive to print with wooden blocks. Consequently the Chinese did not develop the use of movable type. There is no indication that knowledge of the Chinese experiments with movable type reached the West. Thus the invention of movable type in Europe in the fifteenth century was probably an independent development.

Knowledge of block printing did, however, quickly spread beyond the boundaries of China into Japan, Korea, Turkestan, and other countries, finally reaching Western Europe. Just how it reached Western Europe has not been definitely established. The traditional story has it that Marco Polo brought back a printing block on his return to Europe from the East in 1295. Some historians credit missionaries returning from the East as having introduced block printing into Western Europe. Others state that Italian merchants who traveled to China for purposes of trade brought back information about block printing. Again, others believe that knowledge of block printing may have been introduced into Europe through the use of playing cards which were of Chinese origin. Whatever the truth may be in this matter, there is evidence that block printing was practised in Western Europe in the fourteenth century. During the second half of this century playing cards printed from blocks were widely used in both Spain and Germany. Probably the most common use of block printing was for the production of religious prints. The earliest known print of this kind bears the date of 1423 and pictures St. Christopher fording a stream with the child Jesus on his shoulder. Underneath is the couplet:

> Each day that thou the likeness of St. Christopher shall see
> That day no frightful form of death shall make an end of thee.

Such sacred prints with explanatory texts underneath were turned out in large numbers, chiefly for sale or distribution to pilgrims at popular shrines. In addition to the prints bearing a likeness of St. Christopher there were those with representations of other saints, including St. George, St. Bridget, and St. Andrew. Others featured such subjects as the Annunciation, the Nativity, and the Crucifixion. Upon returning from their favorite shrines pilgrims would attach the prints to the walls of their dwellings to serve as daily reminders. Soon various series of such prints were bound into books. They were books to look at rather than to read, the text being subordinated to the picture. In other words, they were a means of teaching Bible stories and legends of the saints to the illiterate. Such block books on at least thirty-three different subjects have survived.

Neither block printing nor the copying of manuscripts by hand were adequate to the demands of the time. Block printing had many serious drawbacks. It could, for example, be used only in the printing of short books. Furthermore, it was a slow and cumbersome method. The blocks had to be carved laboriously by hand and once the carving was completed corrections could be made and errors deleted only by carving a new block. Nor could the scribes make substantial contributions toward supplying the demand for books, despite the fact that certain booksellers hired large numbers of them. The Florentine bookseller Vespasiano da Bisticci, for example, employed as many as fifty at one time. In Florence as a whole there were so many scribes or copyists that they organized a gild. There were also large numbers of scribes in other European cities, particularly in Paris. Nevertheless, the demand for books was increasing much faster than the supply.

What was needed was a method which could produce books quickly in large numbers and at a low cost. In every age in which there was an urgent need for better methods, means were devised to supply them. In this respect the Renaissance period was no exception. All the essentials for an improved method of printing were at hand. One of these was a supply of paper. Like the art of printing itself, paper seems to have originated in China. The Chinese probably had paper made of fibers and cotton cloth long before they used it for printing. There are indications that such paper was produced in China as early as the second century A.D. and perhaps earlier. The art of making such paper seems gradually to have spread westward, for near the end of the eighth century caliph Harun-al-Raschid of Arabian Nights' fame opened a papermill in Bagdad. Before long other factories were opened as far west as Egypt. In Europe paper was available long before the advent of printing and was used as a substitute for parchment in the copying of manuscripts. About the middle of the twelfth century there was a papermill at Fabriano in Italy and during the subsequent period papermaking spread to other countries of Europe. Paper was used for block printing before the invention of movable type. At Strassburg in Germany a papermill was opened in 1430, not very long before movable type was invented. Thus paper was not a problem for the inventor of a better method of printing.

Another essential was an improved ink, one which would adhere to a metal surface and could be transferred to such impressionable materials as paper and parchment. This, too, did not present great problems. The fact that early in the fifteenth century oil was being mixed with pigments for painting probably suggested an improved ink made of lampblack and boiled linseed oil. Also available were screw presses used in making cheese and wine which were easily adaptable to printing. Finally, contemporary metal workers possessed the knowledge needed for the preparation of the proper metal alloys, the skill to cut the dies, and the ability to cast the type. Centuries earlier metal founders had made individual types for affixing seals to documents or for stamping initials on them. William the Conqueror (1066-1087), for example, had wooden and metal stamps made with his monogram on them so that he could impress it on official documents. Manuscripts of the twelfth century have beautiful initials which are so uniform that they are believed to have been impressed by means of stamps or dies. Thus all was in readiness for an improved method of printing. This fact does not, however, minimize the achievement of the inventor or inventors. There were still many problems for which solutions had to be found.

Who Invented Movable Type?

There is no uncertainty about the fact that the improved method of printing was the result of the invention of movable type or separate metal types for each letter which can be used in an endless variety of combinations, but the answer to the question "Who invented it?" is still somewhat controversial. A dozen candidates have at various times been nominated for the honor. More recently, however, the list has been narrowed to two, Laurens Coster of Haarlem in Holland and Johann Gutenberg of Mainz in Germany. The principal statement in support of the claims for Coster is to be found in a history of Holland titled *Batavia* by Hadrianus Junius (Adrian Jung or Young), published in 1588. The story, as related by Junius, has it that one day in 1440 Coster decided to take a walk in the woods near Haarlem and while doing so passed the time cutting letters out of beech bark. Upon his return home he inked the letters and made impressions on paper for the amusement of his grandchildren. The experiment proved so successful that Coster decided to use the idea commercially. He cast type with lead, and later with tin, and aided by his son-in-law, printed whole pages. According to Junius, Coster found printing quite profitable, but he did not enjoy his success very long. He died a short time later and his heirs melted down the type, using the metal in the casting of wine pots.

Junius added another angle to the story when he stated that one night after Coster's death his former helper broke into the printing shop, stole all the tools Coster had left, and secretly fled to Germany. He calls the helper Johann, the implication being that he was the Johann Fust who later became Gutenberg's partner in a printing venture. Junius' story of the invention of printing has all the earmarks of a folk tale. There is not one bit of evidence in support of it from the period in which Coster lived. Junius' claims for Coster were not made until more than a century after the Hollander was supposed to have invented printing with movable type. The weakness of the evidence has caused most serious historians to dismiss the claims in Coster's behalf as unfounded. Mr. Douglas C. McMurtrie who spent much of his adult life in research on the question of the invention of movable type wrote,

"Now that all the evidence in favor of Coster has been subjected to searching scrutiny by many able scholars, it has been found to consist mostly of hearsay and rumor, with nothing conclusive to show that Coster was ever connected in any way with printing or with the invention of the art."

The man who is generally regarded as the inventor of movable type is Johann Gutenberg (*c.*1400-1468). But the evidence that has been presented in support of the claims made in his behalf is rather fragmentary. Beyond the fact that he was born in Mainz little is known about his youth and education. Nor is there any information to show how he acquired the skills in metal work which were necessary for type casting. About 1430 his family which had been involved in political squabbles was expelled from Mainz, and Johann settled in Strassburg. The years Gutenberg spent there appear to have been a period of experimentation during which he worked on various mechanical problems, including the production of a mold for the casting of type. There is definite evidence that in 1438 he entered into an agreement with a trio of men, one of whom was Andreas Dritzehn, to teach them "secret arts." When Dritzehn died before the end of that year, two of his brothers wished to take his place. Gutenberg refused to accept this suggestion, causing the two brothers to file a lawsuit against him. The records of this lawsuit are the first evidence of an activity which is believed to have been printing with movable type. In the records there are references to a press in the house of Andreas Dritzehn and of large and small books. Mention is also made of a mass of "little pieces" that were found in Dritzehn's house after his death. Some biographers believe that the little pieces were individual metal letters which were quite unfamiliar to contemporaries. As for the lawsuit, it ended in a verdict favorable to Gutenberg.

Gutenberg continued to work in Strassburg for some years in affiliation with the gild of goldsmiths, but after 1444 his name no longer appears in the records of that city. When his name does appear it is in the records of his native city of Mainz. There in 1449 or 1450 he entered into an agreement with Johann Fust "for the making of books." Fust, a wealthy goldsmith, was not motivated to enter the printing business by a love of learning, but by the prospect of monetary gain. It is generally believed that the contract was made for the printing of the famous forty-two-line Gutenberg Bible, the name deriving from the fact that there are forty-two lines of type in each column. In any case the project planned was not a minor one as the expenses involved indicate. Fust contracted to advance to Gutenberg the sum of eight hundred Rhenish gulden and to pay him an annual salary. He also agreed to pay such operating expenses as the rent for the printery and the wages of the workmen. Fust further pledged himself to provide funds for the purchase of ink, paper, and other supplies. How large a share of the profits he was to receive is not stipulated. Gutenberg's equipment was to be the security for the loan. All went well for a time, but in 1454 or 1455 the partnership foundered. The cause of the dissension, according to some historians, was that Gutenberg entered into the same kind of contract with a man named Albrecht Pfister. Biographers have conjectured that the second contract was for the printing of the thirty-six-line Bible, called the Bamberg Bible. As proof they point to the fact that Pfister continued after 1458 to print with the type made for the thirty-six-line Bible. (*See Fig. 1.*)

When Fust entered into the pact with Gutenberg, he seems to have believed that the firm would have a monopoly on the art of printing with movable type. Hence Gutenberg's new partnership with Pfister disillusioned him so completely that he brought suit to recover the sum he had advanced together with interest. Gutenberg could have prevented the lawsuit by repaying the sum Fust had invested in the printing venture; this he was unable to do. In this instance the verdict was not in Gutenberg's favor. Being hopelessly insolvent, he was compelled to turn his equipment over to Fust. There are indications that during the court proceedings Gutenberg continued to work on the forty-two-line Bible so that when the verdict was rendered the printing of this book was either completed or almost completed.

Although a number of smaller items such as a wall calendar and fragments of a Latin grammar probably antedate the printing of the two Bibles, the forty-two-line Gutenberg Bible is generally regarded as the first book to be printed with movable type. Unfortunately neither of the two Bibles contains the name of the printer or the date of printing. The claims in behalf of Gutenberg as the printer of the Bibles as well as the inventor of movable type rest on inferences supported to a degree by contemporary writings. Diligent researchers have turned up twenty-eight contemporary references to Gutenberg and his printing activities. Among those who regarded Gutenberg as the inventor of movable type was King Charles VII of France. In 1458 the French king sent Nicholas Jenson to Mainz to obtain from Gutenberg who, according to the contemporary record "had brought to light an invention for printing with metal characters," the secret of his invention. Another contemporary who believed Gutenberg to be the inventor of movable type was Guillaume Fichet, a professor at the Sorbonne who, together with a colleague, was instrumental in introducing printing into France.

During the rest of his life Gutenberg's financial troubles seem to have been chronic. Movable type brought him fame during his lifetime, but did not make him prosperous. He succeeded once more in finding a financial backer who provided him with funds to open another printing establishment. In addition to a number of smaller books Gutenberg's last printing shop printed the *Catholicon* (1460), a large folio volume of 748 pages which was used as a textbook of higher education. Besides sundry information, it contained an elaborate Latin grammar and an etymological dictionary. In the history of typography the significance of the *Catholicon* lies in the fact that the type is about one third smaller than that which Gutenberg used for the forty-two-line Bible. Thus it was possible to print sixty-six lines on a shorter page. The *Catholicon* was probably Gutenberg's last book. After its completion he printed a papal bull promulgated by Pope Pius II; then he retired as a printer. His health, undermined by ceaseless struggle and bitter disappointments, was failing. In 1465 Adolf of Nassau, the archbishop of Mainz, gave Gutenberg a kind of pension by making him an honorary member of his staff, a position which paid him a small income. Three years later, in February of 1468, Gutenberg died under mysterious circumstances and was interred in the Franciscan Church at Mainz. One writer summed up Gutenberg's life in these words, "There is no other instance in modern history, excepting perhaps Shakespeare, of a man who did so much and said so little about it."

The Spread of Printing

Although some uncertainty remains in the minds of a few historians about the invention of movable type, there is none regarding the spread of printing with movable type. Not everyone, it is true, welcomed the new technique enthusiastically. Some scholars and patrons of learning looked upon the new art as a detriment rather than a boon. Trithemius, abbot of Spanheim, deprecated with good reason the lack of a sense of beauty on the part of the printers. He also believed that paper books were not as durable as parchment manuscripts. "A work written on parchment," he wrote, "can be preserved for a thousand years, while it is probable that no volume printed on paper will last for more than two centuries." Owners of rare and costly hand-illuminated manuscripts regarded books produced by the new mechanical process as crude and ugly. Frederick Montefeltro, duke of Urbino, for instance, would not have a printed book in his library. The most determined opponents of the new technique were the scribes who earned a livelihood copying manuscripts. In a number of places they petitioned the authorities to forbid the setting-up of presses or, where they already existed, to banish them from the locality. In Paris where the copyists were a large and influential group they succeeded for a time in preventing the use of printing presses. Even after presses had been set up, the scribes harassed the printers with legal processes until Louis XI intervened. The effects of the invention of movable type were, of course, disastrous for the copyists. It is estimated that whereas there were in 1470 about six thousand men engaged in transcribing manuscripts, a few years later their kind scarcely existed.

All this did not, however, stop the spread of printing with movable type. With incredible speed the pioneer printers carried the new technique to other cities of Germany and to other European countries. Within a quarter-century after the invention of movable type, most of the important commercial and intellectual centers of Germany, Switzerland, the Netherlands, Italy, France, England, Spain, and Portugal had one or more presses. It has been calculated that by 1500 presses had been established in thirteen European countries. Since printing with movable type originated in Germany it is not surprising that German printers were instrumental in introducing the art into other European countries. Soon the presses were turning out large numbers of books in the vernacular as well as in Latin. Neither were Greek and Hebrew books in limited numbers long in making their appearance. It has been estimated that by 1500 no fewer than 30,000 distinct editions were published. Estimates of the total number of printed books and pamphlets vary from six to nine millions. Of this number only about 40,000 copies have survived. The word used by bibliographers to designate such books is incunabula. Most of the books which have survived were printed in such important commercial centers as Venice, Cologne, Nuremberg, Frankfurt, Basel, Antwerp, and Lyons rather than in smaller towns where the distribution facilities were not so good.

The range of subjects covered by the incunabula is a wide one. As already indicated, one of the principal standbys of the early printers was the Bible of which many editions were printed in both Latin and the vernacular languages. The early printers also turned out psalters, books of meditation, and religious tracts and treatises of various kinds. In addition to filling the need for religious publications, the early printers soon turned to works of a secular nature. Prominent among these was a little Latin grammar called *Donatus* after its author Aelius Donatus, a grammar which had tormented hapless schoolboys for about a thousand years. In Germany alone more than twenty editions were turned out during the early decades of printing. Another publication which had a wide circulation was the annual wall calendar, of which two editions appeared before 1460. Notable features of such calendars were the astrological predictions they offered. By consulting them one could learn which days were propitious for love and marriage, for business deals, and for such hardy adventures by the reckless as taking a bath. Other favorites were the popular medical books which prescribed nauseating remedies for a variety of illnesses. What is now called job printing began with the printing of letters of indulgence, papal bulls, religious tracts, and political broadsides.

It was not long after the invention of movable type that printers and publishers turned to the printing of classical and also of vernacular literature. At first only an occasional volume appeared, but near the turn of the century the pace of publication quickened. In addition to the printer who put out an odd volume at long intervals, specialists who devoted themselves largely to the publication of the works of classical authors appeared on the scene. Such specialists were men who possessed a considerable knowledge of the classics and cherished a deep veneration for them. Most of them were also closely associated with the humanist movement. The printing establishment of such specialists was not merely a printing workshop; it was also a kind of literary center where the classics were carefully edited and where scholars congregated to discuss humanism. Consequently fairly accurate texts of such classical works as the orations of Cicero, the odes of Horace, the verse of Virgil and the comedies of Terence were soon available to interested buyers. Before the end of the century a printed edition of the works of Aristotle could also be purchased. The printing of the classics themselves was followed by the publication of commentaries on them and of the works of contemporary humanists. From 1501 to 1520, for example, sixteen of the works of Desiderius Erasmus, the greatest of the northern humanists, were published. As for vernacular literature, the works of Dante, Petrarch, and Boccaccio were also printed soon after the invention of movable type.

The printed books seem to have been eagerly purchased by members of the clergy, humanists, students, and wealthy burghers. The last were an important factor in the spread of printing because they had both the means and the desire to buy books. Although the folk tales, romances, novels, and vernacular poetry held the greatest appeal for the bourgeoisie, those who could afford to do so often purchased treatises on theology, philosophy, mathematics, and other subjects. They did so not because they intended to read or could read the treatises, but because it had become fashionable to have a library. Whereas it had formerly been a status symbol to own manuscripts, the ownership of a considerable collection of printed books now assumed equal significance. This was true in northern Europe as well as in Italy. Consequently merchant princes and wealthy burghers acquired well-stocked libraries of printed books without any intention of ever reading them. The important thing was the prestige which such ownership conferred on them. Sebastian Brant, the German literary figure, used those who bought books for prestige and display as a butt of his satire in his *Ship of Fools*, printed in Basel in 1497. Thus he has one "fool" say, "In the Land of Fools I am in the forefront because I surround myself with books which I neither read nor comprehend."

As the first automobiles were buggies and carriages equipped with mechanical motive power, so the first metal characters were facsimiles of letters made with a pen. Only gradually did printers develop plain letters by omitting the flourishes of the scribes and by modifying them in other ways. The first type form, for which the traditional script was the model, became known as the Gothic type, not related in any way to Gothic architecture. It was an arbitrary name which the Italian humanists of the fifteenth century gave to the script after which it was modelled. During the centuries preceding the Renaissance, the rounded Roman letters had become angular and elongated, characteristics that were carried over to type when Gutenberg chose the Gothic script of missals written by German monks as the model for the type of his forty-two-line Bible. Some of the printers who followed Gutenberg varied the size of type. By and large, Gothic type was used to print sacred or religious books, the marked exception being some of the early law books which were also printed in Gothic type.

The other type form, called Roman, was based on a round form developed by humanists who despised the traditional or Gothic script. In their reaction against everything medieval certain humanists turned to what they regarded as "antique" script because they felt that the use of Gothic script in copying classical works showed a lack of respect for the great minds of antiquity. The script they regarded as antique was actually Carolingian, but it was pre-Gothic. The antique or Roman script exhibited Renaissance characteristics in that its rounded forms harmonized with the rounded classical arches of Renaissance architecture. Students of handwriting have traced the so-called Roman script to an autograph written by Petrarch when he was sixty-five. During the preceding years Petrarch had been modifying his handwriting in the direction of a plain rounded script which he appears to have assumed was the style used by the ancient Roman writers. Florentine humanists cultivated the Roman style with the result that it came into general use in transcribing the works of classical authors. The fact that humanists were among the most regular buyers of classical works probably influenced printers to adopt the Roman form of type. Near the end of the fifteenth century certain Venetian printers sought to revert to Gothic type in the printing of the classics and the works of the early Latin Fathers, but the critical spirit of the Renaissance soon compelled them to return to the use of Roman type.

The Early Period of Printing in Germany

When Fust took possession of Gutenberg's printing plant in 1455 he continued to operate it with the help of Peter Schoeffer who had been Gutenberg's principal assistant and who later married Fust's daughter. The first book the new firm printed was a *Psalter*, a choir-book of psalms and canticles with prayers and liturgical matter. This book, a folio volume of 143 pages, is probably the first book which contains the printer's name, the name of the place where it was printed, and the date of publication. It is also the first book or one of the first to be printed in more than one color. The text was printed in black, with large initial letters in blue and red. The initial letters, 288 in number, were printed with wood blocks which had been exquisitely carved. It amazes the modern reader to learn that only about twelve to twenty copies constituted the first edition, but the book was reprinted many times during the succeeding decades. Historians have referred to it as "the glory of Fust and Schoeffer's press." During the remaining years of Fust's life the firm issued a number of other books, including some editions of the classics. After Fust's death in 1466, Peter Schoeffer operated the business with considerable success until his death in 1502. A superb craftsman, he introduced a number of innovations into the printing of books. Among these were the numbering of the individual pages, the use of title pages, the use of Greek characters for Greek words, and the printing of marginal notes. One of his books, *The Garden of Health* (1485) contained four hundred woodcut illustrations of plants and animals in color. The total number of different books he issued as an independent printer was fifty-nine.

After 1455, the number of journeymen and master printers increased steadily in Mainz, but in 1462 as a result of a political upheaval many of the printers left the birthplace of printing, and other German cities took the lead in the development of printing. In Mainz, however, the printing tradition was kept alive by Johann Schoeffer, son of Peter and grandson of Johann Fust. Most of the books he printed were either classics or studies dealing with classical scholarship. The most notable of his books is a German translation of the writings of Livy (1505) with 214 woodcut illustrations which went through eight editions. The preface contains the following statement regarding the invention of movable type: "In Mainz the ingenious Johann Gutenberg invented the wonderful art of printing in the year of our Lord 1450, after which it was developed and improved by the industry of Johann Fust and Peter Schoeffer in Mainz." This statement by Johann Schoeffer is a tribute not only to his father and grandfather, but also to Gutenberg. Who was in a better position to know the facts about the invention of printing with movable type than the son of the man who had been Gutenberg's principal assistant?

Meanwhile printing presses had been established in many other German cities. The first of these was the city of Strassburg where Johann Mentelin with the help of assistants who were probably trained by Gutenberg opened a printery in 1460. His great work was a Bible about one-third less bulky than the forty-two-line Bible of Gutenberg. This was achieved by the use of smaller type and by judicious abbreviations. Mentelin was the first printer to turn out books for the laity rather than for the clergy, one of his more popular works being Wolfram von Eschenbach's *Parzival* (1477). Another important early German printing center was Nuremberg, the commercial hub of central Germany. Its leading producer of books was Anton Koberger (1445-1513) who raised printing, publishing, and bookselling to the level of big business. At the height of his activity as printer he operated twenty-four presses and employed a staff of more than one hundred men who worked as compositors, editors, proofreaders, bookbinders, and in other capacities. During his printing career he turned out 236 different books remembered for their typographical excellence and lavish woodcut illustrations. He was so determined to have the best possible illustrations that he employed the great Albrecht Dürer and other German artists to sketch them. As a publisher and bookseller he organized his business on an international scale with agents not only in the larger German cities, but also in Paris, Venice, and Rome whence came his greatest competition. His booklists are probably the first publishers' catalogues that were issued.

Koberber's best known work was the *Liber Chronicarum* (1493), better known as the *Nürnberger Chronik* or *Nuremberg Chronicle*, a history of the world from creation to 1493. It is a medieval, and not a Renaissance book, one in which superstition and intolerance stand side by side with engaging stories of saints written in a spirit of naive mystical piety. The volume also has a supplement which contains a full account of the end of the world and the Last Judgment. There is also an intimate study of the Devil, but of the rise of humanism and of the new art in Italy and Flanders there is not a word. A notable feature of the volume is that it contains more than 1800 illustrations.

Three other German cities must be mentioned in passing. The first of these is Cologne where the printers turned out 1300 titles from 1464 to the end of the century. About two-thirds of this number were theological pamphlets. The explanation is that the University of Cologne was at that time a stronghold of orthodox scholastic theology, and many theological dissertations were published in pamphlet form so that the university students could buy them. The one-sidedness of the Cologne publications and the hostility of the university teachers to humanistic learning were later held up to ridicule in the famous *Epistolae Obscurorum Virorum* (Letters of Obscure Men) which will be discussed in a later chapter. (*See page 299.*) The second noteworthy city is Basel which since it did not become a member of the Swiss Confederation until 1501 was still a part of the German domain in the fifteenth century. The most famous of the early printers of Basel was Johann Froben (1460-1527) whose books rank high for fine workmanship and careful editing. For a time the great humanist Desiderius Erasmus served him as editor and proofreader. It was Froben who printed the three works of Erasmus—*Praise of Folly*, *Adagia* (Proverbs), and *Colloquia* (Conversations)—which, excepting the Bible, are generally regarded as the first "best sellers" of the book industry. Froben also had for some years the assistance of the great painter Hans Holbein who later became the court painter of Henry VIII of England.

The most important printing center of northeastern Germany was the city of Lübeck which was at that time the head of the Hanseatic League. Lübeck was not only a thriving book mart; it was also the center from which the art of printing spread to northern and northeastern Europe. Lübeck printers, for example, printed books for both Denmark and Sweden before printing was introduced into these countries. It was also from Lübeck as a starting-point that an attempt was made to introduce the art of printing into Russia. In 1490 the Czar Ivan III sent an embassy to Lübeck to invite printers to come to Russia. One printer (Bartholomaeus Gothan) accepted the invitation and set out for Moscow, but nothing came of the venture. Later it was reported that he was murdered in Russia before he could do any printing. The new art of printing was not introduced into Russia until 1552 when, at the suggestion of Czar Ivan IV (the Terrible), King Christian III of Denmark sent a printer to Moscow to teach the Russians.

The Introduction of Printing into Italy

It was natural that Italy which was then in the full tide of the Renaissance should be the first country outside Germany to appropriate the new typography as the means for the dissemination of knowledge. The attraction of Italy was so great for German printers that they carried the black art to Italy very early. Besides being the mother of Renaissance learning, Italy was a country of prosperous cities and this made it a land of promise for the German printers. Many therefore crossed the Alps to seek their fortunes in Italy. The first two—Conrad Sweynheym and Arnold Pannartz—loaded the essentials for a printing shop on a cart in 1464 and made their way through an Alpine pass with Rome as their destination. En route they stopped to rest in the Benedictine monastery at Subiaco and were invited by the abbot to set up their press within the monastery walls. The first book they printed was a *Donatus* or Latin Grammar which was followed by an edition of Cicero's *De Oratione*. In 1467, however, they decided to move their printing equipment to Rome where over a period of five years they turned out a number of classical and religious works. Although their standard of workmanship was not high and their knowledge of Latin was poor, they did make available in printed form some classics and other works. The fact that they sold their books at the lowest possible price soon involved them in financial difficulties. When their request to the papal court for monetary aid brought no results they dissolved the firm. Their total output after their arrival in Italy was fifty-two different books. Meanwhile other printers had opened printing establishments in Rome and the number gradually increased so that there were thirty-eight by 1500. After 1475 the majority of the printing shops were operated by Italians, most of the German printers having faded out of the picture. Besides numerous theological works the printers of Rome issued eighty editions of the Latin classics before the end of the fifteenth century.

The city of Rome did not, however, have a monopoly on printing in Italy. Within a decade after the first press was set up in Italy printers were active in many parts of that country. The list of places having printing presses at the end of the fifteenth century included seventy-three Italian cities and towns. The rivalry between establishments was intense, with each one trying to surpass the others in the workmanship and elegance of the books it printed. One important progressive step the Italian printers took was the creation of Greek type and the printing of the Greek classics in the original Greek. Italy was also the birthplace of Hebrew typography. During the last quarter of the fifteenth century several shops printed books in Hebrew characters. It has been calculated that before 1500 almost five thousand different titles had been issued by Italian printers.

During the last quarter of the fifteenth century Florence and Milan were the leading printing centers of Italy, but by 1500 Venice had become the capital of the Italian printing business. After the first printers, two brothers from Germany and Nicholas Jenson who had worked in the shop of Fust and Schoeffer in Mainz, opened shops in Venice about 1469, the number of printing establishments increased rapidly. It has been estimated that there were no fewer than two hundred by the end of the century. The classics and works of the early Fathers of the Church predominated among the early books. Soon so many were turned out that the Venetian population could not absorb them, mainly because the large folio volumes were too expensive. The overproduction cast a pall on the printing business. Many presses were shut down and printers were forced into bankruptcy. Smaller and cheaper books were needed, as well as a system which would distribute the books printed in Venice to many parts of Europe. The distribution was achieved by adding books to the stock in trade of the Venetian merchants. Smaller and less expensive books were also produced, and the depression which gripped the printing industry gradually came to an end.

The printer who contributed much toward infusing new life into the book business was Aldus Manutius (1449-1515), one of the great innovators in the history of printing and publishing. Since the Italians of the Renaissance period, as exemplified by such names as Michelangelo Buonarotti and Raphael Santi, preferred to use the given name rather than the family name, Manutius was generally known as Aldus and his press became the Aldine Press. Aldus was not an ordinary printer. Early in life he had acquired a knowledge of Greek and developed a fondness for Greek literature. This was not unusual, for there were many Greeks in Venice. After the fall of Constantinople in 1453 many Greek scholars had migrated to Venice, bringing with them many Greek manuscripts. But the available manuscripts were mostly full of errors and parts of the text were also omitted. There was also a lack of good grammars and lexicons to aid in the study of Greek.

Aldus who was painfully aware that the manuscripts were faulty and the aids to the study of Greek inadequate decided at the age of forty to do something about it. As he put it himself, "I have made a vow to devote my life to the public good. God is my witness that this is my earnest desire. I leave a peaceful life preferring this which is laborious and exacting. Man was not born for pleasures unworthy of an elevated spirit, but for duties which dignify him." The great project he conceived was the publication of the Greek classics in their original language. Up to that time only four Greek classics had been printed with Greek characters. In preparation for the great task Aldus designed his own Greek type, made his own ink known as Venetian Red, and bought high-quality paper from Fabriano, a city which was renowned for the excellence of its paper. More than this, the printing establishment Aldus opened was not an ordinary one. He employed a staff of scholars to edit and collate the manuscripts before his compositors set the type, thereby setting a high standard of accuracy. His first book, published in 1494, was an improved Greek grammar and later he also published a lexicon. His magnum opus was his edition of Aristotle's works, the first volume of which appeared in 1495 and the other four volumes in the years 1497 and 1498. Among the other Greek classics he printed were works by Aristophanes, Sophocles, Herodotus, Xenophon, Euripides, Demosthenes, Plutarch, Plato, and Pindar.

The Greek classics of Aldus were so well received that he turned to other projects. One of these involved the printing of vernacular literature including Dante's *Divine Comedy* and the works of Petrarch and Politian. He also published in Latin works by the contemporary writers Erasmus and Pietro Bembo. His great project, however, was his series of Latin classics. Many of the classics had been printed, as indicated, before Aldus appeared on the scene, but the printing was often poor and the texts were full of errors which had been taken over from the manuscripts. Furthermore, the folio volumes were so large that they could be read only with the use of a desk. Aldus decided to change all this. He and his editors took pains to eliminate every possible error from a manuscript before he printed it. He then designed his own Latin type which became known in Italy as "Aldine" and in France as "Italique" whence the designation "italics." In 1502 the Venetian authorities granted Aldus the exclusive use of the type for ten years. He issued his Latin classics in a new format called octavo which measured only four by six inches and was somewhat smaller than the modern octavo. These editions were pocket-size which scholars and students could carry about with them freely. Finally, Aldus sold his classics at a very low price, a price which was about one-tenth of the price of a contemporary folio volume. Students, scholars, and others who previously had been unable to buy the expensive folio volumes could now enjoy the pleasure of owning one or more Aldines.

Beginning in 1501 the Aldine Press turned out a new volume with great regularity every two months over a period of fifteen years. The total number of editions issued by his press during the lifetime of Aldus was 126. The Aldine books became so popular in northern Europe as well as in Italy that unscrupulous printers issued counterfeit Aldines bearing the name and colophon of the Aldine Press. In Lyons alone fifty-nine spurious volumes were put on the market between 1501 and 1526 as genuine Aldines. In addition to the vexations caused by the pirating of his editions, Aldus was plagued by strikes and by the petty irritations of the daily grind. In a letter to a friend he wrote:

> I am hampered in my work by a thousand interruptions. Nearly every hour I receive a letter from some scholar, and if I undertook to reply to them all, I should be obliged to devote day and night to scribbling. Then through the day come calls from all kinds of visitors. Some desire merely to give a word of greeting, others want to know what's new, while the greater number come to my office because they happen to have nothing else to do. 'Let us look in upon Aldus,' they say to each other; then they loaf in and sit and chatter to no

purpose. Even these people with no business are not so bad as those who have a poem to offer or something in prose (usually very prosy indeed) which they wish to see printed with the name of Aldus. These interruptions are now becoming too serious for me and I must take steps to lessen them.

One of the measures he took was to post a notice on the door of his office which read, "Whoever you are Aldus earnestly entreats you to be brief in stating your business and when you have done so to take your leave promptly. In this way you can be of service as Hercules was to the weary Atlas." Worn out by the toil and vexations of his twenty years as a printer and publisher, Aldus died in 1515. After his death the Aldine Press continued to function under the management of his son Paul and later under his grandson, known as "the younger Aldus."

The Beginnings of Printing in France, England, and Spain

When King Charles VII of France dispatched Nicholas Jenson in 1458 to obtain the secret of printing from Gutenberg his action did not result in the introduction of printing into France. After learning the trade in the Fust-Schoeffer establishment, Jenson, as stated earlier, decided to open a printery in Venice. It remained for two Sorbonne professors (J. Heynlin and G. Fichet) to invite three German printers to set up presses within the confines of the Sorbonne in Paris. The purpose of the two professors in inviting the printers was to give the scholars of the Sorbonne the benefits of the new technique for multiplying books. The German printers started printing in 1470 and during the next two years turned out a score of books, mostly on theology which was the principal subject of study at the Sorbonne. In 1472, however, they left the Sorbonne and opened a shop in the Rue Saint Jacques which thenceforth became the haven of printers. In their new location they printed an edition of the Bible, then dissolved the partnership. One reason for terminating the venture was the growing competition of other printers who were opening shops along the same street. Among these early printers there were so many Germans that printers as a class were called "les Allemands" (the Germans).

Meanwhile in 1473 a German printer named Wilhelm Koenig, better known in France as Guillaume LeRoy, established the first printing press at Lyons, a great commercial city situated on some of the principal trade routes of France. The first Lyons press issued a series of miscellaneous books which included romances of chivalry, folk tales, and fables; also a number of law books for the law school at Lyons. Other printers soon opened establishments and printing flourished so greatly that near the end of the fifteenth century Lyons was for a time rivaled as a printing center only by Venice. The records show that by 1500 more than 160 printers had worked or were working there. Most of the printers of Lyons no longer cast their own type, but purchased it from a type foundry. At the end of the century nearly forty cities and towns had printing establishments; however, when the new technique ceased to be a novelty and the demand for books was satisfied, printing continued to prosper only in the more populous cities.

In the sixteenth century Paris superseded Lyons as France's most important printing center; in fact, as printing suffered a decline in both Germany and Italy before the middle of the sixteenth century, Paris assumed the lead in all of Western Europe in the production of books. Outstanding among the galaxy of printers who appeared was the Estienne family, also known by the latinized form of their name as Stephanus. The founder of the family business was Henri Estienne who from 1502 to his death in 1520 produced 120 different books. All of his books were folio volumes and most of them had a theological cast. He did, however, give some attention to mathematics.

The most distinguished member of the Estienne family was Robert (1499-1559), a scholar of outstanding achievements in the realm of humanism as well as a key figure in the history of printing. His aim as a printer was to spread classical culture by printing accurate classical texts and by selling them at very low prices. He began his career by printing a number of works on grammar and some of the works of Erasmus and of the English humanist Thomas Linacre; then he started his series of Latin classics in which he followed the example of Aldus Manutius in carefully editing the manuscripts and in adopting a small format. He also published editions of the Bible and the New Testament in Latin. Notable is his Greek New Testament in which he set a precedent by dividing the text into verses. Other printers soon followed suit and before long the division of the Bible text into verses became standard practice in the printing industry. Toward the end of his life Robert became involved in some of the religious controversies raised by the Protestant Reformation. After the death in 1547 of King Francis I who had protected him, he and a part of his family quietly moved to Geneva to escape the attacks of certain members of the Sorbonne faculty. In Geneva, Robert spent his last years printing Calvin's *Institutes*, catechisms, and other religious books. His son Robert II, who remained a Catholic, continued to operate the business in Paris.

In England the new art of printing arrived comparatively late. Not until 1477 was the first book printed on English soil. The father of English printing was William Caxton (*c.*1422-1491), translator and man of letters as well as printer. If he had not printed a single book, Caxton would still be an important figure in English literary history because of his translations from French, Dutch, and Latin and because of the prologues and epilogues he wrote for many of the books he printed. An Englishman by birth, Caxton went to the Netherlands as a young man, remaining there for about thirty years, mostly at Bruges. He was successful in business and from 1463 to 1469 served as governor of the Bruges chapter of the Merchant Adventurers, an association of English merchants. During the last years of his stay in

Bruges, Caxton translated into English parts of a French version of a popular medieval romance about the history of Troy. At the urging of friends he finished translating the work during a visit to Cologne in 1471. After observing a printing press at work in Cologne he seems to have conceived the idea of learning the mechanical details of printing for the purpose of making copies of his translation for distribution among his friends. Upon his return to Bruges he entered into a partnership with one Colard Mansion, listed in the gild records of Bruges as an illuminator of manuscripts, for the printing of books. The first book they printed was Caxton's translation which appeared in 1475 under the title *Recuyell of the Historyes of Troye*. It was the first book to be printed in the English language. The second book the Caxton-Mansion press produced was a small volume titled *The Game and Playe of Chesse*, translated from the French by Caxton.

The printing venture having proved a success, Caxton decided to return to England to open a printing establishment there. In London he rented a shop within the precincts of Westminster Abbey where he began to print. He started by printing a Letter of Indulgence and some pamphlets. His first book which was also the first volume to be printed on English soil was *Dictes or Sayings of the Philosophers* (1477), a collection of sayings from classical writers translated from the French by the Earl of Rivers. Thereafter until the time of Caxton's death in 1491 the Caxton Press turned out nearly one hundred books, most of them in English. Since monetary profit was a primary motive, Caxton printed whatever he thought had good sales' prospects. Although he printed law books, schoolbooks, service books for the clergy, and religious treatises, his personal interest lay in what might be called "popular literature," popular with the upper and middle classes. This classification included traditional tales, romances of chivalry from English, French, and Italian sources, and a number of chronicles and histories. Many of these books were translations from foreign languages and therefore new to his countrymen. Caxton himself translated into English more than a score of the books he printed. He also wrote prefaces and postscripts for some and commentaries for others. Among the more notable works he printed in English translations were Boethius' *Consolation of Philosophy*, Aesop's *Fables, Malory's Le Morte d'Arthur*, and the *History of Renard the Fox*. Caxton further printed a number of works by such early English poets as Gower and Chaucer. In addition to printing several editions of Chaucer's *Canterbury Tales*, he printed *Troilus and Cressida* and the *Parlement of Fowles*, Caxton expressed his enthusiasm for the great English poet by placing a memorial tablet over his tomb in Westminster Abbey.

Caxton's books were read and reread; then passed on to other hands until most of them literally fell apart. No copies have survived of some of them and only fragments of others. Those that have survived show that Caxton's technical standards were not as high as those of many contemporary continental printers; nevertheless, the books Caxton printed hold an important place in the history of English literature. Besides giving a wide circulation to works previously known only slightly or not at all, they helped to standardize English usage and to fix the trend of English letters in the direction of popular literature.

While the Caxton Press was turning out books other printers set up presses in London and in various other English cities and towns. The printery at Oxford, for example, printed a number of books during the last decades of the fifteenth century, but only one of them was in English. Other presses, too, centered their attention on learned works, but careful research has shown that a majority of the books printed were in the vernacular. In regard to quantity and quality of output the English printers held a low place. The total number of works printed in the fifteenth century was less than 400, whereas Venice alone printed more than 28,000. The English printers were also slow to adopt what Shakespeare called "the sweet Roman hand," retaining Gothic type for all their subjects until about 1570.

The beginnings of printing with movable type in Spain are vague and controversial. About all that can be said with certainty is that the Germans played a leading role in the introduction of printing into Spain. There are various reasons for the lack of reliable information as to where and when the first press was set up. One is that in Spain, as in Germany, the early printers did not include their names and the place and date of publication in their books. Another reason is that Spain was not unified territorially and had no one capital like London or Paris. The division of the country into regions, states, and provinces generated intense local patriotism which caused historians to claim the honor of having introduced printing into Spain for their provincial capital or part of the country. While some asserted that the first press was set up in Aragon by three German printers, others claimed the honor of having the first press for Valencia, and again others for Barcelona. The dates varied from 1468 to 1474. The book most generally accepted as the first book to be printed in Spain is a collection of hymns to the Virgin Mary, published in Valencia in 1474.

Whatever the truth in the matter of priority, once the new technique of printing had been introduced into Spain it very quickly spread to all parts of the country. By 1500 printing presses were operating in about thirty different places. A German historian who spent years in research has calculated that about 800 editions were printed in Spain during the last quarter of the fifteenth century. Two Castilian cities, Seville and Salamanca, produced respectively 140 and 130 books during this period. Of the 800 works, about 200 were religious and the rest in such secular areas as fiction, poetry, philosophy, mathematics, grammar, and the classics. In 1539 a Seville printer named Johann or Juan Cronberger introduced printing into the New World by dispatching a press to the Spanish colony of Mexico.

One of the problems of authors who wrote books after the invention of printing with movable type was the plagiarization of their works by other printers. In Venice steps were taken early to protect the interests of both the author and his printer. In this respect some of the Spanish cities did not lag far behind. In Salamanca, for example, the beginnings of modern copyright made their appearance almost as soon as the first printing press. Antonio de Nebrija, one of the great Spanish humanists and the man who is credited with the introduction of printing into Salamanca, requested and received from the authorities the exclusive right to publish certain books. Many books printed in Spain after 1510 have the words *Cum privilegio* on the title page, indicating that the authorities had accorded special rights to the author and his printer and that plagiarism was prohibited.

9

The Early Period of Renaissance Painting in Italy

The statement that art reflects the hopes and fears which agitate the mind of man, that it reveals the soul of a society, is as true of Renaissance as of medieval painting. John Addington Symonds expressed it this way: "Painters are but the hands, and the poets but the voices whereby peoples express their accumulated thoughts and permanent emotions." Because of its nature, art is a less comprehensive expression of life than literature; nevertheless, it does express life's significance in terms of the age in which it was produced. Renaissance artists expressed the changing attitude toward the secular. They mirrored in their paintings the deepening interest in earthly life and the new feeling for natural beauty. Their approach has been summed up in the word "naturalism" which, in a general way, meant a more faithful representation of appearances based on careful observation. As a result the representations became less symbolical and more natural, less mystical and more objective, less otherworldly and more secular. Even the supernatural was interpreted in terms of human experience. The gaunt, rigid, and morose figures gave way to more human, kindlier, milder figures. Vital human faces took the place of the stereotyped countenances. Much attention was also given to the expression of such human emotions as joy and grief, happiness and sorrow, hope and despair. Furthermore, the art of portraiture assumed a new importance with the result that figures became individualistic. Special care was also given to the correct representation of dress. Costumes were made authentic down to the smallest detail. The nude or partly nude human body was portrayed with special emphasis on its beauty. Gold backgrounds, which had been a feature of medieval painting, were replaced with natural scenery and scenes from contemporary life. Renaissance painters also made great advances in the technique of perspective and in the use of light and shade (chiaroscuro). In brief, more and more of man's earthly existence became the province of the painter.

The naturalistic representation with its ennoblement of the human form and of everyday life is progressive from the beginning to the culmination of Italian Renaissance painting. From Cimabue to Titian the artists widened their control over their subject matter. Little by little the portrayal of the beautiful progressed until it became an end in itself. Art was no longer primarily "a literature for unlettered laymen" or the expression of otherworldly symbolism, but a means of presenting the beauty of the external world. The fact that artists put more and more emphasis on the natural and the beautiful does not mean that they suddenly turned away from religious subjects. Renaissance painters, and also sculptors, retained many of the traditional religious themes and even added new ones. Such a new theme, for example, was the Holy Family which became very popular. In these and other representations the human and secular aspects of the life of Christ were stressed. While the depiction of scenes illustrating human experiences made for greater poignancy, the increasing emphasis put on the beautiful, the human, and the secular tended to obscure the otherworldly elements which had previously been most prominent in religious paintings. But the paintings of the Italian Renaissance were by no means all religious. During the period in which Masaccio painted his "Expulsion of Adam and Eve from the Garden of Eden," Leonardo da Vinci his "Last Supper," and Michelangelo his "Creation" and "Last Judgment," other painters painted pictures on secular themes. Such pictures were not, of course, illustrations of Christian teachings, but were painted for their own sake.

Although the secular spirit was the primary influence in turning the attention of the painters to nature and mundane life generally, classical art also played a part in changing the attitude toward the natural and the secular. Nineteenth-century historians tended to assign to classical art the major role in the secularization of Renaissance art. Actually the role of classical art was a minor one. The accomplishments of the Graeco-Roman world in painting had been almost entirely forgotten during the Middle Ages, nor did the early Renaissance painters know much about them. The little they knew came not from actual paintings, but from the writings of Pliny and Vitruvius. Some influence may have been exerted on Renaissance painters by the sculptural remains of classical art. Even this influence was in no way decisive. Hence the trend of Renaissance painting would not have been essentially different if there had been no remains of classical art.

One man was an important influence in stimulating interest in nature. He was St. Francis of Assisi (d.1226), founder of the Franciscan Order. St. Francis believed that God reveals himself in the world of nature in no less degree than in the Sacred Scriptures. To him nature was a mirror of the goodness of God. All living creatures he regarded as symbols of divine love. Consequently St. Francis cherished a deep love for all creatures. The birds of the air and the beasts of the field he hailed as fellow servants of God. He expressed his relationship to them in such phrases as "our little sisters, the larks" and "our little brothers, the lambs." St. Francis also felt the same relationship to the elements and the heavenly bodies. Thus he spoke of "our brother, the wind," "our sister, the water," "our brother, fire," and "our sister, the moon." In his "Hymn to the Sun" he wrote:

Praised by His creatures all,
  Praised by the Lord my God
By monsieur Sun, my brother, above all,
  Who by his rays lights us and lights the day,
Radiant is he with his great splendor stored,
  Thy glory, Lord, confessing.

St. Francis' extraordinary love for all created things had a magnetic effect on those with whom he came into contact. For example, Egidio, a member of the Franciscan Order, was carried away by his love of nature to such an extent that he went about kissing trees and rocks. Bonaventura, a follower of St. Francis, wrote verses in which he proclaimed all creatures, even the smallest, his brothers and sisters and called upon vineyards, trees, flowers, and stars to praise God their Creator.

The great love of nature which "the poor little man of Assisi" cherished was an expression of his religious temper, not of the new secularism. His joy was a religious joy, a joy in God the Creator and His creations, not the *joie de vivre* of the worldly circles. His love of nature was rather the culmination of the medieval attitude, expressed by such men as Bernard of Clairvaux who regarded all natural objects as "rays of the Godhead," Honorius of Autun who asserted that "every creature is the shadow of truth and life," and Hugo of St. Victor who wrote, "The whole visible world is like a book written by the fingers of God." St. Francis' philosophy influenced the attitude of his contemporaries and of posterity toward nature. It was more than accidental that the first individualized portraits of the naturalistic trend are those of St. Francis, painted by Giotto near the end of the thirteenth century in the upper Church of St. Francis at Assisi.

A number of Italian schools participated in the development of Renaissance painting, the outstanding ones being those at Florence, Siena, and Venice. It was Florence, however, which held the predominant place in painting as well as in other cultural activities. One of the marked characteristics of many Florentine painters was their versatility. Many achieved distinction in a number of fields of activity. Besides being painters some were also goldsmiths, sculptors, architects, engineers, poets, or scientists. Thus painting was only a partial expression of their genius. Among those who had other interests in addition to painting were Giotto, Verrocchio, Leonardo da Vinci, Raphael, and Michelangelo. Although the Florentine painters did not neglect color, it was in the representation of form that they made the greatest advance. It has been stated that Florentine painting was essentially an art of form. As such it was closely associated with sculpture. The aim of the progressive Florentine painters was naturalistic representation combined with psychological expression. Progress toward the ideal representation was slow, covering a period of about two centuries. For reasons of clarity this development has been divided into three smaller periods.

The First Period of Renaissance Painting in Florence

During the first period, which covered the last years of the thirteenth as well as the fourteenth century, Florentine painters continued to produce traditional representations of scenes from the Bible and the lives of the saints. In these paintings aesthetic values were still subordinated to religious considerations. A few painters who were inimical to the trend toward naturalism went so far as to make their figures deliberately loathsome and grotesque as a means of intensifying the mystical and devotional appeal. But influences were at work which could not be restrained. Those painters who were touched by the new spirit did try to make their pictures more attractive by more naturalistic depiction. They began to humanize their figures. Christ, the Madonna, and the saints became not only more lifelike, but also less stern and forbidding. Some painters also began to include in their paintings, particularly in the backgrounds, some of the beauty of nature. The characteristic form of the period was the religious mural. Practically all the painters devoted themselves to it. In addition they painted altarpieces for churches and private chapels. These altarpieces were painted on wooden panels in tempera (pigment mixed with egg, glue, or milk), for the technique of mixing the colors with oil was still unknown. These altar paintings were fixed in elaborately carved, gilded, and often jeweled frames in groups of three panels, called triptychs, with the central picture portraying Christ or the Madonna and Child, while the side panels were devoted to local patron saints.

Indications of the beginnings of a new sense of natural beauty are evident in the work of a number of painters, two of whom were Cimabue (*c.*1240-1302) of Florence and Duccio (1282-1339) of Siena. In looking for a dramatic scene to mark the beginning of the development of naturalism some art historians have chosen a story related by Vasari, historian of Renaissance painters. According to Vasari, one autumn day in the year 1285 a crowd of joyful Florentines carried Cimabue's "Madonna" in triumph from his studio to the Church of Santa Maria Novella. Nineteenth-century art historians made so much of the incident that many an art lover sought out the church expecting to find a painting beyond comparison. Great was the disappointment when they saw its dim colors and stiff figures. Some were probably inclined to repeat the statement of Nathaniel Hawthorne that the painting should be "borne out of the church in another procession and reverently burned." However, later art critics cast doubt on the veracity of Vasari's story, asserting that the Madonna was painted by Duccio. Whether it was painted by Cimabue or Duccio the painting, which is called the "Rucellai Madonna" and is now in the Uffizi Gallery, does depart in some respects from the medieval tradition. Its figures are more alive. Not only did the painter make the Christ-child more tender and childlike, he also softened the appearance of the Madonna by turning her head to one side. The importance of both Cimabue and Duccio lies not so much in the degree of progress they made in the direction of naturalism as in the fact that they were heralds of the movement. (*See Fig. 2.*)

The first painter to turn sharply in the direction of naturalism was Cimabue's pupil, Giotto di Bondone (1276-1337). Besides being a painter Giotto was also a poet, story-teller, and composer. Young Giotto became so apt at drawing and painting that he soon overshadowed his master. Dante who may have known both painters wrote in his *Divine Comedy:*

> In painting Cimabue thought that he
> Should hold the field; now Giotto has the cry,
> So that the other's fame is growing dim.
>
> (*Purgatorio, Canto XI, 94-97*)

Giotto was fundamentally a teller of sacred stories in pictorial form, but he told his stories more in terms of the secular and the natural than his predecessors had. Turning away from the stiffness and unnaturalness of the traditional Byzantine style, he imbued his figures with greater vitality, posed them in more graceful attitudes, and gave a more natural coloring to the flesh. The types of his figures and the details of their dress he took from individuals he saw about him. Giotto also displayed a greater knowledge of perspective than his predecessors had by giving his scenes more depth and relief. He achieved the impression of depth by setting his buildings diagonally and by filling the background with crowds of spectators. The greatest of his innovations was probably the expression of emotions. Whereas the human features in Cimabue's paintings were still impassive and the attitudes inscrutable, in Giotto's pictures the faces and figures express such emotions as wonder and fear, agitation and grief. In this he had no forerunner either in medieval or classical art.

Although Giotto also painted several panels, his reputation rests on his frescoes, that is, on his paintings in tempera on plastered walls. In them he demonstrated his mastery of dramatic narrative and of psychological expression. Giotto painted three groups of frescoes. The first, which depicts twenty-eight scenes from the life of St. Francis of Assisi, is in the upper Church of St. Francis at Assisi. His interpretation of the life of St. Francis is still mystical, but presented with simplicity and a degree of naturalism. The figure of St. Francis is invested with a warm humanity and a childlike humility which are infinitely more appealing than the austere representations of contemporary painters. The other two groups, one of which is in the Arena chapel at Padua and the other in two chapels of the Church of Santa Croce in Florence, portray Biblical scenes from the life of Christ and the Virgin. In one of the scenes, for example, Giotto painted grief on the faces of the disciples who bend over the Master's body. In the "Presentation of Christ in the Temple" Giotto depicted the Infant as turning from the priest to his Mother with a childlike gesture of fear. The effect of Giotto's representations on his contemporaries may be judged from the fact that less than two decades after his death Boccaccio announced that the painter had opened a new era in the history of painting. "There is nothing in nature," Boccaccio said, "that he could not have represented in such manner that it not only resembled, but seemed to be the thing itself." In the sixteenth century Vasari stated that Giotto had succeeded in restoring art "to a path that may be called the true one." More recently art historians have hailed Giotto as the father of Italian Renaissance printing. (*See Fig. 3.*)

But the statements of Boccaccio, Vasari, and later art historians must not be permitted to mislead one to expect too much in the way of naturalism from Giotto. There is no great gulf between his work and that of his predecessors. His technique and expression are in many respects still medieval. Since his representation of the human body is not based on systematic or scientific study, his figures are not naturalistic in detail. Moreover, they are dressed in garments that are as enveloping as the cowl of a monk; hence there is little indication of bodily action. The settings of his pictures are often merely symbolical. In some of his frescoes there is an obvious contrast between the naturalism of the people and a background constructed of poles, curtains, and unreal buildings, some of which defy the laws of gravity. Even the range of emotions which his figures express is a narrow one. There is no joy in Giotto's frescoes. There is not even a smile on the face of one of his figures. In his paintings life is a very solemn and serious occasion, not something to be enjoyed. It is only when they are contrasted with the works of his predecessors that his paintings reveal Giotto as a key figure in the development of naturalism in Renaissance painting.

After Giotto's death the development of naturalism came to a standstill. A few of his followers did, it is true, produce imitations that are hardly distinguishable from the works of the master. But in the paintings of a host of other painters retrogression manifested itself. These painters, who also tried to imitate Giotto, lacked the ability to measure up to his genius. Hence their figures were not vital and majestic, but lifeless and shapeless. Not until the second period, which covered most of the fifteenth century, was the progress toward natural representation resumed from the point to which Giotto had carried it.

The Second Period of Renaissance Painting in Florence

Whereas Italian Renaissance painting had still been exclusively religious during the first period, it served two masters in the second. In this period, the secular was given a place beside the religious. Supermundane ideas were still given preference and the adornment of houses of worship still remained the highest function of painting, but gradually more and more painters turned to the observation of nature and found natural beauty interesting for its own sake. The result was that an increasing emphasis was put on aesthetic values. For the first time since Christianity supplanted paganism, secular subjects, most of them taken from classical mythology, were used as themes. Such pictures were painted for those who had secular tastes. This group included rulers and princes, wealthy merchants, bankers, and industrialists, and prosperous burghers in general. During the second period Florentine painters made remarkable progress in the development of the technique of painting. A particularly noteworthy achievement was the reduction of the laws of perspective to mathematical formulae. This permitted the painters to make the backgrounds deeper and more natural. Progress was also made in expressing emotions and in making the representations of the human body more symmetrical. It was a period of experimentation and striving rather than one of full achievement. The progress made by the painters during this period opened the way for the masterpieces of the High Renaissance.

The man who may be said to have ushered in the second period in the development of Florentine Renaissance painting was Masaccio (1401-1428). In his work observation of reality plays a greater part than in the work of his predecessors. Very little is known about Masaccio the man. Beyond referring to him as the painter of certain frescoes, contemporary records throw little light on his life. Masaccio achieved his reputation as a painter during a life of less than twenty-seven years. It is interesting to speculate what he might have achieved had he lived longer. He began to paint at an early age and according to the gild records at Florence was an acknowledged master at the age of twenty. In 1426 or 1427 he left Florence for Rome and in 1428 died under circumstances so mysterious that even the place of his burial is unknown.

Masaccio's fame rests on the frescoes he painted in the Brancacci Chapel of Santa Maria del Carmine in Florence. One of the frescoes, "The Tribute Money," based on the Biblical story in the gospel of St. Matthew, shows Jesus surrounded by his disciples who are awaiting his response in various attitudes of expectation. Another fresco, "The Expulsion of Adam and Eve from the Garden of Eden" is noted for its depiction of the nude. Giotto had made no contributions to the representation of the nude, painting it only in such pictures as "The Crucifixion" in which his representation is somewhat feeble. In comparison Masaccio's "Adam and Eve" is extraordinarily natural. Masaccio put his figures in an appropriate environment, accentuated by the play of light and shade. This fresco is also a masterpiece of psychological expression. The two nude figures express the depth of despair over their expulsion. Masaccio's greatest contribution to the development of Italian painting was his treatment of perspective. Whereas Giotto's work still tends to be two-dimensional, Masaccio gave his scenes spaciousness and depth. His backgrounds reach out to the farthest distances for they were scientifically constructed with regard to perspective. (*See Fig. 4.*)

If we can accept the statement of Vasari as a fact, Masaccio's frescoes in the Brancacci Chapel served as a school of perspective, psychological expression, and draughtsmanship for painters of the succeeding period. Many of the painters, including Leonardo da Vinci, Raphael, and Michelangelo, did spend hours studying the frescoes. Some of the later art historians expressed the opinion that for sheer power of expression "The Expulsion of Adam and Eve" is unrivaled even by Michelangelo's frescoes in the Sistine Chapel. To those accustomed to the technical skill of the High Renaissance paintings Masaccio's "Adam and Eve" would probably be a disappointment. The figures are not altogether perfect. Even a cursory examination would reveal that Adam has a crooked leg. The two figures are, nevertheless, the first outstanding examples of naturalistic drawing in the representation of the nude. In comparison with the portrayals of Masaccio's predecessors and contemporaries they throb with life and portray a drama with great intensity.

The next painter who made important advances in the direction of naturalism was Alessandro Filipepi (*c.*1444-1510), better known by his nickname "Botticelli" which means "little barrel." Botticelli was the pupil of Filippo Lippi, the intimate of Lorenzo the Magnificent, and the friend of Michelangelo and Leonardo da Vinci. Of the many contemporary painters he is the only one mentioned by Leonardo da Vinci in his *Treatise on Painting*. Although Botticelli was a painter of considerable technical skill, he was not a superb anatomist. He is distinguished for his mastery in representing movement. Whether his themes are religious or secular, his figures have a vivid sense of life and motion. Many of his light and graceful figures float rhythmically through the air. His use of gauzy draperies serves to enhance the rhythmic grace of the moving limbs. At the Medici court he had the opportunity to meet the poets, humanists, and scholars who frequented it and in his discussions with them he absorbed ideas that go far to explain the secularism and classicism in his paintings. Although he was the official painter of the Medici family, he also worked for others. Together with Ghirlandaio, Perugino, and others, he worked for Pope Sixtus IV from 1481 to 1483 on frescoes in the Sistine Chapel. The frescoes this group painted were later dwarfed by the superlative splendor of Michelangelo's representations in the same chapel. Noteworthy also are the ninety drawings Botticelli made as illustrations for Dante's *Divine Comedy*. These drawings, the execution of which occupied him for many years, have been accorded high praise for their interpretation of Dante's masterpiece.

Botticelli's greatest distinction probably lies in the fact that he enlarged the sphere of art by choosing purely secular subjects from poetry and classical mythology. It was in these secular pictures that his genius found its fullest expression. The two most popular are "Primavera" (Spring) and "The Birth of Venus." Both were originally painted for the decoration of a Medici villa at Castello, but are now in the Uffizi Gallery in Florence. Both paintings claim attention for their sheer beauty as well as for the fact that they represent the flowering of the humanist spirit in painting. As works of art they rank high in the list of the most lyrical and poetical paintings produced by the Italian Renaissance. "Primavera" is the expression of joy at the coming of spring and of the gladness of all nature at that season of the year. The scene is laid in a myrtle bower surrounded by orange trees. The central figure is Venus, with Cupid above her drawing his bow at the three graces who are dressed in flowing, gauzy garments. On the right of the picture is the Goddess of Spring with garlands of flowers and at the extreme left Mercury is picking oranges. Probably more famous as well as more simple in composition is "The Birth of Venus" which shows the new-born Venus, with a sad face, standing lightly on the edge of a shell which amid a shower of roses is being blown toward the shore by two zephyrs, figures whose lightness and visible movement have been the envy of many painters. At the right a maiden waits on the shore with a richly-embroidered mantle to cover the nudity of Venus. (*See Fig. 5.*)

Few painters have suffered greater vicissitudes of fortune. Before he reached middle life Botticelli was recognized as one of the great painters of his age. But after the death of Lorenzo the Magnificent in 1492 his fortunes declined. During this time he came under the spell of Savonarola who was vigorously denouncing sin and the general secularization of life and culture. The death of the fiery reformer in 1498 cast a pall on Botticelli's last years. The secular joys he depicted in "Primavera" were now distasteful to him. His new religiosity is probably best expressed in "The Nativity," the best known work of the last period of his life. Meanwhile his work was being eclipsed by that of Leonardo, Raphael, and Michelangelo. When Botticelli died poor and neglected in 1510 it seemed as if his work had been consigned to oblivion. But in the second half of the nineteenth century John Ruskin and the English Pre-Raphaelites rediscovered the beauty of his paintings and since then his star has been shining brightly in the artistic firmament.

The degree of naturalism in the works of other painters of the period varies, but one can say of all of them that even when the subject is religious the treatment is becoming increasingly secular or naturalistic. The work of Fra Angelico (1387-1455), for example, belongs to the preceding period in its devotion to religion. His primary purpose was still the expression of the life of the soul. But his delight in such colors as heavenly blue, pink, and crimson employed side by side, his mastery of composition in space, and his love of visual beauty in landscapes and flowers as well as in human features set him apart from those who adhered to the traditional symbolism. In the work of Fra Filippo Lippi (1406-1469), imbued as he was with religious feeling, there is a strong leaning toward the secular. His winsome madonnas, painted in glowing colors, express the joy of living. They have been styled "the glorification of an earthly model." His son, Filippino Lippi (*c.*1457-1504), and also Ghirlandaio (1449-1494) and Perugino (1441-1524), painted religious subjects, but treated them in a secular manner. Verrocchio (1435-1488) painted the figures in his "Baptism of Christ" in a somewhat angular style; yet he infused vitality into them. Finally, there is Paolo Ucello (1397-1475) who painted purely secular pictures in addition to religious ones. His is the distinction of painting the first equestrian picture of the Italian Renaissance, a portrait of Sir John Hawkwood, an English adventurer who died in the military service of Florence. Ucello also painted three battle pieces for Cosimo de Medici to commemorate a victorious skirmish of the Florentines against the Sienese.

During the second period the development of naturalism also produced the specialized art of portraiture. Previously Giotto had introduced portraits of a number of his friends into his paintings. In his fresco "Il Paradiso," for example, there is a procession of Giotto's friends, among them Dante. During the second period the practice of introducing the features of contemporaries into compositions became quite common. Thus Masaccio put portraits of himself and a friend among the spectators in "The Tribute Money." Thereafter many painters began to use friends and neighbors as models in their religious as well as in their secular compositions. There were also instances of painters including a portrait of their patron in a picture. Thus Botticelli introduced into his "Adoration of the Magi" two figures which are believed to represent Lorenzo the Magnificent and Savonarola. All this constituted a step toward depriving saintly figures of their supernatural character. Many interesting self-portraits of painters were also preserved in this way. It is generally believed, for example, that the orange-robed figure with the keen eyes and determined jaw in another "Adoration" by Botticelli is a self-portrait of the painter.

Mathematical Perspective

When Giotto made his figures and backgrounds more naturalistic he did not realize that he was initiating a new trend, but the members of a group of artists of the early fifteenth century were not only conscious of the new trend in art, they also formulated principles for the guidance of painters, sculptors, and architects. The nucleus of this group consisted of the architect Brunelleschi, the sculptor Donatello, and the painter Masaccio. Vasari relates many interesting anecdotes of the warm friendship which existed between the three men. At various times other artists associated with the members of the group. The leader of this artistic circle which dominated art in Florence was Filippo Brunelleschi (1377-1446) who besides being an architect was also a painter, sculptor and goldsmith. In preparing designs for buildings Brunelleschi became interested in the problem of proportions or perspective. His interest in perspective was probably excited by the reading of the works of the Roman architect and engineer Vitruvius whose *Ten Books on Architecture* had been the authoritative treatise on architecture since they were written in the first century B.C. So that he could understand the problems involved in perspective, Brunelleschi studied geometry under

Paolo Toscanelli, the great mathematician of that age. What Brunelleschi actually studied was "measurement of proportions" which was later called perspective. According to Antonio Manetti, who wrote the first biography of Brunelleschi several decades after the latter's death, perspective is the science of "the difference of size men see, from afar or close at hand, in such objects as buildings, plains, mountains and landscapes of every kind and every place, and which assigns to figures and other things such size as corresponds to the distance from which they are observed." In other words, perspective is the proportional relationship of objects in space.

Brunelleschi pursued his studies with such diligence and perseverance that he discovered the basic laws of perspective, laws regulating not only the proportions of buildings in architecture, but also figures in painting and sculpture. These mathematical principles were soon applied to painting, sculpture, and architecture. Brunelleschi himself applied his findings to architecture and his friend Donatello carried them out in sculpture. During the course of a long lifetime Donatello consistently elaborated the principles he had learned from Brunelleschi. Masaccio, the third member of the artistic trinity, introduced the new principles into painting. Brunelleschi had not only communicated to Masaccio his discoveries, but had also taught him geometry so that he could apply the principles of perspective. Thus Brunelleschi became the founder of scientific naturalism in painting, that is, of naturalism based on accurate measurement.

Another sculptor who came under the influence of Brunelleschi was Lorenzo Ghiberti (1378-1455). The extent of his indebtedness to Brunelleschi is a matter of debate. Ghiberti, who was a careful observer of nature, wrote in his *Commentaries:* "I introduced into some of my compositions a hundred figures modelled upon different planes, so that the nearer might appear larger and the remoter smaller in proportions." His specific contribution was a mathematical formula for the proportions of the human form. This formula Ghiberti made the basis of beauty. He expressed the idea in the maxim he coined, "Only proportionality makes beauty."

The purpose of the artists in developing a mathematical basis for their art was not solely a desire to achieve verisimilitude in the representation of natural objects. The study of the structure of space fascinated them. When they discovered what they regarded as secrets of nature it gave them great satisfaction. Moreover, they believed that only through the use of mathematical or scientific principles could they surpass the art of classical Greece and Rome. In a more general way the resort to mathematical perspective was an expression of the Renaissance philosophy which saw in mathematics the best means for understanding nature and for the formulation of its ultimate truths. The importance of the laws of perspective in the development of Renaissance art is unquestionable, for it gave the artists definite scientific principles on which they could base their art. Previously a draughtsman was able to prepare a pictorial representation by imitating what he saw, by producing forms from memory or by copying them from other pictures. He needed mathematical principles which would regulate the proportions of objects and their relationship to other objects in a visual space allotted for the representation. Without such guiding principles he could not draw three-dimensional pictures with any high degree of naturalism. In general, without such guiding principles Renaissance art would not have achieved the great heights of excellence it reached. Mathematical perspective was a guarantee of both physical correctness and aesthetic perfection.

The new ideal in art which the members of the group of Florentine artists had realized in their works received its first formal expression in a treatise titled *Della Pittura* (On Painting) by Leon Battista Alberti (1404-1472), the humanist whose interests were as broad as the field of learning. As a member of a family which had played a prominent role in Florentine politics, but had been driven into exile by the opposition of the Abruzzi, Alberti spent the early years of his life outside of Florence. When Cosimo de Medici restored to the Alberti both their property and their civil rights, Leon Battista Alberti returned to Florence in 1434 and immediately joined the circle of artists which Brunelleschi led. What he heard from these artists regarding mathematical perspective intrigued him. After listening to his artist-friends, studying their works, and reading about perspective in the works of classical authors, he wrote his *Della Pittura*. As a mathematician, Alberti was well-equipped for the task. He had also tried his hand at painting and, therefore, understood the problems of the painter. As a humanist he was able to muster support from the classics for the idea of mathematical perspective.

There is little in Alberti's short treatise that was strikingly original. His role was primarily that of popularizer. In the introduction Alberti acknowledges his indebtedness to his friends by dedicating his treatise to them. He wrote in part:

> When I came back from the long exile in which the Alberti have grown old, to this our mother-city, which exceeds all others in the beauty of her monuments, I perceived that many living men, but first of all you Filippo [Brunelleschi], and our dearest friend the sculptor Donatello, and Lorenzo Ghiberti, and Luca della Robbia, and Masaccio have not less talent for genuine and noble work in these arts than any ancient artist of great fame.

But Alberti did organize the ideas he garnered from his association with the artists he named, and from reading Vitruvius and Euclid, into a formula which he applied to painting.

Alberti had a number of reasons for writing *Della Pittura*. First, he wished to acquaint contemporary painters with the basic principles of the new art. The majority of the painters were still employing the traditional methods of the preceding centuries. In his treatise Alberti hoped to state the principles of the new art so clearly that even the untrained would understand it and the experienced painters would adopt it. In this he was not wholly successful because a number of his statements are somewhat obscure. Second, Alberti hoped to improve the status of painters. At that time painters were still craftsmen and as such were members of craft gilds. Alberti sought to free them from gild restrictions which were obstacles to progress and to make them independent artists. Since the use of the new technique of art required a knowledge of geometry and general mathematics, its adoption would raise the standard of education among the painters, thereby putting them on a higher social and intellectual level.

The general idea on which Alberti based his treatise is that the painter's primary function is to portray what he sees in the visible world. This idea is repeated again and again throughout the treatise. It is the idea of a return to nature after a long period during which painters endeavored to produce representations of a supernatural world. Thus it is an expression of the changing attitude toward the world of nature and things secular. Alberti urges the painters to observe nature carefully, particularly the movements of the human body, so that their representations are accurate. The emphasis he puts on the observation of nature is such that it tends to leave the impression Alberti regarded painting as the mere imitation of nature. But the art of painting was more to him. He also stated that a knowledge of mathematics is necessary if one wishes to understand the new art. A painter needs this knowledge, first, to understand what he sees and, second, to be able to make an accurate representation of it. He was so positive in his conviction that he asserted that no painter can paint well without a knowledge of geometry. Hence he urged painters to acquire the necessary knowledge. Only the conscientious application of geometrical principals, he stated, will make it possible for man to improve on nature.

Alberti's little book, completed in 1436, was one of a small number of important treatises on art produced during the Renaissance period. Appearing as it did at a time when new trends were opposing old traditions, *Della Pittura* was an important factor in shaping the taste of the age. When it appeared, the new art had no outstanding representative in painting. In sculpture Donatello and Ghiberti were applying the new principles, and Brunelleschi was introducing them into architecture. Painting had lost its leading figure when Masaccio died in 1428 before he had firmly established the mathematical principles of perspective. Consequently it fell to *Della Pittura* to support the new trend in painting by sponsoring scientific naturalism. After Alberti had set down the principles of the new art in his treatise there was no turning back to medieval methods. Its influence made itself felt in the paintings of the subsequent period. Whereas it modified the work of some painters to a lesser degree, it became for others the authority whose prescriptions must be carried out. For example, the paintings which Fra Angelico produced after the appearance of Alberti's *Della Pittura* clearly show the influence of the treatise on him. Paolo Ucello, whose earlier paintings do not reflect any knowledge of scientific naturalism, came completely under the spell of Alberti's treatise. Writers of treatises on painting during the remainder of the Quatrocento or fifteenth century, including Piero della Francesca and Leonardo da Vinci, borrowed concepts from it. Nor was it forgotten after the invention of printing with movable type. The first printed edition appeared in Basel in 1540.

The most diligent student of mathematical perspective and one of the great mathematicians of the period was Piero della Francesca (1416-1492), a painter by profession. Piero was not a Florentine by birth, but he did launch his career as a painter in Florence. There he met Brunelleschi and Alberti and absorbed many of their ideas. His friendship with Alberti was particularly warm, lasting until the latter's death in 1472. Piero also cultivated the friendship of the sculptor Donatello, with whom he frequently discussed mathematical perspective. In addition Piero made a careful study of Masaccio's frescoes while he was in Florence. The middle years of his life Piero spent in painting frescoes and panels in various Italian cities. He was as gifted a painter as Giotto and Masaccio, but only on rare occasion did he express the full range of his ability. His paintings are largely the expression of his concept of mathematical perspective. This caused Alberti to hail them as the fulfillment of the ideas he had proclaimed in *Della Pittura.*

Many modern critics do not, however, share Alberti's high opinion of Piero's work as a painter. They regard most of his paintings as mere exercises in the application of mathematical principles. They believe that Piero's excessive concern with mathematics has rendered his paintings impersonal and emotionless. Some critics are of the opinion that Piero was so preoccupied with mathematical experiments that he forgot he was painting a picture. The last years of his life Piero spent writing treatises in which he expounded the thesis that the visible world can be reduced to mathematical order. To him perspective was the most important factor in painting. His ideas were carried out to a degree by a number of his Italian pupils. Among the painters of northern Europe Albrecht Dürer, the great German artist, was deeply influenced by Piero's ideas. On his second visit to Italy Dürer either read Piero's treatise or was in close association with someone who had read it.

The most famous artist who discussed the problem of perspective in writing was Leonardo da Vinci. His discussion may be read in his *Trattato della Pittura* (Treatise on Painting) on which he worked spasmodically for many years. Although he started the project when he was about forty and continued working on it at various times during the rest of his life, his *Treatise on Painting* is by no means a finished work. It is rather a series of statements he jotted down on various subjects related to painting. Since the treatise was not published until many years after Leonardo's death, it was not a factor in the struggle between the new art and the traditional forms. When it appeared the new art had already achieved its victory. It is interesting, however, as the statement of a great artist's ideas on the art of painting.

There is little or nothing in the treatise that is definitely new or original. It is based largely on ideas contained in the writings of Alberti, Piero della Francesca, and other fifteenth-century writers.

Leonardo regarded painting as "the science by which visible objects are recreated in a permanent form." In other words, the object of painting is to reproduce the visible world of nature. He frequently advocated the use of a mirror to see if a painting is a faithful representation of nature. "When you wish to know," he stated, "if your picture is like the object you aim to represent, hold a flat looking-glass up in such a manner that it reflects the object you have imitated and compare carefully the original with the copy." Actually Leonardo believed that it was not enough simply to copy from nature the general semblance of things. The representations must be accurate. Objects must be represented with harmonious proportionality. In other words, the relationship of objects one to another must be correct. This, Leonardo believed, can be achieved only through the application of mathematical principles. Only the use of mathematics, he asserted, makes for certainty, for "in them one does not argue if twice three makes more or less than six." "Anyone," he stated, "who discredits the certainty of mathematics is feeding on confusion." Painting and mathematics were so intimately associated in Leonardo's mind that he wrote at the beginning of his treatise, "Let no one who is not a mathematician read my treatise." Again he stated, "First of all I desire a painter to learn geometry." Even the exact representation of the human figure according to mathematical principles was not enough. A good painter must be able to express "what is transpiring in the mind of that figure." In other words, a painting is not good unless it is the outer expression of an inner mental state.

Like Alberti, Leonardo tried to raise the status of both painters and painting. Much of the treatise is devoted to this aim. He would change painting from a manual craft to an intellectual art by proving that it requires a high degree of mathematical knowledge. Leonardo also endeavored to broaden the scope of painting. Up to this time painters had restricted themselves almost entirely to producing representations of the human figure. This was for Leonardo too narrow a scope. He felt that the whole of nature must be the domain of the painter. Accordingly he counseled painters to give careful attention to representations of landscapes and other phases of nature; also to apply themselves to the painting of "clouds, rain, dust, and smoke in their different densities."

10

The High Renaissance in Italian Painting

The third period of Italian Renaissance painting, called the High Renaissance, opened near the end of the fifteenth and continued throughout most of the sixteenth century. After a development of about two hundred years Italian Renaissance painting reached its maturity during this period. It was a time in which the promises of the preceding periods were fulfilled. The great painters of the High Renaissance exhibited a more complete mastery of technique and greater skill in the use of color. The works they produced are in some respects of unsurpassed excellence. So expert were the great artists in the execution of their projects that even the most demanding critics find little to be desired in their masterpieces. Most of the subjects are still religious, but the approach and execution of the artists are definitely secular. Very often religious subjects were to the painter but the means of demonstrating his skill. In the words of John Ruskin, nineteenth-century English literary figure, "The early masters used their powers of painting to show the objects of faith, whereas the later schools used the objects of faith that they might show their powers of painting." After the Florentine painters had exhausted the possibilities of their art, the Venetian painters continued the Italian supremacy in painting for some time. Then a decline set in, and by the end of the century the leadership in painting had definitely passed to the countries north of the Alps.

Leonardo da Vinci

The first of the great figures of this period in point of time was Leonardo da Vinci (1452-1519). Although Leonardo listed painting as his profession, it was but one facet of his many-sided mind. He is the outstanding example of Renaissance versatility. In addition to being a painter he was an engineer, architect, sculptor, writer, and a musician who performed skillfully on the lute. He also conducted experiments in or read treatises on mathematics, anatomy, physiology, geology, botany, chemistry, biology, hydraulics, optics, aeronautics, physics, and mechanics. The scope of his interests is indicated by the contents of his *Notebooks*. Whereas the entries in his *Notebooks* were formerly accepted as original observations and conclusions by Leonardo, scholars now believe them to be mostly notes he jotted down while reading treatises by his contemporaries and by his predecessors. This makes the statements in his *Notebooks* less original, but does not narrow the breadth of Leonardo's interests. King Francis I of France with whom Leonardo spent the last years of his life stated, as recorded by Benvenuto Cellini, "that he did not believe any other man had come into the world who had attained so great a knowledge as Leonardo." Vasari who wrote a little more than three decades after Leonardo's death said the artist was so gifted "that however difficult any subject to which he turned his attention he presently made himself master of it."

Born in the small town of Vinci near Florence, young Leonardo displayed such skill at drawing as a boy that his father sent him to the studio of Andrea Verrocchio who was one of the leading figures in the Florentine world of art. Besides being a sculptor of the first rank in both bronze and marble, Verrocchio was also a painter, goldsmith, engineer, metal worker, musician, and mathematician of note. Thus he was well-equipped to stimulate the mind of young Leonardo. Moreover, Verrocchio's studio was the meeting place of many Florentine intellectuals and artists. It was, therefore, a sort of clearing-house of contemporary ideas, giving Leonardo the opportunity to familiarize himself with the most advanced ideas of the time. During the years Leonardo spent in Verrocchio's studio he not only became a master draughtsman but also cultivated a broad interest in science.

As a pupil of Verrocchio young Leonardo quickly demonstrated his ability as a painter. The story has come down to us that while Verrocchio was painting the "Baptism of Christ" he asked his apprentice to finish an angel in the left-hand corner of the picture. Leonardo did so well that thereafter Verrocchio had him paint more delicate and intricate details in other pictures. At about the age of twenty-one Leonardo became a master in the Gild of St. Luke and opened his own studio in Florence where he remained for the next decade. In 1478 he received a commission to paint the "Adoration of the Magi." The picture which was never finished is now in the Uffizi Gallery. This unfinished work and the "Madonna of the Rocks" were probably his crowning achievements in painting during this period. It was, however, for him a time of intense intellectual activity in science and mathematics. He also made many of his antaomical drawings which demonstrated his profound knowledge of the muscular system. (*See Fig. 6.*)

In 1482 Leonardo entered the service of Ludovico Sforza, the reigning duke of Milan, hoping to find in Milan an ampler outlet for his restless ambition. He remained at the court of Milan as a sort of general factotum for almost seventeen years. Besides serving as "Master of Revels" who directed the festivities, he wrote much of the *Treatise on Painting*, worked on a colossal equestrian statue of Francesco Sforza (the father of Ludovico), constructed large mechanical toys for the amusement of the members of the court, supervised the digging of the Martesana Canal, built a dam across the Po, rebuilt the fortifications of the city, executed designs for public buildings, improved the battering ram then in use, continued his studies in mathematics and anatomy, and carried on investigations in various phases of science. During this period he also painted the "Last Supper," a fresco in the refectory of Santa Maria della Grazia destined to become one of the most celebrated paintings of all time. When the duchy of Milan was invaded and Ludovico was overthrown by the French in 1499, Leonardo returned to Florence where, with the exception of brief intervals, he remained until 1506. His masterpiece of this period is the famed "Mona Lisa." Recalled to Milan in 1506 by the French, he alternated between Milan and Florence for some years; then spent the years 1514 to 1516 in Rome in the service of Pope Leo X. In 1516 Leonardo accepted the invitation of Francis I to come to France where he died in 1519.

For a long time there were dozens, even hundreds of pictures in circulation which bore Leonardo's name, although they had not been painted by him. Modern art critics have, however, reduced the number of authenticated paintings to a small number. The smallness of his output is ascribable to the multiplicity of his interests. His curiosity was so insatiable that it gave him no rest, ever driving him on to new investigations. He found opportunities for inquiry everywhere and in everything. At times his manifold interests crowded upon each other so closely that he did not know which one to follow or which to refuse. Consequently he would often turn feverishly from one pursuit to another without completing the project on which he was working. Hence many of the things he started were never finished. When Isabella d'Este whose portrait Leonardo was sketching about 1500 became discouraged because the artist was making so little progress, she asked one of Leonardo's assistants for an explanation. The answer she received was "His mathematical experiments have withdrawn him from the painting to such an extent that he cannot endure the sight of the brush." Bandello who wrote the interesting account of how the "Last Supper" came to be painted stated: "I have seen him even as the fancy or whim moved him, at mid-day when the sun is at the sign of the Lion, go out from the Corte Vecchia where he was composing that stupendous model of the horse and go straight to the Grazie, and having climbed up on his scaffolding, take the brush, give one or two strokes to one of his figures and then depart as quickly as he came." If he had conserved his energies for painting alone the world might have been enriched by many an additional masterpiece.

Although Leonardo turned to nature for his models, it was not simple, ordinary nature that attracted him, but nature in its subtlest revelations. He achieved the desired effect, first, through a marvelous manipulation of light and shade (chiaroscuro), which constituted one of the fundamental differences between his work and that of his Florentine contemporaries. The second great advance he made was in psychological analysis. In his paintings he portrayed, through facial expression and gestures, the spiritual essence of his subject, fixing the thoughts and emotions of men and women on canvas with a skill seldom if ever equalled. In psychological expression he demonstrated the same mastery Michelangelo did in dealing with the human figure. He already employed this technique in "The Adoration of the Magi," which he started in 1478 but never finished. In the painting the people who surround the Virgin and Child are no longer, as in the painting on the same subject by Botticelli, portraits of friends or patrons; they are the embodiments of the thoughts and feelings excited by the Christ-child.

Leonardo employed the same technique in his "Last Supper," regarded by many as his greatest painting. While all the other artists who depicted the subject, including Giotto, Ghirlandaio, Perugino, and Fra Angelico, treated it in a mystical and symbolical sense, Leonardo's treatment is dramatic. He portrays the effect upon the assembled disciples of Christ's announcement, "One of you shall betray me." The various figures reflect horror, sadness, indignation, pain, silent melancholy, rising anger, timidity, and curiosity, with each one giving outward and visible expression to his inward state through eloquent gestures. The entire composition is set up on a mathematical scale with the distance from one end of the table to the other divided into five equal lengths. While the Master occupies the center space, the four others are occupied by the disciples in groups of three. All the perspective lines of the ceiling and lateral walls converge on the figure of Christ who is the focal point of the picture.

Leonardo also applied the same principles of psychological expression in the "Mona Lisa," now in the Louvre, which is by many critics regarded as the greatest portrait of all time. Probably its most intriguing features are the delicate modeling and the subtle expression. Throughout the centuries this portrait has been the subject of much controversy. While some critics believe it to be the portrait of Mona Lisa, the wife of Francesco del Giocondo (hence it is often called La Gioconda), others contend that it is not a portrait, but an allegory. Leonardo says nothing about it in his writings. Vasari who accepted it as a genuine portrait stated that "Mona Lisa was, indeed, exceedingly beautiful." Of the painting he wrote, "In this portrait there is so pleasing an expression and a smile so sweet that while gazing at it one thinks it rather divine than human." After Leonardo's death the portrait seems to have been largely forgotten, but in the nineteenth century its praises were sung by a number of critics. Théophile Gautier, for example, in 1858 spoke of "the almost magic charm which the portrait of Mona Lisa has for even the least enthusiastic natures." Thereafter such things as the beauty of her hands were extolled, but it was the smile that became the subject of unending discussion, being variously styled as "inscrutable," "clairvoyant," and "enigmatic." One art historian went so far as to state that the smile expresses "the riddle of the eternally feminine." On the other hand, some critics stated that too much has been made of "the insoluble mystery" of the portrait, that the smile was probably evoked on the face of a rather stupid woman by the efforts of the artist to dispel her lethargy. Vasari tells us that singers and dancers were engaged "to prevent Mistress Lisa from looking bored." (*See Fig.* 7.)

Towards the end of his life Leonardo sketched his own portrait in red chalk. The features display the wear and tear of many years of storm and toil. It is the face of a lonely man. All his life Leonardo remained a bachelor and, so far as is known, never had a romance with a fair maiden. Leonardo wrote regarding the necessity of being alone, "If you are alone you belong entirely to yourself; if you are accompanied by one companion, you belong only half to yourself."

Raphael Santi

The second great painter of the High Renaissance was Raphael Santi (1483-1520). Raphael did not, like Leonardo, scatter his energies over many fields of endeavor. During much of his short life he concentrated his attention on painting. Creatively he was a man of lesser stature than Leonardo, Michelangelo, or Titian. He was remarkable for his ability to assimilate the best qualities of other painters. He drew what he regarded as the best features from various sources and combined them into a style of his own. Although he was surpassed in a number of respects by other Florentine painters, his paintings have a singular appeal. In the nineteenth century some critics questioned his high rank in the world of painting, but most continued to regard him as a master of composition. It is the composition in three-dimensional space in which he excelled.

Raphael was, above all, the painter of winsome madonnas. As his art matured, the mystical, otherworldly devoutness which had characterized his early madonnas yielded to a fuller naturalism, one far removed from the conception of the medieval painters who depicted the Virgin apart from secular associations. Raphael's madonnas are affectionate mothers with tender human feelings which are not only comprehensible, but also appeal to the universal human heart. In this respect Raphael stands head and shoulders above his fellow Renaissance painters. He has never been surpassed in the expression of maternal affection. Although the subjects of most of Raphael's pictures are religious, his approach is secular and artistic rather than otherworldly.

As the son of a painter of some reputation in the city of Urbino, young Raphael was familiar with the implements and terms of painting from early childhood. He learned the rudiments of painting from his father; then became an apprentice in the studio of Perugino at Perugia. There is a tradition that Perugino exclaimed after looking at some of the lad's sketches, "Let him be my pupil; he will soon be my master." Toward the end of the nine years the pupil remained with the master, he took such a large part in the execution of the paintings the studio turned out that it is difficult to tell whether the work was Raphael's or Perugino's. Having learned all he could from Perugino, Raphael migrated to Florence where he was deeply influenced by the dramatic style of the Florentine painters. There he had the opportunity to study the bronze gates of Ghiberti and the sculptures of Donatello as well as the paintings of Masaccio, Leonardo, and others. From the works of Masaccio and Donatello he gained greater adeptness in the depiction of the nude and from the paintings of Leonardo he learned psychological representation and the use of light and shade. It was in Florence that he adopted the serene smile which thenceforth graced the countenance of his madonnas. Among his better-known works of this period are the "Madonna of the Grand Duke," "St. George and the Dragon," and "La Belle Jardinière." The last, which is now in the Louvre, is probably the most famous of the madonnas he painted in Florence. Besides showing the Virgin as a tender human mother, it expresses Raphael's love of nature in the plants, flowers, and tufts of grass he painted in the foreground of the picture. (*See Fig. 8.*)

Raphael's style reached its maturity in Rome where he went in 1508, the year in which Michelangelo began to work on the Sistine Ceiling. The unveiling of a part of Michelangelo's masterpiece with its robust figures made a deep impression on Raphael. It is reported that soon after Raphael's death Pope Leo X said to the painter Sebastiano, "As soon as he [Raphael] had seen Michelangelo he gave up Perugino's manner and imitated his as closely as he could." In 1508 Pope Julius II commissioned Raphael to decorate a series of rooms in the papal place which have become known as the "Rooms of Raphael." His representations which include allegories of Theology, Philosophy, Poetry, and Law are the expression of all Raphael had learned of composition and perspective. Some art historians regard these frescoes as the finest expressions of Raphael's genius.

In the painting of madonnas Raphael reached his peak in the "Madonna of the Chair" and the "Sistine Madonna." The former received its name from the fact that the Virgin is seated in a chair with the Child tenderly placing his little face to hers. The scene expresses the joy and blessedness of young motherhood. The "Sistine Madonna," painted on canvas for the monks of San Sisto at Piacenza, depicts the Madonna and Child floating down from heaven on a cloud amidst myriads of cherubs. The Virgin with her large friendly eyes gives the impression of majesty and innocence. The child Jesus, bearing a remarkable resemblance to her, rests in her arms in a simple childlike attitude. St. Sixtus, from whom the picture received its name, kneels in prayer at the left. The kneeling figure on the right is St. Barbara whose face expresses love and charity. This painting which one art historian styled "the revelation of eternal motherhood" was described by Goethe in these words:

> Of mothers the primal type, of women Queen,
> By magic brush portrayed for eye to see.

Raphael is also one of the great portrait painters of the Renaissance period.

Among those who sat for him were many of the important persons of the time. One of his most famous portraits is that of the fiery Pope Julius II who despite his age appears alert and ready for action. Another well-known portait is that of his intimate friend Count Baldassare Castiglione, author of *Il Cortigiano* (The Courtier), a handbook of manners for the high-born. Probably Raphael's greatest achievement in portraiture is the group portrait of Leo X and the cardinals Giulio de Medici (afterwards Pope Clement VII) and Lodovico di Rossi. This group portrait was unique at the time Raphael painted it. In all his portraits Raphael was remorselessly realistic. He put his subjects on canvas as he saw them, without flattery or detraction.

During the years after Raphael came to Rome he reached the height of his career as a painter. By 1512 he had become so famous that he was literally overwhelmed with orders. As his interests were turning more and more to architecture and the recovery of classical remains, he began to rely on his assistants and pupils to meet the demand for his paintings. Often he made only the sketch and put the final touches to a painting. As the demands on his time increased he even permitted his assistants to make the designs. But apart from the work done by his assistants Raphael was one of the most productive painters of all time. No less than 500 paintings are ascribed to him. Every important gallery of Europe and America has at least one Raphael. Despite the fact that he was already overworked, Raphael was appointed architect of St. Peter's in 1515 and in the next year Leo X made him director of Roman antiquities. His biographers have not definitely established how large a role he played in developing the plans for the rebuilding of St. Peter's, but he did leave a written report on the Roman ruins in which he deplored the disregard of the people for them. All this work overtaxed his strength to the extent that he died suddenly in 1520 at the age of thirty-seven. The haunting smile of Leonardo's "Mona Lisa" may have a subtler fascination, the titanic figures of Michelangelo may be more impressive, and the colors of the great Titian more beautiful, but the great charm of Raphael's varied paintings has given them a wide appeal.

Michelangelo Buonarotti

The third great artist of the High Renaissance was Michelangelo Buonarotti (1475-1564). Like Leonardo, Michelangelo was a man of varied gifts. He was a sculptor, painter, architect, engineer, and poet. He did, however, devote most of his attention to painting and sculpture with the result that his achievements in both are of the first order. In his own opinion he was primarily a sculptor and he would often say jokingly that he had imbibed the love of sculpture with the milk of his nurse who was the wife of a stonecutter. The fact that his years of apprenticeship were spent in learning the art of sculpture set its mark deeply upon his future, for his paintings are all in the sculptural style. He could think only in terms of sculptured forms.

Consequently his paintings have been aptly described as "painted sculpture."

Born in the village of Caprese near Florence, young Michelangelo gave evidence of the bent of his mind by sketching with chalk or pencil on anything that was at hand, including the walls of the family home. For a time the father tried to discourage Michelangelo's interest in art, but when all his efforts proved unavailing, he apprenticed his thirteen-year-old son to the painter Ghirlandaio whose studio was at the time regarded as the best school of art in Florence. There young Michelangelo learned the technique of fresco painting which later permitted him to produce his great masterpieces. The agreement his father had made with Ghirlandaio covered a period of three years, but at the end of the first year Michelangelo left his teacher and turned to sculpture. On the recommendation of Ghirlandaio he was admitted to the academy of sculpture Lorenzo the Magnificent had opened in his gardens. There Michelangelo had the opportunity to study the classical statues Lorenzo had assembled. He was also admitted to the Medici circle where he met and conversed with such learned men as Angelo Politian and Marsilio Ficino. During this period Michelangelo also spent considerable time studying and copying the frescoes of Masaccio in the Brancacci Chapel. He further spent time dissecting cadavers in the hospital of Santo Spirito in order to acquire first-hand knowledge of the muscular structure of the human body. After the death of Lorenzo in 1492 Michelangelo accepted commissions for works of sculpture. The two great works of this period were the "Pietà" and the huge statue of David. (*See Figs. 17, 18.*)

By this time Michelangelo's fame had reached Pope Julius II who asked the artist to decorate the ceiling of the Sistine Chapel, one of chapels of the Vatican. Although Michelangelo protested "I am a sculptor. Painting is not my trade," the pope was adamant despite the fact that some members of his court thought that his choice was not a good one. The task assigned to Michelangelo was colossal. Some idea of the size of the design may be gained from the fact that 343 representations of the human form appear on the ceiling, some of them of gigantic proportions. For a time he had assistants to help him prepare the plaster and mix the colors, but his irascibility, which has been ascribed to a bad digestion, made it difficult for him to work with others and for others to work with him. The outcome was that after a time Michelangelo dismissed his assistants and thereafter worked mostly alone. For more than four years he labored unceasingly at the task. Lying on his back on a mattress placed on the scaffold, he would work for hours, sleep for a time and then start afresh. It is reported that he often did not take off his clothes for weeks at a time.

The frescoes on the Sistine ceiling represent the principal scenes of the Book of Genesis from the Creation to the Flood. There are four larger and five smaller fields: I. The division of light from darkness; II. The creation of the sun, moon, and stars; III. The creation of the waters; IV. The creation of man; V. The creation of woman; VI. The temptation and expulsion from

Eden; VII. The sacrifice of Noah; VIII. The deluge; IX. The drunkenness of Noah. The finest of the panels is that depicting the creation of Adam. It represents the instant when Adam comes to life. The sign of the Almighty's creative power is the arm extended toward Adam, a finger of which touches the creature created in His likeness. The figure of Adam, as if in answer to the divine summons, begins to stir, rising slowly to a sitting posture. The head of God with its thick white hair and beard express completely the majesty of which it is to be the image. The figure of the created Adam suggests gigantic strength with its powerful legs and superbly muscular arms. The outstanding characteristic of the ceiling as a whole is what John Ruskin called "the expression of power in visible action." Michelangelo's women are true mates for his men. Although heavy-limbed, they are, nevertheless, thoroughly feminine. When the work was unveiled to the public Michelangelo became at once the first painter as well as the first sculptor of th time, for Raphael, who was later to become his only rival, was then jus beginning his work in Rome. Many art historians of a later time sharec the opinion of contemporaries that the ceiling frescoes in the Sistine Chape are "the highest expression of sublimity in all pictorial art." Unfortunately the ravages of time have robbed the frescoes of much of their brightness.

After the completion of the Sistine ceiling Michelangelo turned again t sculpture which occupied all of his middle life. But in 1535 he became painter once more. In that year Pope Paul III asked him to decorate th north wall above the altar in the Sistine Chapel. The choice of subject seem to have been left to the artist. At the height of his vigor he had chosen t depict the beginning of things; now at the age of sixty his thoughts turne to the Last Judgment. The fresco on which he worked more than seve years is 54 feet, 6 inches high, and 43 feet, 8 inches wide. The central figur is a Herculean Christ, a man of mighty muscular power, young and handsome. Surrounded by prophets, apostles, saints, and martyrs, Christ as th stern Judge has his right hand raised as if he is about to pronounce fina judgment. Underneath, the archangels are blowing their trumpets to awake the dead who are rising from their graves and are moving upward to appea before the Judge. Opposite the ascending dead are the damned, staggerin backward and plunging downward in the writhings of despair to the boa that will carry them over the River Styx into the Inferno. There appears t be no desire in the mass of despairing creatures to help each other, as there i among the blessed. Below stands the figure of Charon emptying his crowde boat, beating the poor wretches down into the fiery lake. Vasari states tha Michelangelo took the idea of Charon from his beloved Dante who describe the boatman of the River Styx:

> Charon, the demon, with the eyes of flame,
> Calls the sad troops, and having gathered all,
> Smites with raised oar the wretch that dares delay.
>
> *Inferno, Canto III*

"The Last Judgment" is a strange mixture of Christianity and paganism, of realism and idealism. The picture as such is awe-inspiring, but not pleasing. Depicting as it does the Last Judgment, it is a terrifying scene, one that might be regarded as the embodiment of Savonarola's fiery threats of retribution. It is a pictorial representation of Thomas of Celano's poem, "The Day of Wrath," which was quoted in an earlier chapter. The one note of tenderness in the picture is the figure of the Virgin Mary whose heart appears torn by the horrors of the scene and whose face is averted as if in pity.

When "The Last Judgment" was unveiled in 1541 the public gazed at it in rapt admiration. It was also heartily acclaimed by contemporary artists. To them the huge writhing and twisting figures appeared to contain the whole grammar of the representations of the human body. The fame of the fresco spread rapidly, attracting people from all parts of Italy, and even from across the Alps, to see it. But the acclamations of contemporaries notwithstanding, "The Last Judgment" does not measure up to the Sistine ceiling in a number of respects. First, it lacks the unity of composition which characterizes the earlier work. Second, it also lacks the freshness of inspiration which the earlier work reflects. Whereas the figures on the Sistine ceiling are spirited and graceful in their attitudes, those in "The Last Judgment" are cumbersome, even swollen and monstrous. In his efforts to achieve the utmost force Michelangelo increased the bulk of his figures beyond the possibility of nature, thereby depriving them of their beauty. In creating this fantastic display Michelangelo entered the path leading to the Baroque.

The one thing that caused some disapproval in the society of Rome, and particularly at the Papal Court, was the nudity of the figures in "The Last Judgment." Among those who disapproved, even before the painting was finished, was Biagio da Cesina, master of ceremonies at the Vatican Court. He voiced the opinion that the painting was "more suitable to adorn a tavern than a consecrated chapel." When this remark reached the ears of Michelangelo he decided to wreak vengeance on the critic by putting his portrait on one of the figures in the nether regions. Biagio at once proceeded to demand from the pope that the likeness be removed, but Paul III reportedly answered, "You know I have received power in heaven and earth, but I have no authority in hell. So I fear you will be obliged to stay there." Something was, however, done about the nudity of the figures. Daniele da Volterra was employed to drape some of them. The gauzy drapery detracted from the grandeur of the painting. Volterra's reward was the title "Il Braghettone," meaning "maker of breeches." (*See Fig. 9.*)

In a general survey of Michelangelo's work as a painter one thing stands out prominently and that is his use of the human figure, draped or undraped, to express beauty and nobility. The language of the human form was, in fact, the language that served all his needs. This is the key to Michelangelo's art. No artist since the Greeks had relied so exclusively on the human figure as his means of expression. Landscape Michelangelo reduced to rudimentary indications. Even drapery was used as an aid in revealing the structure and movement of the human body. Michelangelo seemed bent on proving that every feature, every limb, every attitude of the human body is full of significance. He himself expressed his philosophy in the closing lines of a sonnet to Vittoria Colonna:

> Nor hath God deigned to show himself elsewhere
> More clearly than in human forms sublime,
> Which since they image him compel my love.

Michelangelo's figures, as previously indicated, are not the ordinary human figures. They are representations of primeval power. Even when they are out of proportion they are still full of meaning.

Venetian Painting

Venetian painting had a specific character of its own. Whereas Florentine painting was essentially the art of form, the use of color was the peculiar province of the Venetians. In the paintings of Michelangelo and Raphael the representation of the human form reached heights which could hardly be surpassed. The one road to progress which was still open was the use of color. Form was also important to the Venetian painters, but the use of color was their primary interest. In it they achieved an unrivaled splendor. Hence Venetian painting as a whole is the fullest expression of the Renaissance. The coloring is rich, variegated, and harmonious. It delights the eye and uplifts the mind. In the words of the art historian Bernard Berenson, it "acts like music upon the moods, stimulating thought and memory in much the same way as a work by a great composer." A further difference between Florentine and Venetian painters is that while the former were intellectual or psychological and at times even mystical in their attitude, the Venetian painters were frankly materialistic and sensuous. This is why the Venetian painters have been called "the interpreters of worldly success" and "the poets of sensual beauty."

During the early phases of the Renaissance the Venetians, as previously stated, were too engrossed in commercial and maritime affairs to give much attention to culture. While Giotto, Masaccio, and other Florentines were producing great masterpieces of the Renaissance, there was little activity in Venice in the field of painting. Venetian artists had continued to follow the Byzantine manner. Not until after the middle of the fifteenth century did the first outstanding painters appear on the scene. Venice was then at the height of its prosperity and commercial greatness. Wealthy Venetians were giving themselves over to inordinate indulgence and lavish display as if they were determined to extract the last drop of pleasure from life. The oligarchy which ruled Venice sought to keep the masses happy with glittering pageantry and colorful ceremonial. All this the Venetian painters recorded with their brushes. They are the chroniclers of much that is interesting and colorful in Venetian life.

Although the Venetian painters escaped the compulsions which caused the Florentines to produce mostly representations of Biblical scenes, the Venetians, too, painted many religious subjects. Religious pomp and ceremony were a part of the colorful pageantry of Venetian life. Religious as well as civic holidays were occasions for magnificent ceremonials and gorgeous processions. In their paintings the Venetian artists depicted this religious pageantry in the most pleasing and brilliant manner. Gentile Bellini, for example, painted large canvases depicting the "Procession of Corpus Domini," "Miracles of the True Cross," and "The Preaching of St. Mark." But religion was often little more than a subject on which the painter could exercise his talents. The Venetian painters believed that painting was above all a decorative art, not a means for teaching Christian doctrines. Religious subjects were treated in a serious, but nevertheless a sensuous manner. Madonnas and saints are less the expression of spiritual than of mundane ideals. The models were beautiful women and handsome young men filled with the joy of life. Consequently the Venetian religious paintings charm the sight more than they touch the heart. Their representations were, by and large, something to add to the beauty and enjoyment of life.

The founders of the Venetian school were the brothers Bellini, Gentile (1429-1507) and Giovanni (1430-1516). The technique of the two brothers, who worked independently, constitutes a definite turning-point in the history of Venetian painting. In his paintings Gentile recorded much of the Venetian pageantry of his day, but it was Giovanni who had the wider influence. In his works the Venetian sense of beauty first manifested itself. In his representations of the human body he turned away the harshness and severity of form which characterized the paintings of his predecessors. Furthermore, in his works the depiction of landscapes and atmosphere reached a higher degree of excellence than in any previous Venetian paintings. Giovanni Bellini was also the first of the masters of glowing and brilliant colors which became the distinguishing feature of Venetian painting. It was he who replaced tempera with oil colors. Although he was no longer a young man when the technique of oil painting was brought to Venice, he not only mastered it himself, but also taught it to many pupils. Painters from many parts of Europe came to visit him and to study his paintings. Among these was Albrecht Dürer, the eminent German master, who reported in 1506, "He is very old, but still the best in painting." It was Giovanni Bellini who taught both Giorgione and Titian, the two great figures of the Venetian school. Giovanni's most novel picture is probably "The Feast of the Gods" (now in the National Gallery of Art, Washington, D.C.), an unusually large painting, the subject of which is mythological. Titian later modernized it with a landscape. (*See Fig. 10.*)

The next eminent Venetian painter was Giorgio Barbarelli (1477-1510), better known to posterity as "Giorgione" or Big George. His life, which was short, is enveloped in obscurity. Furthermore, only a few of his works, probably a score, have survived. Nevertheless, Giorgione left his mark in the history of painting. In his works the Renaissance spirit probably achieved its fullest expression in painting. In no other painter was the consciousness of his mission so definite. Giorgione had a decidedly secular cast of mind. Probably no other Renaissance painter cut himself adrift from medieval restraints so completely. His pagan soul reveled in the beauty of nature. He portrayed beauty as he saw it, opening the eyes of his contemporaries to the charms of nature in her most luscious moods. As Vasari put it, Giorgione painted "all that was fairest in the world around him." He combined color and pattern in works of sheer loveliness. The rich glowing colors he used moved lovers of art to label his paintings "symphonies in color." His pictures are sensuous, but not gross. Most of them are filled with poetry, romance, and joy.

"The Giorgionesque fire" was the phrase coined to express the new life he infused into his paintings. His landscapes, based on a careful observation of nature, are as true as they are luxuriant and verdant. Giorgione was one of the first painters to turn to what is now called genre painting. He saw a subtle charm in such little morsels of life as children at play and small groups in conversation. It was, above all, the beauty of the feminine face and form that appealed to him. In the opinion of some art critics he gave to the female nude a freshness and delicacy unsurpassed by any other painter. In "The Tempest" he presented the female form in its voluptuous nudity, while the men are clothed in richly-colored garments. His masterpiece, "The Sleeping Venus" (now in Dresden) presents a beautiful nude with a form of ideal perfection. "To me," Lord Byron wrote, "there are none like the Venetians, especially Giorgione." Giorgione was no less appreciated by his contemporaries. His works were in great demand by the rich Venetians who wished to adorn their homes with cheerful and pleasurable pictures. Unfortunately the plague ended his career at thirty-four. Had he lived longer his influence on the development of Renaissance painting would undoubtedly have been greater. One painter on whose style he did exercise considerable influence was Titian. (*See Fig. 11.*)

Titian

The painting of the Italian Renaissance culminated in the work of Tiziano Vecelli (*c.*1477-1576), better known as Titian. No other painter of the Renaissance united in himself so many qualities of artistic merit. There were painters who excelled in certain phases of painting, but Titian was unsurpassed in his all-around mastery. He combined perspective, drawing, composition, and the use of color with thought and feeling into a great and glowing whole. There was nothing in the craftsmanship of painting that he did not accomplish with ease. Moreover, his was an achievement sustained during a lifetime which approached a century in its length. In his perfect control of the sources of his art, in his universality of subject, and in his masterful serenity he reminds us of that great Renaissance literary figure, William Shakespeare. Titian's mind, like Giorgione's, had a definitely secular bent. His paintings mirror the contemporary Venetian society whose spirit was secular and materialistic. The joy of living and the love of beauty for its own sake never deserted him during his long life. The Venuses he painted during the last years of his life have all the voluptuous charm that characterized those of his early years. Together with the Bellinis and Giorgione, Titian was a pioneer in the painting of landscapes. Many of his paintings have a background of field, wood, hill, and dale. Throughout his long life he painted almost exclusively in oil. The little he attempted in fresco has perished.

Our knowledge of Titian's personal life is so scant that few questions regarding it can be answered with certainty. Even the date of his birth is controversial. Although 1477 is the traditional date, revisionists claim that he was born some time during the years 1488 to 1490. The exquisite landscapes he painted in later life have been ascribed to the fact that he spent his boyhood days in the midst of the beautiful scenery of the Venetian Alps which made an enduring impression on his mind. As a lad Titian showed such interest in painting that his family sent him to Venice to study painting under the brothers Bellini. He was first a pupil of Gentile Bellini, but soon became an apprentice in the studio of Giovanni. During these years he acquired a love of color and the ability to achieve the best effects with it. In this respect not only Giovanni Bellini, but also Giorgione was an important influence. For a time Titian worked with Giorgione. Together they decorated the Fondaco dei Tedeschi (warehouse of the German merchants) in Venice. But Titian saw no future for himself in Venice. In addition to the fact that Giovanni Bellini was the official painter of the Venetian government and, therefore, had a virtual monopoly of all government commissions, Giorgione was popular with many of the wealthy Venetians. Hence Titian decided to make Padua the scene of his activities.

Titian did not, however, remain in Padua long. The sudden death of Giorgione in 1510 caused him to return to Venice. One of the first tasks he performed was to complete the unfinished paintings Giorgione had left. For some time after Giorgione's death Titian continued to paint in the manner of his former colleague. It was only at a later time that he developed a distinctive style of his own. The great turning-point in Titian's career came in 1516 when he was appointed the official painter of the republic of Venice as the successor of Giovanni Bellini who had passed away in that year. One of his first commissions was to paint "The Assumption of the Virgin" for the Church of the Frari (Franciscans). Unveiled in 1518 this painting laid the foundation for Titian's fame, leaving him without a rival in Venice. He now settled down to his painting with a zeal which his fellow Venetians rewarded with a liberal patronage. The volume of his output was such that his paintings soon appeared in considerable numbers in the halls of state and the homes of the wealthy, in churches and in religious institutions. His works were so popular that in 1530 he was summoned to Bologna to paint the portraits of Emperor Charles V and members of his staff who were in Italy at that time. He was not only paid liberally for his work, but in 1533 was also created Count Palatine of the Holy Roman Empire and Knight of the Golden Spur, honors that were truly extraordinary for a painter.

Titian also left Venice temporarily on other occasions. For some years the Papal Court had been trying without success to induce Titian to come to Rome. Finally in 1545 he capitulated and was received with great distinction by Pope Paul III. While he was at the Vatican Titian painted the famous group picture of the pope, Cardinal Alessandro, and Duke Ottavio Farnese. In the winter of 1548 Titian undertook the arduous journey across the Alps to join Charles V and his court at Augsburg. This time he painted not only the well-known portrait of Charles V on the field at Mühlberg, but also portraits of most of the great lords and ministers surrounding the emperor. In addition, he painted the portrait of Philip II which, when sent to England, proved so effective in winning the hand of Mary Tudor. Upon his return to Venice Titian continued to paint as before. Art historians have set the year 1555 as the culmination of his greatness as a painter, although he produced many important works after this time. "The Martyrdom of St. Lawrence," one of the largest and best-known of his works, was probably painted in 1557. During his last years, possibly because of failing eyesight, he worked with masses of color often applied with his fingers. Thus he continued working until he fell a victim to the plague which ravaged Venice in 1576. He was entombed in the Church of the Frari for whom he had painted "The Pesaro Madonna" as well as "The Assumption of the Virgin," two of the most famous of his religious paintings.

Titian seems to have obtained subjects for his mythological paintings from stories and myths of classical antiquity told him by members of the group which frequently gathered in his studio. In some instances the meaning of his paintings is somewhat obscure. An outstanding example of this ambiguity is his famous painting which since about 1700 has been called "Sacred and Profane." An older description referred to it as "Beauty Adorned and Unadorned" and it was also called "The Maidens at a Fountain." It depicts two maidens, one completely dressed and the other largely nude, seated on the rim of a marble fountain. Between them a cupid plays with his hands in the water. The background is a peaceful landscape under a soft blue sky, with a village in the distance. This charming scene has been variously interpreted, but no one has explained to which myth it refers. More apparent are the meanings of such other mythological pictures as "Venus

Equipping Cupid," "The Feast of Venus," and "Bacchus and Ariadne." (*See Fig. 12.*)

Although Titian painted many religious pictures, they do not have the deep religious feeling of Fra Angelico or the impressive spirituality of Christ in Leonardo's "Last Supper." Titian's aim was aesthetic rather than religious. His paramount consideration was sheer earthly beauty. He painted into his religious pictures the life about him and in most instances chose the most favorable elements he saw in nature. His madonnas are typical mothers who have but a slight touch of the saintly. Most of his saints are substantial, comfortable-looking citizens with hardly a suggestion of self-denial or otherworldliness.

A branch of painting in which Titian achieved outstanding excellence was portraiture. He is one of the great portrait painters of all time. His portraits of men are superior to his portraits of women. In painting women he often centered his attention on the hair and the raiment, ignoring psychological factors. The feminine mind was to him something inscrutable. But his male portraits with their dignity and rich coloring are the equal of those of any master and, in the opinion of some critics are unrivaled. Originality and vitality are the twin characteristics of his portraits. Whereas Leonardo idealized his subjects to the extent that his depictions ceased to be true portraits, Titian stayed within the limits of reality even though he did choose the better qualities of his subjects. Posterity is deeply indebted to him for preserving the portraits of so many important personages of the sixteenth century. Titian's patrons included emperors, kings, popes, doges, cardinals, bishops, noblemen and poets. (*See Fig. 26.*)

11

Italian Renaissance Sculpture and Architecture

The influence of classical art was greater in sculpture than in painting. A number of Italian Renaissance sculptors, including Michelangelo, made a careful study of classical remains, paying special attention to the lines and poses of the human body. One can say, therefore, that the study of classical remains probably speeded the development of Renaissance sculpture. It did not, however, radically change the style of the new sculpture. In other words, Renaissance sculpture was not an imitation of classical art. It was an original art, inspired and sustained by the tides of contemporary life. The sculptor, like the painter and the writer, was the medium through which the age spoke. Michelangelo, for example, expressed in his sculpture some phases of the thought and feeling of his time. His work reflects not only the Renaissance interest in anatomy and the beauty of the human figure, but also the spiritual anxiety and restlessness of the period. If there had been no remains of classical sculpture the character of Renaissance sculpture would have been much the same. Such characteristics of Renaissance sculpture as psychological interpretation and deep perspective are definitely unclassical. How little Renaissance sculpture was conditioned by ancient models is shown by the fact that Florence which took the lead in the development of sculpture had in the fifteenth century very few remains of classical art. On the other hand, Rome where there were many ancient monuments played but a small part in the development of Renaissance sculpture. The examples of classical sculpture that were available during the fifteenth century were Roman remains from the decadent third or fourth centuries A.D. Such great works of Greek art as "Apollo Belvedere," "Ariadne," and the Laocoön group were not disinterred until the sixteenth century. Thus whatever inspiration Renaissance sculptors derived from classical models came from the muddy stream of Roman rather than from the purer springs of Greek art.

The history of sculpture in the period from the rise of Christianity to the Renaissance is checkered. Early Christian sentiment did not favor sculpture because it was, as stated earlier, a form in which paganism expressed itself. Some zealots felt that they were doing God's will in destroying statues whose sensuous beauty might induce half-hearted converts to revert to paganism. However, when Christianity became the official religion of the Roman Empire after the conversion of the Emperor Constantine (*d.*337), sculpture became a means for expressing the highest spiritual conceptions of Christianity.

But sculpture was not yet through its troublous times. Having reached a state of bloom, it was withered in the eighth century by the searing blast of the so-called Iconoclastic Controversy. This controversy over the use of religious images began in the Eastern or Byzantine Empire and was inspired in part by the fact that the Koran of the Moslems outlawed all religious images. In 754 a Church Council, meeting at Constantinople, decreed that that the worship of images is not only a corruption of Christianity, but also a revival of paganism. In the Eastern Empire the decision was implemented at once by the destruction of a great number of statues. In the West the decision of the Council of Constantinople was never accepted officially, but it did generate much controversy which limited the production of sculptures during the succeeding period.

A new age of sculpture was ushered in as a result of the construction of Gothic churches and cathedrals in the twelfth century. Sculptured figures either in the form of statues or in reliefs appeared in large numbers in the new churches. Although the ideas represented by the sculptures were high and noble, the appearance of the statues had little aesthetic value. Many of the representations of the human body were almost in the nature of caricatures. Even if the sculptors had aimed at greater aesthetic expression, the chiseling of so many thousands of statues would have left no time for naturalistic representation. Hence the figures tended to assume a sameness. They were long and angular with an exaggerated bend of the body toward one side and a smile which at times became a grimace. Sculptors were, however, beginning to perceive beauty in nature apart from the human figure. This is evidenced by the decorations in such French cathedrals as those of Chartres, Notre Dame de Paris, Amiens, and Rheims, and to a more limited extent south of the Alps. The sculptors employed to decorate these churches turned to nature for their decorative motifs. In the reliefs around the capitals, on the vaultings, and in some instances on the façades, they carved naturalistic representations of animals and plants, flowers and trees, leaves and vines. In the thirteenth century there are indications even in figure sculpture of a new feeling for greater plasticity, for a more natural representation.

If naturalism in sculpture became evident earlier in France than in Italy, it was in the latter country that it reached its fullest development. The work which heralded the rise of naturalism in Italian sculpture was Niccolo Pisano's pulpit in the Baptistery at Pisa (1260). Pisano's pulpit is still medieval in a number of respects. The panels are so crowded with figures that perspective had to be sacrificed. Moreover, his short figures have large heads. But in comparison with the work of his predecessors, Pisano's pulpit was well on the way toward naturalism. Some of the Biblical scenes are interpreted in a manner that is more secular than previous interpretations. Niccolo continued the naturalistic trend in the pulpit for the Duomo of Siena. In the execution of this work he was assisted by his son Giovanni. The style of Niccolo Pisano was influenced by classical remains in Pisa which he studied. Especially important in this respect, as Vasari reported, was a beautiful ancient sarcophagus which is still preserved in the Campo Santo at Pisa. But Niccolo was more than an imitator of classical art. His representations of sheep in his reliefs, for example, show that he was a careful student of nature.

Ghiberti and Donatello

Although the Pisan school started moving in the direction of naturalism, it declined early in the fourteenth century before it had progressed very far. For about half a century no further progress was made; then at the beginning of the fifteenth century Florence boldly assumed the leadership in the forward movement. The predominance of Florence was even greater in sculpture than in painting. Whereas in painting there were other important schools besides that of Florence, in sculpture Florence practically monopolized the field.

The first works of art by a Florentine which made great strides in the direction of naturalism were Lorenzo Ghiberti's famous bronze doors of the Baptistery of St. John the Baptist in Florence. The doors were a votive offering of the Gild of Wool Merchants (*Arte della Lana*) for the delivery of the city from the plague of 1400. To find the best possible artist the city staged a competition in which seven artists participated. Each one was required to make a relief of the "Sacrifice of Isaac" on a piece of metal the size and shape of the door panels. The artists were given a year to prepare their models and at the end of that time the judges decided that Ghiberti's relief was the best.

Ghiberti (1378-1455) started work on his first pair of doors in 1403 and did not finish them until twenty-one years later. Of the twenty-eight panels into which the doors are divided, twenty depict scenes from the life of Christ. On the other eight panels there are scenes from the lives of the four evangelists and four Fathers of the Church. The corners of the doors are decorated with the heads of prophets and sibyls, and each door is framed with a leafy border. When the doors were unveiled in 1424 large crowds came to see them. The next year Ghiberti started work on his second pair of doors which portray the Biblical story from the Creation to Solomon in ten panels. This set of doors on which he worked for nearly thirty years is his great masterpiece. It was of these doors that Michelangelo later said, "They are worthy to be the gates of Paradise." Ghiberti himself wrote, "In modeling these reliefs I strove to imitate nature to the utmost. . . . I sought to understand how forms strike on the eye and how the theoretical part of sculptural and pictorial art should be managed." Some art historians have asserted that nature was not the sole inspiration of Ghiberti. They refer to the close resemblance between the leafy borders of his doors and the carvings of French sculptors in the Gothic cathedrals. However this may be, Ghiberti's doors were studied by many artists of his time and of succeeding generations, and had a great influence on the development of naturalism in both sculpture and painting. (*See Fig. 13.*)

Among those who assisted Ghiberti in casting the bronze doors were the painter Masaccio and a youth named Donato Bardi (*c.*1386-1466), better known by the affectionate diminutive Donatello (little Donato). Beyond the fact that he served his apprenticeship in the shop of a goldsmith before he became Ghiberti's assistant nothing is known of Donatello's early life. Upon leaving the employ of Ghiberti he spent some time in Rome before settling down in Florence to accept commissions as a sculptor. His kindly nature and unfailing readiness to help the less fortunate won him great popularity with the Florentines. To money as such he attached little value. Vasari reported that Donatello "kept what little money he had in a basket suspended by a cord from the roof, and from this all his assistants as well as his friends took what they needed without being expected to say anything about it."

This simple Florentine citizen was a key figure in the development of Renaissance sculpture. While Masaccio was promoting naturalism in painting, Donatello gave naturalism a new impetus in sculpture. His fidelity to nature is exemplified by the prophets and patriarchs, evangelists and saints he executed for the Cathedral of Florence and for the Church of Or San Michele. Each one of his statues is a highly individualized, almost portrait-like representation of a withered old man. Donatello seemed to take pleasure in sculpturing the pronounced features, the protruding bones, the wrinkles and veins of such old men. His efforts to achieve realistic figures did not necessarily produce beauty; in fact, some of his figures are so repellent as to preclude any sensation of pleasure to the observer. One of his works, a statue of Habakkuk for which he used an old man of unattractive features as a model, was quickly nicknamed "Il Zuccone" (the bald head or, literally, the pumpkin head). Donatello copied the features of his model so faithfully that even to him the figure seemed almost alive. He was at times heard addressing the statue in these words, "Speak! The plague take thee, why wilt thou not speak?" But naturalism in itself was not enough for Donatello. He demanded more of art than mere form. Form must convey a message. The outer form, the countenance, and the posture was for him the means of expressing feeling, an inner quality or a state of mind. That his statues did convey a message is attested by Michelangelo's answer when he was asked to express his opinion of Donatello's statue of St. Mark. "I have never seen a figure," he said, "which so thoroughly represents a man of probity."

Donatello's bronze "David" (executed for the courtyard of the Medici palace; now in the Bargello) is inferior to much of his other work. It depicts David as a puny figure in a shepherd's hat, with a small face and arms almost entirely without muscle. Moreover, the weight of his body is unevenly distributed. Nevertheless, this statue is important in one respect. It is generally regarded as the first free-standing statue, one that is not a part of the architecture. His other heroic statues, including those of Joshua, Daniel, Jeremiah, Abraham, St. Peter, St. Mark, St. George, and his marble statue of David were made to occupy niches in the walls of churches. But the bronze "David" was made to stand in a courtyard where it could be looked at from every side. (*See Figs. 14, 15.*)

Donatello's St. George, commissioned by the Gild of Armorers and placed in a niche on the south side of the Church of Or San Michele (1416), is generally regarded as his masterpiece. It is distinguished for its nobility of form, combined with an expression of youth. This figure of a vigilant man of sturdy build, ready to defend others, has been styled the representation of the spirit of citizenship and community life. In executing the statue of St. George, Donatello took sculpture out of its ecclesiastical groove and brought it into close relationship with civic life. This spirit of civic service reappears constantly in Donatello's work. Another example of it is his bronze equestrian statue of the Venetian condottiere Erasmo da Narni, better known by his nickname "Gattamelata."

The Italian Renaissance produced another great equestrian statue, that of the Venetian condottiere Colleone. Having served the republic of Venice for a long period, Colleone left his considerable fortune to the state on condition that an equestrian monument be erected to his memory. After much discussion Verrocchio (1432-1488), a pupil of Donatello, was chosen to make the statue. He worked on it a number of years and at the time of his death had finished the clay model. Leopardi, famed as a bronze caster, did the casting. The dominant impression of the statue is one of strength. It also expresses courage, alertness, and resolution. Perhaps the subtlest touch of genius lies in the fact both horse and rider move together with consummate grace. Verrocchio's naturalism is such that contemporaries offered the criticism that the horse is anatomically too correct. It is somewhat ponderous according to present standards, but it is full of vitality and action, altogether an excellent representation of the warhorse of the period. (*See Fig. 16.*)

Another sculptor who showed an exact knowledge of form was Luca della Robbia (1400-1482). He, too, received some of his training while serving as Ghiberti's assistant. His work does not possess the force and character which marks the sculptures of Donatello, but it, nevertheless, has a wide appeal. He executed reliefs in marble, in bronze, and in glazed terra-cotta, devoting himself particularly to the representation of human features. His faces are characterized by delicacy of feature and sweetness of expression.

Michelangelo the Sculptor

Although sculpture had in the work of Ghiberti and Donatello attained a perfection which it was difficult to equal and in some respects impossible to excel, Michelangelo was to push the sculptor's art to yet greater heights. His art shows a definite progression from his first works to his last. When Michelangelo began his work as a sculptor the realistic style of Donatello dominated the art; hence his first efforts were directed toward making his own sculpture more realistic. His first figures, constructed from direct observation of nature and the study of classical models, are characterized by strength and force; in fact, his statues reveal vitality and force more abundantly than is usual in nature. However, he gradually turned away from photographic realism to a more original technique in which the human figure, as previously stated, became the means of expressing thoughts and feelings, that is, it offered insights into inner realities. Unfortunately the expression was most often one of conflict. Each of his works is an unconscious self-portrait reflecting his moods and his attitude toward the world around him. In his later years this attitude was one of irreconcilability and his moods were bitter. Hence his works of this period express gloom, despair, and disdain for the world. But even so, there is still the representation of strength and force.

The first works of the youthful Michelangelo were a miscellany of statues and reliefs. The work which established his reputation as a great sculptor was the "Pietà," now in St. Peter's at Rome. The contract of 1498 prescribed that Michelangelo was to execute a Pietà with the Virgin holding the dead Christ in her arms. This could be carried out only by a bold disregard of proportions, for a woman could not hold the body of a full-grown man in a position that would be tolerable to the eye. Hence Michelangelo made the body of Christ smaller, thereby producing an effect of childlike helplessness in relation to the larger figure of Mary. Nevertheless, the figure of the dead Christ is a piece of purely realistic sculpture with muscles, cords, and veins showing clearly. While holding the body with her right arm the Virgin gestures with the left as if to say, "Behold my son." The emotion she expresses is not one of grief, but one of infinite love. Most art historians regard Michelangelo's beautiful "Pietà" as the finest example of devotional group sculpture. (*See Fig. 18.*)

Having completed the "Pietà," Michelangelo decided to return to Florence. His reputation was now such that there was no lack of commissions. One of these presented a real challenge. In the courtyard of the Cathedral of Florence there was a huge block of marble out of which another sculptor had many years before that time started to carve a statue, but had succeeded only in disfiguring it. Other sculptors who had since looked at the block, refused to risk the humiliation of failure. When the city officials requested Michelangelo to chisel it into a statue, he accepted the challenge. With only a small wax model to guide him he converted the block into a statue of David, a task which required about two years for its completion. Michelangelo utilized the block of marble so completely that a part of the rough outer surface of the original stone remains on the top of David's head. The statue which because of its height of fifteen feet soon became known as "The Giant," represents the youthful warrior at the moment he says to Goliath, "I have come unto thee in the name of the Lord of Hosts." David's face reflects courage and his neck denotes strength. David's body, which is entirely nude, gives the impression of extraordinary physical beauty, but it is the figure of a long-limbed youth who has not attained his full harmonious physical development. Although Savonarola enthusiasts at first objected to David's nudity, the statue soon became the pride of Florence. After much discussion it was finally placed to the right of the entrance to the Palazzo Vecchio. There it remained until 1874 when it was moved to the Academy of Florence to protect it from damage. Later a marble replica was put in the place Michelangelo's "David" had formerly occupied. (*See Fig. 17.*)

Another famous statue of Michelangelo is his "Moses" which he sculptured between the years 1513 and 1516. The huge seated figure, double life-size, with a long flowing beard, is one of the world's best-known masterpieces. Every motionless limb of Moses is imbued with vitality and the essentials of motion. Like most of Michelangelo's figures it gives the impression of force. In the case of Moses, his stern features, his muscular arms and sturdy legs, and the tables of the law under his right arm, all combine to express an implacable force that crushes and shatters. While some art historians regard "Moses" as the embodiment of Michelangelo's wrath over the political degradation of Italy, others consider it to be an idealized portrait of Pope Julius II for whose tomb it had originally been intended. Whatever it expresses, the statue deeply impressed contemporaries. Pope Paul III was so deeply moved by the sight of it that he exclaimed, "That statue alone is enough glory for one pope." Vasari wrote of the statue, "When Michelangelo had finished it there was no other work, whether ancient or modern, which could equal it." He was particularly impressed by Michelangelo's treatment of Moses' hair, remarking that "one might almost believe that the chisel had become a brush." Condivi, the first biographer of Michelangelo stated that the statue of the mighty lawgiver inspires "both love and terror, as perhaps the man in truth did."

Michelangelo's most impressive achievements as a sculptor are by common consent the Medici tombs in the sacristy of the Church of San Lorenzo in Florence. If he had done nothing more, the six statues of the two tombs would have been enough to rank him among the great sculptors of all time. The original plans called for the erection of six tombs for the outstanding members of the Medici family including Lorenzo the Magnificent, Pope Leo X, and Pope Clement VII, but the project was limited to two tombs for the least significant members of the group, Lorenzo (duke of Urbino) and Giuliano (duke of Nemours). Michelangelo worked on the project intermittently from 1524 to 1532. The figures of Lorenzo and Giuliano, seated in alcoves eight feet from the floor bear little resemblance to the original persons; they are actually embodiments of thought. On the sarcophagi underneath are allegorical figures representing Night, Day, Morning (Dawn), and Evening (Twilight). Night, for example, is represented by a female form in an attitude of deep but uneasy sleep and Day by a powerful male who is in an attitude of arising. Michelangelo did not completely finish his statues. Some critics believe that the "unfinished" head of Day represents a day in the process of taking form. Others point out that this "creative form" does not appear in the clay model which Michelangelo used as a guide.

Some art historians have also made much of the fact that the proportions of the four figures are not correct. A torso may be too long, a head too small, and some limbs are twisted into almost impossible positions. Night, for example, has a torso that is too long and a left leg that is too short. The right leg of Dawn is 15 per cent long than the left, and Day has an unusually deep chest. It is generally believed that the contortions and novel proportions were deliberate and are, therefore, not ascribable to a lack of knowledge or skill on the part of Michelangelo. He was ready to resort to any exaggeration to achieve his purpose which was to express spiritual struggle, suffering, and melancholy. The Medici statues are, in the opinion of most art historians, an expression of the gloom and despair into which he had sunk. His naturally melancholy temperament, soured by dyspepsia and embittered by the thwarting of many of his great projects, was further troubled by the moral degeneration of his time, the impotence of his Italy against foreign invasion, and the decadence of his native Florence. All this many art historians see reflected in his statues. When the statue representing Night was first exhibited, the humanist Strozzi wrote the following verse which according to the custom of the time was affixed to the statue:

> Night, whom you see slumbering here so charmingly
> Has been carved in marble by an angel [Angelo].
> She sleeps, but she is alive; waken her,
> If you will not believe it, and she will speak.

In his answer Michelangelo sounded a note of despair when he wrote:

> Sleep is dear to me, but to be stone is best,
> So long as dishonor and shame last among us;
> The happiest fate is to see, to hear nothing;
> For this reason wake me not, I pray you speak gently.

The Medici figures represent the summit of Italian Renaissance sculpture. With them Michelangelo's career as a sculptor may be said to have come to a close. The same may be said of the period of Renaissance sculpture in Italy. Unfortunately for posterity Michelangelo did not communicate the secret of his technique or of any creative discoveries he may have made to anyone. He did not even train a competent pupil to carry on his ideas. He had imitators who copied his forms, but the inner spirit Michelangelo had expressed was lacking. Italy generally, and Florence in particular, lost the fertility which had caused the arts to flourish.

Benvenuto Cellini

In a survey of Renaissance art the goldsmiths should not be overlooked. Although there had been little demand for their work during the early centuries of the Middle Ages, except by the Church and the courts of rulers, a wider field of activity opened for them as a result of the increase of wealth. Wealthy members of the middle class as well as high dignitaries of church and state displayed a fondness for jewelry, medallions, and other objects created by the skill of the goldsmith. In order to become an expert goldsmith, an apprentice had to learn to work in precious metals and to set precious stones. He had to study enameling, filigree, modeling in wax, baking terra-cotta, and engraving on metals. He also had to acquire some knowledge of drawing, anatomy, chemistry, and architecture. Moreover, an expert goldsmith had to possess inventive power, ability to plot designs, and considerable manual dexterity. The training offered in a goldsmith's shop was so broad and detailed that it was widely regarded as indispensable for a successful career in the various branches of art. Among the leading figures in Renaissance art who received the preliminary training in the shop of a goldsmith were Brunelleschi, Botticelli, Luca della Robbia, and Verrocchio.

The most famous goldsmith of the period was Benvenuto Cellini (1500-1571), a skillful artist who for fertility of invention and delicacy of handiwork was unsurpassed. As the leading goldsmith and jeweler of his day, he received commissions from popes, kings, cardinals, and dukes as well as from members of the wealthy bourgeoisie. But Cellini did not limit his activities to being a goldsmith. One of the most versatile of Renaissance figures, he was also a sculptor, an expert engraver, a master in enameling on gold and in damascening sword blades, a poet of some ability, and the author of one of the most famous autobiographies of all time. Unfortunately most of his art works have disappeared. The magnificent salt-cellar he made for King Francis I of France and a few coins and seals are all of his authenticated works as a goldsmith that are still in existence. Of Cellini's works as a sculptor the statue of Perseus and several busts have survived. Of the jewels he set very few can be traced. Changes of fashion and financial necessity probably caused the owners of the others to melt down the metal and sell the precious stones. (*See Fig. 19b.*)

It is, above all, his autobiography which has kept his memory alive. In writing it he created a monument which has proved more enduring than his works of gold, marble, and bronze. Cellini's autobiography is a valuable record of sixteenth-century life, particularly of "Bohemian" life, in Italy and in France where he lived for some time. In it the brilliant and the sordid, the gay and the brutal, succeed each other with bewildering rapidity. Both famous and infamous persons walk through its pages, including kings and princes, popes and cardinals, artists, friars, and courtiers, bullies, cowards, highwaymen, assassins, fools, and rogues of every kind.

But it is, above all, Cellini who strides through the pages of his autobiography. The record as he put it in writing is a tangled web of truth and falsehood, for when his memory failed him his imagination filled in the gaps. The story is, however, written with a gusto which has lost none of its force with the passing centuries. Most literary historians regard it as a masterpiece of literature worthy of a place beside Cervantes' *Don Quixote* and Rousseau's *Confessions*. Goethe regarded it so highly that he translated it into German. Had Cellini recorded his vices alone or only his virtues, the story of his life would have been ordinary. What gives the book its zest is the uncouth mingling of the two. With astounding frankness he sets down his every act whether it was kindly, generous, mean or brutal. Few people have ever laid bare so completely their innermost thoughts and motives. With equal complacency he discusses his achievements as an artist, his illicit amours, his personal encounters, his visions, his likes and dislikes. The result of his frankness is that the man who emerges from his autobiography is not only an artist skilled in many things, but also a ruffian, a liar, a braggart, a libertine, and an assassin. In his varied love affairs he always treated women without respect and sometimes with brutality.

Cellini's most prominent characteristic as a man was an overwhelming sense of his own importance which expressed itself in braggadocio. His personal vanity was of such proportions that it destroyed his ability to judge his own works with any critical sense. There was no doubt whatsoever in Cellini's mind that he was the first goldsmith of his time and that he ranked no lower than second as a sculptor. In a burst of generosity he conceded that Michelangelo in his prime could possibly have matched Cellini's own "Perseus." He was also boastful of his prowess as a soldier, stating "If I were to tell you minutely all the fine things I did in that infernally cruel business, I should strike the world with wonder." When he encountered the same spirit of braggadocio in others, it nauseated him. His bad temper got him into every kind of trouble; his whole life was a succession of disputes, quarrels, and feuds with the lowly, the near-great, and the great. His overweening ways and his ungovernable temper quickly turned friends into enemies. This fact forced him to travel from place to place. He was so uncharitable that one of his biographers styled him "as vindictive as a viper." His autobiography contains many instances of acts motivated by sheer spite. In addition to the lives he took in warfare, Cellini confesses to three homicides in his autobiography.

But if Cellini's autobiography reveals him as a swaggering ruffian, it also attests to his enthusiasm for art and his sensibility to higher forms of art. It further relates how his projects were conceived and executed. Although he was born in Florence and served his apprenticeship as goldsmith there, his truculence got him into so much trouble that he had to leave his "sweet birthplace," as he calls it. He drifted from place to place, finally settling in Rome where he received commissions from the pope and the dignitaries of the Papal Court. But he soon antagonized so many people that he regarded it as the better part of wisdom to leave Rome. After wandering about Italy for some years he returned to Rome in 1534 upon hearing of the death of Clement VII. It was not long, however, before he lost the favor of the new pope, Paul III. This time he decided to go to France where he hoped to find a patron in Francis I. The French king, however, was preoccupied with other matters, and Cellini soon returned to Italy. Upon his arrival in Rome, he was imprisoned on the charge of having purloined some jewels that had been entrusted to his care. The story of his imprisonment which covered a period of years is fully recorded in his autobiography. Finally released through the intervention of Francis I, Cellini immediately left Italy for France where he produced a number of imposing works. The most notable is the gold salt-cellar, the principal features of which are two nude allegorical figures representing the Sea and the Earth. Around the base there is a border on which Cellini introduced in high relief small figures of Day, Night, Twilight, and Dawn, probably copied on a small scale from the statues of Michelangelo's Medici tombs. (*See Fig. 19a.*)

Cellini's belligerence did not diminish with the passing of the years. He soon excited the enmity of a number of influential persons at the French court with the result that even the interest of Francis I cooled. Finally Cellini's situation became so intolerable that he suddenly left France for Italy. This time he went to Florence where, despite his involvement in quarrels and feuds, he remained until his death. Nine years of this period he spent on his seven-foot bronze statue of Perseus, the work on which his reputation as a sculptor rests. The figure represents Perseus as a gladiator, holding up the gory head of Medusa just after her decapitation. The story of the difficulties he encountered in preparing the mold and casting the statue is told in great detail in Cellini's autobiography. Cellini himself regarded the statue as the masterpiece of a genius, but art critics have not shared his high opinion. The best that has been said of the work is that it represents a high degree of technical excellence. Other critics have pointed out that the thick body and heavy limbs indicate a lack of expert knowledge of the human form. Contemporaries did, however, hail the statue as a great masterpiece, with a number of poets writing odes in both Italian and Latin in praise of it. (*See Fig. 20.*)

The great work of this period was undoubtedly his autobiography. Unfortunately he abruptly ended it in 1562, the year he was married. It would have been interesting to know if his wife was successful in taming his truculence. According to a contemporary record, a sermon was preached at Cellini's funeral in 1571 in which his life, his work, and "his excellent moral qualities" were praised.

Italian Renaissance Architecture

Gothic architecture, one of the highest expressions of medieval spirituality, was not, as previously mentioned, indigenous to Italy. Through the agency of monastic orders such details as the pointed arch, the ribbed vault, and the stained-glass windows were introduced into Italy from France. Thus, for example, in the thirteenth century the Cistercians and the Franciscans built churches with ribbed vaults and pointed arches. It was, however, more the idea of grafting Gothic forms on Romanesque architecture than of domesticating Gothic architecture as such. Hence Italian Gothic architecture was largely an architecture of compromise. At no time did Italian Gothic approach the pure Gothic of France. The Italian architects seemed uninterested in Gothic structural principles. The Roman tradition, though feeble at times, had persisted throughout the Middle Ages, and was active during the period of Italian Gothic style. Even the Roman rounded arch never gave way entirely to the pointed arch, and classical orders and mouldings were used in many modifications. The adoption of classical forms by the Renaissance architects was, therefore, not revolutionary; it was rather a return to native tradition. In another sense it was a phase of "the return to the good ancient manner" which manifested itself in the interest in ancient classics and in classical history and philosophy.

Renaissance architecture was not one unified style; it was rather an ensemble of styles which had in common the use of classical forms. In Renaissance architecture the pointed arch, ribbed vault, and the vertical features were replaced by the rounded arch, the circular dome, Corinthian capitals, and other classical features. Furthermore, whereas Northern Gothic had about it an air of mystery, Renaissance architecture was primarily aesthetic. Its appeal was directed to the eye rather than to the heart, without any suggestion of hidden symbolism. Again, whereas the great Northern Gothic churches and cathedrals are in a general sense expressions of common beliefs, and in some instances collective enterprises, the great works of Renaissance architecture are in large degree expressions of the conceptions of individual architects. Even when, as in the case of St. Peter's in Rome, the building of the structure covered a long period and involved a number of architects, each part reflects the work of an individual. Though some of its greatest monuments are churches, Renaissance architecture found its most typical expression in the field of secular rather than of religious architecture. Its most characteristic structures are palaces, villas, town halls, and civic monuments.

Although Renaissance architecture was indebted to classical forms to a greater degree than painting and sculpture, it was not basically imitative. A group of nineteenth-century critics, headed by John Ruskin, launched the sweeping indictment against Renaissance architecture. It was, they declared, a mere copying of old rather than an invention of new forms. These critics either asserted or implied that Renaissance architects as a whole lacked originality and creative imagination. During the last phase of the Renaissance, architects did, it is true, appropriate with uncritical and indiscriminate enthusiasm the good and the bad features of Roman architecture. For them imitation of classical forms was enough. But this was not true of Renaissance architects before 1550. The early architects studied Roman remains not for purposes of imitation, but to learn how the Romans had achieved the qualities which characterize their architecture. They used the details they borrowed in wholly new combinations, creating with them an architecture different in character and in spirit. Renaissance architecture reflected the spirit of Renaissance Italy no less than did painting and sculpture of the same period. Such buildings as the Cathedral of Florence and St. Peter's of Rome are certainly not imitations of Roman models. Nor were any of the other buildings imitations of recognizable Roman models. In short, Renaissance architecture was a fusion of the old and the new. As such it incorporated new ideas as well as Gothic and Roman elements.

Although indications of a return to Roman forms preceded him, Filippo Brunelleschi (1379-1446) is generally regarded as the architect who ushered in the period of Renaissance architecture. After serving an apprenticeship in the shop of a goldsmith, he entered the competition against Ghiberti in quest of the commission to make the bronze doors of the Baptistery. Despite the fact that he barely missed winning the prize, he decided that architecture offered him better opportunities. He was also induced to become an architect by the hope that he might be able to solve the engineering problem involved in the construction of a dome for the unfinished Cathedral of Florence. The construction of this dome became, in fact, the primary ambition of his life. In preparation for the task he spent several years in Rome where he studied the ruins of Roman architecture. He carefully measured columns and entablatures, making drawings of all the Roman forms he could find. In this way he acquired a good knowledge of Roman architectural principles, methods, and materials. But one looks in vain through the whole range of his works for an instance in which he copied a Roman building.

Securing the appointment as architect to complete the Cathedral of Florence was not an easy task. When he proposed his plan after returning from Rome in 1407, he failed to impress the members of the official committee. They regarded his plan as too daring. Year after year passed without action by the committee. Meanwhile Brunelleschi's plan became the subject of many vigorous discussions not only among the members of the committee but also among the people at large. It was defended by some and openly scoffed at by others. Giovanni di Gherardo, whose advice had been asked by the committee, ridiculed it in a sonnet stating that no man can do the impossible. Finally, after thirteen years of indecision, the committee accepted the plan. Even then its members had so little faith in it that they appointed Brunelleschi's old competitor, the sculptor Ghiberti and also a certain Battista d'Antonio as the colleagues of Brunelleschi in the venture. Although the participation of d'Antonio was only nominal, Ghiberti's role was particularly irritating to the proud Brunelleschi. He, therefore, decided on a ruse to compel Ghiberti's withdrawal. While the workmen were awaiting orders, Brunelleschi feigned illness and turned away all requests for instructions with the reply, "Consult Ghiberti!" The latter, who quickly realized that he was unable to direct the work, resigned, leaving Brunelleschi practically in full charge.

The inherent difficulties were so tremendous that it required fifteen years to build the dome itself. The lantern on top of the dome was not completed until 1467, more than twenty years after Brunelleschi's death. The dome which dominates the city of Florence consists of two shells resting on a drum nearly forty feet high and sixteen feet thick. The construction of two shells not only permitted more magnificent lines than a single shell, it also protected the inner shell and its ceiling decorations from the weather. It was not the shape of the dome since others of similar form had previously been built, but its vast size and boldness of span which constituted an important step in the development of Renaissance architecture. The diameter of the space it covers is 138.5 feet and the height of the dome from the drum is 133 feet. No dome of similar size had been raised since the dome of the Roman pantheon which had a diameter of 142 feet was built by Agrippa in 27 B.C. Furthermore, the use of the drum which raised the dome so that it became the chief feature of the building constituted another important step in the development of Renaissance architecture. (*See Fig. 21.*)

Brunelleschi's dome became at once the pride of Florence and the wonder of the age. Leon Battista Alberti, a fellow architect, wrote in his *Della Pittura* (1435):

> Who is so unfeeling or so envious that he would not praise Pippo [Filippo Brunelleschi], the architect, beholding here a structure so grand, lifted to the heavens, ample to cover with its shadow the whole Tuscan people, erected without aid or framework or multitude of timbers—a work of art in truth, if I judge rightly, such as, deemed incredible in these times of ours, was neither conceived nor known by the ancients?

Many domes have been patterned to a greater or lesser extent after Brunelleschi's dome, including those of St. Peter's in Rome, St. Paul's in London, Les Invalides and Panthéon in Paris, and the Capitol in Washington, D.C.

Although the dome of the Cathedral of Florence is Brunelleschi's greatest and best-known achievement, his other works, designed while the dome was under construction, identify him to a greater degree with the revival of classical forms in architecture. In his churches, including the Florentine churches of San Lorenzo and Santo Spirito, and the Pazzi Chapel of the Church of Santa Croce, suggestions of Gothic influence survive, but the influence of his Roman studies is evident in all his ornaments, moldings, and details. In his palaces and public buildings he reintroduced the use of classical orders and other architectural forms of classical times. Thus, for example, he used a wealth of classical forms in the portico he constructed in front of the hospital of the Innocenti. In general, Brunelleschi demonstrated that classical orders and details can be used with freedom and structural propriety. During his lifetime Brunelleschi met much opposition and was subjected to much abuse, but after his death Florence honored him as one of her greatest sons.

The second great Florentine innovator was Leon Battista Alberti. Alberti, who had a more intimate knowledge of classical antiquity than Brunelleschi, demonstrated his classical appreciation by eliminating from his buildings the last traces of Gothic and by designing them more strictly in accordance with the principles of Roman architecture. Some of the churches he designed include the most literal reproduction of Roman forms yet attempted. His most famous non-ecclesiastical building is the Rucellai Palace in Florence, in the façade of which he incorporated a number of features of the Roman amphitheater. In addition to designing buildings Alberti also wrote *De Re Aedificatoria,* often called *Ten Books on Architecture*, a long treatise which had a wide influence on both theory and practice in architecture. Although Alberti advocated a careful study of classical architecture and held up the works of classical architects as the best models, he was opposed to mere imitation. He advised architects always to introduce something original into their designs. The architect, he stated, must always consider "what improvements might be made in everything he sees . . . he should have the ambition to produce something admirable which may be entirely of his own invention."

In church architecture the culmination was reached in St. Peter's at Rome. Although a number of architects had prepared plans during the second half of the fifteenth century for the rebuilding of St. Peter's, the plan to which it owes its scale and grandeur was drawn up by the Florentine-born architect, Donato Bramante (1444-1514) at the behest of Julius II. Bramante designed the building in the shape of a large Greek cross and execution of the plan was begun in 1506. After Bramante's death in 1514 various architects, including Raphael, supervised the work and devised new plans for the structure. Finally in 1547 Pope Paul III appointed Michelangelo architect and for the next seventeen years the building of St. Peter's absorbed much of Michelangelo's attention. He rejected most of the changes introduced by architects and returned to a kind of simplified version of Bramante's plan. The most striking feature of St. Peter's, its huge dome, was designed by Michelangelo himself, but it was not completed during his lifetime. The design of the dome was to some extent influenced by Brunelleschi's dome on the Cathedral of Florence which was a source of delight to Michelangelo. Although the architects who succeeded Michelangelo modified the plans for the dome only slightly, they did change the plans for the building as a whole. As a consequence of the lengthening of the nave, Bramante's original Greek cross virtually became a Latin cross. The interior has a gigantic order of Corinthian columns crowned with semicircular vaults. The great cathedral was finally completed in 1661 by the architect Bernini who erected the colonnade which encircles the plaza. (*See Fig. 22.*)

Meanwhile Renaissance architecture spread over much of Western Europe. In France, the original home of Gothic architecture, Renaissance architecture encountered greater opposition than in Italy. Nevertheless, the French architects did gradually adopt some of the features of the new style. In church architecture, which was more conservative, such Gothic features as the ribbed vault and the flying buttress were retained. In England Renaissance architecture was opposed by the Tudor style, a variation of Gothic; hence it made little headway until the reign of Queen Elizabeth (1558-1603). In Germany and the Netherlands the Renaissance style was adopted more quickly and employed with greater freedom than in the other countries north of the Alps.

12

The Beginnings of Secular Drama and Music

Medieval Drama

The religious faith of the Middle Ages was reflected most clearly in the drama of the period. It was, in fact, a direct outgrowth of religion, more specifically of the liturgy of the Medieval Church. The birth of this drama was not influenced in any way by the classical drama. Right from the early days of Christianity its adherents denounced the Roman theater because of the pagan and immoral nature of its presentations. The early Fathers, in fact, opposed all forms of worldly amusement. But the Christians had another reason for harboring an antipathy to the Roman stage. The Emperor Nero (d.68 A.D.), in his efforts to destroy Christianity, encouraged the heaping of ridicule on the mysteries of the Christian faith with the result that the proselytes and their way of life were lampooned on the stage. Actors made up as bishops and neophytes (recent converts) burlesqued a conversion even to staging mock baptisms. Furthermore, parodies of martyrdom would be presented in which the dying groans of tortured believers would be presented in such a farcical manner as to evoke laughter. In the light of these facts it is easy to understand why many of the early Fathers inveighed ceaselessly against the theater. After the triumph of Christianity the drama gradually disappeared and the theaters fell into ruin. During the succeeding period there were acrobats, wandering minstrels, masters of sleight of hand, and other entertainers, but the drama was virtually forgotten. And there was no indication that it would ever be revived.

In the tenth century, however, a new form of the drama was born as a spontaneous development within the confines of the Church which had denounced the earlier pagan drama. This new drama is known as the mystery drama or more simply as "the mystery" because it dealt with the central mysteries of the Christian faith. It was performed by priests and other members of the clergy in the church edifice. Hence it has been said that its first stage was the altar and its first actor the priest. The mystery drama originated as an aid to worship and as a means of instruction. The fact that the Mass was everywhere read in Latin rendered it quite unintelligible to most worshippers. If they were to have some knowledge of the basic teachings of the Church, other didactic means were mandatory. Resourceful priests turned to the portrayal of events from the life of Christ through acting. Thus the mystery had its origin as an illustrative episode of the Mass, presented on such holy days of the Church as Christmas, Good Friday, and Easter. Such presentations of scenes from the life of Christ were regarded by the people of the Middle Ages as being more than just instructional aids. They were also believed to be means to assuage the wrath of God and win the favor of the saints. Hence mysteries were often performed in times of pestilence and disaster or as a thank offering to the Deity for having protected the local population from the plague or some other calamity. Mysteries were also staged in honor of the local patron saint.

The mystery which had at first been a single brief scene gradually expanded through the addition of other events from the life of Christ. The gap between Christmas and Easter was filled in with such episodes as the raising of Lazarus and the driving of the money-changers from the Temple. Consequently in time the mystery play included the leading events of the life of Christ. Gradually scenes from the Old Testament were also added. As a result the mystery became so long and unwieldly that it could no longer be staged inside the church edifice. It was, therefore, moved into the cloister or into the square in front of the church. Thus it was divorced from the liturgy and compelled to stand on its own feet, although the religious intent did continue. After the separation of the mystery from the liturgy the tendency developed to replace Latin with the vernacular or language of the people. A further change was introduced when the priests gave up to laymen the acting of the parts. Thereafter burghers, craftsmen, and students assumed the roles in the plays. Gradually the staging of the plays was transferred from the clergy to the laity. By this time the mystery plays were major productions. The task of preparing the script, making ready the elaborate costumes, and training the actors had become too burdensome for the clergy; hence the staging of the mysteries was taken over by town authorities or gild officials. Essentially the mystery was the same wherever it was acted, whether the language was English, French, German, Italian or Spanish. This may be ascribed to the religious unity of medieval Europe, and to the general acceptance of the beliefs and practices of the Roman Church. The differences were largely matters of detail.

Two other forms of the medieval drama were the miracle play and the morality play. Like the mystery play, both received their inspiration and sustenance from medieval religion. Whereas the mystery play was based on sequences taken from the Bible and the miracle play featured the miracles and legends of the saints, the morality play had as its main theme the struggle of good and evil for the possession of man's soul. The original purpose of the three kinds of plays was the same—to instruct the audience in the way of salvation. It was in the mode of representation that they differed. While the mystery and miracle plays portrayed the teachings of the Church symbolically, the morality plays presented them in terms of everyday life, thereby moving in the direction of the secular drama. As painters began to depict the Virgin in the form of a peasant woman or contemporary urban mother, the writers of the morality plays presented good and evil, virtue and vice, in the guise of contemporary persons. Members of the audience might well recognize their neighbors, friends or acquaintances in the representations. They might even see in them a reflection of themselves. The morality play also moved in the direction of the secular drama through the admixture of buffoonery which in the fourteenth century also invaded mystery and miracle plays. One of the favorite devices was the popularization of the Devil or devils. Often, immediately after the loftiest moment in a tragic scene, a pack of little devils would rush in and, to the accompaniment of roars of laughter from the audience, carry off the evildoer to hell. Despite the fact that they were extremely popular, the mystery, miracle, and morality plays seldom rose to the level of literature.

The Birth of the Secular Drama

Renaissance drama offers a notable example of progressive secularization. Two major factors cooperated in producing it. One was the gradual secularization of the religious drama; the other was the influence of the revival of classical drama, particularly the tragedy of Seneca and the comedy of Plautus and Terence. Some historians of the drama have gone so far as to ascribe the origin of the secular Renaissance drama to the study and imitation of the comedy and tragedy of classical times. In the light of recent studies this thesis can no longer be defended. The classical drama was, it is true, an influence in the development. It did provide the rudimentary secular drama with much needed guidance. But the influences which produced the secular drama were at work long before the classical drama began to exert its influence.

For the origins of the modern secular drama it is necessary to go back to the religious drama. It was there that the secular spirit first manifested itself, with the result that the drama became progressively more secular. The secular trend was introduced soon after the mystery drama left the church edifice. In an age of growing secularist influence the lay producers bowed to the popular demand for humor. It was in accordance with the old axiom, "The drama's laws the drama's patrons give." The element of tragedy was already in the drama, but the sharp distinction between comedy and tragedy, so marked in classical plays, was not observed in the medieval drama. An English play of the period is an example of how humor and secular situations were introduced into the religious drama. The scene presents Noah and his ark. When it is time for the spouse of the venerable patriarch to enter the ark, she refuses to do so unless she can take her friends with her. When Noah's patience is exhausted he puts her on board by force, whereupon she rewards him with a sound box on the ear.

Gradually more and more secular materials were introduced until the drama became largely secular with a vestige of religion. In the fifteenth century the religious element in some plays was limited to the appearance of a saint in it. The humor of the rising secular drama was native to the audience, not something borrowed from Greece or Rome. Often it centered in a situation taken from everyday life and presented in considerable detail. An example of an early comedy is the French farce called *The Tub*, with a cast of three characters: husband, wife, and mother-in-law. The wife, aided and abetted by the mother-in-law, prevails upon the henpecked husband to sign an agreement which obligates him to do the housework, all his duties being carefully listed item by item. Soon thereafter the wife falls into a tub in which she was washing clothes and is unable to get out. When her calls summon the husband, he consults his itemized list and then refuses to aid her because it is not one of his listed duties. The mother-in-law now comes to the aid of her daughter, but fails to extricate her from the tub. All the pleas and scoldings of the wife and mother-in-law fail to move the husband. Finally, as the wife grows more and more uncomfortable in her predicament, the husband suggests that since the contract is useless it be torn up. Seeing no other way out of the dilemma, the wife and mother-in-law consent and the masculine prestige of the husband is restored.

Medieval drama was mainly a panorama of successive episodes, lacking plot development and unity. But the elements of modern secular drama were there awaiting a master literary craftsman with the necessary technical skill and imaginative insight to make the best use of them. The final stage in the evolution of the secular Renaissance drama consisted in the separation of comedy and tragedy. Such classical dramas as the comedies of Plautus and Terence and the tragedies of Seneca were an important influence. Many secular plays were presented during the course of the fifteenth century, but it was only in the last decades that the first mature secular dramas appeared. They were, however, only the precursors of the great dramas of the sixteenth century. The farce *Maistre Pierre Pathelin* (1480) is generally regarded as the most artistic comedy that had appeared in France up to that time. A list of the mature comedies of Italy should include Cardinal Bibbiena's *La Calandria* (written about 1490, but not performed until much later), Niccolo Machiavelli's *Mandragola* (1512), and the five comedies of Ariosto (1474-1533). Secular English comedy is usually dated from Nicholas Udall's *Ralph Roister Doister* (*c.*1550) and John Still's *Gammer Gurton's Needle* (*c.*1566). In Germany Hans Sachs (1494-1576), who wrote more than two hundred secular and sacred playlets and dramas, is generally considered "the father of popular German drama." Tragedy also became secular and mature about the same time as comedy. In Italy Politian's *Orfeo*, as stated earlier, is generally regarded as the first secular tragedy. It was the first Renaissance drama to be based on a subject taken from Greek mythology and modeled after the classical Greek drama. In France the foundations for the new tragedy were laid by Etienne Jodelle with *Cleopatra*

(1552) and *Eugene* (1552). English tragedy may be said to begin with Norton and Sackville's *Gorboduc* (1561) which is regarded by some drama critics as a model play and by others as unfit for the stage. Thus the drama which for centuries had served as a means of religious instruction gradually evolved into a vehicle of entertainment. Instead of being esteemed for its religious values it was cultivated for its portrayal of mundane life in both its comic and tragic aspects, for its beauty of style, and for its interpretation of character. In England in the plays of Marlowe and Shakespeare drama was soon to reach a height of excellence which has not been surpassed since that time.

Music in the Middle Ages

Music, like the other branches of culture, was during the Middle Ages the handmaiden of theology. It had, in fact, been an integral part of Christianity right from the birth of this religion. Both the Old and the New Testaments contain many references to music, one of the most important in the New Testament being the announcement of the birth of Jesus by an angelic choir singing "Peace on earth." The singing of psalms, which formed an important part of worship in the synagogue, was taken over by the Christians and incorporated into their worship service. A feature of the psalms was their antiphonal structure with each verse supported by a responsive verse of like character. Gradually chants in the nature of a prayer were also added to the Christian service. In the fourth century the Council of Carthage admonished the church members: "See that what thou singest with thy lips thou believest in thy heart; and what thou believest in thy heart thou dost exemplify in thy life." With the growth of an organized church an elaborate liturgy evolved. During this early period the music of the service was almost entirely vocal; musical instruments were used only rarely. Later the organ became the principal instrument of the church service. The elaborate liturgy was first developed in the Eastern Church. It was St. Ambrose of Milan (333-397), often called "the Father of Ecclesiastical Music in the West," who introduced the antiphonal singing, chants, responses, and hymns of the Eastern Church into Italy. He also composed a number of hymns.

A new era of church music opened with the reign of Pope Gregory I, the Great (590-604). In the history of the Roman Catholic Church, Gregory is celebrated as the great reformer of church music. Soon after becoming pope he ordered that a collection be made of the music used in the church services. Accordingly the antiphons, responses, and offertories were gathered into a collection called *Antephonarius Cento;* they were also revised and a suitable distribution was made to the various Sundays of the church year. The monodic chant (plainsong), sung in unison without any accompanying harmonic support, is still called the Gregorian chant. It is not definitely known whether Gregory personally participated in the work of collecting and revising the music of the Church or whether the work was done in the school of singing (*Schola Cantorum*) which he founded in Rome. After Gregory's death the Gregorian chant was introduced into the other countries of Western Europe. This period, extending into the eleventh century, was the "golden age" of the Gregorian chant, the age in which it became the musical language of Western Europe. It represented the triumph of the spiritual ideal in music and as such was carefully cultivated in the schools of singing. As the language of the soul the Gregorian chant has never been surpassed.

The music of antiquity and the early Church was monodic or homophonous (single-voiced) as contrasted with polyphonous or many-voiced music. Polyphony, which involves the simultaneous and harmonious combination of two or more independent voices or parts, was the great discovery of the Middle Ages. It was a method of adorning the plainsong that eventually revolutionized the entire structure of music. The beginnings of the new method are shrouded in obscurity. It probably developed in France and England. By the end of the tenth century it had become customary to add a second voice to unison singing. This was the first indication of the form that gave occidental music definite characteristics which distinguish it from all other music of the world. After the tenth century the polyphonic tendency gradually penetrated the Gregorian chant effecting a change of musical form. The new method finally developed into counterpoint or "note against note."

Although we have an extensive literature on sacred music from the Middle Ages, prior to the fourteenth century there is hardly a mention of folk or popular music. The censure by ecclesiastical authorities of musicians other than those who devoted themselves to sacred music indicates that there were other types of music. But the cultivation and enjoyment of secular music was regarded by the Church as dangerous because it might turn the attention from the contemplation of otherworldly things to mundane pleasures. Consequently folk or popular music was pushed into the background with the result that every trace of it disappeared. We do, however, have a considerable knowledge of the music and entertainment which the nobility enjoyed. In the large castles there were jongleurs or minstrels, most of whom could also play musical instruments, some as many as four different kinds. They, too, drew down upon themselves the censure of the Church; nevertheless, they increased in number with the passing of time. The twelfth and thirteenth centuries saw the flowering of the songs of the trouvères and troubadours, singers of northern and southern France respectively. Of the two the troubadours were the more important. Actuated by motives of knightly chivalry, they wandered about serenading the noble dames. Most of them were members of the nobility. The fact that the troubadour songs were largely perpetuated by oral tradition explains the many variations of the favorite melodies. Gradually the troubadour song found its way into Italy, Spain, and Germany where it influenced the development of vernacular song and poetry.

The French Ars Nova

During the Renaissance period, music was subject to the same secularizing influences as the other phases of culture. In music, however, the secular elements became visible somewhat earlier than in painting, sculpture, and architecture. The troubadour and trouvère music of the twelfth and thirteenth centuries inaugurated the secular trend which became more definite in the fourteenth century. New forms, styles, and techniques were introduced. These changes can be seen not only in looking back from the present; they were so evident to contemporaries that composers and musicians called the music produced under their influence Ars Nova or the New Art. As Petrarch and Boccaccio believed that a new age of literature had been inaugurated, so the musicians believed they were living in a new age of music. Hence the name "the New Art" for the musical development of the period. The name "Ars Nova" was taken from the title of a musical treatise written about 1324 by Philippe de Vitry, French poet, composer, and friend of Petrarch. In his treatise de Vitry discusses some of the new trends in music and adds some contributions of his own. He was personally responsible for two innovations. First, he probably invented the technique of iso-rhythm, a means of unifying a composition through the use of the same rhythmic pattern, changing only the pitch and the text.[1] Second, he prepared an improved system of notation which clearly indicated the relative strength of notes.

The trend of Ars Nova music was in the direction of secularization and refinement. It was also in the direction of emancipation from the fixed forms of the preceding period. Consequently the Ars Nova music developed largely outside the domain of sacred music. In essence the Ars Nova was the development of new forms to express the growing secular interests. For example, to enable music to achieve the desired effect, composers expanded the tonal space in the higher and lower registers. Instruments were also built on which the higher and lower notes could be played. Thus music became the means of painting in tones man's earthly environment and his reactions to it. More precisely, Ars Nova music was the expression of fourteenth-century man and his joys and sorrows. It is subjective art, an expression of the ideas and experiences of the composers. Many of Philippe de Vitry's compositions, for example, are works of art with a distinctly personal message. They are reflections of the individualism which manifested itself in the other arts. Although there were many unmistakably new elements, one

[1] The opening bars of the Star Spangled Banner are an example of iso-rhythm. "Oh say, can you see" and "by the dawn's early light" have the same rhythm with a different text and a different melody.

must not, however, regard the Ars Nova as a change which rejected the old completely. But the retained medieval components were drastically changed to suit the new purposes. If the changes were not complete, they were also not sudden. The centuries preceding the fourteenth had been a period of preparation for the Ars Nova. Thus the changes were evolutionary, not revolutionary, and in time they became thoroughgoing.

Although the innovations of the New Art found supporters in all the countries of Western Europe, not all composers and musicians accepted them. Like most innovations they caused division. Musicians ranged themselves into two opposing groups, the conservatives and the "moderns." While the conservatives continued to support the old art (Ars Antiqua) or art of the preceding period, the "moderns" allied themselves with the Ars Nova. The most distinguished composer of the French Ars Nova was Guillaume de Machaut (1305-1377) who wrote about half the music which has survived from that period. Although Machaut continued the traditions of the past in his religious music, he freely struck out into new directions in his secular music. In the secular song Machaut developed polyphony to a degree theretofore unknown, expressing himself most freely in the ballade. He regarded music as an art "whose purpose it is to make people laugh, and sing, and dance." This is a definite departure from the old idea that music is a means for exciting otherworldly thoughts and feelings.

Even before Philippe de Vitry wrote his treatise, *Ars Nova,* certain composers who recognized the immense possibilities of the new art sought to infuse new life into the music of the Church by weaving some of the innovations into the fabric of sacred music. This quickly generated considerable opposition among the clergy as well as conservative musicians. Both were determined to keep the New Art from changing the plainsong services and thereby robbing the Gregorian chants of their austere beauty. When their efforts to stop the invasion of the Ars Nova into sacred music failed, they appealed to Pope John XXII for help. The pope responded by issuing from Avignon in 1322 a papal decree regulating the use of polyphony in the church service. He styled the techniques employed by the "moderns" as unsuitable. Certain disciples of the new school, he stated, insist on displaying notes which are new to us, preferring to devise methods of their own rather than to continue singing in the old way. These musicians, he continued, introduce so many new forms that "often they must be losing sight of the fundamental sources of our melodies in the Antiphoner and Gradual." As a consequence of the many innovations, he stated, "devotion, the true end of worship, is seldom thought of." After advocating the casting out of the new forms and methods, he wrote, "We strictly command no one shall henceforth think himself at liberty to attempt such methods or some like them in the aforesaid offices, especially in the canonical Hours or in the solemn celebration of the Mass." Whosoever disobeyed this order was to be punished by suspension from office for eight days.

Although the effect of the pope's decree is not recorded, there is no reason to believe that the order of John XXII was not generally executed. There are some indications that in Florence where innovations were welcomed, and also in Rome, the order of the pope who was in residence at Avignon was not carried out to the letter. On the other hand, almost a century later the pope's prohibition was still a part of the rules upon which the services in the Cathedral of Notre Dame in Paris were based. Thus the Gregorian chant or plainsong was preserved in the service of the Church. In a sense the papal decree of 1322 may be said to have brought about a parting of the ways for secular and sacred music. While the Ars Nova composers turned their attention largely to secular music, the composers of sacred music wrote their works along the lines laid down by the Church. Sacred music continued to develop in its own sphere, although few composers of this period wrote their compositions strictly in accordance with the "stile antiqua." The most sublime heights of sacred music were probably reached in Italy during the High Renaissance in the compositions of Giovanni da Palestrina (1521-1594). He was undoubtedly the greatest composer of sacred music of his time and, in the opinion of some music historians, of all time. His music was chosen by the Council of Trent (1545-1563) as a model of the purest religious style. But even Palestrina could not resist the temptation of writing secular strains into some of his sacred motets and masses. Besides composing sacred music Palestrina was also the composer of madrigals.

The Italian Ars Nova

Meanwhile the influence of the Ars Nova was spreading to other countries of Europe, influencing the development of music in each one to a greater or lesser extent. In other words, the influence was not uniform. In some countries the native traditions offered greater resistance than in others. In Italy, which in the fourteenth century began to play a major role in European music, the Ars Nova stimulated a growing interest in music. Up to this time Italian musicians had not contributed much to the development of polyphony. Interest in music was at such a low ebb that only a few compositions and musical treatises have come down to us from the thirteenth century. In the fourteenth, however, the creative spirit which produced great works in the other branches of the arts also manifested itself in music, stimulating Italian composers to make notable advances. The result was that secular music flowered to an extent undreamed of by the early proponents of the Ars Nova. Italian composers borrowed much from the French movement, but impregnated what they borrowed with the spontaneous lyricism that was characteristic of Italian Renaissance life. They also reduced the complexities of the French Ars Nova movement so that song in all its melodic beauty emerged from the tangled skein of polyphony.

The Italians, as indicated, achieved their most striking success in the field of vocal music. The troubadour songs as well as the Ars Nova movement were an important factor in its development. If the Italian songs were not artistically on a par with the compositions of the troubadours, they were more tuneful and melodious. Whereas the interest of the French Ars Nova had been centered in rhythm and design, the Italian school emphasized melody and color. The French composers were interested more in the intellectual side of music; the major Italian concern was the emotional. Another important factor in the growth of Italian song was the rise of Italian lyric poetry. The new literature in the vernacular supplied much poetry which Italian composers set to music so that the Italians could indulge their love of singing. Very little of the new poetry was overlooked. Among the prime favorites of the composers were the sonnets and canzoni of Petrarch. He undoubtedly heard his poems sung many times. The many poems set to music justified the remark, "Secular music has become the handmaiden of poetry." Some songs were tender, others light, still others humorous, and some obscure. The composers who wrote their own words celebrated many public events in song, including royal marriages or birthdays, peace negotiations, peace treaties, and war victories. Others wrote carnival songs for the gala celebrations and processions staged by some of the Italian city-states. Furthermore, the growth of the folksong during the Renaissance must not be overlooked. This period also saw the rise of popular music in the modern sense.

The most popular forms of song in Renaissance Italy were the madrigal, the ballata, the caccia, and the frottola. The word "madrigal" probably derives from the Italian *mandra*, meaning flock or herd. It was first used to designate a literary form, then applied to the words together with the music. The madrigals of the fourteenth and fifteenth centuries were, as the word "mandra" indicates, pastoral and contemplative in contrast to the gallant and often lascivious French chansons. The first madrigals, usually composed for two and sometimes for three voices, were probably sung without accompaniment, that is, *a cappella*. Before long, however, musical instruments supplied accompaniment for the voice parts. The early madrigals were also quite simple; for example: "In the midst of six peacocks I saw a white one; with a golden crown and languid feathers; so beautiful that my heart softly trembled." The lyrics of later madrigals were somewhat more involved as the following example shows:

> The sun which makes a lily bloom,
> Leans down at times on her to gaze—
> Fairer, he deems, than his fair rays.
> Then, having looked a little while,
> He turns and tells the saints in bliss
> How marvellous her beauty is.
> Thus up in heaven with flute and string
> Thy loveliness the angels sing.

Some of the idyllic madrigals were based on the motif of man's love for woman:

> Hard by a crystal stream
> Girls and maids were dancing round
> A lilac with fair blossoms crowned.
> Mid these I spied out one
> So tender, sweet, so love-laden,
> She stole my heart with singing then:
> Love in her face so lovely, kind,
> And eyes and hands my soul did bind.

The ballata (not related to the French ballade) was originally a song which was sung as accompaniment to round dances. It was sung alternately by a solo singer and by a group. The words usually consisted of a six-line stanza and a two-line refrain. In the ballata there is the same affectation of rusticity as in the early madrigals. One of the most prolific writers of ballate was Angelo Politian, eminent humanist and close friend of Lorenzo the Magnificent. The following is an example of one of his dance songs:

> I went a-roaming, maidens, one bright day
> In a green garden in mid-month of May
>
> Violets and lillies grow on every side
> Mid the green grass and flowers wonderful,
> Golden and white and red and azure-eyed;
> Toward which I stretched my hand, eager to pull
> Plenty to make my fair curls beautiful,
> To crown my rippling curls with garlands gay.
>
> I went a-roaming, maidens, one bright day,
> In a green garden in mid-month of May.
>
> But when my lap was full of flowers, I spied
> Roses at last, roses of every hue;
> Therefore I ran to pluck their ruddy pride,
> Because their perfume was so sweet and true
> With yearning and desire too soft to say.

The caccia, as the Italian word indicates, is a hunting song which is related to the French *chace* and the English *catch*. In it two or three voices, so to speak, chase each other. Although its subject matter was originally a story of a hunt from the assembling of a hunting party to the capture of the quarry, at a later time fishing scenes, battle scenes, and any scenes that lent themselves to vivid description were used. The period of its greatest popularity was the second half of the fourteenth century. The following lines are from a caccia describing a fishing scene, written by the great Italian musician Francesco Landini:

> "Look at the crawfish, look! Look at the fish!
> Catch him, catch him!"
> Isabella began screaming, "Oh! Oh!"

"What's the matter? What's the matter?"
"He bit my toe."
"O Lisa, the fish is swimming away!"
"I've got him! I've got him!"
"Hold on to him!"

The frottola became widely popular in the fifteenth century. In its plural form of frottole the word was used as a class name which included all the secular songs of the period. The frottola was deliberately composed as a lighter form of music and appears to have had its origin in the social atmosphere of the Italian courts. In the early frottole the music consisted of several short sections which were repeated in various arrangements. They were written in three or four parts with the upper part as melody. Often the lower parts were played on instruments. One form of frottole, which must not be confused with the folksong, went down to the masses in much the same manner as the present-day popular songs. Many of the compositions came from the pens of amateur rhymesters who often relied on a patchwork of phrases culled from popular poetry. A large number of these songs, together with the musical settings, have been preserved in the eleven books of frottole collected and published in Venice (1504-1514) by Octaviano Petrucci. A brief summary of the lyrics of two frottole may show how closely they are related to the modern popular songs. In the first the suitor tells the object of his affections that he must part from her much against his will, but that only his body is departing. He is leaving his heart and soul with her. He assures her that the memory of her sweet face will cheer him, offset the discomforts of travel, and hasten his return. In the second frottola the relationship is a different one. The man declares that of his own will he has decided to part from the young lady he had adored. He informs her that if the sight of her once thrilled him, this is no longer true. The one thing he is thankful for is that leaving her causes him no pain. Many similar expressions of love and disillusionment can be found in the popular songs of the present day.

Musical Instruments and Instrumental Music

Another feature of the Italian Renaissance is the progress made in the development of instrumental music. Musical instruments were not, of course, first invented in the Renaissance period. Their use dates back to the dawn of recorded history. The ancient Hebrews had a number of musical instruments. As for the Greeks, their favorite musical instruments were the flute and the chitora, a kind of lyre. During the Roman period, according to Seneca, large-scale musical performances with instruments were often presented. During the Middle Ages, so long as Gregorian music was the predominating type, instrumental music suffered somewhat of an eclipse. But with the rise of secular music more attention was given to instruments. Even then the primary function of the instruments was to provide accompaniment for the song and its relative, the dance. The favorite instruments for this purpose were the *viole* or viol and the lute, but the flute, harp, and portable organ were also used in various combinations. At first the music they provided was more in the nature of improvisation rather than of a definite composition. It was only when instrumental music was recognized as a means of expressing individual feeling and inspiration that it was written down as a definite composition. Gradually the practice developed of playing the music without the singing. The final step was the composition of music for instruments alone. The first instrument for which music seems to have been written in quantity was the lute which was at that time the instrument par excellence for secular music. By the beginning of the sixteenth century, however, considerable music was being written for various instruments.

The instruments mentioned in the preceding paragraph are not the only ones in use during the Renaissance, particularly the later period of it. In addition there were such instruments as the rebec (ancestor of the violin), the psalterium or psaltery (a kind of guitar), the recorder (early flute), the shawm or oboe, drums, the trumpet, the trombone, the bagpipe, and others. In the late Renaissance, wealthy families of the Italian city-states tried to outdo one another not only in the lavish manner in which they decorated their homes, but also in the size of the ensemble they engaged to play for their dances and social affairs. For the indoor entertainment of the aristocracy, stringed instruments were preferred. For music played out of doors, wind instruments were used. This was true of country dances as well as of outdoor entertainments in the cities. In Venice, where most of the functions were staged in the open air, trumpets, trombones, and recorders were used. At the official festivals staged by the city of Florence the music was furnished by pipes, trombones, trumpets, and oboes. Often large numbers of players with various kinds of instruments were assembled to provide music for special events. At the court of Mantua as many as four hundred musicians played at one time. (*See Fig. 23.*)

The center of the Italian Ars Nova music was in northern Italy where secular music was cultivated at the courts of the princes and nobles, and fostered by the governments of the city-states. There were flourishing schools of composers at Padua, Bologna, Ferrara, Rimini, Mantua, Urbino, and other places. But the Florentine composers were the chief exponents of the Italian Ars Nova music. Despite continuing internal political strife and unrest, wars with neighboring towns and city-states, and repeated visitations of the plague, the Florentines pursued the cultivation of music with unmatched zeal, producing a large number of secular compositions. The many festivities offered opportunities for celebrating the occasion in song and the Florentine composers made the most of them by writing songs which show a highly developed sense of both rhythm and melody. The outstanding Ars Nova composer of the Florentine school was Francesco Landini (1325-

1397), called by his contemporaries "Il Cieco" (the blind) or "Francesco degli Organi" (Francesco of the organ). The fact that he lost his eyesight as the result of an attack of smallpox during childhood did not prevent him from studying philosophy, logic, theology, mathematics, astronomy, and music. He also wrote poetry both in the vernacular and in Latin. By his contemporaries he was widely regarded as a man of great learning. His greatest distinction he achieved in music. He performed skillfully on the lute, flute, recorder and, above all, on the organ. As organist in the Church of San Lorenzo in Florence his virtuoso performances made him so famous that he was decorated on a number of occasions. His claim to lasting fame rests on his compositions. In them the Italian Ars Nova music reached its greatest heights. He wrote about two hundred secular works, but many of them have disappeared. Among his compositions that have survived there are many ballate or dance songs, a number of beautiful madrigals, and the lively fishing scene in caccia form (*see page 210*).

After the Ars Nova

Music historians regard the Italian Ars Nova as ending with the fourteenth century. The force of the forward movement had spent itself and northern influences were reasserting themselves. During the succeeding period the northern composers, particularly those of the Netherlands, took the leadership away from the Italians and carried the art of counterpoint to new pinnacles. In this connection the word "Netherlands" (Low Countries) is used in a geographical, not in a political sense. In its geographical sense it included much of northern France as well as the territories which now constitute Belgium, Holland, and Luxembourg. Since it included Holland, Flanders, and Burgundy, the Netherlands schools of music are variously called Dutch, Flemish, or Burgundian. The music is characterized by the same refined grace and harmonious color that distinguishes the paintings of such great Italian masters as Fra Angelico and Fra Lippo Lippi. The works of the composers of this school are also marked by a spirit of lyric happiness, but melancholy is not absent. This music deeply influenced the music of all other countries of Europe. Netherlanders gradually filled the most important positions in the world of music. As a consequence, music began to be more and more alike in the different European countries.

The great master of the early school of Netherlands musicians was Guillaume Dufay (1400-1474). His particular school is often called the Burgundian school because of Dufay's service at the court of Burgundy. As a young man he spent a number of years in Italy studying music and singing in the Papal Choir. The Italian influence is clearly visible in his compositions. He wove many of the ideas of Florentine composers into a mature technique of musical composition. For many years Dufay served as singer and music teacher at the court of Charles the Good, duke of Burgundy, at that time an important cultural center. While there, Dufay wrote some of his best musical compositions. His works include motets and masses as well as purely secular compositions. Especially significant are his chansons which are characterized by spontaneity and charm. The music of Dufay and his followers is soft and mellow. His songs are modern in the sense that they present a picture of the poem and its contents. They mark an advance in expressiveness and melodic charm. An example of a gay and light-hearted chanson is the rondeau "Pour l'amour de ma dulce amye." The music of Dufay's school was organized along such strict lines of construction that it eliminated the improvisations of the previous period. Another change introduced by the Burgundian school was the secularization of the motet to the extent that it became a form of solemn festival music, performed at such events as coronations, the conclusion of peace treaties, and important marriages. Dufay possessed great skill in the composition of such motets and could write them at short notice. Ten years before his death he wrote a motet which, although he planned to have it sung at his deathbed, was actually used at his funeral. In his masses he softened the formerly stern lines by the introduction of familiar secular folk tunes. Thus he was the first to use "L'homme armé" (The Man in Armor) in a mass. Such use of folk tunes in the masses is a good example of the spirit of the Renaissance in that it combines the *joie de vivre* with religious fervor.

In the fifteenth century the influence of the Netherlands music and musical techniques was particularly profound in Italy. During this period there was a close contact between the commercial centers of Italy and the thriving towns of the Low Countries. But this contact was not limited to commerce. Artists and musicians of both countries associated freely and exchanged ideas. The Low Countries possessed a well-developed and prosperous middle class which loved both art and music. Under the patronage of the wealthy burghers both flourished. The musical techniques developed in these towns and at the various courts of the Netherlands were among the exports to Italy. There they became so predominant that what little Italian music was produced was largely devoid of anything new.

The fact that Italian composers were forced into the background did not, however, stifle the Italian interest in music. A natural desire for pleasure by all classes of Italian society kept the musical interest at high pitch. The independent city-states and small principalities took a great pride in promoting the arts. Some states even founded music centers for the cultivation of music. Music was one of the means employed by the Medici to keep the Florentine people happy and unconcerned about political affairs. This was particularly true of Lorenzo de Medici. To encourage the cultivation of music he founded a School of Harmony which was in the nature of a Philharmonic Society. This school attracted musicians from various countries. Lorenzo was himself a musician of no mean ability, performing skillfully on the lute. Many of his poems, particularly those that were obscene, were set to music. Music also added much to the popularity of the festivities and processions of Florence. Most unusual were the carnivals staged before and after Lent which featured torchlight parades with great processions of mummers wearing grotesque masques. Such festivities, enlivened with music, were enjoyed wholeheartedly by all classes of the population. The poems, together with some of the music used for the carnivals which have survived to this day, give us a clear picture of the musical side of the Florentine festivities and entertainments.

Although the cultivation of music was not confined to any one class, it occupied a particularly high place in the social life of the many Italian courts. Baldassare Castiglione in his famous work *Il Cortegiano* (The Courtier, 1528), which contains a colorful account of the social life at the court of Urbino, shows the importance of music in the high society of Italy at his time. It gives us an insight into what was expected from a perfect courtier. He must be not only an able soldier, a gallant, a scholar, a statesman, and a connoisseur of painting, but also an accomplished musician. A knowledge of music was indeed so essential that a gentleman could not be regarded a perfect courtier without it. Castiglione takes great pains to delineate what might be expected from the cultured gentleman in the way of musical accomplishments. A courtier must understand music, have a good singing voice, be able to read music at sight for singing, and "must have skill in like manner on sundry instruments." Castiglione regarded music as "a most acceptable food for the mind," but he repeatedly asserted that in the life of the courtier it must be only a pleasant pastime, not a profession. He also added certain rules of etiquette. For example, a gentleman is counseled to sing only when urged to do so and then not before large gatherings. Women, too, were encouraged to cultivate music, but were advised not to play such unseemly instruments as drums, pipes, and trumpets.

After 1530 the Italian genius reasserted itself, bringing the achievements of the Netherlanders to full flower. In this phase of the Italian musical development Venice was the most important center for sacred as well as for secular music. Venice furnished an ideal environment for the development of secular music; nowhere else in Italy was the interest in mundane joys and pleasures greater at this time. This colorful life with its pomp and pageantry is reflected in Venetian music. The wonderful sense of color which we admire in the paintings of Bellini, Giorgione, and Titian is also manifest in Venetian music. Music and painting are the last great expressions of Venetian life at a time when its political and financial fortunes were declining. Composers turned their attention to such popular songs as the canzoni and frottole, and embodied their gay spirit, sparkling rhythm, and lively color in the madrigal of the sixteenth century. There was instrumental music, too, but it was limited largely to the organ and clavier.

The founder of the Venetian school was Adrian Willaert (1480-1562), a Netherlander who distinguished himself in sacred as well as in secular music. When he wrote a motet in Rome as a young man, the choir refused to sing it because it was not written by a distinguished composer. But it did not take Willaert long to become famous. Soon he was appointed chapel master of St. Mark's, the great Byzantine church in Venice. Thereafter his fame grew rapidly. Among other things he founded a singing school which soon had as alumni many of the outstanding composers of the succeeding period. He was also one of the first to make extensive use of chords in his compositions. But he is particularly famous for writing music for two choirs. About 1500 the Venetians had installed two organs on opposite sides of the nave in St. Mark's. Willaert took advantage of the opportunity to employ two complete choirs which could be used either together or antiphonally. Antiphonal singing was, of course, not new, but polyphonic music that echoed back and forth between the two choirs appears to have been an innovation. Music historians believe that the harmonic quality of this music was probably influenced by the Lutheran choral. The effects produced by the singing of the two choirs were extraordinary. In secular music Willaert is credited with making the sixteenth-century madrigal popular. Some music historians have gone so far as to call him "the father of the sixteenth-century madrigal." This new madrigal became, in fact, the most popular musical form of the sixteenth century. The ancestor of the sixteenth-century madrigal was the frottola; consequently this madrigal has been described as "an ennobled frottola." In 1559 Willaert published a volume of motets and madrigals under the title *Musica Nova*. Many of his mardigals are based on poems by Petrarch.

Music and the Arts

The role of music in Italian life is reflected in contemporary literature. In Dante's writings music is portrayed as one of life's greatest pleasures. Mention has been made earlier of the fact that the poet himself took great delight in both instrumental music and in singing. According to Filelfo in his *Vita Dantis* the author of the *Divine Comedy* "sang suavely, having a clear voice" and also "played skilfully on the organ and lyre." The fact that many of the lines of Dante's great poem testify to his musical knowledge by their rhythm moved Ghiberti to ask, "Who can really describe the suavity and the musical variety of Dante's versification?" If ordinary music gave him so much pleasure, the music of Paradise was to him the highest delight. After hearing the song of hundreds of angels as he met Beatrice at the entrance to Paradise, he wrote, "The sweet song of this earth is but a noise of a thundercloud when compared with the heavenly lyre." While some composers drew inspiration for their compositions from the *Divine Comedy*, others set his ballate and shorter poems to music. When on his journey through Purgatory he met Casella, who had written music for many of his poems, Dante asked his old friend to sing one of the songs which had so often soothed his troubled spirit. Casella obliged by singing a beautiful canzone from Dante's

Convito. So great was Dante's love of music that he could not consign to one of the lower depths of hell Orpheus, the legendary Greek who could move rocks and trees with the music of his lyre. Since Orpheus had lived before the advent of Christianity, Dante could not permit him to enter Paradise, so he put him in the first circle of Inferno. Upon meeting Apollo, the pagan god of music and song, near the gates of Paradise, the poet expressed the wish that he himself could sing as well as the Greek god.

The works of Boccaccio also contain many references to music, but the music is strictly secular. Thus in a beautiful sonnet he describes the singing of Fiametta:

> And when I heard a song as glad as love
> So sweet that never yet the like thereof
> Was heard in any mortal company.
> A nymph, a goddess, or an angel sings
> Unto herself within this chosen place
> Of ancient loves; so said I at that sound.
> And there my lady, 'mid the shadowings
> Of myrrh trees, 'mid flowers and grassy space,
> Singing I saw with others who sat round.

In the introduction to his *Decameron*, discussed in an earlier chapter, Boccaccio makes much of music as one of the principal means of entertainment for the group of young people who left Florence to escape the plague. Every story that the members of the group told during the entire ten days was followed by instrumental music, dancing, and singing. One member of the group played the lute and another the viol. According to Boccaccio both played "excellently well." Then the group began to dance and "fell to singing quaint and merry ditties."

Music was also closely associated with the drama. The so-called "intermezzi" constituted one phase of this association. The intermezzi were brief interludes of musical and dramatic entertainment presented between the acts of morality or mystery plays and later of secular dramas. There was usually no direct connection between the drama and the intermezzi. The latter, often presented with elaborate stage settings and lively music, became so popular with the Italian audiences that in some cases they overshadowed what was supposed to be the main attraction. Contemporary critics were often lavish in their praise of the intermezzi, thereby stimulating the composers of the lively popular music to do their best. Gradually songs and music were employed to make the drama more lively and attractive. Long before the opera was even thought of, music and song played a considerable part in stage presentations as well as in festivities, processions, and social entertainments. Music historians see the first faint traces of opera in *Orfeo*, the tragedy in verse written in 1471 by Angelo Politian.

The enthusiasm of the Renaissance period for classical studies also made itself felt in the field of music. As has been indicated, many of the humanists were musicians and vice versa. For example, Marsilio Ficino, the founder of the Platonic Academy in Florence, often played the lyre before admiring audiences in the palaces of the Medici. Many humanist composers set for themselves the purpose of supplying a modern substitute for the music of classical times. They did not, as did Renaissance sculptors, have actual models that had survived from Greek and Roman times. But the ideas concerning the music of classical times which they found in Plato and other classical writers fascinated them. They learned that Greek music had been patterned after the meter of the verse, that the expression was carefully tuned to the meaning and emotions of the poem. If they did not have actual examples of classical music, they did have classical verses for which they could compose music. Toward the end of the fifteenth century Peter Tritonius set Horace's odes in four-part harmony at the urging of Conrad Celtes who was lecturing on the classics at the University of Ingolstedt. The purpose of setting Horace's odes to music was to make their rhythm more intelligible to the students. These compositions, first published in 1507, became so popular that they were republished several times during the succeeding decades. Musical settings were also composed for verses of Catullus, Martial, and Ovid. But the favorite poet of musicians was Virgil. His poetry proved so fascinating that during the fifteenth and sixteenth centuries composers vied with one another in the use of passages from the *Aeneid* as a basis for their compositions. What appealed to them most was the celebrated "Lament of Dido." No fewer than fourteen composers in Italy and the Netherlands wrote musical settings for it.

The musical interest of the Renaissance period is also reflected in painting. Any good collection of Italian Renaissance paintings demonstrates this. Hundreds of paintings contain musical representations of various kinds. While some depict musical events, others contain reproductions of musical instruments. Besides showing the variety of instruments in use at that time painters often reproduced them with such marvelous exactitude as to fix the details of holding and playing them. Moreover, they also represented such combinations of instruments as were customary at that time. Orcagna's "Triumph of Death" (1368), one of the most beautiful of the early Renaissance paintings, depicts in one corner a scene in which a group of high-born ladies and gentlemen are listening to a young man playing the viol accompanied by a young lady on the psaltery. Orcagna who, like many painters, was also a musician, included musical instruments in his other paintings. One of the most famous musical paintings is "The Concert" in the Pitti Gallery in Florence. This painting, formerly ascribed to Giorgione, suggests a scene from everyday life in which a lively youth in cap and plume presents a street concert with two musicians, one of whom plays a primitive violin and the other a clavicembalo or harpsichord. In religious pictures, angels frequently sing, play musical instruments, or simply hold them in their hands. In Fra Angelico's "Madonna and Child Enthroned" one angel plays a portable organ and the other a lute. In other paintings angels play the psaltery, the harp, the double shawm or oboe, the flute, the trumpet, and other instruments. The most frequently represented instrument was the lute. Even in the heavenly scenes all the instruments the artist introduces are those in use during his life-time. As new types of instruments were developed, they were added to those played or held by the angels. The realism is often so exact that the fingering of the angels on the flute makes musical sense. (*See Figs. 24, 25.*)

Secular music as an art came of age as a result of the invention of printing with movable type. The new printing techniques were soon applied to the printing of music. Previously music had been printed from engraved wooden blocks, but the process was too expensive and cumbersome for wider use. *The Psalter*, printed in 1451 at Mainz by Peter Schoeffer and Johann Fust is generally regarded as the first book containing music. In this book only the text and three lines of the staff are printed. The fourth line was drawn manually in red and the notes were also inscribed by hand. One of the first books in which music was actually printed from type was a missal printed in Milan in 1476. Such printing was, however, restricted to monophonic music. Only in the early sixteenth century was a method devised for printing polyphonic music. A number of printers have been accorded the honor of being the first to print two, three, and four part music. Although he may not have been the first, Octaviano Petrucci was the most successful of the early printers of music. As stated earlier, during the years 1504-1514 he printed in Venice eleven volumes of frottole of which ten have survived. In the succeeding decades other printers of music opened shops in Rome and other Italian cities, and also in various cities north of the Alps, including Paris, Lyons, London, Augsburg, Nuremberg, Strassburg, and Worms. As these presses turned out quantities of prints, music naturally gained a wider circulation than it had enjoyed in the form of manuscripts. It was now ready for distribution throughout Western Europe and the world. (*See Fig. 25.*)

13

Toward the Secular State

Most of the second half of the thirteenth century was a period of comparative peace between the popes and the secular rulers. Earlier in the century Pope Innocent IV (1242-1254) and Frederick II, emperor of the Holy Roman Empire (1215-1250), had waged a bitter struggle. Although Frederick's ambition to conquer Italy was the basic issue, the question of the nature and extent of the authority of the contending parties was soon posed. Frederick who had previously been feuding with the papacy was ready to conclude peace when Innocent IV became pope in 1242, but he felt that the pontiff's terms were arbitrary and unjust. This angered Innocent, causing him to undertake the destruction of Frederick. The pope secretly left Rome for France and there summoned a general council to meet at Lyons (1245). Innocent then proceeded to denounce Frederick before the assembly in unmeasured terms as was customary in the controversies of the age. He accused the emperor of not fulfilling the promises he had made to the Holy See at various times, of violating treaties, of committing sacrilege, and of abetting heresy. The sentence pronounced upon Frederick was excommunication and deposition as emperor and king of Sicily. Frederick responded with a series of recriminations in an open letter. He asserted that since his imperial authority was bestowed on him by God neither council nor pope had any jurisdiction over him. In rebuttal Innocent IV restated the papal claim of the subordination of the secular to the spiritual authority which had been elaborated by his predecessors. As he put it, the authority which Christ had given "to the pontifical chair was not only of a pontifical nature, but also contained a monarchical authority."

After the death of Frederick II in 1250 and of Innocent IV in 1254 the fury of the conflict subsided, but the conflicting claims were not shelved and forgotten. On the one hand, a number of lawyers and polemicists continued to muster support for the claims of the secular rulers and, on the other, theologians and students of canon law collected historical evidence in support of the papal claims. Thus the lines were sharply drawn on both sides, with the ideas of the ecclesiastical jurists pitted against those of the polemicists employed by the secular rulers.

The Emergence of the National State

As the thirteenth century neared its end the conflict between Church and State broke out anew. This time the principal opposition to the papal claims was not offered by one or more emperors. The new opponents of the papacy were rulers of the national states which were emerging to self-consciousness. As they gained strength, they became factors of increasing importance in the realm of international politics. In the thirteenth century the national monarchs were engaged in consolidating their kingdoms territorially and in centralizing in their own hands the administration of the territories of their kingdoms. Since this was done at the expense of the feudal vassals, the royal aims were met with stubborn resistance. The vassals were determined to resist any extension of the royal authority. But the monarchs employed threats and superior force, and even resorted to unscrupulous dealing, to limit the authority of the feudal barons. After crushing the military power of a baron, the monarch would incorporate the lands of his vassal into the royal domains and the national administration would absorb the administrative functions the baron had exercised. In this way the king became the directing head of a compact kingdom which increased in strength as well as in size every time another feudal baron was subdued.

In the struggle against the feudal barons the monarchs had as allies the members of the rising middle class. Merchants, industrialists, bankers, and skilled artisans desired peace and protection so that they could make the most of the opportunities offered by the commercial expansion. They wanted a government strong enough to put an end to the petty baronial wars which were interfering with commerce by keeping the countryside in a state of constant turmoil. They wanted a government that would put an end to the raids highwaymen and robber knights were making on traveling merchants and merchant caravans. Furthermore, they called for the abolition of the plethora of customs duties feudal barons levied on all merchandise that passed through their territories. All this, they believed, could be achieved only by the national monarch; hence they gave him their support. But the benefits were not all on one side. The monarchs needed the middle class as much as the latter needed a strong monarchy. It was from the commerce of the middle class and from the commercial towns that the ruler derived the income in the form of taxes which enabled him to build the army he needed to crush recalcitrant barons who refused to relinquish their political authority. With the income from the duties he levied on trade the monarch also purchased artillery to level the strongholds of robber knights and rebellious barons.

Other important factors in the rise of national states were a common language and a feeling of loyalty called patriotism. A common language was an important bond of unity even though it was not essential. In time the national language became the vehicle of a national literature which excited pride of citizenship. Most effective in the creation of national unity was patriotism or national sentiment. It was the cement which held the national group together. It was also the force which disrupted the theoretical unity of Christendom and undermined the ideal of Christian brotherhood sponsored by the Church. In time national feeling became so strong that it surpassed religion as a motivating force. As each national state demanded the full allegiance of all its citizens, loyalty to the nation state or nationality became a kind of religion which took precedence over the loyalty to a supranational church. The new national patriotism also turned men's minds to secular affairs. The things of this life absorbed more and more of the attention previously reserved for the hereafter.

National unity was not, however, achieved in all the countries of Western Europe. In some the lack of a strong monarchy and a dynamic national feeling permitted the forces opposed to unification to prevail. The ruling idea was that of particularism. The two countries in which a vigorous trend toward unification was absent were Germany and Italy. In Germany a number of factors militated against the achievement of national unity. There was, for example, no strong ruling house in Germany around which a national movement could grow, nor were there well-defined national boundaries. In the west territory frequently shifted to France and back, and on the eastern side the movement of German settlers across the Elbe and the Oder into sparsely-populated Slavic lands kept the boundaries in a state of flux. Probably the greatest obstacle in the way of German unity was an old tradition of the Holy Roman Empire, which perpetuated empty claims to universal rule. A number of emperors cherished the so-called "imperial dream," hoping to restore the old Roman Empire to its pristine glory. In comparison with the imperial dream the establishment of a German national state appeared minor and insignificant.

Despite the opposing factors a considerable patriotic sentiment and feeling of unity did develop about the person of Emperor Frederick I (1152-1190), called Barbarossa or Redbeard. To his people Frederick Barbarossa was a figure of heroic proportions. After his death the legend was current that he had not died, but had retired to a cavern in the Kyffhäuser hills to return at the proper time to lead the German people to unity and greatness. But the surge of German national feeling was short-lived. When Frederick II became emperor in 1215 he sought to make the "imperial dream" a reality by trying to extend imperial rule to Italy and as a result became involved in conflicts with the papacy. While he was thus engaged, the territorial princes of Germany made the most of the opportunity to strengthen their power. As one historian has put it, they not only climbed into the saddle, but also assumed direction of the horse. Thereafter they exerted the decisive influence in the Holy Roman Empire. Thus the rule of Frederick II was a turning-point because the trend toward greater centralization of power was reversed in favor of particularism. Having assumed the direction of affairs in the Holy Roman Empire, the princes and princelings retained it until after the dissolution of the Empire in 1806.

In Italy many people were conscious of being Italians, that is, of living in the Italian peninsula. There was also in some circles a reverence for the glorious past of Rome. Furthermore, the classical tradition, which was more vigorous in Italy than in any other country of Western Europe, implied a common past. In reality, however, Italy was splintered into many fragments. With the exception of the kingdom of Naples which embraced about a third of Italy, the peninsula was divided into small city-states in which particularist feeling reigned supreme. The desire for political unity seems to have been non-existent except in the minds of a few thinkers such as Dante. Venice, Genoa, Pisa, Florence, and other city-states were economic rivals whose feelings toward one another were often characterized by violent hostility. It has been said that the nearer they were located to each other the fiercer the enmity. The purpose of the larger city-states was often to subjugate and exploit the smaller ones or to rob them of their trade. Wars of ambition and pride consumed much of the energy as well as the substance of both sides. In such states politics were being separated more and more from religion and most of the aims were frankly secular and materialistic. In Venice and Padua, for example, the attitude toward the clergy was amazingly modern. Cases involving infractions of the civil laws by clerics were tried in civil, not ecclesiastical courts. This is not to say that the governments of the city-states encouraged heresy or that there was a lack of respect for religion. What it meant was that the governments were moving in the direction of the separation of Church and State.

The two countries which had made the greatest advance toward national unity were France and England. In both countries the process of building compact national states was, it is true, only in an early stage, but the administrative, judicial, and financial systems had been molded sufficiently to serve as a basis for an aggressive national policy. Put in another way, Philip IV of France (also known as Philippe le Bel or Philip the Fair) (1295-1314) and Edward I of England (1272-1307) believed they were strong enough successfully to oppose the papal claims to authority in secular as well as in spiritual matters. The papacy had not denied kings and princes the exercise of their authority; the popes, however, claimed the right to pass judgment on the acts and decisions of the secular rulers according to the moral standards of the Church. The rulers resented what they saw as interference in the affairs of their kingdoms. They did not wish their decisions to be subject to review by the pope. They were confident that they could manage their affairs and make the proper decisions without papal prescription. However much Philip IV and Edward I differed as persons and as rulers, they were at one in opposing pontifical supervision of what they regarded as their personal affairs. Such supervision, they were convinced, was neither in their own best interest nor in the interest of their people. It was this conviction which gave rise to the long conflict with the pope.

It was Pope Boniface VIII, occupant of the papal throne from 1294 to his death in 1303, who took up the cudgels in defense of the papal claims when they were challenged by Philip the Fair and Edward I. As Benedict Gaetani, Boniface had received a good education in both canon and civil law. The bulls and other documents he issued as pope reflect this training. After completing his schooling he entered the service of the papal court and served with distinction over a period of many years. As a cardinal and papal legate he earned the reputation of being a shrewd politician. This reputation weighted the scales in his favor when he was elected pope. The new pontiff decided to restore to the Holy See the prestige it had enjoyed in the time of Innocent III. There was, by and large, nothing new in the assertions with which he hoped to achieve this. The same claims had been stated by earlier popes and clearly formulated by Innocent III. Thus Boniface only reasserted the claims of his predecessors. He was, however, so completely blinded by his determination to strengthen the position of the papacy that he failed to realize that the claims advanced by Gregory VII and Innocent III were at the end of the thirteenth century no longer in accord with the temper of the times. What to him appeared to be the essential truth was not in harmony with the political realities. Profound political changes had taken place since the time of Innocent III.

Boniface also misjudged the situation in other respects. He underestimated the strength of his opponents and their determination to resist the papal claims. Furthermore, he did not realize that he could no longer command the unquestioning obedience of the people of France and England. In the previous conflicts between the popes and the emperors the opinion of the German people had usually been on the side of the popes. Since their patriotism was local, the fact that the popes were restricting the imperial authority did not disturb them. The ruling princes of the many feudal states of Germany seem to have favored the diminution of the emperor's authority. In France and England the situation was different. There the kings were the focus of the new national patriotism; hence the monarchs had the support of their subjects in the conflict with the pope. Large segments of the people regarded the papal claims as encroachments on the rights and interests of their nation. If Boniface had carefully surveyed the situation before issuing his edicts the outcome of the conflict might have been different. As it was, his efforts to enforce the papal claims ended in failure, despite the fact that he defended them with all the arguments and energy he could muster. It should be noted that, in any case, Boniface could not have changed his stand without repudiating the traditions of the papacy.

Boniface VIII and Philip IV: The First Phase

Two immediate issues precipitated the conflict. The first was the desire of Boniface to prevent the outbreak of war between France and England and to prevail on the monarchs of the two countries to lead a crusade against the Turks which would crush them for all time. The second issue was the taxing of the clergy and the estates of the Church for secular purposes by the rulers of France and England without the express permission of the Vatican. When Boniface became pope toward the end of 1294, Philip was making preparations for war against Edward I of England. Being perpetually in need of funds, the French king decided to impose taxes on the clergy and the estates of the Church as well as on the other classes and estates of his kingdom. His legal counselors seem to have advised him that he could do this. It did not, however, meet with the approval of the clergy. When some members of the clergy appealed to Boniface for aid in their efforts to stop Philip from collecting the taxes, the pope took a step which he believed would settle the matter with finality. He issued the bull *Clericis Laicos* in which he emphatically forbade the secular rulers to tax the clergy for secular purposes without the express permission of the pope. All emperors, kings, princes, dukes, and barons, he stated, who demand taxes from the clergy and collect them without first obtaining permission from the Holy See automatically (*ipso facto*) draw down upon themselves the ban of excommunication. Communities which are guilty of the same offense were threatened with the interdict. But Boniface did not stop there. He also threatened with excommunication any members of the clergy who consented to pay the taxes demanded from them by the secular authorities. To make certain that he had left no loopholes, Boniface further stated that those members of the clergy who condone the domination of the clergy by the civil powers are *ipso facto* excommunicated. Finally, he forbade all members of the clergy under threat of deposition to permit the collection of taxes imposed by the civil powers.

There was nothing particularly novel about the claims Boniface made. The Church had long maintained that the right of taxing the clergy was its own prerogative. Both popes and councils had previously asserted that the civil powers have no right to tax the clergy without permission from the ecclesiastical authorities. The Third Lateran Council (1179), for example, claimed immunity from taxation for the clergy and the properties of the Church. The Fourth Lateran Council (1215) decreed that the pope must be consulted even when the members of the clergy wish to make voluntary contributions to the state. The Church had, however, offered no objections when the purpose for which the money was collected was one in which the Church was deeply interested as, for example, the Crusades. What offended many was the position of absolute superiority which Boniface assumed and the arbitrary manner in which he forbade the taxation of the clergy. Philip IV regarded the bull as an unwarranted attack on rights of the crown which he believed to be beyond question. But since the bull did not mention him by name, he did not prepare a formal answer to it. He gave his answer in the form of an order which forbade the export from France of gold and silver, jewelry and negotiable securities, without royal permission. All foreigners residing in France were also ordered to leave the country, an order which was aimed at the delegates of the pope, his nuncios, tax collectors, and all Italians to whom the pope had granted benefices in France.

In cutting off so large a portion of the papal revenues, the export prohibition of Philip dealt a severe blow to the finances of the Holy See. More than this, the enforcement of the prohibition was so complete that it paralyzed banking activities and also trade between Italy and France, threatening ruin to bankers and merchants who were deeply involved in these activities. Hence Italian merchants and bankers seem to have put pressure on the pope to have Philip's orders rescinded. Boniface himself soon felt the effects of the loss of the papal revenues from France. Some weeks after Philip issued his orders, the pope released the first of a series of bulls in which he hoped to prevail on Philip to revoke his orders. In the first bull, *Ineffabilis Amoris* (September, 1296), addressed directly to Philip, Boniface denounced the royal orders as bad advice from evil counselors, but he did adopt a more conciliatory tone than the one which characterized *Clericis Laicos*, pointing out that he had not forbidden the French clergy to make voluntary gifts to the king. In the bulls and letters that followed, the pope continued to threaten and to plead. Thus, for example, he wrote, "Give to the Church, my dearest son, the respect you owe her. . . . If you do not put obstacles in the way of piety, the Church will willingly aid you with her subsidies." But all this left Philip unmoved. Meanwhile Boniface, under the pressure of financial need, had been retreating further and further from the arbitrary stand he had taken in *Clericis Laicos*. Finally, in a bull issued in July, 1297, he recognized the right of Philip to tax the clergy in case of necessity without papal consent. Thus without formally retracting the claims he had made in *Clericis Laicos* Boniface had gradually executed an about-face. Meanwhile Philip remained adamant in his defiance.

Boniface VIII and Philip IV: The Second Phase

It seemed for a time as if the rupture between Boniface and Philip the Fair had been healed. But the outward harmony between the two was short-lived. In the minds of both Boniface and Philip the idea that each was unjustly trying to circumscribe the other's authority still rankled. Boniface, a man of unbending will and unflagging determination, was not inclined to surrender one whit of the authority he believed to be his, and Philip continued to oppose the papal claims of supremacy over the state. Boniface still did not realize how strong the position of the national monarchs was. During the period of outward peace between the two the self-confidence of the pope was bolstered in the year 1300 by the display of religious zeal. This year which had been designated a jubilee year saw vast crowds of pilgrims journey to Rome for the purpose of earning with prayers and offerings the full absolution for their sins which the Holy See had promised them. The wave of religious enthusiasm convinced Boniface that he had the support of the masses of Europe. It made him even more resolute in the assertion of his claims. Refurbishing every weapon in his armory, Boniface again entered the arena to do battle against Philip. As Philip had given further evidence of his disdain of papal authority, the pope appointed Bernard de Saisset, bishop of Pamiers, his legate and sent him to discuss the question with Philip. The fact that a French bishop was willing to serve as papal legate incensed the king to the extent that he refused to see him when he arrived at the royal court. Later when the bishop had returned to Pamiers, Philip had him brought back to Paris where he was tried, convicted of treason and lese majesty, and imprisoned.

Boniface was furious when he heard of the plight of his legate. The proceedings which Philip had instituted against the bishop of Pamiers were an infraction of the laws of the Church which clearly stated that a bishop cannot be tried before a lay court. Boniface reacted by demanding that Philip release the bishop at once. Instead of complying, the French king suggested that the pope strip the bishop of Pamiers of his episcopal dignity and all his clerical privileges. The pope's answer was the bull *Ausculta Fili* in which he forcefully reproached Philip for oppressing the French clergy and restated his right of intervening in the affairs of secular powers. He stated in part, "God, in placing upon us the yoke of apostolic servitude, gave us the right to uproot, destroy, annihilate, dispense, and plant in His name; dearly beloved son, do not allow yourself to be persuaded that you are not subject to the supreme head of the Church, for such an opinion would be folly." Boniface then invited Philip to appear in Rome either in person or by proxy to defend himself against the charge of tyrannical rule over his subjects and of oppressing the Church. Philip responded by summoning representatives of the clergy, nobility, and the Third Estate to meet for the purpose of considering the statements of Boniface and his invitation to Philip. Formerly historians stated that Philip did not present to the assembly (often called the first Estates General) the actual bull *Ausculta Fili*, but an adulterated version in which the claims of the pope were stated in stronger terms. More recently, however, several French historians have offered a defence of Philip against the accusation of forgery. Whatever the truth in the matter, the assembly decided that the pope had no authority to sit in judgment on the king of France. The king himself, in informing Boniface of the assembly's decision, asserted flatly that in secular matters he was subject to no one. "Those who think otherwise," he stated, "are either fools or madmen."

Boniface was not a pope who would surrender easily what he regarded as his God-given authority. Angered by Philip's reply and by the anti-papal propaganda that was being circulated in France, he decided to state clearly and in measured terms the prerogatives which he believed God had vested in the Holy See. The result was the bull *Unam Sanctam* (1302) which is probably the most celebrated assertion of papal authority in history. It is stated in terms of "the two swords, one temporal and the other spiritual." "He who denies," Boniface stated, "that the temporal sword is not in the power of Peter (and the popes who are his successors) has but ill understood the word of our Lord." The temporal sword is to be administered "for the Church" and the spiritual sword "by the Church." "It is fitting that one subject should be under the other; hence temporal authority must be subject to the spiritual power." In other words, "the inferior must be ruled by the superior. . . . Therefore, if the civil power err, it will be judged by the spiritual power, but if the supreme spiritual power err, it can be judged by God alone, not by any man." The papal authority "is not a human, but rather a divine power. . . . Therefore, whoever resists this power which God has ordained resists the ordination of God." The climax is reached in the closing statement which reads. "We, moreover, declare, proclaim, and pronounce that it is absolutely necessary for salvation that every human being be subject to the Roman pontiff."

There was nothing revolutionary or even new in the claims Boniface put forth in the bull *Unam Sanctam*. The claims had, by and large, been made by earlier popes. What is more, they had been widely accepted. But the times had changed, making the claims anachronistic. At the beginning of the fourteenth century the national monarchs, supported by national feeling, refused to accept the papal claims. Philip and his advisers answered the bull by drawing up against the pope a list of accusations which included heresy. They accused Boniface of denying the immortality of the soul because he had stated, "I would rather be a dog than a Frenchman." After making the accusations, Philip suggested that a General Council of the Roman Catholic Church be called for the purpose of passing judgment on the pope and unfrocking him. Boniface, in turn, decided to hurl at Philip the ban of excommunication. He would excommunicate the French king, declare him deposed as ruler of France, and release all Frenchmen from their allegiance to him. The day he chose for the publication was September 8, 1303, but at dawn on September 7 a band of conspirators under the leadership of Guillaume de Nogaret, Philip's vice-chancellor, forced its way into the papal apartments in the pope's native city of Anagni. After the conspirators failed in their efforts to wring concessions from the pope, they considered taking him back to France as a prisoner, but feared the public reaction to a forcible removal of the elderly pope from Anagni. Finally they decided to hold him prisoner in his own palace in order to gain time to plot further moves. Several days later, however, the townspeople of Anagni armed themselves and drove the conspirators out of town.

Boniface was threatened, but not maltreated during the short time he was held prisoner; nevertheless, the shock of the indignities which were heaped on him, and the humiliation he suffered, were too much for his frail health. Broken in spirit, he lived only a short time after his release, passing away on October 11. His death ended the efforts to compel the French government to accept the claims of papal supremacy. By this time it was evident that the spiritual weapons of the preceding period were no longer adequate against an aroused national feeling. Thus the reign of Boniface VIII witnessed the beginnings of the secularization of the national state.

The policy of restricting the papal authority in France which Philip IV had initiated was continued by Charles VII in the Pragmatic Sanction issued in 1438. After a vigorous denunciation of the insatiable cupidity of the papal court at Rome the declaration went on to abolish annates (the first year's income paid to the pope by bishops and others on their appointment to a see or benefice) which were the largest items in the papal taxation. The Pragmatic Sanction also limited the right of appeal to the pope by the French clergy, but did not abolish it completely. Furthermore, in the Pragmatic Sanction the French king limited the papal right of patronage in France. Thenceforth the pope was to exercise only the right of nominating a candidate for a vacant benefice or bishopric. The final decision was reserved for the king. When the Pragmatic Sanction was promulgated the reigning pope, Eugenius IV (1431-1447), naturally protested; so did his successor, Nicholas V (1447-1455). But in 1450 and 1452 assemblies of the French clergy confirmed the Pragmatic Sanction of 1438.

England, Spain, and Papal Supremacy

Meanwhile the papal claims to supremacy had fared no better in England. Like Philip IV of France, Edward I of England was firm in his determination to be free of papal jurisdiction in what he regarded as temporal matters. He, too, believed that the clergy should contribute a part of their wealth to further the purposes of the national state. As he was in need of funds to prepare for war, first against France and then against Scotland, he endeavored to impose a tax on the income the clergy derived from the feudal estates they were administering. The sum requested from the clergy was one tenth of their income. At the same time Edward asked the nobles to pay an additional twelfth of their income and the commoners an additional eighth. But the members of the clergy refused to pay the taxes, taking refuge behind *Clericis Laicos* and pleading that this bull forbade them to pay such taxes under pain of excommunication and deposition. Edward waited for a time hoping that the defiant members of the clergy would consent to being taxed. When they remained adamant in their refusal, he informed those who refused to pay that if they did not relent he would withdraw from them the protection of the civil government. He implemented this threat by notifying all judges to withhold protection. He next ordered the sheriffs to seize and hold all church lands until the members of the clergy consented to pay the taxes levied by the civil government. The means to which the king had resorted proved effective. The recalcitrant clergymen soon relented and thereafter paid the taxes which the king levied on them by his own authority.

When the war between England and France did not break out, Edward marched his army into Scotland (1298). The Scots tried to save their country from conquest by appealing to Pope Boniface for help. The pope replied by sending a declaration to Edward (June, 1299) in which he stated that Scotland was a fief of the Holy See and forbade Edward to molest the Scots in any way. Furthermore, he summoned Edward to appear before a papal tribunal to defend himself for having attacked Scotland. Edward was incensed by the declaration which he regarded as unwarranted interference in English affairs. But instead of answering the pope himself, he called a meeting of Parliament and laid the pope's declaration before it. Parliament considered the declaration of Boniface carefully; then decided by a unanimous vote that Scotland had never been a fief of the Holy See and that the king should not answer the summons to appear before the papal tribunal. It added that if the king wished to appear, the people of England would not permit him to do so. "Never," the Parliament declared, "shall we suffer that our king should submit to such unheard-of demands." In regard to the papal claims of supremacy, Parliament stated that in temporal affairs the king of England is not accountable to the pope or to any other ecclesiastical or temporal judge. The statement of Parliament closed with these words: "Wherefore we reverently and humbly implore Your Holiness benignly to permit our Lord the King peacefully to possess his rights, liberties, customs or laws without diminution or inquietude, that he may take the same unimpaired." The answer was accepted by the pope who was involved in the conflict with Philip IV of France, and in no position to risk open conflict with England.

In other countries, too, the papal claims to overlordship were encountering a growing opposition. No sovereigns were more ardently Roman Catholic than Ferdinand and Isabella of Spain; nevertheless, they resisted every move on the part of the papacy to strengthen its hold on their subjects, and actually succeeded in restricting the papal authority in Spain. In 1482 the so-called Catholic Sovereigns managed to obtain from the pope a renunciation of his patronage in the territories under their rule. They also jealously guarded their own authority by prohibiting in 1493 the publication of a papal bull in their country without their express permission. Even in the Holy Roman Empire the papal authority was gradually being restricted. In

1448, for example, the pope lost part of his patronage in Germany. Further limitation of the pope's authority followed. It must be noted, however, that although the tendency of the secular state to become an end in itself wholly free of outside interference was strong and dynamic, the idea of the complete separation of Church and State was still something to be achieved in the future. The secular rulers were satisfied with relative rather than absolute power. The clergy might continue to administer religious affairs and to a large extent control education, if they would admit that the king had the authority to determine the limits of their jurisdiction.

Secularist Theories

While the national monarchs were consolidating their power and asserting their independence, the pope was also taking steps to fortify his position. For this purpose he engaged experts in canon law to prepare arguments in support of the papal claims. The secular rulers also had a group of lawyers, publicists, and apologists to justify their stand. The inevitable consequence was a great quantity of polemical literature. Among the prominent men who wrote such literature there was one who was not in the employ of either side. The poet Dante was so disturbed by the papal claims and by the contention between the popes and secular rulers that he wrote the treatise *De Monarchia* (1310) in which he argued that the secular powers should be supreme in the realm of secular affairs. This was, as he saw it, the only way in which peace and freedom could be assured. In making these statements Dante had in mind above all the Holy Roman Empire which was little more than the fossilized remains of the original Roman Empire. Dante hoped that new energy could be infused into the Holy Roman Empire so that it would exercise authority in the same degree as the old Roman Empire. This caused him to assert that the emperor's authority was bestowed on him by God and that he, therefore, had a divine mission. Dante called for a sharp division of authority between the emperor and the pope because he believed that both could carry out their mission if each one were supreme in his own sphere.

Dante had a practical reason for supporting the cause of the emperor. He hoped the emperor would become strong enough to establish order and peace in Italy which, divided into many petty states, was weak and strife-torn. In his *Divine Comedy* he wrote of his beloved Italy:

> Ah, enslaved Italy! Thou inn of grief!
> Vessel without a pilot in a great tempest!
> Lady no longer of fair provinces
> But brothel house impure!

Dante was not anti-papal. He felt that the papacy in interfering in secular affairs was not giving full attention to its spiritual functions and was itself becoming secularized. He believed that the secular affairs should be administered by the secular princes whom God had chosen for this purpose. But Pope John XXII did not appreciate Dante's efforts to spiritualize the papacy. The treatise so exasperated him that he ordered it burned in the market place of Bologna in 1329. Papal supporters in general denounced the *De Monarchia.* The opposition to it continued into the sixteenth century and in 1554 it was placed on the Index of Prohibited Books from which it was not removed until the nineteenth century.

The thinker whose ideas constituted a radical departure from the ecclesiastical concept of the state was Marsiglio or Marsilius of Padua (*c.*1275-*c.*1342) whose reputation rests on a unique political treatise titled *Defensor Pacis* (Defender of the Peace). The details of the life of this enigmatic figure are so completely shrouded in obscurity that even the dates of his birth and death are uncertain. The few facts known about his life ascertain that he was born in Padua, spent his early years there, and probably attended the University of Padua. Padua was at that time one of the prosperous city-states of Italy with a government which subordinated everything to commercial aims. This policy caused considerable friction between the clergy and the civil government. One cause of the friction was the clergy's refusal to be taxed like the other citizens of Padua. They even refused as landowners to contribute their share for the upkeep of bridges and dikes. Marsiglio's hostile attitude toward the clergy in his *Defensor Pacis* can be largely attributed to the feud between the clergy and the government of Padua. Although the treatise contains much that is borrowed from Aristotle's *Politics,* it also clearly reflects the developments in the Italian city-states, particularly in Padua. Historians and scholars are generally agreed that many of his ideas are based on experience.

Marsiglio's thought was also molded by other influences. As a young man he appears to have traveled for some time before he settled in Paris where he taught at the University of Paris and for a time served as its rector. At the University he met William of Ockham or Occam (d.1349), the English philosopher who stirred up so much controversy with his nominalist ideas. Regarding the relationship between the papacy and the secular rulers, Ockham asserted that the papacy had no right to claim jurisdiction over the secular governments. Christ himself, he stated, never expressed or claimed such primacy.

Marsiglio's thought was also influenced by John of Jandun, a teacher at the University of Paris who aided him in writing the *Defensor Pacis.* The extent of John of Jandun's assistance is a matter of controversy. Those who ascribe to him a major role point to the fact that he had made a careful study of Aristotle's *Politics* and had even written several treatises on the work. Some scholars have gone so far as to state that John of Jandun wrote the first part of the *Defensor Pacis* and that Marsiglio finished the treatise. On the other hand, more recent historians believe that John of Jandun's role in writing the treatise was a minor one. They assert that the principal ideas of the *Defensor Pacis* were contributed by Marsiglio and are based on his experience in Italian politics.

The event which impelled Marsiglio to write the *Defensor Pacis* was the renewal of the contest between church and state. The two principal personages this time were Pope John XXII and Ludwig or Louis of Bavaria (1314-1347). Both made extravagant declarations in which they claimed prerogatives which neither could enforce. The prolonged contest and its boring reiterations by both sides has been called "a dull epilogue" to the earlier duel between Boniface VIII and the rulers of France and England. Reference is made to it here only in so far as it was the background for the writing of the *Defensor Pacis*. Louis of Bavaria, upon emerging as victor from a desperate struggle against a rival claimant for the so-called German kingship, declared himself a candidate for the emperorship of the Holy Roman Empire. This displeased Pope John who forthwith informed Louis that no one could be a candidate for the imperial crown unless his claims were legitimized by the reigning pope. The pope then demanded that Louis renounce his claims within three months on penalty of excommunication. When Louis refused compliance he was excommunicated early in 1324. It was then that Marsiglio wrote the *Defensor Pacis* with the help of John of Jandun and in the same year released it to the public.

The *Defensor Pacis* is a bold statement of the role of the state at the dawn of an age in which statecraft became a law unto itself. While he was launching an uncompromising attack against the papal claims to jurisdiction over the secular state, he demanded for the state a practical equality which could be established only through a theoretical superiority. Thus his view reversed the importance given to the Church and to the state in the period preceding him. As the title of the treatise indicates, Marsiglio stands as the defender of the peace. The primary object of government, he stated, should be to insure peace for all citizens. Peace was to him "the most indispensable benefit of human society." It can, however, be attained only if all phases of the state function in an orderly manner. So long as the pope and the clergy usurp or strive to usurp secular authority there will be strife and discord. In summing up the content of his treatise Marsiglio stated:

> In our preceding pages we have found that civil discord and dissensions in the various kingdoms and communities is due, above all, to a cause which, unless it be obviated, will continue to be a source of future calamity, namely, the claims, aspirations, and enterprises of the Roman bishop and his band of ecclesiastics, bent upon gaining secular power and superfluous worldly possessions. The bishop of Rome is wont to support his claims to supreme authority over others by the assertion that the plenitude of power was delegated to him by Christ through the person of St. Peter. But in reality no princely authority, nor any coercive jurisdiction in this world, to say nothing of supreme authority, belongs to him or to any other bishop, priest, or cleric.

Marsiglio devoted a large part of the *Defensor Pacis* to his attempts to prove that the papal claims to civil or secular authority are not supported by the Bible. Thus he used what was regarded as the highest authority as a basis for his arguments. He further asserted that the work of saving souls had been enough for the Church and clergy to the time of Constantine, but during the succeeding period pretensions to dominate the secular state appeared. These pretensions, he stated, were based on a grant of civil authority supposedly made in a document known as the Donation of Constantine to Pope Sylvester by Emperor Constantine when he left Rome to establish his capital at Constantinople. When Marsiglio wrote "Some say such a grant was made," he cast doubt on the authenticity of the Donation of Constantine more than a century before Lorenzo Valla proved it to be a forgery.

Some of Marsiglio's ideas were in advance of his time, and were not shared by most of his contemporaries. One historian has called him "the most modern of medieval thinkers." One such idea was Marsiglio's assertion that the people are the real source of power and authority in the state. "The human lawgiver," he wrote, "can only be the whole body of citizens or a majority of them." Since it is in most cases not practical for the people to function as legislators, the task of preparing the laws may be delegated to a small number of experts, but it is within the power of the people to decide whether the laws should be put in force. Even the ruler simply carries out the will of the people. It is, therefore, out of order for the pope to claim jurisdiction over the affairs of the empire and to insist on the right to control the imperial elections. Thus Marsiglio was the herald of a new age of politics. The germs of democratic ideas which he stated in his treatise did not reach their full development until centuries later.

Although many of Marsiglio's ideas were too extreme to be accepted by his contemporaries, opponents of the papal claims to overlordship in all countries of Western Europe eagerly read the treatise. Marsiglio's unsparing attack on papal power which has been described as "the deadliest single assault ever aimed at the papacy" naturally evoked a strong reaction from the Vatican. The authors of the *Defensor Pacis* had foreseen this and for purposes of self-protection had published the treatise anonymously. It was not long, however, before the names of the authors became known. When their identity was discovered Marsiglio and John of Jandun fled for protection to the court of Louis of Bavaria at Nuremberg in Germany, remaining in the service of Louis for the rest of their lives. How Pope John XXII felt about the treatise is indicated by the fact that he excommunicated both authors as "monsters from the depths of Satan and the sulphur-pools of Hell." Pope Clement VI (1342-1352) called Marsiglio "the worst heretic" whose works he had ever read, maintaining that he had found no fewer than 240 heretical statements in the *Defensor Pacis*. That the treatise was widely read may be deduced from the fact that so many manuscripts of it have survived. The first printed edition which appeared in 1517 was read by such reformers as Luther, Calvin, and Thomas Cranmer.

The Completely Secular State of Machiavelli

In Machiavelli's *Prince*, published two centuries after the *Defensor Pacis*, the exaltation of the secular state was carried to new heights. The ideas of the two authors differed in a number of respects. Whereas Marsiglio was interested in the relationship between church and state, Machiavelli sketched his conception of the completely secularized state. Again, whereas Marsiglio purportedly based his views on the Bible, Machiavelli sought to justify his concept of the secular state on grounds of practical expediency. In presenting his thoroughly secular view of statecraft Machiavelli disregarded the whole moral system on which the medieval concept of the state rested. To him the state was an end in itself, completely exempt from any higher law.

Niccolo Machiavelli (1469-1527) was born of parents who were members of the old Florentine nobility. Little is known of his youth except that it was concurrent with the greatness of Florence under Lorenzo the Magnificent. In 1498, after the expulsion of Lorenzo's successor, Pietro de Medici, Machiavelli became a clerk in the Florentine chancery and quickly rose to the position of secretary of the republic. As secretary he not only drew up instructions for ambassadors, but also went on different missions himself, including visits to Cesare Borgia, Louis XII of France, and the Emperor Maximilian of Germany. This gave him a rare opportunity to observe the statecraft of his day. He saw, for example, how the ruthless Cesare Borgia built up his principality out of territories which belonged to others. But in 1512 the Medici were reinstated in Florence by the troops of Charles V of the Holy Roman Empire, and Machiavelli was dismissed from his post. The next year he was tried and imprisoned for participating in a conspiracy against the Medici, but was soon released under sentence to confinement on his little estate. Up to this time Machiavelli had done nothing toward earning for himself a place in the republic of letters. Now, however, he had the leisure and he made the most of it. He wrote a number of books in various fields. They included the two political treatises: *The Prince* and *Discourses on Livy*. His two plays, *Clizia* and *Mandragola*, earned for him a place in the early history of the secular drama. Noteworthy also are *The Art of Warfare* and his *History of Florence*. In addition he carried on a voluminous private correspondence with many outstanding persons of his time.

Although Machiavelli wrote *The Prince* in 1513, he did not publish it during his lifetime. It was not given to the public until 1532, five years after the author's death. While he was composing the treatise Machiavelli wrote to a friend, "Destiny willed that I should be able to speak neither of silk nor of weaving of wool, neither of profit nor of loss; I must speak of the state." When he had finished the treatise he wrote to Francesco Vettori, "I have written a small work on the principalities in which I pour myself out as fully as I can in meditation on the subject . . . when it has been read it will be seen that during the fifteen years I have given to the study of statecraft I have neither slept nor idled." With his thoroughly secular way of thinking, he wrote about politics in a realistic fashion. We must, he said, see what is, not what should be. Actually, however, many of his political maxims were taken from the history of ancient Rome.

Machiavelli's political philosophy is described in the following brief summary: Among the ancient Romans the state was the highest development of civilization. It was the goal of all human endeavor; in fact, it represented the ultimate meaning of life. Everything meaningful and important was centered in it. This order of things was, however, changed by Christianity, more particularly by the Roman Catholic Church. The Church intruded into the domain of the state, creating a sense of opposition to it. This caused an abnormal relationship between church and state. The remedy is the elimination of the influence of the Church from politics and statecraft, so that the state will again be the supreme purpose of all human endeavor, the overriding object of all human morals. Machiavelli felt that the purposes of the state were so important that even morality must not be permitted to stand in the way of their achievement. Every moral consideration may be excluded if expediency demands it. The state and its interests are above all law, civil or ecclesiastical. If the interests of the state demand it, cruelty is a legitimate weapon and hypocrisy an excellent device. There is the much-quoted passage in *The Prince* which reads: "A prince must not keep faith when by doing so it would be against his interest . . . if all men were good this precept would not be a good one, but as they are bad and would not observe their faith with you, so you are not bound to keep faith with them."

Machiavelli's object in writing *The Prince* was to show his countrymen how a weak Italy might be made strong. Previously such Italian states as Venice, Milan, Florence, the Papal States, and Naples had been able to hold one another in check, but toward the end of the fifteenth century Italy had become the battlefield of the great powers of northern Europe. Armies from France, Germany, and Spain fought there to extend the power of their rulers. Machiavelli described the Italy of his time as "more enslaved than the Hebrews, more down-trodden than the Persians, more disunited than the Athenians; without a chief, without order; beaten, despoiled, mangled, overrun; subject to every sort of desolation." In *The Prince* he laid down the principles which, if adopted by a ruler, might make Italy strong. He was so eager to see conditions improved that he denounced the papacy as a danger to Italy and termed Christianity a religion of slaves. What he asked for was not necessarily a unified Italy, as has often been stated. He called for a state powerful enough to put an end to the domination of Italy by the papacy and to free it from the repeated invasions of the French, German, and Spanish armies. Whether such a state would be a republic or a monarchy made little difference to Machiavelli. The peace and freedom of Italy was his primary aim. "This book," the philosopher Hegel wrote of *The Prince*, "has often been cast aside in horror as containing maxims of the most revolting tyranny; yet it was Machiavelli's high sense of the necessity of constituting a state which caused him to lay down the principles on which alone states could be founded under the circumstances."

The absolute secularism of the Machiavellian state, together with the deadly practicality of his principles, violated the idealistic conception of the state which the men of the sixteenth century had been taught; hence *The Prince* excited a storm of indignation. The Church forgave Machiavelli neither his views on Christianity nor his criticism of the papacy. Machiavelli was denounced as an atheist and a villain, and the principles he espoused were vigorously condemned. In some circles *The Prince* became the symbol of everything that was loathsome. The Jesuits of Ingolstadt burned Machiavelli in effigy and Cardinal Pole of England asserted that he was evidently inspired by the Devil. When the Index of Prohibited Books was established by the Roman Catholic Church in 1557, *The Prince* was one of the first books to be listed on it. The Protestants, too, condemned it with equal vigor, ascribing to it, among other things, the Massacre of St. Bartholomew in France (1572). In the Elizabethan drama Machiavelli was portrayed no less then 395 times as the embodiment of villainy.

Despite all this, the maxims and principles proclaimed by Machiavelli became the political realities of the period that followed. Many rulers read *The Prince* assiduously and put some of its principles into practice. The influence of his ideas was so extensive that he has been styled "the father of modern political science." The Emperor Charles V is said to have read the book carefully. Catherine de Medici took a copy of *The Prince* with her when she left Italy to become the wife of the man who later ruled France as King Henry II. The marginal notes in a copy owned by Queen Christina of Sweden (1632-1654) show that she approved many of Machiavelli's principles. In the eighteenth century Frederick II (the Great) of Prussia was a disciple of Machiavelli, although he sought to disguise the fact by an attack on Machiavelli. Napoleon was an admirer of Machiavelli and his principles. During the succeeding period Machiavelli's ideas became an essential phase of modern statecraft.

14

Opening a Wider World

Man's growing interest in the things of this world also expressed itself in a desire for more knowledge of remote lands and peoples. It is one of the most important and most striking manifestations of Renaissance secularism. About the middle of the thirteenth century even the more educated European's knowledge of global geography was only fractional and limited largely to Europe itself. His ideas about far-away lands were vague and often unreliable. The existence of the continents of America and Australia was, of course, quite unsuspected. Vikings or Norsemen, it is true, had visited the coast of North America, but reports of their exploits were not circulated in Europe until a much later time. As for Asia, it was the great unknown continent so far as geographical knowledge was concerned. The same Europeans who were familiar with the history of Greece and Rome had little geographical knowledge of the lands beyond the eastern borders of the Mediterranean. During the Middle Ages the break between Orient and Occident was not complete, but contact was the exception rather than the rule. Very little sound geographical knowledge filtered into Europe from the Far East as a result of these contacts.

Geographical knowledge of Africa was even more restricted. Beyond the narrow strip of territory along the Mediterranean the continent of Africa was "a land of mystery." During the thirteenth century an occasional missionary did penetrate Africa as far as the Sudan, but since geography was not the major interest of the missionaries, their reports contain little geographical information. More attention was given to fantastic tales about the Dark Continent. It was, for example, said that central and southern Africa were inhabited by men without noses, by others without mouths, and by some without heads, the eyes and the mouth being in the chest. One missionary who was sent into the Sudan in the thirteenth century to survey the situation reported, "In that land there is an island in the middle of a great lake and on that island there lives a dragon to whom all people of that island do sacrifice." How limited and imperfect the geographical knowledge of the African continent was is shown by the maps of that time. On them Africa is a shapeless lump with contours which in no way resemble the real Africa.

For geographical knowledge the medieval period prior to the Renaissance was in general a time of stagnation and retrogression. Not only did the science of cartography fall into neglect during the early centuries of the

Middle Ages, but writers also paid little attention to the writings of such ancient geographers as Hipparchus, Eratosthenes, Strabo, and Ptolemy. If one of the Greek geographers had returned to terrestrial life about the year 1000 he would have found that the people of Western Europe had forgotten much of the geographical knowledge they had inherited from the Greeks and learned little that was new. Even the intellectuals were interested in the earth's place in the celestial system rather than in the unknown parts of the earth's surface. Consequently medieval thinkers contributed little to the advancement of geographical knowledge. The geographical lore that was circulating reflected the almost complete lack of first-hand observation. In lieu of actual observation some cartographers gave free reign to their imagination, producing sketches and maps that were anything but accurate. Other cartographers as well as most intellectuals turned to the Bible for their basic geographical concepts. Hence, for example, it was widely believed that Jerusalem was at the exact center of the earth. As proof they had the statement in Ezekiel (5:5) which reads: "Thus says the Lord God, 'This is Jerusalem, and I have set her in the center of the nations, with countries round about her.' "

Even though the medieval knowledge of geography was very limited, the idea of the sphericity of the earth was not foreign to the educated mind. This theory had been developed on philosophical grounds by the Pythagorean school as far back as the fifth century B.C. Thereafter there was probably never a time when this theory did not have supporters. St. Augustine (354-430), for example, believed the earth to be round. Isidore of Seville (*c.*560-636) quoted in his famous encyclopedia writers of antiquity who believed that the earth was a sphere. One such statement reads, "The earth is so named from its roundness (orbis)." The Venerable Bede, English churchman and historian of the eighth century, wrote in his *De Rerum Natura* (On the Nature of Things): "The world is shaped into a perfect globe." The idea was stated again and again by later writers and was even given a place in some of the textbooks.

The theory of the sphericity of the earth did not, however, have the field all to itself. There were men who had other ideas. For example, Cosmas of Alexandria who lived in the sixth century believed the earth to be flat. Having traveled extensively as a sailor and trader before he became a monk, Cosmas became so deeply interested in geography that he constructed a theological system of the universe. In other words, he tried to harmonize geographical knowledge with the teachings of the Bible as he understood them. His acceptance of the phrase, "the four corners of the earth," in a literal sense caused him to denounce as blasphemous the idea of the sphericity of the earth. On his map he represented the earth as a great rectangle, twice as long as it is wide. "The figure of the earth," he stated, "is lengthwise from east to west and breadthwise from north to south." Besides citing religious arguments against sphericity, he also adduced what he regarded as "common sense" arguments against it. He stated that the idea of the earth being a sphere is ridiculous because while some men would be walking upright on one side of the earth those on the other side would be walking upside down.

Expanding Geographical Horizons

About the middle of the thirteenth century the geographical horizons of the people began to expand considerably. Previously the Crusades had given impetus to land travel when many crusaders and a large number of pilgrims journeyed to the Holy Land. No new lands were, however, discovered during this period. But after the middle of the thirteenth century geographical knowledge did expand on a broad scale. The new knowledge came from various sources such as the accounts of diplomatic missions, missionaries and travelers who visited Asia. Their destination was usually the court of one of the Mongol Khans. Early in the thirteenth century Ghenghis Khan embarked on a career of conquest which from 1206 to 1227 extended Mongol rule over a vast territory extending from the Far East to the Dnieper River. His successors continued moving westward until in 1240 the Mongol hordes swept into Poland, Hungary, and Silesia. A combined force of Poles and Germans which tried to stop the Mongol tide was crushed in the battle of Liegnitz (1241). When the news of this defeat became known, Europe was seized by "the Mongol terror," a great fear that the Mongol wave would inundate all of Europe. But the Mongols suddenly decided, for reasons that are still a matter of conjecture, to move their forces back into Asia. The Mongol terror having subsided, some of the European leaders conceived the idea of enlisting the aid of the Mongols against the Turks who were advancing on Europe through Asia Minor. Both the heads of states and the head of the Church sent out missions to explore the possibilities for establishing friendly relations which, it was hoped, would lead to the conversion of the Mongols to Christianity. In both missionary and diplomatic efforts, members of the Franciscan order played leading roles.

The first mission was sent out in 1245 by Pope Innocent IV. Its leader was Giovanni Carpini (often called John of Plano Carpini), a Franciscan monk. The journey was one to test the mettle of the most courageous. The corpulent, sixty-three-year-old Carpini and his companions endured almost incredible hardships before they finally reached the court of the Great Khan at Karakorum in Mongolia. Although the reception by Kuyuk who was Great Khan at the time was not unfriendly, the mission failed to effect a diplomatic rapprochement between the Vatican and the Mongol ruler. But on his return after an absence of two years Carpini wrote an interesting account of his experiences which gave Europe its first glimpse of life in Central Asia. In it he told the Europeans of the high level of craftmanship in Cathay (China) and of its wealth in gold and silver as well as in grain, wine, and other products. This account did not fail to excite the interest of the commercial classes. Carpini's geographical descriptions of the lands he visited are, on the whole, quite accurate.

A few years later a missionary group under the leadership of William Rubruck, a Franciscan from northern France, journeyed to the court of the Great Khan after rumors had been circulated that several Mongol leaders had either become converts to Christianity or had expressed a willingness to become converts. The missionaries carried with them a letter to the Great Khan from Louis IX of France (St. Louis) who not only supported the idea of converting the Mongols, but also hoped to enlist them as allies in the fight against the Moslems. Rubruck and his companions left Constantinople in 1253. Crossing the Black Sea, they journeyed through the northern Crimea, then eastward, thereby avoiding some of the hardships suffered by their predecessors. The missionaries received a friendly welcome at the court of the Great Khan, but the mission was no more successful than the previous one had been. They not only failed in their efforts to convert the Mongol leaders; they were also unsuccessful in their endeavors to enlist the Mongols as allies of Christian Europe. Like Carpini, Friar William wrote of his experiences. It is a fuller account than that written by his predecessor. Among the interesting things he mentions is the use of paper money by the Cathayans or Chinese. "The common money of Cathay," he wrote, "consists of pieces of cotton paper about a palm in length and breadth," with an imprint on it resembling the seal of the Great Khan. He also pointed out that in their language "a single character embraces several letters, so as to form a whole word."

The most famous medieval traveler was Marco Polo (*c.*1254-1324), a Venetian. Marco's father Niccolo and his uncle Maffeo were enterprising merchants whose travels took them as far as the court of Kublai Khan who was at that time the ruler of the great Mongol empire. No sooner had they returned in 1269 than they began to make preparations for a return to Peking in northern China where the Great Khan's headquarters were now located. This time they took with them young Marco who was about seventeen. They left Venice by ship in 1271 sailing to Acre at the eastern end of the Mediterranean. From there they followed caravan routes through Persia and Afghanistan, after which they crossed the great plateau of Central Asia. At Peking they were cordially welcomed by Kublai Khan who asked them to enter his service. Kublai was particularly impressed by Marco's intelligence and discretion. After the young Italian learned the languages of the East, the Great Khan sent him on missions to various parts of Asia. The Polos remained in Kublai's service for almost two decades before he reluctantly permitted them to return to Venice.

If Marco Polo had settled down in Venice to the life of a prosperous merchant, posterity might never have known the story of his experiences. As it was, he became the captain of a Venetian galley in one of the wars against Genoa. In 1298 the Genoese roundly defeated the Venetian fleet, burning 66 galleys, capturing 18 others, and taking 700 prisoners, one of whom was Marco Polo. During an imprisonment of less than a year Marco related his experiences to a fellow prisoner variously called Rusticiano or Rusticello who wrote them down in pidgin French which at the time seems to have been a kind of "international vernacular." The importance of the narrative for the history of geography lies in his descriptions of the places he had either visited or heard about, including China, the island of Zipangu (Japan), India, Tibet, Java, Sumatra, and Ceylon. His descriptions reveal an enthusiastic interest, a keenness of observation, and a fullness of knowledge. But when he adds hearsay to what he saw he displays a typically medieval gullibility. To cite just one example, he includes the tale of the roc, a bird so large that it laid eggs the size of a hogshead and had feathers that were thirty feet long. This bird was so powerful that it could pick up a large elephant with its talons, carry it to a great height and drop it, after which it would descend to devour the carcass at its leisure.

The Travels of Marco Polo became so popular that they were soon translated into most of the principal European languages and also into a number of dialects as well as into Latin. The fact that 338 manuscript copies are still in existence gives some indication of the large number of copies that must have been made. After the invention of printing with movable type, editions were printed in all the principal languages of Europe. To Marco Polo's contemporaries and to the succeeding generations *The Travels* proved fascinating because they revealed Asia to the Western world, the Asia which had theretofore been little more than a name. The accounts of Carpini and Friar William did, it is true, precede *The Travels of Marco Polo*, but they were never made available to the general public in the way Marco's account was. Not only did the spirit of adventure which fills the book fascinate more people, the descriptions also broadened the mental horizons of those who read it and increased their knowledge of geography. In short, Marco Polo taught the people of Western Europe to think in terms of a wider world. But his narrative left a number of questions unanswered. One of these was, "Are there any large bodies of land eastward of Japan?" He does state that there are thousands of islands east of Japan, but throws no light on the existence of the continent of America. Furthermore, *The Travels* contain no information on the question, "Is Africa circumnavigable?" Marco discusses the east coast of Africa and also the neighboring islands of Zanzibar and Madagascar; he even discusses the African trade in slaves and ivory, and describes the natives of East Africa as having kinky hair, flat noses, and thick lips. However, of the possibility of sailing around the southern tip of Africa he says nothing. Europe had to wait two centuries before the question was answered conclusively.

After the visits of the Polos to the Far East other travelers followed in their footsteps. The knowledge that their reception would be friendly caused missionaries, traders, and travelers who had the wanderlust to undertake the long journey. Upon their return some wrote accounts of their experiences, while the others circulated by word of mouth stories of the great riches and fabulous things they had seen, thereby stimulating further interest in the mysterious lands of the East. But the situation in Cathay changed when the descendants of Kublai Khan were driven out of Peking in 1368. Thereafter visits to China again became rare.

Other important sources of geographical knowledge were some of the writers of Greek and Roman antiquity. During the revival of interest in classical literature, humanists and cartographers did not overlook the geographical discussions of such ancients as Strabo, Hipparchus, and Eratosthenes, but the writer whose treatise on geography exerted the greatest influence was Claudius Ptolemaeus, better known as Ptolemy, a geographer, astronomer, and mathematician who lived in Alexandria during the second century A.D. In the libraries of Alexandria, Ptolemy had access to the writings of Greek geographers and what he learned from them he supplemented with information obtained from traders and travelers. The final result was the treatise titled *Geography* which appears to have attracted little attention in the Middle Ages until it was translated from Greek into Latin in 1410. Since it was superior in many respects to medieval discussions on geography it was widely read and accepted by scholars, cartographers, mariners, and others.

Although Ptolemy's world map did give definite form to the theory of a spherical earth, his execution was very faulty. His outlines of the Roman Empire were quite correct, but he lacked the knowledge to sketch the outlines of distant regions with any degree of accuracy. In doing so he either relied on the erroneous knowledge of Greek cartographers or he resorted to his imagination. Consequently his map contains some fundamental errors. One of these is that he underestimated the circumference of the earth by more than one-sixth. Ptolemy probably took the measurements from the writings of Greek geographers. Another error was his exaggeration of the size of the land body which stretches from the Atlantic coast of Spain to the edge of Asia. The result was that on his map Asia extends much farther into the ocean now called the Pacific than it really does. Since the existence of the American continent was unknown the over-size Asia created the illusion that eastern Asia is not far from Western Europe. It was this idea which encouraged Columbus to sail westward across the Atlantic in the hope of reaching Asia. Ptolemy also included in his map a vast southern continent, one end of which was joined to Africa and the other to China making the Indian Ocean a land-locked sea. This conception ruled out the possibility of circumnavigating the African continent in order to reach the Indian Ocean. Ptolemy's errors persisted until they were exposed by actual explorations. Thus it was in many instances necessary for the explorers to unlearn what Ptolemy had taught them.

Important as the accounts of travelers, missionaries, and ancient writers were for the extension of geographical knowledge, the major source of such knowledge was actual exploration. In the first decades of the fifteenth century the Canary and Madeira Islands were discovered or rediscovered; then the explorers began to press on toward previously unknown regions. The discoveries that followed were of such magnitude that the period in which they were made has ever since been known as "the Great Age of Discovery." A combination of economic, religious, and political motives provided the impulse. The motive which overshadowed all others was the desire to find a direct route to the riches of Cathay and India. It was an incentive which motivated some of the nations north of the Alps for almost two centuries. All the other nations of Europe wished a share in the trade in spices and oriental luxuries which was the source of the wealth of the Venetians, "the lords of the gold of all Christendom."

The great voyages of discovery were made possible by the invention of new and improved aids to navigation. During the early Middle Ages mariners had only the sun and the north star to guide them in clear weather; when the sky was overcast they had to fall back on instinct. So long as maritime activities were restricted to the Mediterranean, this was not too serious, but better aids to navigation were necessary for voyages on the open ocean, out of sight of land. Such aids appeared in response to the need. The most important one was the compass. Although the first known mention of the compass dates from the twelfth century, the principle on which the compass is based—a lodestone (magnetic stone) or a piece of iron magnetized by contact with the lodestone will direct itself to point to the geographical north—appears to have been known much earlier. In its simplest form the compass was a water compass, that is, a lodestone or a magnetized piece of iron would be placed on a stick or reed floating in a vessel of water. Historians have called attention to the fact that frequent references are made in some of the early Nordic sagas to a lodestone (Leidarstein) floating in a container. It has even been suggested that when the Norsemen penetrated the Mediterranean in the ninth century to found colonies in Calabria and Apulia, they took to Italy the knowledge of the basic principle of the compass. However this may be, a simple form of the compass was probably used in the Mediterranean by both Christians and Arabs as early as the eleventh century. In its improved form, a magnetized needle was mounted on a pivot attached to a card marked with thirty-two points of direction. Mariners who had such a compass no longer found it necessary to stay in sight of land during cloudy weather. They could now boldly venture out into the uncharted ocean.

There were also other improved aids to navigation. One of these was the astrolabe, an instrument for measuring the altitude of heavenly bodies. Its history goes back to ancient Greece where it was used by astronomers, physicists, and travelers to make observations of the altitude of the sun or the north star, observations which enabled the observer to compute the hour of the day or night. Since the instrument was portable it lent itself to adaptation for use on shipboard. The time of its adaptation is unknown, but by the fifteenth century the device was standard equipment for all ships. It enabled the mariner not only to calculate the time, but also to establish the latitude of the place of observation. In principle it is probably a forerunner of the modern sextant. Ships were also improved in many ways. The old galleys, propelled mainly by oars, were preferred in the Mediterranean for their reliability and independence of wind. But such ships were obviously unsuited for exploration in rougher waters. By 1400 the Venetian and other shipbuilders were constructing large galleons whose broad beams gave them greater stability. These ships which were dependent on sails for motive-power were more seaworthy and more commodious, so that they could carry larger cargoes. The practical equipment of the mariner was also supplemented by better maps and by the portolani or coast charts based on the experiences of pilots, mariners, and merchants. As new knowledge was gained the portolani were changed to bring them into a closer relation with reality.

The Quest for a Sea Route to the Indies

The nation which took the lead in the exploration of unknown regions was Portugal, a small unified kingdom. Portugal had achieved territorial unity in the second half of the thirteenth century and with it a high degree of internal peace. Hemmed in to the north and to the east by territories which later became a part of Spain, the Portuguese were cut off from trade with the European states by land routes, so they turned to the sea. The small country had a number of distinct advantages for a maritime career. In addition to its geographical location at the south-western corner of the continent, it had a long coastline on the Atlantic with some excellent harbors. Furthermore, all the longer rivers of Portugal flow into the Atlantic and some of the country's principal cities are situated at or near their mouths. Portugal also had a commercial class which had grown prosperous from the trade in salt, wine, olive oil, and other commodities, and was interested in further expansion of trade and larger profits. Another factor which fostered expansion was the crusading spirit kept alive by the wars with the Moors of North Africa. In 1415 this crusading spirit found expression in a great expedition of some two-hundred ships and 20,000 men against the Moorish stronghold of Ceuta, the African counterpart of Gibraltar. The capture of Ceuta after bitter fighting gave the Portuguese a base for trade and for further expansion.

After the Portuguese success in taking Ceuta, a great leader took charge of the Portuguese program of expansion. He was Prince Henry the Navigator (1390-1460), a younger son of King John I of Portugal. Young Henry who had been raised in the tradition of knighthood displayed great courage during the assault on Ceuta and was knighted on the field of battle. His experiences at Ceuta kindled his deep interest in Africa which caused him to study every possible map and chart he could obtain and to gather information from traders who had crossed the Sahara with caravans laden with African and oriental merchandise. What he learned convinced him to send out expeditions to explore the west coast of Africa. After his return to Portugal Prince Henry retired from the court and set up his headquarters at Sagres on Cape St. Vincent, the rocky tip of southwest Portugal which overlooks the Atlantic. There he gathered a group of mathematicians, astronomers, cartographers, instrument makers, and experienced pilots. The outstanding member of the group was probably Jayme of Majorca, whose name appears in the records as Mestro Jacome, of whom the chronicler Barros says that he was "a man very learned in the art of navigation and the construction of charts and instruments." While the members of this group studied the best available information on the regions marked out for exploration, at the nearby port of Lagos stout ships were being built and fitted out for the planned explorations.

Prince Henry was impelled to send out his expeditions by a combination of religious, patriotic, and economic motives. As Grand Master of the Order of Christ he was interested in finding a field for the missionary activities of the order. He also wished to ascertain the extent of the Moorish dominion in Africa to determine if it would be feasible to strike at the Moors from the rear. A further motive was Prince Henry's desire to make contact with the fabled Presbyter or Prester John who was widely believed to be the ruler of a great Christian state. Some historians believe that the existence of Coptic Christianity in Abyssinia gave rise to the fable. As for Prince Henry, he hoped to find Prester John not only for purposes of trade, but also to enlist his aid in the fight against the Moors. With the passing of time the expansion of trade became more and more the dominant motive.

In 1420 Prince Henry sent out the first expedition to explore the west coast of Africa and during the remaining years of his life he dispatched a number of others to continue the explorations southward. He himself did not accompany his seafarers, but remained at Sagres to plan and direct the maritime enterprises, earning for his successful efforts the title, "the Navigator." If one of his expeditions turned back because of baffling currents, shoals, and adverse winds, Henry would prevail on his mariners to try again, urging them to penetrate deeper into the unknown. Besides the actual difficulties there were also imaginary terrors of the deep which were very real to the superstitious sailors. But Henry persisted in his encouragement and exhortations with the result that his mariners continued to press on. As they returned with more knowledge of the African coast Prince Henry's interest became more intense and his hopes for important discoveries stronger. Hence he sent out more expeditions. In 1446 one of his expeditions passed Cape Verde (so named because of its green appearance), 1500 miles down the coast of Africa. By the time of his death in 1460 Prince Henry's explorers had almost reached the Gulf of Guinea, some two thousand miles from the Straits of Gibraltar.

The immediate result of the Portuguese explorations was the establishment of trade with the natives in such things as ivory and gold, but this was followed before long by the capture and sale of the natives themselves. Upon receiving various reports about the natives from his mariners, Prince Henry asked one of his captains to bring back some natives. When an expedition brought back ten naked Africans of both sexes in 1441, the Portuguese quickly decided that Africa was an almost inexhaustible source of cheap labor. The prospect of making vast profits from the trade in humans caused a group of shipowners to request from Prince Henry permission to engage in the traffic in African slaves. Six caravels were immediately sent out in quest of Africans. The contemporary chronicler Azurara tells how the heavily-armed members of the expedition made raids on African villages, capturing as many natives as possible and killing those who resisted capture. The expedition finally returned to Portugal with 235 Africans who were then equally divided among the four sponsors of the expedition and Prince Henry. In the distribution husbands and wives were separated and children were torn from their parents. Whatever qualms of conscience the Portuguese slave traders may have had were stilled by the thought that physical mistreatment was but a small price for eternal salvation. As Azurara put it, the African "had previously lived in perdition of soul and body without knowledge of the holy faith." Thus the Portuguese inaugurated modern Negro slavery which, before it was finally abolished, resulted in the enslavement of many millions of Africans and the killing of millions of others who resisted.

After the death of Prince Henry, interest in further exploration lagged for a time, although the trade which had been started along the African coast was continued. No further exploring expeditions were sent out until after the accession of King John II in 1481. The Portuguese continued to press southward until in 1486 an expedition headed by Bartholomew Diaz sailed around the southern part of the African continent into the Indian Ocean. The feeling that they had finally discovered the route to India was expressed in the name the Portuguese gave to the southernmost point of Africa, the Cape of Good Hope. Even then unsettled internal affairs prevented them from immediately making the most of the discovery of Bartholomew Diaz. Finally in 1497 an expedition of four ships under Vasco da Gama followed the route around the Cape of Good Hope and after a voyage of more than a year reached Calicut in India. The reception which awaited the Portuguese was anything but friendly. The Arabs who had up to this time controlled the trade between the East and Europe stirred up opposition to the Europeans. This made it necessary for Vasco da Gama to leave Calicut and repair to a neighboring city where he collected a cargo of spices and also rubies and other precious stones before he started his homeward voyage. In Lisbon which he reached in September, 1499, he and his men received a triumphal reception. Prince Henry's dream of finding an all-water route to India had become a reality. When the cargo was sold, it yielded sixty times the cost of the expedition, but of the four ships which had started out only two returned and the price in human life and suffering was staggering. Vasco lost his own brother and more than half the members of his crew, most of them becoming victims of the dread disease of scurvy.

The discovery of the sea route to India was fraught with tremendous consequences. It meant, first of all, the establishment of a direct contact between Western Europe, on the one hand, and India and the Spice Islands, on the other. The Portuguese could now transport spices and oriental luxuries from the East directly to Lisbon. It broadened the scope of commerce from European to transoceanic. Second, the discovery of the all-water route broke the monopolistic hold of the Arab traders on the trade between the Far East and the Mediterranean. Third, as a result of the discovery, the center of trade shifted from the Mediterranean to the Atlantic. The Mediterranean which for many centuries had been the main artery of trade now became a side-street. This change gradually spelled the doom of Venetian prosperity as the flow of oriental goods through Syria and Egypt was diverted by the Portuguese. It has been calculated that during the first two decades of the sixteenth century the supply of spices available to the Venetians was reduced by 75 per cent. No longer did the Venetians send galleys loaded with oriental merchandise to Flanders and England. These countries now purchased their spices and oriental luxuries from Lisbon. It must be noted, however, that the Venetian decline did not take place suddenly; it was a slow process. Fourth, for the Portuguese the discovery of the all-water route to India and the Spice Islands meant that the lucrative trade in spices passed temporarily into their hands. Finally, the discovery of the Cape route meant for Portugal the beginning of a colonial empire. Thus the achievement of Vasco da Gama was truly epoch-making.

The Great Idea of Columbus

While the Portuguese were pressing southward along the west coast of Africa toward the Cape of Good Hope and the Indian Ocean, Christopher Columbus struck out across the Atlantic on a westward course. He was not the first explorer to venture in that direction; it is probable that a number of hardy explorers preceded him. There is, in fact, a considerable literature on pre-Columbian explorations in the Atlantic. Claims have been advanced in behalf of many explorers or exploring groups from Ireland, Poland, Scandinavia, North Africa, the Basque country, Portugal, and other places. It is even alleged that a Buddhist priest from China and a group of settlers crossed the Pacific in the fifth century, landing on the coast of what is now California. In the sixth century St. Brendan is supposed to have sailed to America from Spain. During the succeeding centuries others are alleged to have crossed the Atlantic. It is claimed that two expeditions sailed about two decades before Columbus set sail. One of these, sent out by King Christian of Denmark in 1472, is said to have reached the St. Lawrence River and the other, headed by a Polish navigator named Szkolny, is said to have reached the coast of Newfoundland about 1476. Some of the many claims that have been advanced may have merit, but in most of them the real and imaginary are intermingled in such a way that they cannot be separated. In brief, the evidence presented is not conclusive enough to warrant a general acceptance.

Of the so-called pre-Columbian explorations it is the exploits of the Vikings or Norsemen which are most widely accepted; in fact, an account of their adventures is included in most textbooks on American history. According to the Norse sagas (in the *Hawk's Book* and the *Flatev Book*) the ship of Bjarni Herjulfson, a friend of Eric the Red who colonized Greenland, was blown off its course while he was sailing from Iceland to Greenland about 986. After some days Bjarni and his men found themselves approaching a wooded shore, but they did not land. During the succeeding days they saw land again on several occasions. On his return to Greenland Bjarni related his experience to Eric the Red and his son, Leif Ericson, also known as Leif the Lucky. About 992 the latter borrowed Bjarni's ship and with a crew of about thirty-five men set sail for the land Bjarni had sighted. The first stretch of coast this expedition saw was so rocky that Leif called it Helluland (Stone Land). Proceeding southward the expedition found flat timberland at the mouth of a river. The location was so inviting that the men decided to build houses and spend the winter there. Later they reported that the salmon in the river and in the sea were larger than any they had ever seen before. They also found vines laden with grapes, a discovery which caused them to name the district Vinland. After further explorations in the following spring, the expedition returned to Greenland.

Subsequently other voyages were made to North America. Leif's brother Thorwald made several to the camp Leif had established, one group spending several winters there. There are indications that further voyages were made during the centuries that followed. Trade may even have been carried on between Greenland and the natives of North America. In 1963 a Norwegian archeologist discovered in northern Newfoundland the remains of a settlement which according to the most competent authorities had been a Norse settlement. Further evidence was added in 1965 to support the pre-Columbian discovery of America when Yale University announced the finding of a map of the world, made in 1440, on which North America appears. Moreover, on the map there is a notation regarding the visits of Bjarni and Leif Ericson to Vinland. If the Runic inscriptions on the Kensington Runestone, found in Minnesota in 1898, are authentic, and archeologists and linguists believe they are, a fourteenth-century Norse expedition penetrated as far inland as that state. According to the inscriptions, after ten members of the party of thirty were massacred the rest withdrew to Vinland in 1362. Three axes, two spears, two fire steels, two swords, two ceremonial halberds, and thirteen other implements dating back to the fourteenth century were also found in the vicinity. Many of these articles as well as the Runestone are now in the Runestone Museum at Alexandria, Minnesota.

If Columbus was not the first to discover America, his discovery was the first to have vast consequences. The exploits and adventures of the Norsemen did not become common knowledge in Europe until the nineteenth century. Their achievements were something outside the mainstream of European history. If the Norse discoveries had any influence on thought and action in Western Europe, it was slight. Neither did any other discoveries which may have taken place stimulate important developments. In contrast, reports of the discoveries of Columbus quickly circulated throughout Europe and soon the New World not only became part of European thought, but also stirred the Europeans to action. Thus it was Columbus who gave America to Europe. The path he opened between Europe and the New World was a permanent one. Other explorers and also fortune-hunters soon set out along the same general path, taking back to Europe great quantities of silver and gold which alleviated the scarcity of precious metals that had existed for centuries. This new supply of precious metals infused new energy into the bloodstream of commerce, industry, and capitalism. Groups of settlers followed in the wake of Columbus' first voyage and later crossed the ocean in increasing numbers to establish European communities in the New World. The social and political experiments conducted in these communities had rich significance for the social and political development of various states in Europe. Finally, many of the communities in the New World combined into the United States of America, a move of incalculable significance. It can, therefore, be said that the discoveries of Columbus opened a new era in history.

In turning to Columbus the man, the first question that presents itself is, "Who was he?" The answers have been many and varied, a large proportion of them reflecting the preconceptions and prejudices of those who conceived them. A number of nations have claimed the discoverer as a native son. The issue becomes somewhat amusing when one book offers "unassailable evidence" that Columbus was a Portuguese by birth, a second one presents "indisputable evidence" that he was born in Spain, and a third flaunts the title, "Christopher Columbus was a Greek and his real name was Nikolaos Ypshilantis from the Greek island of Chios." In addition attempts have been made to prove that Columbus was by birth an Irishman, a Frenchman, and an Armenian. It would not be surprising if some ingenious writer were to claim that Columbus was actually an American who went to Europe to discover America for the Europeans. But all attempts to provide him with a nationality other than Italian have failed. The weight of the evidence supports the claim that he was born in Italy. The controversy does not, however, end there. No fewer than sixteen cities of Italy have claimed the honor of being the birthplace of Columbus; however, the consensus of opinion among dispassionate scholars is that he was born in Genoa. As one historian has put it, "The evidence for Genoa is overwhelming." The Spanish historian Salvador de Madariaga gave the story of Columbus a new twist when he asserted in his *Christopher Columbus* (1940) that, although Genoa was the birthplace of Columbus, his parents were Spanish immigrants of the Jewish faith and that Columbus later became a "converso" (convert) who rendered lip-service to Christianity in order to be free to pursue his goals. The proofs the Spanish historian adduced in support of his contention are, however, based on opinion rather than on concrete evidence.

But the uncertainty regarding the facts of the life of Columbus is not limited to the question of his origin; it runs through the entire story of his life up to the time of his first voyage in 1492. Almost every point in the traditional version of his life, based on the biography of his son Fernando and on that of Bishop Bartolomé Las Casas who knew Columbus, has been questioned. The only thing many of those who have assailed the Columbus story have in common is a desire to undermine the traditional. Even the character of Columbus has been the target of determined attacks. Whereas the traditional story exalted Columbus as a man of great nobility of soul, some revisionists have pictured him as a greedy, selfseeking charlatan. It has been asserted that he had no higher ambition than personal gain. Again, while traditionalists deplored the treatment he received from King Ferdinand of Spain, revisionists have asserted that both Ferdinand and Isabella displayed extraordinary forbearance in their dealings with him. It has even been claimed that when he embarked on his first voyage he was only returning to a continent he had previously discovered. The issue may be summed up by stating that some have asserted that Columbus was an Italian but not a hero, others that he was a hero but not an Italian, and again others that he was neither a hero nor an Italian. The end result is that there are few facts in the life of Columbus which are not controversial.

Columbus himself is partly responsible for the controversies that have raged about the details of his life. He revealed so little about himself that he has been called "the embodiment of reticence." In all his writings he never mentioned his father, his mother, or his wife. Even his son Fernando was uncertain about his father's birthplace. When Columbus did refer to his early life he at times made conflicting statements. It has been suggested that he did so to conceal a "secret." In general Columbus had a penchant for telling tall tales and for spinning yarns which had no foundation in fact, but which caused confusion and controversy among his biographers. Most of the available documents are too unreliable and the difficulty of deciphering them is so great that they offer the widest scope for interpretation and misinterpretation. Consequently the hundreds of books that have been written on the life of the discoverer have failed to solve the riddle of Columbus.

It thus becomes necessary to accept tentatively the statements which dispassionate scholars have found most plausible. For example, various years have been designated as the year in which Columbus was born, but the best informed opinion has it that the year was 1451. His father Domenico Colombo, a wool weaver by trade, named his son Cristoforo or Christopher, an appropriate name in the sense that St. Christopher is the patron saint of travelers. Later when Columbus settled in Spain he hispanicized his name calling himself Cristóbal Colón. At an early age Christopher became an apprentice in his father's shop and therefore had little, if any, time for formal education. Later he did, however, acquire some knowledge of Latin and also learned Portuguese and Spanish. The fact that toward the end of his life he wrote Italian so poorly and Spanish so well has been used as an argument to bolster the contention that he was born in Spain. Christopher early felt the lure of the sea, and as a young man of about nineteen exchanged the life of a wool weaver for that of a seafarer. The first voyages on which he went were in the Mediterranean. Later he was on ships that sailed along the Atlantic coast. On one of these voyages the Genoese ship on which he was sailing was attacked off Cape St. Vincent in the Atlantic by a hostile fleet and set on fire. In order to save his life Columbus leaped into the water and using a large oar to buoy himself up swam to the Portuguese shore. He soon reached Lisbon where his brother Bartholomew had a small shop in which he sold nautical charts. A few months later Christopher was on a Portuguese ship sailing northward to England or Ireland, a ship which may have sailed north of Iceland on the return voyage. In the Portuguese service he also seems to have made a trading voyage to the west coast of Africa.

It was during these years that he conceived his great idea of reaching the East by sailing westward. At no time did he entertain the idea of discovering a new continent. What he hoped to find was a short route to the old continent of Asia, more specifically to Zipangu (Japan) and Cathay (China). It is not known whether he conceived the idea himself, whether it was communicated to him by another person or whether it was suggested to him by a book, a letter, or a map. The idea that the shortest route to the Orient was westward across the Atlantic was based on two errors. First, Columbus greatly underestimated the circumference of the earth and, second, he overestimated the extension of Asia eastward into the ocean now called the Pacific. The combination of the two errors gave him the impression that the distance from Portugal to Japan was only about 2400 nautical miles. He expected Japan to be about where Florida is. The errors on which Columbus based his calculations were in wide circulation at that time. They were, as previously stated, an essential part of Ptolemy's geographical thinking. After the discovery of Ptolemy's *Geography* in the first decade of the fifteenth century they were restated almost verbatim by a Frenchman, Cardinal Pierre d'Ailly, who was interested in geography. Near the end of the third quarter of the century Paolo Toscanelli (1397-1482), a Florentine physician and cartographer who had long been interested in the idea of a westward route to Asia, embodied his ideas in a letter and a map which he sent to Cardinal Martins in Lisbon. Toscanelli advocated the idea of sailing "from Lisbon in a straight line toward the west" to reach the land of the Great Khan where "they may gain gold, silver, precious stones, and spices." In some unknown manner Columbus managed to get possession of a copy of the letter and the accompanying map. If the letter and map did not suggest the idea to him, they at least strengthened his conviction that the plan was feasible. Whatever the source of Columbus' idea, the fact remains that the discovery of America was prompted by a monumental error in calculation.

The Execution of the Plan

The conviction that the western route to the Orient was the shortest soon became an obsession with Columbus. Thereafter he worked with unremitting zeal for the realization of his dream. He began to believe that he was the chosen instrument of Divine Providence to carry out the mission of discovering the westward route. Biographers, however, have suggested that this idea as well as his talk about converting the heathen were merely window dressing to aid him in getting the money he needed to carry out his project. The primary motive of Columbus was undoubtedly the hope of getting some of the wealth of Asia. Buoyed by this prospect, Columbus began to seek financial support for his great venture. He decided to offer his plan to Portugal, where he was living at the time. But he failed to excite the interest of government officials in his project. Undiscouraged, he managed by dogged persistence to get an audience with King John II of Portugal. The king listened attentively as Columbus endeavored to persuade him that the Orient could be reached by a shorter route than the one around Africa which the Portuguese were trying to find at that time. King John who was not unsympathetic to the plan, turned it over to a commission for further study. After some consideration the members of the commission voted against accepting it, calling Columbus an impractical visionary. King John was hardly free to override the veto of his commission since he had already put his country deeply into debt by the exploration of the west coast of Africa, so he too rejected the plan.

After the failure of his efforts to obtain the backing of the Portuguese government, Columbus crossed the border into Spain. There he was successful in getting an audience with Queen Isabella through the intervention of a friendly Franciscan friar. Upon hearing the plan of Columbus, Isabella, like King John of Portugal, submitted it to a commission. Like the Portuguese commission, the Spanish commission sent the ruler an unfavable report. However, instead of rejecting the plan Ferdinand and Isabella kept Columbus in Spain by paying him a small pension. At the time the Spanish sovereigns were hardly in a position to give serious consideration to the plan as they were preoccupied with internal problems, particularly the war against Granada, the last Moorish stronghold in Spain. Then, too,

Columbus' demands for personal rewards were rather exorbitant. He de manded not only the title of Admiral of the Ocean Sea, but also the positio of governor-general of all lands he might discover and the further title o Viceroy, both titles to be hereditary. Furthermore, he demanded for himsel 10 per cent of all gold and precious stones that would be obtained eithe through mining or through trade with the Asiatics. Columbus hoped an waited for five or six years. Finally in January of 1492 Granada fell. Eve then nothing further transpired for some weeks regarding his plan. Bu just as Columbus was about to leave for France to offer his plan to Kin Charles VIII he was notified that Ferdinand and Isabella had decided t support the plan on his terms.

During the succeeding weeks three ships were fitted out in the har- bor of Palos. The largest was the Santa Maria, estimated to have been abou 90 feet long. The other two, the Niña and the Pinta were somewha smaller, having a length of about 65 to 70 feet. Columbus chose the larg- est, but also the slowest of the three ships as his flagship. The member of the three crews, about ninety in number, were almost all Spaniards All preparations having been completed, the three ships sailed out of the harbor of Palos on the morning of August 3, 1492, in the direction of the Canary Islands. There the expedition remained three weeks while the rudde of the Pinta was being repaired and fresh water and provisions were being put on board. Then the small fleet set sail on a course due west. The ex- pedition encountered no severe storms or prolonged calms; nor did the crews suffer from a shortage of water or provisions. Their only troubles were of a psychological nature. As the ships moved farther and farther from Spain the courage of some of the men began to falter. In three weeks they had sailed farther than Columbus had estimated the distance from Spain to Asia to be without seeing any land. Despite the prospects of great rewards and the efforts of Columbus to calm their fears, the crew members decided on October 10 that if no land were sighted in three days they would turn back. As the ships sailed on, the crew members saw such indica- tions of the proximity of land as floating branches and flocks of birds and finally about 2 A.M. on October 12, 1492, a lookout sighted land.

What Columbus saw before him when daylight came was an island which the natives called Guanahani, but which he named San Salvador. Various islands have been suggested, for the description fits almost any one of the Bahama Islands. The one most generally accepted as the first island sighted is Watling Island. In any case, Columbus was convinced that he had reached the eastern fringe of Asia, that the island he had discovered was one of the 2700 islands which, according to Marco Polo, formed the ap- proach to Japan and the mainland of Asia. He believed the natives of the islands to be Asiatics, as the name Indians indicates. The idea is also per- petuated in the name West Indies, Indies being the name used to designate the general territory of Japan, China, and India. After claiming San

Salvador in the name of the Spanish crown, Columbus pressed his search for Japan and China. When he reached the northeastern coast of Cuba he was so certain he had found Cathay that he sent emissaries inland to deliver a letter from the Spanish sovereigns to the Great Khan. The mission returned, of course, without finding the Great Khan. Instead it found natives smoking cigars, that is, dry herbs rolled in a leaf. According to Columbus' journal, smoking the herb made the natives immune to fatigue. Consequently tobacco was introduced into Europe as a medicament having miraculous curative qualities rather than as "a solace for fallen human nature."

Next the expedition of Columbus discovered the large island which now contains Haiti and the Dominican Republic. Because the climate and the trees reminded him of Spain, Columbus named the island Hispaniola (Little Spain). On it, however, he found no rich cities or palaces and temples roofed with gold, but only scantily-clad natives living in a most primitive manner whose total wealth consisted of the few gold trinkets they wore. Columbus had planned to continue his search for Zipangu and Cathay, but when the Santa Maria was wrecked on a reef on Christmas Day, he decided to return to Spain. He was so firmly convinced he had found a short route to Asia that he was eager to carry the news to the Spanish sovereigns. Upon his arrival in Spain large crowds turned out to hail him as a hero and to gaze at the six Indians in native dress he had brought back. At Barcelona Ferdinand and Isabella received him with great ceremony and bestowed on him the titles of "Admiral of the Ocean Sea" and "Viceroy of the Indies," commissioning him to organize a second expedition. It was his great hour of triumph. The only fly in the ointment was his failure to bring back some of the vast wealth he had hoped to find.

The strange paradox of the career of Columbus is that he never did achieve what he set out to do. Not only did he not find a short route to Asia, he did not find any western route to the Indies despite the fact that he made three further voyages of discovery. On his second voyage he searched for the land of the Great Khan in the vicinity of Cuba. When he returned to Spain in 1496 it was clear to almost everyone but Columbus that the islands he had discovered were not Asia. On his third voyage he touched the mainland of South America which he believed to be the great island Marco Polo reported as lying to the southeast of Asia. From the natives near the isthmus of Panama he learned about a great ocean on the other side of the isthmus. To find this ocean which Columbus believed to be the Indian Ocean was the purpose of his fourth and last voyage. He spent some months sailing along the coast of Central America in search of a non-existent strait before he was forced by leaking ships and bad provisions to abandon the search.

In 1504 Columbus returned to Spain in failing health and deeply discouraged by his failure to reach Cathay with its reputed wealth. Furthermore, Ferdinand and Isabella had lost confidence in him even before he embarked on his final voyage. Now Isabella was on her deathbed and Ferdinand would have nothing to do with him. Without hope of being given another opportunity to find the wealth of Asia, Columbus spent the remaining months of his life trying to collect the share of the trade with the New World which the Spanish sovereigns had promised him. It was all to no avail. Actually he was not suffering from want, but from neglect. He died at Valladolid in May, 1506. After his death he became the "forgotten man" until the memory of his deeds was revived by his son Fernando in the biography he wrote of his father.

When the continent Columbus had discovered was named, fate decreed that it should be given the name of another. The man after whom it was named was Amerigo Vespucci (1451-1512), the latinized form being Americus Vespuccius. Amerigo was a Florentine merchant who about 1491 was sent to Spain as an agent of the Medici family. He was in Spain when Columbus sailed on his first voyage and he was also there when the great discoverer returned in 1493. The explorations of Columbus excited in him such a keen interest in navigation and discovery that in 1497 he sailed as navigator with a Spanish expedition on a visit to the New World. Two years later he repeated the experience and in 1501 joined a Portuguese expedition sailing in the same direction. On these voyages he may have reached Central America and possibly South America. Subsequently in 1504 Amerigo wrote a series of letters in which he described the New World, referring to it as "a continent." In some unknown manner these letters came into the possession of the German cartographer Martin Waldseemüller who in 1507 published a Latin translation of them in his *Introductio Cosmographiae*. Waldseemüller also sketched a map of the new continent and labeled it "America." Actually he applied the name only to the southern part of the continent, but the name was quickly accepted as a designation for the whole continent.

On the homeward voyage after his first visit to the New World Columbus sailed into the harbor of Lisbon, ostensibly to escape the fury of a storm. While he was in Portugal the Admiral of the Ocean Sea could not resist the opportunity to boast about his discoveries to King John II who had rejected the plan Columbus had presented to him. The Portuguese king reacted by claiming for his country all the lands Columbus had discovered. When Ferdinand and Isabella were apprised of this they petitioned the pope to confirm the rights of Spain to the lands their emissary had discovered. In May 1493, Pope Alexander VI responded by promulgating a bull which drew a line of demarcation a hundred leagues west of the Azores and of the Cape Verde Islands, allotting to the Spanish crown all lands west of this line which were not in the possession of a Christian king. The Portuguese, however, objected vigorously to this division. Representatives of the two nations finally negotiated the treaty of Tordesillas which the pope confirmed in 1506. In placing the line of demarcation 370 leagues west of the Cape Verde Islands this treaty assigned Africa and Asia to the Portuguese and accorded to Spain the American continent with the exception of Brazil which was on the Portuguese side of the line. The other nations respected or ignored the line as it suited their interests and purposes.

The Beginnings of Colonial Empire

The Portuguese went to India as traders, not as colonizers. The idea of founding an empire did not furnish the original impulse for the hazardous undertaking. Circumstances rather than preconceived ideas induced them to adopt the role of colonizers. A share of the spice trade did not satisfy them; they wanted an absolute monopoly. To achieve this goal, they built factories or warehouses along the coast to which the natives could conveniently bring commodities for the purpose of selling them to the Portuguese. But the hostility of the Moslems whose hold on the spice trade had been broken and the antagonism the Portuguese aroused among the natives by their imperious conduct made it necessary to fortify the trading posts and to garrison them with armed Portuguese.

The task of trying to maintain a monopoly of the spice trade put too great a strain on the limited manpower resources of a nation as small as Portugal. Some of the Portuguese fighting men fell in combat, and others became victims of malaria, cholera, scurvy, dysentery, and other diseases. By 1525 the shortage of manpower reached a point at which it became necessary to induct convicts and boys into the armed forces. The colonial administration tried the expedient of marriage alliances between Portuguese men and native women, but it did not prove very successful. Such marriages produced half-breeds who were neither Portuguese nor native and as such were not an asset to the Portuguese administration. Back at home in Portugal the vast profits of the spice trade were breeding corruption in high places and impairing the efficiency of the colonial administration as well as of the internal administration. That the Portuguese were able to maintain their hold on the spice trade as long as they did was due in large measure to the powerful Portuguese fleet. Gradually this too lost its effectiveness, enabling other nations to appropriate a major part of the spice trade. In general, Portuguese power in India slowly crumbled under the persistent attacks of the Dutch and the English.

In Brazil the Portuguese were more successful, but the profits of the Brazilian trade were not nearly so large. In 1500 Pedro Alvarez Cabral took possession of Brazil for the Portuguese crown when his ships touched the coast of South America while on the way to India. There are indications, however, that the existence of Brazil was known to the Portuguese before Cabral "discovered" it. As the Portuguese found only poor natives there, they showed little interest in it. At one time they even considered withdrawing from it. Its function during the early years was to serve as a site for Portuguese penal colonies. Later settlers did begin to migrate there in considerable numbers, among them many Jews who were seeking a refuge from religious persecution. Toward the end of the sixteenth century the cultivation of sugar cane also attracted settlers. It has been estimated that by the end of the sixteenth century there were about forty thousand Portuguese in Brazil. One of the first towns to be founded there was Rio de Janeiro (1567).

While the Portuguese were struggling to maintain their monopoly of the spice trade, the Spaniards were busy exploring and founding settlements in the vast territories which had been allotted to them in the division of the non-Christian territories of the globe. After establishing settlements on various islands off the eastern coast of the American continent, including those presently called Haiti and San Domingo, Jamaica, Puerto Rico, and Cuba, the Spanish conquerors, customarily called conquistadores, turned their attention to the mainland. When Ponce de Leon set out in search of the fabled land of perpetual youth, he discovered a land he called Florida, but did not establish a settlement because of the determined opposition of the natives. Spanish rule in Florida was not definitely established until 1565, the year in which St. Augustine was founded. Previously in 1513 Balboa, after hearing from the natives about the great ocean on the other side of the isthmus of Panama, made his historic march across the isthmus through malarial swamps and almost impenetrable jungles, until he saw before him the great expanse of water which Magellan later named the Pacific. This discovery proved beyond doubt the fact that the new continent was not a part of Asia.

But there were even more romantic exploits in the offing, the first of which was the conquest of Mexico. After an expedition sent to the mainland by the governor of Cuba reported that it had found people with a higher civilization than any discovered up to that time, Hernando Cortez in 1518 led an expedition on the epic march into Mexico. Upon reaching the mainland he founded a settlement called Vera Cruz and then began his march into the interior. It was not a large expedition, but the fact that the conquistadores had cannons and horses gave them an important psychological advantage. Not only cannons but also horses had previously been unknown on the American continent. When Montezuma, the ruler of the Aztecs, who dominated the native tribes of Mexico, heard of the arrival of the strange men with the strange animals, he went out to meet them and tried to dissuade them from continuing their march to the Aztec capital by giving them presents of gold. The gifts, however, only excited the cupidity of the Spaniards, causing them to advance more quickly. The sight of the Aztec capital on the spot where Mexico City stands filled the Spaniards with amazement. The great buildings of solid masonry on an island surrounded by water at first caused many of the Spaniards to think it was a vision. But the reality of the concrete fortifications caused the

Spaniards to consider how they could capture it with so small a force. The problem was solved for them by Montezuma who again tried to propitiate the Spaniards by inviting them into the city. This did not, however, please the Aztecs who proceeded to depose Montezuma and to fight so fiercely that the Spaniards withdrew from the city. The arrival of reinforcements from Cuba some time later and the recruitment of a large force from native tribes who wished to be free of the Aztec yoke enabled Cortez to take the Aztec capital by force of arms. Soon Cortez was the master of Mexico. From Mexico City he sent out expeditions to the north and the south with the result that the Spaniards extended their rule over the entire region from northern Mexico to Panama.

The conquest of Mexico was soon followed by the conquest of Peru. When Columbus on his last voyage touched the American continent in the vicinity of the isthmus of Panama, the natives told him and his men about a land to the south where there was gold in great abundance. Later Balboa and his men heard similar stories. The man who found this land called Peru was Francisco Pizarro who had accompanied Balboa on his march across the isthmus of Panama. Although his first attempt in 1524 failed, the second one met with success. He landed a small force of two hundred men and fifty horses along the coast and then started the march toward the capital of the Incas, a conquering minority which had subjugated the natives of a wide area. As the invading force advanced Atahualpa, the ruler of the Incas, came to meet it and was at once taken prisoner. He paid a large ransom in good faith, but instead of releasing him the Spaniard put him to death after a mock trial. Without their leader the Incas were unable to offer effective resistance and were soon overwhelmed. Then the Spaniards plundered the Inca temples and palaces, collecting vast quantities of gold. When the news reached Spain, adventurers in large numbers flocked to South America. Before long the large area now occupied by Peru, Ecuador, Bolivia, and northern Chile was Hispanicized. Other explorers penetrated the region now divided between Argentina and Paraguay where settlements were also founded. Thus Spain established a great colonial empire in the New World. According to an official report, there were by 1574 more than two hundred towns and settlements in Spanish America.

While the conquistadores were searching for precious metals another Spanish adventurer named Fernando Magellan proved by a practical experiment not only that the earth is round, but also that there is a vast expanse of ocean between the New World and Asia. Leaving Seville in 1519, Magellan struck out across the Atlantic, sailed down the coast of South America, through the treacherous straits which bear his name into the ocean he named the Pacific because of the calm weather his expedition found there. By the time he reached the Pacific the original fleet of five ships had shrunk to three, one having foundered on the rocks and another having furtively returned to Spain. On the Pacific the ships sailed three months and twenty days without sighting land. During this time the men suffered terribly from scurvy due to the lack of fresh food. Finally the ships reached the islands later named the Philippines after King Philip II of Spain. There Magellan was killed in a quarrel with the natives (April, 1521), but the survivors continued the voyage to Borneo, the Spice Islands, and around the Cape of Good Hope into the Atlantic. In 1522 the last remaining ship sailed into the port of Seville after a voyage which lasted more than two years. This first circumnavigation of the globe is one of the most impressive maritime feats of all time. Besides exposing once and for all the fallacy of Columbus that the West Indies were near Asia, this voyage also gave Europeans some general idea of the earth's circumference. But the results in terms of commerce and colonization were negligible. The one concrete result was the establishment of Spanish dominion over the Philippines after a struggle lasting more than a century.

The other countries of Western Europe did not at once enter the contest for colonies. It was not the division of the non-Christian world between Portugal and Spain by Pope Alexander VI which restrained them. They were either split up into small fractions which made them too weak to contest the division or they were too preoccupied with other matters. Germany and Italy were too splintered to undertake any great commercial or colonial ventures against the opposition of the Iberian powers. Both countries did not join in the scramble for colonies until after they achieved national unity in the second half of the nineteenth century. The Dutch, too, were not ready because the group of provinces in which they lived lacked solidarity. Later a more united Netherlands would challenge both Spain and Portugal.

As for England, near the end of the fifteenth century it was just emerging from a series of disastrous wars (Hundred Years War and the War of the Roses). As the victor in the battle of Bosworth which ended the War of the Roses Henry VII (1485-1509), the first of the Tudor line of sovereigns, was crowned king of England. Henry was so busy consolidating his rule and replenishing the royal coffers that he had little time and less money to engage in maritime or colonial adventures. But private interests did finance and send out a number of small expeditions in the hope that they might share in the wealth the Portuguese and Spaniards were garnering. As early as 1497 a group of Bristol merchants sent out Giovanni Caboto, better known as John Cabot, an Italian merchant who had settled in England, in a small ship with a crew of eighteen. Like Columbus, John Cabot labored under the delusion that he could reach Asia by sailing due westward. He sighted the coast of America in the vicinity of Newfoundland, but saw nothing to convince him that he had reached Asia. A second voyage was no more fruitful. The only practical result of his voyages was the exploitation of the Newfoundland fishing banks which he had discovered on his first voyage. His son Sebastian, believing that he could circumvent the land mass his father had found, set out some years later in search of a northwest passage to Asia, but was forced to turn back by the masses of ice he encountered. After him others made futile attempts to find such a passage to the northwest and also to the northeast.

The immediate successors of Henry VII did not display any greater interest in exploration and colonization. They regarded other matters as more worthy of their attention. Portugal and Spain had already established themselves in the better colonial areas and the others were regarded as valueless for the time being. Although Henry VIII did not embark on any colonial ventures, he did greatly strengthen his naval forces. The royal navy, which at the time of Henry VIII's accession had a total of only seven ships, boasted no fewer than fifty-three at the time of his death. His son Edward VI, a mere boy when his father died, was king only a few years and his half-sister, Mary, was preoccupied with internal matters during her brief occupancy of the throne. It was during the reign of Queen Elizabeth I (1558-1603) that England became a real power on the seas, and the idea of colonization was given some consideration. During the early years of her reign the search for a northwest passage was continued. Probably the best known attempts to find such a passage are the three voyages of Martin Frobisher (1576-1578). During the same period a group of English mariners, often called Elizabethan seadogs, were actively attacking Spanish shipping as a means of getting their share of colonial wealth. Prominent among the seadogs were Sir John Hawkins and Sir Francis Drake. In 1577 the latter embarked on the second circumnavigation of the earth, returning to England with a cargo of spices, silks, precious stones, and precious metals. The success of Drake's voyage emboldened a group of English merchants to send fleets of ships directly to India and the Spice Islands. After the first attempt was frustrated by storms, the second proved successful, paying the financial backers a profit of 100 per cent. This was followed in 1600 by the founding of the East India Company, the greatest empire building corporation in English history. Meanwhile a number of unsuccessful attempts were made to establish English settlements in the New World. Finally in 1607 the Virginia Company succeeded in founding the first permanent settlement on the James River.

While the Portuguese and Spaniards were making their early voyages of discovery, the French monarchy had its eye on Italy, hoping to extend French dominion over at least a part of the Italian peninsula. It was an attempt at empire-building within the confines of Western Europe. This ambition embroiled the French kings in wars with other European states. Later the controversies and conflicts stirred up by the Protestant and Catholic Reformations absorbed the attention of the French rulers. Private interests, however, sent expeditions to explore the possibilities of sending fishing expeditions to the Newfoundland banks. During the succeeding years fleets of fishing boats were sent out each year. King Francis I (1515-1547), was interested in sharing in the wealth of the Orient to the extent that in 1524 he sent out Giovanni Verrazano, a Florentine, to search for a northwest passage. A decade later he sent out Jacques Cartier for the same purpose. Upon discovering the mouth of the St. Lawrence, Cartier was certain it was the long sought passage to China. In the following spring he sailed up the St. Lawrence until his way was barred by rapids. Cartier was so sure that the rapids kept him from reaching China that he named them La Chine (China) or Lachine. Thereafter the French government did nothing further until the reign of Henry IV (1589-1610). In 1604 the French founded settlements at Port Royal in Nova Scotia and in 1608 at Quebec. These settlements opened a new era which saw the progressive development of New France in America.

15

The Dawn of Modern Science

After the humanist reaction against the Middle Ages, historians neglected the medieval period as a time devoid of achievements. Medieval science, a field which appeared barren, was regarded as particularly unworthy of careful investigation. In writing surveys of the history of science, scholars would discuss the contributions of the classical period, then continue the narrative with a discussion of science in the sixteenth century, as if the intervening period were a blank page. The scientists of the sixteenth and seventeenth centuries were depicted as men of genius who quickly laid the foundations of modern science without help from precursors. Even in the nineteenth century when historians began to make a careful study of various phases of medieval civilization, scholarly investigation of medieval science lagged far behind. Recent historiography has, however, made amends for the long neglect. Although much remains to be done, diligent investigators have shown that the Middle Ages made substantial contributions to the development of natural science.

Natural Science in the Early Middle Ages

When the foundations of their empire began to crumble the Romans exerted little effort to preserve for posterity the scientific knowledge passed on to them by the Greeks. They themselves had made few original contributions to the philosophy of science. Since their primary interest was in engineering and practical affairs, the philosophical discussions of nature held no strong attraction for them. Greek science remained something imported, something exotic. But not all knowledge of Greek science was lost even temporarily. In the first century A.D. Pliny the Elder (23-79) compiled his *Natural History* containing citations from nearly five hundred different works. The subjects included were astronomy, geography, anthropology, zoology, botany, medicine, and mineralogy. For more than a thousand years this compilation was the largest known collection of nature knowledge. During this period scholars found Pliny's *Natural History* a most important source of information. Another important compilation was the *Etymology* of Isidor of Seville (560-636) which contained knowledge of all kinds from astronomy to medicine. For centuries scholars of Western Europe had to rely largely on such compilations for their knowledge of natural science.

Among the early Christians there was no great desire to understand what was happening in nature round about them. Their interest was centered in preparation for "the kingdom of the Lord" which they believed might be inaugurated at any moment. St. Paul, for example, regarded Greek ideas on natural science as something irrelevant to the primary purpose of life. There was little, if anything, in the teachings of such early Church Fathers as Tertullian (155-222), St. Jerome (340-420), and St. Augustine (354-420) to induce Christians to study nature except for otherworldly and medical purposes. St. Augustine expressly deprecated the study of natural phenomena except for purposes of salvation and health. In his *Confessions* he wrote, "Men seek out the hidden powers of nature which to know profits not and wherein men desire nothing but knowledge." "We should rest content," he wrote in the treatise *On Faith*, "to be ignorant of the mysteries of the heavens and the earth." In the early Middle Ages generally there was little desire to pursue scientific inquiry for its own sake. The observations that were made were almost entirely for religious, astrological, or magical purposes. There was a widespread belief in the magical properties of nature, a belief shared by such outstanding scholars as Isidore of Seville. Those who believed in astrology, and there were many, were convinced that the heavenly bodies have an influence on human life; hence astrologers scanned the heavens to ascertain the varying positions of the planets. For the believers the realities of nature had a religious meaning. Their purpose in observing them was to find symbolical illustrations of Christian teachings. The spots on the moon, for example, were believed to be symbols of the stain of sin which came into the world as the result of Adam's fall. The wind was regarded as symbolic of the existence of the Holy Ghost.

If the scholars of the Christian world ignored the scientific traditions of the Greeks, this was not true of the learned men of the Arab world. After the foundations of the Arabian Empire of Islam had been laid in the seventh century, the Arabs conquered Persia, Asia Minor, and northeastern Africa, and began to penetrate into Spain. From the Syrians who had preserved much of the learning of the Greeks by translating Greek works into their own language, the Arabs obtained many manuscripts which they translated into Arabic. Additional Greek manuscripts were procured from the Greeks of Constantinople. Arab scholars studied these works carefully and often added detailed commentaries. Important centers of Arabic learning were Bagdad and Basra in the Near East, Toledo and Córdoba in Spain, and Palermo in Sicily. One of the subjects which held a special interest for the Arabs was optics. It is believed that they may have been the first to make lenses. They were also interested in astronomy to the extent that they built observatories for the purpose of studying the heavens. A third field of interest was medicine, and the Arabs made important contributions toward its advancement. But their greatest influence was undoubtedly in the realm of mathematics. They contributed to the development of algebra and the founding of trigonometry. Above all, they developed the system of Arabic numerals which originally came from the Hindus. This system with its symbol for zero was greatly superior to the system of Roman numerals. Its adoption in Western Europe during the later centuries of the Middle Ages was a great boon to expanding commerce, industry, and banking.

Meanwhile interest in a more definite knowledge of the natural world was gradually increasing among Christian scholars of Western Europe. They were beginning to ask questions about natural phenomena. Having no other body of detailed knowledge at hand they turned to Greek science and to the Arab commentaries on science for their answers. The life of Adelard of Bath, an Englishman of the twelfth century, is a good illustration of the growing interest in Greek and Arabic science. Aspiring to encompass the whole field of learning and particularly mathematics and natural science, Adelard visited Arabic countries for the purpose of gaining a first hand knowledge of Arabic learning. Upon his return he was urged by his friends to disclose some of the new ideas he had absorbed. He responded by writing *The Mirror of Nature*, a purported conversation between him and his nephew. At the beginning of his work Adelard listed seventy-six topics for discussion, among them "How and why the globe of the earth is held up in the middle of the air," "Why the waters of the sea are salty," "Whence the ebb and flow of the tides come," "Where thunder and lightning come from," "What food the stars eat if they are animals," "Why certain beasts chew the cud, and certain others not at all," "Whether beasts have souls," "Why men are not born with horns or other weapons," and "Why plants are not produced from water or air, or even from fire, as they are from the earth."

The Introduction of Greek Science

In the twelfth century Arabic, Jewish, and Christian scholars began to supply the demand for more knowledge of nature by bringing in Latin versions of Arabic translations of Greek writings on science; in some cases the Latin translations were made directly from Greek texts. At the same time the commentaries on these texts by learned men of the Arab world were also introduced into Western Europe. In this way almost all of the scientific works of the ancients were made available in Latin translations to the scholars of Western Europe by the middle of the thirteenth century. Although many of the Latin translations were clumsy, full of errors, and even contained interpolations unrelated to the basic subject, Greek scientific knowledge and the ideas of the Arab commentators did reenter the mainstream of European thought. Among the works on science which became available were those of Aristotle, Ptolemy, and Galen. As a result of their acceptance, medieval science became largely the science of the ancients modified by the commentaries of Arab scholars. While astronomy was greatly influenced by the ideas of Ptolemy, and medicine by the writings of Galen, the general view of science was based on the works of Aristotle. The works of these writers remained the basic textbooks in the universities for centuries. According to present standards the quantity of scientific knowledge was not large, nor was the quality high. But the assimilation of classical ideas on science, supplemented by what the Arabs had added, was new and interesting. It was a development which not only quickened the interest in natural science, but also speeded the advance of science.

Among the classical writings which stimulated a wider interest in natural science those of Aristotle (384-322 B.C.) were outstanding. Aristotle, the greatest of Greek scientists, is the father of scientific method, inductive as well as deductive. His contributions have earned for him an important place in the history of science. Several of his works are still highly esteemed by scientists. Prior to the twelfth century he was known in Europe only through the excerpts from his works which had been included in such collections as those of Pliny and Isidore of Seville. The only works of Aristotle that were known during the period before the twelfth century were his writings on logic which Boethius (480-524) had translated. In the twelfth and thirteenth centuries the other works of Aristotle were restored to Western Europe in Latin translations, some from Arabic and others from Greek manuscripts. In the twelfth century Latin translations of his *Physics*, his *De Coelo* (On the Heavens), and the first books of his *Metaphysics* were brought into Western Europe, probably from Toledo in Spain. During the early part of the next century Aristotle's *History of Animals* as well as the last books of *Metaphysics* made their appearance in Latin. In many monasteries and most universities these writings were copied and carefully studied. So many found his answers convincing that Aristotle became "the philosopher." By some he was hailed as the greatest of masters whose statements were absolutely authoritative. Gradually every phase of medieval thought, including philosophy, education, politics, and natural science, came under the influence of Aristotle's ideas. In natural science his views of nature and of the universe became the framework on which the whole of medieval science rested.

According to Aristotle, scientific investigation is a twofold process, the first being inductive and the second deductive. Although many of his observations were keen and many of his inferences acute, other deductions, some of them expressed in the form of generalizations, were not sound. For example, Aristotle, like Plato, taught that all matter is composed of four elements: earth, air, fire, and water in different proportions. These elements possess four primary qualities: hot, cold, moist, and dry. Accordingly earth was cold and dry, air was hot and moist, fire was hot and dry, and water was cold and moist. Since the elements were believed to exist in varying proportions in metals, the possibility presented itself of changing the proportions and thereby transmuting base metals into precious metals.

One result was that the alchemists, those who endeavored to effect the transmutation, devoted much time and effort to the search for the fabled Philosopher's Stone which was believed to possess the magic power to transmute metals. Astrologers also found in Aristotle's works support for their claims that the heavenly bodies influence human destinies, in fact, astrology came to be regarded as a legitimate part of natural science. By providing sustenance for astrology, alchemy, magic, and superstition, the writings of Aristotle retarded the development of such sciences as physics and chemistry for centuries. In time, as the sciences developed, Aristotle's ideas became obstacles in the path of progress which had to be removed to permit further advance.

When Aristotle's writings were first introduced into Western Europe they were sternly opposed in some circles and reading them was forbidden because Aristotle's ideas were at variance with the teachings of the Church on a number of points. It was feared that his writings might undermine the faith of those who read them. The scholar who did more than anyone else to make Aristotle's writings acceptable was Thomas Aquinas (1225-1274), a Dominican monk and the author of the monumental *Summa Theologica* in which scholasticism reached its highest level. In this great work Aquinas constructed a rational synthesis of knowledge in which he incorporated the science and logic of Aristotle together with philosophy and theology. Aquinas believed that there could be no basic difference between natural truth and revealed truth. The ultimate purpose of all knowledge was, in his opinion, the eternal salvation of mankind. Accordingly he decided to make Aristotle's ideas subservient to Christian theology. As authority for this he had the words of St. Paul (II Cor. 10:5): "Bringing into captivity every understanding unto the obedience of Christ." A careful study of Aristotle's writings convinced Aquinas that there was general agreement between the ideas of the Greek philosopher and the teachings of the Church, and he turned to specific points of disagreement. One of these was Aristotle's assertion that matter is eternal. This conflicted with the Christian idea of God as a creator who had created matter out of nothing. The question had already been considered by the Jewish philosopher Maimonides (1135-1204) whose account was current in Christian circles. Maimonides decided that Aristotle was actually referring to creation. Aquinas accepted this interpretation, thereby eliminating one point of difference. Other differences were glossed over or simply ignored as being of no great significance. Thus St. Thomas Aquinas established a working harmony between the statements of Aristotle and the teachings of the Church.

The final result of the efforts of Aquinas was a closely-knit synthesis of natural and revealed knowledge in which the former served as an aid to the latter. The inter-relationship of science and theology was so close that, as Descartes complained at a later time, it was almost impossible to disagree with Aristotelian science without appearing to contradict the teachings of the Church. Furthermore, the close union of natural and revealed knowledge had the effect of delaying the separation of science from theology and metaphysics. On the other hand, the synthesis of St. Thomas helped to open the way for the new science by demonstrating the regularity, uniformity, and intelligibility of nature. What natural science needed in order to advance was a new approach, a new methodology. In stressing the uniformity and constancy of nature the first step had been taken in the direction of the experimental method. Even this method was not entirely foreign to Aquinas. He himself stressed the importance of experience, but not as strongly as his contemporary Albertus Magnus.

The Beginnings of the Experimental Method

After the appearance of the Latin translations of the Greek and Arabic scientific treatises many scholars turned their attention to natural science. During the remainder of the twelfth century they were too busy absorbing the contents of the various treatises on physics, medicine, astronomy and other subjects to consider the question of methodology, that is, of an orderly approach to or systematic arrangement of the new knowledge. Gradually, however, some of the leading thinkers recognized that the methodological approach was a necessary preliminary step toward an understanding of the differences between natural science and other forms of knowledge, and of such questions as the relationship of theory and practice within natural science itself. In various centers of learning, and particularly in the universities of Oxford and Paris, leading thinkers applied themselves to the problem of methodology. Most successful was a group of Franciscan scholars at Oxford University. This group made some definite contributions to the advancement of scientific thought.

The founder of the Oxford group, and the thinker whose ideas were decisive for the members of the group, was Robert Grosseteste (*c.*1175-1253), an Englishman by birth. After studying theology, medicine, and law at the universities of Oxford and Paris, Grosseteste became rector of the Franciscan school at Oxford and in 1235 was elevated to the episcopate, becoming the bishop of Lincoln, the diocese which included Oxford University. During the time he was able to spare from his official duties Grosseteste wrote many treatises and tracts on an encyclopedic range of subjects which included philosophy, ethics, theology, agriculture, geography, and natural science. Grosseteste's interest in natural science had definite theological implications. Although he regarded "revealed truth" as the purest form of truth, he saw no conflict between "natural truth" and "revealed truth." The study of natural science was, therefore, to him a branch of theology. It was a further means of discovering God and his ways.

The fact, however, that he regarded science as the handmaiden of theology did not prevent him from making important contributions to the development of natural science. Thus he explained the shape of the rainbow by attributing it to the refraction of light. He also suggested the use of lenses to magnify small objects. More important for the future of natural science was his advocacy of the use of the experimental method as a necessary method of verification. The experimental method was not something new. It was known to the Greeks and Arabs, and was used in contemporary technology. Neither was Grosseteste the only thinker of his time who was interested in the experimental method. In the first half of the twelfth century, for example, a certain Bernard Silvestris had written a treatise on astronomy titled *Experimentorius*. But Grosseteste appears to have been the first thinker of his time to show in a number of his writings how questions of natural science can be answered through the use of the experimental method.

Grosseteste made a further contribution by emphasizing the application of mathematical, particularly geometrical, principles in the study of natural science as a means of understanding its phenomena. Such geometrical abstractions as lines, circles, and triangles, he stated, are also abstract principles of physical things and can, therefore, supply the general principles for explaining the facts of natural science. He even went so far as to say that it is impossible to understand the physical world without the application of geometrical principles. This idea, too, was not original with Grosseteste. He probably found it in Greek treatises on science. The Greeks had tried to express not only optics and astronomy but also biology and medicine in geometrical terms. Geometrical demonstration is, in fact, the great Greek contribution to the history of science. Grosseteste was so busy with reading and writing in addition to his official duties that he had little opportunity to use his knowledge in practical experiments. The ideas he enunciated did, however, influence the thinking of scholars and scientists of his time and of the succeeding period, including William of Ockham, John Peckham, Thomas Bradwardine, and Roger Bacon.

The best known member of the Oxford group is undoubtedly the Englishman Roger Bacon (1214-1294). Many writers of the nineteenth and early twentieth centuries greatly overstated his importance in the history of science, depicting him as a genius who was so far ahead of his time that he stood alone among his contemporaries. Various inventions, including gunpowder and spectacles, have without reason been ascribed to him. He has been credited with foreseeing the invention of the steamship, the automobile, and the airplane. By some writers he has also been styled "the father of the experimental method." The truth is less spectacular, but still interesting. After showing real promise as a student at Oxford young Bacon continued his studies at the University of Paris and also lectured there. How widely he read in classical, early medieval, and contemporary works is reflected in his writings. His interests were as broad as the field of knowledge at that time. About 1215 Roger Bacon returned to Oxford and several years later joined the Franciscan order. In his early writings he subjected the learning and the methodology of his time to such sharp criticism that it brought him under suspicion of heresy and resulted in his being forbidden by the head of the order to write for public circulation. But Bacon appealed to Pope Clement IV who prior to his elevation to the papacy had been papal legate to England where he had learned of Bacon's ability. Clement permitted him to write, injunctions by Bacon's superiors notwithstanding. Bacon responded by writing the triad of works which made him famous: the *Opus Majus* (*c.*1267), the *Opus Minus* (1267), and the *Opus Tertium* (1267-1268). In these works he expounded his ideas on natural science and other phases of the knowledge of his time. In 1278 the head of the Franciscan order condemned Bacon's books because they contained "suspected novelties" and for the next fourteen years Roger Bacon was not permitted to write. Thereafter he started writing a compendium of theological knowledge, but died before he could carry out much of the project.

Roger Bacon was in some small respects ahead of his time, but in general his ideas reflect the interests of other natural scientists of the period. In his study of optics he appears to have made a small contribution to the knowledge of reflection and refraction. He was also probably one of the first of his time to realize that light does not move instantaneously, but with a definite velocity. On the whole, however, his ideas on optics were those of Robert Grosseteste. Bacon also espoused the experimental method, going so far as to insist that without careful experimentation science was but verbiage. In his writings he urged the use of the experimental method again and again with such statements as "It alone has the means of finding out perfection" and "Without experimentation nothing can be adequately known." In all this he is, however, not an original thinker, but a disciple of Grosseteste. His explanation of the rainbow which he used to demonstrate the value of the experimental method is undoubtedly based on ideas he appropriated from Robert Grosseteste. In a general sense Bacon's conception of experience and the experimental method is thoroughly medieval. Knowledge in his opinion derives from three sources: the Sacred Scriptures, the observation of the senses, and "inner experience" or divine illumination. The purpose of observation and experimentation is not to discover new truths, but to find support for, and elucidation of, the truths which have been revealed in the Bible. Bacon was firmly convinced that every truth which might be discovered in nature could be found in the Bible.

Despite the fact that Bacon emphasized the use of the experimental method as a means of ascertaining truth, he himself exhibited an amazing credulity in accepting many tales without verifying them. Thus he asserted his belief in the existence in Europe of flying dragons on which Ethiopians, who were reported to have come to Europe for this purpose, rode by means of saddles and bridles. In typical medieval fashion Bacon also believed in the miraculous powers of precious stones, certain herbs, and certain metals. Another instance of his amazing credulity is his account of a woman who had not partaken of food for twenty years. His unfounded reputation as an inventor is based on a letter in which he speaks of ships propelled by machines, carriages which move with incredible speed without animals, and a flying machine which can be made to fly by beating the air with artificial wings. He further mentions a small device which can lift great weights and another which enables man to walk in seas and rivers. Bacon does not, however, claim to have invented the devices he mentions. They were, he stated, made in antiquity. The one exception is the flying machine. Regarding it, Bacon said that he knew a man who had thought how to make one. Bacon's letter is important as an indication of what contemporary technologists were trying to invent.

While Grosseteste and Roger Bacon were discussing scientific methodology at Oxford, the members of a group of Dominicans at the University of Paris were also busy studying and discussing problems of natural science. The leading spirit of this group was Albertus Magnus (Albert the Great), born Albert of Bollstädt (1206-1280). Albert was a man of prodigious learning whose intellectual attainments were the admiration of contemporaries. He taught at the University of Cologne and at the University of Paris, earning for himself the reputation of being one of the great teachers of his time. His voluminous writings included treatises on philosophy, metaphysics, logic, and natural science. Although he was both an avid reader and a commentator of Aristotle, sparing no effort to interest his contemporaries in the teachings of the Greek philosopher, Albert was not uncritical in his approach. "Whoever believes that Aristotle is a god," he wrote, "must also believe that he never erred; but if he believes that Aristotle was a man, then he was just as liable to err as we are."

Like Grosseteste and Bacon, Albert the Great was an advocate of the experimental method. He took great pride in pointing out that some of his work was based on direct observation. In his *De Vegetabilibus,* a catalogue of trees, plants, and herbs known at that time, he wrote, "All that is here set down is the result of our own experience or has been borrowed from authors of whom we know that they wrote what their personal experience confirmed; for in these matters experience alone makes for certainty." In his *De Animalibus* Albert sought to show that he did not accept information on the basis of mere authority by adding such notations as "I experienced this" and "But I have not experienced that." Albert's writings contain some acute observations on the physiology of plants. Centuries later the great German naturalist Alexander von Humboldt was amazed at both the breadth and depth of Albert's knowledge. Although his observations did not lead to novel conclusions, his activities did promote the study of natural science.

The fact that Albertus Magnus was a harbinger of the age of experimental science must not be permitted to obscure the fact that he was medieval in his general outlook. He, too, regarded all knowledge, including natural science, as the servant of theology. He believed that the branch of knowledge which best supported theology was the most noble. Like Roger Bacon he was also medieval in his credulity. He asserted, for example, that a person who annoints his body with the fat of a lion will put all animals to flight. He also believed that cancer could be cured by the application of lion's blood. His emphasis on the experimental method as a means of establishing certitude did not keep him from believing medieval cosmographical lore. He believed, for example, that there were three zones in the air, with the middle one inhabited by the Devil and his evil angels. It is in this zone that storms and tempests of various kinds are brewed and hail and snow are generated. From there the demons also send forth thunder, lightning, and other natural terrors which fill the hearts of men with fear. He was also uncritical in his acceptance of such reports as that "of a trustworthy person" who claimed he saw three hundred ducks, over one hundred geese, about forty hares, and a large quantity of fish in an eagle's nest, all this being required to satisfy the ravenous appetites of the young eagles. Nevertheless, the contributions of Albert the Great as well as those of Robert Grosseteste and Roger Bacon were of no mean importance in stimulating interest in natural science. Above all, they demonstrate that scholasticism was not the sterile movement many historians have pictured it.

It should also be pointed out that during the Middle Ages the experimental method was used by alchemists, inventors, engineers, skilled artisans, and others. Alchemists used it, for example, in their efforts to transmute base metals into precious metals. Inventors, engineers, and skilled artisans conducted countless experiments in their quest for better inventions, better products, and better techniques. Experimentation produced the three great inventions: gunpowder, the compass, and printing with movable type. It also produced better instruments for the observation of the heavens, better tools for the sculptor, better pigments for the painter, better instruments for the musician, and better techniques for the architect and the builder. In commerce and banking it resulted in better ships, in better methods of calculation, and in better business techniques. Such uses of the experimental method, however, were isolated ventures which did not result in the establishment of experimentation as the basic method in natural science.

Natural Science in the Fourteenth and Fifteenth Centuries

Although Robert Grosseteste, Roger Bacon, and Albertus Magnus opened the way for the acceptance of the experimental method, the natural scientists who followed them were slow to accept it. The authority of tradition was still too great, and astrology and alchemy still had too firm a hold even on educated minds to permit so radical a change. Put in another way, the synthesis of theology and science which had been forged early in the Middle Ages still held and the laws prescribed by theology, "the queen of the sciences," were still basic. The principal function of natural science was still to serve theology.

Nevertheless, the fourteenth and fifteenth centuries were not a period devoid of scientific progress as many students of history formerly believed. This was demonstrated beyond a vestige of doubt early in the twentieth century by the French historian Pierre Duhem in a number of treatises. Progress in the direction of the study of nature for its own sake, it is true, was slow and at times almost imperceptible, but there was progress. While the same old ideas were being restated again and again, new ones were making their appearance. Philosophers and scientists were turning to nature for the answers to questions the Church and Aristotle had not answered. Some turned directly to nature and others approached it through the medium of mathematics. Despite the stubborn opposition of tradition, progress was, on the whole, peaceful. Most of the scientists of the time were members of the clergy and as such maintained an attitude of respect for the Church and its teachings. The differences between science and theology did not engender open conflict until the second half of the sixteenth century.

In the fourteenth century the universities of Oxford and Paris continued to be the outstanding centers of scientific progress. The principal subject of study was dynamics, the branch of physics which treats of the action of force in motion. At both universities the motivation for the study of dynamics was dissatisfaction with the explanations given by Aristotle. The Oxford group was composed of mathematicians who applied mathematical principles to motion. The leader of this group was Thomas Bradwardine (1290-1394), probably the most skillful mathematician of his time. His treatise, titled *On the Properties of Velocity in Motion* (1329), was one of the earliest attempts to describe motion in mathematical terms. During the succeeding decades at least three of his students wrote treatises in which they developed some of the master's ideas. The members of the Oxford group were not, however, interested in experimental science; their interests were strictly mathematical. They were completely indifferent to the empirical implications of their mathematical analyses.

The mathematical concepts which the members of the Oxford group developed were applied to specific problems by the group at the University of Paris. The most important member of the Paris group was Jean (also called John) Buridan (*c.*1297-1358), a scholastic philosopher. During the thirty years he taught at the University of Paris, Buridan spent much time studying dynamics. His great contribution was the theory of impetus. He defined impetus in terms of velocity and quantity of matter, stating that impetus varies with the size and weight of a moving body and the velocity imparted to it. He further stated that the impetus given to a body would last indefinitely if it were not diminished by resistance. This resistance he defined as "something tending to an opposed motion." One of the special

problems to which Buridan applied his theory was the acceleration of free
falling bodies. What is now known as the force of gravity he defined
the force which increases the impetus of the body on which it acts. Burida
also applied his theory to the movement of the celestial bodies. The con
clusion he reached was that in this case the impetus is of a permaner
nature and that it emanated from God. The general framework of h
thought was still Aristotelian, but his studies of motion mark the beginnin
of a shift in the direction of the physics of Galileo and Newton. Althoug
his explanation of gravitational force was still somewhat crude, it did in
clude the fundamental concepts.

After his death, Buridan the natural scientist seems to have been quickl
forgotten. The memory of the man himself was kept alive, first, as th
originator of the story of the ass which starved to death because it wa
unable to decide between two equal bundles of hay and, second, by
story in a poem of the fifteenth-century French poet François Villo
which depicts Philip V of France as ordering Buridan to be tied in
sack and thrown into the Seine because he was involved in a love affai
with Philip's queen. Both stories are probably apocryphal. But if Burida
the natural scientist was forgotten, his ideas were not. The developmen
of them by his successors resulted in the complete undermining of th
Aristotelian formulation of the problem of motion. Prominent among thos
who perpetuated his ideas were Albert of Saxony, bishop of Halberstad
(d. 1390), who did make some small contributions of his own. Thus he
mentions, for example, the possibility that the speed of falling bodies i
proportional either to the distance or the time of the fall, but he did no
decide between the two. More important is the fact that his book titled
Questiones, in which he restated the ideas of Buridan, was printed in Italy
early in the sixteenth century. Some students of Galileo's life believe tha
he derived his knowledge of fourteenth-century dynamics from this
volume.

Probably the most important of Buridan's successors was Nicole Oresme
(1320-1382), a French bishop who as a student at the University of Paris
had worked in close cooperation with Buridan. Like Buridan and Albert
of Saxony, Oresme wrote a commentary on Aristotle's *De Coelo et de Mundo*
(On the Heavens and the Earth) in which he expressed ideas which were
at variance with those of the Greek philosopher-scientist. Oresme also served
the cause of scientific advance by denouncing in several of his works certain
magical and astrological practices. From the long discussion in Professor
Thorndike's *History of Magic and Experimental Science* Oresme emerges a
shrewd critic of astrology, but a believer in other forms of pseudo-science.
In his studies of impetus, Oresme altered some of Buridan's concepts
of the nature of impetus and added some of his own views. After careful
investigation of fourteenth-century concepts of motion, both the French

historian Pierre Duhem and the German historian Ernst Borchert asserted that Oresme arrived at a concept of impetus remarkably close to the modern theory. They further stated that in developing his idea of impetus he foreshadowed some of the discoveries of Copernicus, Galileo, and Newton.

Oresme has been styled a precursor of Copernicus because he expounded the so-called diurnal theory which had come down from the Greeks. According to this theory the earth, situated in the center of the universe, revolves on its axis once every twenty-four hours. Oresme, however, had been preceded in the revival of this old Greek theory by Buridan, Albert of Saxony, and others. Buridan, for his part, listed five reasons in favor of the diurnal theory and five against the hypothesis of a rotating earth, then decided it was more reasonable to adhere to the traditional view of a fixed earth. Albert of Saxony, on the other hand, took a different position, asserting that it is impossible to disprove the rotation of the earth. All this demonstrates that modern science was not ushered in suddenly, but was the result of an evolutionary development covering centuries.

By the beginning of the fifteenth century northern Italy had become the important center of scientific activity. The University of Padua and other schools, including the universities of Bologna and Pavia, had assumed the leadership in the study of natural science. In Italy, as in northern Europe, Aristotelianism was still the basis for the study of science, but there was a difference. In northern Europe, Aristotelianism adhered to the synthesis Thomas Aquinas had forged between science and theology. In Italy this brand of Aristotelianism survived only in the monasteries. In the schools the commercial and secular atmosphere was prevalent. This was particularly true in the University of Padua where there was a strong anti-clerical feeling. The science taught and studied there was not a theologically oriented science, but a science nourished by the Greek and Arab traditions. The approach to science was, in a word, secular. As in the fourteenth century, special attention was given to methodology and the relationship of mathematics to science. There was also a continuity of subject matter. The velocity and acceleration of falling bodies to which so much attention had been devoted in the previous century remained one of the leading questions. The interest in the general subject of dynamics is indicated by the printing in Italy of two treatises on the subject in 1482, one by Oresme and the other by Albert of Saxony. Among those who studied at the University of Padua and later achieved distinction in science or mathematics or both were the scientist Nicholas of Cusa, the mathematicians Peurbach and Regiomontanus, and the mathematician and astronomer Nicholas Copernicus. The University of Padua remained the leading center for the teaching of a secularly oriented science right down to Galileo (1564-1642).

The fifteenth century was neither a period of startling innovations in science, nor did it produce many outstanding personalities in the field of science. Progress was made largely through the elaboration of traditional ideas and the modification of old methods and approaches. It was a period during which the old was assimilated and the way was opened for the seemingly spectacular innovations of the sixteenth and seventeenth centuries. The outstanding scientific figure during the middle decades of the century was Nicholas of Cusa or Nicholas Cusanus (1401-1464). Nicholas was born at Cues or Cusa in Germany, attended the famous school of the Brethren of the Common Life at Deventer where Erasmus, the great humanist, was later a pupil, and after spending a year at the University of Heidelberg matriculated at the University of Padua. His studies at Padua included mathematics, natural science, philosophy, and law. Upon completing his formal education he entered the service of the Church, rising rapidly to the cardinalate. Nicholas was one of the most highly respected personages of his time both as an ecclesiastical official and as a man of learning. Above all, he was a prolific writer on many subjects. Historians of mathematics have commended him for his "good attempts" to square the circle. In his botanical studies Cusanus observed that the earth in which plants are growing lost weight, inferring that this weight was gained by the plants. He also believed that plants gain weight from something they take out of the air. Nicholas of Cusa further suggested that air has weight, a somewhat novel idea at that time.

Nicholas of Cusa is remembered primarily for his theory of the universe. He vigorously opposed the Ptolemaic idea that the earth is fixed in the center of the universe. The universe cannot, he argued, have a definite center or circumference, for if it did it would be something limited and not a universe. He believed that since the earth is not the center of the universe, it must move. "To my mind," he wrote, "the earth revolves on its axis once in a day and a night." For this statement he has been styled "a precursor of Copernicus." But this is true only in a limited sense as he still had the sun revolving. Incidentally, Nicholas also believed the other heavenly bodies to be inhabited in the same way as the earth. He even speaks of dwellers on the sun. His conclusions were not based on scientific reasoning, but on metaphysical grounds. Nicholas of Cusa did see, however, that differences were developing between theological and scientific viewpoints; hence he forecast the approaching clash between the proponents of theology and those of science. In the sixteenth century the astronomer Johann Kepler frequently cited the opinions of Nicholas of Cusa whom he called "my divine Cusanus." Nicholas of Cusa profoundly influenced the thinking of Giordano Bruno (*c.*1548-1600) through his assertion that the earth is subject to the same laws of matter and motion as the other bodies in the universe.

Leonardo da Vinci as a Scientist

The scientific writings of the fourteenth and fifteenth centuries consider problems which Copernicus, Galileo, Newton, and others were to solve at a later time. Many of the scientists no longer accepted Aristotle as the final authority in natural science. Turning to nature and mathematics, they began to probe things with their own intelligence. In doing so they began to look at evidence from the scientific rather than from the theological point of view. Although such scientists did succeed in increasing the general fund of knowledge, their discoveries were largely isolated instances and did not meet with general acceptance. Nevertheless, these discoveries were important because each one put tradition to a test, thereby helping to create the milieu which produced modern science. As new discoveries were made, it became evident that the synthesis between science and theology was breaking down and that the interests of science and theology were beginning to diverge. These changes augured the complete separation of science from theology. In brief, science was beginning to go its own way along a path which led to a status of its own as an autonomous study, that is, a study which has its own aims and its own principles of investigation.

How far science and technology had progressed by the end of the fifteenth century, and also the nature of the problems scientists were trying to solve, can be learned from the *Notebooks* of Leonardo da Vinci whose achievements as an artist were discussed in an earlier chapter. The man who is probably most famous as the painter of the "Mona Lisa" and of the "Last Supper" is also an important, if somewhat over-rated, figure in the history of science. As Leonardo grew older he devoted more and more time to science and engineering, and less and less to art. Contemporaries pointed out that he was more in demand as an engineer and scientist than as an artist. His insatiable curiosity led him into almost every phase of science, including anatomy, astronomy, botany, geology, and physics. The one exception was chemistry which in his time was still largely alchemy, and, therefore, akin to quackery. It should be noted, however, that Leonardo's interest in science was, first of all, that of the artist who desires a first-hand knowledge of nature, so that he can paint more accurately. Second, Leonardo's interest was that of an engineer who desires to know about the structure of things. Unfortunately he dissipated his energies by restlessly turning from one field to another before he found real solutions for the problems he had been considering.

Leonardo's *Notebooks* are filled with notations, observations, plans, and designs of many kinds. They contain, for example, sketches of various machines for both civilian and military use. There are drawings of a lathe, a rolling mill, a mechanical excavator, a machine for polishing mirrors, a hygrometer for measuring moisture in the atmosphere, an anemometer

for measuring the velocity of the wind, and a pendulum for clocks. Th
Notebooks further contain plans for a girder bridge, designs for a du
system of roads at different levels, plans for irrigation systems, and sketch
of a system of canal locks which under his supervision were actually con
structed. There is also a sketch of a flying machine which was to be pro
pelled by the manipulation of wings. The idea of flying seems to hav
fascinated Leonardo to the extent that he spent considerable time observin
the flight of birds in the hope that he would discover the secret of fligh
Other interesting sketches in his *Notebooks* are those of a mortar fo
hurling bombs which explode in the air, a machine for shooting arrow
in quick succession, and an "armored chariot" which one historian ha
dubbed "the forerunner of the modern tank." In the *Notebooks* a sub
marine is mentioned without further details lest "the evil nature of men
might employ it to "practice assassination at the bottom of the sea." Finally
the *Notebooks* contain a series of magnificent anatomical drawings. Th
purpose of the drawings was not medical, but artistic. Leonardo felt tha
a more precise knowledge of human and animal anatomy would result i
more perfect artistic representations. He made no analysis of what he saw
he simply recorded it.

The statements Leonardo jotted down in his *Notebooks* deal with many phases of science. There are statements which prescribe experimentation as the only proper approach to science, as, for example, "Those sciences are vain and full of errors which are not born from experiment, the mother of all certainty" and "Whoever in discussion adduces authority uses not intellect but rather memory." There are also many allusions to the application of mathematical principles to science. One statement reads: "No human inquiry can be called science unless it pursues its path through mathematical exposition and demonstration." Regarding astronomy there are such statements as "The sun does not move" and "The earth is a star." A statement on the forces now associated with gravity reads: "Every force desires to descend to the center by the shortest way." Statements on geology argue against the widely accepted idea that the fossil remains of shells found on mountain tops of northern Italy were carried there by the waters of the Flood at the time of Noah; Leonardo ascribes their presence at such high altitudes to geologic upheavals in bygone ages.

A careful reading of the contents of the *Notebooks* leaves unanswered the question, "How many of the ideas were original with Leonardo and how many did he cull from works of his and the preceding period?" In the answers to this question the pendulum of opinion has swung from one extreme to the other. Whereas many nineteenth-century historians and biographers believed the contents of the *Notebooks* to be original outpourings of Leonardo's mind, recent historians have gone so far as to doubt that more than a few, if any, of the ideas were original with him. After Leonardo's death in France in 1519, Francesco Melzi, his assistant, took the *Notebooks* to Milan where contemporaries who saw them commented on their bulk. A few scientists were permitted to read them, but after Melzi's death in 1570 they seem to have been forgotten. More than two centuries later Napoleon Bonaparte took some of the *Notebooks* to Paris. After the Peace of Vienna in 1815 most of them were returned to Milan. They were the subject of considerable discussion during the next decades, but were not published until late in the nineteenth century. Although many of the pages had undoubtedly been lost, more than 5300 still remained. When the contents of the *Notebooks* appeared in print, historians and scholars accepted them as the original product of Leonardo's thought and observation, hailing Leonardo as the most original genius of all time. The French historian Michelet, for example, dubbed Leonardo "the Italian brother of Faust."

Studies of the progress of science in the fourteenth and fifteenth centuries by twentieth-century historians resulted in a more moderate estimate of Leonardo's ability. These historians assert that the extravagant estimates of Leonardo's ability were due to a lack of knowledge of the progress of science and technology during the centuries before he appeared on the scene. They further state that a study of the writings on science and technology which appeared during the fourteenth and fifteenth centuries reveals that there is little, if anything, new in the *Notebooks*. Hence they question whether he contributed anything to the theory of science or invented anything that was practical. They point to the fact that the man who in the nineteenth century was regarded as the greatest inventive genius of all time was so devoid of inventive ability that he was unable to invent a technique for preserving his two great frescoes, the "Last Supper" and the "Battle of the Standard." Whereas the latter disappeared completely, the "Last Supper" became a ghostly remainder of one of the great paintings of all time. Investigators further point out that the hygrometer which is discussed in the *Notebooks* was previously described by Nicholas of Cusa and Leon Battista Alberti. They also trace other devices which Leonardo sketched or discussed to inventors who preceded him. Leonardo's references to a flying machine modeled after the flight of birds and his mention of a submarine recall the statements of Roger Bacon. Girolamo Cardano (1501-1576), philosopher, physician, and magician, reported that Leonardo actually constructed a flying machine but failed to make it fly.

The sources of many of Leonardo's theoretical ideas have also been found. There is, for example, nothing in Leonardo's statements on the application of mathematical principles to scientific knowledge which had not been stated by Robert Grossetest, Nicholas of Cusa, and others. The idea that the sun does not move was stated and restated by a number of scientists who preceded Leonardo. The explanation in the *Notebooks* as to why fossils of marine life may be found on the tops of mountains was previously given by Albertus Magnus and Albert of Saxony. The statements on dynamics in the *Notebooks* add nothing to the discussions of this subject by Jean Buridan, Albert of Saxony, and Nicholas Oresme. It has been suggested that the ideas on gravity which Leonardo jotted down in his *Notebooks* were taken from a treatise by Albert of Saxony, a copy of which was found in Leonardo's library after his death. The Italian scholar Edmondo Solmi early in the twentieth century published a list of more than two hundred books and manuscripts from which he believed Leonardo collected his ideas, and more sources have been added since then. There is nothing in the *Notebooks* to show that the contents are anything but notes Leonardo jotted down while reading. It was customary at that time for men of learning to keep such notebooks in which they entered ideas and statements they found interesting and illuminating. Furthermore, there is nothing in the *Notebooks* to indicate that they were meant for posterity. The notes were jotted down in helter-skelter fashion without any attempt at organization. Moreover, they were written with the left hand from the right side of the page to the left, without punctuation and with many abbreviations and cryptic allusions. This alone is enough to discourage all but the most determined.

The real value of the *Notebooks* lies in the fact that they show how far science and technology had progressed by Leonardo's time. They reveal which questions were occupying the minds of the scientists and which devices engineers and technologists had invented or were trying to invent. They show that science was becoming an autonomous study with a meaning of its own, a meaning which was definitely secular. When Leonardo advocated the use of the experimental method he did not, like Roger Bacon, do so because he hoped to find natural truths which support revealed religion. To him scientific knowledge was important in itself. He saw in scientific knowledge the means to a better life on earth. It was in this respect that he differed from most earlier natural scientists. It was this attitude toward science which ushered in the age of modern science.

Heliocentric Versus Geocentric

The dominant theory of the universe during the centuries preceding the sixteenth was geocentric (earth-centered). It is known as the Ptolemaic theory, so named after Claudius Ptolomaeus, or Ptolemy (*see page 243*). After studying the writings of Greek scientists, in particular those of Hipparchus and Aristotle, in the second century A.D. Ptolemy elaborated his theory in a work of thirteen volumes titled *Mathematical System.* Later this voluminous study became known as the *Almagest*, a combination of Greek and Arabic words meaning "the greatest." About the year 800 the *Almagest* was translated into Arabic and carefully studied and annotated by Arabic men of learning. The Arabs then transmitted the theory, together with some additional observations of their own, to western Christendom. Toward the end of the twelfth century the *Almagest* was introduced into Europe in a Latin translation so that the learned men of Christendom could study it for themselves.

Ptolemy expounded his theory in great detail. In it the spherical earth is located at the exact center of the universe which occupies a limited space. Furthermore, in Ptolemy's theory the earth is fixed and immovable with the sun, moon, and the planets revolving about it. As for the stars, they are, according to Ptolemy, spots of light in a huge canopy or dome which is arched over everything. In the *Almagest* Ptolemy elaborated the whole theory with subtlety and skill. All in all, it was a grandiose attempt to explain the universe. Ptolemy argued so convincingly that his theory was accepted by even the most learned. First of all, the idea of a stationary earth seemed to correspond with the perception of the senses. Second, the idea of a motionless earth seemed to be in accord with the teachings of the Scriptures. A favorite text which was often quoted in support of the concept of an immobile earth was the first verse of Psalm 93 which reads: "The world is so established that it cannot be moved." Third, the idea that the earth is in the center of the universe was in harmony with the homocentric ideas of the theologians. They believed that since the universe had been created to fulfill man's needs, it was proper that the central position be assigned to the earth, the abode of man. The idea was clearly stated by Peter Lombardus (1100-1160) when he wrote: "Just as man is made for the sake of God, in order that he may serve Him; so the universe is made for the sake of man, that it may serve him; therefore man is placed in the center of the universe, that he may both serve and be served." It should be stated, however, that Thomas Aquinas' acceptance of the Ptolemaic theory was not unqualified. Although he agreed that the earth must be the center of the universe, he cautioned that the Ptolemaic theory was only a supposition which had not been demonstrated. But his followers, the Thomists, overlooked the master's word of caution with the result that the Ptolemaic theory became a part of Thomist philosophy.

Since Ptolemy's theory was wholly unsupported by scientific evidence in the modern sense, it was gradually undermined in the sixteenth and seventeenth centuries by scientists who collected data by observing the movements of the heavenly bodies. The first to take a long step toward demolishing Ptolemy's geocentric theory and replacing it with a heliocentric (sun-centered) theory was Nicholas Koppernick (1473-1543), better known as Copernicus, the Latin form of his name. Copernicus, who is often called the founder of modern astronomy, was born in the little town of Thorn in Polish Prussia. The question as to whether his ancestry was Polish or German is still controversial. After the elder Copernicus died in 1483, an uncle who was bishop of Ermeland took charge of the education of young Nicholas. He sent Nicholas to the University of Cracow to prepare him for a career in the Church. The young student spent a year there; then expressed a desire to continue his studies at one of the Italian universities The uncle made this possible by appointing his nephew a canon in the cathedral chapter of Frauenburg in his native land. The chapter gave him permission to continue his studies in Italy, and the income from his position was sufficient for his needs. The next decade (1496-1506) Nicholas spent at the universities of Bologna and Padua where he pursued studies in law, theology, philosophy, mathematics, astronomy, and medicine. His interest in the Ptolemaic theory seems to have been stimulated by Domenico di Novara, professor of astronomy at Bologna, who publicly questioned the accuracy of Ptolemy's calculations.

In 1506 at the age of thirty-three Copernicus returned to his homeland where he settled down at Frauenburg, remaining there for the rest of his life. Besides carrying out his duties as canon, he served as physician for the members of his chapter and also ministered to the poor. His spare time Copernicus devoted to astronomy which became the great interest of his life. His first objection to the Ptolemaic theory was its complexity. Since he believed that nature always carries out its laws in the simplest way, it seemed strange to him that Ptolemy had the large sun revolving about the small earth. In his search for a solution to the problem he turned to the writings of the Greek astronomers where he found that a number of them attributed motion to the earth. He also received permission to place on the wall surrounding the precincts of the cathedral a platform from which he made observations of the movements of the celestial bodies. But his instruments were poor and his eyesight weak. For the most part Copernicus achieved his results inside his study through the application of mathematical principles to the movements of heavenly bodies. In his search for astronomical truth Copernicus put aside the religious considerations which had motivated the conclusions of most of his predecessors. Believing that religion should be outside the sphere of astronomy, he relegated it to its own domain of piety and spirituality. It is for this reason that his work has been described as the full crystallization of the idea that astronomy must be an autonomous science.

The result of his years of study was a manuscript, titled *De Revolutionibus Orbium Coelestium* (Concerning the Revolutions of the Heavenly Bodies), in which he elaborated his heliocentric theory placing the sun, not the earth, in the center of the solar system. The planets of this solar system, including the earth, revolve around the sun. The rising and setting of the sun is a consequence of the daily rotation of the earth on its polar axis. The earth not only rotates on its polar axis once every twenty-four hours; it also revolves around the sun in 365 days and a fraction.

Having expounded his heliocentric theory of the universe Copernicus time and again postponed publication of his manuscript because he feared the reaction would be hostile. As he himself wrote, "The book has lain in my study not merely nine years, but four times nine." He did, however, cir-

:ulate a resume of his findings among his friends. Meanwhile he also con-inued his studies for the purpose of strengthening his conclusions. Finally n 1540 Georg Joachim, a Wittenberg mathematician who preferred to be :alled Rheticus, prevailed on him to put aside his fears and to permit oublication of his manuscript. Before sending it to the printer, Copernicus dedicated the work to Pope Paul III, expressing the hope that his studies would be useful to the Church. While the book was being printed Copernicus became ill, and he received a copy of it only a few hours before his death. In it the heliocentric system was not, however, presented to the public as a revolutionary truth. Without consulting Copernicus, Andreas Osiander, a mathematician and Lutheran theologian to whom the task of supervising the printing had been entrusted, wrote a preface at the last moment in which he stated that the work was being offered to the public as a mathematical hypothesis, not as a statement of fact. He wrote in part:

> Scholars will be surprised by the novelty of the hypothesis proposed in this book which supposes the earth to be in motion about the sun which is fixed. . . It is not necessary that such hypotheses should be true or even probable. . . . If astronomy admits principles, it is not for the purpose of affirming truth, but to give a certain basis for calculation.

Osiander's statement did not reflect the attitude of Copernicus who in his dedication to Paul III had written: "I am so pleased with my conclusions as not to weigh what others will think about them."

A theory so revolutionary that it toppled man from his throne in the center of the universe could not fail to excite widespread opposition. Even most of the mathematicians, astronomers, and scientists in general rejected it. Some mathematicians and astronomers did, it is true, accept it, but they were a small minority. One of these was Copernicus's friend Rheticus who was, however, not permitted to teach the heliocentric theory at the University of Wittenberg, a Lutheran stronghold, but had to continue teaching the Ptolemaic system. Theologians generally condemned it as being contrary to the teachings of the Bible. Luther, for example, as reported in his *Tischreden* said, "The fool is trying to turn the whole science of astronomy upside down. But, as the Holy Scriptures state, Joshua commanded the sun to stand still and not the earth." Calvin denounced the Copernican theory as a foolish superstition, adding "Who will venture to place the authority of Copernicus above that of the Holy Spirit?" In the Roman Catholic Church the heliocentric theory did not at first evoke official condemnation, for others before Copernicus had attributed motion to the earth, among them Nicholas of Cusa. But as the real import of the Copernican theory became apparent, condemnations were heard on all sides. When Giordano Bruno, the bold and fiery philosopher-scientist who was burned as a heretic in Rome (1600), accepted the heliocentric theory as the basis of his philosophy, it was officially denounced by the Church. The Roman Inquisition formally de-clared in 1615, "The proposition that the sun is the center and does not revolve about the earth is foolish, absurd, false in theology, and heretical because expressly contrary to Holy Scripture." It also denounced the proposition that the earth revolves about the sun and is not the center of the universe as "absurd, false in philosophy, and from the theological point of view opposed to the true faith." The next year Copernicus' *De Revolutionibus Orbium Coelestium* was put on the Index of Prohibited Books where it remained for about a century and a half.

Although Copernicus did make the earth revolve about the sun, he still retained some of the false notions associated with the Ptolemaic theory. One was the axiom that heavenly bodies move in exact circles and that their motion is uniform. "It is impossible," Copernicus stated, "that a single heavenly body should move unequally in its orbit." This view had been held by astronomers of antiquity and also by astronomers who preceded Copernicus. Two successors, however, were instrumental in disproving this idea of uniform circular motion. The first of these was Tycho Brahe (1546-1601), a Danish astronomer for whom the king of Denmark built an observatory on the island of Hven. For twenty years Tycho observed the movements of the planets, using his observations to prepare astronomical tables. Although he lacked such instruments as the telescope and the astronomical clock, his observations were amazingly accurate. Whereas the observations of the ancient astronomers could be depended on within a degree, those of Tycho Brahe were accurate to the sixtieth part of a degree. In other words, Tycho Brahe's observations were nearly sixty times more accurate than those of the ancient astronomers. Paradoxically, although Brahe had rejected the heliocentric system of Copernicus in favor of the geocentric system of Ptolemy, his careful observations became the means for disproving the concept of uniform circular motion of the planets and for proving the correctness of the heliocentric theory.

After Tycho Brahe's death in 1601 his former assistant Johann Kepler (1571-1630), a German, continued the work of studying the motion of the planets. Since poor eyesight prevented him from making direct observations of the planets, he devoted himself to a careful analysis of Tycho's recorded observations, deducing from them the law of planetary motion which is known as Kepler's Law. Kepler's findings completely demolished the Aristotelian theory of the uniform circular motion of the planets. On the positive side Kepler demonstrated mathematically that the orbit of the planets is definitely elliptical. Moreover, he established that the ellipses are not uniform, but that they vary from almost circular to highly elliptical. Among the larger planets Venus has the most circular orbit and Pluto the most eccentric. The publication of Kepler's findings in his *Epitome of Copernican Astronomy* (1616) is an important milestone in the establishment of the Copernican system.

But the heliocentric theory was still not ready for general acceptance. The next scientist whose discoveries strengthened it was the Italian physicist, astronomer, and mathematician Galileo Galilei (1564-1642). Galileo accepted the Copernican system because it explained phenomena which could not be explained in any other way. When the news reached him of the invention of the telescope in the Dutch Netherlands, probably by Hans Lippershey, an optician, Galileo constructed a telescope which magnified about thirty-three times. The instrument was crude according to modern standards; nevertheless, Galileo was able to make discoveries with it which supported the Copernican theory. He became such an enthusiastic follower of Copernicus that he ridiculed those who refused to give up the Ptolemaic theory. Because of this he was ordered by officials of the Roman Catholic Church to desist from further advocacy of the Copernican theory. Galileo submitted, but quietly continued his astronomical studies. In 1632 he published his findings in *Dialogue Concerning the Two Chief Systems of the World.* Galileo hoped to escape censure by stating his ideas in the form of a dialogue. His support of the heliocentric theory was, however, so obvious that he was summoned before the Inquisition in Rome and there compelled to abjure as contrary to the teachings of the Bible the theory that the sun stands in the center of the solar system with the earth revolving about it.

There still remained a major objection to the Copernican theory which was frequently voiced by its opponents. If it were true that the earth is revolving with great velocity, the opponents stated, objects on the earth's surface would be hurled into space. Copernicus had not given a satisfactory explanation as to why this does not take place. In the year after Galileo's death a child was born in England who was to provide the answer. He was Isaac Newton (1643-1727) whose discoveries in mathematics and science rank him as one of the great intellects of all time. His discovery of the law of gravity is undoubtedly the best known of his achievements. He was, of course, not the first to study the problem. Most of the philosophers and scientists since Plato had speculated on the force now called gravitation. It remained for Newton, however, to discover the basic law of gravitation. His discovery was not made during a momentary flash of insight; it was the result of a long and careful study of the mathematics of motion. He himself stated that he discovered the law of gravitation by "thinking about it ceaselessly." Even after he made the discovery he continued to work on the problem for years before he consented to publish his findings. He did so in his *Principia* (The Mathematical Principles of Natural Knowledge) (1687), one of the great works in the history of science. The essence of the law of gravitation, as stated in the *Principia* is that "the attraction between any two bodies is proportional to the square of the distance which separates them." It was this law which, by putting order into what previously had been confusion, finally gave certitude to the heliocentric theory Copernicus had published almost a century and a half earlier.

16

The Renaissance in Germany

The Northern Renaissance

The term Northern Renaissance is employed here to designate the manifestations of the Renaissance in the countries north of the Alps. The Northern Renaissance was not merely, as has been stated, an extension of the Italian Renaissance. In its earliest stages it was an indigenous growth. The influence of the Italian Renaissance made itself felt at a later time to rekindle the interest in the new culture which in most of the areas of Northern Europe had been stunted by economic depression, destructive wars, and recurring epidemics of the plague. One of the first areas of Northern Europe in which indications of a new cultural trend appeared was the area occupied by the southern provinces of the Netherlands. In the thriving towns of these provinces, particularly in the Flemish towns, there was a prosperous middle class whose members enjoyed life. They found special delight in the rising secular music and in the paintings which, although religious in subject, reflected their interest in the things of this life. Under their patronage both painting and music flourished in the fifteenth century. The trend toward a more secularized portrayal is clearly evident in the paintings of Jan van Eyck. These paintings, which were executed during the early decades of the fifteenth century, are characterized by a naturalism unmatched in Italian painting up to that time.

At the opening of the fourteenth century it appeared for a time as if France would play the leading role in the Renaissance drama. During the preceding period the French had held the leadership in the development of art, letters, and learning. In Gothic architecture France had expressed the soul of medievalism more passionately than any other country of Europe. During the last stages of this development, naturalism began to manifest itself in the carvings of such cathedrals as Amiens, Rheims, Chartres, Rouen, and Paris. In literature the thirteenth century and the early part of the fourteenth were the heyday of the fabliaux (comic satirical tales in verse) which expressed the attitudes and feelings of the rising bourgeoisie. France also produced the troubadours and the secularist troubadour songs which were an inspiration to many poets, including Dante and Petrarch. The French Ars Nova opened a new era in the history of music by turning music into secular paths and inspiring composers of France and other counries to write secular as well as sacred music. There was also a growing nterest in the writings of classical authors among the learned men of France. In addition to all this, the preceding period had witnessed the rise of a prosperous middle class, the members of which could have served as patrons of a new culture.

But French culture did not fulfill its promise. The buds of the new culture soon withered. By the middle of the fourteenth century France had ceded its cultural leadership to Italy. Economic depression, plague, and a long series of wars blighted French artistic, literary, and intellectual endeavors. Even before the outbreak of the so-called Hundred Years War with England (1337-1453) the economic recession which spared few areas of Northern Europe had made inroads into the French economy. Then came the great hostile armies of England and its allies, inflicting ruin on many parts of the country. Since France was the battlefield for most of the fighting, some parts of it were devastated again and again. The series of wars was not only more protracted, but also more destructive than the feudal wars of the preceding period. Instead of small groups of knights, great national armies were pitted against each other. Commerce was sharply curtailed, industrial production was greatly reduced, and agriculture was disrupted in the provinces invaded by the hostile armies. In the provinces which were repeatedly scourged by the invaders, many peasants abandoned their holdings which reverted to forest and wasteland.

There was also a general population decline. Although it can be ascribed in some part to the heavy loss of life in the Hundred Years War, the real culprit was the Black Death of 1348, one of the most terrible epidemics of all time. It is believed that the Black Death originally came from Central Asia whence it moved westward to Constantinople and was then carried to Italy. The carriers were fleas living on rats. In all of Europe the disease found fertile ground for diffusion at a time when society still lacked a sense of personal hygiene. It seems to have spread most rapidly in overcrowded towns in which there was no proper sanitation. In spreading death and desolation over Europe it assumed various forms. The pneumonic form seems to have been the more deadly and the bubonic form the most common, the latter being characterized by buboes or swellings in the armpits or groin. From Italy the Black Death moved northward into France, then into Central Europe and England. One contemporary chronicler believed that a ship brought the plague to France. Since most ships were infested by rats, this may well be true. The medical men of the time could neither account for its spread nor did they develop an effective remedy for it. Formerly historians estimated the loss of life at one half or even as high as two-thirds of the population. Recent investigators have reduced the number of the victims to about one-fourth of the population. Even this is a tremendous loss. It was a loss which opened the way for greater economic deterioration. Further lives were claimed by recurrences of the plague in milder forms. Both the population decline and the economic depression seem to have reached their lowest point during the decades from 1380 to 1420, after which the trend turned upward. By the end of the fifteenth century France had recovered most of its population and much of its prosperity.

England, too, was the scene of economic recession during much of the fourteenth and fifteenth centuries. Not only did the tempo of economic development become slower, but after a time a depression set in which for many decades held the country in a viselike grip. The economic depression also seems to have cast a pall on the development of learning and culture, for the period was barren of great literature and great art. Practically all statistics available to historians show that the decline became evident, first of all, in agriculture. Since England was predominantly an agricultural country, the slump affected the entire economy and reduced the national wealth as a whole. Among the symptoms were a drop in agricultural production, a slackening demand for land, and a falling-off of land values. The area under cultivation also contracted sharply. The land hunger which in the thirteenth century had brought about the reclaiming of marginal and waste lands for cultivation no longer existed. Poorer agricultural areas were being systematically abandoned in favor of more fertile ones. The agricultural depression seems to have continued until about 1460 when conditions took a turn for the better.

There is no simple explanation for the depression which paralyzed the English economic life for so long a period. English economic historians tend to regard the population decline as the principal cause. As the agricultural expansion and increased production of the twelfth and thirteenth centuries are explained in terms of a rising population, so the contraction of the area under cultivation and the lower agricultural production is ascribed to a falling population and a decreasing demand for agricultural products. In England, as in France and other European countries, the Black Death seems to have accelerated the decline which some historians believe had set in earlier. The plague first struck London where it swept through the slum districts, but did not spare the well-to-do classes. From London it spread to other parts of England, claiming more victims in some districts than in others. While the mortality was very high in some agricultural villages, it was very low in others; in fact, the plague bypassed some villages completely. The mortality seems to have been particularly high in monasteries and among the clergy. It has been estimated that the mortality among the clergy who exposed themselves to fleabites by visiting those stricken by the plague was 40 per cent. Some English historians believe that the mortality rate of the peasants was not much lower. They point to the careful studies which show that in the three Cambridgeshire villages the Black Death claimed the lives of 47 per cent of the population and that the mortality rate was even higher in other villages. It has been calculated that in 1349 the English mortality was fifteen times the normal rate. Even after considering the fact that the plague affected some villages less severely, these historians believe that the overall loss was one-third of the population.

The losses of 1349-1350 alone do not explain the population decrease. Even the heavy loss of life in the great battles of the Hundred Years War does not account for the continuing decline. Further light is thrown on the situation by the fact that the plague epidemics recurred at regular intervals of seven or eight years. If the toll they took was not so large as in 1349-1350, their effect was to depress the population so that it could not recoup the losses and expand beyond the mark it had reached when the decline started.

But the recession was not confined to agriculture. It affected every phase of economic activity. The English foreign trade slumped badly. With the exception of London and several other cities, the English trading centers, seaports as well as of inland towns, lost much of their trade. A series of causes combined to bring this about. English trade with Scandinavia dwindled to practically nothing as the English traders were forced out of the Baltic by the merchants of the Hanseatic League. English trade with Picardy, Normandy, Brittany, and Aquitaine became a casualty of the Hundred Years War. Trade with other countries was disrupted by French privateers who were ever on the lookout for English merchant ships which they might capture as prizes of war. In general, the English lost so much of their foreign trade that they had to start rebuilding it practically from scratch when the war ended. Economic recovery began late in the fifteenth century and continued to develop under the Tudor monarchs into a great upsurge which was accompanied by a rising interest in humanism, painting, music, and literature.

Neither did Germany escape the great recession. In a number of respects the economic conditions were much like those in England and France. The agricultural decline which appears to have set in before the visitation of the Black Death was aggravated by the heavy loss of life. The question of how many victims the plague claimed in Germany cannot be answered with any greater exactness than the question regarding the loss of human life in England and France. Contemporary records report such losses as 40,000 in Vienna, 14,000 in Strassburg, and the same number in Basel. Even if they are reliable, such statistics are of little help in any effort to arrive at a total figure. Suffice it to state that the mortality rate seems to have been about the same as in England and France. Another parallel was that the plague recurred again and again in somewhat milder forms. The total number of epidemics from 1350 to the end of the century was fourteen.

The damage to the German economy was as severe as in the other countries. It was most marked in agriculture. Since there were fewer cultivators, the area of land under cultivation was smaller. Much land which had been cultivated in the thirteenth century became waste land. The prices of agricultural products, and especially of grain fell considerably. The wave of colonization which had pushed the German frontiers eastward to the Vistula and along the Baltic shores to the Gulf of Finland during the two preceding centuries ceased abruptly after the Black Death had ravaged Germany. An indication of the hard times in the towns was the great increase in the number of destitute citizens. There was little recovery in agriculture before the middle of the sixteenth century, but in the towns and cities both industry and trade began to exhibit a new vitality during the second half of the fifteenth century. It was in the thriving towns and cities that the secular spirit grew stronger and an interest in the culture of the Italian Renaissance began to manifest itself. However, both the secular spirit and the interest in the new culture had only a brief period in which they could develop. Early in the sixteenth century the Protestant Reformation followed by the Catholic Reformation turned the cultural interests back into religious channels and temporarily curbed the growth of secularism.

During the first half of the fifteenth century Italian Renaissance ideas filtered into the countries north of the Alps, but the wars, economic depression, and generally unsettled conditions militated against the creation of a Renaissance movement. But the situation changed in the second half of the century. Not only did the economic conditions improve; the intellectual and artistic climate became propitious for the acceptance of the new ideas. Students who regarded Italy as the Promised Land of Scholars and an El Dorado of Learning journeyed there in larger numbers to attend such universities as those at Padua and Bologna or went to hear the lectures of teachers whose fame had reached the northern countries. What they saw and heard excited in them an interest in the new culture. When they returned to their homelands they carried with them the inspiration of the Italian Renaissance and became instrumental in disseminating the new knowledge. At the same time, journeymen painters and full-fledged artists were visiting Italy to see and study the works of great Italian painters. Conversely, while students and artists from Northern Europe were traveling to Italy, Italian humanists and painters visited the countries north of the Alps. Some of them even settled there. By the end of the fifteenth century a considerable number of Italian humanists were teaching Latin and lecturing on classical literature in foreign countries. In this way a love of the classics, a knowledge of the new techniques in painting and the new forms in Italian literature, and some of the secular spirit of the Italian Renaissance were introduced into Germany, France, England, and Spain.

Not all men of learning, literary figures, humanists, and artists, however, accepted the ideas, forms, and attitudes imported from Italy. It might be said that the reactionaries were many and the "moderns" few in number. Even those who approved the new ideas and techniques rarely resorted to uncritical imitation of the Italians. In Italy the ideas were regarded as part of the national tradition, as the revival of an earlier stage of Italian civilization; in the northern countries they were something imported. Native traditions offered a strong resistance to the acceptance of the secularist philosophy and the new aesthetics of the Italian Renaissance. Consequently those who did make use of the new ideas applied them only in part. The end result was a culture based on native traditions with Renaissance ideas superimposed on them. In each country the new culture mirrored the tastes and interests of the people. The fact that the native traditions of each country were different gave the Renaissance manifestations of each country a peculiar character.

The Renaissance manifestations of the northern countries were generally less secular than the culture of the Italian Renaissance. This was true in a greater degree in Germany, England, and Spain than in France where the court of Francis I displayed a brilliant secularism wholly in keeping with the secular spirit of the Italian Renaissance. But even in the countries in which the motivation was still largely religious the secular spirit was expressing itself to a greater or lesser extent in all phases of culture. It is, of course, most evident in secular music, drama, and literature, but it also left its mark in painting even when the subjects were religious. Portrait painting was definitely secular and before long genre painting (scenes from everyday life) made its appearance. In humanism, too, there was a secular strain.

When the Italian influence made its appearance in the northern countries it did not stimulate a great outburst of artistic activity. In the realm of art its effect was greatest in painting. In sculpture little was produced that was outstanding and in architecture the Renaissance style modified rather than replaced the traditional architectural forms. In literature it stimulated the rise of humanism and the growth of national literatures.

Divided Germany

The collective government of the group of states which occupied geographical Germany was the Holy Roman Empire. It was called Roman because some believed it was a continuation of the old Roman Empire which had been disrupted by the Germanic invasions. Various explanations have been given for the use of the word "Holy" in the title. One explanation is that the empire was called "Holy" because of its close association with the Church. Another and more plausible explanation is that it was added to the title by emperors to assert their independence of papal sanctions. The first known use of the word in combination with empire dates from 1034 when the lands ruled by the Emperor Conrad II were designated a "Holy Empire." The use of the whole title "Holy Roman Empire" seems to have come into use about the middle of the thirteenth century. Nevertheless it signifies to most historians the political organization which dates from the coronation of Charlemagne on Christmas Day in the year 800 and which continued its dreary existence until Napoleon administered the *coup de grâce* in 1806. At times it is also called the "Medieval Empire." For the purposes of this chapter its connection with Germany during the Renaissance period is of major importance.

One of the broader differences between the histories of France and Germany is that in France the central government grew stronger during the later centuries of the Middle Ages and particularism or localism gradually merged into a wider national feeling, while in Germany the reverse took place. There the central government grew weaker, and particularism gained strength. As a result, by the end of the fifteenth century France had achieved a high degree of national unity, but Germany was still an aggregation of more than three hundred small states. Furthermore, while the French monarchy was hereditary, that of Germany was elective. The election principle was not bad in itself; it was the manner in which the king (who was then crowned emperor by the pope) was elected that prevented the rise of a strong national government. Originally the right to choose the German king, that is, the future emperor, had been vested in all freemen. As time passed, however, this right was exercised only by the leaders or higher nobility; then it was restricted further until the number of the electors dropped to seven. The number was fixed at seven in 1356 by the Golden Bull (so named after the imperial seal or bulla on the document) promulgated by the Emperor Charles IV. Of the seven electors, three were ecclesiastical princes. They were the archbishops of Mainz, Treves (Trier), and Cologne. The four secular princes were the king of Bohemia, the duke of Saxony, the margrave of Brandenburg, and the count palatine of the Rhine. Just why the right of being electors was vested in these seven dignitaries is still somewhat of a mystery.

Thenceforth until the Holy Roman Empire expired in 1806 the emperor was chosen by the college of electors set up by the Golden Bull. When an emperor died the archbishop of Mainz would summon the electors to meet at Frankfurt for the purpose of electing the next one. A candidate needed a minimum of four votes to be elected. So that no disputes would arise regarding the number of electors the Golden Bull declared the lands of the secular electors to be indivisible and the succession to them was limited to males according to the right of primogeniture. The Golden Bull granted the electors such special privileges as the right of coinage and the right to pass legal judgments from which there was no appeal. All this added greatly to the power and prestige of the electors, but weakened the position of the emperor, making the establishment of a strong central authority impossible. The electors jealously guarded their own rights and privileges, missing no opportunity to curtail those of the emperor. Since the electors were not constrained to choose a member of the House of Habsburg, the competition for the office could be spirited. Candidates found it necessary on occasion to insure their election with bribes of money, grants of land, or the assignment of certain revenues. The best known instance was probably the election in

1519 of Charles V who, as mentioned earlier, had to borrow such large sums of money from the Fugger Bank for bribery purposes that he was in financial straits for many years to come.

Much controversy has been generated among German historians by the question, "To what extent did the identification of the German monarchy with the imperial idea influence the course of German history?" Some German historians have gone so far as to state that it spelled the doom of the idea of national unity. This position is undoubtedly extreme. On the other hand, the fact that certain emperors borrowed the idea of universal rule from the old Roman Empire and then endeavored to translate at least a part of it into reality certainly did influence the course of German history. For example, the efforts of the Emperor Frederick II (1215-1250) to extend the imperial rule over much of Italy resulted in the neglect of Germany and presented the German princes with an opportunity to establish particularism more firmly. Consequently the constitutional developments which took place in Germany occurred within the particularist states, and did not point in the direction of a national state.

In general, the ideals of holiness and universal rule suggested by the title "Holy Roman Empire" were little more than lofty pretense. The propagation of holiness was certainly not a primary aim of the practical administrators of the empire. Moreover, there was little about the empire that could be called Roman beyond the fact that its administration was based in large part on Roman law and the emperor was customarily crowned in Rome. Even the latter was not always carried out. From the coronation of Henry VII in 1312 to that of Charles V in 1519, only three emperors were duly crowned in this way. As for the claims to universal rule, they had lost what little meaning they may once have had. In the case of the original Roman Empire the claim was based on the fact that the Romans ruled most of the then known civilized world. But the emperors of the Holy Roman Empire had no such basis for their claim. Since England, France, Italy, Spain, and Portugal no longer recognized the dominion of the Holy Roman Empire, its real boundaries had shrunk so that by the fourteenth century they included only Germany. This was even indicated in the title which in the fifteenth century was changed to "Holy Roman Empire of the German Nation."

When Frederick III of the House of Habsburg became emperor in 1452 the power of the princes and princelings was so firmly established that he could hardly hope to strengthen his position at their expense. The only way in which he and his successors could enhance their power was by adding to their own hereditary lands. They were successful in adding considerable territory to the holdings of the House of Habsburg by dynastic marriages, but they still lacked the power to overcome the particularism in Germany. Despite these problems, Frederick III still clung to the hollow pretension of universal rule. One reason may have been his desire to offset French pretensions to leadership in Europe. Another may have been his unwillingness to surrender the vain hope of extending his rule in the direction of universality. Whatever his real motives may have been, Frederick III proudly displayed on his family escutcheon the device AEIOU which stood for "Austriae est imperare orbe universo" or "Alles Erdreich ist Oesterreich untertan," the English version being "Austria's empire is over the universe." In reality the empire for which he claimed the rule of the world was in a pitiful state. It was racked by dissension and was slowly disintegrating. The emperor himself, his pretensions notwithstanding, was little more than a figurehead.

Some interesting attempts were made during the reign of Emperor Maximilian I (1493-1519) to reform the constitution of the empire. The reforms were sponsored in the Reichstag or Diet (composed of the emperor's feudal vassals) by a group of ecclesiastical princes who had the support of the lay princes. The reformers had no desire to strengthen the authority of the emperor. Their aim was to put an end to the disorders and petty wars which were keeping the country in a state of constant turmoil. They also endeavored to stop the flouting of the decrees issued by the Diet. Among those who were guilty of flagrantly ignoring the decrees of the Diet were the Imperial Cities, cities which were free of feudal overlordship and owed allegiance only to the emperor. Their excuse was that they were not obligated to carry out the decrees because they had no proper representation in the Diet. This was remedied even before Maximilian became emperor. In 1489, four years before he was elected, a Diet was summoned to meet in three divisions. The first was composed of the seven electors, the second of the ecclesiastical and lay princes of the empire, and the third of representatives of the Imperial Cities. Each group conducted its deliberations apart.

Having reinforced the Diet through the addition of representatives of the Imperial Cities, the reform party presented its program for strengthening the machinery of government to a meeting of the Diet in 1495. The members of the Diet obliged by voting acceptance of a number of the suggestions. First of all, the Diet proclaimed a perpetual peace (Landfriede) in the empire, hoping that it would put an end to the wars between the rulers of the states. Second, it created an imperial court of justice (Reichskammergericht) to which all disputes between feudal states and feudal lords were to be referred in order to prevent private wars. This court was composed of sixteen judges chosen by the states and a presiding judge or president appointed by the emperor. It was permanently established at Frankfurt and continued to function until the Holy Roman Empire was dissolved in 1806. Third, the Diet voted that it be summoned annually so that it could enforce obedience to its decrees. At the session of the Diet which convened in 1515 the reform party continued its efforts with the result that measures were adopted for better policing of the empire. The empire was to be divided into ten administrative districts or "circles," in each of which there was to be a standing force to suppress wars, feuds, and disorders. Each circle was also to have a council charged with the duty of seeing that the decrees of the Diet and the judgments of the Reichskammergericht were carried out. The Diet also voted an imperial tax which was called the Common Penny to provide the emperor with funds to maintain the Imperial Court. When Maximilian petitioned the Diet to establish a permanent military force or standing army, his request was voted down overwhelmingly because a standing army would have strengthened the emperor's position.

The reforms were, however, more apparent than real. When all was said and done, they accomplished very little. The electors, princes, and representatives of the cities were unable to put aside their selfish considerations long enough to adopt measures that would have set up a central government strong enough to enforce peace and order in the empire. With no means to compel acceptance of its decisions the Imperial Court established by the Diet was singularly ineffective. Its jurisdiction had been limited from the start by granting some of the greater princes special privileges which exempted their courts from the jurisdiction of the Imperial Court. The smaller princes ignored judgments of the Court which were not to their liking. Furthermore, the tax voted by the Diet for the purpose of financing the Court was so unpopular that many princes did not even try to collect it. In 1505 the Common Penny tax was replaced by a lump-sum tax levied on the cities and feudal princes, but even this was collected only on rare occasions. Even the plan to divide the empire into ten administrative districts was not carried out in its entirety. As for Maximilian, he had in the beginning sanctioned some of the reforms in the hope that the Diet would reciprocate by voting him the men and money he needed for a large military force. When his hope did not materialize, he not only withdrew his support; he went so far in 1497 as to set up his own court which functioned in direct competition with the Reichskammergericht. Thus the opportunity to strengthen the government of the empire and the position of the emperor was missed. Germany remained weak and divided until the conglomeration of states was welded into a strong national state in the nineteenth century.

To the credit of Maximilian it must be stated that he increased both the hereditary domains and the prestige of the House of Habsburg by propitious marriages. He concluded for his son Philip the Handsome a marriage alliance with Joanna, daughter of Ferdinand and Isabella which was later to unite the rule of Spain and the Holy Roman Empire in their son, Charles V. Maximilian himself had increased the territorial possessions of the house of Habsburg by his marriage in 1477 to Mary of Burgundy who had inherited the duchy of Burgundy and the Netherlands on the death of Charles the Bold, duke of Burgundy. Later Maximilian and Mary did lose Burgundy to the French, but they managed to retain the Netherlands.

In things of the mind Maximilian stood between the Middle Ages and the Renaissance. Although the influence of the Italian Renaissance was making itself felt in Germany during his youth, his education was still medieval in spirit. He was a man of the Renaissance only in the breadth of his interests and in his desire to achieve every possible earthly distinction. In founding the University of Vienna he did, however, include in its faculty teachers of the humanities. This university grew so rapidly that at the time of Maximilian's death in 1519 more than 5,000 students were enrolled in it. He was succeeded as emperor of the Holy Roman Empire by his grandson, Charles V.

German Humanism

In Germany the influence of Italian humanism made itself felt early in the fifteenth century. Not only did students return from Italy with an interest in humanism; the seeds of humanism were also sown on German soil by two important church councils, the Council of Constance (1414-1419) and the Council of Basel (1431-1448). At these councils church representatives from the northern countries came into close contact with humanists from Italy. Two of the more famous humanists who attended the Council of Constance were Poggio Bracciolini and Manuel Chrysoloras. Prominent among the humanists who were present at Basel was Aeneas Sylvius Piccolomini who later became Pope Pius II. These and other humanists impressed the northern representatives with their learning, exciting in some an interest in classical literature. Another factor in the dissemination of humanistic knowledge was the printed book. There was, of course, considerable interest in classical literature before Johann Gutenberg invented printing with movable type. Nicholas of Cusa, for example, collected a library of classical manuscripts before the classics appeared in print. But the availability of accurately printed copies of classical masterpieces acted as a stimulant to arouse a wider interest.

The purpose of the German humanists in studying the classics was still largely religious. By and large, they did not read the classics for their pagan content. Jakob Wimpheling (1450-1528), German humanist and educator, stated the issue in these words, "Without doubt it would be deplorable if we were to propagate by means of the classics a pagan way of judging and thinking as has often happened in Italy." Another humanist, Johann Trithemius (1462-1576) stated that the classics should be read "to amass therefrom in imitation of the Church Fathers precious seeds appropriate to serve the development of Christian knowledge." In the studies of the German humanists, the Bible and the writings of the Church Fathers had a place beside the classics. They often used the knowledge of Greek to find new truth and beauty in the New Testament. The same was true of Hebrew and the Old Testament. They critically examined various texts of the Bible for errors and aberrations. This study resulted in the publication of the Old Testament in the original Hebrew, of the New Testament in the original Greek, and of the whole Bible in a new Latin translation.

But German humanists did not concern themselves in a large degree with the hereafter. They did not hold heated discussions or write long theological dissertations on the destiny of man. They did not go beyond the boundaries of practical morality in their philosophy. Their domain was the Here and Now; their viewpoint was human and secular. In a broader sense their aim was the betterment of human existence on earth. They hoped to raise the moral standards of their time and to promote general enlightenment. All this, they believed, could be accomplished through a more widespread study of the classics. The leaders of German humanism were also advocates of freedom of thought. They have been described as "the most conscious workers for freedom of thought among all humanists of the sixteenth century." But the freedom of thought they advocated stopped short of the right to criticize or contradict the dogmas of the Church. One reason why Erasmus and other German humanists refused to join the Protestant movement was that they did not share the view of those who saw in Luther the protagonist of a new era of intellectual freedom. They feared that the violent religious partisanship would destroy such freedom of thought as they had. They also feared that their cultural program to enlighten mankind and raise the standard of morals through the study of the classics would be shipwrecked in the sea of religious controversy. As Erasmus put it, "Where Lutheranism rules there is an end of letters." As it turned out their fears were not unfounded. The Reformation proved to be the rock on which humanism foundered.

It was in education that the German humanists exerted their greatest influence. They were instrumental in effecting reforms in both the methods and content of education. The keynote of their educational aims was sounded by Rudolf Agricola who stated, "Regard as suspect all you have been taught hitherto. Ban and cast away as an imposture anything and everything that professes to be knowledge unless the title can be vouched for by the evidence of the great writers of old." Even Erasmus could not have broken more abruptly with medieval tradition in education. Many of the German humanists believed that every curriculum should include courses in both Latin and Greek, so that each person can both read and understand the Latin and Greek classics. "Within these two literatures," Erasmus wrote, "are contained all the knowledge which we recognize as of vital importance to mankind." Thus the German humanists regarded the classics as the best available educational means. "A man who is ignorant of letters," Erasmus stated, "is no man at all."

As a result of the efforts of the humanists many so-called Latin schools were founded in which Latin and the Latin classics became the staple of education, and in the existing schools more attention was given to the study of the Latin classics. Greek was taught to a more limited extent, but its study gradually became more popular in the German universities. At first the study of the classics was not given an enthusiastic reception in many universities. Conservative educators feared lest the pagan writings might make the students less enthusiastic about Christianity. Gradually, however, the study of the classics became a part of the curriculum of most of the existing universities. Among the first to feature the classics were the universities of Tübingen, Heidelberg, and Frankfurt. A number of new universities were also founded on a humanistic basis. The University of Vienna, founded by the Emperor Maximilian in 1497, made the study of the classics a prominent feature. Some of the humanists attracted large audiences to their lectures. Once they were established in the German universities, classical studies remained the core of the curriculum until the nineteenth century.

The first outstanding German humanist was Rudolf Agricola (1443-1485), a man of extraordinary gifts as a classicist and musician. Erasmus said of him that "he was the first to bring to us out of Italy a breath of higher culture." This is an overstatement, but Agricola did through his charming personality and his reputation as a teacher help to make classical studies popular in German universities. Because he was so successful in exciting a wide interest in the classics, his influence in Germany has been compared with that of Petrarch in Italy. As a young man he spent many years at various Italian universities, becoming an enthusiastic humanist. Upon his return to Germany he was appointed professor of classical literature at the University of Heidelberg where his popularity attracted many students from near and far. His knowledge of the classical languages and of the classics was prodigious. His Latin poetry was so elegant that contemporaries compared him with Virgil. One of his scholarly achievements was the translation of the Hebrew Psalms into Latin. He was exceptional among the humanists in that he also wrote in German. He even suggested that the classics be translated into German so that the common people could read them. Agricola died at the age of forty-two, just when his intellectual powers were at their peak.

The recognized leader of German humanism during the last years of the fifteenth century was Johann Reuchlin (1455-1522), one of the great humanists of the Northern Renaissance. He was the ablest Greek scholar of his time and had no peer among Christians as a Hebrew scholar. Moreover, at the early age of twenty he published a Latin dictionary that was much superior to existing dictionaries. It became so popular that it passed through thirty editions in twenty years. Reuchlin visited Italy twice, returning both times with a heightened enthusiasm for the classics, particularly the Greek classics. As a teacher he infused some of this enthusiasm into the students who came in large numbers from near and far to hear his lectures. Probably his greatest contribution was his revival of the study of Hebrew in the German universities. In this respect his *De Rudimentis Hebraicis* was epoch-making. "Hebrew," he stated, "is simple, uncorrupted, holy, terse, and vigorous. It is the language in which God confers directly with men."

Reuchlin's interest in Hebrew literature involved him in a bitter controversy which raged for many years. In 1509 Johann Pfefferkorn, a convert from Judaism to Christianity, sought to prove his zeal for his adopted religion by advocating the destruction of all Hebrew literature, including the Talmud. The only exception he made was the Old Testament. Pfefferkorn even received the approval of the Emperor Maximilian for his plan, but when Reuchlin's opinion was asked he vigorously opposed it. This caused the theological faculty of the University of Cologne, composed largely of Dominicans, to support Pfefferkorn's plan as vigorously as Reuchlin opposed it. Jakob von Hochstraten, the leader of the group, became so incensed that he denounced Reuchlin's statements as heretical and cited him to appear before the tribunal of the Inquisition. Reuchlin was successful, however, in having the case transferred to the Papal Curia in Rome. No verdict was rendered for many years; finally in 1520 during the growing furor aroused by Luther's rebellion Reuchlin was ordered to remain silent on the matter. Thereafter the controversy gradually subsided and Reuchlin spent the remaining years of his life in peace.

One of the interesting features of the controversy was the literature it produced. Soon after the controversy reached the boiling point many prominent figures wrote letters to Reuchlin assuring him of their support. These letters were collected and published under the title *Epistolae Clarorum Virorum* (Letters of Illustrious Men) as a means of winning further support for the cause. In 1514 the first part of a companion piece titled *Epistolae Obscurorum Virorum* (Letters of Obscure Men) was given to the public, the second part appearing several years later. This collection of letters has been regarded by many as one of the great satires of all time. Historical scholarship has not definitely established the identity of the authors of the more than a hundred letters. It is generally believed that the humanist Johann Jäger (who assumed the pretentious Latin name of Crotus Rubeanus) wrote the first series of letters. Later Ulrich von Hutten, humanist, writer of popular German poetry, and advocate of political as well as intellectual freedom, confessed indirectly to writing many of the letters of the second series. The letters were purportedly written by Dominican monks who discuss in them their opinions, experiences, mode of life, attitude toward the opposite sex, and ideas of education. Actually the letters pour satire on the obscurantist pedantry and endless quibbling of the scholastics and on the ignorance, superstitions, and antiquated methods of instruction of the monks. In mimicry of the barbarous style of the monks the letters were written in a Latin jargon often called dog-Latin. Jakob von Hochstraten and Pfefferkorn are both ridiculed in many letters. Throughout the impression is created that the members of the Cologne group who opposed Reuchlin were hostile to learning and progress. The following is an excerpt from Letter No. 26 of the second part:

> I now write to ask your reverence what opinion you hold concerning one who on a Friday, that is on the sixth day of the week—or on any other fast day of the week—should eat an egg with a chicken in it? You must know that we were lately sitting in an inn having supper and were eating eggs when on opening

one I saw that it contained a young chicken. This I showed to my comrade who at once said to me, "Eat it quickly before the innkeeper sees it, for if he does, you will have to pay a Caroline or a Julius for a fowl. . . . In a second I gulped down the egg, chicken, and all. And then I remembered it was Friday. Then I said to my crony, "You have made me commit a mortal sin in having me eat flesh on the sixth day of the week." But he asserted that it was not a mortal sin, not even a venial one, averring that such a chickling is regarded merely as an egg until it is born. He told me, too, that it is just the same as the case of cheese in which there are sometimes grubs, as there are in cherries, peas, and new beans; yet all these may be eaten on Friday, and even on Apostolic Vigils. But innkeepers are such rascals that they call them meat. Most earnestly do I entreat you to resolve the question I have propounded.

The *Epistolae Obscurorum Virorum* were read not only in Germany, but throughout Europe with shouts of laughter. Curiously enough, Reuchlin frowned on the letters written in support of his cause because he disapproved of the coarseness to which the writers resorted in some instances.

Desiderius Erasmus

The most prominent humanist not only in Germany but north of the Alps was Dutch-born Desiderius Erasmus (1466-1536), variously called "the educator of Europe," "the most influential scholar of his age," "the prince of humanists," and "the high priest of humanism." Ulrich von Hutten called him "the German Socrates" and the humanist Mutianus of Gotha stated, "Erasmus surpasses the measure of human gifts. He is divine and must be worshipped in pious devoutness." Actually Erasmus was not an impeccable Latinist; nor was he the equal of Reuchlin as a Greek scholar. It was his deep love of the classics, the breadth of his interest, the keenness of his wit, and the charm of his personality which gave him preeminence among contemporary men of letters. Regarding his love of the classics, Erasmus himself said that he could not read the writings of Cicero "without sometimes kissing the book and venerating a pure heart." His knowledge of his native Dutch was rather limited; in fact, he had little use for it since he thought, spoke, and wrote in Latin and liked to think of himself as a citizen of the world. During most of his adult life he did not remain long in any one place, but continued to travel from country to country despite his delicate constitution and chronic lack of funds. His wanderings took him to various parts of Germany, Switzerland, Italy, France, and England.

Erasmus started life in Rotterdam, Holland, where he was born in 1466. The fact that he was born out of wedlock caused him to draw a veil of secrecy over his early years. Although it is reported that his father, Gerard, became a monk while Erasmus was a child, this did not result in the neglect of the boy's education. He received some preliminary instruction; then at the age of nine he was enrolled in the famous school of the Brethren of the Common Life at Deventer. This school, which had already given the study of the classics a prominent place in its curriculum, numbered among its teachers several who had an enthusiastic interest in the classics and who were able to kindle this interest in the mind of the son of Gerard. It was the boy's great interest in Latin and the Latin classics which at a later time impelled him to latinize his name to Desiderius Erasmus.

At Deventer young Erasmus also received the religious bent which he retained throughout life. The religion of the Brethren of the Common Life was mystical. It stressed the good life rather than dogma, the inner spirit rather than external rites and outward observances. This religion impressed itself so deeply on the mind of Erasmus that it became the essence of his mature life. It explains why unyielding dogmatism, stereotyped formalism, and ritualistic sacramentalism had no place in his religious philosophy. It further explains why this undogmatic theologian waged incessant war against the primacy of dogma. Erasmus later wrote, "If one wishes to attain that peace, that concord, which is the ideal of our religion, one must speak as little as possible of the definition of dogma, and permit free and personal judgment to each on many points." Erasmus' religion which he called "the philosophy of Christ" was an ethical religion which was slanted in the direction of this life. An English historian wrote, "It is inexact to speak of him as a religious thinker unless we add he was unable to divorce religion from what many consider secular activities." (W. G. More, *Hibbert Journal*, XXXIV [1936], p. 525). Everything Erasmus wrote at a later time was to a greater or lesser extent an expression of the religious ideas he absorbed at the school of the Brethren of the Common Life.

At about the age of twenty-one Erasmus entered an Augustinian monastery near Gouda and was later ordained a priest. He was, however, unable to adjust himself to the monastic routine of prayer, penance, and fasting. He gradually developed a strong anti-monastic feeling which he expressed repeatedly in his later writings. But monastic life did give him the opportunity to continue his studies and indulge his love of the classics. Nevertheless, he was quick to seize the opportunity to leave the monastery when it presented itself after he had been there six years. It came when the Bishop of Cambrai, attracted by Erasmus' attainments as a Latinist, offered him the position of private secretary. Little is known about the relationship between the bishop and his secretary beyond the fact that the latter did not hold the position long. The year 1495 saw Erasmus studying at the University of Paris which was still a stronghold of scholasticism. He soon became disgusted, however, with the scholastic learning he found there, regarding it as a form of obscurantism which had no connection with reality. It was to him, as one historian has put it, "a nightmare of quiddities and quoddities." In 1498 Erasmus made his first journey to England where he met most of the prominent Englishmen of the day. The two men who influenced him most were John Colet and Sir Thomas More. In Colet, who later became famous as dean of St. Paul's, Erasmus found a kindred spirit. The two not only shared a love of the classics, their religious attitudes also had much in common. After their first meeting a friendship developed which was life-long. Erasmus paid Colet this tribute: "When I listen to my friend Colet it seems as if I am listening to Plato himself." Equally great was his veneration for Thomas More, humanist, statesman, and author of *Utopia*. "When," Erasmus asked, "did nature mold a disposition more gentle, enduring, and happier than his?"

Erasmus' visit to England was a turning-point in his life. At the age of thirty-three he had written very little and was unknown outside of certain humanistic circles. At the suggestion of his friends Colet and More he now devoted himself with ardor to the study of Greek. Shortly thereafter he wrote to a friend, "I have given my whole soul to Greek learning, and as soon as I get money I shall buy Greek books, and then clothes." In 1506 he was able to fulfill the dream of every humanist, that of visiting Italy. Since he had already published two books he was known to Italian humanists who received him cordially. He spent almost a year in Venice before going to Rome. While in Italy he had a number of opportunities to teach at Italian universities. He could also have had ecclesiastical appointments, but he turned down all offers because he loathed the idea of being subject to ecclesiastical or academic routine. Although Italian humanism as a movement was already in an advanced stage of decline, he seems to have found the intellectual climate of Italy congenial. Soon after leaving Italy he wrote, "There one enjoys sweet liberty, rich libraries, the charming friendship of writers and scholars, and the sight of ancient monuments." In 1509 he was back in England again, remaining there this time for about five years. He taught Greek at Cambridge University for a time and could have kept the position permanently had not the *Wanderlust* seized him again.

Meanwhile a number of Erasmus' books had appeared. Five or six of the many books he wrote or edited were events in the history of European culture. Their underlying purpose was reform. Erasmus saw that the life of contemporary society, including that of the Church, was overlaid with superstition, venality, corruption, and immorality, all of which he believed to be rooted in ignorance. His purpose was to dispel this ignorance with education. The evils afflicting society, he was certain, would yield to "the civilizing influence of knowledge," particularly to the knowledge found in the classics. On this aim he concentrated all the powers of his mind. His first book, titled *Adagia* or *Adages* (1500) was a collection of proverbs culled from the classics, with a commentary on each one. This book made Erasmus at once the leader of those interested in the "new learning." During the years that followed many revised and enlarged editions of the *Adagia* were published. Whereas the first edition contained only about eight hundred adages from Latin literature, in its final form the book was a collection of 4251 proverbs from Greek as well as from Latin sources, all of them elucidated with a detailed commentary. Erasmus' second noteworthy book was *Enchiridion Militis Christiani* (Handbook of the Christian Knight) which appeared in 1502. In it Erasmus gave to the world his concept of religion. "I wrote the *Enchiridion*," Erasmus stated, "to remedy the error which makes religion depend on ceremony and observance of bodily acts, while neglecting true piety." Its popularity continued through the centuries and even in the twentieth century it has appeared in new translations and new editions.

Erasmus' most popular book was *Encomium Moriae* or *Praise of Folly* (1511). It won for him a place among the great satirists of all time. Much of it was probably written in the house of Sir Thomas More during the visit to England in 1509. The title is believed to be a playful pun on More's name and the book is also dedicated to him. Although Erasmus spoke of *The Praise of Folly* as something light he had dashed off for the amusement of his friends, it is a deeply serious book. Underneath the apparently light humor the book is a severe indictment of contemporary society, a biting satire on the evils of contemporary life. In it he lashes with a sharp tongue the greed and misrule of the princes, the gross superstitions of the masses, the venality of the clergy, the immorality of the monks, the traffic in indulgences and pardons, the worship of relics and images, and the ignorance of the scholastics. A special target for his barbed shafts are the scholastics whom he attacks because of their penchant for magnifying trifling matters at the expense of important ones and for their tiresome disputes over futile questions. He taunts them with such questions as, "If Christ had appeared in the form of an inanimate substance would he have been able to preach his gospel?" and "What would Peter have consecrated if he had celebrated the Eucharist while Christ was still alive?" The ex-monk also castigates what he regards as the foibles and follies of the monks, going so far as to ridicule the common belief that monastic life is meritorious and that one can win God's favor by ascetic practices. In a serious vein he also scourged those who foment war. "What is more foolish than to undertake it," he asked, "especially when both parties are sure to lose more than they get?" War he regarded as the antithesis of everything Christian.

Soon after *The Praise of Folly* appeared, it was known and read throughout Europe. The demand for it was so great that it went through several editions in a few months. In 1514 Froben, the famous printer of Basel, issued an edition for which the artist Hans Holbein sketched the illustrations. It has been calculated that twenty-seven editions appeared during the lifetime of Erasmus. Before long the book was also translated into many of the European vernacular languages. Probably no other book of the time with the possible exception of the Bible attained such a circulation. Contemporaries reported that those who could read, read it and those who could not, listened while others read it aloud. More than a century later John Milton wrote,

"Everybody here in Cambridge is reading it." During the centuries that followed *The Praise of Folly* was not consigned to the limbo of forgotten books. A number of new translations have been made and many new editions have been published in the twentieth century.

Erasmus continued his attacks on the evils and shortcomings of contemporary society in his *Colloquies* (1516). The *Colloquies* and *The Praise of Folly* are the two books through which Erasmus exercised the most permanent influence. In the *Colloquies* his wit is just as sharp as in *The Praise of Folly*, but his philosophical scope is broader and deeper. The *Colloquies* were received so enthusiastically that the first printing of 24,000 copies was sold out in months. This is amazing in a period before the rise of modern advertising and distribution techniques. Erasmus may, therefore, be said to have written the first best-sellers of modern times. He was also one of the first writers to reap the full benefits of printing and to earn a living by his literary labors. Writing at a time when Latin was still the common language of learning he was able to reach a wide European public.

Erasmus' contribution to scholarship was his version of the Greek New Testament (1516), the first edited Greek text of the New Testament to appear in print in the Western world during the Renaissance. Actually Erasmus' text left much to be desired. One historian has called it "amazingly bad." The collating and editing seems to have been done somewhat hurriedly because reports had reached the printer Froben in Basel that a similar work was being prepared in Spain under the direction of Cardinal Ximenes. The Greek New Testament of Ximenes was ready as early as 1514, but was not published until 1520 as part of the *Complutensian Polyglot* which contained the whole Bible. Nevertheless, the *Greek New Testament* of Erasmus was significant because it opened the way for biblical criticism. The Greek text in the version of Erasmus was accompanied by a new Latin translation of the New Testament in which many of the errors and aberrations which had crept into the Vulgate or official version over a period of a thousand years were exposed.

During the last years of his life Erasmus spent much of his time in Basel where Froben, the humanist printer, published most of the books he wrote, translated, or edited. Erasmus labored unremittingly to the end. Besides writing short treatises on a variety of subjects, including education, the classics, and the need for peace, he also translated a number of Greek classics and writings of the Greek Church Fathers into Latin. In addition he carried on a voluminous correspondence with many outstanding personages. This collected correspondence is now an important source for the study of contemporary life. In 1536 Erasmus died in Basel at the age of seventy. As a man of many talents and interests, he was, above all, a social reformer whose primary concern it was to improve the life of his time by eliminating from it everything that was obsolete, fraudulent, or foolish.

The Beginnings of Modern German Literature

For the German language the period of the Renaissance was a time of transition from the Middle High German to the New High German language which Lessing, Schiller, and Goethe later used as a vehicle to raise German literature to its greatest heights. The German literature of the Renaissance period was also transitional in that it reflects the passing of the old order and the beginning of a new one. It is a literature motivated in large measure by secular interests. As in the other countries of Western Europe it was the townspeople who provided the cultural impetus for the rise of the new literature. Before the intensified secularism was expressed in a literature written particularly for the rising bourgeoisie, the more literate members of the middle class turned to the secular legends and romances. These tales featured the exploits of knights errant who succored the weak, protected women and children, and always emerged as victors from every contest. But as the armored knight was becoming obsolescent so the courtly romances were losing favor. The interests of the people were turning from the realms of the imagination to the realities about them. Hence the great popularity of satirical literature which dealt with life as they saw it and lived it. To satisfy the new tastes middle-class writers wrote for middle-class readers. It was for the most part a realistic, not an idealistic literature like the courtly romances.

German literature did not, however, reach its full bloom in a short period of time, like Italian literature in the fourteenth century and English literature in the sixteenth. Practically all the German literature of the Renaissance period was popular rather than belles lettres. Scholarly works were written in Latin because most of the learned men of the time regarded German as undeveloped, inelegant, and unfit for the expression of learned thoughts. The use of German in the classroom also seemed preposterous to them; hence all lectures in the universities continued to be given in Latin. Many of the German humanists even regarded their German names as barbarous. Accordingly they translated them into Greek or Latin. Schwarzerd (black earth) became Melanchthon and Huysman (peasant) was changed to Agricola. German as such was relegated to the masses who used it in the affairs of everyday life.

An outstanding example of popular literature is Brant's *Narrenschiff* (Ship of Fools), a long poem which has been styled "the most famous poem of its time." It was published in 1494, some years before the appearance of Erasmus' *Praise of Folly* and it was, of course, written in German. Its author, Sebastian Brant (1458-1521) is a good example of Renaissance versatility, for he was a lawyer and professor of law at the University of Basel, an artist, humanist, poet, civic leader, and man of practical affairs as well as of broad learning. Like Erasmus he was animated by a desire for reform, and the *Narrenschiff* was his means for achieving it. The device he employed as a framework for his poem was that of a weather-beaten ship freighted with fools, sailing past *Schlaraffenland* (land of idlers) on the way to *Narragonien* (land of fools) to which Brant would consign all fools. The public to which he obviously addresses the poem is the prosperous middle class of the German cities.

Brant had a keen sense for charlatans, rogues, knaves, and their ilk. Each fool on the ship represents a fault, vice, weakness, or folly of human nature. On all these fools he pours denunciation, contempt, and scorn. Among the hundred fools he parades before the reader are pedants, gamblers, idlers, gluttons, drunkards, exploiters of others, slaves of fashion, and lazy students who employ every bit of cunning they can muster to avoid study. He is particularly caustic of women who sit at the gaming table to

> Rattle the dice early and late
> Forgetful of their proper state.

There is also a section on church-goers who attend church services because it is the fashionable thing to do or because they have a fine dog or hawk to display. Even the members of the clergy do not get away unscathed. Clerical delinquencies are scored, idle monks are excoriated, and the clergy in general are admonished to lead better lives. Brant's droll word pictures have been likened to the paintings of the English artist Hogarth, because there is a moral earnestness behind the jest and satire. Although Brant shared with Erasmus the opposition to moral stupidity and mental sloth, his philosophy was not progressive like that of Erasmus. Brant was a conservative and in some ways a reactionary. Thus, for example, he denounced the new philosophies which bordered on heresy.

Brant's *Ship of Fools* had a tremendous popular appeal. Not only did its humor and satire please the public; it was probably the first book printed in Germany which dealt with contemporary affairs. In this connection it contains the earliest known reference in literature to the discovery of America by Columbus. A special feature of the early German editions was a series of woodcuts, many of which were sketched by Brant himself. All this assured it a wide circulation. The first edition was followed by eight further editions in a short period of time. Everywhere in Germany it was read, discussed, quoted, and there were even a number of imitators. *The Ship of Fools* became so widely known that at least one noted preacher (Geiler von Kaisersberg) based a series of sermons on it in 1499. Erasmus who referred to Brant as "the incomparable" may even have conceived the idea of writing *The Praise of Folly* after reading *The Ship of Fools*. The circulation of Brant's poem was not, however, limited to Germany and Switzerland. With *Das Narrenschiff* Germany entered the stream of European literature for the first time. A Latin translation, published in 1497, made it available to learned circles throughout Europe. During the years 1497 to 1499 three free translations were made into French, translations that were more in the nature of adaptations. It was also translated into other languages of Western Europe, including English, Dutch, Low German, and Flemish.

The most winsome figure in German Renaissance literature is Hans Sachs (1494-1576), the happy cobbler of Nuremberg. Destined from early youth to be a craftsman, he was, nevertheless, sent to a Latin school where he developed interests in humanism, history, and literature which he retained throughout life. At the age of fifteen he was apprenticed to a shoemaker and, after learning the craft, became a journeyman and a master shoemaker; he then settled down in Nuremberg to ply his trade and to write. For the next sixty years he recorded in verse almost everything he saw, read, or heard, leaving more than six thousand separate pieces at the time of his death. His writings include songs, poems, dialogues, and dramas, all of them replete with his shrewd and humorous observations of life. Whatever he wrote is saturated with unfailing good humor, contagious gaiety, unlimited kindness and magnanimity, and a zest for life. The ideals he held up before his contemporaries were honesty, decency, kindness, and civic spirit.

Hans Sachs is, first of all, the most celebrated of the Meistersinger (mastersingers) who were the successors of the Minnesinger (singers of love), young knights who rode from castle to castle to sing the praises of noble ladies to the accompaniment of the lute. In contrast the Meistersinger were craftsmen of the rising commercial towns who organized singing groups or gilds. Since recreation was very limited, such singing societies were during the fifteenth century founded in most German towns. These singing groups sang at various festivities and also staged annual singing contests, thereby encouraging popular song. Gradually, however, hard and fast rules were set up regarding form, rhythm, and manner of presentation which hampered the free development of popular music. Richard Wagner in his comic opera *Die Meistersinger* gives an excellent idea of the pedantic importance they attached to the observance of the rules. Those who wished to become masters in the gild of Meistersinger were required to compose an original song, a requirement which was hardly an obstacle for Hans Sachs; during his lifetime he composed no fewer than four thousand. Hans Sachs was not only the most celebrated, he has also been called the last of the Meistersinger. The period of his life marked the heyday of the movement, and although it lingered on after his passing, the spirit had gone out of it.

Hans Sachs wrote poems on all possible subjects. His favorite stories were Biblical episodes and legendary tales, but he also wrote poems which mirror the burgher life in the midst of which he lived. Whatever the subject on which he was writing, Hans Sachs never expressed indignation. He always maintained his sense of humor and his poetic composure. A characteristic example of his treatment of legendary tales with simple humor is the poem in which he relates the story of St. Peter and the goat. One day while he was walking, St. Peter met the Lord. He told the Lord that he was greatly disturbed over the prevalence of evil in the world in which conditions were so bad that knavery was passing for rectitude and the pious were suffering great injustice. Human relations, he said, reminded him of life in the sea where one fish swallowed the other. Peter intimated to the Lord that if he were given permission to rule the world for a year he would see that order was established and justice would triumph. At this point an emaciated peasant woman in a torn dress approached, driving a young goat before her. Seeing the Lord, she complained to him that she had to work hard in the fields all day to feed herself and the many mouths in the family and in addition had to mind the frolicsome young goat. The Lord at once suggested to Peter that he show pity by taking charge of the goat for a day. Peter who saw in the situation an opportunity to demonstrate his ability, eagerly accepted the Lord's assignment. But he soon found the task a trying one.

The frisky goat, of sportive mind,
Soon left St. Peter far behind.
Never stopping a moment at any place
It led the good saint a merry chase
Across the meadow, hither and yon
As poor old Peter kept plodding on.
Up one hill and down another
Bleating, crying for its mother,
Through brush and briars, around the trees
While Peter did sigh, and pant, and wheeze.
All day beneath the scorching sun
The tireless goat continued to run
Arousing in Peter great indignation
And wetting his clothes with perspiration.
Finally evening came, the goat was caught
And safely to its mistress brought.
The Lord greeted Peter with a smile
Knowing he had covered many a mile.
"Peter," he said, "are you still intent
On ruling the world and its firmament?
If minding a goat your mettle has tried
How could you rule a world so wide?"
Peter replied, "Dear Lord of mine!
Take back the scepter that is thine!
It was for me by no means play
To rule a goat for one short day;
It must be infinitely worse
To regulate the universe."
The Lord then said, "Your words are true!
Let each his proper duty do
And leave the world in the command
Of one Supreme Almighty hand."

Hans Sachs also holds a high place among those who prepared the way for the modern German drama. Historians of literature refer to him as "the father of the German folk drama." He wrote more than two hundred dialogues, short plays, tragedies, and comedies. In the field of drama he is best remembered today as the author of seventy-five *Fastnachtspiele* (Carnival or Shrovetide Plays). Plays of this type made their appearance in the fifteenth century and were at first presented, as the name indicates, on the day or days preceding Ash Wednesday which ushers in the Lenten season. The early *Fastnachtspiele* were basically religious, but humorous improvisations and other farcical and secular materials were gradually added until the plays were largely secular with religious remnants. Jests, pranks, and gestures were often coarse, the degree of coarseness being governed by the taste of the audience. In the beginning many of the jests and gestures were improvisations by the players; in time, however, the actors were provided with carefully written dialogue, many plots being based on incidents taken from daily life.

The *Fastnachtspiele* of Hans Sachs show a marked improvement over those of earlier and contemporary playwrights. Among other things they display an improved technique of playwriting. His first plays, it is true, were mere dialogues, but his technique shows a steady improvement. When the city of Nuremberg opened its playhouse in 1550 Hans Sachs began a series of plays designed for the stage rather than for an improvised theater in a private house. In doing so he transformed the *Fastnachtspiel* from a formless dialogue to a well-constructed play with a complicated plot. Besides being superior in construction, Sachs' plays were also based on better materials. In addition to the Bible, the sources of his materials were classical literature, history, and the vast store of legends and anecdotes that were available to him. Several of his early plots were suggested by Brant's *Ship of Fools* and for thirteen others he was indebted to Boccaccio's *Decameron* which he read in a German translation. Hans Sachs did, however, carefully Germanize everything he borrowed from foreign sources. The plays of Hans Sachs further display a sharper delineation of character than other *Fastnachtspiele*. This improved characterization undoubtedly stems from his remarkably deep insight into human nature. His dialogue is more natural; the language is that which Sachs heard in the street and in his shop. This quality of naturalness makes his plays vivid folk pictures of sixteenth-century life. The dialogue of Sachs's plays is also more wholesome than that of the ordinary play of his day. Although some of his lines are earthy, he carefully avoided the offensive materials with which many of his predecessors and contemporaries filled their plays.

If Hans Sachs had felt the pulse of modern life, he might have become the creator of the modern German drama. Since he did not, he is only a forerunner of it. The spirit which pervades his plays is still in a large degree medieval. A good example of his use of medieval materials is his play *The Wandering Scholar from Paradise*. In the plot a wandering scholar comes upon a peasant woman who is still mourning her departed first husband although she already has a second one. She confides to the wandering scholar that her second husband is the worst of misers.

> He rakes and scrapes the pence together
> And keeps me on a sorry tether.

The wandering scholar, seeing an opportunity to benefit from the situation, convinces the dull-witted woman that he has just returned from a visit to Paradise where he found her first husband in dire need of money and clothing. He related emphatically that her husband, having only his shroud, was unable to attend festive gatherings for the lack of proper clothing. The woman is so deeply moved that she gives the wandering scholar her second husband's best clothes and also his savings, imploring the stranger to take them to her first husband as speedily as possible. When the miserly second husband returns from the field to find that his wife has given away his savings and his best clothing, he quickly mounts his horse and rides furiously in pursuit of the wandering scholar, hoping to recover his precious possessions. Upon hearing the sound of hoofs and seeing a horseman approach, the wandering scholar hides his bundle of clothing in a thicket; then steps out with an air of innocence to meet the peasant. The latter stops in his breathless pursuit to ask the wandering scholar if he has seen a young man with a bundle of clothing. The wandering scholar replies that a young man answering the description had just entered a nearby swamp to avoid detection. Hope wells up in the peasant's breast. Asking the wandering scholar to hold his horse, he rushes into the swamp in search of the man who has his money and clothing. No sooner is the peasant out of sight than the wandering scholar retrieves the bundle of clothing, mounts the horse, and rides away, leaving the peasant to his misery. How will the peasant account to his wife for the missing horse? He is equal to the situation. He tells her that he gave the horse to the wandering scholar to enable him to return to her first husband in Paradise so much more quickly.

During the lifetime of Hans Sachs religious controversy had gradually absorbed the intellectual interests and energies of the German people. As a result the Renaissance had come to an end in Germany. Many secular trends were temporarily reversed in the direction of medieval otherworldliness. While humanistic knowledge was being used for polemical purposes, literature became an instrument of religious partisanship. Thus, just when it was showing signs of coming into its own, German literature was blighted by the winds of religious controversy. The non-religious German literature of the succeeding period was anemic and spiritless.

17

The Renaissance in France

The Lure of Italy

There has been considerable controversy regarding the extent of Italian influence on French Renaissance culture. Whereas some historians have advanced the theory that most of the ideas and forms of the French Renaissance were imported from Italy, others who are more nationalistic have asserted that France's debt to Italy was a small one. The latter insist that the French Renaissance was constructed on a French foundation and that almost all the materials used to build the superstructure were French. They further assert that the little the French did borrow from Italy corrupted the French cultural traditions. The truth probably lies somewhere between the two extremes. On the one hand, it is easy to show that most of the Renaissance manifestations in France are not servile imitations of the Italian Renaissance. For example, François Rabelais, one of the great literary figures of the French Renaissance, owed little to Italy. This is also true of other French writers, artists, and humanists. On the other hand, those who brush aside the Italian influence as insignificant are doing violence to the facts of history. Many French writers, humanists, and artists either borrowed from or were inspired by Italian culture. The French sculptor Jean Goujon, for example, made no secret of the fact that he needed the inspiration of Italian artists. Others also made no effort to conceal the source of their inspiration. But in most instances the borrowed ideas were subjected to a subtle transformation before they were incorporated into the native cultural strains. Thus French Renaissance culture represents a fusion of Italian and French ideas and forms. In art, Flemish influence was also a factor of importance.

Although Renaissance ideas and ideals had been filtering into France from Italy for some time, the flow was speeded by the expeditions three French kings led into Italy. The first of the trio, and also the first French ruler to come under the spell of Italy, was Charles VIII who ruled France from 1483 to 1498. Having inherited from Louis XI a fairly compact kingdom with a large army and substantial revenues, Charles looked outside of France for worlds to conquer. A dreamer of grandiose dreams, he believed that France was too small a stage for the part he hoped to play in European affairs. He would achieve glory by embarking on a great foreign venture. His aim was to conquer Italy; then push on to crush the Turks before returning home to have his brow wreathed with laurel and to be hailed as the conquering hero who had saved Western Christendom from the threat of the infidel. He proceeded at once to collect a large force, asserted a claim to the kingdom of Naples, and in October, 1494, led an expedition across the Alps. His force was a formidable one. It was composed of a large corps of artillery, 3600 cavalrymen, and 21,000 infantrymen. Since the Italian states were not prepared to offer resistance to so powerful an army, Charles VIII and his expedition were able to march the whole length of the peninsula practically unmolested. It was jestingly said that the only weapons needed were pieces of chalk to mark the doors of the houses in which the troops were quartered each night.

When the expedition reached Naples Charles VIII assumed the rule of that kingdom without striking a blow. Before long, however, some of the Italian states recovered from the shock of the French invasion. Venice, Milan, and the Papal States formed the so-called Holy League against the efforts of Charles VIII to conquer Italy and were soon joined by King Ferdinand of Spain. Upon being apprised of this, Charles decided to return to France at once to avoid being cut off from the Alps by the forces of the Holy League. As it was his army found it necessary to fight a sharp but indecisive battle in northern Italy before it was permitted to recross the Alps into France. A short time later the troops which Charles had left in Naples as a holding force were driven out, leaving Charles without an inch of territory to show for his efforts.

Although the expedition of Charles VIII was not a military success, it did excite in the king and some of his troops a lively interest in some phases of Italian civilization. The stay of the expeditionary force in Italy was so brief that the Frenchmen had time for little more than a quick glance; nevertheless, they were impressed by what they saw, particularly the spacious and well-lighted residences of the wealthy, the well-planned gardens, the monuments, sculptures, and paintings, and the growing fashion of portraiture. Charles himself who was not devoid of interest in art and learning gave some practical help toward the introduction of the Renaissance by taking to France in his army-train a number of Italian artists and men of learning, including the sculptor Guido Mazoni and the architect Fra Giocondo. Charles also brought home from Italy tailors, embroiderers, perfumers, cabinet makers, and gardeners. Among the inanimate objects in the royal baggage were books and manuscripts, paintings and sculptures, tapestries and furniture, jewelry and ornaments of various kinds. The interest in things Italian which the expedition of Charles VIII aroused caused larger numbers of students, humanists, and artists to visit Italy for the purpose of learning about Renaissance civilization at first hand. At the same time Italian artists and humanists followed those who had entered France with King Charles. More Italian artisans also settled in France "to ply their crafts after the manner and customs of Italy," as the French chronicler

Philippe de Commines put it. The sculptor Guido Mazoni executed a number of works, among them the sculptures for the tomb of Charles VIII which was destroyed during the Revolution of 1789. Fra Giocondo and his associates drew the plans for a number of buildings and the Italian gardeners who accompanied Charles VIII to France laid out Italian gardens featuring plots of flowers surrounded by hedges of boxwood and yew.

Louis XII who became king after the death of Charles VIII in 1498 displayed much more administrative ability in the internal affairs of the realm. By eliminating unnecessary expenses and extravagances at his court he was able to reduce taxes. He is quoted as saying, "I would rather see the courtiers laugh at my avarice than to have the people weep at my extravagances." During his reign France prospered to the extent that by the end of his reign in 1515 the royal income had almost doubled. But in his foreign policy Louis XII was no wiser than Charles VIII had been. He, too, succumbed to the lure of Italy. Whereas Charles VIII had laid claim only to the kingdom of Naples, Louis XII claimed both Naples and Milan. Furthermore, he met with little difficulty in occupying them with his army. Again, as in the case of Charles VIII, the occupation of Italian territory aroused widespread opposition, involving Louis in quarrels with the pope, with Ferdinand of Spain, with the Emperor Maximilian, with Venice, and with Henry VIII of England. In the end he failed as dismally as his predecessor. Beyond turning Italy into the cockpit of the sixteenth century his efforts achieved nothing. When he died in 1515 France held no more territory in Italy than it had at the death of Charles VIII.

Louis XII's expeditions into Italy did, however, intensify French interest in Italian life and culture. King Louis himself cherished an admiration for certain phases of the Italian Renaissance. One of the first things he did on reaching Milan was to go to Santa Maria della Grazie to see "The Last Supper" which Leonardo da Vinci had just completed. The painting made such a profound impression on him that, it is reported, he inquired of his engineers if it were possible to transport the entire wall to France without damaging the painting. Louis also tried to persuade Leonardo to accompany him to France, but the artist had other commitments. The French king did, however, take into his employ a number of lesser painters and architects.

Francis I and His Aims

The reign of Francis I (1515-1547) saw the Renaissance reach its zenith in France. One of the more important reasons for this was the king himself. He personally sought to promote the development of French culture in every possible way. He was, for example, the great patron of artists and writers. He also built a number of magnificent palaces, thereby giving employment to architects, painters, and sculptors. His example served to excite the interest of many great nobles and members of the high bourgeoisie. As ruler of

France he did not measure up to his predecessor, for he detested unromantic administrative affairs. His disposition was such that he could not apply himself to anything for any length of time. Although he claimed for himself the right of deciding all important matters, the actual conduct of affairs was largely carried on by his ministers and favorites. On occasion considerable influence in the affairs of state was wielded by women, particularly by his sister Margaret of Navarre and by the reigning mistress of the moment. As king his great ambition was self-aggrandisement. To this aim everything else, including the practice of religion, was subordinated.

As a person Francis was willful and selfish to an extraordinary degree. He was badly raised by a doting mother, Louise of Savoy, who idolized him, calling him "my lord" and "my Caesar." During the years of his youth she indulged his every whim with the result that when he grew up he devoted himself to self-indulgence. One French historian has described him as "a large eater, a heavy drinker, and an even better sleeper." His love affairs, which were many, at times became scandalous. His sister, Margaret of Navarre, has described two of his early affairs in the twenty-fifth and forty-second stories of her *Heptameron.* His biographers report that after an illicit affair with the wife of one of his ministers or courtiers he usually stopped at a church on the way home to ask divine forgiveness. Among his better qualities was the friendliness of his bearing. He was accessible to all, a charming conversationalist, and often his gayety was "the life of the party" at court gatherings. As a young man he took great pleasure in riding, hunting, and jousting. Later he fought on the field of battle like a medieval knight. This was the man who, in a sense, was the embodiment of the French Renaissance. His education was good enough for him to take an interest in the French language and even to write French verse of a sort. Later, although he never made a careful study of the classics, he also evinced considerable interest in humanism. For reasons of personal prestige he surrounded himself with artists and men of learning. He even found pleasure in discussing art, the classics, and philosophy with them. (*See Fig. 26.*)

With his predecessors Francis I shared the hope of extending French rule over Italy. Undeterred by their failures, he led an expedition into Italy to oppose the forces of the league which had been founded to curb the ambitions of the French kings. In the battle of Pavia (October, 1515) Francis won so complete a victory that the enemy forces retreated in disorder and Milan capitulated without offering resistance. Francis could not, however, make the most of his victory as he had to return to France where important matters were awaiting his attention. It was only the first round in the contest for Italy. Charles V, emperor of the Holy Roman Empire and king of Spain, also had designs on Italian territory. Gradually collecting a powerful army in northern Italy, Charles attacked the forces of Francis at Pavia in 1525. This time the story had a different ending. Francis not only left the flower of his army, some six thousand men, dead on the field of battle, he himself was also taken prisoner. At this time he wrote to his mother who was regent in his absence, "Nothing remains to me but honor and life." Charles V sent his prisoner to Madrid where he held him in close confinement and treated him with calculated contempt. The purpose was, of course, to get Francis to agree to terms that were to the liking of the captor. But the sympathy of Europe was with the French king and there was a great outcry, in which Erasmus joined, against the indignities the emperor was heaping on Francis. This finally caused Charles to conclude the treaty of Madrid with his unfortunate captive early in 1526 and to release him. In one of the provisions of the treaty, Francis renounced all his claims to Italian territory. Although he had no intention of abiding by his agreement, his later efforts to reassert his claims came to nothing.

Francis I and the Renaissance

When Francis returned to France after leading his first expedition into Italy, he brought back a number of artists and men of learning, among them the great Leonardo da Vinci. By this time Leonardo was over sixty and in failing health, but he was still a stately figure and Francis regarded him as a great prize. The veteran master and the assistants and students who accompanied him to France were assigned a small chateau at Cloux near Amboise as a residence. There Leonardo spent the last years of his life occupying himself with various engineering problems and also doing some painting. The latter was extremely difficult because his right hand was partially paralyzed. Two pictures of this period were "Leda" which was never wholly finished and "Pomona" (goddess of gardens) of which only a copy has survived. Francis I was very fond of Leonardo and visited him frequently. Benvenuto Cellini reported that Francis was fascinated by the intellectual powers of the Italian master. "Since his [Leonardo's] genius," Cellini wrote, "was as varied as it was great, and since he had some knowledge of both Greek and Latin letters, King Francis, violently enamored of his great talents, took so great a pleasure in hearing him discourse there were few days in the year when he was separated from him." The king also purchased in Italy some of the paintings Leonardo had executed. Two of these were the "Virgin of the Rocks" and the "Mona Lisa" (*La Belle Gioconde*) which are now in the Louvre. It is, therefore, not hard to believe that Francis was deeply moved when advised of Leonardo's death. But the king of France was not the only one to mourn. Francesco Melzi, Leonardo's assistant, wrote to Giuliano da Vinci, brother of Leonardo: "The loss of such a man is mourned by everyone, for Nature cannot create his like again." His remains were entombed in the Church of St. Florentin at Amboise and later removed to the chapel of Blaise.

Another artist Francis had the pleasure of welcoming to France was Benvenuto Cellini. After his arrival, Cellini was much annoyed by a long delay while the king decided what he wanted the artist to do. He was further nettled because Francis offered him a lower annual salary than he had paid Leonardo. Finally Cellini decided to visit the Holy Land, but Francis sent in pursuit a group of men who convinced the sculptor-goldsmith to return. The most famous of the works of art he executed during the remainder of his stay was the salt cellar with the two nude figures which he made for Francis. Cellini discusses this work in great detail in his autobiography. But Cellini's penchant for antagonizing people soon involved him in many quarrels, in lawsuits, and in several duels. Francis who regarded Cellini as a genius overlooked all the involvements until the artist incurred the enmity of the Duchess d'Etampes, the king's mistress. When Cellini was advised that he had aroused the royal anger, he finally realized that he had overstayed his welcome; hence he quickly and quietly departed for Italy.

The king's penchant for building magnificent palaces was an important factor in the development of French architecture. What he saw on his first visit to Italy moved him to order the construction of palaces at Fontainebleau, Saint Germain, and Chambord. He also began the reconstruction of the palace of the Louvre. It should be mentioned, however, that Italian influences did not predominate in these buildings. Italian Renaissance features did find a place in the architectural plans, in the ornamentation of the facades, and in the interior decorations, but in the main the structures were traditionally French. This compromise between the old French and the new Renaissance forms and elements set the style until the middle of the sixteenth century. The example which Francis set was followed by many noblemen. From one end of France to the other, Renaissance chateaux replaced the old feudal fortresses. Unfortunately most of the chateaux built at that time have disappeared.

Besides encouraging the development of the arts, Francis was also instrumental in promoting the growth of humanism. This he did, for example, by encouraging native humanists and by inviting foreign humanists to settle in France. Francis tried to induce Erasmus to add lustre to the royal court, but "the prince of humanists" preferred freedom and peace to becoming involved in court intrigues or to engaging in controversy with the Sorbonne, the theological branch of the University of Paris. Francis further aided the cause of humanism by encouraging native printers to print classical works and by advising French humanists to import the classical works they could not find in France. The royal envoys were instructed to make the most of any opportunity to acquire rare manuscripts. That the royal orders were not without results is demonstrated by the fact that in 1541 the French ambassador to Venice sent the king four boxes of manuscripts. Francis even sent a special agent to search for manuscripts in Constantinople, Syria, and Egypt. The manuscripts and books the agents collected were added to the royal library at Fontainebleau which was later incorporated into the Bibliothèque Nationale in Paris. The greatest of Francis' contributions to the advancement of humanism was the founding of the Collège de France, a school which specialized in the teaching of Latin, Greek, and Hebrew as preliminary to the study of the classics. Although the Sorbonne fulminated against the plan to cultivate humanism, labeling the school "a nursery for heretics," the king was firm in protecting the new institution which flourished as the number of professorial chairs gradually increased and mathematics and science were added to the curriculum.

In imitation of some of the Renaissance courts in Italy, Francis also displayed much pomp and ceremony at his court. After seeing the splendid courts of the more prosperous rulers in Italy the French king became determined that his court must be more brilliant than any court in Italy. He was so successful in achieving his aim that his court became by far the most brilliant in all of Europe. It was also the largest court any European monarch had ever put on display. Nobles who had lost their feudal rights were given a new purpose in life, that of serving as decorations at the royal court. Some received high-sounding titles and performed special duties. The Grand Chamberlain, for example, had charge of the royal bedchamber. He had four assistants called First Lords-in-Waiting, and there were also Lords of the Bedchamber whose number varied from twenty to fifty-four. The queen had her noble attendants with highsounding titles, and there were others for the princes and princesses. So that the nobles could afford to dress extravagantly Francis distributed pensions and gifts with a lavish hand. In dress and ornamentation he himself set the style with clothes made of the finest fabrics, embellished with gold and silver; even his buttons and hooks were made of pure gold. His courtiers tried to imitate this extravagant dress.

At the royal court the women were second only to the king as primary objects of glorification. They were the king's special court decorations. Francis shared the opinion of the chronicler Pierre de Brantôme who said, "A court without women is like a garden without flowers." On formal occasions the ladies of the court wore costly dresses of velvet and silk, or gold and silver cloth, embroidered or brocaded, and often in flamboyant colors. At times the matter of dress was carried to ludicrous lengths. For example, for her marriage to the duke of Cleves the king's niece, who was thirteen at the time, wore a dress of cloth of gold which was so heavy that she had to be carried into the church. Such spectacles impressed the French masses, but they were also a source of much merriment and satire.

State affairs were celebrated with magnificence on a grand scale. When Francis I and Henry VIII of England met for the first time (1520), their meeting place in France (between Guinès and Ardres) was decorated so lavishly that it had since become known as "the Field of the Cloth of Gold." No less than three hundred tents decked inside and out with gold cloth were erected to house the courtiers and attendants of the French king. For the occasion Francis himself wore a mantle of gold and over it a cape of gold leaf set with diamonds and rubies. On his head he wore a velvet beret ornamented with precious stones. The nobles attending the king changed their attire twice each day and at the great balls at night they appeared in fantastically decorated dresses. The display of such magnificence in dress moved one chronicler to remark that the French nobles had all their possessions on their backs.

Francis was so restless that he could not stay at one place for any length of time. It has been said that the king followed his whim and that the court followed the king. As a result the members of the court led a sort of nomad life, constantly moving from town to town, from camp to camp, from feast to feast. When the members of the court moved from place to place they were accompanied by their staffs. Benvenuto Cellini reported that "the king in time of peace travels with upwards of twelve hundred horses and a retinue of several hundred persons." Although the courtiers rode on the horses, the myriad of servants proceeded on foot. It must have been a motley procession. If at nightfall the caravan arrived at some place where there were only a few houses, tents had to be erected. This moving from place to place did not inflict hardships on the king, for a group of his servants always preceded him by some hours to prepare his accommodations. They carried with them the king's bed, his bedroom furniture, and also oriental rugs and draperies. As the chronicler Brantôme put it, "Whether he is in a village, in a forest or at the assembly he is treated as though he were in Paris." But the courtiers complained bitterly about the hardships and the expense of this gypsy-like existence. Foreign ambassadors who were obliged to accompany the king also grumbled loudly.

Margaret of Navarre and the Heptameron

The central female figure of the French Renaissance was Margaret or Marguerite of Navarre, the sister of Francis I. Raised and educated with her brother, she received an education which was unusual for a woman in that age. She had a taste for literature and a lively appreciation of the arts. She could read Latin freely and, it is reported, also read some of the works of Plato and the Greek dramatists. Her mother, Louise of Savoy, also taught her Italian, enabling her to read Dante's *Divine Comedy* and Petrarch's sonnets in Italian. Margaret also possessed a poetic gift which won for her a place in the history of French literature. She wrote so much poetry on so many different subjects that one critic referred to her output as "poetry unlimited." Her poetry reflects the influence of both Dante and Petrarch. When Francis ascended the French throne in 1515 she quickly became one of the brightest stars of the court firmament. She was gay in speech, joyous in spirit, and physically attractive in her prime. She had many admirers and was married twice. Her title Margaret of Navarre derives from her marriage to King Henry of Navarre who ruled a small country bordering on the Pyrenees, and who later became Henry IV of France.

Like Francis I, Margaret did much to encourage the development of arts and letters in France. It was probably she who kept her brother's interest at high pitch during his later life. While she was in Navarre her court was the most celebrated literary center of her time. She welcomed most of the men of letters from learned intellectuals to popular poets. She was their friend and protector. Not a few of them enjoyed her patronage in the form of a pension or employment on her household staff. When the poet Clement Marot showed his sympathy with the religious reformers too openly and was denounced as a heretic by the faculty of the Sorbonne, it was Margaret's plea to her brother which secured his release. Besides giving the poets and literary men of her time oral encouragement, she carried on a wide correspondence with other men of learning. Among the latter was Erasmus who in a letter to her expressed his admiration of her many gifts.

The literary work of Margaret of Navarre which is most widely remembered is the *Heptameron* (Seven Days), a collection of stories in imitation of Boccaccio's *Decameron.* The framework employed by Margaret was clearly borrowed from Boccaccio. A group of five noble ladies and five noblemen who have spent some time in the Pyrenees are unable to return to their homes because of rains, swollen rivers, and floods, so they whiled away the time telling stories. Margaret had hoped to emulate Boccaccio in the number of tales she included in her work, but ill health forced her to conclude the project after she had written seventy stories. Hence, whereas the story-telling continued for a period of ten days in the *Decameron,* it ended after seven days in the *Heptameron.* One difference between the two works is that the characters in the *Heptameron* are on a higher social level than those in the *Decameron.* Margaret herself stated in the prologue to her work that her stories differ from those of the *Decameron* in that she endeavored to tell the truth. Like the stories of Boccaccio those of Margaret are at times witty, and often coarse and lascivious. This cannot, however, be ascribed to youthful folly, for Margaret was a mature middle-aged woman when she wrote the *Heptameron.* It is not easy to believe that the same mind which conceived religious poems whose every line breathes devotion could have produced the profane, gross, and at times grotesque stories of the *Heptameron.* The licentiousness of the stories coupled with a strange concern for religion, and also occasional ventures into freethinking, give the work a definite Renaissance flavor.

Margaret's purpose in writing the *Heptameron* appears to have been to provide reading matter for her brother Francis whom she adored and whose health was failing. In the *Heptameron* she repeatedly pictures him as the embodiment of chivalric courage and extraordinary magnanimity. Her admiration for her brother is such that she even commends him for stopping at a church for prayer on his way home from an illicit affair with the wife of a friend. Some literary critics feel that her purpose of writing to amuse her brother explains the coarseness and licentiousness of her tales. They are qualities which Francis seemed to enjoy in the literature he read. To Margaret's credit it must be said that she tried to offset the gross and licentious adventures she related by advocating faith in God, denouncing corruption, and moralizing on various subjects. The literary grace of the stories is such that it has convinced certain critics that some of the professional writers Margaret befriended had a hand in the writing of the book.

French Humanism

The French humanists who achieved prominence were but a small group in comparison with the Italian humanists; yet their influence stirred a wide interest in the classics with the result that classical learning became the basis of higher education in the liberal arts. The purposes of French humanism, like those of German humanism, were largely religious. This was due to the persistence of religious traditions and to the lack of such secular sponsorship as that of the Medici and Sforza which Italian humanism enjoyed. Consequently Greek and Hebrew were largely used by professional scholars in a critical approach to the Greek New Testament and Hebrew Old Testament. Even this met with opposition. A group of theologians, including many members of the Sorbonne faculty, opposed the critical approach to the New Testament because they feared it might breed heresy. For example, the publication in 1550 of Robert Estienne's edition of the Greek New Testament was greeted with a storm of disapproval. But French humanism was not entirely devoted to religious purposes. There were many men of learning, such as Rabelais and Montaigne, who read the classics for their content.

French humanism, embracing the study of both Latin and Greek classics, did not become a full-fledged movement until the end of the fifteenth century. There were, however, a number of prominent humanists in France at the end of the fourteenth and during the early fifteenth century. One of these was Nicholas de Clemanges (1367-1437) who has been called "one of the fathers of the humanist movement." His interests were limited to the Latin classics and his purpose in reading them was to improve his Latin style and his ability as an orator, for he was one of the great preachers of that time. His favorite classical writer was Cicero. He read Cicero's *Orations* so many times that he could repeat many of them from memory. Another prominent early humanist was Jean de Montreuil (1354-1418) who learned his humanism in Italy where he met many of the humanists of that time. His great hero among Italian humanists was Petrarch. In France his great enthusiasm for the classics was instrumental in arousing the interest of many. If the two foregoing humanists formed the first generation, there was no second one. Interest in humanism seems to have declined for a time. Perhaps the last and most devastating phase of the Hundred Years War which ended in 1453 was fatal to the interest in the classics. After the war ended, however, and normal conditions began to prevail, a renewed interest manifested itself. Students began to travel to Italy in larger numbers to study humanism, and Italian humanists crossed the Alps to visit France. Among the latter was Pico della Mirandola who remained in Paris from 1485 to 1488.

Meanwhile the study of Greek and the Greek classics had assumed increasing importance. A number of French students had returned from Italy with a knowledge of Greek early in the fifteenth century, but it was not until after the Hundred Years War that French universities began to offer courses in Greek and the Greek classics. The first or one of the first universities to introduce the study of Greek into its curriculum was the University of Paris where Gregorias Tifernas, who had studied under Chrysoloras, taught Greek for a time beginning in 1456. Once the study of Greek was established on a wider scale, it was no longer used merely for Biblical scholarship or for the study of the early Church Fathers. Knowledge of Greek became a cultural distinction or a status symbol. Members of the wealthy bourgeoisie spared no expense to get the best possible teachers of Greek in order to give their offspring the benefit of a knowledge of Greek. According to contemporary accounts Girolamo Aleandro who taught Greek in Paris in 1508 had as many as two thousand students in his audience. By this time France was training its own Hellenists so that it could become independent of teachers from Italy and Greece. Some idea of the breadth and depth of Greek studies may be gained from the fact that during the first half of the sixteenth century many Greek works were printed in France. It has been calculated, for example, that from 1526 to 1550 no fewer than 116 editions of one or more works of Aristotle were turned out by the French press, 64 of them in Paris.

The most distinguished Greek scholar of the day, as Erasmus was the ranking Latinist, was Guillaume Budé or Budaeus (1468-1540). The French humanist Dolet called him "the light of his age." Not until he was twenty-six did Budé begin to study Greek; then he became so interested in the beauty of the language and the literature that he decided to achieve a mastery of both. It is reported that he became so absorbed in the study of Greek that he forgot to appear for his wedding. Greek language and literature remained his real love for the rest of his life. In his correspondence with Erasmus, Budé often wrote long passages in Greek, but Erasmus contented himself by replying with an occasional Greek word or phrase. Budé's reputation for learning soon attracted the attention of King Francis I. Besides using Budé as a court ornament, King Francis sent him on various diplomatic errands and employed him as a secretary. It was Budé who drew up the plans for and played the leading part in the establishment of the Collège Royal (Collège de France). Through his writings Budé won great intellectual prestige for France. In 1515 he published a treatise on the monetary systems of Greece and Rome with a detailed discussion of antique coins and their variations in purchasing power. This treatise, which made a profound impression, was probably the first detailed study on economic history by a French scholar. Budé also wrote an important study on the importance of the classics and history in an educational curriculum, but as Budé wanted to avoid comparison with a similar study by Erasmus he did not publish his work. It was, however, given to the public after his death. Another work, his *Commentaries on the Greek Language* (1529), is a monumental study which contains more than seven thousand critical discussions of problems in Greek grammar with quotations from the works of many Greek authors. Budé also wrote a number of other treatises on linguistics and translated treatises on a variety of subjects from Greek into Latin so that more people could read them.

The most prominent French humanist during the middle decades of the sixteenth century was Robert Estienne whose activities as a humanist and printer were discussed in Chapter 8. After the middle of the century the attention which had previously been devoted to humanism was largely absorbed by the religious controversy aroused by the Reformation.

The Rise of Secular Literature in France

Whereas the troubadour songs of love and adventure were the forerunners of much of the lyric poetry of the Renaissance, it was the fabliaux which ushered in the period of realistic literature. The fabliau is a short comic tale in verse dealing with real or possible situations. Most of those which have survived come from northern France and are invariably written in eight-syllable couplets. The first fabliaux seem to have appeared in the twelfth century, but most of them were written in the thirteenth century and in the early part of the fourteenth. The underlying purpose of the composers was entertainment, more specifically laughter. Many were probably written by professional entertainers (jongleurs), and others were composed by wandering scholars, renegade monks, and unfrocked priests. They were recited in taverns or before gatherings of townspeople to provide pastime for the long winter evenings. The more clever narrators would on occasion write new fabliaux or refurbish old ones.

The comedy of the fabliaux is of a somewhat satirical nature occupying itself with every rank or class from the peasant to the king. The leading character in most of the stories is *la femme* and the mainspring of the action is love of a baser sort. A favorite theme is the faithless and cunning wife who outwits the jealous, but stupid husband. On occasion, however, the tables are turned in favor of the husband as in the fabliau in which he disguises himself as a priest and hears his wife's confession. A typical plot depicts a wife, surprised by the unexpected return of her husband, hiding her lover under a tub she had borrowed from a neighbor. At the psychological moment the neighbor appears and demands the return of his tub. The wife is, however, equal to the situation. She extricates herself from the dilemma by bribing a passerby to shout "Fire!" In another fabliau the wife hides her lover behind the door when her husband returns unexpectedly. As the husband enters the wife asks him, "What would you do if you found a man in the house?" Drawing his sword the husband replies, "Kill him." To this the wife responds, "Oh no you wouldn't! I'd fling a cloak over your head like this, and he would escape." The lover takes advantage of the situation to do so. Another favorite subject is man's greed. Again and again in the fabliaux man encompasses his downfall because he is unable to control his greed for worldly goods.

Although written as simple and unpretentious verse, the fabliaux contain all the elements of the modern short story. Prose writers widened and deepened the plots, put them into prose form, and the result was the modern short story. Boccaccio, for example, borrowed the plots for a number of his *Decameron* stories from fabliaux. Chaucer took not a few of the *Canterbury Tales* directly from fabliaux. In Germany Hans Sachs was indebted to the fabliaux for some of his plots. But it was in France that the fabliaux exerted the greatest influence. There they preceded and paved the way for much of the secular Renaissance literature. They established a trend which led directly to the collection of tales known as *Les Cent Nouvelles Nouvelles*, to the *Heptameron* of Margaret of Navarre, and Rabelais' *Gargantua* and *Pantagruel*. Later Molière built his farce *Le Médecin Malgré Lui* on a plot taken from the fabliau "Vilain Mire" (Peasant Doctor). The humorous tradition was also kept alive by La Fontaine who appropriated the story of Gombert, the miller's wife, from a fabliau.

In the field of lyric poetry the fourteenth century was not a fruitful age. The greatest poetic figure of the century was Guillaume de Machaut (1300-1377) whose place in the history of music has been discussed in Chapter 12. At his death he left 80,000 lines of verse, most of it in manuscript form. His best known work is *Voir Dit* (1363) in which he takes the reader into the world of his personal experiences. As Dante had his Beatrice and Petrarch his Laura, Machaut had his Péronnelle. As a young lady of seventeen she feel in love with him as a result of reading his poetry and a long correspondence followed. Much of the poetry Machaut wrote during the later years was addressed to her. One of his verses reads:

White as the lily, than the rose more red,
Outshining far the ruby of the East!
To see your peerless beauty being led
White as the lily, than the rose more red
So charmed am I straightway my heart is sped
Humbly to serve you where true love holds feast.
White as the lily, than the rose more red
Outshining far the ruby of the East!

The idyl ended quite suddenly when Péronnelle finally met the gouty old poet. In his time Machaut was highly esteemed as a master of lyric poetry and ranked beside Petrarch. Chaucer paid Machaut the compliment of imitating him in *The Book of the Duchess.*

The last half of the fourteenth and much of the fifteenth century were, as stated earlier, a period of recurring epidemics, almost constant war, and economic depression. The thoughts and troubles of this time found expression in the poetry of François Villon (*c.*1431-1463), vagabond, burglar, and careless "Bohemian." In his poetry he broke so completely with tradition that some literary historians have called him "the first modern poet." Much of his poetry is trivial, obscure, and awkward, but the remainder earned for him a high rank in the history of French poetry. He is the most personal of poets, he himself being the principal subject of his poetry. Born into a poor family whose name was Montcorbier, François borrowed the name "Villon" from a benefactor. He received a good education, earning the degrees of Bachelor of Arts and Master of Arts at the University of Paris. But during this time he became a member of a gang which engaged in street brawls, thievery, robberies, and other disreputable acts. In 1455 Villon killed a priest in a street brawl, but was pardoned because his victim had struck the first blow and before dying had asked for mercy for his attacker. Several years of quiet followed during which he wrote *Les Lais* (The Legs), known as *Petit Testament.* Soon he was in trouble again. In 1457 he was arrested as a member of a gang which stole a large sum of money from the Collège de Navarre, but was released when Louis XI proclaimed a general amnesty at his accession in 1461. During the succeeding months he wrote his *Grand Testament.* In 1562 he was, however, arrested for participating in a street brawl and this time sentenced to be hanged in chains. While awaiting execution Villon wrote the macabre, but much admired "Ballade des Pendus" which has also been called "Epitaph in the Form of a Ballad." It reads in part:

Yea, we conjure you, look not with disdain,
Brothers, on us, though we to death were done
By justice. Well you know, the saving grain
Of sense springs not in every mother's son.

. . . .

We are whiles scoured and soddened of the rain
And whiles burnt up and blackened of the sun;
Corbies and pyets have our eyes out ta'en,
And plucked our beard and hair out one by one.
Whether by night or day rest have we none:
Now here, now there, as the wind shifts its stead,
We swing and creak and rattle overhead,
No thimble dented like our bird-pecked face.
Brothers, have heed and shun the life we led:
The rather pray, God grant us of his grace!

(*Translation by John Payne, 1874*)

But Villon managed to cheat the gallows. Influential friends succeeded in having the sentence commuted to banishment from Paris for ten years. At this time he dropped out of sight completely; so that nothing is known of the time and manner of his death.

Villon's *Petit Testament* and *Grand Testament* are autobiographical. Their importance lies in the fact that they present a real flesh-and-blood human being for the first time in the history of French literature. The verses he left relate the story of his crimes, misfortunes, sufferings, and degradations. He offers no feigned repentance for his life of crime, ascribing his evil deeds to his weakness, his inability to keep from sinning. In his time his poetry enjoyed a popularity rarely granted to the works of living poets, but today his verses are not easy to understand because most of the places and things to which they refer have disappeared. Nevertheless, some of Villon's verses have continued to enjoy a considerable popularity. Literary historians have suggested that Villon was the model for Rabelais's description of Panurge. In the nineteenth century Villon's verses fascinated many literary men, among them Victor Hugo and Robert Louis Stevenson. Swinburne translated a number of Villon's ballads into English. Probably the best known translation is that of the "Ballad of Old-Time Ladies" by Dante Gabriel Rosetti, rendered with the doleful refrain: "Where are the snows of yesteryear?"

The first definitely secular and popular work of prose literature was not circulated in France until about 1460 or shortly after the conclusion of the Hundred Years War. It was *Les Cent Nouvelles Nouvelles*, a work of uncertain authorship. The plots of the hundred short humorous tales were not new. Many of them were taken from fabliaux and from the *Facetiae* of the Italian humanist Poggio Bracciolini. In addition to other evidence, the fact that there are one hundred stories points to the influence of Boccaccio's *Decameron* which had been translated into French in 1414. Written in everyday French, these comic tales are more impersonal and also more indecent than those of Boccaccio. They were most avidly read by the bourgeoisie whose interests and feelings they portray. In the first half of the sixteenth century other such collections appeared, culminating in the *Heptameron* of Margaret of Navarre.

François Rabelais

François Rabelais (*c.*1490-1553) was the first French writer of popular prose whose writings reflect undeniable genius. Literary historians regard him as the real creator of the modern French novel. As a representative of the Renaissance he embodies in his person more Renaissance trends and tendencies than any other figure of the time. First, he exhibited a real zest for life on this earth, which to him was worth while for itself. He believed that each individual possesses in an eminent degree the ability to enjoy the pleasures of mundane existence. His writings display more gusto for life than those of any other prose writer of the Renaissance. Second, the range of Rabelais's knowledge, like that of other prominent figures of the Renaissance, was encyclopedic. He surveyed the whole field of knowledge then known, including theology, jurisprudence, astronomy, botany, chemistry, and medicine. Besides acquiring a thorough knowledge of French, he studied Latin, Greek, Hebrew, Italian, and Spanish. He associated and corresponded with the most learned men of his day, including Erasmus and Budé. The breadth of his knowledge has been compared with that of Goethe. Whereas Goethe's culture was delicate, that of Rabelais mirrors the coarseness of his time. But Rabelais had a deep sense of humor which Goethe lacked. Third, Rabelais shared the contempt with which many leading thinkers of the Renaissance regarded the so-called "Gothic ages." His distaste was especially strong for asceticism, mysticism, scholasticism, and formalism. Fourth, Rabelais was also a staunch advocate of progressive education, urging that real knowledge rather than forms and words be imparted to the young. Fifth, his ideas and ideals reflect a strong belief in man's inherent goodness and in his infinite possibilities for improvement. Like the Italian Pico della Mirandola, Rabelais was convinced that man can make of himself whatever he desires to be. Finally, Rabelais manifested a certain indifference to organized religion. In this he followed in the footsteps of many Renaissance thinkers. Although he did not leave the Roman Catholic Church in which he was born and ordained a priest, it is certainly no exaggeration to state that he was not a good Catholic. His writings leave the impression that he regarded Christianity as an outworn religion. In his criticism of religious abuses he included Calvin and his followers as well as the Roman Catholic Church. His own religion has been defined as "a vague, but not cold or unemotional deism."

Researchers have found only limited facts regarding Rabelais' life. This is equally true of the other two great literary masters which the sixteenth century produced, Shakespeare and Cervantes. There is enough information on Rabelais, however, to present a fair conception of his life. Although it is known that he was born at Chinon which he called "the garden of France," the date of his birth is still a subject of controversy. As a young man he became a Franciscan friar and was later ordained a priest. During this period he developed a passion for study which remained with him for the rest of his life. Two letters to Guillaume Budé which have survived show that the head of the Franciscan Order was disturbed because young Rabelais read so omnivorously. He sought to check the young friar's ardor by confiscating some of the books that were suspect, but later returned them. Rabelais soon chafed under the rules and restrictions the order imposed on its members. The scathing criticism he later poured on monasticism has been ascribed to the experiences of his early years. In 1524 he was given permission to leave the Franciscan Order to join the Benedictines. As a Benedictine monk, however, he was still unhappy and after several years took "French leave" from the monastery to wander about the country for some time. The year 1530 saw him studying medicine at Montpellier and two years later he was a practising physician at a hospital in Lyons.

The years from 1532 to Rabelais' death in 1553 were filled with manifold professional and literary activities. Besides his work as a physician he gave lectures on the works of Galen and Hippocrates, often demonstrating his knowledge by dissecting cadavers before his classes. He also edited a volume of Hippocrates's *Aphorisms* and an edition of Galen's *Ars Parva*. In 1532 he also started writing *Gargantua* and *Pantagruel*, the books which made his name immortal. There has been much controversy regarding Rabelais' reasons for writing them and whether he wrote the first book of *Pantagruel* before he wrote *Gargantua*. The writing of these books was not the primary purpose of his life, but rather an avocation, perhaps a means of relaxation. When the day's work was done he would sit down to give free rein to his fancy and then put his thoughts on paper with a genial exuberance. The two names "Gargantua" and "Pantagruel" were not unknown before Rabelais; in fact, both names had appeared in several books of small literary value shortly before Rabelais began writing. Of the five books which comprise Rabelais' romance, one is devoted to Gargantua and the other four to Pantagruel. The book of *Gargantua* and the first book of *Pantagruel* were probably written in 1532. The second and third books appeared during the succeeding years and the fourth book was not published until eleven years after the death of Rabelais. For this and other reasons doubt has been cast on the authorship of the fourth book of *Pantagruel*. The first book of the five relates the story of the birth, education, and exploits of Gargantua, a man of gigantic proportions and an enormous appetite from which the adjective "gargantuan" derives. Pantagruel, the son of Gargantua, is also a giant with an appetite which matches that of his father.

The books of *Gargantua* and *Pantagruel* are a strange medley of satire, humor, buffoonery, coarseness, encyclopedic erudition, and common sense. They have been called more witty, more unclean, more caustic, more penetrating than any other books of the time. As regards humor, they rank among the wittiest books of all time. Even their coarseness is probably unsurpassed in the history of literature. It must be stated, however, that if Rabelais was coarse, he was never prurient. His offense is one against good taste, not against morals. But to say that Rabelais was a mere merry-andrew who wrote down the burlesque adventures of Gargantua and Pantagruel just for fun would be to ignore the real Rabelais. His buffoonery and coarseness of expression disguised his real purpose which was to pour scorn and censure on the opinions and errors, follies and foibles, crimes and evils of the day. He denounced and satirized in a spirit not unlike that of Erasmus, by whom he was greatly influenced. In order to make his indictments more devastating he drew on the whole of classical and contemporary learning for contributions to his arsenal of mockery. While handing out his uncommon good sense and wise counsel he also wielded the dunghill pitchfork. It was the technique he adopted to escape the penalty for attacking corruption and inefficiency in high places. Although the coarse humor repelled some, others read it and shook with laughter, at the same time realizing the biting satire inherent in it. Whereas Erasmus wrote in Latin which only a few could read, Rabelais employed the French vernacular which the masses, the bourgeoisie, and the upper classes could understand.

In his books Rabelais aims his satirical shafts at many targets. Among those he attacks are fanatics, pedants, bigots, and medical quacks. He scores the imperialistic ambitions of princes, the arid disputations of the schoolmen, and the despoilers of religion. But he reserved the sharpest attacks for the monks and friars whom he chided for their sloth, their filth, their ignorance, their arrogance, and their intolerance. "They are," he wrote, "contemptible drones, useless to society. They mock God with their ave's and litanies recited by rote, and they have no better occupation than to make love to their neighbors' wives." He also derided the religious superstitions which they turned into a source of personal profit. "Go home," Grandgousier, the father of Gargantua, enjoins the pilgrims, "abandon these vain journeys and live as the apostle bids you." In the *Book of Gargantua* Rabelais also presents a picture of his ideal monastery. It is the Abbey of Thélème where the members of both sexes are admitted and the basic rule is "Fais ce que tu voudras" (Do what you wish to do). Rabelais was convinced that well-bred, well-educated, and unrestrained persons not only shun vice, but are also impelled to live a virtuous life.

The most constructive contributions Rabelais made were probably in the field of education. His ideas on education are original and forceful, and in some respects anticipated modern scientific methods. Starting from the premise that scholastic education was obsolescent and a waste of time, he proposed a broader and more practical system. His curriculum would, in addition to languages, include astronomy, mathematics, geography, history, philosophy, law, and elementary medicine. Noteworthy also is the fact that he put special emphasis on physical education. His purpose, in short, was to educate youth in such a way that it would "not be ignorant of anything that exists." In looking back to the recent past he found that considerable progress had already been made. Thus he wrote:

> The old learning is now restored. The ancient languages, without which it is a shame for anyone to call himself learned, are studied again: Hebrew, Chaldean, Latin. There are correct and beautiful editions printed, an art invented in my own age by divine inspiration, as much as on the other hand artillery is the invention of the devil. All the world is full of learned men and wise teachers, large libraries; and I believe that never in the time of Plato, Cicero, or Papinian, has there been such a convenience for study as one sees now. . . . I see brigands, executioners, and vagabonds now who are more learned than the doctors and preachers were when I was young.

Rabelais was also optimistic about the future. He predicted the rise of a new spirit of inquiry inspired by the determination to discover the truth. He had a strong faith in scientific progress, a progress based on observation and experiment.

The caustic wit, the biting satire, and the unbridled obscenity made the *Books of Gargantua and Pantagruel* popular with the members of all classes. The *Book of Gargantua*, for example, was purchased so avidly that Rabelais was moved to state, "More copies of it have been sold in two months than there will be of the Bible in nine years." As the other books appeared they were also widely read. In present-day France, public interest in the *Books of Gargantua and Pantagruel* is limited because Rabelais's French is archaic. In England a number of excellent translations have kept alive the interest in Rabelais' books. In the English-speaking world generally Rabelais' work is better known and more frequently read than any other work of the French Renaissance. As for Rabelais himself, he is ranked among the great literary masters of all time by practically all literary historians. In his knowledge of human nature Rabelais was probably surpassed only by Shakespeare. Panurge, Grandgousier, and Father John as well as Gargantua and Pantagruel have become definite types in literature.

French Literature in the Second Half of the Sixteenth Century

The most prominent literary figure during the later decades of the sixteenth century was Michel de Montaigne (1533-1592). Like Rabelais, Montaigne was a social critic; in fact, some of the criticisms Rabelais leveled at the social order were developed further in Montaigne's *Essays*, the work which made him famous. The best way to know Montaigne is to read his *Essays*, for they are a rich revelation of the man, particularly of his intellect. As he put it, "I am myself the subject of my book." When King Henry III told the author that he liked his book, Montaigne replied, "Then your majesty must like me, for my book is myself." The *Essays* reveal their author's opinions and tastes, likes and dislikes, in considerable detail. He states, for example, that he prefers white wine to red, that he derives pleasure from scratching his ear, and that he can relax better with his legs raised. Few writers have revealed their minds in their writings so completely. But the *Essays* are not a systematic autobiography. The bits and pieces of self-revelation must be put together like the pieces of a jig-saw puzzle. Montaigne was convinced that in portraying himself he was writing about all mankind since "every man has within himself the whole form of human nature."

Who was this man who revealed himself in so detailed a fashion in the *Essays*? He was the grandson of a bourgeois merchant who achieved nobility through the purchase of the Chateau Montaigne and its estates. It is from these holdings that the title "de Montaigne" derives. Michel's father, Pierre, had his own ideas regarding the education of his son. He decided, for example, that his son must not be subjected to sudden nervous shocks; hence a musical instrument was played at the boy's bedside each morning to awaken him. The father further decreed that his son must learn Latin before he learned French. To achieve this he engaged a German teacher who could not speak French. Furthermore, all members of the household were ordered to address him only in Latin. "It is not to be imagined," Montaigne wrote, "how great a boon this was for the whole family. In this way my father and mother learned enough Latin to understand it and so did those of the servants who were with me most." As a teenager he left the parental roof to study law and upon the completion of his studies his father obtained a magistracy for him. In 1557 he became a member of the Parlement of Bordeaux, thus occupying at the early age of twenty-four a seat on the bench of a supreme court of justice. At the age of thirty-five he became the lord or seigneur of Montaigne as a result of the death of his father and older brothers. Soon thereafter he seems to have conceived the idea of doffing the long robes of justice for the purpose of retiring to his estates, as he put it, "to pass in repose as much of my life as remained to me." This resolution he carried out in 1571 at the age of thirty-eight. Montaigne explained his retirement from public life in this way: "I would shun not so much the throng of men as the importunity of affairs." Montaigne, it appears, had a distaste for his judicial functions. Furthermore, as a man of broad tolerance he disliked the religious fanaticism which animated some of the magistrates at Bordeaux.

Most of the rest of his life Montaigne spent on his estates. The principal events of his life after his retirement were a visit to Italy, one or two journeys to Paris to arrange for the publication of his *Essays*, and his mayoralty of Bordeaux which was forced on him against his wishes. The rest of his time he largely spent in the famous circular tower-room of his chateau, a room which was decorated with quotations from the classics and mottoes of various kinds. It was in this room that he wrote his *Essays*. Montaigne's purpose in writing them was not to achieve fame. He merely wished to record his thoughts and opinions for his friends. Writing the *Essays* was thus an outlet for the thoughts he garnered from the books he read and for the opinions he developed during his meditations. It was only after the first two books of *Essays* were published in 1580 that their favorable reception by the public convinced him of their value. The fact that his *Essays* are in a sense his intellectual autobiography does not mean that he himself is the subject of every essay. Actually the range of topics on which he wrote is a very wide one. Some of the titles of his *Essays* are: "The Custom of Wearing Clothes," "On Idleness," "On the Education of Children," "On the Useful and the Honorable," "On some Verses of Virgil," "On the Inequality that is between Us," "Observations on Julius Caesar's Methods of Making War," "On Smells," "On Pedantry," and "On War Horses."

Montaigne's *Essays* reflect various Renaissance trends. One of these is his deep interest in the classics. Few, if any, of the scholars of the Renaissance period possessed so broad and thorough a knowledge of the Latin classics. The classical writers were for him the great authorities on all questions concerning life on earth; hence the plethora of quotations from the classics in support of his statements. Montaigne's interest in mundane life was profound. Like Rabelais he believed that this life is worth while for itself. He even advanced a step beyond Rabelais when he attempted to interpret life in secular terms without recourse to religious and metaphysical literature. But Montaigne did not share the optimism of the early Renaissance leaders. At the time Montaigne wrote his *Essays* it was clear that the idea of a golden age which was to be ushered in by the new education and culture had been a mirage. Two of the most prominent characteristics of his day were bigotry and intolerance on the part of both Protestants and Catholics. Religious frenzy was running amok, venting itself in tortures, brutalities, and finally the massacre of St. Bartholomew (1572). In a world of fanaticism and strife when blind adherence to factional dogmatism was demanded, Montaigne sought inner freedom and peace of mind in introspection and self-analysis.

Montaigne's *Essays* hold a high place in the history of literature. They taught his contemporaries and future generations the delights of the essay. Among the French literary figures whose writings reflect Montaigne's ideas were La Rochefoucauld, Molière, and La Fontaine. Although Pascal detested Montaigne as a pagan, he read the *Essays* until Montaigne's ideas became his own. Montesquieu and Rousseau regarded Montaigne as a great master. The sixteenth-century essayist was a precursor of Rousseau in at least one respect. He believed that man was happy in his primitive state and that his happiness was gradually undermined by the rise of artificial conventions. In referring to the American Indians, for example, he stated, "They are governed by the laws of nature, as yet but little corrupted by ours." Soon after Montaigne's death his *Essays* were translated into a vivid and picturesque Elizabethan English by John Florio. There is in the British Museum a copy of this translation with what may be Shakespeare's autograph on the fly leaf. In any case, Montaigne's *Essays* inspired many lines in Shakespeare's plays from *Hamlet* to *The Tempest*. Sir Francis Bacon used Montaigne's title for his own essays and in his first essay quotes Montaigne with a reference to the source of his quotation. The influence of Montaigne's *Essays* also made itself felt across the ocean in America. Two men upon whom they made a deep impression were Thoreau and Emerson. Upon discovering a copy of them in his father's library the latter wrote, "It seemed to me as if I had written the book in some former life, so sincerely it spoke to my thought and experience."

To many readers the name "Montaigne" suggests "the great sceptic." More scepticism has, in fact, been ascribed to him than is justified by the facts. He did question all established dogmas, but he did not repudiate them. The fact that he refrained from rejecting any of them may possibly be attributed to his desire for personal safety in an age in which heresy hunters were ever on the watch. Montaigne has been styled everything from a good Catholic to an avowed agnostic. It is, however, impossible to put a definite label on his thoughts, for he was not a systematic thinker. What can be stated is that articles of faith and dogma no longer occupied the center of his thinking. The human capacity to know the truth appeared to him so weak that he sought to avoid dogmatic assertions and extreme judgments while retaining strong convictions of his own.

In poetry the work of the Pléiade reflected the humanist influence. The Pléiade came into existence when seven poets with kindred ideas about poetry decided to join forces in order to effect a literary revolution. The name by which the group is known derives from the Pleiades, a constellation of seven stars. The members of this group aimed to give French poetry refinement and to improve the French language so that it could serve as the vehicle for the new poetry. The observation that Italian poets had studied classical poetry as a means of giving their own work greater refinement and quality of style caused them to advocate the same method to raise French poetry to a higher level. The motive power behind their aims was their enthusiasm for classical culture and their admiration for Italian poetry. They would replace such traditional forms as rondeaux and ballades with odes, sonnets, epics, and epigrams. It was through their efforts that the alexandrine or twelve-syllable line became the principal meter of French poetry. The program of the group was stated in Joachim du Bellay's *Défense et Illustration de la Langue Française* (1549), the first French work of literary criticism. In it he urged his fellow countrymen to attain for French literature the same greatness achieved by the Italians and to employ the same methods. The poverty of the French language, he stated, is no valid excuse for failing to create a distinguished literature, because French can equal Greek and Latin in richess and dignity if additions to its vocabulary are made from other languages. He also urged French poets to choose subjects from the history of their country so that France may have a French *Iliad* and *Aeneid*. Although du Bellay's work was verbose, it was written with an enthusiasm which made it the guidebook of poets during the succeeding centuries.

The brightest star in the Pléiade constellation was Pierre de Ronsard (1525-1585). When he was a boy his father chose for him the life of a courtier and soldier, but at the age of sixteen a severe illness left him partially deaf, causing him to abandon his career and turn to classical studies and to the writing of poetry. His rise to fame was rapid. In 1550 he published his *Odes*, two years later *Amours de Cassandre*, followed by *Amours de Marie* and the first book of *Hymnes* in 1555. In 1560 he brought out the first edition of his complete works. After the accession of Charles IX in 1559 Ronsard had been appointed the official poet of the king. At the command of Charles IX he undertook the writing of an heroic poem titled "Franciade" in which he related for France, as Virgil had for Rome, what he believed to be the story of the founding of the French kingdom. Charles IX was so delighted with the poem that he heaped rewards and honors on the poet. At the death of his royal patron in 1574, Ronsard lost his position as official poet. He spent the remaining years of his life on a country estate writing poetry. The tranquillity of field and forest coupled with his deep interest in nature inspired him to write about nature as well as about men. Some of his songs were addressed to the birds and insects he saw about him. Flowers also occupy an important place in his poetry.

Seldom, if ever, have poems been received with such enthusiasm. Ronsard was applauded as "the prince of poets" by princes, kings, and queens, and the general public. Laudatory statements regarding the poet and his work were extravagant. There was the assertion, for example, that his birth in 1525 had more than compensated France for the defeat at Pavia in the same year. A literary critic wrote that he would rather have written one of Ronsard's odes than to receive the duchy of Milan as a gift. Montaigne asserted that Ronsard had equalled the ancients and carried French poetry to perfection. Ronsard's poetry was also praised outside France. Queen Elizabeth of England was so deeply moved by it that she presented a valuable diamond to the poet. Mary Stuart sent him a statuette bearing the inscription, "To Ronsard the Apollo of the Fountain of the Muses." When Ronsard died in 1585 at the age of sixty-one he was widely mourned and praised. But fifteen years later the poet whose literary supremacy had been unquestioned during his lifetime was practically a forgotten man. Other literary figures were in the limelight. Forgotten was the fact that he was "the father of the French ode" and that he had opened the way for his successors. Not until the appearance of Victor Hugo in the nineteenth century did France produce a poet whose lines equalled the melody, simplicity, and grace of Ronsard.

18

The Renaissance in England

The Tudor Monarchy

Although there were harbingers of the coming of the Renaissance in England prior to the accession of the Tudors, the English Renaissance, by and large, ran its full course during the Tudor era, which began with the accession of Henry VII in 1485 and ended with the death of Elizabeth I in 1603. Five Tudor rulers occupied the royal throne during this period with each reign reflecting the diverse character of the ruler. The Tudor monarchs were not all persons of great ability. While some were able, others failed to understand the problems and issues which confronted them. Nevertheless, the authority of the English crown reached its greatest heights in the Tudor period. In financial matters the Tudor rulers were largely independent of Parliament, except for the extra cost of war. In legislation their power was limited by the necessity of gaining Parliament's consent. In this they were so extraordinarily successful that historians speak of a "Tudor despotism."

The first ruler of the Tudor line was Henry VII (1485-1509) who, so to speak, won the crown by defeating Richard III in the battle of Bosworth Field (1485), in which the latter lost his life. According to the traditional story, Richard III wore his crown into battle; after the battle one of Henry's supporters found it under a bush and forthwith placed it on Henry's head while the victorious army acclaimed him king. Since Henry's claim to the crown was rather weak he proceeded at once to summon a meeting of Parliament for the purpose of confirming his accession. The battle of Bosworth was the last of the Wars of the Roses (1455-1485), so named because the two houses contending for the English throne had roses as their symbols. The symbol of the house of York was a white rose and that of the house of Lancaster a red rose. After becoming king, Henry Tudor, who was the head of the house of Lancaster, strengthened his position considerably in 1486 by marrying Elizabeth of York, heiress to the Yorkist claims. Consequently the offstring of the union inherited the claims of both houses.

Henry VII was not an idealist. His actions were not motivated by a lofty theory of kingship. He was an opportunist and a realist, and his aims were simple. As the founder of the Tudor dynasty he sought to consolidate his hold on the throne and to make the kingship secure for his heirs. As a king

Henry VII was hardly a romantic figure. He was, however, industrious, patient, and shrewd. Furthermore, he was somewhat thrifty, at times even niggardly. Economy was forced on him by the fact that the royal treasury was empty at his accession. Careful management was necessary if he was to remain largely independent of Parliament. If his was not a personal popularity, Henry VII did gain the approval of the English people. They welcomed his efforts to restore law and order after the long period of intermittent wars. Those who disturbed the peace were dealt with severely. Among those instigating uprisings were Yorkists and Yorkist sympathizers who were not placated by the marriage of Henry and Elizabeth of York. Henry also rendered harmless the great barons who were not ready to surrender their authority to a centralized national government. The task of forcing the feudal barons into submission was made easier by the heavy loss of life among the nobility during the Wars of the Roses. Against the barons whose holdings enabled them to maintain a considerable number of armed retainers for purposes of private warfare or to intimidate local authorities, Henry invoked the statutes against "livery and maintenance" which prohibited the keeping of liveried retainers. Upon those who did not obey promptly, Henry imposed heavy fines which achieved two purposes. They impoverished the unruly barons so that they could no longer maintain large numbers of armed men, and they filled the royal treasury. If any were so brash as to resist, the king's artillery which was a royal monopoly would level their strongholds.

In his struggles with the barons Henry relied on the middle class for support; in fact, he broke with tradition by choosing a number of non-noble counselors to supplant noble advisers. The only nobles who held high office during Henry's reign were relatives of the royal family. Henry also aided the cause of the middle class by fostering the expansion of commerce and industry. By the end of his reign the Tudor monarchy was so firmly established on the English throne that his son Henry VIII, in whose veins Yorkist as well as Lancastrian blood flowed, was able to succeed him without a contest. Henry VII also left a full treasury to his son who at once proceeded to enjoy it with the abandon of a *nouveau riche*.

The many-sided interests of Henry VIII (1509-1547) stamped him as a man of the Renaissance. In addition to a knowledge of English which enabled him to draft telling state papers, he had a command of Latin which elicited the praise of Erasmus. He could also carry on a conversation in French and Spanish. Furthermore, Henry VIII was well versed in theology, an accomplished musician, and an athlete of considerable skill. During the early years of his reign he devoted much time to archery, wrestling, horsemanship, jousting, and tennis. All in all, he was probably the best-educated and most accomplished ruler to occupy the English throne up to that time. As a person he was genial in his youth, but later selfishness, arrogance, frustration, dissipation, and disease made him ill-tempered, callous, and even brutal. He failed so often that his role in life has been described as "a lesson in how not to do it." Many of his failures can be attributed to his desire for personal glory. His colossal arrogance often blinded him to the realities of a situation. His ambitions to become the arbiter of Europe, for example, came to naught. Actually he was frequently tricked by sovereigns whose abilities were much less than his own. Furthermore, his financial policy was hardly a success. The wealthiest ruler in Europe at his accession, he was during the later years of his reign in such desperate financial straits that he found it necessary to debase the coinage. Despite all his failings and shortcomings, he did, however, retain to the end much of the popularity with which he started his reign.

Henry VIII's best-known shortcoming was undoubtedly his inability to maintain stable marital relations, a failure which greatly affected the future of English history. His first wife was Catherine of Aragon, daughter of Ferdinand and Isabella and widow of Henry's older brother, Arthur, who had died soon after he married Catherine. The marriage of Henry and Catherine was arranged for political purposes and a special papal dispensation was necessary to legitimize it. Over a period of seventeen years Catherine bore Henry five children, all of whom died in infancy except Mary who later became queen. Desirous of leaving a male heir to the throne, Henry in 1527 ordered Cardinal Wolsey, his chief minister, to obtain from Pope Clement VII an annulment of the marriage on the ground that marriage with a brother's widow is contrary to God's law. There were other considerations which entered into Henry's desire to terminate the marriage: Catherine was an ailing melancholy woman; and the king had fallen passionately in love with Anne Boleyn, an attractive maid of honor at his court. Henry's request created a serious predicament for the pope. To grant the request, it would have been necessary for him to declare invalid the papal dispensation which permitted the marriage. Furthermore, Pope Clement who was at that time the virtual prisoner of Charles V, nephew of Catherine of Aragon, did not dare to offend the emperor. For failing to get the marriage annulled Cardinal Wolsey was dismissed in disgrace and stripped of his wealth. The next year (1530) he died a broken man.

Henry did not, however, discard his plan for having his marriage annulled. He now took matters in his own hands. In 1532 he succeeded with the sanction of the pope in raising Thomas Cranmer to the dignity of archbishop of Canterbury and soon thereafter the new archbishop presented the case to an archiepiscopal court which declared that Henry had never really been married to Catherine. The breach with Rome was completed in 1534 when Parliament at Henry's request passed the Act of Supremacy which declared the king to be the only supreme head of the Church of England. Thus the tie which had joined the English or Anglican Church to the papacy was cut and the Church of England became an independent institution. Since there was a strong anti-clerical feeling in England at the time, there was no widespread opposition. In substituting himself for the pope as the head of the English Church Henry had no intention of establishing Protestantism in England, for he prided himself on his orthodoxy. At his behest Parliament in 1539 passed the Act of the Six Articles which reaffirmed transubstantiation, celibacy of the clergy, auricular confession, and other doctrines. But he made a few concessions to Protestant feeling, including authorization of the use of an English Bible in the churches. Being in need of money and regarding the monasteries as strongholds of papal influence, he did dissolve and despoil the monastic establishments. In 1536 he closed all monastic establishments having less than twelve residents and in 1539 the remaining monasteries met the same fate. All the properties of the monasteries were sold, the receipts going into the royal treasury.

In the meantime Henry's marital adventures had not produced the male heir he was determined to have. Even before the archiepiscopal court had annulled his marriage to Catherine he had secretly married Anne Boleyn. By the time the marriage was made public Anne was already with child. The birth of the child was a great disappointment to Henry, for it was a girl, the future Queen Elizabeth. His affection for Anne soon cooled when she did not bear him a son. Moreover, his disappointment turned him into a Bluebeard. Anne was accused of infidelity and beheaded by a swordsman from France. A short time later he married Jane Seymour who did bear him a son later known as Edward VI. When the queen died shortly after Edward's birth, Henry showed no interest in another matrimonial alliance. He was satisfied that he had a son. Before long, however, it became apparent that Edward was weak and sickly, and might not even survive long enough to succeed his father. So Henry began looking for a fourth wife. At the suggestion of Thomas Cromwell, his chief minister, he chose Anne of Cleves, a German Protestant princess. When she arrived in England Henry found her so unattractive that he at first refused to go through with the marriage ceremony. He finally consented, but after the marriage did not trouble to take the bride home. For his part in urging the marriage Thomas Cromwell was dismissed and later sent to the block. After this marriage was dissolved, Henry married his fifth wife, Catherine Howard. A short time later she was detected in an intrigue with a former lover and beheaded. With Catherine Howard out of the way Henry married his sixth wife, Catherine Parr (1543), who managed to survive him. (*See Fig. 27.*)

By this time Henry VIII was prematurely old and his body was racked by disease. His character had gradually deteriorated, turning him into a callous and arrogant egotist who relentlessly cut down all those who did not submit completely to his will. The list of those he sent to the block or to the gallows in addition to two of his wives is imposing, the most notable being Sir Thomas More. In 1547 the king himself died at the age of fifty-five. Henry left his nation economic confusion resulting from his debasement of the coinage, and seething discontent among the agricultural population whose arable lands were being converted into pasture lands for sheep-raising. On the other hand, Henry did leave England a strong navy. He also left a sickly son and two daughters, both of whom had been declared legitimate by Parliament.

Edward VI, who was king of England from 1547 to 1553, was only nine when he succeeded his father. Much has been made of the fact that he was a precocious boy with a deep interest in the affairs of his kingdom. This did not, of course, give him maturity. Since his father had permitted him to be brought up as a Protestant, he wished to see Protestantism firmly established in England. The actual conduct of affairs was in the hands of a Regency Council, appointed by Henry VIII before his death, in which there were supporters of both the old religion and the new. The dominant figure was the young king's uncle, Edward Seymour, duke of Somerset who was made "the protector" of Edward VI. Somerset who also had Protestant sympathies took the lead in replacing the use of Latin in the mass. The First Prayer Book (1549) imposed on all churches an order of service in English. As a statesman Somerset had good intentions; unfortunately, however, he lacked the ability to provide solutions for the problems Henry VIII had left unsolved. Consequently he was forced in 1550 to step down in favor of the duke of Northumberland, an able, though often unscrupulous person. Under the leadership of Northumberland, who sided with the more extreme Protestants, the Second Prayer Book was prepared and issued in 1552. This book revised many of the teachings of the Roman Catholic Church. The changes were made so suddenly that they confused the English people. So much attention was given to the religious question that other matters were neglected. In 1553 the frail king fell victim to tuberculosis and was succeeded by his half-sister Mary.

Mary (1553-1558) who became queen at the age of thirty-seven was a devout Catholic who regarded the reestablishment of Roman Catholicism in England as her special mission. During her reign, all the religious changes the Protestants had made were nullified by a repeal of the legislation that had been passed, Latin mass was reinstated, and the supremacy of the papacy over the English Church was restored. This did not, however, satisfy Mary. She was determined to uproot and stamp out Protestantism completely. A Parliament in which Catholic sentiment predominated obligingly reenacted (January, 1555) the statute which permitted the burning of heretics, and the consigning of Protestants to the flames began. The first six months saw the burning of more than fifty, many of whom had been leaders in the reform movement. Thereafter the burnings continued at a slower pace until the end of the reign. Far from eradicating Protestantism the persecutions probably strengthened the movement, even though they did frighten many into outward conformity.

The last years of Mary's reign were not a happy period for her. In 1554 she married her Spanish cousin Philip II, a marriage which was unpopular in

England. Whereas she loved her husband with a dog-like devotion, Philip did not return her affection. To him she was just a pawn in the great game of European politics. She fervently hoped the marriage would produce an heir so that her half-sister Elizabeth who had Protestant leanings would not succeed her as ruler. But religious and succession troubles were not the only ones that plagued her. Before her accession she had been so completely preoccupied with religious matters that she learned little about the needs of her country, and after becoming queen she was still out of touch with the political and economic currents of her time. This caused her, among other things, to neglect the English navy. Hence when the French attacked Calais early in 1558 the English lost this last fragment of territory on the continent because they were unable to send reinforcements to the beleaguered garrison. The loss of Calais was a severe blow to the English queen. This loss, added to the realization that she was not leaving an heir who would continue her religious policies, that her husband had deserted her, and that she was practically without friends, cast a pall on the last months of her life. She died in November, 1558.

The Elizabethan Age

The short reign of Mary was followed by the long reign of Elizabeth I (1558-1603), years of great achievements and far-reaching progress for the English. In honor of the "Virgin Queen" the period has been named "the Elizabethan age." At the time of her accession Elizabeth was twenty-five, fairly tall and slender, with a face that was pleasing rather than pretty. Endowed with an astute mind, she received an education which in its breadth reflected the Renaissance interests. She learned Latin and some Greek, and acquired a sufficient knowledge of French and Italian to carry on conversations with foreign ambassadors. As a girl she also developed considerable skill in playing the lute and viol. Her naturally keen mind was further sharpened in the school of adversity. Since her mother Anne Boleyn was beheaded and her father showed little interest in her, she had to learn to fend for herself. During the reign of her half-sister Mary who mistrusted her, Elizabeth had lived in an atmosphere of suspicion. This mistrust was nourished by a number of attempts to dethrone Mary and enthrone Elizabeth. To save herself from the block Elizabeth had to walk circumspectly and act prudently. For a time she was imprisoned in a room of the Tower of London from which she could see the spot where her mother and others had been decapitated. At that time the slightest indiscretion would have been fatal to her. She managed to save herself by eschewing involvement in politics, and by self-control and self-reliance.

As a woman Queen Elizabeth exhibited the Renaissance love of dress, display, and personal adornment. Having been compelled by fear of her half-sister to dress in the plainest fashions before her accession, she was free as queen to revel in gorgeous apparel and glittering jewelry. She took great delight in adorning herself with many kinds of ruffs, embroideries, laces, combs, brooches, and bracelets. She herself did not spend much on articles of personal adornment; her wardrobe was largely stocked by those attending her court. It is reported that at her death she left more than a thousand dresses. A list of gifts presented to her by the Earl of Leicester in 1571-1572 includes one which may have been the first watch bracelet. She may also have been the first English queen to wear silk stockings. Elizabeth's love of display was fortified by an almost incredible vanity. She never tired of compliments, although she must have known that they were not sincere. Her thirst for flattery was so insatiable that she demanded it from those who surrounded her. As her weakness for personal admiration was a matter of common knowledge, many took advantage of it to rise in her good graces. Elizabeth seems to have been so inordinately proud of her hands, which contemporaries described as being "very white and very beautiful," that in the presence of prominent visitors she was wont to put on and take off her gloves hundreds of times in order to call attention to them. But all the personal adornment did not hide the fact that there was in her makeup a definite masculine strain. She could display a most unfeminine hardness and coarseness. Her overbearing temper frequently vented itself in a torrent of cuss-words that even the proverbial fishwife would have found it difficult to match.

There is a general consensus of opinion among the biographers of Elizabeth that she was an able ruler who by temperament was fitted to cope with the problems of her position. An important factor in her success was the choice of able advisers, but even more important was the fact that most of her policies were in accord with the wishes of her people; in fact, she identified herself so completely with her subjects that their wishes became her own. Her people responded by affectionately calling her Good Queen Bess.

One of the first problems to which Elizabeth's government turned its attention was the religious question. Elizabeth does not seem to have developed any deep religious feelings. What she aimed at was to allay the animosities which had been aroused during the preceding reigns. Thus, she decided to steer a middle course. When Parliament met in 1559 it cooperated with her. After repealing some of the reactionary laws enacted during Mary's reign, it passed a new Act of Supremacy which declared the crown supreme in ecclesiastical as well as in civil matters. Elizabeth did, however, refuse the title "Supreme Head of the Church" because she thought it might give offence. She contented herself with the title "Supreme Governor of the Church." Parliament also passed an act which made a modified version of the Second Prayer Book the only legal form of common worship. The acts passed by Parliament at that time have determined the character of the Anglican Church to the present. Their immediate effect was to give England some degree of religious peace until the question of Puritanism became a major issue.

In her foreign policy Elizabeth endeavored to avoid open declarations of war. One of the first things she did upon becoming queen was to end the war with France in which England had lost Calais, thereby opening the longest period of official peace since the thirteenth century. For a time she kept her two principal adversaries, France and Spain, from attacking England by tactics which included bare-faced prevarication and playing off one against the other. Elizabeth showed herself to be such a consummate master of the art of double-dealing that the Spanish ambassador was moved to state she must have "a hundred thousand devils in her body." When Philip II of Spain, after much goading by English seamen, did finally send his "Invincible Armada" against England, the English navy supported by a large number of privateers captured or destroyed some of the Spanish ships and forced the rest to seek safety in flight (1588).

The reign of Queen Elizabeth was, in general, a time of national glory on the sea. It was during this period that the foundations for England's maritime greatness were laid. The daring exploits of Sir Francis Drake, Captain John Hawkins, and others prepared the way for the great role England was to play as a colonial power. After efforts to find a northwest or northeast passage failed, English seamen and merchants decided to exploit such opportunities for trade as were at hand. One of their moves was to contest the monopoly the Portuguese held on the spice and luxury trade. The result of such activities was a tremendous expansion of English trade. The English merchant marine increased with a rapidity theretofore unknown. English industry also made great advances. Foreigners who might found new industries were encouraged to migrate to England. As a consequence new industries were established, notably glass-making, paper-making, the manufacture of cutlery, and the manufacture of new kinds of textiles. At the same time, quiet and prosperity were also restored to the rural districts where the enclosure of land for sheep-farming had during the previous reigns dispossessed many tenants and agricultural laborers, causing great distress and much unemployment. Under Elizabeth, laws were passed to rectify matters and much of the surplus labor was reemployed. The overall picture in the Elizabethan age was one of growing prosperity.

The English victory over the Spanish Armada in 1588 marked the high-point of Elizabeth's personal power and glory. During the last years of her reign an opposition party was formed in Parliament for the purpose of curbing the power and authority of the ruler. Since Elizabeth was an aging woman the opposition did not put too much pressure on her, but its formation foreshadowed the contest between Parliament and the Stuarts. As for Elizabeth, the trials and troubles of her long reign had taken a heavy toll of her strength. She sought to hide the ravages of time by greater magnificence in dress and by endeavoring to dance with her former vigor at court affairs, but in the privacy of her apartments she was a fretful and often melancholy woman in failing health. Early in her reign Parliament, expressing concern over the succession, had urged her to marry. The queen did not seem to be able, however, to make a final choice. Much has been written to explain the fact that she did not marry, but the various explanations are largely based on conjecture. Without husband, children or close relatives, without the counsel and friendship of most of the faithful ministers who had served her during the early part of her reign, Elizabeth spent her last years as a lonely spinster. Her death on March 24, 1603, closed the Tudor era. One of the last acts of her life was to designate as her successor her cousin King James VI of Scotland, the first English ruler of the Stuart line.

English Literature of the Renaissance Period

The culture of the English Renaissance, like other Renaissance cultures, was a fusion of the old and new. Like the cultures of the other countries north of the Alps, it also bears the stamp of Italian influence. The English Renaissance was, however, unique in a number of respects. It produced no noteworthy sculpture and no native painters who rank with the better painters of Western Europe. In architecture the great period of development, inspired by Inigo Jones, did not begin until the seventeenth century. On the other hand, the sixteenth was a rich century in the history of English music, both sacred and secular. More composers turned out more music during the period than during the entire previous history of England. This upsurge of music was closely linked with the rise of English poetry. As Shakespeare expressed it:

> If Music and Sweet Poetry agree
> As they must needs, the sister and the brother,
> Then must the love be great, 'twixt them and me,
> Because thou lovest the one and the other.

The English Renaissance also put the study of the classics on a new footing and produced some outstanding humanists, notably Sir Thomas More, the author of *Utopia*. It should be noted, however, that in England humanism was a form rather than a spirit; hence antiquity did not become the living world it was to the Italian humanists. Although the more prosperous classes of English society imitated the Italians in dress and manners, the great enthusiasm for life which manifested itself in certain strata of Italian society did not assert itself in England. But, whereas in the fifteenth century the best English minds were still occupied with religious questions in the otherworldly sense, in the sixteenth century a secular spirit slowly pervaded the intellectual life of the nation.

The supreme glory of Renaissance England is the splendor of its secular literature. After promising beginnings in the fourteenth century, the rise of English literature was stunted by the upheavals caused by war, epidemics, and economic depression. Not until the reign of Henry VIII did a gradual revival set in; then during the last quarter of the sixteenth century there was a sudden surge of literary production, a surge so unprecedented that the period is called "the golden age of English literature." The literary output of poets, dramatists, and prose writers was so profuse that it can be compared only with the Cinquecento (the artistic outburst in Italian painting and sculpture during the sixteenth century). Of the scores of literary figures who appeared on the scene many won enduring fame, and a few wrote works of such outstanding excellence that they must be ranked with the great literary figures of all time. The overall result was that England which as late as 1570 was poorer in its vernacular literature than France and in some respects than Spain, and immeasurably poorer than Italy, had by the death of Queen Elizabeth in 1603 produced a literature which could stand comparison with that of any people in any age.

A feature which distinguishes most of the secular literature of the English Renaissance is its strong sense of reality. This feeling represents a break with the literature which moved in an atmosphere of the supernatural and in the realm of fancy. The primary task this new literature set for itself was the depiction of human life in terms of secular interests. It no longer points to the next world as the purpose and goal of all human strivings; nor is it filled with supernatural miracles. The great miracle is mundane life in itself; hence the vitality of Elizabethan literature is thoroughly mundane. It is not, however, indifferent to evil. Through faithful representation it preaches the moral life very eloquently. Despite the fact that authors borrowed forms, plots, and ideas from Italian and French literature, the final product is in most instances essentially English. In the case of Petrarch's sonnets, a number of English poets, it is true, composed poetry that is little more than an obvious imitation of the Italian poet. It is about such poets that Sir Philip Sidney (1554-1586), Elizabethan poet and novelist, wrote:

> You that do dictionary's method bring
> Into your rhymes running in rattling rows,
> You that poor Petrarch's long deceased woes
> With new-born sighs and denizened wits do sing;
> You take the wrong ways!

Sidney, Spenser, Shakespeare, and others naturalized the Petrarchian sonnet so completely that it became the English sonnet, a sonnet which has more feeling, elasticity, and beauty than the sonnets of the imitators of Petrarch. But even Petrarchism, despite its artificiality, enriched English literature with new forms, moods, and expressions.

Although the literature of the preceding period contains various secular strains, it is in the writing of Geoffrey Chaucer (1340-1400) that manifestations of the Renaissance spirit are evident. These writings not only usher in a period of Italian influence; they also depart from the ascetic attitudes to ally themselves with the various interests of the secular world. In these writings Chaucer stands as a man of the world, one who is willing to take the world as he finds it. His earthly and sometimes earthy tales sound no heavenly fanfare. The spirit that pervades them is a buoyant zest for life. Every aspect of life, happy and sad, moral and immoral, is literary material for him. He regarded it all with an insatiable curiosity, an unflagging keenness, a complacent amusement, and an unwavering tolerance. Francis T. Palgrave, the nineteenth-century English poet, stated it this way:

> To paint
> With Nature's freshness what before him lies;
> The knave, the fool, the frolicsome, the quaint;
> His the broad jest, the laugh without restraint,
> The ready tears, the spirit lightly moved;
> Loving the world and by the world beloved.

Chaucer's primary purpose in writing was to entertain, to amuse. For him the depiction of the here and now was sufficient.

Little more is known about Chaucer's life than about the life of Homer. The known facts pertain almost entirely to his official career. Starting as a royal valet, young Chaucer gradually rose to the position of royal squire at the court of King Edward III. By 1373 he was a person of such importance that the king sent him to Italy as a member of a commission to negotiate a trade agreement with Genoa. Shortly thereafter he went to Italy a second time for the purpose of conducting business for the king in Florence. As a reward for his faithful services Chaucer was, it appears, appointed Controller of the Great Customs of the port of London, collecting customs on wool, skins, and leather. He continued to hold this post until the year of his death which was probably 1400. Thus writing was for him not the main business of life, but an avocation pursued whenever a busy life permitted. Chaucer's statement in *The House of Fame*, in which he describes himself as going straight home after balancing his accounts in order to read and write until his eyes glazed, can be taken as a literal description. The fact that few of his longer works were completed in design and execution can undoubtedly be ascribed to his manner of working. Nevertheless, he left behind more than 32,000 lines of verse and a far from inconsiderable quantity of prose.

Chaucer drew the plots upon which he based his writings from many sources. He seems to have read everything he could lay his hands on and also to have listened attentively to any stories that were being circulated. In his earliest writings the fabliaux and French romances of chivalry were an important source of ideas, but after his visits to Italy, Italian literature became the major influence. On his first visit he seems to have become acquainted with the writings of Dante, Petrarch, and Boccaccio. The vivifying effect of these writers is evident in everything he wrote after his return. It was from Boccaccio's writings that he borrowed most freely, although there is no evidence that he had read the widely known *Decameron*. Chaucer's first important work, *Troilus and Cressida*, a novel in verse, is based on the story he found in Boccaccio's *Filostrato*. He also took ideas and plots for some of his other works from Boccaccio. As he wrote, Chaucer gradually progressed from medieval allegory to modern realism.

Chaucer's *Canterbury Tales*, a series of tales in verse about everyday life in England, are his crowning achievement. Dryden said of them, "Chaucer took into the compass of his *Canterbury Tales* the various manners and humors of the whole English nation." As a framework for his tales Chaucer used the idea of a group of pilgrims journeying to the shrine of St. Thomas at Canterbury. To relieve the tedium of the journey the various members of the party relate their legendary experiences punctuated with lively jests. Among the principal characters are the Knight, the Shipman, the Prioress, the Miller, the Man of Law, the Pardoner, and the Wife of Bath. The *Canterbury Tales* earned for Chaucer the honor of being the first great delineator of character in English literature. Possessing an intimate knowledge of human nature, Chaucer sketched his characters in such a way that they are flesh-and-blood men and women who bare their very selves with utter abandon. The Pardoner, for example, who is evil to the core, offers pardons for sale and fake relics to kiss. Then there is the Wife of Bath who is Rabelaisian long before Rabelais and as amoral as Shakespeare's Falstaff. With unashamed frankness she states her views on matrimony and relates her marital adventures. The entire picture is one of pitiless realism. It is for his realistic portrayal of secular interests that Chaucer is remembered.

Among the successors and imitators of Chaucer there was not one poet who approached him in poetic stature. Many literary historians have stated that the English muse was silent for more than a century after Chaucer's death. This is not literally true. There was no dearth of poets or poetic writings. During the fifteenth century many poets composed verses. The scarcity was one of poetic talent. The poetry of that period is remembered only by specialists in the literary history of that time. The conditions and general atmosphere of the time were not, it seems, propitious for the writing of great poetry. Signs of a rejuvenation of poetry became evident, however, after the Tudors restored order, and prosperity began to return to the nation. Even then the growth of secular literature was retarded by the religious controversy which arose when Henry VIII severed the ties which joined the English Church to the Church of Rome. Some idea of the religious confusion that existed may be gained from the fact that the official religion of England changed four times from 1535 to 1560. Not until after Elizabeth and her Parliaments provided a religious settlement that was acceptable to a majority of the English people did secular poets in greater number give eloquent voice to their poetic sentiments. Even then there was little indication of the tremendous upsurge that was to take place during the last decades of the century.

The problem of accounting for the great burst of creative energy during the reign of Elizabeth is not a simple one. The explanation most frequently offered is that the political, economic, and social conditions were extremely favorable for the writing of great poetry, drama, and prose. This explanation does not, however, offer any clues to the specific factors involved. Among these was the comparative peace, both religious and national, which prevailed during Elizabeth's reign. Another factor was the steadily increasing prosperity. The opulence of the age was reflected in the realm of literature. Furthermore, the age of Elizabeth was one of intense emotion and daring action. While the former expressed itself in sonnets and other poetic forms, the spirit of daring and enterprise, exemplified by the raids of the Elizabethan seamen and the defeat of the Spanish Armada, also found expression in the new literature. Not to be overlooked is the fact that the queen herself inspired much poetry. Her romantic virginity coupled with the pomp and pageantry surrounding her and her delight in poetry made her a natural subject of verse. She was praised and glorified under many different names with a fervor usually reserved for the adoration of the Virgin Mary. The poets who did not sing the praises of the Virgin Queen addressed their verses to some other "virgin" at the court of Elizabeth. Outstanding among the courtly poets until his death in battle at the age of thirty-two was Sir Philip Sidney (1554-1586) whose sonnets express subtle perception of love's effects.

The great efflorescence of poetry is usually dated from the publication in 1579 of Edmund Spenser's *Shepheard's Calendar*, the first great pastoral in English. Although skillfully written, its archaic language kept it from being more widely read. Other works by Spenser followed, culminating in his masterpiece, *The Faerie Queene* (1593). Among other things, Spenser contributed much to the development of the English sonnet. English poetry attained further greatness in the long poem titled "Hero and Leander" (1593), the first part of which was written by Christopher Marlowe. Then there are the two long poems of William Shakespeare, "Venus and Adonis" (1593) and "The Rape of Lucrece" (1594), in which he probes the mystery of human nature. As for shorter poems, there are the sonnet sequences of Drayton and of Daniel, and the sonnets of Shakespeare which appeared in 1609. The production of poetry was so prolific that it would require many pages to list only the names of the poets and the titles of their works.

Poetry was but a fraction of the literary production of the Elizabethan age. The secular dramas which appeared toward the end of the sixteenth century constitute one of the richest collections of all time. The playwrights of the period took the existing English drama and gave it a form which made it the enduring possession of the ages. The first of this group of dramatists was Christopher Marlowe (1564-1593). After studying at the University of Cambridge, young Marlowe went to London where the first part of his tragedy *Tambourlaine* was produced in 1587. His career as a playwright was of brief duration. In 1593, at the age of twenty-nine, he was killed in a tavern brawl. During the brief period of his activity Marlowe wrote not only *Tambourlaine*, but also *The Jew of Malta*, *Edward the Second*, and *Doctor*

Faustus, the last being generally regarded as his masterpiece. It is interesting to conjecture what he might have written if he had lived to a ripe old age. Marlowe gave the English drama new direction by putting human passion on the stage. In each of his dramas there is a commanding personality impelled by a consuming desire for power. In *Tambourlaine* it is the desire for power through the force of arms, in *The Jew of Malta* Barabas would achieve power through wealth, and *Doctor Faustus* would gain power through infinite knowledge. The plays are tragedies in the sense that all three leading characters are destroyed by their ambitions. Marlowe's dramas left a lasting imprint on English literature. Particularly noteworthy was their influence on Shakespeare. There are echoes and imitations of Marlowe in Shakespeare's plays and poems. For example, Shakespeare's *Merchant of Venice* is unquestionably indebted to Marlowe's *Jew of Malta*. In *As You Like It* Shakespeare both quoted and addressed Marlowe.

The death of Christopher Marlowe left the field of drama to William Shakespeare who overshadowed his contemporaries and obscured them. Shakespeare is not only the greatest figure in English literature; he is also the greatest dramatist of all time. Since our knowledge of Shakespeare is so scanty he does not live for us as a person in the same way as Henry VIII and Queen Elizabeth do. Aside from his writings we know little or nothing regarding his temperament and tastes, the nature of his beliefs, and the extent of his knowledge. The scantiness of the existing information has caused some critics to doubt that Shakespeare was really the author of the poems and dramas which bear his name. One should keep in mind, however, that only sixteen years after Shakespeare's death John Milton accepted him as the author of the Shakespearean dramas. In general, the weight of the existing evidence tips the scales heavily in favor of Shakespeare.

Difficulty and struggle marked Shakespeare's early years with a company of players in London; he probably was a player of minor parts before he became a recognized actor and director. But success, wealth, and fame came after he turned to writing plays. *Romeo and Juliet*, his first play, was an instant success. In the succeeding period he wrote the series of great plays which included *Midsummer Night's Dream*, *Merchant of Venice*, *Merry Wives of Windsor*, *Much Ado About Nothing*, *As You Like It*, and *Twelfth Night*. At the turn of the century the first of his four great tragedies appeared. In succession they were *Hamlet*, *Othello*, *King Lear*, and *Macbeth*. After this period of pessimism he entered a happier time as reflected in his final plays *Cymbeline*, *Winter's Tale*, and *The Tempest*. Having written the last play, he put away his pen and retired to Stratford where he lived as a wealthy, respected citizen until his death in 1616 at the age of fifty-two.

In his writings Shakespeare was a man of the late Renaissance. Everything he wrote reflects the time in which he lived. In the words of Ben Jonson he was "the soul of the age." He is the great analyst of mundane life, more specifically of the rich and manifold life of the Elizabethan age. To him this life is a combination of smiles and tears, but he does not concern himself with the hereafter. The spirit of his writings is thoroughly secular. Tolstoy called him "the champion of secular life." Shakespeare, for example, wrote in *Twelfth Night:*

> What is love? 'tis not hereafter;
> Present mirth hath present laughter;
> What's to come is still unsure.
> In delay there lives no plenty;
> Then come kiss me, sweet and twenty,
> Youth's a stuff will not endure.

Shakespeare's plays, of course, contain many medieval strains that were a part of the life of his time. On the other hand, one can hardly call a man who had Shakespeare's abounding zest for life an ascetic or a religious mystic. His love of life and interest in secular knowledge were ends in themselves. There is not the slightest evidence that he suppressed desire or eschewed the joy of life in order to gain entrance into the "Heavenly Jerusalem." He was wholly a citizen of this world. Like Rabelais, Shakespeare derived pleasure from the contemplation of everything that is human, even what some regard as obscene. He was like Homer in that he presented scenes from life without pushing himself into them. His prescribed task was to observe and record. The mere fact in itself he regarded as sufficient.

Like the Renaissance artists and some of the Renaissance writers, Shakespeare exalted man. Some of his leading personages are like the powerful figures of Michelangelo. Among these are Hamlet, Othello, Lear, and Macbeth who speak unforgettable lines. Like the Italian philosopher Pico della Mirandola, Shakespeare regarded man as a godlike creature who can raise himself to great heights. In the words of Hamlet, "What a piece of work man is! how noble in reason! how infinite in faculties! in form and moving how express and admirable! in action how like an angel! in apprehension how like a god! the beauty of the world! the paragon of animals!" In order to achieve godliness, however, man must use his god-given reason, Hamlet says in his last soliloquy:

> Sure, He that made us with such large discourse,
> Looking before and after, gave us not
> That capability and godlike reason
> To fust in us unused.

Shakespeare's poetry and plays are linked with the Italian Renaissance in many respects. If all the scenes that are laid in Italy, all the Italian characters, and all the materials culled from Italian sources were deleted, the content of his plays would be greatly diminished; in fact, the list of his plays would be shorter. To show the extent that Italy stimulated Shakespeare's imagination it is necessary only to mention *The Merchant of Venice*, *Two Gentlemen of Verona*, *Othello. Romeo and Juliet*, *The Tempest*, and *The Winter's Tale*. Besides being deeply indebted to Italy, Shakespeare also owed much to classical literature. His interest in and reverence for the literature of the ancients is amply demonstrated by the many classical allusions which are scattered throughout his plays. His knowledge of classical antiquity was probably gained largely from translations and secondary sources. This does not mean, however, that his interest in classical lore was not absorbing. Whereas in Marlowe's opinion the classical world stood preeminently for beauty, for Shakespeare it represented wisdom and power as well as beauty.

English prose-writing started much later than English poetry and drama, because the humanists preferred Latin to English for the expression of serious thoughts. An outstanding example of this preference is Sir Thomas More who wrote his *Utopia* in Latin. Hence whereas both English poetry and drama had a tradition dating back for centuries, English prose was by the middle of the sixteenth century only in the early stages of its development. One important factor in the rise of English prose as well as in the enrichment of the thought of the English people was the translation of masterpieces from other languages into English. William Caxton, the printer, set the precedent by translating works from French and other languages into English. Later the humanists translated many Latin and Greek works into English. It has been calculated that no fewer than sixty-eight Greek works were translated into English between 1560 and 1600. Probably the most famous of all translations was Lord North's version of Plutarch's *Lives* based on a French edition. This translation, rendered in a vigorous, lucid, and rhythmic style, served Shakespeare as an important source of material. Further noteworthy influences in the development of English prose were the English versions of the Bible and the Book of Common Prayer. Then there were translations from the Italian, notably Sir Thomas Hoby's version of Castiglione's *Il Cortegiano*, a book of manners for the high-born which enjoyed a considerable popularity among the members of the upper classes. Also worthy of mention is John Florio's translation of Montaigne's *Essays*. Among the books that were written in English, those of Richard Hooker on the history of the Church and Francis Bacon's *Essays* (1593) greatly influenced the development of English prose. In fiction the short stories from Italy, particularly those of Boccaccio, stirred considerable interest in England. They were both translated and imitated. As examples of realistic fiction they were in large part responsible for establishing the realistic trend in England. In Elizabethan England realistic fiction reached the highest point of its development in the novels of Thomas Deloney (*c.*1542-*c.*1600) who wrote racy descriptions of English middle-class life. Thereafter interest in novels declined until it was revived by Daniel Defoe (1660-1731).

Secular Music in the English Renaissance

The Renaissance period has also been called a golden age of English music. English sacred music reached new heights, and the rise of secular music gave English composers new opportunities and new resources. Secular music, it is true, moved within limits which seem narrow to present-day musicians, but within these limits it was wonderfully alive. England was known throughout Europe for the verve and excellence of its music. Moreover, the interest in music was not restricted to professional musicians; it was as broad as the nation. Erasmus stated on the basis of his long stay in England, "The English could lay claim to being the best looking and the most musical, and to setting the best table in Europe."

The music of the English Renaissance was primarily vocal music. Its origins go back to the early folk songs and folk dances, back to the time before secular music developed a distinctive style of its own. Gradually, however, secular music developed along lines which set it apart from religious music. One such step was, for example, taken when John Dunstable (d.1453), the leading English composer of the first half of the fifteenth century, used the six-three chord as a distinguishing feature of his secular music. In the sixteenth century English music developed so rapidly that while most of the other European countries looked to the Netherlands for their composers, music teachers, and court musicians, England produced musicians in such numbers that it could well have supplied its own needs. However, since it was fashionable to employ foreign musicians, England, too, had its quota. But foreign musicians did not greatly change the style of English music, for English composers adhered tenaciously to national traditions.

The principal form of secular vocal music in sixteenth-century England was the madrigal, introduced into the country by Italian musicians. In England, however, the word madrigal had a broader meaning. It included a variety of songs variously called canzonets, airs, or simply songs. The eminent composer William Byrd published some of his madrigals under the title *Psalms, Songs and Sonets,* and the composer Thomas Morley called his first published collection of madrigals *Canzonets* with the subtitle *Little Short Songs.* The early madrigals were polyphonic, that is, they had parts for two or more voices up to and including six. Many of the English madrigals are based on verses composed by sixteenth-century poets, including Spenser, Marlowe, and Ben Jonson. This in itself gave the English madrigal a distinctive character. The music, too, with its fulness of melody was in the English tradition. Thus England was the only country north of the Alps to develop its own national form of the madrigal. The richness of the harvest of madrigals in the Elizabethan age is indicated by the thirty-six volumes of madrigals from the period 1588 to 1624 that were published from 1913 to 1924 under the title *The English Madrigal School.* In spirit some of the madrigals are gay and lighthearted, while others are sad. On the one hand, a madrigal might extol the virtues of the Morris dance (a folk dance) or describe the frolicking on May Day and, on the other, it might express sorrowful emotions. Purely instrumental music was still in its infancy in sixteenth-century England, but it did develop rapidly during the last decades.

Noteworthy is the fact that many English country dances date from the Tudor period. As madrigals were written to satisfy the widespread love of singing, so dances were composed for those of all classes who derived pleasure from dancing.

The great name in English music of the sixteenth century is William Byrd (1542-1623) who towered above contemporary English composers and won a place beside the best European composers of his time. The eminent American musicologist Paul Henry Lang has ranked Byrd as the most imposing figure of the English Renaissance, second only to Shakespeare. Byrd stands as the great example of Renaissance versatility in music. He not only excelled in every form of music, both sacred and secular, known at that time, but he also opened new paths for others to explore. His contemporaries esteemed him so highly that they bestowed on him the title "Father of Musick" which musicologists later changed to "father of British music." In sacred music his reputation rests on his three great Masses. As a composer of masses he has been ranked with the Italian composer Palestrina. In the realm of secular music Byrd is best remembered for the beauty of his madrigals and for the excellence of his instrumental compositions. He earned for himself an important place in the history of vocal music by converting the polyphonic madrigal into a type of song for solo voice with accompaniment by a string quartet. Byrd was also a pioneer in composing purely instrumental music. His forty-two compositions for the virginal and his pieces for viol quartets contributed much to the development of instrumental music. Byrd's work as a composer was supplemented by that of his student Thomas Morley (1557-*c.*1603) who also wrote madrigals and instrumental pieces for the virginal. Morley published a number of volumes of madrigals with three, four, and five voice parts.

One of the reasons for the popularity of music in England was that the Tudor rulers were music-lovers. Henry VII had musicians at his court because he enjoyed music. He also saw to it that his children were properly educated in music. The Book of Privy Purse expense shows, for example, that in 1501 he purchased a lute for his eldest daughter, Margaret, who was twelve at the time and who later became queen of the Scots. His son and successor Henry VIII received such a thorough education in music that he learned to play the virginal, the flute, and the recorder. Later he also composed five songs for four voices, twelve three-part songs, and a number of instrumental pieces for three and four viols. Henry VIII was particularly fond of light and lively dance music, including the jig, the hornpipe, the pavane, the galliard, and the domp or dump. An inventory taken at Westminster Palace in 1542 lists twenty-five lutes, eleven viols, seven gitterns or guitars, fourteen virginals, two clavichords, sixty-five flutes and almost as many recorders, fifteen shawms (a woodwind instrument), a variety of clarinets, and one bagpipe.

The interest in music which Henry VIII had stirred by his example was not stifled during the reigns of Edward VI and Mary. Court musicians employed by Henry VIII also served Edward VI. From a diary kept by Edward VI it appears that the young king played on the lute before the French ambassador to display his skill as a musician (1551). Queen Mary, despite her piety and a disposition that was at times dour, enjoyed secular music. There is no evidence to show that she discharged the musicians who had served the royal court during the reigns of her father and her half-brother; in fact, during her reign provisions were made for the cultivation of secular music of the most popular type. Mary herself played the lute and the virginal with considerable skill. There is a recorded complaint by the Venetian ambassador that the queen did not display her skill often enough.

During her girlhood Elizabeth learned to play several musical instruments, developing particular skill in playing the virginal. As queen she often played rounds on it to relieve the tedium of her position. She was so inordinately proud of her skill that she asked foreign ambassadors if their queen played as well as she. Elizabeth's staff of household musicians included seventeen trumpeters, six sackbutists (the sackbut was a forerunner of the trombone), six viol players, two lutenists, two harpists, two virginal players, and three drummers. The queen derived so much pleasure from the sound of trumpets and drums that dinner was usually announced by twelve trumpeters and two drummers "who made the hall ring for a half hour together." Elizabeth was also the subject of, and inspiration for, many madrigals. Composers glorified her under such names as Gloriana, Pandora, and Cynthia. She is also the heroine of Thomas Morley's famous collection of madrigals titled *The Triumphs of Oriana*. This elaborate tribute consists of twenty-six madrigals linked by the common refrain:

> Then sang the nymphs and shepherds of Diana
> Long live fair Oriana.

Ironically the printed copies of the madrigals were not distributed until after the queen's death because she disliked the name Oriana.

Although the royal court with its musicians was an important center for the cultivation of music, it was not the whole story. One need make only a superficial study of life in Tudor England to realize how widespread the interest in music was. The members of the nobility followed the example of the Tudor rulers insofar as they were financially able to do so. Those who could not afford to employ professional musicians became amateur musicians or encouraged members of their immediate family to study music. As prescribed by Castiglione's *Courtier* many gentlemen learned to read music at sight and to carry a part in madrigal or catch singing. Women, for their part, learned to play the lute, the viol, or the virginal. As the sixteenth century moved toward the Elizabethan age it became customary for guests to bring their music books for a round of singing after dinner. According to

Thomas Morley in his *Plain and Easy Introduction to Practical Music* (1597) any man or woman who could not carry his or her part in group singing might well elicit such comment as, "How was he (or she) brought up?" Among the members of the middle class the interest in music was equally great. In regard to music as in other respects the bourgeoisie imitated the nobles. The interest in music extended beyond the home. At Oxford and Cambridge, for example, students would gather for recreational singing after study hours. Furthermore, many craft gilds organized singing groups which met after working hours. Singing was also a common pastime in many shops, so that all from the apprentice to the master could indulge their love of song. Considerable attention was also given to music, and particularly singing, in primary and secondary schools. In many schools it was customary for the music master to take his pupils on singing walks over the fields and through the woods.

The interest of the Elizabethan age in music is reflected in Shakespeare's poems and plays. The great dramatist seems to have assumed that music was a matter of common knowledge, for his plays abound in references which only a person familiar with the art can appreciate. Thirty-two of his thirty-seven plays contain references to music and musical instruments, many of them in the form of witticisms. The instrument which supplied him with the most metaphors was the lute. He wrote, for example, "Nay, but this jesting spirit which is now crept into a lute string, and now governed by stops." Again, "O, you are well-tuned now, but I'll set down the pegs that make this music." There is a broader reference to music in "The Rape of Lucrece":

> My restless discord loves no stops or rests;
> A woeful hostess brooks not many quests.
> Relish your nimble notes[1] to pleasing ears,
> Distress like dumps when time is kept with tears.
> These means, like frets upon an instrument,
> Shall tune our heart-strings to true languishment.

In general. Shakespeare's references to music are those of a knowledgeable amateur. His songs, of which there are many in his plays, represent the secular form of the art which for so long had been the servant of religion. There is a happy strain in most of the songs, but in some instances they are very solemn. The titles include such as "Where is Sylvia?", "Blow, Blow Thou Wintry Wind," "Tell Me Where is Fancy Bred?", "Sigh No More," "Hark, Hark the Lark," "It was a Lover and His Lass," and "Come Away, Come Away, Death." In Shakespeare's plays there are also more than three hundred stage directions regarding music. In all of them, however, there is not one that calls for music of the "Te Deum" or "Sanctus" type.

[1] "Nimble notes" was a term used to designate brilliant music. A dump, as stated earlier, is a dance.

English Humanism

In England, as in France and Germany, humanism received its first impulse from Italy. But in England humanism did not become the fashion in as wide a circle as it had in Italy. At first the study of the classics was confined to a relatively small group of scholars and later it became an important part of the curriculum of some primary and secondary schools and of most universities. Its introduction into the schools, which took place gradually over a long period of time, changed the character of education by putting greater emphasis on secular and less on religious aims. Much attention was given to the study of Latin because of its vocational value. A knowledge of it was a necessary preliminary to the study of law, medicine, and the learned professions generally. The Greek language and Greek thought, on the other hand, were studied for their cultural value, an important exception being the study of the Greek New Testament by theologians. The early humanists, and particularly the Oxford Reformers, most of whom were educators as well as scholars, had a firm faith in the enlightenment value of the classical writings; hence they regarded the study of the classics as the best means for effecting reforms in education, religion, government, and society in general.

Humanism was not, as has often been stated, introduced into England rather suddenly near the end of the fifteenth century by the group of scholars known as the Oxford Reformers. Like all cultural movements, English humanism was the fruit of a period of development. Italian humanism did, however, take root comparatively late in England. For this the wars, epidemics, and economic depression as well as England's geographical isolation were responsible. After its introduction, its growth was undoubtedly slowed by the conservative nature of English culture. When the Italian humanist Poggio Bracciolini visited England (1419-1422) he found a lack of interest in Italian humanism. He wrote to a friend that he was able to find "few lovers of learning and those few were barbarous, skilled rather in quibbles and sophisms than in letters." What Poggio meant was that they were imbued with the spirit of scholasticism. He further stated, "There are few ancient books and these are greatly inferior to our own."

The first Englishman who displayed a lively appreciation of Italian humanism seems to have been Humphrey, duke of Gloucester (1391-1447), younger son of King Henry IV. Duke Humphrey's interest in Italian learning appears to have been stimulated, above all, by the works of Petrarch and Boccaccio. As his interest developed he employed Italian humanists as secretaries and also carried on a correspondence with other Italian humanists. Furthermore, with the help of his Italian friends he started a collection of manuscripts of classical writings. But his greatest contribution to the establishment of humanism in England was his donation of classical manuscripts to Oxford University where there was a scarcity of such manuscripts. His first gift of 129 manuscripts was followed by a second of 134. Later he gave the university his entire collection. Among these manuscripts were many translations from Greek into Latin which had been made at his request by his Italian friends. Like Petrarch, Duke Humphrey could not read Greek, but he was deeply interested in Greek life and thought.

The scholar who is generally credited with reviving interest in the Greek language and Greek thought in England is William Selling (also spelled Sellying or Celling) (d.1494), a Benedictine monk. As a young man Selling spent the years from 1464 to 1467 in Italy, the wellspring of humanism. The prominent humanists whose lectures he heard at Padua, Bologna, and Rome excited in him a deep enthusiasm for classical studies. Selling achieved a mastery of Greek which he used to translate at least one work from Greek into Latin. He also became a collector of classical manuscripts, taking a number of them back to England. Upon his return home he taught Greek in the schools at Canterbury for several years and in 1472 became prior of St. Augustine's monastery at Canterbury. There he made his most important contribution by inspiring his monks with his ardor for learning, making his monastery a center of Hellenic studies. Some historians believe that it was Selling's example which was responsible for the addition of courses in the Greek language and in Greek thought to the curriculum of Oxford University. His most distinguished pupil was Thomas Linacre who later became one of the Oxford Reformers. Selling probably taught young Linacre Greek before the latter entered Oxford University. In 1486 Linacre accompanied Prior Selling who was sent to Italy by Henry VII as envoy to the papal court. Linacre remained there more than a decade, spending some of the time studying Greek under the great Italian humanist Angelo Politian, the protege of Lorenzo de Medici.

In the last quarter of the fifteenth century the interest in humanism gradually increased. More foreign scholars visited England and what was of greater importance, more English students traveled to Italy to drink at the fountains of humanistic knowledge. Humanistic studies, however, were pursued more as a series of individual efforts than as part of a movement. It was not until the appearance of the Oxford Reformers near the turn of the century that humanism entered the professional stage. The outstanding members of the Oxford group which sponsored what in England was called the New Learning were William Grocyn (1446-1519), Thomas Linacre (1460-1524), John Colet (1466-1519), and Sir Thomas More (1478-1535). Erasmus, too, was affiliated with the group during his visits to England.

Grocyn, Linacre, and Colet had during the last decade of the fifteenth century studied in Italy where they had developed a keen interest in humanism. Upon their return to England they all taught at Oxford, giving special attention to the Greek language and Greek thought, and imparting to their students some of the enthusiasm which had been kindled in Italy.

Humanism and scholasticism which up to that time had stood side by side now began to diverge with the former becoming a study in its own right in the schools and universities. At the same time humanism was also gained a place in the curriculum of Cambridge University where Erasmus helped to introduce the study of Greek. From that time onward, humanistic studies gradually displaced scholastic learning in other English universities. The process, however, was slow, covering a considerable period. For the members of the Oxford group, humanism was not only an experience in good letters, but also a training for an active and successful mundane life. It was more than this. The Oxford Reformers also regarded humanism as the means for educational and religious reform. They would make the classics the new basis for a liberal education, thereby toppling scholasticism from its high place in education. In this they were not disappointed. They further hoped that the moral ideas of the ancient philosophers would cleanse religion of superstition. In this, however, they were disappointed. The Oxford Reformers also had another reason for learning Greek. They regarded a knowledge of this language as the key to understanding the New Testament. In general, the Oxford Reformers exerted a broadening influence on the entire field of knowledge.

The educational reforms of John Colet are worthy of special consideration. After teaching at Oxford for some years, he was appointed dean of St. Paul's Cathedral in London. It was there that he made his greatest contribution to the establishment of classical learning in English education. He did this by founding St. Paul's Grammar School, the first school in England devoted expressly to classical studies (New Learning). He also set a precedent by choosing as trustees for this school the Company of Mercers, thereby putting it under lay management. The example set by Colet soon inspired others to open schools on the model of St. Paul's. It has been calculated that sixty such schools were opened during the reign of Henry VIII and about the same number during the short reign of Edward VI.

Sir Thomas More and His Utopia

By all odds the most famous of the English humanists is Sir Thomas More, author of *Utopia*. After receiving his preliminary schooling in London where he was born, young Thomas entered Oxford University. There he came under the influence of Grocyn, Linacre, and Colet. Thomas' developing interest in humanism soon distressed his father, the barrister Sir John More. He not only wanted his son to enter his own profession, but he also feared that the study of the pagan classics might undermine his son's religious orthodoxy. Hence the father removed young Thomas from Oxford and entered him at New Inn in London to begin the study of law. Two years later he became a student at Lincoln's Inn. In the practice of law More was so successful that he was soon ranked with the best lawyers of England.

He did not, however, lose his interest in classical studies. What little time he could spare from a busy life was devoted to humanistic pursuits. He himself said, "I get only that time which I steal from sleep and meat." These were the happiest years of his adult life. His work, his studies, his children, and his friends were sources of much pleasure to him. Later Erasmus lived for a considerable time in the midst of More's family. It is reported that when the two men met for the first time Erasmus greeted More by saying, "You are either More or nothing," to which the latter replied, "You are either Erasmus or the Devil." The fast friendship which followed resulted in a translation into Latin of parts of the writings of Lucian, the Greek satirist, a work in which the two humanists collaborated. (*See Fig.* 27.)

In 1518 More became a member of the staff of King Henry VIII. For some time both the king and Cardinal Wolsey had been urging him to do so, but More had no taste for the life of a courtier. When he finally did consent, he wrote to his friend Bishop Fisher, "I have come to Court extremely against my will." As a member of the Privy Council he was in close contact with Henry VIII. Both the king and his first wife, Catherine of Aragon, were very fond of him and he was frequently invited to dine with the royal couple. In 1529, when Cardinal Wolsey lost the king's favor for failing to have Henry's marriage to Catherine annulled by the pope, More was chosen to succeed him as Lord Chancellor of England. The three years during which he held the office were not a happy time for Sir Thomas. The arguments that were advanced to justify the annulment of the king's marriage did not in the opinion of More carry conviction, and he frankly communicated this to the king. Henry VIII, who could not brook opposition, never forgave his Chancellor. In 1532 illness gave More an excuse for resigning his office. He retired to private life, but the vengeful king did not permit him to end his life in peace. Henry demanded that More take the oath of supremacy which declared the king to be "the only supreme head in earth of the Church of England." When Sir Thomas refused he was tried for treason, convicted, and sentenced to death. Henry did nothing to save the life of his former close friend and faithful servant. The extent of his mercy was to change the mode of execution from hanging to decapitation. More faced death calmly in July, 1535. It is reported that when he arrived at the scaffold erected on Tower Hill in London he said to the guards escorting him, "Assist me up; in coming down I shall shift for myself." As his neck was placed on the block he said to the executioner, "Wait till I put my beard aside, for it hath done no treason." But the king's spirit of vengeance was still not satisfied. As a warning to others, More's head was fixed on a pike set up on London Bridge. Furthermore, Henry exercised his right to confiscate the property of one condemned for treason. Lady More was evicted from the house in the Chelsea district of London and the property was bestowed on Henry's young daughter Elizabeth who retained ownership of it for the rest of her life. As for More, in 1935 the Roman

Catholic Church conferred on him the supreme honor by raising him to sainthood.

The book of Sir Thomas More which has kept his memory alive is his *Utopia*, a title which literally means "no place" or "nowhere." Originally written in Latin, the treatise is a dialogue between the author and one Raphael Hythloday who supposedly had accompanied Amerigo Vespucci on his voyages to the New World. The first part of More's *Utopia* is an indictment of the social order in Europe, and particularly in England. In it he lays bare some of the evils afflicting contemporary society. One of the major evils is that of corrupt government. He denounces rulers for not ruling justly. Many princes, he states, are so busy waging ruthless wars in an effort to enlarge their dominions that they have no time to devote to the welfare of their subjects. Another major evil is the misuse of private property, a misuse which leads to the oppression of the poor by the wealthy. As an example of this, More cites the inclosure by the landlords of arable land and common pasture for purposes of sheep-raising, thereby causing the eviction of many peasant cultivators and much unemployment. At the end of Book I, Hythloday asserts that all the social evils previously discussed could be eliminated if all property were held in common. He then promises to show in Book II that this is possible.

In Book II More presents his concept of an ideal Commonwealth in the form of Utopia. It is a thoroughly secular concept, one which recreates the hopes of the Garden of Eden. It is located in the lands or islands of the New World visited by Amerigo Vespucci whose description More had read. The commonwealth of Utopia is, in More's words, "so different from the manner of our government which is based upon the right of private property." In it the common welfare prevails over the interests of the individual. The principal feature of Utopia is the absence of private property. Everything is held in common. Money is used only in transactions with other nations. The principal source of income is agriculture, with the working day limited to six hours. A national system of education offers instruction to all Utopians of both sexes, but higher education is restricted to the most gifted. All living quarters are uniform and there are no locks on the doors. War is outlawed in Utopia except for self-defense and there is a broad toleration of religious beliefs. Another interesting feature is the ban on use of cosmetics. Furthermore, if two people contemplate marriage they are permitted to examine each other in the nude in order to make certain that neither has a physical defect which might cause marital unhappiness. In general, all citizens live together as brothers and sisters. In describing his ideal commonwealth More emphasizes that it is "not possible for all things to be well unless all men are good." In the case of the Utopians the good life is possible because they are living in a state of "uncorrupted nature."

The two works usually mentioned as furnishing More with the germ of his concept of an ideal commonwealth are Plato's *Republic* and St. Augustine's *City of God*. More refers to Plato's *Republic* in his work and it is recorded that he also made a careful study of *The City of God* either before or while he was writing *Utopia*. It is easy, however, to exaggerate More's indebtedness to the two works. He had his own concept of an ideal commonwealth. There are many important differences between More's *Utopia* on the one hand and Plato's *Republic* and St. Augustine's *City of God* on the other. One such difference, for example, is inherent in the attitude toward war. Although St. Augustine ascribed war to man's fall from grace, that is, to sin, he did permit resort to arms as a means of forcing dissenters into line. The Utopians, on the contrary, never resort to force to change dissent to assent. As for Plato, his ideal republic is a combination of peace and war. His professional soldiers belong to one of the two highest ruling classes. The Utopians, however, abhor war as a school of unnatural cruelty, as the negation of everything that is good. Every activity in Utopia is organized on a peaceful basis. Whereas Plato regarded hunting as excellent training for warfare, it is to the Utopians inhuman debauchery of human nature.

More's criticism of conditions he saw about him was so pointed that he did not dare to publish his *Utopia* in England. The first edition, published at Louvain in the Netherlands in 1516 under the supervision of Erasmus, was an immediate success; in fact, its success was not far short of that enjoyed by Erasmus' *Praise of Folly* four years earlier. A second Latin edition was published in France in 1517 with a preface by the French humanist Budé. The next year a third edition was put out in Basel with illustrations by the painter Hans Holbein. Before long the book became a classic, appearing in many languages in many countries. By the middle of the sixteenth century it appeared in German, Italian, and French translations. Finally in 1551 an English translation was also put out in England. During the next two centuries it went through forty-four editions and since then has continued to evoke considerable interest. It has been of special interest to those who look toward a better society. The adjective "utopian" is used to designate all plans for and all literature dealing with an ideal society which is theoretically attractive, but impossible to translate into reality. All attempts to establish such a society before Marxian socialism appeared are lumped under the term "utopian socialism."

After More's death English humanism developed at a much slower pace. This was due in large part to the fact that many of the best minds became involved in the religious controversies which followed Henry VIII's break with Rome. Humanism, however, became progressively more secular. Whereas Dean Colet feared the possible effect of the pagan classics on Christian readers, Roger Ascham (1515-1568), Cambridge humanist and tutor of Elizabeth Tudor, regarded the classics as a treasury of practical knowledge for everyday life second only to the Sacred Scriptures.

19

The Renaissance in Spain

Spain Under Ferdinand and Isabella

During much of the Middle Ages most of Spain was under the rule of the Moslems or Moors. The opportunity of conquering Spain was offered them when the government of the Christian Visigoths who had settled in Spain at the beginning of the Middle Ages began to decline. The Moorish invasion began in 711 when a force of Arabs and Berbers (indiscriminately called Moors in Spain) under the leadership of Tarik took Gibraltar, a name which is a corruption of Jabal-al-Tarik meaning the "mountain of Tarik." The invaders then continued their advance until most of the Iberian Peninsula was under their control. They did, however, permit the Christians to retain the territory along the northern rim of the peninsula. In addition there were scattered groups of Christians in isolated valleys. Although the Moors did endeavor to convert the Christians to Mohammedanism, they were tolerant enough to permit those who refused to become converts to remain Christian upon payment of a fee. The tolerant rule of the Moors also attracted many Jews to Spain. During the centuries that followed a vigorous intellectual life developed in a number of centers. For example, many manuscripts dealing with Greek science were translated into Arabic and special attention was given to the study of mathematics, optics, and medicine. In general this Arabic civilization left an indelible mark on the civilization of Spain.

The tide turned again in favor of the Christian population when the political organization of the Moors began to disintegrate in the second half of the eleventh century. What had been a centralized government under a caliph gradually broke up into small states, and the Christians began to reconquer some of the territory their ancestors had lost in the eighth century. Progress was slow and was often achieved at a high cost in blood. But the Christian forces persisted, managing finally by 1266 after a determined effort to reduce the holdings of the Moors to the kingdom of Granada which they continued to hold for more than two centuries. The fact that the campaign of reconquest was conducted in the spirit of a crusade tremendously affected the future history of Spain. It intensified the religious feelings of the Spanish people to the point of fanaticism which, in turn, led to the persecution and suppression of other faiths and the expulsion of their adherents.

In the meantime another contest had begun. This one was between particularism and national unity. It was not easy to overcome the particularist feelings which were nourished by a variety of political, economic, and social factors, one of which was the diversity of language. Although, as in the other countries of Western Europe, Latin was the language of the Church, the universities, and the law, the language of the people varied according to the district in which they lived. In addition to the many local dialects there were five major languages: Castilian, Catalan, Basque, Arabic, and Portuguese. Nevertheless, the many smaller territorial units were gradually incorporated into larger ones. The stronger states absorbed neighboring territories until the whole of the Iberian Peninsula, except Granada, was included in four states: Portugal, Castile, Aragon, and Navarre. Portugal, which early displayed a strong particularist spirit, managed by the middle of the fifteenth century to gain enough strength and wealth to prevent its absorption. Castile, which was by far the largest of the other three states, embraced roughly the central regions of the Iberian Peninsula. The territory of Aragon, which was in the eastern and northeastern part of the peninsula, extended southward from the Pyrenees. The little kingdom of Navarre straddled the Pyrenees with territory to the north and to the south.

A new period in the history of what is now called Spain was ushered in by the marriage of Ferdinand, heir to the crown of Aragon, and Isabella, heiress to the crown of Castile. The marriage did not bring about an actual political union of the kingdoms, for, as provided by the marriage contract, each kingdom retained its separate laws, institutions, and tariff boundaries. The two kingdoms had no institutions in common except the Spanish Inquisition which was established some years after the marriage. But the marital union did result in a common foreign policy which caused the other European states to regard Castile and Aragon as a single power which they called Spain. After the death of Ferdinand and Isabella the rule of the two kingdoms was joined in the person of their grandson Charles.

After Isabella succeeded to the Castilian throne in 1474, and Ferdinand to the throne of Aragon in 1479, one of their aims was to consolidate the royal power in their respective kingdoms and to establish peace and order. In Castile, for example, the enforcement of law was so lax that the country was on the verge of anarchy. During the preceding reign the royal authority had declined to the point where the laws were openly flouted by the great nobles who terrorized the royal judges and even collected and kept royal revenues. Highways were infested with bandits who preyed on travelers, especially on traveling merchants. As a means of restoring respect for law and the authority of the crown the new sovereigns revived the Santa Hermandad (Holy Brotherhood), an association which had been founded in the thirteenth century to restore peace and order in certain districts. The members of the Santa Hermandad, functioning as a kind of royal constabulary, made short shrift of bandits and other lawbreakers. The same organization was used to enforce law and establish the authority of the crown in Aragon. In the struggle against the rebellious nobles, Ferdinand and Isabella had the support of the members of the middle class. This support the bourgeoisie willingly gave in return for the preservation of order which they needed to conduct their business. The sovereigns, for their part, needed the revenues they were collecting in the form of customs duties imposed on the expanding commerce. Hence they endeavored to promote the growth of commerce by improving highways, encouraging the holding of fairs, and by replacing adulterated and debased coins with coins of standard value.

A further aim of Ferdinand and Isabella was to make Spain a country of one religion. In religious matters both sovereigns were ardent champions of the Roman Catholic faith. They were so zealous in behalf of it that Pope Alexander VI bestowed on them the title "The Catholic Sovereigns." Their efforts to establish religious uniformity had a further purpose beyond extending the sway of the Roman Catholic faith. They saw in religious unity a means of binding together their scattered territorial possessions. The first step in the direction of religious unity was to break the Moorish hold on the kingdom of Granada. This was finally achieved in 1492 after a decade of fierce resistance by the Moors. The capitulation of Granada marked the end of the long struggle between the Christians and the Moslem Moors which had been waged intermittently for almost eight centuries. Although the Catholic sovereigns promised the Moors free exercise of their religion, the promise was not implemented. Pressure was soon exerted on the Moors to compel them to accept Christianity. When the Moors of some districts of Granada rose in protest, the Spanish government declared that the uprising had nullified the terms of the treaty. In 1502 a royal decree ordered all Moors either to become converts to Christianity or to leave the country. While some remained as Moriscos, as the converts were called, others decided to emigrate even though it meant the confiscation of their property. Since the Moors were, by and large, industrious subjects who had learned various skills and whose morals were on a par with those of the Christians, the emigration of a large number of Moors was a loss Spain could ill afford.

The forcible conversion or expulsion of the Moors was only a single phase of the plan of Ferdinand and Isabella to make Spain a land of one faith. In the same year they also moved against the Jews. Whereas the long struggle had engendered hostility toward the Moors, no such struggle had taken place against the Jews. Among the major sources of ill-feeling toward the Jews was their stubborn resistance to all efforts to convert them to Christianity. Another source of opposition was the success achieved by Jews in the business world where they served the society of their time as merchants and money-lenders, and also as physicians. Even the rulers and the members of the court turned to Jewish money-lenders when they were in financial straits. The success of Jewish merchants and bankers in amassing wealth excited both envy and hostility in some circles. The center of the opposition appears to have been in the population at large where agitators stirred up anti-Semitic feelings. At first this feeling vented itself in sporadic attacks on the homes of wealthy Jews by mobs who ransacked and plundered them. Some of these attacks even degenerated into pogroms in which many Jews lost their lives. To escape such persecutions and threats, some Jews became *conversos*, known as Maranos, but the majority adhered to their old faith. Meanwhile various persons were urging Ferdinand and Isabella to force the remaining Jews either to become converts or to leave the country. After the fall of Granada in 1492 the Spanish rulers decreed that within a period of four months all Jews of whatever age or sex must under penalty of death and confiscation of property either become conversos or leave Spain. The number of converts has been estimated as being in the hundreds of thousands. How many left Spain is still a debatable question. In any case their departure added greatly to the loss Spain suffered through the expulsion of the Moors.

The conversion of the Jews and Moors who decided to stay in Spain failed to mollify public feeling. It was widely believed that many of the conversions were not sincere, that many of the neo-Christians who accepted Christianity outwardly were furtively observing the rites of their ancestral religion. The suspicions seem to have been especially strong regarding the Maranos. Many Maranos experienced little difficulty in adjusting themselves to their new religion and a limited number even succeeded in achieving distinction in the Roman Catholic Church. One such example is that of a former rabbi who became bishop of Burgos. There are also many instances of the intermarriage of such neo-Christians with members of the old Spanish nobility. Impecunious nobles did not spurn the opportunity to get a large dowry for a son or daughter by concluding a marriage alliance with a member of a wealthy Marano family. Such marriages were so common that in some parts of Spain there was hardly an aristocratic family without an admixture of Jewish blood. On the other hand, it is self-evident that many, even most, of the conversions effected by forcible means were not sincere. Many outwardly accepted Christianity so that they could stay in Spain, but in the privacy of their homes practised crypto-Judaism, observing every jot and tittle of the Jewish laws. Except for the fact that they had their children baptized, attended mass, and outwardly observed Christian rites, they were as Jewish as they had been before. Hence the popular conception that many Maranos were hypocritical Jews was not without justification. As Jews the Maranos had not been under the jurisdiction of the Church and were thus not liable to be accused of heresy. Now it was another matter. As Jews they had been infidels, but as Maranos they were heretics and as such subject to investigation by the dread Inquisition, a tribunal for the searching out and punishment of heresy.

During the period just prior to the accession of Ferdinand and Isabella there had been considerable agitation in certain lay and ecclesiastical circles for the introduction of the Inquisition into Spain. This demand was repeated after Isabella became queen of Castile in 1474. At first she was too busy with the problem of establishing law and order in Castile, but as early as 1478 she approved the sending of a petition to the Vatican for permission to establish such a tribunal. Pope Sixtus IV granted the request in a special bull and the so-called Spanish Inquisition was subsequently set up in both Castile and Aragon. Although the most obvious purpose of the Spanish Inquisition was to cleanse the taint of heresy from the lifeblood of the Church, this was not the whole story. The Spanish Inquisition was also an instrument of the crown for the enforcement of absolute rule. To the Catholic Sovereigns heresy was more than a crime against the Church; it was also an offense against the monarchy which had forbidden heresy. The rulers believed that those who rejected some of the teachings of the Church were also inclined to be disloyal to the government. Furthermore, the Inquisition was also a means for replenishing the royal treasury. The rulers had the right to claim two-thirds of the property of any person convicted of heresy and they did not fail to exercise the right. This goes far toward explaining why the wealthy were more frequently accused of heresy.

During the first months of its existence the Spanish Inquisition moved slowly, but once it was established in Seville (1480) it unleashed its full fury against the wealthy Maranos and Moriscos. Soon its reputation was so sinister that the very mention of it struck terror into many hearts. Some of the inquisitors were so fiendishly zealous that Pope Sixtus IV found it necessary to reprove them. In 1482 he wrote a letter to the Spanish sovereigns in which he stated that the unrestrained zeal against heretics seemed to be motivated by "ambition and greed for earthly possessions." But the admonition of the pope fell on deaf ears. Ordinarily the inquisitors aimed at obtaining a personal confession of guilt. If the confession was not voluntary the inquisitors could resort to torture. The tortures were so terrible that few could stand up under them. In Seville alone over a period of eight years the tribunal condemned some seven hundred persons to death by burning. In some instances as many as fifty were burned at one time. During the same period such lesser punishments as monetary fines, imprisonment, consignment to the galleys, and elaborate public penance were imposed on about five thousand others. The number of cases in which the accused was not found guilty was small. In Spain as a whole about two thousand were condemned to death during the fifteen years (1483-1498) Torquemada was inquisitor general and grand inquisitor, to say nothing about the many thousands who were punished in other ways. The efforts of the Spanish Inquisition to uncover heresy continued until it was abolished in 1834.

The piety of the Catholic Sovereigns and their zeal in the eradication of heresy did not, however, incline them to permit papal interference in the affairs of their kingdoms. Throughout their reigns they jealously guarded the royal prerogative in both ecclesiastical and secular matters. When the pope wished to appoint a foreigner to a Spanish bishopric, the Spanish rulers objected so vigorously that he abandoned the idea. In 1482 they succeeded in obtaining from the pope a renunciation of his right to choose candidates to fill vacancies in Spanish bishoprics. They further circumscribed the pope's authority in Spain by decreeing that papal bulls must not be introduced into the country without their permission.

Before her death in 1504 Isabella named as her successor her daughter Joanna or Juanna (often called Juanna la Loca or Joanna the Mad), specifying that if her daughter should be incapacitated Ferdinand was to rule Castile. Joanna, who had earlier shown signs of mental instability, was so distraught when her mother died that Ferdinand assumed the rule of Castile. However, Joanna's husband, Philip the Fair of Habsburg, son of Maximilian I of the Holy Roman Empire, contested Ferdinand's assumption of the rule of Castile. The latter stepped back in favor of his son-in-law who took up the reins of government with the title King Philip I of Castile. A man of quite ordinary mental endowments, the handsome Philip was too busy pursuing pretty women to give much attention to governmental affairs. His rule was short-lived. In 1506 he died so suddenly at the age of twenty-eight that it was rumored he had been poisoned. Since his death further unhinged Joanna's mind, causing her to sink into a deep melancholy, Ferdinand again assumed the rule of Castile. Just before his own death in 1516 Ferdinand despatched a force to overrun that part of the kingdom of Navarre which lies south of the Pyrenees. Thus the entire Iberian Peninsula with the exception of Portugal was united under one rule.

Charles V and Philip II

Ferdinand's successor as the ruler of all of Spain was Charles (1500-1558), the son of Joanna and Philip the Handsome. On the maternal side he was the grandson of Ferdinand and Isabella and on the paternal side of Emperor Maximilian I and Mary of Burgundy. From both sides he inherited vast territories. His title as ruler of Spain was Charles I, but he later became Emperor Charles V of the Holy Roman Empire and is generally known as Charles V. Ten years before the death of Ferdinand of Spain Charles had inherited the Netherlands and Franche-Comté (the county of Burgundy). It was there that he spent most of the next decade. When he was apprised of the death of his grandfather Ferdinand, Charles waited more than a year before he went to Spain to claim the crowns of Castile and Aragon. His reception was hardly enthusiastic. The fact that he was a foreigner who could not speak Spanish did not endear him to his Spanish subjects. Neither did the fact that he was accompanied by a group of Flemish courtiers who acted as his advisers and to whom he gave many of the most lucrative offices in the Church and in the state. His Spanish subjects believed that the offices should have been given to Spaniards, not to greedy foreigners who would drain the country of gold.

Further objections were raised when Charles became a candidate to succeed his grandfather Maximilian as emperor of the Holy Roman Empire. The Spanish people wanted their ruler to center his attention on the problems of their country and had no desire to become entangled in the affairs of Germany. The Cortes (representative body) of Castile and also that of Aragon finally voted him the subsidies he requested, but only under protest. Charles then went to Germany where he was elected emperor in 1519 and crowned in the next year. At the age of twenty he was the ruler of a vast empire which, in addition to the Habsburg territories of Germany, included Spain, the Netherlands, Franche-Comté, the kingdom of Naples and Sicily, a number of ports and fortified trading stations in Africa, and the immense Spanish possessions in the New World.

Relations between Charles and his Spanish subjects improved after his return to Spain in 1522. Having gained some experience in statecraft, he made a greater effort to please his subjects. The Spanish people, for their part, responded by accepting the imperial destiny which Charles imposed on them and which created a more intimate relationship between the affairs of Spain and those of Europe. Spain, as the heart of the great empire of Charles, furnished the lion's share of men and money to wage the wars in which Charles became involved. Charles's first war with France was a military success. As stated in Chapter 17, his army roundly defeated the forces of Francis I of France at Pavia in Italy (1525) and took the French king captive. Although peace was concluded, war with France broke out anew in the thirties. In 1537 Charles sent an army into Provence, but a determined French resistance compelled it to withdraw. A further war was waged against the Turks who were moving into Eastern Europe. In 1529 they made Hungary a Turkish province; then attempted to take Vienna. With the help of Polish reinforcements, the imperial army forced the Turks to lift the siege of Vienna and withdraw. Later Charles became involved in hostilities with the Protestant League in Germany, defeating the Protestant army at Mühlberg (1547). His victory, however, failed to settle the religious question in Germany; in fact, none of his wars solved any major problems.

Spain did, it is true, have its hour of greatness under Charles V; it was regarded as the dominant power of Europe. Some contemporaries even believed Spain to be the greatest power on earth. It was said that "when Spain moves the whole world trembles." But its greatness was more apparent than real. Spain's shortlived supremacy was achieved at a tremendous price in blood and money. The wars of Charles V were so costly that they drained Spain of much of the treasure which flowed in from the New World. If the silver mines of Peru had not poured such vast quantities of the precious metal into the royal coffers, Charles would have been in serious financial difficulties during the last decade of his reign. Since Spain derived little if any benefit from the wars, they were a prodigal waste of men and substance. It would have been better for the future of Spain if Charles had centered his attention on the economic development of this country.

By the middle of the century Charles was becoming discouraged and depressed. Most of the old problems were still far from being solved. The Turks were still a menace to Europe, the religious question in Germany had not been settled, his second war with France had not gone well, and in Italy the people of the territories ruled by Charles were restive. In addition new troubles were brewing in other directions. During his last years the emperor's health was also failing. Complications were added to the gout from which he had suffered for many years. Convinced that he could no longer bear the burdens of empire, he abdicated the crowns of Castile and Aragon, the rule of the Netherlands, and the throne of the kingdom of Naples in favor of his son Philip II in 1556. He also made an unsuccessful attempt to secure for his son the succession to the imperial dignity of the Holy Roman Empire. Having shifted the burden of ruling the vast Spanish empire to the shoulders of his son, Charles retired to a Spanish monastery where he spent the last months of his life walking in the garden, feeding the birds, and tinkering with clocks. He died in 1558. Later his remains were entombed in the Escorial.

The biographers of Philip II (1527-1598) have projected various images of him in their biographies. Those with Dutch or Protestant sympathies have pictured him as a cruel and despotic bigot. Some English biographers have presented him as a misguided ruler who sought to overwhelm their country with his "Invincible Armada." Biographers who sympathize with Philip's aim of preserving orthodoxy by suppressing what the Church and the Inquisition regarded as heresy have depicted him as a man of great religious fervor. But others, in addition to sympathetic biographers, have held him in high esteem. Among these most of his Spanish subjects must be included. Their esteem was rooted in the fact that he was thoroughly Spanish and that his aims coincided with their wishes. To them he was Philip the Prudent. As a person Philip was serious, even somber, with a haughty bearing. Whereas his father could be jovial on occasion, Philip was always cold and reserved in public. Only in the privacy of the royal apartments does he seem to have displayed any feeling of humanity. He must have been capable of some degree of affection, for each of his four wives loved him deeply. Some of his biographers have relieved the starkness of the portrait they painted in words by asserting that he was devoted to children and loved flowers. Philip's hero was his father whom he imitated in many ways. Unfortunately Philip lacked his father's ability. He also lacked the vigor his father displayed during much of his life; such pastimes as jousting and hunting had little attraction for him.

As ruler Philip took great delight in the exercise of his royal authority. He was convinced that God had bestowed this authority on him and that he was accountable only to God. In making decisions he was so obstinately self-willed that he was almost impervious to the influence of others. He was so distrustful and suspicious of his ministers that he feared to delegate authority to them. He, therefore, tried to do as much of the work of administration as he could. He was, however, so lacking in discretion that he spent much of his time on trivial matters, while his ministers were attending to more important ones. His aim as a ruler was twofold. First, he would reestablish the universal power of the Roman Catholic Church, and second, he would make Spain the greatest power of his day. He failed to achieve either aim. He did, however, succeed with the help of the Inquisition in maintaining religious unity in Spain. Regarding religious deviation as a form of resistance to royal authority, he felt that it was his duty to use all the resources of his country to stamp it out. But, while he was insisting that every subject accept the teachings of the Church unquestioningly, he was so jealous of his royal prerogative that, like his predecessors, he refused to permit the pope to interfere in the affairs of his empire beyond the degree he thought proper.

At the time of the abdication of Charles V Spain was the predominant power in Europe and during most of Philip's reign it was able to maintain its ascendancy by virtue of the fabulous riches which the mines of the New World were producing. During these decades, however, the prosperity and prestige of the country were being slowly undermined. This was in part due to the manner in which Philip solved or tried to solve the problems confronting him. For example, when the Moriscos of Andalusia, one of the most industrious segments of the Spanish population, rose up to demand redress of certain grievances, Philip drowned the revolt in blood (1568-1571) and then scattered the Moriscos over all of Spain preliminary to their expulsion by his successor in 1609. This uprooting of the Moriscos was an important factor in the disruption of the Spanish economy.

In foreign affairs Philip was not unsuccessful during the early part of his reign. He vigorously pursued the war against France, which he had inherited from his father, with the result that the Spanish forces won two notable victories, Saint Quentin (1557) and Gravelines (1558). Thereafter Philip and Henry II of France made a treaty of peace so that both could devote more attention to eradicating the Protestant heresy. In the naval war against the Turks, Spain and its allies scored an impressive victory at Lepanto (1571). A large fleet of about 250 ships composed of contingents from Venice, Rome, and Florence as well as from Spain sailed under the command of Don John, illegitimate son of Charles V, to attack the Turks. The two fleets met at Lepanto in the Gulf of Corinth and after hours of bloody fighting Don John's fleet sank or captured many of the Turkish ships and forced the rest to seek safety in flight. Dissension which broke out among the Christian allies prevented them from making the most of the victory. Meanwhile the Turks had recovered from the defeat and had again taken the offensive.

Philip failed miserably in his attempts to conquer England and to suppress revolt in the Netherlands. The story of Philip's difficulties with England began with his marriage to Queen Mary (1554), arranged by his father who believed such a union would be advantageous to Spain. But the marriage of the spinsterish and sickly Mary, who was thirty-eight, and of Philip, a widower of twenty-six, was anything but a success from the Spanish point of view. When Philip failed to make England a Spanish appendage during Mary's lifetime, he became an unsuccessful suitor for the hand of Queen Elizabeth. He never forgot this rebuff. In addition the daring Elizabethan seamen began to prey on Spanish commerce, particularly on the Spanish treasure ships transporting precious metals to Spain from the New World. Philip also nourished a desire to punish Elizabeth for the execution of Mary, Queen of Scots, and, above all, he wished to reestablish Catholicism in England. All this caused him to assemble and fit out the "Invincible Armada" and to send it against England. Its destruction by the English, aided by storms, was not only a personal calamity for Philip; it was also a severe blow to Spanish prestige. The most vexing of Philip's problems was the revolt of the Netherlands, brought about by Philip's efforts to stamp out Protestantism. Charles V had adopted repressive measures against Protestantism in the Low Countries, but since he was born in the Netherlands and cherished a great affection for them, his measures did not excite revolt. Philip was, however, a foreigner and during his reign Protestantism was more widespread. When he with his characteristic determination to suppress heresy enforced the edicts against it with greater severity, a rebellion broke out (1566) which Philip with all the vast resources of his empire was unable to suppress. The Dutch fought on doggedly until their independence was recognized in the seventeenth century.

The last years of Philip's life were not a happy time. Not only had he failed to suppress the revolt of the Dutch and to crush the English; he also looked with dread toward the future because of the weakness of his son who was to succeed him as Philip III. In addition a lingering illness was sapping his energy. He accepted all as the will of God and sought relief from his disappointments in the construction of the Escorial which he had promised his father he would build. As the location for the huge building, which has been variously described as "a pile of granite" and "a clumsy mass with a central dome," Philip chose the bare windswept Guadarama mountains some distance from Madrid. Besides serving as a mausoleum for the Spanish kings and queens, the Escorial contains a church, a monastery, and royal apartments in which Philip II spent the last months of his life. For its embellishment Philip employed Spanish and foreign artists, also importing sculptures and paintings as well as building materials, tapestries, and candelabra from various parts of Europe. The structure was finally completed in 1595 and in the spring of 1598 Philip was carried there on a litter to await death. After months of almost indescribable pain which he suffered with his customary impassivity, his joyless life came to its end in September, 1598.

By the time of Philip's death signs of a decline were apparent in many phases of Spanish life. This decline, as it continued, terminated Spanish hegemony in Europe, relegating Spain to the rank of a second-rate power. The causes of this decline were so numerous and so complex that only some of the important ones can be listed here. One was the drain on the national finances caused by the fruitless attempts of Charles V and Philip II to dominate Europe. Another cause was the sharp drop in revenue from the American colonies. This was a result not only of a decline of the trade with the colonies, but, above all, of a reduced output of the Peruvian silver mines. A further cause was the inflation which had resulted earlier from the influx into Spain of gold and silver from Mexico and Peru. The rise of the prices of goods manufactured in Spain handicapped manufacturers and merchants in the competition for foreign markets. This and other factors caused a general decline of Spanish industry. In Seville, for example, the number of looms turning out silk and woolen cloth dropped from 16,000 during the reign of Charles V to 400 in 1621. Both trade and industry were also hampered by the technological backwardness of the Spanish people. As early as 1513 Guicciardini wrote, "Spaniards are thought to be shrewd and intelligent, but they are not good in liberal and mechanical arts." During the sixteenth century the other European countries outstripped them in technological advance.

There were also other causes of Spanish decadence which must not be overlooked. Among these was the decline of agricultural production. Two reasons for this were the widespread use of arable land as sheep meadows and the expulsion of the Moriscos. Soon Spanish agriculture was unable to meet the demand for food and the nation became dependent on northern and eastern Europe for grain. A cause of the decline which has frequently been emphasized by historians was the widespread aversion to honest labor among the Spanish people. This was true not only of the higher nobility, but also of the hidalgos or lesser nobles. Work was beneath their dignity. Consequently many hidalgos lived in a state of poverty and sloth. Moreover, their contempt for labor quickly filtered down to the lower classes. A further cause of decline was the lack of a vigorous growing middle class. Under Ferdinand and Isabella the Spanish middle class had flourished, but had begun to decline in both prosperity and numbers under Charles V. The decline was due in part to the fact that some members of the middle class managed to join the noble class, thereby enhancing their social standing and gaining exemption from certain taxes. During the reign of Philip II the deterioration of the middle class was steady. A final cause of the decline of Spain was the weakness of its rulers. The successors of Phillip II were both weak and incompetent. Hence when the Spanish decline gained momentum there was no strong hand to stem the tide. But in spite of the political and economic decline, the first decades of the seventeenth century were a golden age of Spanish culture.

The Spanish Renaissance

The question as to whether there was a Renaissance in Spain has been widely debated among historians. While some have asserted that Spain did not experience a Renaissance, others have stated emphatically that it did. Among the former was a group of German historians who published their works during the early decades of the twentieth century. Judging the case on the basis of arbitrary definitions of the Renaissance, members of this group made such statements as, "The Iberian Peninsula did not really experience a Renaissance." One historian published a book titled *Spain, the Land Without a Renaissance*. Even in Spain this idea was widely accepted. More recently, however, opinion has shifted; historical facts support the positive side. The same forces and influences which created the Renaissance in Italy were active in Spain, and they did leave their mark on Spanish life and culture.

One must bear in mind, however, that since the conditions the Renaissance forces encountered in Spain were different, the results they achieved were not the same as in Italy. Conditions were much more favorable in the Italian peninsula for the growth of a secular spirit. Whereas the tradition of a thoroughly secular Roman civilization was cherished in Italy, it had largely been extinguished in Spain. The great tradition in Spain was the long struggle of the Christians against the Moslem Moors. This struggle which had at times taken the form of a crusade had deeply ingrained the otherworldliness of Christianity in the hearts and minds of the Spanish people. It had engendered a religious fervor which the state as well as the Church helped to keep dynamic. In short, the otherworldly spirit was much more tenacious in Spain than in Italy. Medieval traditions were so firmly intrenched that there was no repudiation of the Middle Ages. Spanish humanists, artists, and writers did not, like Petrarch and other Italian leaders, regard the Middle Ages as a period of intellectual darkness. They were too deeply rooted in the Middle Ages. Architects, for example, continued to build cathedrals and churches in the Gothic style, giving little consideration to the classical elements in the Renaissance style. Furthermore, while scholars and philosophers of other countries were turning away from, even denouncing scholasticism, Spanish thinkers were developing it.

All this does not mean, however, that the Renaissance forces and influences did not make themselves felt in Spain. If they did not succeed in creating a thoroughly secular culture, they did substantially modify the existing culture. Scholars, artists, poets, novelists, and dramatists included secular ideas and Renaissance forms in their works; in fact, in some phases of culture the spirit and subject matter as well as the mode of expression became largely secular. This was achieved without rejecting religious or national traditions. By blending new secular ideas with old traditional concepts, poets, novelists, dramatists, and artists produced something new which was representative of the spirit of the Renaissance. In doing so they broadened the scope of Spanish thought and enriched Spanish culture.

The principal sources of inspiration from the outside were Flanders and Italy. Since Flanders became a part of the great Spanish Empire with the accession of Charles V, the contact between Spain and Flanders was close. There was also a close relationship between Spain and Italy. The crown of Aragon had long ruled Sicily, Naples, and Sardinia; during the reign of Ferdinand and Isabella, Castilian troops were also sent to southern Italy. Charles V expanded the Spanish rule by adding Milan to his domain after the defeat of Francis I of France at Pavia (1525). Thus Spain ruled a large part of the Italian peninsula. Thousands of Spanish administrators and soldiers were deeply impressed by what they saw and heard in Italy and upon their return to Spain told their fellow countrymen about it. Italian universities, particularly Bologna, attracted many Spanish students who carried back to Spain an interest in Italian Renaissance culture. Many Spanish artists visited Italy to study the art treasures of that country. Conversely, Italian humanists and artists who visited Spain were also active in disseminating humanistic and artistic knowledge. Groups of Italian actors who toured Spain and presented their plays in many towns had a considerable influence on the development of the Spanish drama.

Spanish scholars, writers, and artists were not indiscriminate borrowers. They did not accept an idea simply because it was Flemish or Italian. There was, in fact, a strong reluctance in Spain to adopt or imitate anything that had originated in a foreign country. When they did borrow they were careful to accept only aspects of the new Renaissance culture which did not extend beyond the limits set by the rigorous Roman Catholic orthodoxy or which did not violate national traditions. This helps to explain why there is in the Spanish Renaissance so little evidence of the neo-paganism of the Italian Renaissance. The religious, intellectual, and artistic climate of Spain did not foster the growth of neo-paganism. This also goes far in explaining why Spanish literature is free of the obscenity which abounded in some of the writings of the Italian Renaissance.

The Spanish Renaissance was, by and large, a plant of slow growth. First, the stubborn resistance of the old to the new slowed the secularization of life and culture. Second, Spanish Renaissance culture did not enjoy the same patronage as the culture of the Italian Renaissance. In Italy a number of popes, many petty despots, and members of the upper middle class were munificent patrons of humanists, artists, and literary men. In Spain there were no popes and the interest of the rulers was absorbed by other matters. Then, too, near the middle of the sixteenth century the upper middle class began to show symptoms of a bad case of anemia. Although some nobles did pose as patrons of the arts, their patronage was neither generous nor liberal-minded. Queen Isabella did, it is true, encourage humanists whose work promised to bolster religious orthodoxy, but in other respects her influence was restrictive and even repressive. For these and other reasons Spain lagged behind the other countries of Europe in the development of a Renaissance culture. In Spain the first significant signs of Renaissance influence did not appear until the reign of Ferdinand and Isabella. Thereafter the pace of the development was so slow that Spanish Renaissance culture did not reach its zenith until the early decades of the seventeenth century.

The Rise of Secular Literature

Renaissance Spain produced a rich and abundant secular literature. The principal language of this literature is Castilian. After the establishment of a semblance of political unity in the rule of Ferdinand and Isabella, Castilian gradually became the national literary language of Spain, while Catalan, Galician, and other dialects lost their importance as literary media. Thus Spanish literature came to mean Castilian literature. In creating the new literature, novelists and short-story writers looked more and more to everyday life for their inspiration, and poets sang of earthly love, some of them taking the Italian poets as their models. The two Italian poets who exercised the greatest influence on Spanish poetry were Dante and Petrarch. The latter in particular caught the fancy of the Spanish poets with his canzoni and his sonnets to Laura. Some idea of the popularity of Petrarch's poetry in Spain may be gained from the fact that during the Renaissance period more than 300 translations of his poems into Spanish were made.

The two most prominent poets of the so-called Italian school which flourished in the first half of the sixteenth century were Juan Boscán (1493-1542) and Garcilaso de la Vega (1501-1536). Boscán who was a nobleman became interested in Italian poetry while he was serving in the army of Charles V in Italy. His enthusiasm for it was such that he decided to use Italian forms in writing Castilian poetry. Despite vigorous denunciation by poets of the old school, he continued to write sonnets. His ninety sonnets helped to make the Italian sonnet popular in Spain. Boscán also made a number of translations from Latin and Italian into Spanish, the best known being his translation of Castiglione's *Il Cortegiano* into excellent Spanish. Garcilaso was the greater poet of the two. Like Boscán he was a nobleman who became interested in Italian poetry while serving with the forces of Charles V in Italy. He wrote only thirty-eight sonnets, but they are of high quality. When he died at the age of thirty-five from a wound he sustained while fighting with the forces of Charles in France, his widow published his sonnets together with those of Boscán in one volume (1543). The publication of his collection of sonnets is one of the important events in the early history of Spanish literature. It opened the way for the flood of Spanish poetry that followed.

In the realm of the novel the first significant realistic work was the *Tragicomedie de Calisto y Melibea* which gradually became known as *La Celestina* or simply *Celestina,* after the crafty old bawd who dominates the action. Published in 1493, this vivid and interesting novel ushered Spanish fiction into the Renaissance. Its characters are real human beings moving in a secular environment with motives that are wholly secular. Actually *La Celestina* is a novel in the form of a play, but in the original form there were so many acts that it did not lend itself to stage presentation. As a novel it is the first in the history of Spanish literature to offer the reader a sustained narrative instead of a series of unrelated episodes in the style of the romances of chivalry. Much ink has been spilled over the question of the authorship of *La Celestina.* There are indications that the first act was written earlier than the rest of the work and that it was "discovered" by one Ferdinand de Rojas, a lawyer, who wrote fifteen additional acts. In a later edition appearing in 1502 the number of acts was increased through interpolations to twenty-one.

The plot of *Celestina* is a simple one, even more simple than that of Shakespeare's *Romeo and Juliet* which parallels it in some respects. While searching for a lost falcon, Calisto, a handsome young nobleman, walks into a garden where he sees beautiful Melibea, daughter of a noble family, and falls in love with her at first sight. His love is so passionate that when he is asked if he is a Christian he answers, "I am a Melibean! I worship Melibea, I believe in Melibea, and I love Melibea." Modesty, however, causes her to repulse his advances. At the suggestion of a servant Calisto turns for aid to Celestina, a crone of many professions, including those of a prostitute, a procuress, a compounder of potions, and a master of the arts of witchcraft. Her basic philosophy was "Come what may, we are here to enjoy life." Celestina, who manages to gain admittance to Melibea's house in the guise of a peddler of needlework materials, succeeds in persuading her to respond to her lover's suit. A series of clandestine meetings between the two lovers follows. After one of these meetings Calisto misses his footing while climbing down a ladder from her window and falls to his death. Melibea is so distraught that she joins Calisto in death by hurling herself from the tower of her house. Meanwhile tragedy has struck in another direction. During a quarrel between Celestina and two of Calisto's servants over the division of the money they received for their plotting Celestina is killed by the servants who are, in turn, put to death for their crime.

Celestina is one of the great works of Spanish literature. Many historians of literature rank it as second only to Cervantes' *Don Quixote.* In Spain it inaugurated the trend to base fiction on real life. Its influence was, however, not limited to Spain. It was also of primary significance in the development of European fiction and the European drama. One literary historian has styled *Celestina* "the first true novel to appear in Europe." Historians of the drama regard it as probably the first work to contain the essentials of the modern drama. Its greatness lies in the richness of its prose, the fluency of its style, its realistic approach, its skillful depiction of human passion, and above all, its unhampered portrayal of human character. The characters who play the various parts are among the most sharply etched in all literature. Celestina herself, for example, is a true Renaissance type. She is so realistically depicted that it is easy to accept her as a product of the Renaissance environment. This is true also of the disreputable group of servants and prostitutes who surround her.

The popularity of *Celestina* both in Spain and in Western Europe is attested by numerous reprints, adaptations, and separate editions. In Spain alone the presses turned out more than fifty editions in the sixteenth century. Cervantes who felt that *Celestina* was rather too human, nevertheless called it "a divine work." The great dramatist Lope de Vega treated the same theme in his novel *Dorotea*. *Celestina* was the first Spanish work to have such a tremendous vogue in Europe generally. Its wide circulation gave Spanish literature an international status. Within a short time it was translated into all the major languages of Western Europe. In England it was also adapted to the stage in various forms. How deeply Shakespeare was indebted to the story of *Celestina* in writing *Romeo and Juliet* and *All's Well That Ends Well* is a matter of conjecture.

During the decades after the publication of *La Celestina* a new type of fiction developed. It was the picaresque novel, the most typically Spanish of all Renaissance literary forms. The word "picaresque" probably derives from *picaro*, a word of uncertain etymology. It has been translated into English as "rogue." Accordingly the picaresque novel deals with roguery. Its cast of characters is composed largely of persons who subsist by defrauding others. They are rogues and wretches who might be found along the highways and in the slums of Spanish towns. As a group they include unscrupulous valets, army deserters, soldiers back from the wars, renegade monks, cutthroats, pickpockets, and vagrants of every kind and description. The novels are vigorously realistic with their scenes laid in actual life and the characters are familiar types. Their most outstanding feature is the mordant and at times malicious satire they pour on all classes of contemporary society. The picaro or social outcast saw life from below and took delight in pricking many bubbles of Spanish pride.

Many of the personages in *La Celestina* had picaresque characteristics, but the book which is generally regarded as the first full-fledged picaresque novel, and in many ways the best of the series, is *The Life of Lazarillo de Tormes*, published in three different places in 1554. It was published anonymously and all scholarly efforts over the centuries have failed to identify the author. Under the guise of being a record of the fortunes and misfortunes, adventures and misadventures of the rogue Lazarillo, this short novel expresses truths that many were thinking, but feared to utter. Moreover, it subjected many phases of contemporary Spanish life to devastating criticism. The persons in the novel were familiar types of that time. As a realistic masterpiece it ranks with *Celestina* and *Don Quixote*. The popularity of *The Life of Lazarillo* was immense. It was read by members of all classes, high and low, clergy and laity. In a short period of time it went through no fewer than twelve editions. Because of the criticism the novel leveled at the clergy and the sale of indulgences it was put on the Index of Prohibited Books in 1559. Thereafter it was printed in Spain either surreptitiously or in expurgated form. Its influence was disproportionate to its small size. Its autobiographical form set the pattern for the many picaresque novels that followed.

In one sense the picaresque novel was a reaction against the romances of chivalry which had come into vogue later in Spain than in the other countries of Western Europe and then retained their popularity through most of the sixteenth century. These fantastic tales with their preposterous array of fabulous characters were the offspring of the legends of King Arthur and the Knights of the Round Table. As their popularity increased they became more and more extravagant and absurd in their portrayals. They have been described as a combination of the unreality of fairy tales and the bombast of melodrama. The romances of chivalry featured innumerable knightly duels in which the hero is invariably victorious, and also the slaying of giants, wild beasts, and dragons by the hero. Furthermore, the hero goes out to right wrongs and to protect innocent women. By spreading a taste for realism *The Life of Lazarillo de Tormes* and the picaresque novels of the succeeding period dealt the romances of chivalry a crippling blow and later Cervantes administered the *coup de grâce* in his *Don Quixote*.

Miguel de Cervantes

Miguel de Cervantes Saavedra (1547-1616) was the greatest novelist of the Spanish Renaissance and remains one of the great names in the history of literature. Cervantes was a contemporary of Shakespeare, but except for the fact that the two great literary figures died in the same year within a few days of each other, there are few parallels in their lives. Shakespeare's gifts matured early. He began writing plays and poetry when he was a young man. By the age of forty he was at the height of his power and before he was fifty he went into retirement. There is no evidence to show that he experienced any serious setbacks in his career. Cervantes, on the other hand, had to struggle against unfavorable odds. Success came to him late in life. Had he died at the same age as Shakespeare, his name would be unknown today. The years before Cervantes' great work appeared were for him a period of disappointments, hardships, and poverty. When he turned to writing as a career he was a battered soldier.

In the case of Cervantes, as with many other literary figures of the Renaissance period, there is a dearth of information regarding his personal life. More is known, however, about the life of Cervantes than about that of

Shakespeare. Most literary historians believe that he was born at Alcalá where Cardinal Ximenes had earlier founded the university noted for its humanistic studies. Since the parents of Cervantes were proud but impoverished hidalgos, young Cervantes received but little formal education. He did, however, develop a thirst for knowledge which he endeavored to satisfy by reading. His writings indicate that he was an omnivorous reader. He further rounded out his knowledge by adventure, travel, and his general contact with the world around him. At about the age of twenty-one, Miguel became a member of the retinue of Monsignor Acquaviva, who had been sent to Spain as papal legate, and accompanied him to Rome. There young Cervantes came into contact with the thought of the Renaissance. Although the Italian Renaissance was by this time in its last stage, Renaissance ideas were still in the air. Michelangelo had passed from the scene only about four years before Cervantes' arrival and Benvenuto Cellini was still among the living. How much of the remaining Renaissance thought Cervantes absorbed it is impossible to state. Whatever effect his stay in Italy may have had on his thinking, he did in his writings evince a leaning toward antiquity and humanism.

About 1570 Cervantes obtained a release from his post to enlist in a Spanish regiment which was being recruited for service against the Turks. This regiment joined the combined naval forces of Spain, Venice, Rome, and Florence under the command of Don John (Juan), the half-brother of Philip II. It was this great naval force which in 1571 defeated and scattered the Turkish fleet at Lepanto. Cervantes fought with conspicuous bravery until he sustained three gunshot wounds and fell in a faint. A disfigured left hand was the mark of battle he carried with him throughout life. After the battle of Lepanto, Cervantes participated in several other expeditions against the Turks which were failures from the outset. Finally he decided to return to Spain. Armed with recommendations of merit and bravery from leading Spanish commanders, Cervantes boarded a Spanish galley for the homeward voyage. But the galley was captured by Moorish pirates after bitter fighting and Cervantes was taken to Algiers where he spent five memorable years in captivity. During these years the threat of torture and death did not discourage him from planning a series of escapes, all of which miscarried. The respect of the Moors for his daring and bravery was such that he escaped severe physical punishment. As a result of the intervention of prominent Spaniards on his behalf the Spanish government finally ransomed him and he was permitted to return to Spain.

Cervantes quickly discovered upon his arrival that the victory of Lepanto had faded into the past and that he was a kind of social outcast compelled to join the crowds of ex-soldiers, picaros, and beggars who thronged the streets of Spanish cities. His future looked anything but promising. During the years that followed he eked out a precarious existence at various occupations, at times doing menial labor. For a while he held a government post as tax collector, but his unbusinesslike methods got him into difficulties and he was sent to jail. Biographers of Cervantes believe that he conceived the idea of *Don Quixote* while he was in prison. He did not, however, act on it at once. He wrote occasional verses and in 1584 gave to the public his *Galatea*, a pastoral novel. Next he threw himself heart and soul into writing plays. He would free the Spanish stage from the banality and vulgarity which he believed was threatening to overwhelm it. Although some of his plays were performed, it gradually became evident even to Cervantes himself that his future did not lie in the theater. When the dramas of Lope de Vega completely overshadowed the work of all other playwrights, Cervantes turned to the writing of *Don Quixote*. The necessity of keeping the wolf from the door left him only evenings and odd moments for writing, but he persevered and finally in 1605 published the first part of his great novel in a bulky volume titled *The History of Don Quixote de la Mancha*. This was followed in 1613 by his *Exemplary Tales*, a collection of twelve short stories. These tales later inspired Sir Walter Scott to become a writer of fiction. The second part of his *Don Quixote* did not appear until 1615, the year before Cervantes' death. On April 23, 1616, he "put his foot into the stirrup and rode off into the great unknown." There is no record of his last resting place.

Although Cervantes was prouder of having participated in the victory of Lepanto than of having written *Don Quixote*, it is on the latter that his fame rests. The adventures of "a knight" and his squire form the framework of the long novel. Its principal character is Don Quixote, a country gentleman (hidalgo) whose mind had become unhinged from reading too many romances of chivalry. Clad in a suit of rusty armor and mounted on a spavined, swaybacked steed which he affectionately named Rosinante, Don Quixote rides forth into the world to restore the lost ideal of chivalry. He plans to right wrongs, fight giants, kill dragons, protect the innocent and, in general, win chivalric honor. As he proceeds along the roads his warped mind transforms ordinary wayfarers into warriors, giants, and monsters. In his eagerness to perform great deeds he even tilts at windmills which he believes to be giant living creatures. Throughout all his adventures, however, Don Quixote remains brave, dignified, and courteous. As his squire he chooses Sancho Panza, an unschooled but in many ways shrewd peasant who is deeply attached to his master. Whereas Don Quixote is idealistic with an overwrought imagination, Sancho Panza is earthy with his interest centered in food, drink, and a good sleep. Sancho's conversation is spiced with many peasant proverbs. Together Don Quixote and Sancho Panza get into many ludicrous and at times painful situations. At the end Don Quixote's sanity is restored, he foreswears the reading of romances of chivalry, and dies penitent.

In the introduction to his novel Cervantes states that his sole purpose in writing it is "to destroy the authority and influence which the romances of chivalry have in this world and with the public." Cervantes believed that the false and foolish romances, written by authors who permitted their imaginations to run wild, were being accepted as real by many readers and that such acceptance was severing the last ties between literature and reality. In an effort to destroy the influence of the romances of chivalry Cervantes set out to parody them and to heap ridicule on them. It is the opinion of a number of literary historians that Cervantes' purpose was broader than his declaration, that *Don Quixote* is actually a sweeping satire on life in contemporary Spain. They believe that his statement of purpose was a device to forestall accusations which might excite the interest of the Inquisition. Whatever the truth in the matter, Cervantes aimed not merely to destroy the influence of the romances of chivalry; he would turn literature in general back to reality from its fantastic flights of fancy. He believed that it was time to doff the shining armor of the Middle Ages and to consider contemporary life and its problems. In this he was the antithesis of Sir Walter Scott who at a later time sought to revive the spell of chivalry. Cervantes was propounding a new attitude more clearly stated than that of Rabelais. In proclaiming that literature must have its roots in reality Cervantes was, above all, the voice of the Renaissance. Of all his works *Don Quixote* is the one which is most closely affiliated with the thought of the Renaissance, but there are flashes of the Renaissance spirit in his other writings.

The success of *Don Quixote* was immediate and outstanding. The literary critics of the day, it is true, showed little enthusiasm for it, but this was offset by the interest of the Spanish people at large. Copies of *Don Quixote* found their way into the modest homes of the lower classes as well as into the palatial houses of the wealthy. It is reported that in towns and villages groups of citizens would assemble for the purpose of having one member read aloud to them from Cervantes' novel. Many of those who could read eagerly read it themselves. The adventures filled some with delight, made others laugh aloud, and caused a few to weep. Edition after edition flooded the country so that the book was soon known throughout Spain. Unfortunately Cervantes derived little in the way of a monetary return from his great novel because he had signed away most of his rights in the contract with his publisher. The book did, however, make him famous. During the last years of his life his name was on many Spanish lips and has remained there ever since.

But the interest in *Don Quixote* was not limited to Spain. Its appeal was, and still is, universal, as is that of the dramas of Shakespeare. Within a short period of time it was translated into all the major languages of Europe and, as in Spain, it delighted many readers of all classes. One reason for its popularity is undoubtedly its juxtaposition of humor and pathos. Not to be overlooked is the fact that the action takes place in real life. It is, however, its broad humanity which appeals most strongly to many readers of all classes. Neither Chaucer nor Tolstoy exhibited a deeper or broader humanitarian feeling.

The contributions of *Don Quixote* to the history of literature are many. From it, for example, the word "quixotic" derives. Another contribution is the creation of the two immortal characters, Don Quixote and Sancho Panza. If Cervantes had done nothing more than this, the civilized world would owe him a debt of gratitude. The mentally-disturbed but noble and courteous knight and his paunch-bellied and spindle-shanked squire are truly original creations. But Cervantes contributed much more. As a forerunner of the modern novel, *Don Quixote* opened the way for the libraries of fiction that were to follow. The influence of Cervantes on the development of the modern novel was so broad and so deep that it has not been completely measured. During the centuries since it was published *Don Quixote* inspired many masterpieces of fiction. Fielding, Dickens, Flaubert, and Dostoievsky were some of the great writers who were influenced by it.

The Beginnings of the Secular Drama

The Spanish secular drama, like the secular drama in other countries of Europe, is an outgrowth of the medieval religious drama. The pattern of secularization was also much the same. In Spain, however, the secular elements may have been introduced into the religious drama earlier than in France and Germany. As early as the thirteenth century, opposition developed to the participation of the clergy either as actors or directors of plays which included farcical secular materials. A code of law promulgated in Castile about 1260 during the reign of Alfonso X states specifically:

> Neither shall they [the clergy] be makers of buffoon plays that people may come to see and if other men present them, members of the clergy should not come to see them, for such men do many things that are low and reprehensible. Nor, moreover, should such things be presented in the churches; they should be cast out in dishonor, without punishing those engaged in them. For the Church of God was made for prayer and not for buffoonery.

The law did not, however, prohibit the presentation of tableaus in the churches to illustrate doctrines or commemorate the festivals of the church year. In addition to tableaus, *autos sacramentales* or one-act religious plays could also be presented as a means of explaining the mysteries of the faith.

The transitional period from the religious to the secular plays seems to have been much longer in Spain than in France or Germany. In other words, the plays which contained both religious and secular scenes and elements were presented over a longer period of time. Whereas in France and Germany the task of staging plays after they outgrew the confines of the churches and churchyards was assumed by the gilds or the town officials, in Spain they were presented by groups of strolling players who traveled from place to place. Since little scenery was used, a crude stage could be set up without much difficulty wherever there was space to accommodate the crowds of people who congregated to see the productions. The plays were loosely constructed, ill-proportioned, and full of repetitions, with little elegance of speech and harmony of plot. But to the largely illiterate populace they were a favorite diversion in an age when the opportunities for diversion were few. Both the ecclesiastical and civil authorities seem to have tolerated with slight protests the commingling of the secular and the sacred. But they did vigorously oppose, and not always successfully in the pre-Inquisition period, the staging of certain plays called *juegos de escarnios* which openly burlesqued the mass and other sacred rites of the Church. It was not until late in the fifteenth century that some of the plays became almost entirely secular. A few Spanish humanists, appalled by the formlessness of the existing plays and the vulgarity of the performances, tried to write plays modelled after Roman comedies or Greek tragedies, but such plays had little appeal for the Spanish masses. The popular play was more spontaneous, a reflection of the beliefs and aspirations of the people.

The first outstanding playwright in the history of the Spanish secular drama was Juan del Encina (*c.*1460-*c.*1529) who has variously been called "the father of the Spanish secular drama" and "the true founder of the secular theater in Spain." He also wrote much poetry and was a distinguished musician. Encina called his dramatic compositions "representations." Actually they were dialogues in verse form. The lines were acted as well as spoken. In all of his so-called plays there is singing and in one dancing, foreshadowing the coming of the later secular drama. Many of Encina's plays are religious, written to commemorate Christmas and other religious holidays, others are definitely secular. For example, he took the shepherds from the story of the Nativity and completely secularized them, presenting them as human beings who speak in a rustic dialect and discuss their everyday problems. In one of his plays a shepherd falls so desperately in love that he commits suicide when his love is not requited. In some of the scenes there is also much humor. Encina's early dramatic compositions were written for presentation in palaces and the homes of the rich, but after he published nine of them in 1496 they became public property and were performed in many parts of Spain by strolling players. The total number of his "representations" has been set as high as 170. Encina spent some years of his life in Rome where he served Pope Alexander VI and also Leo X as musician in the papal chapel. His contact with the Italian Renaissance caused him to put more action into his plays and to secularize the dialogue more completely. In one of his secular plays titled *The Shepherds Who Became Courtiers* Encina satirized the courtly manners and praised the simple life of the shepherd and peasant in such lines as the following:

> But look ye, Gil, at morning dawn,
> How fresh and fragrant are the fields;
> And then what savory coolness yields
> The cabin's shade upon the lawn
> And he who knows what 'tis to rest

Amidst his flocks the livelong night,
Sure he can never find delight
In court, by courtly ways oppressed.

Encina's "representations" are more notable for their secular content than for their dramatic merit. They make no pretense to a plot and are lacking in dramatic spirit. Spirited dramas did not make their appearance until Lope de Vega began to write. The period from the death of Encina about 1529 to the last decade of that century was one of experimentation in the various forms and theories of the drama. The dramatists of this period, including Cervantes, endeavored to find out which dramatic form had the greatest appeal for Spanish audiences. In this way they prepared the public for the coming of the "new drama" of Lope de Vega. By combining what he regarded as the best features of the drama in the period which preceded his activity as a playwright, Lope produced plays which enabled him to dominate the Spanish theater during his lifetime.

Lope de Vega (1562-1635), whose full name was Lope Félix de Vega Carpio, was born in Madrid of poor parents. At a very early age he demonstrated that he was a child prodigy. It is reported that he composed verses before he could write them down. At the age of five he could read Latin as well as Spanish and when he was ten young Lope translated Latin verse into Spanish verse. He was only twelve when he wrote his first play, continuing thereafter to write both poetry and plays in the intervals between his studies, travels, and service as a soldier. As a young man Lope became a proficient musician and was also adept at fencing and dancing. Handsome, accomplished, and temperamental, he led a flamboyant and, at times, tumultuous life. Twice he served in the armed forces of Spain, the first time he enlisted as a soldier in an expedition against Portugal and later in 1588 joined the "Invincible Armada." His galley was one of the few to return to Cadiz after the defeat. His mature life was a succession of love affairs, some of which were rather unsavory. The fact that he married twice only meant that his wife of the moment had to share his love with his mistresses. The philosophical principle underlying Lope's actions, one which he expounded in a number of his plays, was "Love excuses all things." Later in life, after the death of his second wife, he took holy orders in a burst of piety, but he did not permit this to restrict his amours. One biographer in attempting to show his virtues stated that Lope loved his numerous legitimate and illegitimate children. Unfortunately most of them died before reaching maturity.

Lope's life as a playwright and poet was one long success. He was one of the most prolific writers in the history of literature. Cervantes called him "the marvel of nature." Lope de Vega wrote sonnets, odes, lays, madrigals, ballads, epics, pastorals, hymns, stories, novels, and above all, plays. There are few forms of the drama which he did not attempt. He wrote comedies, tragi-comedies, tragedies, and religious plays. His inventiveness and command of versification were prodigious. Plays flowed from his pen like water bubbling out of a spring. One of his disciples credited him with writing 1800 full-length plays and 400 one-act religious plays (*autos sacramentales*). The number is probably exaggerated. According to more sober estimates he wrote between 700 and 800 full-length plays and an indeterminate number of *autos sacramentales*, all of them in good verse. Lope himself stated that more than a hundred were written at the rate of one in twenty-four hours. Others were written in a period of two days. At least once in his life he wrote five plays in fifteen consecutive days. He was spurred on to do this by the great demand for his work. Managers of theaters took every full-length play he wrote. Lope not only reaped a golden harvest from the plays; he also became famous in Spain. Of all the plays he wrote, only about four hundred have survived.

Lope was indifferent to the classical unities. He mixed the tragic and the humorous, the sad and the gay, the serious and the ludicrous in such a way that the French drama critics of a later time were horrified. But his dramas were spirited. He moved from episode to episode, from complication to complication, with such great facility that his plays were seldom uninteresting. His plays were so popular that the work of all other Spanish playwrights was pushed into the background. This popularity has moved some Spanish writers to compare Lope with his contemporary, William Shakespeare. But although Lope wrote many more plays than the Bard of Avon, Shakespeare's work is much superior. Lope's plays are characteristically Spanish and lack universality. He never created a character with the timeless appeal of Hamlet or Macbeth. Hence while Shakespeare's plays are the common property of civilized nations, those of Lope are little known outside the Spanish-speaking countries. In Spain, however, Lope was a great influence. There he created the national drama, setting the direction in which the drama was to move after his death. During the succeeding century no Spanish playwright made a significant change in Lope's methods. Even Calderón did not attempt any form of drama which Lope had not previously tested. After Calderón the decadence which had previously stunted many phases of Spanish life began to weigh heavily on literature and the drama.

Spanish Humanism

The humanistic impulse which emanated from Italy left its mark in Spain as well as in the other countries of Western Europe. It quickened the interest in ancient writers and in classical knowledge. This interest was not limited to court circles. Humanistic studies were introduced into Spanish universities and the University of Alcalá was founded expressly for the study of ancient writings. The classics were read widely in the original and in such Spanish translations as existed. One reason for reading them was to enjoy the elegance of their style. They were also quoted by theological as well as by profane writers. But Spanish writers were careful not to quote anything from the classics which might conflict with the teachings of the Church. Strict limits for the activities of the humanists were prescribed by Spanish orthodoxy, aided by the Inquisition. Moreover, there was no relaxation of discipline for the benefit of the humanists as there was at times in Italy. Everything might be investigated or questioned except the orthodox faith. There were such unorthodox humanists as Luis Vives (d.1540) and Juan de Valdés (d.1541), but they did most of their work outside Spain. Thus the study of the classics was not an end in itself. Spanish humanism was, as it had been in the Middle Ages, largely the servant of theology and its basic purpose was the strengthening of the faith. Accordingly the outstanding achievements of Spanish humanism were in the field of Biblical scholarship.

The influence of Italian humanism did not enter Spain with a rush. It filtered in over a long period of time, stimulating humanist interests in many parts of the country. During the early decades of the fifteenth century Italian humanists visited Spain and Spanish students went to Italy to study humanism. As a result humanistic studies were pursued by individual scholars. There was, however, no humanistic movement as such. But humanism was on the way. Although the major attention was devoted to the Latin classics as the numerous translations from Latin into Spanish indicate, the study of Greek was not neglected. Among the students of Greek during this period was Ferdinand de Córdoba whom the Italian humanist Lorenzo Valla praised highly in 1444. The systematic teaching of Greek was not introduced into the University of Salamanca until about 1490.

The beginning of Spanish humanism as a movement is generally dated from the return to Spain from Italy in 1473 of Antonio de Nebrija (1441-1522), the greatest of the early Spanish humanists. During the succeeding period the full import of Italian humanism was felt in Spain. Nebrija became disgusted with the barbarous Latin of his teachers at the University of Salamanca and vowed that he would change this. He journeyed to Italy where he studied at various universities for ten years. Upon his return to Spain he was at once recognized as Spain's greatest scholar. His personal influence was tremendous. In addition to teaching with distinction at the universities of Salamanca and Alcalá, he wrote a number of influential books. In 1481 he published his *Grammatica Latina*, the first good Latin grammar to be published in Spain. This book was an important factor in improving the quality of Spanish Latinity. Another important work of Nebrija was his Spanish-Latin and Latin-Spanish dictionary which soon became an indispensable aid to Spanish scholars. At the behest of Queen Isabella who was working to make Castilian the common language of Spain, Nebrija wrote a grammar of the Castilian language (1492) which was probably the first scientific grammar of any of the vernacular languages. Thus Nebrija served a definitely secular purpose.

The best known Spanish humanist of the period is Cardinal Ximenes or

Jimenez (1436-1517). Ximenes was not only a high official in the Church and in the government, he was also a distinguished scholar, a patron of learning, and a person of high character whose mode of living was ascetic. After holding various ecclesiastical positions he was chosen in 1492 by Queen Isabella to be her confessor. This was a position of great prestige as Isabella was wont to consult her confessor on both ecclesiastical and civil matters. Ximenes soon won the confidence of the queen and in 1495 she appointed him archbishop of Toledo, the highest ecclesiastical office in Spain, with a large income which he used for philanthropic purposes. Ximenes also served the Inquisition as Grand Inquisitor for Castile. In this capacity he sought to protect the innocent from prosecution by the Inquisition. One of those whom he protected against such prosecution was the humanist Antonio de Nebrija. Ximines was further appointed chancellor of Castile by Isabella and reached the pinnacle of his career as a statesman when after Isabella's death he served as regent in Castile during the minority and absence of Charles V.

Cardinal Ximenes made two significant contributions to the development of Spanish humanism. First, he founded the University of Alcalá with his personal funds. This university, which opened its doors to students in 1508, quickly became the principal center of humanistic studies in Spain. His second great contribution was his sponsorship of the Polyglot Bible (*Complutensian Polyglot*). Realizing that many errors had crept into the Latin Vulgate, the official version of the Church, over the centuries, Cardinal Ximenes combed Europe for the best possible manuscript of this version; then assembled at Alcalá a corps of scholars and linguists, including Nebrija, to edit it. The result of their labors over a period of fifteen years was the Polyglot Bible, published in six folio volumes (1514-1520). In this Bible the Latin version of the Old Testament is accompanied by Hebrew and Chaldaic versions printed side by side. The New Testament was printed in Latin and Greek. The inclusion of the Hebrew, Chaldaic, and Greek versions stimulated critical inquiry by inviting comparisons. All in all, the printing of the Polyglot Bible was a major achievement of Spanish humanism. After Nebrija and Ximenes other noted humanists appeared in Spain, but humanism increasingly came under the influence of mysticism and the Counter-Reformation.

20

Northern Renaissance Art

Although Italy was preeminently the home of Renaissance art, the artists of the countries north of the Alps also created many great masterpieces. But, since the medieval religious spirit persisted longer in the northern countries than in Italy, most phases of art were subject to medieval discipline longer. In the fine arts Gothic architecture and Gothic sculpture retained their sway longer than in Italy. There were, however, notable exceptions. In the so-called Burgundian school several sculptors turned out naturalistic sculptures some decades before the Renaissance spirit inspired northern painters. It was in painting that the greatest changes took place. In the early stages of the Northern Renaissance the changes were largely in the realm of technique. Except in portraiture, the old religious subjects retained their status during the fifteenth century, and religious education and edification continued to be the primary purpose of painting. The pagan tradition was not so vivid in Northern Europe as it was in Italy. Earlier Greek and Roman mythology had been overshadowed by Teutonic mythology which, in turn, had given way to Christian themes. When the northern painters did turn to secular themes, many of them depicted scenes from everyday life. This type of painting, called genre painting, originated in the Netherlands. What the painter portrayed was the commonplace, the natural, or something close to nature. This they did with a quaint originality which made their paintings interesting. The subjects, whether a beggar, children at play, or an old woman threading a needle, were portrayed by the painters with the zest of a Raphael or a Michelangelo. The artists bestowed on their paintings all the grace and skill they could muster, thereby contributing much to the ennoblement of mundane life.

What was new in the early stages of Northern Renaissance painting was the mode of treatment. Traditional subjects were portrayed in secular terms, that is, in terms of the visible world. Representation became more and more naturalistic. Figures and scenes were presented as they appeared to the eye. As in Italy, ordinary human beings served as models for Christ, the Virgin, saints, and angels. Moreover, they were portrayed in a familiar environment and in human attitudes. Painters depicted cherubs picking flowers, fondling animals, and playing with fruit like ordinary children. The German painter Albrecht Dürer in one of his paintings of the Holy Family seated the Virgin and Child in the midst of a barnyard and surrounded them with animals and all kinds of rural accessories. Many of the northern painters were more meticulous in their attention to minor details than most of the Italian painters.

The changes inaugurated by the Northern Renaissance painters were not the result of an arbitrary decision on their part. They were a reflection of the changing taste of the people, particularly of the members of the middle class. The naturalistic art of the Renaissance appeared and grew with the middle class. In the Netherlands and in Germany, for example, the middle-class burghers were a somewhat dull lot with limited interests. Their primary interest was the accumulation of wealth. As a conservative group, they continued to adhere to the faith of the Middle Ages, but a deeper interest in mundane life had been added. The wealth they were accumulating and the luxuries they were enjoying made life more pleasant and interesting. This explains the dualism of northern painting. Although its themes were at first otherworldly, the mode of expression was secular. Thus it represented the scale of values and the way of life of the new middle class.

It should be pointed out that there was much less fresco painting in the countries north of the Alps than in Italy. During the early period of the Northern Renaissance the Church was, just as in Italy, the great patron of the arts. But the churches built in accordance with the northern Gothic style did not because of their many large windows have wall spaces adequate for fresco painting. Furthermore, the cold and damp climate of Northern Europe made the preservation of frescoes even more difficult than in Italy. The northern painters of the early Renaissance therefore painted their pictures on wooden panels, most of which were used as altarpieces and for the general decoration of the churches. With the passing of time, however, as the subjects as well as the treatment became secular, more and more painters put their representations on canvas.

Flemish Painting

In painting a definite trend toward naturalism manifested itself in the Netherlands early in the fifteenth century. Although life in the prosperous semi-independent cities or communes with which the country was studded was less flamboyant than in Florence and Venice, the citizens took much the same interest in mundane life as the citizens of the Italian cities, enjoying with zest many of the good things life had to offer. Hence the painters portrayed as much of the contemporary scene as their subjects permitted. Not only were figures represented as living human bodies; they were also dressed in costumes of that time. Special attention was given to coiffures, jewelry, and other accessories, and to the depiction of fur and the texture of fabrics. Landscapes and architecture, furniture, draperies, and carpets were also rendered with the minutest care. As most of the Flemish painters looked at the bright side of life, their colors are bright and harmonious, their landscapes sunny, their trees in bloom, and their flowers brightly-colored. It all adds up to a glorification of nature and earthly existence.

The forerunners of the Flemish painters were the illuminators of manuscripts, also call miniaturists. In the Netherlands they did their best work in the fourteenth century, reaching the highpoint in both skill and output during the last half of the century. They decorated the margins of manuscripts with exquisite designs of foliage, birds, and such insects as butterflies and caterpillars. They also painted in miniature a wide variety of scenes from daily life as well as biblical scenes. Their work had a wide appeal among the people. The influence of the illuminators on painting was so definite that the panel paintings of the "Adoration of the Lamb" by Jan van Eyck have been called "minatures made larger."

The traditional story, generally accepted over a period of almost five centuries, has it that the Flemish school of painting was founded by two brothers, Hubert (d.1426) and Jan van Eyck (1390-1441). It was believed that these two painters jointly produced the "Adoration of the Lamb," noted for its naturalistic representation. This work is regarded by art critics and historians as the first great masterpiece of the Northern Renaissance. As one historian put it, the "Adoration of the Lamb" is "the luminous dawn of Renaissance painting in northern Europe." In the traditional story Hubert is credited with choosing the subject of the work, sketching the designs, and spending the last years of his life painting some of the panels. These assumptions are based on the inscription which is on the frame, "The painter Hubert van Eyck, greater than whom there is none to be found, started this work. Jan, his brother and follower, finished it at the behest of Jodocus Veydt in 1432." Historians believed that the inscription was written by Jan van Eyck and that he finished the paintings by working on them at various intervals between the time of Hubert's death in 1426 and the year 1432.

In the 1930's, however, a great controversy developed in the art circles of Belgium over the van Eycks. The fact that the "Adoration of the Lamb" is the first great masterpiece of the Northern Renaissance was not questioned. The basic question in the controversy was, "Was there ever a Hubert van Eyck?" While the Belgian historian M. E. Renders was carrying on research for a biography of Hubert his suspicions were aroused when he found no mention of Hubert or his studio in the municipal archives of Ghent. In continuing his research he discovered that the inscription on the frame had been written in 1616, not in 1432 as the traditionalists believed. Further research convinced him that Hubert was a myth created to claim for Ghent the honor of being the cradle of Flemish painting, that Hubert was invented to prove that a painter was active in Ghent before Jan van Eyck launched his career as an artist in Bruges (1425).

Other art critics and historians joined in the search for evidence that was either pro or con, thereby stimulating a lively controversy. Although the revisionists produced cogent arguments for their claim that Hubert was a mythological character, the conservatives remained unconvinced. They staunchly defended their claim that Hubert was a real person. Further complications developed when some revisionists posed such questions as "Since Hubert is a figment of the imagination, who painted the 'Adoration of the Lamb'? Did Jan paint it by himself or did some unknown person do the preliminary work?" In 1951 the Belgian government appointed a special commission to study the whole problem. After a year of investigation the committee issued a preliminary report which was disappointing to the revisionists because it did not categorically assert that Hubert was mythical. There was, in fact, no mention whatsoever of Hubert in the report. But the final report did settle the controversy in favor of the revisionists.

The "Adoration of the Lamb," which was painted for one of the chapels of the Church of St. Bavon in Ghent, is not a single painting. It is a series of twenty panels, each one of which is complete in itself and also a part of a larger concept. The overall subject is the reconciliation of mankind with God through the sacrifice of Christ, the Lamb of God. In its technique of representation it is far in advance of anything that had been produced in Italy up to that time. The great central figures are portrayed in terms of material rather than spiritual wealth; they impress through the richness of their raiment. The Eternal Father, for example, is attired in the garb of a rich earthly ruler. On his head there is a tiara studded with a profusion of jewels. His costly mantle which completely envelops his form is bordered with a double row of pearls and amethysts and fastened with a large jeweled brooch. In form the Eternal Father is a man with a broad forehead, dark eyes, and a short black beard. On the panel to the left of the Eternal Father there is a representation of the Virgin Mary and to the right one of St. John the Baptist. The Virgin, in her gown of blue, also wears a jeweled tiara. Her long blond hair flows in waves on her shoulders and in her graceful hands she holds a book. On the lower central panel there is a picture of a lamb standing on an altar with blood flowing from its side into a chalice. This scene is set in a southern landscape with palm, cypress, and orange trees against a background of green hills receding into the distance. On the right there is a city in the background, probably a representation of the Heavenly Jerusalem. Two other panels portray Adam and Eve, and still others singing and music-making angels. Not to be overlooked are the two panels bearing portraits of the donors of the altarpiece, Jodocus and Isabella Veydt, depicted with pitiless realism.

All of the twenty panels are painted with a conscientious attention to detail previously unknown in panel painting. For example, the verisimilitude with which the glittering jewels in the tiaras of the Eternal Father and the Virgin Mary are rendered is amazing. The same is true of the elaborate designs of the brooches and clasps on their garments. Then, too, the carvings on the choir stalls of the singing angels are painted with an incomparable regard for detail. This careful attention to realistic detail is also visible in the depiction of the towers of the New Jerusalem and the landscape generally. It has been said that a single leaf was as important to the painter as the composition of the whole tree. The panels reflect a keenness of observation that has been admired by posterity. Much time was spent on details which the medieval painters regarded as unworthy of their attention. But the work is not mere imitation of nature. Alongside the unrivalled realism there is, except in the portraits of Jodocus and Isabella Veydt, the idealism of the concept which the paintings as a group portray. Unfortunately all of the panels of the great masterpiece were not kept intact. During the Napoleonic wars the French confiscated them and carried them to the Louvre, but with the return of peace in 1814 they were returned to Ghent. However, only the four central panels were restored to their original place. The rest were stored in the basement whence they disappeared, finally turning up in the Berlin Gallery and in the Academy of Brussels.

Besides being a pioneer in naturalistic portrayal, Jan van Eyck was also among the first to recognize and exploit the potentialities of oil pigments, thereby opening the way for the splendid art of oil painting. Jan van Eyck was not, however, the inventor of oil paints or oil painting. The art of blending oil with colors appears to have been no secret in the Byzantine Empire as well as in Western Europe. It has been suggested that the Italians did not use this medium because the only easily available oil in Italy was olive oil which did not dry easily. The oil used by Jan van Eyck was linseed oil. A new medium was needed to give paintings greater resistance to the influence of the northern climate than was inherent in the tempera colors prepared with the use of egg whites. Jan van Eyck found the answer in oil. This not only gave his paintings greater durability, but also enabled him to achieve a workmanship and beauty of color that had been impossible with the use of tempera. The new medium gave paintings a lustre which suggests translucent enamel. In Italy Giotto and his successors did not enjoy the advantage of using oil pigments. Tradition has it that the art of oil painting did not reach Italy until about 1473 when knowledge of it was carried to Venice by the painter Antonello da Messina who had studied in Flanders. The first of the greater Italian painters to use it were the Venetian brothers Gentile and Giovanni Bellini. Thereafter its use spread to other parts of Italy. It was, for example, essential to the easel painting of Leonardo da Vinci. As for the Venetian painters, it would be difficult to imagine their brilliant colors apart from the use of the oil medium.

After finishing the "Adoration of the Lamb" Jan van Eyck continued to paint until his death in 1441. The most famous of his portraits is "Arnolfini and His Wife" (1434), now in the National Gallery of London. Arnolfini was an Italian merchant who had settled in Bruges and taken a wife. In the painting the newlyweds are standing in their bedroom, with a bed on the right. On the left there is an open window which offers a distant view. According to an inscription on the painting Jan set up his easel in the bedroom. What he saw he painted with the utmost precision. Among the details he included are scenes from the passion of Christ on the frame of the mirror hanging on the back wall; also the reflection in the mirror. Not to be overlooked are the quilted fabric of the wife's robe, the chandelier with the candles burning, and the carvings on the bedposts, on one of which there is an image of St. Margaret, patron saint of newlyweds. The work as a whole is a masterpiece which exhibits a skillful use of color, superb technical execution, and a precise knowledge of light and shade. Another outstanding work is Jan's portrait of his wife Margaret (1439), now in the Bruges Academy. Margaret was not a beautiful woman and Jan did not flatter her in his portrait. It is a further example of keen observation and of exact rendering of color, texture, and atmosphere. The careful attention to minute details which carried Jan's work to new heights also imposed limitations on his work. Jan was so intent on capturing every detail of what he saw that he overlooked the soul of the persons he was painting. (*See Fig. 28.*)

Although the beginnings of Flemish painting seem to have been largely indigenous, many Flemish painters of the last decades of the fifteenth century and of the early decades of the sixteenth came under the spell of the Italian Renaissance. The Italians had almost from the beginning set up for themselves certain standards of beauty applicable to the general design of a painting as well as to the human form. Moreover, they stressed unity of action, subordinating detail to general harmony. In their representations they brought nature into harmony with their preconceived ideas of beauty, employing it for the expression of abstract thought. The Flemish painters, on the other hand, had no ideals of beauty, of form, or of design. Their primary aim was to hold a mirror up to nature, to reproduce the world about them in minute detail. Their love of their mundane environment was such that they asked for nothing more. It was not a matter of concern to them that the human form as they portrayed it with narrow shoulders, disproportionately small head, and long limbs was somewhat awkward, although the modeling of the face was remarkably good. During the period of the High Renaissance, however, many Flemish painters visited Italy where they were fascinated by the magic of Leonardo's brush, the charm of Raphael, and the greatness of Michelangelo. Upon their return they incorporated in their paintings many of the things they had seen and the techniques they had learned. Some paintings were so evidently imitations that they were devoid of originality and spontaneity. As one art historian has put it, "There was not enough Flanders in them to make them Flemish and not enough of Italy to make them Italian." But the Italian influence was far from being the evil some nationalist historians have styled it. The Flemish painters learned much from the Italians. Thorough assimilation of the knowledge they gained from the Italians enabled the Flemish and Dutch painters of the seventeenth century to produce some of the great paintings of all time.

One of the first painters whose works definitely show Italian influence was Quentin Metsys (also Matsys or Massys) (1466-1530) of Antwerp which by the end of the fifteenth century had become the leading art center as well as the great commercial and banking center of the Netherlands. Metsys was the first important member of the Antwerp school, and his work made a deep impression on future generations of Flemish painters. His work is characterized by a largeness of vision, a fine sense of color, good craftsmanship, and skill in the use of chiaroscuro. The Italian artists who exerted the greatest influence on him were Leonardo da Vinci and Raphael. The subtlety of expression he gave his madonnas probably derives from Leonardo and their oval faces are reminiscent of the madonnas of Raphael. Something new in the work of Metsys is the large scale of his figures. For example, in his masterpiece, "The Descent from the Cross," painted for one of the chapels of the Cathedral of Antwerp, the figures are life-size. Whereas small panels like those of Jan van Eyck were acceptable in the fifteenth century, the sixteenth demanded paintings which could be clearly seen from all parts of large churches. Metsys was also one of the earliest genre painters. In this respect his work represents the transition from the spirituality of fifteenth-century painting in the Netherlands to the secular qualities of the sixteenth. Two good examples of his genre painting are "Banker and His Wife" and "Courtesan and the Old Man." These are not portraits, but satires bordering on caricature. In addition to his interest in painting, Metsys also had a deep interest in humanistic culture. As the friend of Erasmus and Sir Thomas More he painted the portraits of both men.

Although there were among the successors of Metsys some who were intent on imitating Italian painters as fully as possible, there were also others who drew their inspiration from native sources. Prominent among the latter was Pieter Bruegel or Brueghel (1520-1569) who carried out in full some of the ideas for a popular art Metysys had foreshadowed. Born and raised in the village of Bruegel which later became a part of Holland, he spent the years of his activity as a painter in Antwerp and Brussels. Thus Bruegel represented both the northern and the southern provinces of the Netherlands, one of the last to do so before the regions separated into two distinct groups of provinces. Like most painters of his time he visited Italy, but Italian art which by this time was decadent did not impress him. What interested him most was the beauty of the Alpine landscape and of the natural scenery of southern Italy, a beauty which is reflected in his early paintings. To keep the wolf from his door upon his return to Antwerp, Bruegel took employment with the firm of an engraver, Jerome Cock, and during the months that followed made a series of remarkable sketches for engravings. During this period Bruegel frequently visited nearby villages where he joined in the pastimes, dances, and festivities of the peasants. He made many sketches of what he saw and later used them for the series of paintings which established him as the great painter of peasant life. Never before had peasant life been painted with such richness, vigor, and truth. Particularly noteworthy are his portrayals of wedding feasts and peasant dances. His scenes vary from the happy and pleasant to the coarse and harsh. (*See Fig. 29.*)

Bruegel did not, however, limit himself to peasant scenes. He was also a pioneer in the painting of majestic landscapes which have been called the fountainhead of all landscapes painted during the succeeding centuries. Bruegel also painted a number of pictures on religious subjects, but his treatment of them is thoroughly secular. It has been said that he portrayed religious subjects in terms of contemporary peasant life. During the last years of his life, which he spent in Brussels, Bruegel associated with a group of liberal humanists. The influence of this group is reflected in the psychological emphasis of his last paintings. In 1568, for example, he painted "The Blind Leading the Blind" which is probably a satire on the religious controversies of his day. Bruegel's most successful disciple was his own son Pieter II or Pieter the Younger. The styles of father and son are so much alike that it is difficult to decide whether certain unsigned paintings were executed by the father or by the son.

Flemish painting reached its epitome in the work of Peter Paul Rubens (1577-1640). His work embodies the progress made by Flemish painters since the time of Jan van Eyck. Whereas many of his predecessors were merely imitators of the Italians, Rubens assimilated the elements he borrowed from the Italians, and effected a marvelous synthesis of Italian techniques and Flemish tradition. Orders for paintings came from the Church, the court, civic groups, and from wealthy members of the bourgeoisie. The demand was so great that Rubens hired a staff of assistants to help him meet it. Over a period of three decades his studio turned out more than two thousand paintings, many of them of colossal size. The range of subjects included portraits, landscapes, genre, and religious pictures. But there was little of the spiritual in his religious pictures. Religious subjects were for Rubens merely the means for displaying his techniques and brilliant color schemes. Decorative effect was always paramount. Rubens' mature work, produced during the early decades of the seventeenth century, belongs to the Baroque Period during which the simplicity of the Renaissance was replaced by affectation and excessive ornamentation.

Renaissance Art in France

Naturalism in art made its appearance in France earlier than in Italy. Whereas in Italy the first manifestations of a naturalistic trend are to be found in the sculpture of Niccolo Pisano (1220-1284) after the middle of the thirteenth century, in France the craftsmen and stonemasons of the first half of the thirteenth century were close observers of nature as is indicated by the foliage that twines about the capitals of the columns in the French Gothic cathedrals. A tendency toward naturalistic representation is also visible in some of the sculptured figures, particularly those of the deeply-recessed porches at Chartres and Bourges. Even more naturalistic are the figures in the Rheims Cathedral. But it must be noted that the naturalism in Gothic art which reached its apogee in the thirteenth century was a naturalism in detail. The representation as such was still purely symbolical and the overriding consideration was still spiritual effect. During the fourteenth century this naturalism lost its spontaneity and became a reiteration of old formulas.

If the art interests in Paris and surrounding territories were still medieval, there was a definite trend toward naturalism in the works of the Burgundian school which had its headquarters at Dijon, the capital of Burgundy. Since the ruler of Burgundy was also the ruler of the Netherlands, Burgundy was joined to the Netherlands by political ties rather than to Paris. Only later was Burgundy incorporated into France. The Burgundian school was founded by Philip the Bold (1342-1404), duke of Burgundy, who gathered about himself in the capital of his prosperous duchy a number of artists from France, Flanders, and Holland. The most prominent figure in this group was Claus Sluter (*c.*1345-1406), a sculptor whom some art historians have styled "the Michelangelo of the North." Sluter lived long before Michelangelo appeared on the scene and his figures were still a far cry from those of Michelangelo, but he was one of the earliest apostles of naturalism in art. Although little is known of his background, it is believed that his ancestry was Dutch. Contemporaries called him "Sluter of Haarlem." As a sculptor he stands poised between the Gothic and Renaissance styles. His statues are undoubtedly the best portrait sculpture which had appeared up to that time. He demonstrated an ability to individualize his figures that was unparalleled in that age. Any estimate of his masterpieces must take into consideration the fact that when he had completed his life-work Ghiberti was only starting his career and Donatello was just entering young manhood. Even the famous "Adoration of the Lamb" painted by Jan van Eyck (1432) was not finished until more than a quarter century after Sluter's death. The dignity, the naturalism, and the intense individualism of his figures give Sluter rank among the major sculptors of Europe. (*See Fig. 30.*)

Sluter demonstrated his ability in three monumental works: the tomb of Philip the Bold, the portal of the abbey at Champmol, and "The Well of the Prophet." Philip the Bold, enjoying a large income from his prosperous territories, decided to build at Champmol, just outside Dijon, a monastery which in magnificence would outrank all others. Since it was originally his intention that the abbey should also serve as mausoleum for himself and his descendants, he commissioned the sculptor Jean de Marville to erect a magnificent tomb in it. But when de Marville died while working on the project, Claus Sluter assumed the task of completing it. The raised sarcophagus upon which lies the recumbent effigy of Philip was surrounded by statuettes representing a procession of ecclesiastics, choir boys, and mourners, each one having a distinctive personality. Next Sluter executed a series of statues for the portal of the abbey. This group of sculptures depicted the presentation of the abbey by Duke Philip and Duchess Margaret to the Virgin and the patron saints of the Carthusian order, John the Baptist and St. Catherine. The individualization of each figure, particularly the head and posture, is more definite than any known work of sculpture previously executed in northern Europe. Philip is presented as a real, not as an idealized, personality. The statue of the Duchess Margaret is an unflinching portrait, stocky with a prominent double chin, arrogant rather than attractive. The Virgin is a husky contemporary woman carrying her child on her hip as was the custom of peasant women. The statues of John the Baptist and St. Catherine are also realistic, modeled after contemporary figures. Although the abbey was demolished during the French Revolution of 1789, the statues were preserved in the museum at Dijon. Sluter also executed the six figures for "The Well of the Prophets," also called "The Well of Moses" after the most striking figure. These figures, representing Moses, David, Jeremiah, Zachariah, Daniel, and Isaiah, were grouped about the well in the courtyard of the abbey. The massive figures were men of this world with each one proclaiming his individuality in feature and figure. Sluter gave careful attention to such minute details as veins and wrinkles. He was in advance of his age not only because of his naturalistic representation, but also because his statues dominated the architecture; in the Gothic cathedrals statuary served only to enrich the architectural composition. Two and a half centuries later Rembrandt used Sluter as the model for his "Apostle Matthew."

One of the first artists in France proper whose work displayed a definite tendency toward realistic representation was Jean Fouquet (died *c.*1480), painter of miniatures, portraits, and altarpieces. Until 1904 when an exhibition of Fouquet's works was held, art historians regarded him only as a great miniaturist, but the portraits and panels that were sent in from various parts of Europe clearly demonstrated his skill in other phases of painting. His style was influenced by the work of Jan van Eyck and also by the works of Italian painters which he studied while visiting Italy; nevertheless, he managed to absorb both influences so completely that his style was characteristically his own. As court painter to Charles VII and Louis XI he painted a number of notable portraits, one of them being that of Charles VII himself. His miniature work includes the illumination for Chevalier's *Très Riches Heures* (The Book of Hours) and of a French edition of Boccaccio's *Decameron.* He also illustrated an edition of Josephus' *History of the Jews* which is now in the Bibliothèque Nationale in Paris. In his works French miniature painting reached its highest excellence. In *The Book of Hours,* for example, his illustration for December pictures a group of hunters in gay attire with their dogs closing in on a boar against a background of colorful fall foliage. The smallest details are rendered with great precision. In his larger portraits Fouquet portrayed individual characteristics with great skill, bestowing on his subjects an extraordinary vitality. Since Fouquet's art is a courtly art, his work epitomizes the spirit of the court circles. As an artist he surveyed life from the heights occupied by persons of the highest rank, but he depicted what he saw with the realistic outlook of the bourgeoisie of which he was a member. Fouquet was the first French artist of the Renaissance period whose reputation extended beyond the boundaries of his country. Specimens of his miniatures can be seen in museums in various parts of Europe.

But the example set by Fouquet did not inspire other artists to produce works of equal skill. Conditions in France, it seems, were not conducive to the development of great art apart from the Gothic tradition. When Guiliano de Medici visited France early in the sixteenth century he was appalled by the lack of culture at the French court. Upon his return to Florence in 1507 he reported that the only hope of raising the culture of the French barbarians to a higher level lay in the prospect that M. d'Angoulême would succeed Louis XII. In 1515 M. d'Angoulême did ascend the French throne as Francis I and immediately devoted some attention to raising the cultural standards of his court and his people. As stated in an earlier chapter, he invited artists and humanists to come to France, imported great paintings into France from Italy, and founded a school of decorative arts at Fontainebleau. But his efforts did not produce great art. Such artists as Leonardo da Vinci, Andrea del Sarto, and Benvenuto Cellini were men of such extraordinary ability that they had little in common with the French artists of that time. Furthermore, the paintings Francis I imported from Italy were of such high quality that the French painters lacked the skill to emulate them. Consequently they turned to the study and imitation of the works of inferior Italian painters. Another unfavorable factor was the desire of Francis to create a great art in France quickly, without a period of development. This spurred French artists to turn out works which were mere imitations or the products of undigested Italian influences combined with native traditions. Such art bore the stamp of artificiality. If portrait painters are excepted, it can be said that the reign of Francis I did not produce one painter who ranks high in the history of European art.

The two outstanding portrait painters of the period were Jean Clouet (d.1545) and his son François Clouet (d.1584). Jean's title at the royal court was Groom of the Chamber, but the services he rendered were those of court painter. As court painter he produced only eight paintings, his other portraits being crayon sketches. Jean was succeeded by his son François who achieved even greater renown. The Clouets did not paint their portraits from life. They are based on sketches which they made of their subjects. So great was the demand for portraits that more than fifty artists borrowed this technique from the Clouets. Sketching portraits with crayons was much in vogue during the reign of Francis I. Original sketches were often copied many times and distributed as photographs are today. This was true not only of the portraits of the king and queen, but also of members of the court and the bourgeoisie. Such portraits were commonly bound into albums to be preserved as family treasures. Although many of these crayon portraits have disappeared, thousands have survived, preserving for posterity the features of most of the outstanding personages of that time. (*See Fig. 31.*)

In sculpture sixteenth-century France had two noteworthy figures in Germain Pilon (d.1590) and Jean Goujon (d.1580). Pilon is probably best known for his "Les Trois Grâces" (The Three Graces) which have become widely familiar through reproductions. The three figures in graceful poses, representing perfect womanhood, were designed by Pilon to support an urn which was to contain the hearts of King Henry II and Catherine de Medicis, but the plan was never carried out. Of the two sculptors, Jean Goujon is a more important figure in the history of French sculpture. In the Louvre his works are exhibited in a special room called the Salle de Jean Goujon. In the center of the room stands Goujon's famous "Diana and the Stag" so named because it also includes a stag and two dogs. Diana is nude except for a light drapery over her right leg and her hair is dressed in coils after the contemporary manner of the French court. In all his works Goujon showed great skill in displaying the nude in such a way that it does not give offense. To a certain extent Goujon followed the long-drawn proportions of the human figure affected by certain Italian sculptors in which the hands and feet are longer than in nature. Probably equally as well-known as "Diana and the Stag" are the bas-reliefs he executed for the *Fountaine des Nymphs*, perhaps better known as the *Fountaine des Innocents*. These bas-reliefs were added to the thirteenth century fountain when it was reconstructed in his time, but in 1812 they were removed to the Louvre for safe-keeping. The rhythmic grace of his figures and the purity of their lines represent a fusion of classical and Renaissance styles. (*See Figs. 32, 33.*)

German Renaissance Painting

In the development of Renaissance art, Germany lagged far behind Italy and the Low Countries. Painting, sculpture, and architecture continued much longer to express otherworldly aspirations. Even in such cities as Nuremberg and Augsburg which had grown prosperous from trade and industry the medieval spirit persisted longer than in the Flemish towns. Among the German artists of the fifteenth century there was little consciousness of the developments in the direction of secularism and naturalism that had taken place in Italy and the Netherlands. Painters were still craftsmen whose function it was to paint devotional pictures for the Church and for noblemen and burghers who wanted and could afford them. In general, painters were not regarded as highly in Germany as they were in Italy. When Albrecht Dürer left Venice in 1493 on his return journey to Germany he is reported to have said, "Here I am a gentleman; at home I am only a parasite." In painting devotional pictures Germans adhered largely to the traditional methods of representation. Their figures were still angular and stiff; their paintings were overcrowded and lacked unity; the backgrounds still displayed a complete lack of understanding of aerial perspective. Furthermore, most of their work was poorly executed and the coloring was crude. There was also a lack of artistic consciousness and aesthetic standards. The aim of the painter was not technical excellence; it was the representation of piety. This backwardness of German art cannot be ascribed to a dearth of artists. It was due mainly to the fact that the attitude of those who bought the paintings was still medieval. The patrons of art had not as yet developed a taste for secularized art.

When the secular spirit did begin to assert itself, it found little room for self-expression in sculpture and architecture. German sculpture and architecture did not experience the stimulating influence of classical art which was such an important factor in Italy. Neither were the German sculptors and architects greatly affected by the secular trend in Italian art. Hence the attitude of German sculptors remained medieval, and German architects continued to build churches in the traditional German Gothic style. Early in the sixteenth century, however, the secular spirit of the Renaissance manifested itself in painting, drawing, woodcut designing, and engraving on metal. During this period the graphic arts rose to heights they had not previously attained in Germany. The flowering of the graphic arts was, in fact, so prodigious that the Germans could in some respects teach the Italians.

The artist who dominated the art of the German Renaissance was Albrecht Dürer (1471-1528), painter, draughtsman, woodcut designer, engraver, and author. His interests were so broad and his thirst for knowledge so insatiable that he has in these respects been compared with Leonardo da Vinci. "He who works in ignorance," Dürer wrote, "works more painfully than he who works with understanding." He was a man of great charm, nobility of mind, and earnestness of purpose. Born in Nuremberg, a free city of the Holy Roman Empire, he remained a citizen of his native city throughout life. He was so proud of Nuremberg that he referred to it as "that venerable city, my fatherland" and when he signed his name he usually added the words, "noricus civis" meaning citizen of Nuremberg. Since Germany was at that time broken up into many political fragments, such a display of local patriotism was not unusual. Dürer's affection for Nuremberg which was also the birthplace of Hans Sachs was so deep that he could not bring himself to leave it when he received tempting offers from other cities.

Young Albrecht very early demonstrated great skill in drawing. His father who was a goldsmith wanted him to continue the family tradition, and after his son had completed his elementary education he took him into his shop as an apprentice. What Dürer learned in his father's shop aided him in his later work, but he had a mind of his own. He wanted to be a painter. When at the age of thirteen Albrecht sketched a self-portrait the father was so impressed that he apprenticed his son to Michael Wohlgemuth who was not much of a painter, but who made a good living painting stereotyped devotional pictures. Possessing but little skill himself, Wohlgemuth did not have much to teach young Dürer. One cannot help conjecturing what it would have meant for Dürer's future if he had had a good teacher. On completing his apprenticeship, Dürer set out on his travels (Wanderjahre) as a journeyman to gain experience before settling down as a master painter. In his absence his father had arranged a marriage for him with a certain Agnes Frey whose great attraction was a dowry of two hundred florins. According to his friends the marriage was unfortunate for the artist. Not only was Agnes something of a shrew; she also had no appreciation of art and therefore evinced little interest in her husband's career. It is therefore not surprising to learn that he soon left his bride to embark on a journey to Venice.

Two years later Dürer was back in Nuremberg devoting himself to painting, woodcut designing, and engraving. During the next decade he produced many of the works for which he is famous. In 1505, however, his friend Willibald Pirckheimer, humanist and official of the city of Nuremberg, lent him the money for a second visit to Venice. His closest friend among the Venetian painters was Giovanni Bellini who despite his age was still the most prominent painter in Venice. While Bellini encouraged Dürer to continue painting, other painters were critical of his ability. They felt that the man who had already achieved a European reputation as an engraver and woodcut designer should concentrate his efforts on these arts. They told him that his style as a painter was not sufficiently naturalistic and classical, also that he was not a good colorist. To show them that he could paint well Dürer executed an altarpiece, "The Festival of the Rose Garlands," for the chapel of the German merchants living in Venice. This painting reflected Italian influence in a number of ways, but it also revealed the painter's Teutonic origins. Dürer himself was pleased with it, but his Italian critics for whom it was not naturalistic and classical enough disparaged it.

In his work as a painter Dürer combined medieval and Renaissance, Teutonic and Italian elements. His main concern was still the salvation of the soul. In his opinion, painting had a twofold purpose: service to the Church and the preservation of "the form of men after their death." Accordingly he painted religious pictures and portraits. In his early religious paintings the human form was still somewhat angular and there was a tendency to overcrowd his compositions with detail. This is undoubtedly the way he was taught to paint by his teacher. But Dürer gradually overcame many of his early limitations. His work after his second visit to Italy clearly reflects the influence of the Italian painters. As a colorist he did not, however, achieve a high rank. Art critics have described his coloring as gaudy and hard, and affording "little pleasure to the eye accustomed to color effects." His outstanding merit is his draughtsmanship, his mastery of line.

Although Dürer's active career covered a period of about thirty-five years, his output of paintings was not large. Some have disappeared; the total number of those now known is between forty and fifty. It has been suggested that Dürer did not paint more pictures because he found woodcut designing and engraving more remunerative. There is, for example, the case of the "Coronation of the Virgin," also called the "Heller Madonna" after the man who ordered it. After Dürer devoted much time and energy painting the picture, he had difficulty collecting the fee from Jacob Heller, a rich merchant of Frankfurt. The compensation he received was so small that he thenceforth allotted more of his time to woodcut designing and engraving. Besides the "Heller Madonna" and "Festival of the Rose Garlands" he painted such pictures as the "Adoration of the Magi" (now in the Uffizi Gallery in Florence) and "Adoration of the Trinity," an altarpiece for a Nuremberg almshouse. Probably his greatest religious painting is "The Four Apostles" (1526) on two panels, an extremely simple representation in comparison with the elaborate detail of his early paintings. This painting Dürer presented to the city of Nuremberg as a token of his gratitude. As a painter Dürer is at his best in his portraits. They represent the spirit of the Renaissance in a much greater degree than his other paintings. Probably his most famous portrait is the self-portrait he painted at the age of twenty-eight. It shows him dressed like a dandy in a black and white costume bordered with gold, his long honey-colored locks flowing down on his shoulders. Another famous portrait is that of Emperor Maximilian I. Dürer did not paint portraits of Erasmus and Pirckheimer, but he did leave woodcut drawings of them.

Far greater is the volume of work he turned out as a draughtsman, designer of woodcuts, and engraver of copper plates. All in all more than a thousand drawings, designs, and engravings have been preserved. The subjects include plants and animals, mythological scenes, religious pictures, costume designs, portraits, and studies of the human figure. Dürer is particularly famous for his sensitive drawings of hands; one of his most famous sketches is the "Praying Hands." All of his drawings testify to his keen observation of nature, to his extraordinary manual skill, and to his originality of execution. His earliest woodcut designs were illustrations for Sebastian Brant's *Narrenschiff* and for an edition of the plays of Terence. Probably the best known of his woodcuts are the illustrations for the Apocalypse or Book of Relevation. The most familiar of these scenes is that of the "Four Horsemen." No description can convey the dramatic power of this composition. Under a baleful sky four grim riders come charging from some mysterious land behind the ken of human knowledge, carrying their woes onward into an unseen future while trampling down merchants, burghers, women, monks, and peasants. Last rides the figure of death, represented by a withered old man with eyes staring in their sockets. It is one of the masterpieces that established Dürer's reputation as a woodcut designer.

Dürer's achievements as an engraver of copper plates are equally distinguished. With some exceptions he used woodcuts to illustrate religious subjects, while employing copper plates for mythological and secular subjects. An example of his early copper engraving is his "Hercules" which portrays the mythological figure confronted by the necessity of choosing between two figures personifying Virtue and Vice. The two figures are so realistic that it is quite evident which is Virtue and which is Vice. Other famous engravings include "Melancholia," "The Knight, Death, and the Devil," and "St. Jerome in His Study." In these engravings Dürer reached the height of his mastery. The prints made from the copper engravings quickly attained a wide circulation in other countries of Europe as well as in Germany. Some of them were copied and imitated by foreign engravers. It has been stated with some justification that Italian engravers borrowed more from him than he borrowed from Italian painters. (*See Fig. 34.*)

During the last years of his life Dürer devoted much time studying the mathematical or scientific approach to art, specifically to painting. The major stimulus to study the mathematical approach to art seems to have come from Jacopo dei Barbari of Venice who spent some time in Germany where he was known as Jacob Walch. "He showed me the figures of a man and a woman," Dürer wrote, "which he had drawn according to a canon of proportions." On his second visit to Italy Dürer discussed with Italian painters some of the treatises on the mathematical basis of art which had been written by such artists as Brunelleschi, Alberti, Piero della Francesco, and Cennini. At this time he conceived the idea that it was his mission to disseminate this knowledge in Germany. Such knowledge, he was certain, would insure a glorious future for German art. But on his return to Germany after his second visit to Italy Dürer became so immersed in his practical work that he was unable to give much attention to the theoretical side of art.

Finally in 1525 he published a treatise titled *Measurements and Proportions*. In the broader sense it is an introduction to geometric measurement of space as well as to mathematical proportions. Some months before his death he began working on a second treatise on the mathematical basis of art, this one being titled *Four Books of Human Proportions*. In it he set up a canon for a human figure of absolutely correct and harmonious proportions, the correctness of which could be established by mathematical measurements. As he stated in the introduction to the second part, "I will in this book teach how to measure out the human figure with a rule." He developed his formula to the point where the human figure was divided into six hundred mathematical parts. But Dürer did not demand that all figures be painted according to his formula. "We are," he wrote, "considering the most beautiful figure conceivable." As a student of nature he knew that nature does not make any two individuals alike. Hence he demonstrated how the proportions may be altered for the portrayal of "large, long, small, stout, broad, thick, narrow" and other kinds of figures.

It was while he was working on this treatise that Dürer suddenly passed away in the spring of 1528. In a moving eulogy Willibald Pirckheimer said, "Why hast thou suddenly left thy sorrowful friend and hastened away with rapid steps never to return again? It was not granted to me even to touch thy dear head or to grasp thy hand and say a last word of farewell to thee." But the memory of Albrecht Dürer has not died; in fact, his fame has increased with the passing of the centuries. He himself said of his work, "I am convinced that others will come who will write on these matters and paint better than I do, for I know the true value of my works and their faults. Would to God that I might see the works and learn the art of the great artists to come." Dürer's dream of a more magnificent German art did not materialize. Other German artists came, but none surpassed him.

Painting in Renaissance England

Native-born English painters did not respond to the stimulus of Italian or Flemish painting. During the Renaissance period, as stated earlier, England did not produce one painter whose name stands out in the history of European art. Whatever noteworthy paintings England had during this period were painted by foreign artists. The royal accounts show that a number of Italian and Flemish artists were employed at the royal court during the reign of Henry VII, but what they painted is largely a mystery. Although Henry VIII invited Raphael and Titian to make England their home, both refused. A number of foreign painters did, however, spend some time in England.

By far the greatest and most productive foreign painter who settled in England was Hans Holbein the Younger (1497-1543). Holbein's activities as a painter were so international that three countries can claim him as a citizen. He was born in Germany in the free city of Augsburg which was hardly less important as a commercial center than Nuremberg. His father, Hans Holbein the Elder, taught his son drawing and painting. In this respect young Holbein had one advantage over Dürer. Holbein the Elder was not as deeply immersed in medieval tradition as Michael Wohlgemuth, the teacher of Dürer. Hence Holbein, the Younger, did not have so much to unlearn at a later time. Having completed his training, young Hans saw no prosperous future for himself in Augsburg. As the elder Holbein found it difficult to support his family on his meager income as a painter, Hans migrated to Basel, a small city in Switzerland. A highlight of his stay in Basel was his association with Erasmus. One of the first things Holbein did was to draw eighty-three pen-and-ink sketches to illustrate Erasmus' *Praise of Folly* which the Froben Press in Basel published. He also sketched or painted a series of portraits of Erasmus. Like most of the important artists and humanists of his day, Holbein made the journey to Italy. What he saw there had an important influence on his development as a painter. Above all, it gave him a better sense of composition and perspective.

Meanwhile the situation in Basel had become less favorable for artists. The religious struggle between Protestants and Catholics was stifling the interest in art. As Erasmus put it in a letter to Quentin Metsys, "Here the arts are torpid." Holbein who found it increasingly more difficult to support his family finally decided to leave Basel. The last work he painted in Basel was the "Madonna of Burgomaster Meyer," one of Holbein's great religious masterpieces. This altarpiece received its name from the fact that it was ordered by the burgomaster and portrays him and his family in adoration of the Virgin. Having completed the altarpiece, Holbein decided to go to England, probably at the suggestion of Erasmus who gave him a letter of introduction to Sir Thomas More. On the way Holbein stopped at Antwerp to discuss art with Quentin Metsys. When he reached London he was cordially received by Sir Thomas More and his friends; in fact, he seems to have spent most of the time he was in England as the guest of Sir Thomas. Besides painting portraits of More and also a group picture of the More family, he was kept busy painting the portraits of a number of influential members of the English court. During this period (1526-1528) he saved so much money that he decided to return to his family in Basel. But he found conditions there much the same as they had been when he left for England. About the only work he was able to find was the painting of frescoes in the town hall. He also painted in oil on paper the widely-known "Portrait of an Artist's Family" which depicts his wife Elsbeth, his son, and his daughter in life-size figures (now in the Basel Museum). In 1532 lack of work impelled him to return to England. (*See Fig. 27.*)

This time Holbein remained in England for the remainder of his life, except for several brief visits to the continent. As Sir Thomas More was now in disfavor with Henry VIII, Holbein had to look in other directions for commissions. For a time he worked for the German merchants in the Steelyard, painting two large murals in the dining room. In addition he painted the portraits of some of the wealthy merchants who had their headquarters in the Steelyard. Gradually, however, he moved back into the court circle where he painted the portraits of a number of prominent figures, including that of Chancellor Thomas Cromwell, the successor of Sir Thomas More. In 1535 Henry VIII took him into his service as court painter and gave him a studio in Whitehall Palace. One of Holbein's primary tasks was to paint portraits of Henry VIII. It was not an easy assignment. He had to be exceedingly careful lest he antagonize the burly king and be sent to the block. For these portraits he designed the king's costumes down to the last detail, including jewelry, pendants, and even the buckles on the royal robes.

When Holbein was not preoccupied with the king's business, he spent his time painting portraits or making portrait sketches of both men and women surrounding the king. Some of his more famous portraits are those of Jane Seymour, Catherine Howard, and Edward VI as a child. When, after the death of Jane Seymour, Henry began to entertain ideas of a new matrimonial alliance, Holbein was sent to Brussels to paint the portrait of Christina, duchess of Milan, a widow of sixteen who was the daughter of the king of

Denmark and the niece of Emperor Charles V. Holbein's portrait is regarded as one of his best, a masterpiece of grandeur and simplicity; but Christina did not become Jane Seymour's successor. Next Holbein was dispatched to paint the portrait of Anne, duchess of Cleves, who had been suggested as a candidate by Chancellor Thomas Cromwell. This portrait gave rise to the legend that Holbein made the portrait so flattering that Henry VIII fell in love with Anne after seeing it and decided to marry her. Whatever may be the true story, Henry found her repulsive when he saw her in person. In 1543 when Holbein at the age of forty-six was at the height of his creative ability he suddenly fell victim to the plague. (*See Figs.* 27, 35.)

Although the craftsmanship of some of Holbein's religious pictures is superb, he is best known as one of the great portrait painters of all time. His portraits are distinguished by a certainty of draughtsmanship and an unusual skill in the use of rich and harmonious colors, and are characterized by exquisite taste and judgment. Furthermore, Holbein executed his portraits with diligence and exactness, giving the most careful attention to detail. Although he stressed realistic portrayal, his ultimate aim was delineation of character. He was eminently successful in expressing the inner thoughts of his subjects with the brush. Few artists have had the ability to make character so visible. In this and in other respects Holbein's portraits have an affinity with those of Leonardo da Vinci and other great portrait painters.

Holbein was the real founder of the English school of portrait painting. England would be much poorer artistically if he had not settled there. In his portraits and sketches of prominent figures of the English court he made his period live as no previous period had lived in English history. Painters of the succeeding period tried to imitate his mastery of portraiture, but none could equal it. The next great figure in English painting was Sir Anthony Van Dyck (1599-1641) who did not appear on the scene until the seventeenth century. He, too, was a foreigner.

Spanish Renaissance Painting

Renaissance Spain did not produce any outstanding figures in architecture, sculpture, or music. The contributions which Spain made to the arts were in the field of painting, but even there the number of noteworthy artists is small. The principal outside influences on Spanish painting came from Flanders and Italy. Of the two the Flemish influence was the first to make itself felt. A number of Flemish masters who migrated to Spain bequeathed their manner of painting to their Spanish successors. A large number of Flemish paintings were also imported into Spain by merchants or were painted to order by Flemish painters for Spanish patrons. From the reign of Ferdinand and Isabella through the sixteenth century, Italian masterpieces were the great source of inspiration for many Spanish painters. Interest was centered particularly in the works of the painters of the Italian High Renaissance, more specifically of Leonardo da Vinci, Raphael, Michelangelo, and Titian. It was even suggested that the artistic excellence of these Italian painters be set up as a goal for Spanish painters to achieve. The range of subject matter of the Spanish painters was not, however, as broad as that of the Italians. For example, the Spanish painters rejected mythological themes. Although paintings on mythological subjects by Titian were given places in the Escorial, most Spanish painters carefully eschewed subjects from Greek or Roman mythology. Furthermore, Spanish painters did not follow the example of the Italians in portraying the human body in the nude. The artistic climate of Spain was not propitious for the depiction of the nude.

Since the Roman Catholic Church, the members of the orthodox royal court, and nobles with religious preoccupations were the principal patrons of the Spanish painters, the subjects of most of the paintings were of a religious nature. Portraits were the great exception. In the sixteenth century, portraiture became a flourishing art. The first of the great Spanish portrait painters was Alonso Sanchez Coello (1515-1590) who learned the art of portraiture in the studio of a Flemish artist and from a careful study of Titian's portraits. Consequently his early portraits were a blending of the Flemish and Italian manner. But Sanchez Coello was no mere imitator, for he developed certain techniques of his own. Appointed court painter in 1571, he became the close friend and companion of Philip II. During the succeeding years Sanchez Coello painted many portraits of his royal patron in various poses, but most of them were destroyed by a fire in the Prado. The full-length portrait of Philip II which survived is notable for its rich color and exquisite rendering of the texture of the king's costume. In his studio adjoining the palace Sanchez Coello also executed many portraits of members of the royal family and persons who frequented the court. The best known of these portraits is probably that of Philip's pathetic son Don Carlos, the ill-starred hero of Schiller's tragedy. In all his portraits Sanchez Coello took great pains to achieve a verisimilitude of jewelry, laces, brocades, and fabrics. He was, however, superficial in some respects. Art critics have pointed out that most of the hands he painted are of the same pattern. Nevertheless, his portraits gave a decided impetus to portrait painting with the result that other artists followed in his footsteps. Sanchez Coello's portraits are the direct precursors of the great portraits of Velasquez.

The religious paintings of the period of the Spanish Renaissance reflect the atmosphere which prevailed at a time when the Inquisition was compelling religious conformity. They are somber in tone, medieval in subject, passionately ascetic, mystical, and otherworldly in spirit. During the early stages of the Renaissance the drawing was crude and the manner of representation was generally backward in comparison with the paintings that were being turned out in most of the other countries of Western Europe. Many Spanish painters deliberately retained the archaic angular style because they regarded it as more pious. Gradually, however, the mode of representation became more secular. Exposure to Flemish and Italian influences caused many Spanish painters to move in the direction of naturalism. More and more they incorporated the beauty of nature in their paintings. Secular Renaissance forms and styles were imposed on the traditional subjects. Despite the fact that the Spanish painters borrowed the technique and adopted the manner of Flemish and Italian painters, the finished product was not the same. Spanish painting had a distinctive character of its own. Even when the Spanish painter endeavored to depict a subject with the frankest realism, the finished work had about it an aura which transcended nature. It has been stated that Spanish art is the most mystical and at the same time the most realistic form of art. Religious subjects were rendered in terms of daily life so that they would be more appealing and more comprehensible.

It is not easy to establish the beginnings of the naturalistic trend in Spanish painting, for Spain did not have a Masaccio, a Jan van Eyck, a Dürer, a Fouquet, or a Holbein. The Spanish painter who best represents the trend toward naturalistic depiction is Juan Fernandez Navarete (1526-1572) who was called "El Mudo" because he was a deaf-mute, a serious illness in early childhood having robbed him of his hearing. After learning the rudiments of drawing and painting, he followed the example of other Spanish painters by going to Italy to continue his studies. In Venice where he spent most of his time Navarete came under the influence of the school of Titian; in fact, he may have been a pupil of Titian himself. The influence of Titian is apparent in El Mudo's use of color and to a lesser extent in his drawing. When Philip II was building the Escorial he recalled Navarete from Italy and commissioned him to execute a number of paintings for the new structure. His first important painting, "Baptism of Christ" (now in the Prado), shows the influence of his Italian training. Thereafter his paintings became more characteristically Spanish. For the minor altars in the Escorial he painted eight saints and evangelists in a realistic manner. He also painted a number of pictures for the upper cloisters, including a "St. Jerome," an "Adoration of the Shepherds," and a "Nativity."

Navarete's best known picture is probably his "Martyrdom of St. Jerome" which depicts the tortures of the saint with a merciless realism. It is reported that when one of the court officials insulted him, El Mudo took his revenge by painting the face of the official on the figure of one of the torturers. In general his pictures are noted for naturalistic depiction, bright colors, bold designs, and mastery of chiaroscuro. His early death in 1572 was lamented by Lope de Vega in his "Laurel de Apolo." Lope believed that Navarete was the Spanish painter who best rivaled the Italian masters. His adoption of the Italian styles set the example for many Spanish painters who followed him. In his use of color, chiaroscuro, and naturalistic design, El Mudo was a forerunner of the great Spanish masters who appeared at a later time.

The best known Spanish painter of the late sixteenth century and the early part of the seventeenth is Domenico Theotocopuli (*c.*1547-1614) who was either born in Crete or was the son of Greek parents living in Venice. As his name was difficult for the Spanish tongue he was called "El Greco" (the Greek) and has been known by this name ever since. El Greco is a controversial figure. While some art historians have ranked him with Velesquez and Goya as the great trinity of Spanish painting, others have accorded him a lesser rank. The Spanish painter Palomino (d.1728) took an intermediate stand when he stated, "What he could do well none could do better and what he did badly none could do worse." El Greco learned his art in Italy and may even have studied under Titian. About 1576 he journeyed to Spain where he settled in Toledo. One of the first pictures he painted there was his "Stripping of Christ," painted for the cathedral of Toledo. This work shows El Greco's "Venetian manner" at its best. It is noted for its careful realistic drawing and its warmth of color. But thereafter El Greco gradually abandoned the Venetian manner for a style peculiarly his own. Not many years after he settled in Spain Philip II ordered him to execute for the Church of the Escorial a painting titled "The Martyrdom of St. Maurice." The king who had been led to expect something Titianesque was greatly disappointed when he saw the painting. Although he paid El Greco the agreed stipend, Philip did not have the painting hung in the Escorial Church, but relegated it to an obscure place. El Greco, having forfeited the royal favor, returned to Toledo to live and paint in comparative quiet until his death in 1614.

As El Greco grew older his manner of representation became increasingly eccentric and at times verged on the grotesque. One art historian has styled this "the pathological degeneration of El Greco." His colors became harsh and he introduced weird gleams of light into his paintings. He also exaggerated the lines of his drawings, elongating and twisting the human figures in utter disdain of reality. Yet the heads and faces he put on these figures are remarkable for their naturalism. As indicated, his eccentricities have by some art historians been ascribed to a mental illness which supposedly afflicted him. Curiously enough, his observations were quite sane, however, when he was painting portraits, of which there are nine in the Prado. While painting pictures that were not portraits El Greco became so obsessed with his eccentricities that he believed only he could paint. Pacheco reported that when he visited El Greco in 1611 the latter stated during a discussion of Italian art that Michelangelo is "a good man but doesn't know how to paint."

Art historians are generally agreed that one of his earlier paintings, "The Burial of Count Orgaz," painted for the Church of Santo Tome in Toledo, is El Greco's masterpiece. It is based on the legend that when the pious count died in 1323 St. Stephen and St. Augustine came down from heaven and with their own hands carried him to the tomb. The two saints are the central figures as they support the body which is being lowered. The contrast between the youthful St. Stephen and the venerable St. Augustine with a mitre on his head is striking. Priests and monks surround the tomb and in the background there is a group of nobles whose faces are portraits of contemporary noblemen. The firmament above is open, showing Christ, the Virgin, and a host of angels receiving the soul of the departed count. The painting is a strange combination of realism and mysticism. Since realism was at the time of El Greco's death the dominant note in Spanish painting, the eccentric El Greco had few disciples.

Bibliography

1 *The Renaissance: The Word and the Concept*

THE RENAISSANCE PROBLEM. There are two good brief statements of the problem of the Renaissance: *The Renaissance: Medieval or modern?* (1959), edited by K. H. Dannenfeldt, and *The Renaissance Debate* (1965), edited by Denys Hay. The standard longer account is W. K. Ferguson's *The Renaissance in Historical Thought* (1948) which covers the interpretations of the Renaissance during the last five centuries. The same author has also written a solid survey of the fourteenth and fifteenth centuries under the title *Europe in Transition, 1300-1520* (1962). Professor Ferguson has collected in *Renaissance Studies* (1963) eleven papers which were previously published separately. *The Horizon Book of the Renaissance* (1962), edited by J. H. Plumb, is a well-edited and lavishly-illustrated volume of special studies on various phases of the Renaissance. Emil Lucki's *History of the Renaissance* (5 vols., 1964) incorporates many recent findings of historical scholarship; the volumes discuss respectively economic history, religion, education and thought, literature and art, and politics and political thought. *Renaissance and Revolution: The Remaking of European Thought* (1966), by Joseph A. Mazzeo, is an extensive treatment of two writers of the sixteenth century (Machiavelli and Castiglione) and two of the seventeenth (Bacon and Hobbes). There are some interesting and informative studies in *Studies in Medieval and Renaissance History* (2 vols., 1963-65), edited by William M. Bowsky. M. M. Checksfield's *Portraits of Renaissance Life and Thought* (1965) offers essays on ten personages of the Renaissance, including Erasmus, More, Francis I, Montaigne, and Cervantes. On cultural trends *From the Renaissance to Romanticism: Trends in Style in Art, in Literature, and Music, 1300-1830* (1962), by Frederick B. Artz, is filled with many keen observations. There are a number of works on the Renaissance by groups of historians as, for example, *The Renaissance Reconsidered* (1964), by L. Gabel and others. Another is *The Renaissance: A Reconsideration of the Theories and Interpretations of the Age* (1961), edited by T. Helton. Then there is *The Renaissance: A Symposium* (1962) offering six essays read at the Metropolitan Museum in New York City in 1953. Finally there is a paperback titled *Facets of the Renaissance* (1963), a series of papers read at the University of California in 1956. There are a number of illuminating essays on Renaissance subjects in *The Dawn of Modern Civilization* (1962), edited by Kenneth A. Strand. Neal W. Gilbert's *Renaissance Concepts of Method* (1960) is a valuable scholarly study.

ITALIAN RENAISSANCE. J. H. Plumb's *Italian Renaissance* (1961) is a brief, well-written, stimulating survey. *The Italian Renaissance in Its Historical Background* (1961), by Denys Hays is an able and enlightening discussion of the Italian Renaissance and its background. Will Durant's *Renaissance: A History of Civilization in Italy, 1304-1576* (1953) is a well-written popularization with excellent portraits of some of the leaders, but it lacks unity and interpretation. H. Vaughan's *Studies in the Italian Renaissance* (1930) is a series of lively lectures. *The Italian Renaissance* (1962), edited by E. F. Jacob, is a series of studies by sixteen British historians whose ideas on the Renaissance differ widely. Jakob Burckhardt's *Civilization of the Renaissance in Italy* (originally published in German in 1860) is time-worn and badly scarred from the attacks of critics, but is still informative if read with discretion (various English translations). Another nineteenth-century work which can still be read with profit is John Addington Symond's *Renaissance in Italy* (7 vols., 1875-86). The same author has also published *A short history of the Renaissance in Italy* (1894) which has been widely read. Walter Gundersheimer's *Italian Renaissance* (1965) is a recent brief readable survey.

Special Studies. *The Philosophers of the Italian Renaissance* (1964), by Paul O. Kristeller, is a series of stimulating lectures on the writings of eight philosophers. Professor Kristeller has republished his penetrating articles in two paperbacks: *Renaissance Thought I: The Classic, Scholastic, and Humanist Strains* (1961) and *Renaissance Thought II: Papers on Humanism and the Arts* (1965). B. L. Ullman has also republished the series of scholarly articles he wrote for various periodicals in one volume titled *Studies in the Italian Renaissance* (1955); unfortunately the book was published in Rome. A third historian who has written a number of valuable studies for learned periodicals is Herbert Weisinger. Some of these are "Ideas of history during the Renaissance," *Jour. of the Hist. of Ideas,* 6 (1945), 415-435: "The Renaissance theory of the reaction against the Middle Ages as a cause of the Renaissance," *Speculum,* 20 (1945), 461-467; and "Renaissance accounts of the revival of learning," *Studies in Philology,* 14 (1948), 105-18. Ernst Cassirer's much discussed treatise *The Individual and the Cosmos in Renaissance Philosophy* is now available in an English translation by M. Domandi (1963), rewarding but not easy reading. M. P. Gilmore's "Freedom and determinism in Renaissance historians," *Studies in the Renaissance,* 3 (1956), 49-60, is a brief provocative study. Cecil Roth's *The Jews in the Renaissance* (1965) is a well-written account by a British historian. For an approach to the Renaissance from another side there is Kenneth M. Setton's "The Byzantine background of the Italian Renaissance," *Proceedings of the American Philosophical Society,* 100 (1956), 1-76.

Renaissance Readings. *The Renaissance Philosophy of Man* (1948), edited by E. Cassirer, P. O. Kristeller, and J. H. Randall, offers some well-chosen selections from the writings of Renaissance philosophers with critical comments. *The Renaissance and the Reformation* (1965), edited by Donald Weinstein, is a useful collection of source material. *The Portable Renaissance Reader* (1953), edited by J. B. Ross and M. M. McLaughlin, offers a broad selection of readings illustrative of the Renaissance in northern Europe as well as in Italy. *A Renaissance Treasury* (1953), edited by Hiram Haydn and J. C. Nelson, is a collection of excerpts from the writings of representative figures of the Renaissance. *Literary Source-Book of the Renaissance,* (2nd ed., 1903), edited by M. Whitcomb, illustrates the intellectual side of the Renaissance in Italy and Germany.

2 *The Role of the Medieval Church*

Middle Ages. Some of the better surveys of the Middle Ages are Sidney Painter's *History of the Middle Ages* (1953); John L. LaMonte's *World of the Middle Ages* (1949); J. R. Strayer's *Western Europe in the Middle Ages* (4th ed., 1959); C. W. Hollister's *Medieval Europe: A Short History* (1965); Carl Stephenson's *Medieval History,* revised by Bryce Lyon (4th ed., 1963); and Norman Cantor's *Medieval History: The Life and Death of a Civilization* (1963). *Medieval People* (10th ed., 1963), by Eileen Power, and *Life in Medieval France* (rev. ed., 1957), by Joan Evans, contain much interesting information on the life of the period. S. Painter's *Medieval Society* (1951) offers a broad discussion of feudal society. For a more detailed account there is G. G. Coulton's *Life in the Middle Ages* (4 vols. in 1, 1930), a rich and varied fund of knowledge. *The Medieval Mind* (2 vols., 1919), by H. O. Taylor, is somewhat antiquated but still eminently useful. The same author has also written *Thought and Expression in the Sixteenth Century* (2nd ed., 2 vols., 1930) and *The Emergence of Christian Culture in the West,* edited with foreword by K. M. Setton (1958). *The Portable Medieval Reader* (4th printing, 1955), edited by J. B. Ross, contains many illuminating excerpts from medieval writings.

The Medieval Church. Marshall W. Baldwin's *The Medieval Church* (1953) is a good brief introduction to the subject. The same author has also written *The Medieval Papacy in Action* (1950). Roland H. Bainton has also written a brief survey under the title *The Medieval Church* (1961). There are two lucid longer accounts by A. C. Flick, *The Rise of the Medieval Church* (1909) and *The Decline of the Medieval Church* (2 vols., 1930). There is a good discussion of the Medieval Church in K. S. Latourette's *History of Christianity* (1953). Other useful volumes are Margaret A. Deansley's *History of the Medieval Church* (1925) and L. H. Hertling's *History of the Catholic Church* (1959). James A. Corbett's *The papacy* (1956) is a good brief survey. For a somewhat longer account there is *The Development of the Papacy* (1952), by H. Burn-Murdoch.

THOUGHT and PHILOSOPHY. *The Mind of the Middle Ages, 1300-1500* (3rd ed., 1958), by Frederick B. Artz, is a good one-volume survey of medieval learning and culture. The standard history of medieval philosophy by a Catholic historian is Etienne H. Gilson's *History of Christian Philosophy in the Middle Ages* (1955). Another valuable survey is David Knowles' *Evolution of Medieval Thought* (1962). Another important volume by the same author is *Saints and Scholars: Twenty-five Medieval Portraits* (1962). For a fresh approach to some medieval problems there is Gordon Leff's *Medieval Thought* (1958). *Molders of the Medieval Mind: The Influence of the Fathers of the Church on Medieval Schoolmen* (1944), by Frank Cassidy, is an informative study of medieval education. *Perspectives in Medieval History* (1963), edited by Katherine F. Drew, contains five essays by eminent historians emphasizing the continuity between medieval and modern times. The social organization and the underlying theories are ably discussed in Bede Jarrett's *Social Theories of the Middle Ages* (1942). Helene Wieruszowski's *The Medieval University* (1966) is a penetrating concise study. The two longer standard accounts are Charles H. Haskins' *The Rise of Universities* (1923) and H. Rashdall's *The Universities of Europe in the Middle Ages* (3 vols., rev. ed., 1936). Pearl Kibre's *The Nations in the Medieval Universities* (1948) is a sound painstaking study.

SPECIAL STUDIES. *The Idea of Usury* (1949), by Benjamin N. Nelson, is a concise but penetrating discussion. Howard R. Patch's *The Other World According to Descriptions in Medieval Literature* (1950) is an interesting fact-crammed volume. Another informative study is Marcus Dods' *Forerunners of Dante: An Account of Some of the More Important Visions of the Unseen World* (1903). A third informative volume is *Medieval English Conceptions of Hell* (1960), by R. C. Sutherland. On Satan there is M. J. Rudwin's scholarly study *The Devil in Legend and Literature* (1931). The same author has also selected and edited *Devil Stories: An Anthology* (1921). One of the best accounts is *The Devil: An Historical, Critical and Medieval Study* (1929), by M. Garcon and J. Vinchon. The stories of Caesarius of Heisterbach are available in an English translation under the title *The Dialogue on Miracles,* translated by H. von E. Scott and C. C. S. Bland (2 vols., 1929).

3 *The Intensification of the Secular Spirit*

MISCELLANEOUS STUDIES. For discussions of the new science, literature, painting, sculpture, architecture, and music see the bibliographies for the pertinent chapters. This should also be done for economic and political developments. A good short introduction to the influence of Innocent III is Sidney R. Packard's *Europe and the Church under Innocent III* (1927). There is a good brief discussion of Innocent III in D. C. Somervell's *Critical Epochs in History* (1923). There is also a good longer biography of Innocent III in English by L. Elliott-Binns (1931). *Roman Law in Medieval England* (1909), by P. Vinogradoff, is the best concise study on the subject. Another informative volume is James Hadley's *Introduction to Roman Law* (1893).

RENAISSANCE EDUCATION. There are good brief discussions of Renaissance education in H. G. Good's *History of Western Education* (2nd ed., 1960); John E. Wise's *History of Education* (1964); and William Boyd's *History of Western Education* (7th ed., 1965). An enlightening discussion of culture and education in the age of the Renaissance is available in R. F. Butt's *Cultural History of Education* (2nd ed., 1955). William H. Woodward has written an entire volume on Renaissance education titled *Studies in Education During the Age of the Renaissance* (1924). There is a longer discussion of medieval education in *The History and Philosophy of Education: Ancient and Medieval* (1940), by Frederick Eby and Charles F. Arrowood. Education is regarded from a special point of view in George Jackson's *The Privilege of Education: A History of Its Extension* (1918). There is a biography of Vittorino in English by a sister of

Notre Dame (otherwise unnamed) titled *Vittorino da Feltre: A Prince of Teachers* (1908). "Education in Dante's Florence," by Charles T. Davis in *Speculum*, 40 (1965), 415-35, is a short informative discussion. On the education of the aristocracy, there is the brief scholarly discussion by J. H. Hexter, "The education of the aristocracy in the Renaissance," *Jour. of Mod. Hist.*, 22 (1950), 1-20. For an informative chapter on Castiglione see Ralph Roeder's *The Man of the Renaissance* (1933). Castiglione's famous treatise, *The Courtier*, is available in a number of English translations.

Savonarola. Probably the best impartial biography of Savonarola is Roberto Ridolfi's *Life of Girolamo Savonarola*, translated from the Italian by C. Grayson (1959), which cuts through the mass of legends. Another informative account is M. de la Bedoyere's *The Meddlesome Friar: The Story of the Conflict Between Savonarola and Alexander VI* (1957), a brief study of the two men. An older standard account of Savonarola and his age is P. Villari's *Life and Times of Girolamo Savonarola*, translated by L. Villari (2 vols., 2nd ed., 1909). There are two well-written popular biographies: *Savonarola: A Study in Conscience* (1930), by Ralph Roeder, and *A Crown of Fire: The Life and Times of Girolamo Savonarola* (1960), by Pierre van Passen.

4 *The Social and Economic Background of the Renaissance*

General Surveys. H. Pirenne's *Economic and Social History of Medieval Europe* (1936) is a judicious survey by a distinguished historian. Another good survey is J. W. Thompson's *Economic and Social History of the Later Middle Ages* (1931). H. Heaton's *Economic History of Europe* (2nd ed., 1948) is a sound readable survey. The most comprehensive work is the *Cambridge Economic History of Europe* (3 vols., 1941-63), edited by J. H. Clapham, M. M. Postan, Eileen Power, and others, detailed and readable. P. Boissonade's *Life and Work in Medieval Europe* (1927) contains much useful information. *An Essay on Western Civilization in Its Economic Aspects* (2 vols., 1910), by William Cunningham, is a mine of valuable information. L. B. Packard's *Commercial Revolution* (1927) is a good brief introduction to the expansion of commerce. Clive Day's *History of Commerce* (rev. ed., 1922) contains some interesting chapters on commerce in the age of the Renaissance. Henri Pirenne's *Medieval Cities* (2nd ed., 1939) is a readable account by a recognized authority on the subject. *Urban Civilization in Pre-Crusade Europe* (2 vols., 1965), by Irving A. Agus, is a study of town life in northeastern Europe which contains important new information. *Medieval Technology and Social Change* (1962), by Lynn White, is an interesting and provocative account. There are a number of books which contain good scholarly discussions of the early history of capitalism. Some of these are Henri E. Sée's *Modern Capitalism: Its Origins and Development* (1928); J. A. Hobson's *Evolution of Modern Capitalism* (1926); and H. Pirenne's *The Stages in the History of Capitalism* (1953). On agriculture there are two authoritative works, Nellie Neilson's *Medieval Agrarian Economy* (1936) and B. H. Slicher van Bath's *Agrarian History of Western Europe* (1963), which survey agrarian life over a period of thirteen centuries. There is a useful collection of readings in *A Source Book for Medieval Economic History* (1936), edited by R. C. Cave and H. H. Coulson. For further references see W. K. Ferguson's "Recent trends in the economic history of the Renaissance," *Studies in the Renaissance*, 7 (1961), 7-26. There is excellent background material in Volume 1 of Emil Lucki's *History of the Renaissance* (1964), titled *Economy and Society*.

Depression. There are a number of references to the economic depression of the fourteenth and fifteenth centuries in Volume 2 of the *Cambridge Economic History of Europe*. The best study is "The economic depression of the Renaissance" by R. Lopez and H. A. Miskimin, *Economic Hist. Rev.*, Ser. 2, vol. 14 (1961-62), 408-26. The depression is also discussed in H. Pirenne's *Economic and Social History of the Middle Ages* (1936). For Italy there is C. M. Cipolla's "The trends in Italian economic history in the later Middle Ages," *Econ. Hist. Rev.*, Ser. 2. vol. 2 (1949), 181-4. A. R. Lewis' "The closing of the medieval frontier, 1250-1350," *Speculum*, 33 (1958), 475-83, points to a population decline. J. M. W. Bean's "Plague, population, and economic decline in the later Middle Ages," *Econ. Hist. Rev.*, 5 (1933), 423-50.

NORTHERN EUROPE. *The Netherlands* (1946), by B. Landheer, is a good survey. Herman van der Wee's *The Growth of the Antwerp Market and the European Economy* (3 vols., 1963) is a detailed scholarly account of the history of the great sixteenth-century emporium. The best account of the herring fisheries is James T. Jenkins' *The Herring and the Herring Fisheries* (1927). There is also a popular account by W. C. Hodgson titled *The Herring and Its Fishery* (1957), not always reliable. On banking at Bruges there is R. de Roover's interesting and scholarly study, *Money, Banking, and Credit in Medieval Bruges* (1948). Unfortunately the best and most up-to-date accounts of the Hanseatic League are in German. One of these is Fritz Rörig's *Vom Werden und Wesen der Hansa* (1940). Two useful accounts in English are *The Hansa: Its History and Romance* (1929), by E. Gee Nash, and *The Hansa Towns* (1895), by Helen Zimmern. An important study in English is John A. Gade's *The Hanseatic Control of Norwegian Commerce During the Late Middle Ages* (1951). A. R. Bridbury's *England and the Salt Trade in the Late Middle Ages* (1955) is an informative study on one phase of English trade.

MONEY AND BANKING. *The Evolution of Money* (1964), by R. J. Ederer, contains a good background for banking. Two other informative volumes are Norman Angell's *The Story of Money* (1929) and E. Cornwall's *The Story of Money* (1938). The functions of the early banks are ably discussed in A. P. Usher's *The Early History of Deposit Banking in Mediterranean Europe* (1943). A more comprehensive survey is N. F. Hoggson's *Banking Through the Ages* (1926). The most detailed survey is J. W. Gilbert's *History, Principles, and Practice of Banking* (2 vols., 1907). On banking in northern Europe there is Richard Ehrenberg's *Capital and Finance in the Age of the Renaissance* (reprint, 1963), which deals particularly with the age of the Fugger family. *Jacob Fugger the Rich* (1931), by Jacob Strieder, is a solid biography of the great merchant and banker of Augsburg. A valuable book on a related subject is C. F. Trenerry's *The Origin and Early History of Insurance* (1926). *Papal Revenues in the Middle Ages* (2 vols., 1934), by W. E. Lunt, is the definitive study on the subject in English.

5 *Renaissance Italy*

GENERAL STUDIES. J. P. Trevelyan's *Short History of the Italian People* (4th ed., 1956) and L. Salvatorelli's *Concise History of Italy*, translated by B. Miall (1940), are two good surveys. Useful as an introductory survey is *A Short History of Italy* (1963), edited by H. Hearder and D. P. Waley. Broader in content is Decio Pettoello's *Outline of Italian Civilization* (1932). For a more detailed study of the political history of the Renaissance period consult Henry B. Cotterill's *Italy from Dante to Tasso* (1919). Two other well-written and fairly reliable volumes are John Addington Symonds' *Renaissance in Italy: The Age of the Despots* (3rd ed., 1920) and O. Browning's *The Age of the Condottieri* (1895). On the city-states there is the lively discussion by M. V. Clarke titled *The Medieval City-State: An Essay in Tyranny and Federation in the Later Middle Ages* (1966). Maud F. Jerrold's *Italy in the Renaissance: A Sketch of Italian Life and Civilization in the Fifteenth and Sixteenth Centuries* (1927) is a good overall survey of Renaissance Italy. *Renaissance Italy: Was It the Beginning of the Modern World?* (1958), edited by Gene A. Brucker, is a collection of interesting excerpts on the subject from the works of Renaissance writers.

VENICE. One of the better surveys of Venetian history is Charles E. Yriarte's *Venice: Its History, Art, Industries, and Modern Life* (1896). There is a more recent brief survey by Selwyn J. C. Brinton titled *Venice: Past and Present* (1925). The fullest account of Venetian history is P. G. Molmenti's *Venice: Its Individual Growth from Its Earliest Beginnings to the Fall of the Republic* (6 vols., 1906-8). Such older histories as Francis Marion Crawford's *Venice* (2 vols., 1908) and Horatio R. Brown's *The Venetian Republic* (1902) may still be used with profit. *Venetian Ships and Shipbuilders of the Renaissance* (1934), by Frederic C. Lane, is an interesting and well-written treatise. The same author has also written *Andrea Barbarigo, Merchant of Venice, 1418-1449* (1944) based on Barbarigo's papers, and *Venice and History*

(1966), a collection of papers on Venetian history. James C. Davis' *The Decline of the Venetian Nobility as a Ruling Class* (1962) throws much light on one phase of Venetian history.

FLORENCE. The best general survey of Florentine history is F. Schevill's *History of Florence* (1936). Another good survey is Edmund G. Gardner's *Florence and Its History* (1953). There is also a useful older account by Francis A. Hyett titled *Florence: Her History and Art to the Fall of the Republic* (1903). For a discussion of Florence during the age of the Renaissance consult Paul G. Ruggieri's scholarly treatise, *Florence in the Age of Dante* (1964). Gene A. Brucker's *Florentine Politics and Society, 1343-1378* (1962) is a sound readable account of one of the most complex periods in Florentine history. *A City that Art Built* (1936), by August C. Krey, is a stimulating essay on the city of Florence; also published in the same author's *History and the Social Web* (1955). Another good discussion of the relationship between the city and the art it produced can be found in George Bierman's *Florence and Her Art* (1921). *The Builders of Florence* (1907), by James W. Brown, is a useful older study. Charles C. Bayley's *War and Society in Renaissance Florence: The De Militia of Leonardo Bruni* (1961) provides a critical text of the *De Militia* of Bruni, one of the most eminent humanists of Florence. Gene A. Brucker's "Sorcery in early Renaissance Florence," *Studies in the Renaissance*, 10 (1963), 7-24, is an interesting discussion of one phase of Florentine life.

THE MEDICI. Gene A. Brucker's "The Medici in the fourteenth century," *Speculum*, 32 (1957), 1-26, is a concise informative study. *Lives of the Early Medici as Told in Their Correspondence* (1910), by J. Ross, is an important source of information on members of the Medici family. *The Medici* (2 vols., 1909; single-vol. ed., 1932), by C. F. Young, is interesting and readable, but not always trustworthy. The best short account is F. Schevill's *The Medici* (1960). There is a good biography of Cosimo de Medici by C. S. Gutkind (1938) and an older one by R. D. Ewart (1889). There are two interesting introductory surveys of Lorenzo and his rule: Edward Armstrong's *Lorenzo de Medici and Florence in the Fifteenth Century* (reprint, 1923) and Cecilia M. Ady's *Lorenzo dei Medici and Renaissance Italy* (1962). There is also a good longer popular biography by David Loth titled *Lorenzo the Magnificent* (1929). *Florentine Merchants of the Age of the Medici* (1932), edited by Gertrude R. B. Richards, throws light on a phase of Florentine economic life. *The Rise and Decline of the Medici Bank* (1963), by R. de Roover, is the definitive account of the Medici institution. For an account of how the Medici rulers entertained the Florentines see Alois M. Nagler's *Theatre festivals of the Medici*, translated by G. Hickenlooper (1964). *Art Treasures of the Medici* (1963), by Antonio Morassi, demonstrates the interest of the Medici rulers in art.

ROME. W. Miller's *Medieval Rome from Hildebrand to Clement VIII, 1073-1600* (1904) is a general survey of the history of Rome. Daniel Waley's *The Papal States in the Thirteenth Century* (1961) is a well-documented study which fills a distinct need. *The Golden Days of the Renaissance in Rome* (1907), by Rodolfo Lanciani, discusses life and culture in Rome and is a mine of interesting information. On the contributions of the popes there is John L. Paschang's *The Popes and the Revival of Learning* (1927), an important study by a Roman Catholic. *The Life and Pontificate of Leo the Tenth* (4 vols., 1805), by William Roscoe, contains much valuable information. Another valuable study is Herbert M. Vaughan's *The Medici Popes* (1908). There is an interesting account by Vespasiano da Bisticci (whose active career covered the first four decades of the sixteenth century) titled *Renaissance Princes, Popes, and Prelates: Lives of Illustrious Men of the Fifteenth Century*, with an introduction by M. P. Gilmore (1963).

OTHER CITY-STATES. *The story of Milan* (1908), by D. Noyes, is a careful introductory survey. Another important study is Dorothy Muir's *History of Milan under the Visconti* (1924), *Pisa in the Early Renaissance: A Study of Urban Growth* (1958), by David Herlihy, deals with the problems of a city-state in a critical period. On Padua J. K. Hyde's *Padua in the Age of Dante: The Social History of an Italian City-State, 1256-1328* (1965) is a first-rate treatise. On Siena there is F. Schevill's *Siena: The History of a Medieval Community* (1964).

6 *The Rise of Italian Literature*

SURVEYS AND SPECIAL STUDIES. J. H. Whitfield's *Short History of Italian Literature* (1960) and J. S. Kennard's *Literary History of the Italian People* (1941) are two good introductory surveys. For a somewhat fuller account there is E. H. Wilkins' *History of Italian Literature* (1954). The most comprehensive and detailed survey is Francesco de Sanctis' *History of Italian Literature*, translated by Joan Redfern (2 vols., 1931). Useful for certain phases of Italian literature is Domenico Vittorini's *High Points in the History of Italian Literature* (1958), a series of 23 essays. The same author has also written *The Age of Dante* (1957) which is a concise survey of the culture of the early Italian Renaissance. For a discussion of literature on a broader scale there is B. Weinberg's *History of Literary Criticism in the Italian Renaissance* (2 vols., 1961), a painstaking scholarly survey. Another important volume is Vernon Hall's *Renaissance Literary Criticism: A Study of Its Social Content* (1945). There is also a brief discussion in the same author's *Short History of Literary Criticism* (1963). A further valuable study is J. B. Fletcher's *The Literature of the Italian Renaissance* (1934). Ernesto Grillo's *Early Italian Literature* (2 vols., 1920) and A. Gaspary's *History of Early Italian Literature to the Death of Dante* (1901) offer detailed discussion of the beginnings of Italian literature. *In Praise of Love* (1948), by Maurice Valency, is a good introduction to the love poetry of the Renaissance. Another important study is John C. Nelson's *The Renaissance Idea of Love* (1958). A further valuable special study is *The Renaissance Idea of Wisdom* (1958), by Eugene F. Rice, Jr. Then there is *Wit and Wisdom of the Italian Renaissance* (1964), by Charles Speroni, interesting and enlightening.

DANTE. Among the more recent readable scholarly biographies of Dante are Michele Barbi's *Life of Dante*, edited by P. Ruggiero (1954); J. B. Fletcher's *Dante* (reprint, 1965); Paget Toynbee's *Dante Alighieri* (1962); and T. G. Bergin's *Dante* (1965). Karl Vossler's *Medieval Culture* (2 vols., 1958) has the subtitle *An Introduction to Dante and His Times*, scholarly but far from easy reading. *Essays on Dante* (1964), edited by Mark Musa, and *Dante: A Collection of Critical Essays* (1965), edited by John Frederick, are penetrating and informative. Another important volume is Charles S. Singleton's *Essay on the Vita Nuova* (1958). Charles Williams' *The Figure of Beatrice: A Study of Dante* (1957) is a competent study. Two of the best recent discussions of the *Divine Comedy* are Allan Gilbert's *Dante and His Comedy* (1963) and Irma Brandeis' *Ladder of Vision: A Study of Dante's Divine Comedy* (1962). The latter has also edited *Discussions of the Divine Comedy* (1961). J. B. Fletcher's *Symbolism in the Divine Comedy* (1921) is still valuable. Francis Fergusson's *Dante's Drama of the Mind* (1953) seeks in Dante's religious thought the meaning of Dante's work. U. Limentani's *Fortunes of Dante in the Seventeenth Century* (1962) discusses the attitude of the century toward Dante's works. *Dante in English Literature, 1380-1844* (2 vols., 1909), by Paget Toynbee, is a monumental scholarly work.

PETRARCH. E. H. Wilkins' *Life of Petrarch* (1961) is the best biography of Petrarch, scholarly and up-to-date. Professor Wilkins has also written a number of other works on Petrarch including *The Making of the "Canzoniere" and Other Petrarchan Studies* (1951); *Studies in the Life and Work of Petrarch* (1955); *Petrarch's Eight Years in Milan* (1958); and *Petrarch's Later Years* (1959). *Petrarch and His World* (1963), by Morris Bishop, is a first-rate biography. There is also a fairly sound popular biography by H. C. Hollway-Calthorp titled *Petrarch and His Times* (1907). The fullest life of Petrarch in English is E. H. R. Tatham's *Francesco Petrarca, 1304-1347* (2 vols., 1925-26). There are a number of informative essays on Petrarch in T. E. Mommsen's *Medieval and Renaissance Studies*, edited by Eugene F. Rice, Jr. (1959). Siegfried Wenzel's "Petrarch's accidia," *Studies in the Renaissance*, 8 (1961), 36-48, is a lively discussion of Petrarch's concept of sentiment which he called *accidia*. The poems and letters of Petrarch are available in many English translations.

BOCCACCIO. There are a number of English translations not only of the *Decameron*, but also of other works by Boccaccio. *The Life of Giovanni Boccaccio* (1930), by

Thomas C. Chubb, is one of the better biographies. Two other useful biographies are Edward Hutton's *Giovanni Boccaccio* (1910) and F. MacManus' *Boccaccio* (1947). There is a good short discussion of Boccaccio the short-story writer in J. W. Krutch's *Five Masters* (1959). *Boccaccio's Defence of Poetry* (1898), by Elizabeth Woodbridge, and Charles G. Osgood's *Boccaccio on Poetry* (1930) offer detailed accounts of Boccaccio's concept of poetry. Gordon R. Silber's *The Influence of Dante and Petrarch on Certain of Boccaccio's Lyrics* (1940) discusses one phase of Boccaccio's relationship with the two other members of the literary trio. *Nature and Love in the Late Middle Ages: Cultural Context of the* Decameron (1963), by Aldo D. Scaglione, throws much light on one aspect of the *Decameron.* The influence of the Decameron on Chaucer is discussed in Jonathan B. Severs' *The Literary Relationship of Chaucer's Clerke's Tale* (1942). On Boccaccio's influence in Spain there is C. B. Bourland's *Boccaccio and the Decameron in Castilian and Catalan Literature* (1905).

7 *Italian Humanism*

PRE-RENAISSANCE HUMANISM. *The Renaissance of the Twelfth Century* (1927), by Charles H. Haskins, has long been the standard account, but is now antiquated in some respects. Another important volume by the same author is *Studies in Medieval Culture* (2nd ed., 1958). There are three shorter studies of the surge of interest in the classics during the twelfth century: W. A. Nitze's "The so-called twelfth-century Renaissance," *Speculum,* 23 (1948), 464-71; Eva M. Sanford's "The twelfth century: renaissance or proto-renaissance," *Speculum,* 26 (1951), 635-42; and Urban T. Holmes' "The idea of a twelfth-century renaissance," *Speculum,* 26 (1951), 643-51.

ITALIAN RENAISSANCE HUMANISM. *The Dawn of Humanism in Italy* (1947), by Roberto Weiss, is a good study by an English historian. W. J. Bouwsma's *The Interpretation of Renaissance Humanism* (1959) and Hanna H. Gray's "Renaissance humanism," *Jour. of the Hist. of Ideas,* 24 (1963), 497-514, are two brief provocative discussions. There is a good longer account in R. R. Bolgar's *The Classical Heritage* (1964). Another longer account is G. Toffanin's *History of Humanism,* translated from the Italian (1954), but it overemphasizes religious factors in Italian humanism. There is also a penetrating discussion in H. O. Taylor's *Thought and Expression in the Sixteenth Century* (1930). Probably the fullest account is in J. E. Sandys' *History of Classical Scholarship* (3 vols., 1906), outdated in some respects. *The World of Humanism, 1453-1517* (1952), by M. P. Gilmore, is a well-done survey of a limited period. For advanced students, a recent treatise on the half-century from 1480 to 1530 is A. Chastel's *Age of Humanism* (1964). *The Classics and Renaissance Thought* by P. O. Kristeller (1955) is a series of four stimulating lectures on the relationship of humanism to philosophy. Not to be overlooked are two first-rate scholarly treatises by Hans Baron, an eminent Renaissance historian: *The Crisis of the Early Italian Renaissance* (2 vols., 1955) and *Humanistic and Political Literature in Florence and Venice at the Beginning of the Quattrocento* (1955). For further references see P. O. Kristeller's "Studies on Renaissance humanism during the last twenty years," *Studies in the Renaissance,* 9 (1962), 7-30.

SPECIAL STUDIES. *Petrarch, Scipio, and the Africa: the Birth of Humanism's Dream* (1962), by Aldo S. Bernardo, is a good study of Petrarch the humanist. L. Martines' *The Social World of the Florentine Humanists, 1390-1460* (1963) is an authoritative discussion of the social and economic status of humanists. *Adversity's Noblemen: The Italian Humanists on Happiness* (rev. ed., 1965), by Charles Trinkaus, is first-rate. The same author has also written "A humanist's image of humanism," *Studies in the Renaissance,* 7 (1960), 90-125, a well-written account of one humanist's idea of humanism. Two other enlightening articles in the same periodical are Aldo Scaglione's "The humanist as scholar and Politian's conception of the humanities," 8 (1961), 49-70, and Guido Kisch's "Humanistic jurisprudence," 8 (1961), 71-87. Two significant treatises on the revival of the study of Greek are *The Greek Anthology in Italy* (1935), by J. Hulton, and *Greek Scholars in Venice: Studies in the Dissemination of Greek Learning from Byzantium to Western Europe* (1962), by D. J. Geanokoplos. *The Fall of Constantinople,*

1453 (1965), by S. Runciman, is a fresh account of one of history's spectacular events and its aftermath. K. H. Dannenfeldt's "Renaissance humanists and the knowledge of Arabic," *Studies in the Renaissance*, 2 (1955), 96-117, is an enlightening discussion of a neglected subject. An equally enlightening discussion is Leo Spitzer's "The problem of Latin Renaissance poetry," *Ibid.*, 2 (1955), 118-38. A valuable study of another phase of humanist activity is B. L. Ullman's *Origins and Development of Humanistic Script* (1960). In *Humanists and Artists: Six Studies in the Renaissance* (1963) M. P. Gilmore takes a fresh look at familiar situations and documents, a first-rate study.

OTHER HUMANISTS. There is an older biography in English of Poggio by William Shepherd titled *The Life of Poggio Bracciolini* (reprint, 1837) which offers much information on the life of the enthusiastic collector of manuscripts. English translations of Poggio's *Facetiae* are available in several editions. One phase of Poggio's interest in manuscripts is discussed by B. L. Ullman in "Poggio's manuscripts of Livy," *Classical Philology*, 28 (1933) 282-88. For Ficino there is P. O. Kristeller's penetrating treatise *The Philosophy of Marsilio Ficino* (1943). Valla's treatise is available under the title *The Treatise of Lorenzo Valla on the Donation of Constantine*, translated by C. B. Coleman (1922). There is an interesting chapter on Valla in Lloyd W. Eshleman's *Moulders of Destiny: Renaissance Lives and Times* (1938). *The Humanism of Coluccio Salutati* (1963), by B. L. Ullman, is a careful study based on the manuscripts that had been in Salutati's library. A closer knowledge of Politian may be gained from *The Memoirs of Angelus Politianus*, translated and edited by W. P. Gresswell (1805). Charles Trinkaus' "Humanist treatises on the status of the religions: Petrarch, Salutati, Valla," *Studies in the Renaissance*, 11 (1964), 7-45, is an acute study of three important humanist treatises.

8 *The Invention and Spread of Printing with Movable Type*

GENERAL STUDIES. Pierce Butler's *The Origins of Printing in Europe* (1940) is a good introductory volume. There is another sound scholarly account in *The Invention of Printing in China and Its Spread Westward* (2nd ed., 1955), by T. F. Carter and L. C. Goodrich. *Printing in the Fifteenth Century* (1940), by George Winship, is a good survey of the century. Broader in scope and more detailed is G. H. Putnam's *Books and Their Makers in the Middle Ages* (2 vols., 1962). *The Book: The Story of Printing and Bookbinding* by D. C. McMurtrie (2nd ed., 1943) is a first-rate account based on a lifetime of study and research. The same author also published *The Golden Book: The Story of Fine Bookmaking* (1927). S. H. Steinberg's *Five Hundred Years of Printing* (1959) covers the period from Gutenberg to the middle of the twentieth century with emphasis on the technical phase. *The Printed Book of the Renaissance* (1950), by E. P. Goldschmidt, offers a brief discussion of the effect of printing on the spread of learning. *The Emergence of Printing and Publishing as a Trade* (1955), by Rudolf Hirsch, is a useful short study. Not to be overlooked is *The Student History of Printing* (1930), by Merritt W. Haynes.

SPECIAL STUDIES. Two books by D. C. McMurtrie should be put at the head of the list: *The Dutch Claims to the Invention of Printing* (1928) and *Wings for Words: The Story of Johann Gutenberg and His Invention of Printing* (1940). *The Gutenberg Documents*, translated into English and edited by Karl Schorbach (1941), offers practically all the evidence in the case. Another important volume is *Gutenberg and the Strassburg Documents of 1439* (1940), by W. Fuhrmann. Robert C. Proctor's *The Printing of Greek in the Fifteenth Century* (1900) is an enlightening study. *Printing Types: Their History, Forms and Use* (2 vols., 1962), by Daniel B. Updike, is the standard account of the subject. This writer knows of no comprehensive study in English of the spread of printing in Germany. The subject is, however, discussed in many of the books listed in the preceding paragraph. There is also no comprehensive English survey of the early period of printing in France, but there is much material in the general surveys. For Spain and Portugal there is Konrad Haebler's *The Early Printers of Spain and Portugal* (1897).

ITALY AND ENGLAND. There are a number of good books in English on the introduction of printing into Italy. Two of the best are G. Biagi's *Books in Italy During the Fifteenth and Sixteenth Centuries* (1929) and W. D. Orcutt's *The Book in Italy During the Fifteenth and Sixteenth Centuries* (1928). Another informative volume is T. L. DeVinne's *Notable Printers of Italy During the Fifteenth Century* (1910). For Venice there is Horatio F. Brown's *The Venetian Printing Press* (1891). An older and still valuable biography is W. Blades' *The Life and Typography of William Caxton* (rev. ed., 1882). There are also two useful volumes by E. G. Duff: *William Caxton* (1905) and *Fifteenth-Century English Books* (1917). *The Prologues and Epilogues of William Caxton* (1928), edited by J. B. Crotch, are invaluable for an insight into Caxton's mind. The importance of Caxton's work for English literature is discussed in Nellie S. Aurner's *Caxton: A Mirrour of Fifteenth-Century Literature* (1926). For those who want a more comprehensive survey of printing in England there is Henry B. Plomer's *Short History of English Printing, 1476-1808* (1900). The best English account of Robert Estienne is Elizabeth Armstrong's *Robert Estienne, Royal Printer: An Historical Study of the Elder Stephanus* (1955).

9 *The Early Period of Renaissance Painting in Italy*

GENERAL. Bernard Berenson's *Italian Painters of the Renaissance* (rev. ed., 1952) is a well-written sophisticated survey with illustrations (also as paperbacks without illustrations). *Creators of the Renaissance* by L. Venturi and R. Skira-Venturi (Volume 1 of *Italian Painting,* 3 vols., 1950-52) is an authoritative study of Italian Renaissance painters. C. H. M. Gould's *Introduction to Italian Renaissance Painting* (1957) is a good introduction. Another good introductory volume is H. Wölfflin's *Classic Art: An Introduction to the Italian Renaissance* (1952). For an excellent discussion of the beginnings of Renaissance painting see F. Bologna's *Early Renaissance Painting* (1964). Another competent discussion of Renaissance painting may be found in Volume 1 of F. M. Godfrey's *History of Italian Painting* (2 vols., 1965). E. Panofsky's *Studies in Iconology: Humanistic Themes in the Art of the Renaissance* (1939) offers a philosophical interpretation of the great works of Renaissance art. Those desiring a brief and simple introduction to the theory of Italian art will find it in Anthony Blunt's *Artistic Theory in Italy, 1450-1600* (1959). *Dictionary of Italian Painting* (1965), edited by E. Hazan, is a valuable aid to students. Volume 1 of *A Documentary History of Art* (2 vols., 1947), edited by E. G. Holt, contains some interesting extracts from the writings of Renaissance artists. For a scholarly discussion of the art of the period preceding the Renaissance consult Charles R. Morey's painstaking survey titled *Medieval Art* (1942) or H. Focillon's *Art in the West in the Middle Ages* (2 vols., 1963). There is much interesting information about Italian painters in G. Vasari's *Lives of the Painters, Sculptors, and Architects* (4 vols., 1927; also condensed editions).

SPECIAL STUDIES. *Painting in Florence and Venice after the Black Death* (1965), by Millard Meiss, is an able discussion by an art critic. *Vision and Design: The Art of Florence* (1920), by Roger E. Fry, is a judicious analysis by an eminent student of art. Basil de Selincourt's *Giotto* (1905) is a useful biography. C. Semenzato's *Giotto* (1964) is a brief readable discussion. *Giotto* (1960), by Eugenio Battisti, is a longer scholarly biography. There is another life of Giotto by Cesare Gnudi (1959) with good illustrations. Two other valuable studies on Giotto are *Giotto and Assisi* (1960), by M. Meiss, and *Giotto: The Peruzzi Chapel* (1965), by L. Tintori and E. Borsook. *Masaccio* (1964), edited by Palma Viardo, is an informative brief discussion. *All the Paintings of Masaccio* (1962), edited by Ugo Procacci, is indispensable for a better knowledge of Masaccio's paintings. *Botticelli* (1962), by D. Formaggio, and *Botticelli* (1957), by Giulio C. Argan, are two good biographies. Other important discussions of Botticelli and his paintings are *Botticelli* (1961), edited by Lionello Venturi, and *Sandro Botticelli* (1953), edited by F. Hartt.

MATHEMATICAL PERSPECTIVE. *Art and Science* (1949), by Adrian Stokes, is an illuminating study of mathematical perspective as illustrated by Alberti, Piero della Francesca, and Giorgione. There is a lucid discussion of Alberti in A. Blunt's *Artistic Theory in*

Italy, 1450-1600 (1959). Kenneth M. Clark's "Leon Battista Alberti on painting," *Annual Italian Lecture of the British Academy* (1944) is an illuminating brief discussion. Alberti's treatise *On Painting* is available in an English translation by John R. Spence (1956). Cennino Cennini's *Treatise on Painting* (translated in 1844) is an informative treatise by a fifteenth-century painter. Leonardo da Vinci's treatise *Thoughts on Art and Life* is available in English translation in various editions and under various titles. One such edition is *The Art of Painting* (1957).

10 *The High Renaissance in Italian Painting*

Leonardo as Artist. Probably the best short discussion of Leonardo the artist is Kenneth M. Clark's *Leonardo da Vinci: An Account of His Development as an Artist* (1963). There is a valuable older study by Edward MacCurdy titled *Leonardo da Vinci The Artist* (1932); it is packed with facts about Leonardo but some of the superlatives must be discounted. L. H. Heydenreich's *Leonardo da Vinci*, translated from the German (1954), contains a good account of Leonardo the artist. D. Merezcovski's *Romance of Leonardo da Vinci* (1964) is a popular romantic biography. Richard Friedenthal's *Leonardo* (1960) is a pictorial biography. Other informative works include *Leonardo da Vinci* (1964), edited by G. Castelfranco, and L. Goldscheider's *Leonardo da Vinci* (1953). For further references see the bibliography for Chapter 15.

Raphael. Luciano Berti's Raphael (1961) and Emma Micheletti's *Raphael* (1962) are two fairly sound and readable biographies. A good older biography is Edward McCurdy's *Raphael* (1917). For a more detailed study of the great artist there is Oskar Fischel's *Raphael* (2 vols., 1948), comprehensive and painstaking. Two valuable illustrated volumes are *All the paintings of Raphael* (1962) and *All the Frescoes of Raphael* (1962), both edited by Ettore Camesasca. Charles J. Holmes' *Raphael and the Modern Use of Classical Tradition* (1933) is an informative study of one phase of Raphael's painting.

Michelangelo. Adrian Stokes' *Michelangelo: A Study in the Nature of Art* (1956) is one of the best introductions to Michelangelo's art. For those desiring a simple straight-forward biography there is M. Saponaro's *Michelangelo* (1951). L. Goldscheider's *Michelangelo* (4th ed., 1962) is a careful analysis of Michelangelo the painter, sculptor, and architect. An older, well-written, and still valuable biography is John Addington Symonds' *Life of Michelangelo Buonarotti* (1936 and various other editions). More recent readable biographies are A. Bertram's *Michelangelo* (1964); Elizabeth Ripley's *Michelangelo* (1953); C. H. Morgan's *Life of Michelangelo* (1964); and S. Alexander's *Michelangelo the Florentine* (1957). The most detailed and definitive work is Charles de Tolnay's *Michelangelo* (5 vols., 1943-60; another in preparation). Robert J. Clements' *Michelangelo's Theory of Art* (1961) is one of the best overall studies. The same author has also written a careful study titled *The Poetry of Michelangelo* (1965). Another valuable volume is *All the Paintings of Michelangelo* (1962), edited by Enzo Carli. *Michelangelo: A Self-Portrait* (1964), edited by R. J. Clements, and *The Letters of Michelangelo* (2 vols., 1963), edited by E. H. Ramsden, throw much light on Michelangelo the man. Other important studies are M. Salinger's *Michelangelo: The Last Judgment* (1955) and John Arthos' *Dante, Michelangelo, and Milton* (1964).

Venetian Painters. M. Valecchi's *Venetian Painting* (1962) and P. Erlanger's *Venetian Painting from Bellini to Veronese* (1954) are two of the better studies of Venetian painting. Another good account is B. Berenson's *The Venetian Painters* (various editions). H. H. Powers' *Venice and Its Art* (1930) is an interesting and informative volume. For Giovanni Bellini there are two good older biographies, one by Roger E. Fry (1901) and the other by George Hay (1908). Two other important books on Bellini are Edgar Wind's *Bellini's "Feast of the Gods": A Study in Venetian Humanism* (1948) and Millard Meiss' *Giovanni Bellini's "St. Francis"* (1963). There is a penetrating discussion of Giorgione in A. Stokes' *Art and Science* (1949). *All the Paintings of Giorgione* (1964), edited by Luigi Coletti, is a comprehensive survey with illustrations. Other important works are *Giorgione* (1965), edited by L. von Baldass, and L. Venturi's

Four Steps Toward Modern Art (1956). One of the best biographies of Titian is Hans Tietze's *Titian: Painting and Drawing* (2nd rev. ed., 1951). There is a good short life of Titian by Denys Sutton (1962). Other good biographies include Elizabeth Ripley's *Titian* (1962); G. Bovini's *Titian* (1965); and D. Cocchi's *Titian* (1958). *All the Paintings of Titian* (1964), edited by F. Valcanover, is a valuable introduction to the study of Titian. On the early Venetian painters there is F. Godfrey's *Early Venetian Painters, 1416-1495* (1955) with 56 plates.

11 *Italian Renaissance Sculpture and Architecture*

SCULPTURE. *Studies of Italian Renaissance Sculpture* (1950), by W. R. Valentiner, with 250 illustrations, is a good introductory survey. Another good introduction is Eric R. D. Maclagan's *Italian Sculpture of the Renaissance* (1935). A third important study is John Pope-Hennessey's *Introduction to Italian Sculpture* (3 vols., 1962) of which Volume 2 and a part of Volume 3 are devoted to the Renaissance. *Nicola Pisano* (1935), by G. H. and E. R. Crichton, tells the story of the beginnings of Renaissance sculpture. Richard Krautheimer's *Lorenzo Ghiberti* (1956) offers an expert analysis of the man and his work. Of Donatello there are two competent studies, *The Sculpture of Donatello* (2nd ed., 1963), by H. W. Janson, and *Donatello* (1965), by Giorgio Castelfranco. *All the Sculpture of Donatello* (1964), edited by Luigi Grassi, is an invaluable aid to a sound knowledge of Donatello's work. The same is true of *All the Sculpture of Michelangelo* (1962), edited by F. Rissoli.

ARCHITECTURE. R. Wittkower's *Architectural Principles of the Age of Humanism* (reprint, 1952) is a penetrating analysis of Renaissance architecture and traces the relationship between architecture and humanism. A somewhat older important study is Corrado Ricci's *Architecture and Decorative Sculpture of the High and Late Renaissance in Italy* (1923). Geoffrey Scott's *Architecture of Humanism* (2nd rev. ed., 1929; now as paperback) is a lucid discussion of the Principles of Renaissance architecture. *Four Changes of Renaissance Style* (1955), by W. Sypher, discusses the changes in art and literature. There is also a brief readable survey by B. Lowry titled *Renaissance Architecture* (1962). *The Architecture of the Renaissance in Italy* (rev. ed., 1927), by W. J. Anderson, is still useful. James Ackerman's *The Architecture of Michelangelo* (2 vols., 1961) is the definitive study of Michelangelo the architect. Peter Murray's *The Architecture of the Italian Renaissance* (1963) is a well-organized and well-informed survey.

12 *The Beginnings of Secular Drama and Music*

DRAMA. One of the best surveys of the history of the drama is Brander Matthews' *The Development of the Drama* (1934). Two other useful volumes are *An Introduction to the Drama* (1927), by Jay B. Hubbell, and *The Development of the Dramatic Art* (1960), by Donald C. Stuart. Most comprehensive and detailed is *The Drama: Its History, Literature and Influence on Civilization* (22 vols., 1903-04), edited by Alfred Bates and others; one or more volumes are devoted to each European country. *A History of the Theatre* (1961), by Edmund Fuller, and *A History of the Theatre* (1955), by G. Fredley and J. A. Reeves, contain some interesting information on the history of the early theater. Karl Young's *Drama of the Medieval Church* (2 vols., 1933) is a mine of information on the medieval drama. Older but still eminently useful is E. K. Chambers' *The Medieval Stage* (2 vols., 1903). P. K. Kretzmann's *The Liturgical Element in the Earliest Forms of the Medieval Drama* (1916) discusses the early stages of the drama. Leicester Bradner has written two concise provocative studies on Renaissance drama: "The rise of the secular drama in the Renaissance," *Studies in the Renaissance*, 3 (1956), 7-22 and "The Latin drama of the Renaissance," *Ibid.*, 4 (1957), 31-70. *The Braggart in Renaissance Comedy: A Study in Comparative Drama from Aristophanes to Shakespeare* (1954), by D. C. Boughner, summarizes and analyzes a large number of plays and is pleasant reading. More limited but equally interesting is *An*

Anthology of English Drama Before Shakespeare (1952), edited by Robert B. Heilmann. Other important works are D. M. Bevington's *From Mankind to Marlowe: Growth of Structure in Popular Drama of Tudor England* (1962); W. L. Wiley's *The Early Public Theatre in France* (1959); and M. T. Merrick's *Italian Comedy in the Renaissance* (1960).

Music. There are two interesting and readable as well as sound surveys of the history of music: *Music in History: The Evolution of an Art* (1940), by Howard D. McKinney and W. R. Anderson, and *Music in Western Civilization* (1941), by Paul Henry Lang. H. Prunières' *New History of Music* (1943) is a good survey which puts special emphasis on French music. Gustave Reese's *Music in the Middle Ages* (1940) is the standard account of the subject. The same author has also written *Music in the Renaissance* (rev. ed., 1959) which is equally authoritative. Another important volume is A. Harman's *Medieval and Early Renaissance Music* (1958). Equally valuable is N. C. Carpenter's *Music in the Medieval and Renaissance Universities* (1958). *Music of the Renaissance in Italy* (1934), by E. J. Dent, emphasizes the development of modern harmony. There is also a lively popular account by Nesta de Robeck, *The Music of the Italian Renaissance* (1928). M. F. Bukofzer's *Studies in Medieval and Renaissance Music* (1950) is an informative series of essays. The best account of the development of musical instruments is Curt Sachs' *History of Musical Instruments* (1941). The same author has also written the best history of the dance under the title *World History of the Dance* (1937). *The Italian Madrigal* (3 vols., 1949), by Alfred Einstein, is the definitive work on the subject. Willi Apel's "The early history of the organ," *Speculum*, 23 (1948), 191-208, is an informative scholarly study. W. H. Rubsamen's *Literary Sources of Secular Music in Italy c. 1500* (1943) throws much light on the writing of popular music. *Guillaume de Machaut* (1954), by Sigmund Levarie, is an interesting brief biography of the French musician and poet. *Source Readings in Music History: From Classical Antiquity Through the Romantic Era* (1950), selected and annotated by Oliver Strunk, is a good anthology of selections from the writings of musicians and thinkers. *Musica Nova* (1964), edited by H. Colin Slim, devotes 130 pages to reproductions of Renaissance music. Invaluable for the understanding of sixteenth-century music is Edward E. Lowinsky's *Tonality and Atonality in Sixteenth-Century Music* (1961), with a foreword by Igor Stravinsky. *The Renaissance* (1965), by Oliver Strunk, is a well-chosen collection of source readings in the music history of the Renaissance.

13 *Toward the Secular State*

Political Thought. One of the best surveys of political thought of the period is C. H. McIlwain's *The Growth of Political Thought in the West: From the Greeks to the End of the Middle Ages* (1932). Equally good are the pertinent chapters of George H. Sabine's *History of Political Theory* (2nd ed., 1950). Another good brief introduction is J. B. Morrall's *Political Thought in Medieval Times* (1958). The standard longer account is *A History of Medieval Political Theory in the West* (6 vols., 1909-35), by R. W. and A. J. Carlyle. Two other useful surveys are *The Church and the World in Idea and History* (1909), by W. Hobhouse, and *Church, State, and Christian Society* (1940), by G. Tellenbach. Arthur L. Smith's *Church and State in the Middle Ages* (1913) is one of the best books on the subject. Not to be overlooked is Ewart K. Lewis' *Medieval Political Ideas* (2 vols., 1954). Brian Tierney's *The Crisis of Church and State, 1050-1300* (1964) is a solid readable study. *The Growth of the Papal Government in the Middle Ages* (1955), by Walter Ullman, is a very learned book which surveys the growth of papal government from the fifth century to the twelfth. On political thought in the sixteenth century there is J. W. Allen's painstaking survey *A History of Political Thought in the Sixteenth Century* (2nd ed., 1941).

Special Studies. On the relationship of Frederick II and the popes see *Frederick the Second* by Ernst Kantorowicz, translated from the German by E. O. Lorimer (1931). There are two biographies of Boniface VIII in English and both are favorable to him. One is Luigi Tosti's *History of Pope Boniface VIII and His Times* (1911) and the other, Thomas S. Boase's *Boniface VIII* (1933). The best short study is F. M. Powicki's "Boniface VIII," *History*, n.s.8 (1934), 307-29. Sister Mildred Curley's *The Conflict between Boniface VIII and Philip the Fair* (1927) is written from the Catholic viewpoint, but with a high degree of impartiality. On Dante's political ideas there are many short and longer treatises. Two of the better ones are A. P. d'Entreves' *Dante as a Political Thinker* (1952) and C. T. Davis' *Dante and the Idea of Rome* (1957). Alan Gewirth has written a painstaking scholarly study on the *Defensor Pacis* under the title *Marsilius of Padua and Medieval Political Philosophy* (1951). The same author has also translated and edited the *Defensor Pacis* (1956). There is an earlier translation by C. W. Previté-Orton (1928) with an introduction. An older study of Marsiglio's work by E. Emerton (1920) is still rewarding reading.

MACHIAVELLI. The literature on Machiavelli is so vast that only a few works can be listed. *The Statecraft of Machiavelli* (1955), by Herbert Butterfield, is a concise and readable study. Another important study is F. Chabod's *Machiavelli and the Renaissance*, translated by D. Moore (1954), interesting and suggestive. One of the better biographies of Machiavelli is that by J. H. Whitfield (1947) who supports the traditional concept of Machiavelli. Roberto Ridolfi in his biography of Machiavelli, translated by C. Grayson (1963) describes Machiavelli as an ordinary peaceful citizen. There is a good older biography by G. Prezzolini (1928). The background of *The Prince* is sketched by A. H. Gilbert in *Machiavelli's "Prince" and Its Forerunners* (1938). *Machiavelli and Guicciardini: Politics and History in Sixteenth-Century Florence* (1965), by Felix Gilbert, is a major study which shows how new political ideas emerged in sixteenth-century Florence. Two other scholarly studies by the same author are "The humanist concept of the prince and the 'Prince' of Machiavelli," *Jour. of Mod. Hist.*, 11 (1939), 449-83, and "The concept of nationalism in Machiavelli's Prince," *Studies in the Renaissance*, 1 (1954), 38-48. Felix Raab's *The English Face of Machiavelli* (1964) shows how widely *The Prince* was read in England and how it influenced English thought. *Machiavelli: The Chief Works and Others*, translated and edited by Allan H. Gilbert (3 vols., 1961), is one of the better editions of Machiavelli's writings in English.

14 *Opening a Wider World*

MISCELLANEOUS. Charles E. Nowell's *The Great Discoveries and the First Colonial Empires* (1954) is a brief judicious survey. *Travel and Discovery in the Renaissance, 1420-1620* (2nd ed., 1955), by B. Penrose, is a vivid account of interesting explorers and places. *The Great Age of Discovery* (1937), edited by A. P. Newton, offers a series of chapters by specialists in specific fields. Other important studies are James B. Scott's *The Era of Discoveries* (1933) and John H. Parry's *The Age of Reconnaissance* (1963). Leo Bagrow's *History of Cartography* (1964) surveys the art of map-making from antiquity to the eighteenth century. Two other enlightening studies are *They Put Out to Sea: The Story of the Map* (1943), by Roger A. Duvoisin, and *Explorers' Maps: Chapters in the Cartographic Record of Geographical Discovery* (1958), by R. A. Skelton. *Voyages of Great Pioneers* (1929), edited by Vincent T. Harlow is a book of excerpts from the writings of great explorers and contemporaries. W. E. Washburn's "The meaning of discovery in the fifteenth and sixteenth centuries," *Am. Hist. Rev.*, 68 (1962), 1-21, is a critical reexamination of the discoveries of the Age of Discovery. Frederic C. Lane's "The economic meaning of the invention of the compass," *Am. Hist. Rev.*, 68 (1963), 605-17, is a lively informative study. In *Essays on Tartar History* (1963) Boris Ischboldin surveys the history of the Tartars. In *The Century of Discovery* (1966) (Volume 1 of *Asia in the Making of Europe*) Donald Lach traces the influence of sixteenth-century Asia on Western Europe. *Marco Polo's Predecessors* (1943), by Leonard Olschki, is a readable and informative short study. The account dictated by Marco is available in English translations under such titles as *The Adventures of Marco Polo; The Book of Ser Marco Polo the Venetian;* and *The Curious and Remarkable Voyages and Travels of Marco Polo.* Maurice Collis' *Marco Polo* (1950) and Henry H. Hart's *Venetian Adventurer* (1942) are two interesting biographies of the Venetian.

Portuguese Explorations. Edgar Prestage's *The Portuguese Pioneers* (1933) is an authoritative account of Portuguese explorations during the period of Portuguese primacy. *European Beginnings in West Africa, 1454-1578* (1937), by J. W. Blake, and *Portuguese Voyages to America in the Fifteenth Century* (1940), by Samuel E. Morison, are two sound scholarly studies of individual phases of Portuguese explorations. Elaine Sanceau's *Henry the Navigator* (1947) is a carefully-done account of the life and work of the Portuguese prince. The same author has also written *The Land of Prester John* (1944). There is a good older biography by C. R. Beazley (1895). The entire period is surveyed by J. Oliveira Martins in *The Golden Age of Prince Henry the Navigator*, translated by J. J. Abraham and W. E. Reynolds (1914), at times brilliant but not always trustworthy. K. G. Jayne's *Vasco da Gama and His Successors* (1910) contains much biographical material on Portuguese leaders. H. H. Hart's *Sea Road to the Indies* (1950) is a lively popular account. Two older scholarly works which discuss Portuguese activities in India in considerable detail are R. S. Whiteway's *The Rise of Portuguese Power in India* (1899) and F. C. Danvers' *The Portuguese in India* (2 vols., 1894). For those who desire to penetrate more deeply into the relations between the Portuguese and the natives of the newly-discovered lands there are three studies by C. R. Boxer: *Four Centuries of Portuguese Expansion, 1415-1825* (1961); *Race Relations in the Portuguese Colonial Empire* (1963); and *Portuguese Society in the Tropics* (1965).

Pre-Columbian Discoveries of America. E. Reman's *The Norse Discoveries and Explorations in America* (1949) is a careful and comprehensive study. *The Lost Discovery: Uncovering the Track of the Vikings in America* (1952), by F. J. Pohl, argues that the Norsemen were neither the first nor the last pre-Columbian explorers. Gwyn Jones has retold in lively fashion the stories of the Viking adventures in *The Norse Atlantic Saga* (1963). P. H. Sawyer's *Age of the Vikings* (1963) is an up-to-date re-evaluation of the Viking discoveries. New support has been given to the account of the Norse discoveries by a map purportedly sketched by the Norsemen. It was published under the title *The Vinland Map* (1965), edited by R. A. Skelton and others.

Columbus and Amerigo. One of the better biographies of Columbus is H. H. Houben's *Christopher Columbus: The Tragedy of a Discoverer*, translated by J. Linton (1936). Samuel E. Morison has written a long popular biography of Columbus titled *Admiral of the Ocean Sea* (2 vols., 1942), also published in condensed form as a paperback (1947). S. de Madariaga's *Christopher Columbus* (1939) endeavors to prove that Columbus was the son of Jewish parents. *The Legacy of Christopher Columbus* (2 vols., 1949), edited by O. Schoenrich, contains some valuable source materials on the life and activities of Columbus. Another useful source of information is *Select Documents Illustrating the Four Voyages of Columbus* (2 vols., 1930-32), translated and edited by Cecil Jane. *America and the New World: Life and Times of Amerigo Vespucci* by G. Arciniegas, translated by Harriet de Onis (1955), is a critical discussion of the traditional view of Amerigo and a defense of him. There is also a well-written popular biography of Amerigo by Stefan Zweig titled *Amerigo: A Comedy of Errors in History* (1942).

English Explorations. The definitive work on the Cabots is James A. Williamson's *The Voyages of the Cabots and the English Discovery of North America under Henry VII and Henry VIII* (1929). Other important works by the same author are *A Short History of British Expansion* (new ed., 2 vols., 1930); *The Founding and Growth of the British Empire* (2nd ed., 1933); and *The Age of Drake* (1938). J. A. Williamson has also written a good short life of Drake (1951) and a first-rate biography of Hawkins (1950). On the beginnings of English overseas trade there are two books by Eleanor M. Carus-Wilson: *Medieval Merchant Venturers* (1954) and *The Overseas Trade of Bristol in the Later Middle Ages* (1937). Another informative study is Gordon Cownell-Smith's *Forerunners of Drake* (1954) which offers an account of the trade with Spain in the early Tudor period. There is also a brief account of English explorations in North America by F. T. McCann titled *English Discovery of America to 1585* (1953). The story of England's struggle to break the power of the Portuguese in India is ably told in W. Foster's *England's Quest of Eastern Trade* (2 vols., 1933).

SPANISH DISCOVERY AND EXPANSION. Roger B. Merriman's *Rise of the Spanish Empire in the Old World and in the New* (4 vols., 1919-34) is the best comprehensive account of Spanish exploration and colonization in the New World. For those who desire a shorter survey there is Bohdan Chudoba's *Spain and the Empire, 1519-1643* (1952), based on a careful study of the Spanish archives. E. G. Bourne's *Spain in America* (1904) is still useful. There is also a series of provocative essays on Spanish colonization by P. S. Zavala titled *New Viewpoints on the Spanish Colonization of America* (1943). *The Spanish Main* (1935), by P. A. Means, is readable and well-documented. W. H. Prescott's *History of the Conquest of Mexico* can still be read with profit in the carefully edited editions. One such edition is *Prescott's Histories: The Rise and Decline of the Spanish Empire,* selected and edited by Irwin R. Blacker (1963). *Bernal Diaz: The Conquest of New Spain,* translated by M. Cohen (1964), is a new translation of a vivid account by one of the soldiers of Cortes. Another interesting account by a contemporary is *Cortes: The Life of the Conqueror of Mexico by His Secretary,* translated and edited by L. B. Simpson (1964). *The Aztecs under Spanish Rule, 1519-1810* (1964), by Charles Gibson, is an illuminating study which has the clash of cultures as its central theme. Henry R. Wagner's *Spanish Voyages to the Northwest Coast of America in the Sixteenth Century* (1929) is an interesting account of Spanish explorations along the coast of California. *The Exploration of the Pacific* (2nd ed., 1947), by J. C. Beaglehole, tells the story of explorations from Magellan to Cook. A. S. Hildebrand's *Magellan* (1925) and E. F. Benson's *Magellan* (1929) are readable and reasonably sound biographies. *Magellan's Voyage Around the World: Three Contemporary Accounts,* translated and edited by C. E. Nowell (1963), makes three of the best contemporary sources available. Among the better studies of the Spanish conquests is F. A. Kirkpatrick's *The Spanish Conquistadores: The Story of the Conquest of the New World* (1963).

15 *The Dawn of Modern Science*

SCIENCE AND SCIENTIFIC THOUGHT. Charles Singer's *History of Scientific Ideas to 1900* (1959) and W. C. Dampier's *Shorter History of Science* (1957) are good introductory surveys. A third useful survey is Herbert Butterfield's *The Origin of Modern Science, 1300-1800* (rev. ed., 1963). Giorgo de Santillana's *The Origins of Scientific Thought* (1961) traces the rise of scientific ideas since the sixth century B.C. One of the best of the more recent histories of science is A. C. Crombie's *From Augustine to Galileo: The History of Science* (rev. ed., 1963). This work is also available in paperback (2 vols., 1961), Volume 2 having the title *Medieval and Early Modern Science.* Two important books by George Sarton are *The Appreciation of Ancient and Medieval Science During the Renaissance* (1955) and *Six Wings: Men of Science in the Renaissance* (1957). Marie Boas' *Scientific Renaissance, 1450-1630* (1962) is useful, but does not go back far enough. *A History of Science, Technology and Philosophy in the Sixteenth and Seventeenth Centuries* (2 vols., 1961), by A. Wolf, is a sound and valuable work. On the Middle Ages there are Lynn Thorndike's monumental *History of Magic and Experimental Science* (6 vols., 1923-41) and *Science and Thought in the Fifteenth Century* (1929). Charles H. Haskins' *Studies in the History of Medieval Science* (1955) can be read with profit. *Readings in the Literature of Science* (1959), edited by W. C. Dampier, and *Roots of Scientific Thought* (1957), edited by P. Wiener and A. Noland, offer readings on some of the basic concepts of science.

SPECIAL STUDIES. W. P. D. Wightman's *Science in the Renaissance* (2 vols., 1963) is a comprehensive, painstaking study. Three brief provocative discussions are C. Doris Hellmann's "Science in the Renaissance," *Renaissance News,* 8 (1955), 186-99; Marie B. Hall's *The History of the Sciences* (1964, Aids for Teachers of History); and Harcourt Brown's "The Renaissance and the historians of science," *Studies in the Renaissance,* 7 (1960), 27-42. J. H. Randall's *The School of Padua and the Emergence of Modern Science* (1961) is a careful and informative study. Another important study is Francis R. Johnson's *Astronomical Thought in Renaissance England* (1937). *The Development of Physical Theory in the Middle Ages* (1954), by James A. Weisheipl, is a brief carefully-done survey. M. Claggett's *The Science of Mechanics in the Middle Ages* (1959) is the best account of the subject. On the influence of Aristotle see F. von Steenbergen's *Aristotle in the West: The Origin of Latin Aristotelianism*, translated by L. Johnson (1955). A further important study is Max Jammer's *Concepts of Force: A Study in the Foundations of Dynamics* (1957). *The Medieval Science of Weights* (1952), by Ernest Moody and M. Claggett, is a first-rate study. William S. Fowler's *Development of Scientific Method* (1965) is a study of prime importance. Charles R. Schmitt's "Aristotle as a cuttlefish: the origin and development of a Renaissance image," *Studies in the Renaissance*, 12 (1965), 60-72, is an interesting as well as enlightening brief study.

Individual Scientists. *Robert Grosseteste and the Origins of the Experimental Method* (1963), by A. C. Crombie, throws much light on the beginnings of the new science. For a more comprehensive study of Grosseteste see *Robert Grosseteste: Scholar and Bishop* (1955), by D. A. Callus. On Aquinas there is James A. McWilliams' *Physics and Philosophy: A Study of St. Thomas' Commentary on the Eight Books of Aristotle's "Physics"* (1945). D. B. Durand's "Nicole Oresme and the medieval origins of modern science," *Speculum*, 12 (1941), 167-85, is a study of first-rate importance. J. H. Randall's "The place of Leonardo da Vinci in the emergence of modern science," *Jour. of the Hist. of Ideas*, 14 (1953), 191-202, should be required reading for everyone who regards Leonardo as a great inventive genius. For Leonardo's contributions see the histories of science by A. C. Crombie and W. C. Dampier previously listed. For an English version of the *Notebooks* see *Leonardo da Vinci's Notebooks*, translated and arranged by Edward McCurdy (1906). Robert Friedenthal's *Leonardo* (1960) is a pictorial biography of Leonardo.

From Copernicus to Galileo. H. Kesten's *Copernicus and His World* (1945) is a good popular biography. Another lively biography is *Sun, Stand Thou Still* (1947), by A. Armitage. T. S. Kuhn's *Copernican Revolution* (1957) is sound and interesting. On the effect of the Copernican teachings there is Dorothy Stimson's *The Gradual Acceptance of the Copernican Theory of the Universe* (1917). *The Life and Times of Tycho Brahe* (1948), by J. A. Gade, is a lively and authoritative study. *Johannes Kepler: Life and Letters* (1952), by Carola Baumgardt, centers its attention on Kepler the man but includes translations of some of his letters. For Kepler's place in the history of science see *Johannes Kepler* (1931), a series of papers published by the History of Science Society to commemorate the tercentenary of Kepler's death. On Galileo there is F. Namer's *Galileo: Searcher of the Heavens*, translated by S. Harris (1931), a work of painstaking research. *Galileo and Freedom of Thought* (1938), by F. S. Taylor, is an informative study. *The Crime of Galileo* (1955), by Giorgio de Santillana, is a comprehensive treatise which contains much new material. H. C. King's *History of the Telescope* (1955) is an informative study. *Galileo Reappraised* (1965), edited by Carlo L. Golino is a book of five essays which contribute new insight into the life, thought, and achievements of Galileo.

16 *The Renaissance in Germany*

The Northern Renaissance. Unfortunately there is no comprehensive study of the Northern Renaissance in English. Two books by the Dutch historian Johan Huizinga throw much light on cultural developments. The first, *The Waning of the Middle Ages* (1954), discusses life, thought, and art in France and the Netherlands at the dawn of the Renaissance. The other is *Men and Ideas* (1959), a series of collected studies, some of which are devoted to Renaissance problems. For art see the bibliography for the last chapter. *Change in Medieval Society: Europe North of the Alps,* c. *1050-1500* (1964), edited by Sylvia L. Thrupp, is an informative book of readings. There is a broad discussion of Renaissance thought in H. A. Enno von Gelder's *The Two Reformations: A Study of the Religious Aspects and Consequences of Renaissance and Humanism* (1961); one of the reformations is that effected by the humanists. The cultural contact between Italy and the countries north of the Alps is illustrated in George B. Parks' *The English Traveler in Italy* (2 vols., 1954), of which Volume 1 covers the period to 1525. *John Free: From Bristol to Rome in the Fifteenth Century* (1955), by R. J. Mitchell, relates the experiences of an English student in Italy. *Prose and Poetry of the Continental Renaissance,* translated and edited by Harold H. Blanchard (1949), contains excerpts from the works of Erasmus, Rabelais, Montaigne, and Cervantes as well as from Italian writers. T. M. W. Bean's "Plague, population and economic decline," *Economic History Review,* 5 (1963), 423-50, is a study of first-rate importance. An important study limited to England is Charles F. Mullett's *The Bubonic Plague and England* (1956) which covers the period from the Black Death to the nineteenth century. Another illuminating study of epidemics is *History of Epidemics in Great Britain* (new ed., 1964), by Charles Creighton. On the question of rising and declining population there is J. C. Russell's painstaking study, *Late Ancient and Medieval Population* (1958).

German Political and Economic History. Three of the best brief surveys of German history are Ralph Flenley's *Modern German History* (new ed., 1965); S. Steinberg's *Short History of Germany* (1945); and J. K. Dunlop's *Short History of Germany* (1957). There is a somewhat fuller account in J. E. Rodes' *Germany: A History* (1964). The fullest account is in the early chapters of Volume 1 of Hajo Holborn's *History of Modern Germany* (1954). *The Holy Roman Empire in the Middle Ages: Universal State or German Catastrophe?* (1966), edited by R. E. Herzstein, is an anthology of excerpts illustrating different points of view. The best study of medieval Germany is G. Barraclough's *The Origins of Modern Germany* (1947). *Sixteenth-Century Germany* (1959), by Gerald Strauss, is an able survey. Marian Andrews' *Maximilian the Dreamer* (1913) is a lively popular biography.

German Humanism. Roberto Weiss discusses in his *Spread of Italian Humanism* (1964) how the humanist spirit entered Germany. *The Age of Erasmus* (new ed., 1963), by P. S. Allen, is a good survey of humanist activities. The standard biography of Reuchlin is L. Geiger's *Johannes Reuchlin* (1871). In English S. A. Hirsch has in his *Essays* (1905) "John Reuchlin, the father of the study of Hebrew among the Christians" and "John Pfefferkorn and the battle of books." There is also a chapter titled "Reuchlin and the humanists" in William Cowan's *Pre-Reformation Worthies* (1897). On Conrad Celtes, another key figure in German humanism, there is Lewis W. Spitz's first-rate study *Conrad Celtes, the German arch-humanist* (1957). The same author has also written *The Religious Renaissance of the German Humanists* (1963).

Erasmus. Preserved Smith's *Erasmus* (1923) is one of the best biographies of the Dutch humanist. Most sympathetic to its subject is J. Huizinga's *Erasmus* (1924), a somewhat nationalistic biography. Albert Hyma's *The Youth of Erasmus* (1930) is a good discussion of the formative influences in the early life of Erasmus. Margaret M. Phillip's *Erasmus and the Northern Renaissance* (1950) is, in the words of the author, "primarily intended for the use of beginners in Renaissance studies." Louis Bouyer's *Erasmus and His Times,* translated by Francis X. Murphy (1951), presents a Catholic view of Erasmus. In his *Praisers of Folly: Erasmus, Rabelais and Shakespeare* (1963) Walter Kaiser makes some interesting comparisons. In *Erasmus, Tyndale and More* (1950) W. E. Campbell shows how the three men differed in dispositions, tastes, and achievements. The more popular works of Erasmus are available in various hardcover and paperback editions. For example, *Erasmus and the Humanists,* translated and edited by A. Hyma (1930), contains selections from the writings of Erasmus and from the *Letters of Obscure Men.* A hardcover edition of *The Praise of Folly,* edited by Hendrik Willem van Loon, was published in 1942. The first complete English translation of *The Colloquies* since 1725, edited and translated by Craig R. Thompson, was published in 1965. Outstanding among the paperbacks is *Essential Works of Erasmus,* edited by W. T. H. Jackson (1965), which contains *The Praise of Folly,* some *Colloquies,* and various letters from famous contemporary persons. There are many important scholarly articles in learned periodicals which for reasons of space cannot be listed here.

German Literature. One of the best brief surveys of German literature is Ernst Rose's *History of German Literature* (1961). John G. Robertson's *History of German Literature* (rev. ed., 1962) is crammed with facts, but lacks readability. Still eminently useful is Kuno Francke's *History of German Literature as determined by Social Forces*

(1905). *Medieval German Literature* (1962), by Maurice O. Walsh, contains a good account of the beginnings of German literature. Another enlightening study is Eric Blackall's *Emergence of German as a Literary Language* (1959). Jethro Bithell's *Germany: Companion to German Studies* (5th ed., 1955) contains much information on German learning and culture. There is an English edition of Brant's *Ship of Fools,* translated into rhyming couplets by Edwin H. Zeydel (1944). Eli Sobel's *Sebastian Brant, Ovid, and Classical Allusions in the "Narrenschiff"* (*California University Publications in Modern Philology*, vol. 36, no. 12, 1952) links Brant with the Renaissance humanists. Many of Hans Sachs' dramas and poems have been translated into English. Two examples are *Seven Shrovetide Plays,* translated by O. U. Ouless (1930), and *The Strolling Clerk from Paradise,* translated by Philip Wayne (1935). Unfortunately there is no biography of Sachs in English. A useful study in English is Walter French's *Medieval Civilization as Illustrated by the Fastnachtspiele* (1925). *Drama in Renaissance Germany and Switzerland* (1961), by Derek Van Abbé, is a brief informative study of a neglected period.

17 *The Renaissance in France*

Political and Economic History. There is a good survey of the political and economic life of the period in L. Battifol's *Century of the Renaissance,* translated from the French by E. F. Buckley (1925). Among the better surveys of French history are A. L. Guerard's *France* (1946) and J. Bainville's *History of France,* translated by A. and C. Gauss (1926). For those desiring a fuller account there is J. R. Macdonald's *History of France* (3 vols., 1915), not always in harmony with the latest research. The definitive biography of Louis XI is Pierre Champion's *Louis XI* (2 vols., 1929). J. E. Neale's *Age of Catherine de Medici* (1959) is a masterly study. Not to be overlooked are J. Russell Major's *The Deputies to the Estates General in Renaissance France* (1960) and *Representative Institutions in Renaissance France, 1421-1559* (1960), scholarly and enlightening.

The French Renaissance. Henry Hornik's "Three interpretations of the French Renaissance," *Studies in the Renaissance*, 7 (1960), 43-66, is a provocative brief discussion. Older but still authoritative studies by A. Tilley are *The Dawn of the French Renaissance* (1918); *The French Renaissance* (1919); *Studies in the French Renaissance* (1922); and *Literature of the French Renaissance* (2 vols., 1904). Bernard Weinberg's *Critical Prefaces of the French Renaissance* (1950) is a collection of prefaces from the works of twenty-four authors with a commentary on each. Edith Sichel's *Women and Men of the French Renaissance* (1903) is a well-written popular discussion. *The Gentleman of Renaissance France* (1954), by W. L. Wiley, is a careful study of the life of a French gentleman and of the forces that created him. On Francis the First as the focus of the French Renaissance there is Jehanne d'Orliac's *Francis I: Prince of the Renaissance* (1932). Francis Hackett's *Francis the First* (1935) is a lively popular biography. *Marguerite of Navarre* (1935), by Samuel Putnam, is a readable and informative biography. There is also a good brief essay on Margaret in M. B. Ryley's *Queens of the Renaissance* (1907).

French Humanism. A good history of French humanism in English is something to be desired. There is a brief lucid discussion of French humanism in Volume 1 of *The Cambridge Modern History*, p. 575 *sq.* and a longer account in Volume 3 by A. Tilley titled "French humanism and Montaigne," pp. 53-72. Frances A. Yates' *The French Academies of the Sixteenth Century* (1947) is an important study. Linton C. Stevens' "The contributions of French jurists to the humanism of the Renaissance," *Studies in the Renaissance, I* (1954), 92-105, is a penetrating study which broadens the concept of French humanism. First-rate, too, is E. F. Rice, Jr., "The humanist idea of Christian antiquity: Lefèvre d'Etaples and his circle," *Ibid.*, 9 (1962), 126-60. *John Calvin: A Study in French Humanism* (1931), by Quirinius Breen, discusses another side of French humanism in an expert manner. For a further discussion of Calvin's relationship to French humanism see Charles Trinkhaus' "Renaissance problems in Calvin's theology," *Studies in the Renaissance*, 1 (1954), 59-80. Robert Estienne is discussed as both humanist and printer in Elizabeth Armstrong's *Robert Estienne* (1954).

French Literature. Among the better surveys of French literature are Geoffrey Brereton's *Short History of French Literature* (1962); L. Cazamian's *History of French Literature* (1955); and W. Nitze's and E. Dargan's *History of French Literature* (3rd ed., 1938). On the earliest French literature there is Urban T. Holmes' *History of Old French Literature from the Origins to 1300* (1937). *Forerunners of the French Novel: An Essay on the Development of the Nouvelle in the Late Middle Ages* (1955), by James M. Ferrier, is an enlightening study on the beginnings of the French novel. Hilaire Belloc's *Avril: Essays on the Poetry of the French Renaissance* (1945) contains essays on both Villon and Marot. On Villon there are a number of careful studies including Winthrop H. Rice's *The European Ancestry of Villon's Satirical Testaments* (1941); Cecily Mackworth's *François Villon: A Study* (1947); and Edward F. Chaney's *François Villon in His Environment* (1946). There is an interesting essay on Villon in Philip B. Barry's *Sinners Down the Centuries* (1928). *François Villon: His Life and Times* (1916), by H. de Vere Stackpole, is a more detailed life. There are many translations of Villon's poetry including *The Complete works of François Villon*, translated by J. U. Nicolson (1931). Translations of some of Villon's poetry by A. C. Swinburne, Dante Gabriel Rosetti, and others have been collected in *The Lyrics of François Villon*, with an introduction by Léonie Adams (1933). Important for a knowledge of both music and the theater is Howard M. Brown's *Music in the French Secular Theater* (1963).

Rabelais and Montaigne. There is no dearth of biographies of Rabelais. One of the best of the more recent ones is J. C. Powys' *Rabelais* (1952). For those who wish a well-written popular biography there is D. B. W. Lewis' *Doctor Rabelais* (1957). M. P. Willcock's *Laughing Philosopher* (1951) is a brief critical study aimed at those who use Rabelais to prove fanciful theories. The most scholarly biography, though somewhat dry at times, is Jean Plattard's *Life of Rabelais*, translated by L. B. Roche (1930). More readable is *Rabelais* (1929), by A. J. Nock and C. R. Wilson. Another good readable biography is Samuel Putnam's *Rabelais* (1929). A. C. Keller's "Pace and timing in Rabelais's stories," *Studies in the Renaissance*, 10 (1963), 108-125, is a brief enlightening discussion. *Rabelais and Music* (1955), by N. C. Carpenter, is an expert analysis of Rabbelais' interest in music. One of the more recent studies of Montaigne is Donald M. Frame's *Montaigne's Discovery of Man* (1955) which discusses Montaigne's philosophy of life. André Gide's *Montaigne* (1939), a penetrating study by an eminent French historian, is now available as a paperback. Edith Sichel's *Montaigne* (new ed., 1911) is a simple readable life. A Lamande's *Montaigne*, translated by A. van Duym (1928), is at times rather sentimental. In his *Representative Men* Ralph Waldo Emerson wrote an essay on Montaigne which is still worth reading. Montaigne's *Essays* are available in English in many editions, one of them being *Selected Works of Montaigne*, edited by Donald M. Frame (1953). Another edition is titled *Autobiography*, edited by M. Lowenthal (1956). For the educational theories of Rabelais and Montaigne see K. A. Sarafian's *French Educational Theorists* (1935).

18 *The Renaissance in England*

Political, Economic and Social History. Two of the better surveys of English history are G. M. Trevelyan's *History of England* (rev. ed., 1937) and W. E. Lunt's *History of England* (4th ed., 1957). *Medieval England* (1958), edited by A. L. Poole, is a series of essays by a group of eminent historians. Another important volume is George O. Sayles' *The Medieval Foundations of England* (1948). *The Tudor Revolution in Government* (1954), by G. R. Elton, discusses the change in method and principle introduced by the Tudors. For a good summary of the economic conditions in England see Volume 1 (1934) of E. Lipson's *Economic History of England*. Another useful survey is J. Clapham's *Concise Economic History of Britain to 1750* (1957). One of the best surveys of social history is G. M. Trevelyan's *English Social History* (2nd ed., 1946). Two other informative surveys are G. G. Coulton's *Social Life in Britain from the Conquest to the Reformation* (1939) and John Finnemore's *Social Life in England* (rev. ed., 1955). There are a number of first-rate accounts of the Tudor period including *Tudor England* (2 vols., 1955), by David Harrison; *The Tudor Age* (1954), by J. A. Williamson; *The Tudor Period* (1956), edited by R. Edwards and L. G. Ramsey; *England under the Tudors and Stuarts* (1935), by Keith Feiling; and *Tudor and Stuart Britain* (1964), by R. Lockyer. There is also an informative paperback by S. T. Bindoff titled *Tudor England* (1962). For further references see *Bibliography of British History: Tudor Period* (2nd ed., 1959), edited by Conyers Read.

THE TUDORS. *The Tudors* by Conyers Read (reprint, 1953) is a good introductory account. Another informative volume is *The Tudors and Stuarts* (1940), by M. Reese. C. W. Williams' *Henry VII* (1937) is the best shorter biography of the first Tudor king. *Henry VIII* by A. F. Pollard (new ed., 1951) is the best scholarly life of Henry VIII. There is a brief well-written popular biography by Helen Simpson (1934) and a somewhat romanticized longer popular life by Francis Hackett (1945). Notable among the more recent semi-popular and popular biographies are J. J. Bagley's *Henry VIII* (1963); J. Bowle's *Henry VIII* (1965); and H. B. Morrison's *Private Life of Henry VIII* (1965). *Mary Tudor* (2nd ed., 1953), by Hilda M. Prescott, is sympathetic and judicious. J. E. Neale's *Elizabeth* (1934) is the authoritative life of the "Virgin Queen." Another important life is J. Clapham's *Elizabeth of England*, edited by E. P. and C. Read (1951). There are also two lively and well-written popular biographies: Katharine Anthony's *Elizabeth* (1929) and M. Waldman's *Elizabeth* (1933). *The Elizabethan Age* (2 vols., 1950-55), by Alfred L. Rowse, covers a wide range of topics. A somewhat less detailed survey is J. B. Black's *The Reign of Elizabeth* (2nd ed., 1959). Roy C. Strong's "Queen Elizabeth as Oriana," *Studies in the Renaissance,* 6 (1959), 251-60, tells the story of the glorification of Good Queen Bess in poetry by her admirers.

THE ENGLISH RENAISSANCE. *The English Renaissance: Fact or Fiction?* (1952), by Eustace M. W. Tillyard, is a series of lectures in support of the idea of an English Renaissance. *The English Renaissance* (2nd ed., 1952), by Vivian de Sola Pinto, deals largely with literature but has a chapter on music and some useful general observations. James Lees-Milne's *Tudor Renaissance* (1951) discusses a broad variety of subjects. *Thought and Culture in the English Renaissance* (1956), edited by Elizabeth M. Nugent with an introduction by Douglas Bush, is a collection of readings, some of which are interesting and others dull. *The Renaissance Man* (2nd ed., 1955), by Dorothy and Charlton Ogburn, is an interesting brief analysis. Ruth Kelso's *Doctrine for the Lady of the Renaissance* (1956) deals primarily with the English Renaissance. It is the counterpart of her *Doctrine for the English Gentleman of the Sixteenth Century* (1929). Another phase of social life is ably discussed in Arthur B. Ferguson's *Articulate Citizen and the English Renaissance* (1965). John Baxton's *Sir Philip Sidney and the English Renaissance* (1954) shows how he, his family, and friends played an essential part in the flowering of the English Renaissance. John R. Hales' *England and the Italian Renaissance* (1954) traces the development of the Italian Renaissance in England. More limited in subject but equally important is A. Lytton Sells' *The Italian Influence in English Poetry from Chaucer to Southwell* (1955). Older but still eminently useful is Lewis Einstein's *The Italian Renaissance in England* (1902). Italian influence in the Elizabethan age is ably discussed by J. L. Livesay in *The Elizabethan Image of Italy* (1963). L. B. Wright's *Middle-class Culture in Elizabethan England* (new ed., 1963) is a well-documented and enlightening account. *The Renaissance in England* (1966), edited by J. V. Cunningham, is a book of readings, many of which are not even remotely connected with the Renaissance.

ENGLISH LITERATURE. *A Literary History of England* (1948), edited by A. C. Baugh, is a crisply-written comprehensive survey. For the Tudor period there is *English Literature in the Sixteenth Century* (1954), by Clive S. Lewis in *Oxford History of English Literature,* an authoritative survey. Another valuable survey is Esther C. Dunn's *Literature of Shakespeare's England* (1936). Hardin Craig's *The Enchanted Glass: The Elizabethan Mind in Literature* (1936) is a unique and illuminating study. *The Renaissance in England* (1954), edited by H. E. Rollins and H. Baker, is a useful anthology. On poetry Douglas Bush's *English Poetry: The Main Currents from Chaucer to the Present* (1952) is a good survey. Other important studies by the same author are *Mythology and the Renaissance Tradition in English Poetry* (1932); *Classical Influences in Renaissance Literature* (1952); and *Preface to Renaissance Literature* (1964). Herbert C.

Wright's *Boccaccio in England from Chaucer to Tennyson* (1957) illuminates one phase of Italian influence. *Essays on Elizabethan Drama* (1956), by Thomas S. Eliot, is a good introduction to the drama of the period. *Elizabethan Lyrics: A Critical Anthology* (1953), edited by Kenneth Muir, is a useful aid.

CHAUCER, MARLOWE, AND SHAKESPEARE. One of the best biographies of Chaucer is G. G. Coulton's *Chaucer and His Times* (1957); it supplies the background for understanding the *Canterbury Tales. Geoffrey Chaucer* (1958), by John L. Lowes, is a short biography by a distinguished Chaucerian scholar who depicts the literary climate of the age. Another important book by the same author is *Chaucer and the Development of His Genius* (1934). Other informative volumes are John S. Tatlock's *The Mind and Art of Chaucer* (1950), and *Chaucer's World* (1948), by Edith Rickert. *The Tragical History of Christopher Marlowe* (1942), by John E. Bakeless, is the definitive study of the dramatist. Somewhat shorter but equally good for an understanding of Marlowe is F. S. Boas' *Marlowe: A Biographical and Critical Study* (1940). Other readable and informative biographies are Philip Henderson's *Christopher Marlowe* (1952) and Paul H. Kocher's *Christopher Marlowe* (1946). *Marlowe and the Early Shakespeare* (1953), by Frank W. Wilson, traces the intellectual relationship between the two great dramatists. Peter Alexander's *Shakespeare Primer* (1952) is a good general introduction. For a somewhat fuller account there is Max M. Reese's *Shakespeare: His World and His Work* (1954). On Shakespeare and the Renaissance see Dorothy and Charlton Ogburn's *The Star of England: William Shakespeare, Man of the Renaissance* (1953) and James A. K. Thomson's *Shakespeare and the Classics* (1952). Another valuable study is *Shakespeare and the Nature of Man* (1942), by Theodor Spencer. Other important volumes are Kenneth J. Spaulding's *The Philosophy of Shakespeare* (1954); F. Halliday's *Shakespeare in His Own Age* (1964); and Ruth Anderson's *Elizabethan Psychology and Shakespeare's Plays* (1927). Invaluable is H. C. Goddard's *The Meaning of Shakespeare* (1951) which is the fruit of a lifetime of study.

MUSIC IN ENGLAND. Ernest Walker's *History of Music in England* (3rd ed., 1952) is a good survey. Another useful account is Henry Davey's *History of English Music* (2nd ed., 1921). M. F. Bukofzer's *Studies in Medieval and Renaissance Music* (1950) contains some interesting information on English music. "Music: a book of knowledge in Renaissance England" by C. L. Finney, *Studies in the Renaissance*, 6 (1959), 36-63, is a well-written informative article on the role of music in Renaissance England. John Stevens' *Music and Poetry in the Tudor Court* (1961) is crammed with interesting facts. Another important study is Walter C. Woodfell's *Musicians in English Society from Elizabeth to Charles I* (1953). Joseph Kerman's "The Elizabethan motet: a study of texts for music," *Studies in the Renaissance*, 9 (1962), 273-308, elucidates one phase of music. For information on individual composers see William H. Hood's *Tudor Composers* (1925). On the use of music on the stage there is George Cowling's *Music on the Shakespeare Stage* (1913). The most thorough study of Shakespeare and music is John H. Long's *Shakespeare's Use of Music* (2 vols., new ed., 1961). Other useful studies are Christopher Wilson's *Shakespeare and Music* (1922) and Louis C. Elson's *Shakespeare in Music* (1901). The background of Tudor music is ably surveyed in Frank L. Harrison's *Music in Medieval Britain* (1958). Joseph Kierman's *The English Madrigal* (1962) is the definitive study on the subject.

ENGLISH HUMANISM. *The Renaissance and English Humanism* (1939), by Douglas Bush, and *Humanism in England During the Fifteenth Century* (2nd ed., 1957), by Roberto Weiss, are two good penetrating introductions. Fritz Caspari's *Humanism and the Old Order in Tudor England* (1954) is a first-rate analysis of the social and educational ideas and ideals of the time. *England and the New Learning* (1937), by Leonard Elliott-Binns, is a brief discussion of the impact of classical learning. *Humphrey, Duke of Gloucester* (1907), by Kenneth H. Vickers, is a careful biography of one of the key figures in the introduction of humanism into England. *John Colet and Marsilio Ficino* (1963), by Sears Jayne, presents a new interpretation of Colet's thought. F. Seebohm's *Oxford Reformers* (3rd rev. ed., 1914) is a careful analysis of certain thought-currents of the English Renaissance. M. M. Mahood's *Poetry and Humanism* (1950) and Harold A. Mason's *Humanism and Poetry in the Early Tudor Period* (1960) are two informative discussions of the relationship between humanism and poetry. H. Lathrop's *Translations from the Classics into English from Caxton to Chapman, 1477-1620* (1933) conveys some idea of the interest in the classics. *Classical Myth and Legend in Renaissance Dictionaries* (1956), by D. T. Starnes and F. W. Talbert, centers its attention on English works, a mine of information.

THOMAS MORE. *More's Utopia and His Social Teachings* (1929), by W. E. Campbell, contains some illuminating reflections. *More's Utopia: The Biography of an Idea* (1965), by J. H. Hexter, is an important contribution to a better understanding of a complex and controversial figure. Russell A. Ames' *Citizen Thomas More and His Utopia* (1949) is a well-organized and clearly-written study of More's work. H. W. Donner's *Introduction to Utopia* (1945) offers a good approach to the *Utopia*. R. W. Chambers' *Thomas More* (1935) is a first-rate biography. Two more recent well-done popular biographies are *The Story of Thomas More* (1955), by John Farow, and *Sir Thomas More* (1954), by Leslie Faul. *The Lyfe of Sir Thomas More, Knighte* by William Roper, edited by James M. Cline (1950), is a biography of More by his son-in-law written shortly after More's death. More's *Utopia* is available in English in a variety of editions. A complete English edition of More's works, edited by Edward Surtz, S. J., and J. H. Hexter, is in preparation. More's correspondence is well presented in *The Correspondence of Sir Thomas More*, edited by E. F. Rogers (1945). Two important painstaking studies, *Utopia: The Praise of Wisdom* (1957) and *The Praise of Pleasure: Philosophy, Education and Communism in More's Utopia* (1957), both by Edward Surtz, S. J., attempt to lay bare More's real intent.

19 *The Renaissance in Spain*

SPAIN UNDER FERDINAND AND ISABELLA. One of the best shorter surveys of Spanish history is Rafael Altamira's *History of Spain*, translated by Muna Lee (1940). A more recent concise survey is Harold V. Livermore's strongly factual *History of Spain* (1958). There is a good account of the period in J. H. Elliott's *Imperial Spain, 1469-1716* (1964). An older but still valuable account is *Spain's Greatness and Decay* (3rd rev. ed., 1940), by M. A. S. Hume. R. T. Davies' *The Golden Century of Spain, 1501-1621* (reprint, 1954) is a readable account which is antiquated in some respects. J. H. Mariejol's *Spain of Ferdinand and Isabella*, translated by B. Keen (1961), is a judicious and well-written account by an eminent Spanish historian. William H. Prescott's *History of the Reign of Ferdinand and Isabella* (3 vols. 1838) is still the most comprehensive account of the period. Isabel L. Plunket's *Isabel of Castile and the Making of the Spanish Nation* (1919) is still the best of a group of inadequate biographies. The standard history of the Spanish Inquisition is H. C. Lea's *History of the Inquisition in Spain* (4 vols., 1906-07), a monumental work of scholarship. A useful shorter study of the Inquisition is F. Vacandard's *Inquisition* (1908), written from the Catholic point of view. Cecil Roth's *The Spanish Inquisition* (1937) is a readable popular account. The same author has also written *The History of the Maranos* (1937). H. C. Lea's *The Moriscos of Spain* (1901) is the standard account of the subject. A. A. Neuman's *The Jews in Spain* (2 vols., 1948) is a careful study of the life and culture of the Spanish Jews.

CHARLES AND PHILIP II. In his *Spain under the Hapsburgs* (Volume 1, *Empire and Absolutism, 1516-1598* (1964), John Lynch ably surveys the political developments of the period. Karl Brandi's *Charles V*, translated by C. V. Wedgwood (1939), is the definitive biography. Although written many decades ago E. Armstong's *Emperor Charles V* (2 vols., 1902) is still unsurpassed in some respects. For those who desire a readable shorter treatment there is W. L. McElwee's *The Reign of Charles V* (1936). B. Chudoba's *Spain and the Empire, 1519-1643* (1952) is a valuable study of Spanish policies. *The Character of Philip II: The Problem of Moral Judgments in History* (1963), edited by J. C. Rule and J. J. TePaske, presents a brief informative collection of excerpts from various historical writings on the subject. M. A. S. Hume's *Philip II of Spain* (1897; several reprints) is still a first-rate scholarly biography. J. H. Mariejol's *Philip II* (1934) is a carefully-done life despite its subtitle "the first modern king." David Loth's *Philip*

II (1932) and Charles Petrie's *Philip II* (1963) are lively popular biographies. M. A. S. Hume's *Philip IV: Spain in Decadence* (1907) tells the story of Spain's decline. *The Armada* (1959), by Garrett Mattingly, is a lively account of Philip II's great fiasco. Robert H. Schwobel's "Coexistence, conversion, and the Crusade against the Turks," *Studies in the Renaissance*, 12 (1965), 164-87, is a significant discussion of the Turkish problem.

THE SPANISH RENAISSANCE. Little has been written on the Spanish Renaissance in English. The best account in English is Aubrey F. Bell's "Notes on the Spanish Renaissance," *Revue Hispanique*, 80 (1930), 319-652, factual but lacking interpretation. David Hannay's *The Later Renaissance* (1898) has a number of mediocre chapters on the Spanish Renaissance. There is a chapter titled "The Renaissance in Spain" in *The Heritage of Spain: An Introduction to Spanish Civilization* (1943), by Nicholson B. Adams. Spanish culture of the Renaissance is also discussed in E. Allison Peer's *Spain: A Companion to Spanish Studies*, revised and enlarged by R. F. Brown (5th ed., 1956). There are also discussions of the culture of the golden age in Henry D. Sedgwick's *Spain: A Short History of its Politics, Literature and Art* (1925).

SPANISH HUMANISM. David Rubio's *Classical Scholarship in Spain* (1934) is a concise but informative survey of the interest in the classics. Ximenes role in the Spanish Renaissance is described in P. R. Lyell's *Cardinal Ximenes and the Making of Spain* (1934). R. Schevill's *Ovid and the Renaissance in Spain* (1913) is a real contribution toward understanding Spanish humanism. *A College Professor of the Renaissance: Lucio Marineo Seculo among the Spanish Humanists* (1937), by C. Lynn, offers an interesting glimpse of one phase of the Spanish Renaissance. Aubrey F. Bell's *Luis de Leon: A Study of the Spanish Renaissance* (1925) is a detailed scholarly study which presents the intellectual background of the period. *Man of Spain: Francis Suarez* (1940), by Joseph H. Fichter, is a careful well-documented study which throws much light on Spanish humanism. "The Elaboration of Vives' Treatise on the Arts" by William Sinz, *Studies in the Renaissance* 10 (1963), 68-90, is a concise and well-written scholarly study. Otis H. Green's *Spain and the Western Tradition: The Castilian Mind in Literature from "El Cid" to Calderón* (3 vols., 1963-65) is a monumental work of scholarship.

SPANISH LITERATURE. Ernest Merimée's *History of Spanish Literature*, translated and revised by S. G. Morley (1931), is one of the best surveys. Equally good and more up-to-date is *A New History of Spanish Literature* (1961), by R. E. Chandler and K. Schwartz. Another well-written and judicious survey is Gerald Brenan's *The Literature of the Spanish People* (1952). J. Fitzmaurice-Kelly's *New History of Spanish Literature* (1926) is no longer new but still useful. *Dictionary of Spanish Literature* (1956), edited by Maxim Newmark, is eminently useful for reference purposes. A. F. Bell's *Castilian Literature* (1938) is an able account. Clara L. Pluvey's *The Book Called Celestina* (1954) and Stephen Gilman's *The Art of La Celestina* (1956) offer lucid and lively discussions of the first great Spanish work of the Renaissance. *Celestina* is available in a number of English translations; one of the more recent is that by Phyllis Hartnoll (1959). For the influence of *Celestina* in England see J. G. Underhill's *Spanish Literature in the England of the Tudors* (1899). Two other scholarly works on Spanish influence are M. A. S. Hume's *Spanish Influence on English Literature* (1905) and Gustav Ungerer's *Anglo-Spanish Relations in Tudor Literature* (1956). On Boccaccio's influence in Spain there is C. B. Bourland's *Boccaccio and the Decameron in Castilian and Catalan Literature* (1905). The picaresque novel is ably discussed in F. DeHaan's *Outline of the History of the Novela Picaresqua* (1903) and F. W. Chandler's *Literature of Roguery* (2 vols., 1907). Low-priced paperback editions of the *Life and Adventures of Lazarillo de Tormes* in English are available. In *The Petrarchan Sources of "La Celestina"* (1961), A. D. Devermond discusses the indebtedness of the author of *La Celestina* to Petrarch.

CERVANTES AND LOPE DE VEGA. W. J. Entwistle's *Cervantes* (1940) is one of the better biographies of the Spanish novelist. Equally well-written and scholarly are the biographies by J. Fitzmaurice-Kelly (1917); A. F. Bell (1947); and G. MacEóin (1951). Bruno Frank's *A Man Called Cervantes*, translated by H. T. Lowe-Porter (1935), is a well-written popular biography. Still one of the best studies on Lope de Vega is R.

Schevill's *The Art of Lope de Vega* (1918). Another first-rate study is *Lope de Vega and the Spanish Drama* (1902), by J. Fitzmaurice-Kelly. Two other important volumes are H. J. Chaytor's *Dramatic Theory in Spain* (1925) and H. A. Rennert's *The Spanish Stage in the Time of Lope de Vega* (1909). On the period preceding Lope there is J. P. W. Crawford's *Spanish Drama Before Lope de Vega* (1937). Not to be overlooked is E. C. Riley's *Cervantes' Theory of the Novel* (1962) which demolishes the idea that Cervantes was a careless writer and relatively untutored.

20 *Northern Renaissance Art*

NORTHERN ART: THE NETHERLANDS. The best interpretative survey of northern art is *The Art of the Renaissance in Northern Europe in Its Relation to the Contemporary Spiritual and Intellectual Movements* (1945), by Otto Benesch. Frank J. Mather's *Western European Painting of the Renaissance* (1948) contains much useful information but is antiquated in some respects, one being the Van Eyck problem. *Early Netherlandish Painting; Its Origins and Character* (2 vols., 1953), by Erwin Panofsky, is a detailed study by an eminent art historian. One of the most lucid accounts of Flemish painting is *Flemish Painting* (1957-58), Volume 1 by Jacques Lassaigne titled *The Century of Van Eyck*, and Volume 2 by J. Lassaigne and Robert L. Delevoy titled *From Bosch to Rubens*. R. L. Delevoy has also written *Early Flemish Painting* (1963). Another good survey is Max J. Friedländer's *From Van Eyck to Bruegel*, translated from the German by M. Kay (1956). On individual painters there is much information in Horace Shipp's *The Flemish Masters* (1954). Not to be overlooked is Roger E. Fry's *Flemish Art: A Critical Survey* (1927), a penetrating analysis by a distinguished art historian. *Flanders in the Fifteenth Century: Art and Civilization* (1960), by Lucie Ninane and others, discusses art in terms of the civilization which produced it. In his *The Van Eyck Problem* (1954) Maurice W. Brockwell exposes the myth of Hubert van Eyck. On Bruegel there is a longer biography by R. L. Delevoy (1959) and a series of brief discussions and 16 plates, edited by W. Stechow (1954). *Bruges: The Cradle of Flemish Painting* (1964), by François Cali, is an interesting brief discussion of Bruges as an art center.

BURGUNDIAN AND FRENCH ART. For a discussion of Sluter and his work see Ruth M. Tovell's *Flemish Artists of the Valois Courts* (1950). There is also a discussion of Sluter in René Huyghe's *Art and the Spirit of Man* (1962). For a general background of northern art see André Chastel's *Age of Humanism* (1963) which discusses the changes humanism effected in art and culture generally. The same author has also written *Art in France*, Volume 1 (1960), which is a sound and readable survey. There is also a good survey by Anthony Blunt titled *Art and Architecture in France, 1500-1700*, (new ed., 1957). For a more detailed account see Volume 1 of *French Painting* by Albert Chatelet and Jacques Thuillier, entitled *From Fouquet to Poussin* (1963). Roger E. Fry's *French, Flemish and British Art* (1951) is an expert analysis and interpretation. Those who are interested in the background of Renaissance art should consult Joan Evans' *Art in Medieval France, 987-1498* (1948), a good non-technical introduction. There are a number of readable scholarly biographies of Fouquet including Klaus G. Perls' *Jean Fouquet* (1940) and Paul Wescher's *Jean Fouquet and His Time* (1947). On Goujon there is an older English biography titled *Jean Goujon: His Life and Work* (1903).

GERMAN ART. There is so far as this writer knows no good up-to-date survey of German art in English. There are discussions of German art in Jethro Bithell's *Germany: A Companion to German Studies* (2nd ed., 1955). Some of the outstanding German painters are discussed in Helen A. Dickinson's *German Masters of Art* (1914). Probably the best recent treatise is Alfred Stange's *German Painting* (1950) which covers the fourteenth, fifteenth, and sixteenth centuries. Erwin Panofsky's *The Life and Art of Albrecht Dürer* (2 vols., 1943; also one-vol. ed.) is the definitive biography of the German artist. T. S. Moore's *Albert Dürer* (1905) and Frederick Nuechter's *Albrecht Dürer* (1911) are useful older lives with selections from Dürer's writings.

English Art. For those desiring a general survey there is Richard S. Lambert's *Art in England* (1938). William Gaunt's *Concise History of English Painting* (1964) and Michael Kitson's *English Painting* (1964) are two brief readable surveys. More limited in scope but more detailed in its discussions is Ellis K. Waterhouse's *Painting in Britain, 1530-1650* (1961). James Lees-Milne's *Tudor Renaissance* (1951) contains some interesting discussions of English Renaissance art. Another useful book is Aymer Vallance's *Art in England During the Elizabethan and Stuart Periods* (1908). On Tudor artists see Erna Auerbach's *The Tudor Artists: A Study of the Painters in the Royal Service from Henry VIII to the Death of Elizabeth* (1954). The background of English Renaissance painting is ably discussed in Margaret Ricket's *Painting in Britain: The Middle Ages* (1954) and Joan Evans' *English Art, 1307-1461* (1949). The most detailed scholarly biography of Holbein is A. B. Chamberlain's *Hans Holbein the Younger* (2 vols., 1913). There is an interesting study by A. Bruce titled *Erasmus and Holbein* (1936).

Spanish Art. Jose Gudiol's *The Arts of Spain* (1964) is a lucid survey with 162 illustrations. Two other informative volumes are *Spanish Painting* (1938), by E. Harris, and Philip Hendy's *Spanish Painting* (1946). A fuller and more recent survey is Jacques Lassaigne's *Spanish Painting* (2 vols., 1952) of which Volume 1 covers the period to El Greco. On the Renaissance period itself there are two readable carefully-done volumes: Carmen Gómez-Morino's *Spanish Painting: The Golden Century* (1965) and A. Cirici-Pellicer's *The Golden Age of Spain* (1961). The most comprehensive and detailed account of Spanish painting is Chandler R. Post's *History of Spanish Painting* (12 vols. in 18, 1930-58). *Art and Architecture in Spain and Portugal and Their American Dominions, 1500-1800* (1961), by George Kubler and Martin S. Soria, is a first-rate survey. Oskar Hagen's *Patterns and Principles of Spanish Art* (rev. ed., 1948) is a stimulating discussion of the types and the underlying principles of Spanish art. M. Legendre's *El Greco* (1947) is a judicious appraisal of the Spanish painter. A more recent careful biographical and critical study is Paul Guinard's *El Greco*, translated by J. Emmons (1956).

Index